Animal Gazetteer

2nd edition
2009

The Dictionary Project, Inc.
Sullivan's Island, SC 29482

Printed and made in the U.S.A.
ISBN 1-934669-05-9

He that plants trees loves others besides himself.

English proverb

My son Lewis and I were driving to his preschool class when he shouted, "Mom, stop! Turn back! You have to make them stop cutting down that forest! They are destroying the animals' habitats."

"I wish I could make them stop cutting down the trees," I told him, "but I can't. Someone owns that land and they are building a shopping center there."

That was eight years ago. I didn't want to see Lewis become apathetic. I loved his zeal to protect habitats of the birds and lizards and insects in our town. I did not teach him this--- he was only four—and I wanted him to feel the same sense of urgency to protect our planet when he was fifty. In my heart I knew that if I did nothing to protect the habitats of the animals in our community and on our planet, he would learn from my example to feel powerless. So I wrote this book to help children understand their roles as stewards of their environment and to help them see that if they do not protect the habitats of animals, these animals will be gone forever.

Mary French

March 6, 2007
Sullivan's Island, SC

We want to thank the people who gathered the information in this book:

Laura Dimmick
Anya Marsalek Leveille
Wanda Parker
Karan and Siddarth Rai

from the following government websites.

www.ciafactbook.gov

www.icunredlist.org

http://www.ozonelayer.noaa.gov/science/basics.htm

http://ga.water.usgs.gov/edu/watercycle.html

the websites for the 50 United States

We are grateful for the data that these agencies have collected and provided to the public so that we can make decisions based on factual information.
We appreciate all suggestions, ideas and contributions.
Please write to us, to let us know what you would like to see in the next edition of the *Animal Gazetteer*.

www.TheDictionaryProject.com

Cover Design by Jay Fletcher

ABCDEFGHIJKLMNOPQRSTUVWXYZ

Table of Contents

abcdefghijklmnopqrstuvwxyz

A

a [ā] *article*, used to indicate one before a noun

a-ba-cus [ăb′ə-kəs] *noun*, a frame holding parallel rods with beads, used for doing arithmetic

ab-a-lo-ne [ăb′ə-lō′nē] *noun*, a shell sea mollusk animal whose shell is lined with mother-of-pearl

a-ban-don [ə-băn′dən] *verb*, to leave or give up completely, to walk away from

a-bate [ə-bāt′] *verb*, to gradually become less in amount or degree

ab-bre-vi-ate [ə-brē′vē-āt′] *verb*, to shorten, to cut down, to contract

ab-di-cation [ăb′dĭ-kā-shŭn] *noun*, a surrender, abandonment

ab-do-men [ăb′də-mən] *noun*, the digestive system in the body, belly

ab-duct [ăb-dŭkt′] *verb*, to kidnap

ab-er-ra-tion [ăb′ə-rā′shən] *noun*, a departure from what is right, correct or natural

a-bet [ə-bĕt′] *verb*, to encourage or assist, especially in wrongdoing

ab-hor [ăb-hôr′] *verb*, to withdraw in disgust or horror

a-bide [ə-bīd′] *verb*, 1) to put up with, tolerate 2) to wait patiently for 3) to withstand

a-bil-i-ty [ə-bĭl′ĭ-tē] *noun*, 1) capability, power or knowledge 2) skill, expertise

a-ble [ā′bəl] *adjective*, having the strength or knowledge to do something

ab-nor-mal [ăb-nôr′məl] *adjective*, irregular, unusual, peculiar

a-board [ə-bôrd′] *preposition*, on, in, upon (a ship)

a-bode [ə-bōd′] *noun*, home; a place of residence; a habitation

a-bol-ish [ə-bŏl′ĭsh] *verb*, to do away with entirely

ab-o-li-tion [ăb′ə-lĭsh′ən] *noun*, complete destruction

a-bom-i-na-ble [ə-bŏm′ə-nə-bəl] *adjective*, detestable, odious

ab-o-rig-i-ne [ăb′ə-rĭj′ə-nē] *noun*, a primitive native

a-bor-tive [ə-bôr′tĭv] *adjective*, unsuccessful, fruitless, unfinished

a-bound [ə-bound′] *verb*, to overflow, to prevail, to exist in large numbers

a-bout [ə-bout′] *adverb*, 1) concerning 2) approximately 3) here or there, everywhere

a-bove [ə-bŭv′] *adverb*, 1 at a higher level, *preposition*, 2) over, in a higher place

a-bra-sion [ə-brā′zhən] *noun*, a wearing away or rubbing that causes scratches

a-bridge [ə-brĭj′] *verb*, to shorten by using fewer words

a-bridg-ment [ə-brĭj′mənt] *noun*, abbreviation, shortening

a-broad [ə-brôd′] *adverb*, in a foreign country, overseas

ab-rupt [ə-brŭpt′] *adjective*, happening without warning, suddenly

ab-scess [ăb′sĕs′] *noun*, an accumulation of pus due to an infection from bacteria

1

ab-sence [ăb'səns] *noun*, 1)the state
of being away from someplace or
someone 2) lack

ab-sent [ăb'sənt] *adjective*, missing,
not present, unavailable

ab-sent-mind-ed [ăb'səntmīn'dĭd]
adjective, forgetful, not paying
attention

ab-so-lute [ăb'sə-loot'] *adjective*,
complete, perfect, total

ab-solve [əb-zŏlv', -sŏlv'] *verb*, to
pardon, to forgive

ab-sorb [əb-sôrb', -zôrb'] *verb*,
1) to soak up a fluid or moisture
2) to hold someone's attention
3) to dissolve a debt completely
and accept the loss 4) to assimilate
information

ab-sorb-ent [əb-sôr'bənt] *adjective*,
absorbing moisture, fluid or light
rays

ab-stain [ăb-stān'] *verb*, to
deliberately avoid doing something

ab-sti-nence [ăb'stə-nəns] *noun*, the
act of depriving oneself of some
indulgence, voluntary denial

ab-stract [ăb-străkt'] *adjective*,
difficult to describe or qualify

ab-surd [əb-sûrd', -zûrd'] *adjective*,
outrageous, silly, untrue

ab-surd-i-ty [əb-sûrd'ĭt ē] *noun*, that
which is ridiculous or
unreasonable

a-bun-dance [ə-bŭn'dəns] *noun*,
large quantity, plenty

a-bun-dant [ə-bŭn'dənt] *adjective*,
plentiful, more than enough

a-buse [ə-byoo's] *noun*, 1) hurtful
treatment, *verb*[ə-byooz'], 2) to
hurt someone or something
intentionally

a-bu-sive [ə-byoo'sĭv, -zĭv]
adjective, using insulting words or
bad treatment

a-but [ə-bŭt'] *verb*, to border upon,
to be next to or touching

a-bys-mal [ə-bĭz'məl] *adjective*,
1) immeasurably bad
2) bottomless

a-byss [ə-bĭs'] *noun*, a very deep
crack in the earth, a bottomless
gulf, a deep chasm

ac-a-dem-ic [ăk'ə-dĕm'ĭk] *adjective*,
1) of or relating to an education in
the arts 2) having no practical
importance

a-cad-e-my [ə-kăd'ə-mē] *noun*, a
school offering specialized
training and education

ac-cel-er-a-tion [ăk-sĕl'ə-rā'shən]
noun, an increase in the speed of
something

ac-cent [ăk'sĕnt'] *noun*, 1) the sound
and tone of a foreign language,
verb, 2) to emphasize a sound or
letter when pronouncing a word
3) to emphasize something

ac-cept [ăk-sĕpt'] *verb*,
1) to agree with 2) to receive

ac-cep-tance [ăk-sĕp'təns] *noun*, the
act of receiving something
graciously

ac-cess [ăk'sĕs] *noun*, a way to get
to a person, place, or thing

ac-ces-si-ble [ăk-sĕs'ə-bəl]
adjective, easy to reach or use,
approachable

ac-ces-so-ry [ăk-sĕs'ə-rē] *noun*,
1) an accomplice, connected as a
subordinate 2) an article or
decoration worn to complete an
outfit, such as a belt, scarf, hat,
etc.

ac-ci-dent [ăk′sĭ-dənt] *noun*, 1) an incident involving bodily injury or death 2) a mistake

ac-claim [ə-klām′] *verb*, to applaud, to announce with great approval

ac-cli-mate [ə-klī′mĭt] *verb*, to change or adjust to a different temperature or environment

ac-com-mo-date [ə-kŏm′ə-dāt′] *verb* 1) to adapt or make fit 2) to do a favor 3) to provide lodging

ac-com-mo-da-tion [ə-kŏm′ə-dā′shən] *noun*, an adaptation, an adjustment made to assist someone

ac-com-pa-ny [ə-kŭm′pə-nē] *verb*, to go with, to join

ac-com-plice [ə-kŏm′plĭs] *noun*, someone who goes along with something, usually something wrong

ac-com-plish [ə-kŏm′plĭsh] *verb*, to finish, to complete a task or reach a goal

ac-com-plish-ment [ə-kŏm′plĭsh-mənt] *noun*, something done, a goal that has been reached, a finished task

ac-cord [ə-kôrd′] *noun*, 1) mutual agreement, *verb*, 2) to be in harmony, to conform

ac-cor-di-on [ə-kôr′dē-ən] *noun*, a musical instrument that is played by fingering a keyboard on one side and squeezing bellows in and out on the other side

ac-cost [ə-kôst′] *verb*, to approach abruptly and speak to first

ac-count [ə-kount′] *noun*, 1) an explanation, a statement of money or inventory, *verb*, 2) to give a reason, to explain

ac-crue [ə-krōō′] *verb*, to be added on to, to increase

ac-cu-mu-late [ə-kyōōm′yə-lāt′] *verb*, to collect, to amass

ac-cu-mu-la-tion [ə-kyōōm′yə-lā′shən] *noun*, gathering a quantity of something

ac-cu-ra-cy [ăk′yər-ə-sē] *noun*, exactness, correctness, precision

ac-cu-rate [ăk′yər-ĭt] *adjective*, having no mistakes

ac-cu-sa-tion [ăk′yōō-zā′shən] *noun*, a claim that someone has done something wrong

ac-cuse [ə-kyōōz′] *verb*, to say someone has committed an offense or crime

ac-cus-tom [ə-kŭs′təm] *verb*, to become familiar with something through use or habit

ace [ās] *noun*, 1) a playing card 2) a fighter pilot who was shot down

ache [āk] *noun*, 1) a painful or sore spot, *verb*, 2) to hurt, to feel pain

a-chieve [ə-chēv′] *verb*, to do what one sets out to do

a-chieve-ment [ə-chēv′mənt] *noun*, something that a person has done to reach a goal

ac-id [ăs′ĭd] *noun*, a chemical substance soluble in water, sour in taste, that reddens litmus paper

ac-knowl-edge [ăk-nŏl′ĭj] *verb*, 1) to look at someone and speak to him or her 2) to admit the truth

ac-knowl-edg-ment [ăk-nŏl′ĭj-mənt] *noun*, 1) admission, recognition of an achievement 2) an expression of thanks

a-corn [ā′kôrn′, ā′kərn] *noun*, the seed of an oak tree

3

a-cous-tic [ə-kōō′stĭk] *adjective*, of or relating to the ability to carry a sound without distortion

ac-quaint [ə-kwānt′] *verb*, to cause to know or be aware of someone or something

ac-quaint-ance [ə-kwān′təns] *noun*, a person with whom one is familiar

ac-qui-esce [ăk′wē-ĕs′] *verb*, to submit, to consent, to agree

ac-quire [ə-kwīr′] *verb*, to get or to buy, to gain possession of

ac-qui-si-tion [ăk′wĭ-zĭsh′ən] *noun*, something gained or acquired

ac-quit [ə-kwĭt′] *verb*, to render a verdict that an accused person is not guilty of a crime, to exonerate

ac-quit-tal [ə-kwĭt′l] *noun*, a setting free from a charge, a finding of "not guilty"

a-cre [ā′kər] *noun*, a plot of land measuring 43,560 square feet

ac-ri-mo-ny [ăk′rə-mō′nē] *noun*, bitterness or caustic temper or speech, bad feelings

ac-ro-bat [ăk′rə-băt′] *noun*, a person skilled in tumbling or in using gymnastics equipment

ac-ro-nym [ăk′rə-nĭm′] *noun*, a word formed from the initial letters of a series of words, e.g. AIDS: *Acquired Immune Deficiency Syndrome*

a-cross [ə-krôs′, ə-krŏs′] *adverb*, 1) from one side of a place to the other, *preposition*, 2) on the opposite side from something

act [ăkt] *noun*, 1) something that has been done, a deed 2) a part of a play containing different scenes,

verb, 3) to pretend to be something or someone 4) to behave 5) to carry out, to perform

ac-tion [ăk′shən] *noun*, 1) something done 2) the process of doing

ac-tive [ăk′tĭv] *adjective*, 1) always busy doing something 2) taking part

ac-tiv-i-ty [ăk-tĭv′ĭ-tē] *noun*, state of action, energy, a task

ac-tor [ăk′tər] *noun*, a male or female performer in a play, a film or television program

ac-tu-al [ăk′chōō-əl] *adjective*, real, existing in fact

ac-tu-al-ly [ăk′chōō-əl-ē] *adverb*, really, truly, in reality

a-cu-i-ty [ə-kyōō′ĭ-tē] *noun*, keenness, as of thought and vision

a-cute [ə-kyōōt′] *adjective*, 1) sharp, pointed, keen, sensitive 2) describing an angle formed by intersecting lines that is less than 90 degrees

A.D. abbreviation for the Latin words **Anno Domini**, the time after the birth of Christ

ad-age [ăd′ĭj] *noun*, a proverb or a saying with a moral message

ad-a-mant [ăd′ə-mənt] *adjective*, inflexible, unyielding

a-dapt [ə-dăpt′] *verb*, to change to fit the environment

ad-ap-ta-tion [ăd′ăp-tā′shən] *noun*, a change to improve the way things work

add [ăd] *verb*, 1) to put together with something else 2) to count

ad-der [ăd′ər] *noun*, a snake with a poisonous bite, a viper

ad-dict [ə-dĭkt'] *noun*, someone who has a strong habit or a physical despendency, as for drugs

ad-dic-tion [ə-dĭk'shən] *noun*, a dependency, such as a physical craving for a drug

ad-di-tion [ə-dĭsh'ən] *noun*, 1) the act of putting or joining things together 2) an annexation

ad-di-tion-al [ə-dĭsh'ən-əl] *adjective*, added on, extra

ad-dress [ə-drĕs'] *noun*, 1) the location of something, usually the street number, city, and state, *verb*, 2) to speak or write to someone 3) to direct in writing, as in a letter 4) to speak to an audience, as in a speech

a-dept [ə-dĕpt'] *adjective*, proficient, expert, highly skilled

ad-e-quate [ăd'ĭ-kwĭt] *adjective*, just enough, sufficient, all right

ad-here [ăd-hîr'] *verb*, to hold, to be attached, to stick to

ad-her-ent [ăd-hîr'ənt] *adjective*, 1) sticking securely, *noun*, 2) a supporter or follower

ad-he-sive [ăd-hē'sĭv, -zĭv] *noun*, a sticky substance that holds things in place

a-dieu [ə-dyōō', ə-dōō'] *noun and interjection*, farewell, goodbye

ad in-fi-ni-tum [ăd ĭn'fə-nī'təm] *adverb*, to infinity, endlessly

ad-ja-cent [ə-jā'sənt] *adjective*, next to, lying near or touching

ad-jec-tive [ăj'ĭk-tĭv] *noun*, a word that describes a person, place or thing

ad-join [ə-join'] *verb*, to be next to and connected to something

ad-journ [ə-jûrn'] *verb*, to put off a meeting until later, to postpone

ad-just [ə-jŭst'] *verb*, to reposition or reset something

ad-just-a-ble [ə-jŭst'ə-bəl] *adjective*, capable of being arranged or altered

ad-just-ment [ə-jŭst'mənt] *noun*, a minor modification or change

ad lib [ăd lĭb'] *verb*, to make up words or actions at the moment, not before

ad-min-is-ter [ăd-mĭn'ĭ-stər] *verb*, 1) to look after or tend 2) to distribute, to disperse 3) to manage, to run

ad-min-is-tra-tion [ăd-mĭn'ĭ-strā'shən] *noun*, those who are empowered to make decisions, management

ad-min-is-tra-tor [ăd-mĭn'ĭ-strā'tər] *noun*, a person authorized to carry out certain duties

ad-mi-ra-ble [ăd'mər-ə-bəl]*adjective*, excellent, deserving the highest praise

ad-mi-ral [ăd'mər-əl] *noun*, the highest ranking officer in the navy

ad-mi-ra-tion [ăd'mə-rā'shən] *noun*, appreciation, esteem

ad-mire [ăd-mīr'] *verb*, 1) to look up to someone, to revere 2) to look at with pleasure

ad-mis-si-ble [ăd-mĭs'ə-bəl] *adjective*, that may be allowed

ad-mis-sion [ăd-mĭsh'ən] *noun*, 1) access, admittance 2) acknowledgment, confession

ad-mit [ăd-mĭt'] *verb*, 1) to allow someone to enter 2) to acknowledge as true

a-do[ədōō]*noun*, fuss, excitment

a-do-be [ə-dō'bē] *noun*, 1) a type of clay or the sun-dried bricks made from it, 2) a home made with baked mud, usually in the Southwest

ad-o-les-cent [ăd'l-ĕs'ənt] *noun*, a teenager

a-dopt [ə-dŏpt'] *verb*, 1) to use someone else's idea 2) to make someone a member of your family, legally

a-dore [ə-dôr', ə-dōr'] *verb*, to like or love very much

a-dorn [ə-dôrn'] *verb*, to decorate, to add beauty, to embellish

a-drift [ə-drĭft'] *adverb*, out in water or space without means of control, drifting

a-dult [ə-dŭlt'] *noun*, a grown person or animal

ad-vance [ăd-văns'] *adjective*, 1) ahead of time, done beforehand, *noun*, 2) a positive change, progress *verb*, 3) to move forward

ad-van-tage [ăd-văn'tĭj] *noun*, something that helps a person

ad-van-ta-geous [ăd'văn-tā'jəs,] *adjective*, profitable, useful, beneficial, favorable

ad-vent [ăd'vĕnt'] *noun*, the arrival of someone or something

ad-ven-ture [ăd-vĕn'chər] *noun*, 1) a bold or hazardous undertaking, 2) an exciting or extraordinary experience

ad-verb [ăd'vûrb] *noun*, a word that tells how, when, or where something is done

ad-ver-sar-y [ăd'vər-sĕr'ē] *noun*, a rival, foe, or opponent

ad-verse [ăd-vûrs'] *adjective*, opposed, hostile

ad-ver-si-ty [ăd-vûr'sĭ-tē] *noun*, hard times, trouble

ad-ver-tise [ăd'vər-tīz'] *verb*, 1) to announce publicly 2) to try to sell something by promoting it

ad-ver-tise-ment [ăd'vər-tīz'mənt] *noun*, a notice or short film about something that is for sale

ad-vice [ăd-vīs'] *noun*, counsel, opinion given for acceptable conduct, guidance

ad-vis-a-ble [ăd-vī'zə-bəl] *adjective*, proper, recommended, prudent

ad-vise [ăd-vīz'] *verb*, to suggest to someone what to do, to inform, to recommend, to counsel

ad-vis-er [ăd-vī'zər] *noun*, one who advises, one who gives counsel or information

ad-vo-cate [ăd'və-k t'] *noun*, 1) one who pleads the cause of another or himself, [ăd'və-kāt'] *verb*, 2) to defend, to urge, to support, to endorse

aer-i-al [âr'ē-əl] *adjective*, pertaining to or inhabiting the air

aer-o-bic [â-rō'bĭk] *adjective*, requiring the presence of free oxygen to live

aer-o-dy-nam-ics [âr'ō-dī-năm'ĭks] *noun*, the science of the movement of flying bodies in air

aer-o-sol [âr'ə-sôl'] *noun*, a gaseous suspension of fine particles, a mist

aer-o-space [âr'ō-spās'] *adjective*, having to do with the atmosphere and space

aes-thet-ic [ĕs-thĕt'ĭk] *adjective*, relating to beauty or the arts

aggravate

af-fair [ə-fâr'] noun, matter, concern, business of any kind

af-fect [ə-fĕkt'] verb, 1) to act upon to bring about a change 2) to move the feelings of someone 3) to pretend to do something

af-fec-ta-tion [ăf'ĕk-tā'shən] noun, insincerity, pretense

af-fec-tion [ə-fĕk'shən] noun, tenderness, warmth, love, devotion, kindness

af-fec-tion-ate [ə-fĕk'shə-nĭt] adjective, feeling or showing love

af-fec-tion-ate-ly [ə-fĕk'shə-nĭt-lē] adverb, showing love and care

af-fi-da-vit [ăf'ĭ-dā'vĭt] noun, a written declaration, an oath

af-fil-i-ate [ə-fĭl'ē-āt'] verb, to closely connect or associate with someone or groups of people

af-fil-i-a-tion [ə-fĭl-ē-ā'shən] noun, an association, a connection

af-fin-i-ty [ə-fĭn'ĭ-tē] noun, a feeling of attraction to a person or thing

af-firm [ə-fûrm'] verb, to approve, to confirm, to endorse

af-fir-ma-tion [ăf'ər-mā'shən] noun, a solemn pledge

af-firm-a-tive [ə-fûr'mə-tĭv] adjective, 1) being positive and helpful, noun, 2) a word or phrase expressing a positive reply

af-flict [ə-flĭkt'] verb, to hurt, to torment, to cause pain

af-flic-tion [ə-flĭk'shən] noun, state or cause of distress, pain or misery

af-flu-ence [ăf'lōō-əns] noun, an abundant supply, wealth

af-ford [ə-fôrd'] verb, to have enough money to buy something

a-float [ə-flōt'] adjective, on or above the water, buoyant

a-fraid [ə-frād'] adjective, scared

Af-ri-ca [ăf'rĭ-kə] noun, one of the seven continents, surrounded by the Atlantic and Indian Oceans, containing 12.7% of the world's population

af-ter [ăf'tər] adverb, 1) following, next, preposition, 2) behind

af-ter-math [ăf'tər-măth'] noun, the end result, outcome, consequence

af-ter-noon [ăf'tər-nōōn'] noun, time between noon and evening

af-ter-ward [ăf'tər-wərd] adverb, later

a-gain [ə-gĕn'] adverb, once more

a-gainst [ə-gĕnst'] preposition, 1) in opposition to 2) in contact with, touching 3) in the other direction, opposite

age [āj] noun, 1) the amount of time something has lived 2) a particular period of time, verb, 3) to grow or cause to become old

aged [ā'jĭd] adjective, old

a-gen-cy [ā'jən-sē] noun, an organization designed to distribute funds and services to people

a-gen-da [ə-jĕn'də] noun, a list of items that need attention

a-gent [ā'jənt] noun, 1) a person who represents a group 2) a force of change

ag-gran-dize [ə-grăn'dīz'] verb, to make greater in power, rank or riches

ag-gra-vate [ăg'rə-vāt'] verb, to make worse, to annoy

7

ag-gre-gate [ăg′rĭ-gĭt] *noun*, the sum total of a group of things

ag-gres-sion [ə-grĕsh′ən] *noun*, anger in an attack

ag-gres-sive [ə-grĕs′ĭv] *adjective*, forceful, likely to attack

ag-ile [ăj′əl, -īl′] *adjective*, swift, nimble, able to move easily

ag-i-tate [ăj′ĭ-tāt′] *verb*, to shake up

ag-i-ta-tion [ăj′ĭ-tā′shən] *noun*, confusion, frenzy, excitement

ag-nos-tic [ăg-nŏs′tĭk] *noun*, a person who believes that the human mind cannot comprehend the beginning of the universe or the existence of God

a-go [ə-gō′] *adverb*, in the past

ag-o-ny [ăg′ə-nē] *noun*, very bad physical or emotional pain

a-gree-a-ble [ə-grē′ə-bəl] *adjective*, easy to get along with

a-gree-ment [ə-grē′mənt] *noun*, a mutual understanding

ag-ri-cul-ture [ăg′rĭ-kŭl′chər] *noun*, the science and art of cultivating soil and growing crops

a-head [ə-hĕd′] *adverb*, 1) in front, preceding 2) into the future

aid [ād] *noun*, 1) a form of help 2) assistance, support, *verb*, 3) to help or assist

aide [ād] *noun*, an assistant, a helper

ail-ment [āl′mənt] *noun*, a sickness,

aim [ām] *noun*, 1) target, direction 2) intention, purpose, goal, *verb*, 3) to point toward a target when ready to throw something, fire something, or take a picture

air [âr] *noun* 1) the mixture of gases surrounding the earth 2) an

appearance or atmosphere, *verb*, 3) to refresh or ventilate

air-borne [âr′bôrn′] *adjective*, carried by or through the air

air-craft [âr′krăft′] *noun*, a machine capable of flying

air force [âr′fôrs′] *noun*, a group of soldiers trained to fight and destroy using aircraft

air-plane [âr′plān′] *noun*, a flying machine used to transport people or cargo moving through the air by means of motor driven propellers or engines and kept aloft by the upward thrust of the air on its fixed wings

air pol-lu-tion [âr - pə-loō′shən] *noun*, particles that contaminate the air and make it unsafe to breathe

air-port [âr′pôrt′] *noun*, a place where aircraft land and take off

aisle [īl] *noun*, the passageway between seats in a bus, auditorium, church, etc., or between shelves in a store

a-jar [ə-jär′] *adjective and adverb*, slightly open

Al-a-bama [ăl′ə-băm′ə] *noun*, one of the southern United States the capital is Montgomery. The state flower for **Alabama** is the camellia and the motto is "We dare to defend our rights."

a-lac-ri-ty [ə-lăk′rĭ-tē] *noun*, 1) cheerful willingness or readiness 2) speed

a-larm [ə-lärm′] *noun*, 1) a feeling of fear or danger 2) a programmed sound to awaken persons from sleep or warn of danger, *verb*, 3) to worry or frighten

a-las [ə-lăs′] *interjection*, an expression of pity or concern

Alas-ka [ə-lăs′kə] *noun*, one of the 50 United States located in the North. The capital city is Juneau. The state flower of **Alaska** is the forget me-not, and the motto is "North to the Future."

al-ba-tross [ăl′bə-trôs′] *noun*, a large bird with long narrow wings found near the ocean, especially in the South Seas

al-bi-no [ăl-bī′nō] *noun*, a person or animal lacking pigmentation, and therefore extraordinarily pale

al-bum [ăl′bəm] *noun*, 1)a book that holds a collection of pictures, stamps or autographs 2) a collection of recordings

al-che-my [ăl′kə-mē] *noun*, medieval chemistry that attempted to turn ordinary things into gold

al-co-hol [ăl′kə-hôl′] *noun*, 1) an intoxicating beverage, such as wine, beer or liquor, the result of fermentation 2) an organic compound used as an antiseptic

al-co-hol-ic [ăl′kə-hô′lĭk] *adjective*, 1) containing alcohol as an ingredient, *noun*, 2) a person with the disease of alcoholism

al-der-man [ôl′dər-mən] *noun*, a member of a city council

a-lert [ə-lûrt′] *adjective*, 1) awake and ready to act, *noun*, 2) a warning of danger

al-fal-fa [ăl-făl′fə] *noun*, a plant in the pea family

al-ga [ăl′gə] *noun*, *plural*, **algae**, an organism, often one-celled, that continuously divides itself, with no root or stem that lives in water

al-ge-bra [ăl′jə-brə] *noun*, a branch of mathematics in which the expressions of quantity are in symbols that express general relationships

a-li-as [ā′lē-əs] *noun*, an assumed name, a fake name, incognito

al-i-bi [ăl′ə-bī′] *noun*, the plea of having been elsewhere at the time a crime was committed

al-ien [ā′lē-ən] *adjective*, 1) strange, wholly different in nature, *noun*, 2) a person from another country

al-ien-ate [āl′yə-nāt′] *verb*, to separate, to make hostile

a-light [ə-līt′] *verb*, to come from, to get off

a-lign-ment [ə-līn′mənt] *noun*, 1) arrangement in a line 2) the condition of cooperation

a-like [ə-līk′] *adjective*, 1) similar, *adverb*, 2) in the same manner

al-i-men-ta-ry [ăl′ə-měn′tə-rē] *adjective*, supplying nourishment

al-i-mo-ny [ăl′ə-mō′nē] *noun*, an allowance given to a spouse for his or her support after a divorce

a-live [ə-līv′] *adjective*, 1) living, not dead 2) active, moving

al-ka-li [ăl′kə-lī′] *noun*, any soluble substance having marked basic qualities as a mineral salt or mixture of salts that can neutralize acids and turns litmus blue

all [ôl] *adjective*, the whole of, any, 2) *adverb*, 2) completely, totally, *pronoun*, 3) everyone, the whole thing

al-lay [ə-lā′] to ease, to calm, to appease

al-le-ga-tion [ăl′ĭ-gā′shən] *noun*, the statement of something that is to be proved, an accusation

al-lege [ə-lĕj′] *verb*, to urge as a reason, to assert, to suggest

al-le-giance [ə-lē′jəns] *noun*, strong support of something, an obligation to a government or ruler, loyal support

al-le-go-ry [ăl′ĭ-gôr′ē] *noun*, a story with a moral in which characters are used as symbols, a fable

al-ler-gy [ăl′ər-jē] *noun*, an abnormal reaction to substances in the environment such as pollen, dust or insect bites

al-le-vi-ate [ə-lē′vē-āt′] *verb*, to lighten or lessen pressure

al-ley [ăl′ē] *noun*, a very narrow road between buildings

al-li-ance [ə-lī′əns] *noun*, a partnership based on trust, common objectives, etc.

al-li-ga-tor [ăl′ĭ-gā′tər] *noun*, a large reptile that lives near water and is a carnivore

al-lit-er-a-tion [ə-lĭt′ə-rā′shən] *noun*, repetition of the beginning sound, e.g., *Peter Piper picked a peck of pickled peppers*

al-lo-cate [ăl′ə-kāt′] *verb*, to set something aside for a special use

al-lot [ə-lŏt′] *verb*, to divide something and then to give someone his or her portion

al-lot-ment [ə-lŏt′mənt] *noun*, the portion given to each

al-low [ə-lou′] *verb*, to permit someone to do something

al-low-ance [ə-lou′əns] *noun*, a definite sum granted, an abatement or deduction

al-loy [ăl′oi′] *noun*, a substance composed of two or more metals mixed together

al-lude [ə-lood′] *verb*, to hint or suggest indirectly

al-lu-sion [ə-loo′zhən] *noun*, an indirect reference, knowledge of something not actually mentioned

al-ly [ə-lī′] *noun*, 1) someone who helps you fight against someone else, a person or group who has the same purpose or cause, *verb*, 2) to unite, to join

al-ma ma-ter [ăl′mə mä′tər] *noun*, a school from which a person has graduated

al-ma-nac [ôl′mə-năk′] *noun*, a book containing a calendar and certain statistics

al-might-y [ôl-mī′tē] *adjective*, having very great power

al-mond [ä′mənd] *noun*, a nut-like kernel of the fruit of the almond tree

al-most [ôl′mōst′] *adverb*, nearly, not quite

alms [ämz] *noun*, *plural*, money or items given to charity

a-lo-ha [ə-lō-ha′] *noun and interjection*, Hawaiian word used for greeting or parting

a-lone [ə-lōn′] *adjective and adverb* without others, singular

a-long [ə-lông′] *adverb*, 1) following the length of something from end to end 2) moving forward 3) as a companion, *preposition*, 4) over, through, by the course of

a-loof [ə-l oof] *adjective*, 1) reserved in social relationships, *adverb* 2) away in place or time

a-loud [ə-loud'] *adverb*, in a clear voice that can be easily heard

al-pha-bet [ăl'fə-bĕt'] *noun*, the letters of a language arranged in customary order

al-pha-bet-i-cal [ăl'fə-bĕt'ĭ-kəl] *adjective*, arranged in the same order as the letters of the alphabet

al-read-y [ôl-rĕd'ē] *adverb*, even now, before a certain time

al-so [ôl'sō] *adverb*, in addition, too

al-tar [ôl'tər] *noun*, a table in a holy place where religious rites are performed

al-ter [ôl'tər] *verb*, to change

al-ter-a-tion [ôl'tə-rā'shən] *noun*, a change or an adjustment

al-ter-nate [ôl'tər-nāt'] *verb*, to take turns, to switch off

al-ter-na-tive [ôl-tûr'nə-tĭv] *adjective*, 1) other, *noun*, 2) something you can choose

al-though [ôl-thō'] *conjunction*, supposing that, notwithstanding

al-ti-tude [ăl'tĭ-tōod'] *noun*, extent upward, the height of something measured in relation to a reference level, such as sea level

al-to [ăl'tō] *noun*, a singing voice between tenor and soprano

al-to-geth-er [ôl'tə-gĕth'ər] *adverb*, wholly, completely, including everyone, united

al-tru-is-tic [ăl'trōo-ĭs'tĭk] *adjective*, unselfish, concerned about others

al-u-mi-num [ə-lōo'mə-nəm] *noun*, a very soft silver metal made chiefly of bauxite ore

al-ways [ôl'wāz] *adverb*, at all times, forever

am [ăm] *verb*, the part of the verb *be* used with **I**

a.m. in the morning, the hours between midnight and noon, from the Latin ante meridiem "before midday"

a-mass [ə-măs'] *verb*, to collect, to accumulate

am-a-teur [ăm'ə-tûr'] *adjective*, 1) for enjoyment rather than money, not professional, *noun*, 2) someone who is not paid for doing something but does it for pleasure

a-maze [ə-māz'] *verb*, to surprise or bewilder

a-maze-ment [ə-māz'mənt] *noun*, a state of surprise, awe, wonder

am-a-zon [ăm'ə-zŏn'] *noun*, a mythical female warrior

am-bas-sa-dor [ăm-băs'ə-dər] *noun*, an appointed official who represents his or her country in another country

am-ber [ăm'bər] *noun*, the fossilized sap from a pine tree

am-bi-dex-trous [ăm'bĭ-dĕk'strəs] *adjective*, capable of using either hand with equal ease

am-bi-ence [ăm'bē-əns] *noun*, the environment, the atmosphere in a room or building

am-big-u-ous [ăm-bĭg'yōo-əs] *adjective*, capable of more than one interpretation, unclear

am-bi-tion [ăm-bĭsh'ən] *noun*, a strong desire to achieve

am-bi-tious [ăm-bĭsh'əs] *adjective*, wanting to have power, driven to achieve

am-biv-a-lent [ăm-bĭv′ə-lənt]
adjective, having conflicting
emotional attitudes

am-bul-ance [ăm′byə-ləns] *noun,* a
vehicle equipped to carry the
injured or sick

am-bush [ăm′bŏŏsh] *noun,* a
surprise attack

a-mel-io-rate [ə-mēl′yə-rāt′] *verb,* to
improve a deplorable condition

A-men [ā-měn′, ä-měn′] *interjection,*
an expression of approval, to say I
agree

a-mend [ə-měnd′] *verb,* to correct,
to change generally for the better

a-mend-ment [ə-měnd′mənt] *noun,*
a change made in a bill or motion

a-men-i-ty [ə-měn′ĭ-tē] *noun,* a
courtesy, a thoughtful action of
consideration, a convenience

A-mer-i-ca [ə-měr′ĭ-kə]*noun,* a
country in North America with a
democratic form of government

A-mer-i-can In-di-an [ə-měr′ĭ-kən
ĭn′dē-ən] *noun,* the people whose
ancestors lived in North America
for thousands of years

am-e-thyst [ăm′ə-thĭst] *noun,* a
purple or bluish-violet stone

a-mi-a-ble [ā′mē-ə-bəl] *adjective,*
friendly, easy to get along with

a-mid [ə-mĭd′] *preposition,* among,
surrounded by

am-mo-nia [ə-mōn′yə] *noun,* a
colorless compound of hydrogen
and nitrogen

am-mu-ni-tion [ăm′yə-nĭsh′ən]
noun, rockets, bombs and bullets
used in loading or charging guns
and rifles

am-ne-sia [ăm-nē′zhə] *noun,* loss of
memory

am-nes-ty [ăm′nĭ-stē] *noun,* a pardon
that absolves or discounts past offenses

a-mong [ə-mŭng′] *preposition,*
between, surrounded by

a-mount [ə-mount′] *noun,* 1) a sum,
the total number 2) quantity, mass,
verb, 3) to add up

am-phib-i-an [ăm-fĭb′ē-ən] *noun,*
1) a cold-blooded animal living
both on land and in the water
2) an airplane designed to take off
on the water or on land

am-phib-i-ous [ăm-fĭb′ē-əs]
adjective, able to live or operate
on land or in water

am-phi-the-a-ter [ăm′fə-thē′ə-tər]
noun, a theater with seats all
around the stage or arena

am-ple [ăm′pəl] *adjective,* abundant,
plentiful, more than enough

am-pli-fy [ăm′plə-fī′] *verb,* to
increase in size, to make louder

am-pu-tate [ăm′pyŏŏ-tāt′] *verb,*
to cut off

am-u-let [ăm′yə-lĭt] *noun,* a good
luck charm, a talisman

a-muse [ə-myŏŏz′] *verb,* to entertain
or delight, to make someone smile

a-muse-ment [ə-myŏŏz′mənt] *noun,*
entertainment, a distraction

an [ən; ăn when stressed] *article,* used
instead of a in front of a vowel

an-aer-o-bic [ăn′ə-rō′bĭk] *adjective,*
able to live only in the absence of
free oxygen

a-nal-o-gous [ə-năl′ə-gəs] *adjective,*
similar, comparable, resembling

a-nal-o-gy [ə-năl′ə-jē] *noun*, an explanation based on resemblances between different objects or cases

a-nal-y-sis [ə-năl′ĭ-sĭs] *noun*, a thorough examination

an-a-lyze [ăn′ə-līz′] *verb*, to examine critically elements or constituent parts

an-ar-chist [ăn′ər-kĭst] *noun*, a person who rebels against the established order or laws

an-ar-chy [ăn′ər-kē] *noun*, a lawless condition of society, chaos

a-nat-o-my [ə-năt′ə-mē] *noun*, the study of the structure of people, animals or plants

an-ces-tor [ăn′sĕs′tər] *noun*, a person from whom one is descended

an-ces-try [ăn′sĕs′trē] *noun*, family members or ethnic descent

an-chor [ăng′kər] *noun*, 1) a heavy piece of metal on the end of a rope or chain lowered into the water to keep a boat from drifting, *verb*, 2) to secure or fasten firmly, to fix in place

an-cient [ān′shənt] *adjective*, belonging to a remote period of time, very old

and [ənd, ən; ănd when stressed] *conjunction*, a word that adds or joins other words

an-ec-dote [ăn′ĭk-dōt′] *noun*, a short story or fact of an interesting nature

a-ne-mi-a [ə-nē′mē-ə] *noun*, a condition marked by a low red blood cell count

an-e-mom-e-ter [ăn′ə-mŏm′ĭ-tər] *noun*, an instrument to measure the force or speed of wind

an-es-the-sia [ăn′ĭs-thē′zhə] *noun*, the loss of sensation or consciousness, especially when caused by anesthetic

an-es-thet-ic [ăn′ĭs-thĕt′ĭk] *noun*, a substance that causes loss of sensation or consciousness

an-gel [ān′jəl] *noun*, 1) a messenger of God 2) a kind, loveable person

an-ger [ăng′gər] *noun*, feelings of hostility and hurt, a desire to fight or argue

an-gle [ăng′gəl] *noun*, 1) the shape made when two lines or planes intersect 2) a point of view, *verb*, 3) to fish with a hook and line

an-gry [ăng′grē] *adjective*, feeling extreme emotion due to hurt feelings, hostile

an-guish [ăng′gwĭsh] *noun*, extreme pain either of body or mind, acute suffering, deep sadness

an-i-mal [ăn′ə-məl] *noun*, a living creature that is not a plant

an-i-mate [ăn′ə-māt′] *verb*, to inspire with energy, to enliven

an-i-mos-i-ty [ăn′ə-mŏs′ĭ-tē] *noun*, a feeling of hatred leading to opposition, hostility

an-kle [ăng′kəl] *noun*, the joint connecting the foot to the leg

an-nals [ăn′əlz] *noun*, records, history, chronicles, accounts

an-neal [ə-nēl′] *verb*, to subject to high heat, with subsequent cooling, for the purpose of softening thoroughly and making less brittle

an-nex [ə-nĕks′] *noun*, 1) a building added onto a larger building, *verb*, 2) to add on, to attach a smaller thing to something larger

an-nex-a-tion [ăn′ĭk-sā′shən] *noun*, the territory or thing that has been added

an-ni-hi-late [ə-nī′ə-lāt′] *verb*, to reduce to nothing, to destroy entirely, to obliterate

an-ni-ver-sa-ry [ăn′ə-vûr′sə-rē] *noun*, a day celebrated each year to remember something important from the past

an-no-tate [ăn′ō-tāt′] *verb*, to write comments or explanatory notes

an-nounce [ə-nouns′] *verb*, to give notice of the arrival of something, to proclaim, to declare

an-nounce-ment [ə-nouns′mənt] *noun*, 1) act of making something publicly known 2) a printed notice

an-noy [ə-noi′] *verb*, to disturb or irritate, to bother

an-noy-ance [ə-noi′əns] *noun*, anything that irritates

an-nu-al [ăn′yōō-əl] *adjective*, 1) occurring once a year, *noun*, 2) a plant that lives for one year

a-noint [ə-noint′] *verb*, to baptize, to purify, to sprinkle with oil or holy water

a-nom-a-ly [ə-nŏm′ə-lē] *noun*, an irregularity, a deviation from the normal, one of a kind

a-non-y-mous [ə-nŏn′ə-məs] *adjective*, of unknown name

an-o-rex-i-a [ăn′ə-rĕk′sē-ə] *noun*, a lack of appetite and inability or refusal to consume food

an-oth-er [ə-nŭth′ər] *adjective, and pronoun*, 1) an additional, one more 2) someone else

an-swer [ăn′sər] *noun*, 1) a reply to a question, *verb*, 2) to make a response, to reply

ant [ănt] *noun*, a small insect that lives in colonies, known for its social order and industry

an-tag-o-nist [ăn-tăg′ə-nĭst] *noun*, one who opposes with active resistance, an opponent

Ant-arc-ti-ca [ănt-ärk′tĭ-kə] *noun*, one of the seven continents in the world, the area containing the South Pole

an-te-ced-ent [ăn′tĭ-sēd′nt] *adjective*, going before, preceding

an-te-lope [ăn′tl-ōp′] *noun*, a wild animal, similar to a deer, which runs fast and usually has antlers

an-ten-na [ăn-tĕn′ə] *noun, plural*, **antennae**, 1) the sensory organ of an insect or crustacean 2) wire supported in the air for directly transmitting and receiving electromagnetic waves

an-them [ăn′thəm] *noun*, a song or hymn of praise

an-thro-po-log-ist [ăn′thrə-pŏl′ə-jĭst] *noun*, a student of the history and science of mankind

an-thro-po-mor-phic [ăn′thrə-pə-môr′-fĭk] *adjective*, having human form or characteristics

an-ti-bi-ot-ic [ăn′tĭ-bī-ŏt′ĭk] *noun*, a substance such as penicillin, effective in fighting destructive microorganisms and used for treatment of diseases

an-tic-i-pate [ăn-tĭs'ə-pāt'] *verb*, to look forward to

an-ti-dote [ăn'tĭ-dōt'] *noun*, 1) a remedy to counteract poison 2) anything that counteracts evil

an-tip-a-thy [ăn-tĭp'ə-thē] *noun*, a strong dislike, a natural aversion

an-ti-quat-ed [ăn'tĭ-kwā'tĭd] *adjective*, old-fashioned, obsolete

an-tique [ăn-tēk'] *adjective*, 1) old-fashioned, from another time, *noun*, 2) something made long ago and valued for its age

an-ti-sep-tic [ăn'tĭ-sĕp'tĭk] *adjective*, 1) clean, sterile, *noun*, 2) a substance that tends to prevent harmful effects of bacteria growth

an-tith-e-sis [ăn-tĭth'ĭ-sĭs] *noun*, the exact opposite

ant-ler [ănt'lər] *noun*, one of a pair of branched horns on the head of a deer

an-to-nym [ăn'tə-nĭm'] *noun*, a word that has the opposite meaning to another

anx-i-e-ty [ăng-zī'ĭ-tē] *noun*, uneasiness of mind, concern about future events

anx-ious [ăngk'shəs] *adjective*, worried, concerned, nervous

any [ĕn'ē] *adjective*, 1) some, an uncertain number, quantity, volume or degree 2) every 3) one

an-y-bod-y [ĕn'ē-bŏd'ē] *pronoun*, any person

an-y-one [ĕn'ē-wŭn'] *pronoun*, anybody

an-y-thing [ĕn'ē-thĭng'] *noun*, something

an-y-way [ĕn'ē-wā'] *adverb*, 1) no matter what happens, in any case, 2) haphazardly, in any fashion

an-y-where [ĕn'ē-hwâr'] *adverb*, in, at, or to any place

a-part [ə-pärt'] *adverb*, separately in place or time

a-part-ment [ə-pärt'mənt] *noun*, rooms or a part of a building where someone lives

ap-a-thy [ăp'ə-thē] *noun*, lack of interest or concern

ape [āp] *noun*, 1) a large mammal similar to a monkey without a tail, for example, a gorilla, chimpanzee, etc., *verb*, 2) to copy, to imitate

aph-o-rism [ăf'ə-rĭz'əm] *noun*, a statement of truth, an adage

a-poc-a-lyp-tic [ə-pŏk'ə-lĭp'tĭk] *adjective*, prophetic, pertaining to revelations about the end of the world

a-pol-ogize [ə-pŏl'ə-jīz'] *verb*, to say you're sorry for what you have done, to express regret

a-pol-o-gy [ə-pŏl'ə-jē] *noun*, an explanation by way of asking for forgiveness

a-pos-tle [ə-pŏs'əl] *noun*, any person zealously advocating a cause

a-pos-tro-phe [ə-pŏs'trə-fē] *noun*, a mark (') used to indicate an omission of a letter, i.e. *I'll*, or letters, or to denote the possessive case i.e. *Kara's*

ap-o-thegm [ăp'ə-thĕm'] *noun*, a pithy, compact saying, a proverb

a-poth-e-o-sis [ə-pŏth'ē-ō'sĭs] *noun*, deification, glorification, making into a god ap-pall [ə-pôl′] *verb*, to fill with horror or dismay, to shock

ap-pa-rat-us [ăp′ə-ră′təs] *noun*, equipment, a collection or set of implements for a specific purpose

ap-par-el [ə-păr′əl] *noun*, clothing, garments

ap-par-ent [ə-păr′ənt] *adjective*, capable of seeming or appearing to be evident, easily understood

ap-par-ent-ly [ə-păr′ənt] *adverb*, clearly, evidently, obviously

ap-pa-ri-tion [ăp′ə-rĭsh′ən] *noun*, a ghost, a phantom

ap-peal [ə-pēl′] *noun*, 1) the proceeding by which a case is brought to a superior court for reexamination or review 2) a request, *verb*, 3) to plead, to ask urgently 4) to seem attractive

ap-pear [ə-pîr′] *verb*, 1) to come into view unexpectedly 2) to seem to be

ap-pear-ance [ə-pîr′əns] *noun*, 1) the act of appearing or becoming visible 2) the way something or someone looks

ap-pease [ə-pēz′] *verb*, to satisfy or often by granting demands

ap-pel-lant [ə-pĕl′ənt] *noun*, one who asks for a judicial decree

ap-pel-la-tion [ăp′ə-lā′shən] *noun*, a name or title

ap-pen-di-ci-tis [ə-pĕn′dĭ-sī′tĭs] *noun*, inflammation of the appendix

ap-pen-dix [ə-pĕn′dĭks] *noun*, 1) information added to a section at the end of a book 2) a small tube-like part growing out from the intestine

ap-pe-tite [ăp′ĭ-tīt′] *noun*, craving, the desire for food

ap-plaud [ə-plôd′] *verb*, to show approval especially by clapping hands together in praise

ap-plause [ə-plôz′] *noun*, praise for someone, usually expressed by clapping hands

ap-ple [ăp′əl] *noun*, the firm-fleshed, round, juicy fruit of an apple tree

ap-pli-ance [ə-plī′əns] *noun*, an apparatus or device, a machine

ap-pli-ca-ble [ăp′lĭ-kə-bəl] *adjective*, relevant, appropriate

ap-plic-ant [ăp′lĭ-kənt] *noun*, one who makes a request, a petitioner

ap-pli-ca-tion [ăp′lĭ-kā′shən] *noun*, 1) work or effort 2) a use 3) a form used to make a request

ap-pli-que [ăp′lĭ-kā′] *noun*, ornamental patterns put on textiles

ap-ply [ə-plī′] *verb*, 1) to seek or ask 2) to put on 3) to pertain to

ap-point [ə-point′] *verb*, to choose for a job

ap-point-ment [ə-point′mənt] *noun*, 1) a meeting, a date, a rendezvous 2) a selection, a nomination

ap-prais-al [ə-prā′zəl] *noun*, value or worth, assessment

ap-praise [ə-prāz′] *verb*, to evaluate something to establish its worth

ap-pre-ci-ate [ə-prē′shē-āt′] *verb*, 1) to recognize the value of something, 2)to increase in value

ap-pre-ci-a-tion [ə-prē′shē-ā′shən] *noun*, grateful recognition

ap-pre-hend [ăp′rĭ-hĕnd′] *verb*, 1) to arrest a criminal 2) to anticipate

with anxiety, dread, or, fear
3)to understand
ap-pre-hen-sion [ăp′rĭ-hĕn′shən]
noun, 1) the ability to understand
2) fear, anxiety, dread
ap-pren-tice [ə-prĕn′tĭs] *noun*, a
novice or learner who works with
a master to learn a skill
ap-prise [ə-prīz′] *verb*, to give notice
to, to inform
ap-proach [ə-prōch′] *noun*, 1) a way
of dealing with something, 2) the
way that leads to a place, *verb*,
3) to move toward
ap-proach-able [ə-prō′chə-bəl]
adjective, friendly, nice, easy to
talk to
ap-pro-pri-ate [ə-prō′prē-ĭt]
adjective, 1) suitable, proper, [ə-
prō′prē-āt]*verb*, 2) to allocate, to
set aside for a purpose
ap-pro-pri-a-tion [ə-prō′prē-ā′shən]
noun, a setting apart for a
particular purpose
ap-prov-al [ə-prōō′vəl] *noun*,
1) praise 2) the go-ahead or okay
to proceed, permission
ap-prove [ə-prōōv′] *verb*, to say that
something is favorable
ap-prox-i-mate [ə-prŏk′sə-mĭt]
adjective, 1) almost accurate or
exact, near, [ə-prŏk′sə-māt]*verb*,
2) to estimate or guess
ap-prox-i-mate-ly [ə-prŏk′sə-mĭt-lē]
adverb, closely, nearly
ap-pur-te-nance [ə-pûr′tn-əns]
noun, something connected but
not as important, accessory
A-pril [ā′prəl] *noun*, the fourth
month of the year, having 30 days

a-pron [ā′prən] *noun*, a cover worn
over the front of one's clothing to
protect it
ap-ro-pos [ăp′rə-pō′] *adjective*,
appropriate, pertinent
apt [ăpt] *adjective*, 1) suited to,
fitting, 2) likely or almost certain
ap-ti-tude [ăp′tĭ-tōōd′] *noun*, natural
ability, fitness, talent
a-quar-i-um [ə-kwâr′ē-əm] *noun*, a
container, usually with glass sides,
to keep animals or plants in water
a-quat-ic [ə-kwăt′ĭk] *adjective*,
occurring on or in the water
aq-ue-duct [ăk′wĭ-dŭkt′] *noun*, a
passage used to bring water from
a distant source
aq-ui-fer [ăk′wə-fər] *noun*, an
underground geologic formation
in which the cracks in rock, sand,
soil, or gravel are filled with water
Ar-ab [ăr′ə-b] a native or inhabitant
of Arabia, 2) any of a Semitic
people originating in Arabia
Ar-a-bic [ăr′ə-bĭk] *adjective*,
1) relating to the Arab language and
culture, *noun*, 2) the Semitic
language of the Arabs
ar-bi-ter [är′bĭ-tər] *noun*, a judge, an
umpire or referee, a mediator
ar-bi-trar-y [är′bĭ-trĕr′ē] *adjective*,
chosen without any qualifications
ar-bi-tra-tion [är′bĭ-trā′shən] *noun*,
the hearing and determination of a
matter in dispute by a third party
ar-bor [är′bər] *noun*, a place shaded
by trees or shrubs
arc [ärk] *noun*, a segment of a circle,
a curve in an arch
arch [ärch] *noun*, a curved part of a
structure sometimes supporting.

weight above it, as in bridges,
doorways, etc

ar-chae-ol-o-gist [är′kē-ŏl′ə-jĭst]
noun, an expert in the study of
past civilizations and ancient
cultures, mainly through digging
up remains

ar-chae-ol-o-gy [är′kē-ŏl′ə-jē] *noun*,
the study of ancient things made
by man from an earlier civilization

ar-cha-ic [är-kā′ĭk] *adjective*,
antiquated, ancient, very old

arch-bish-op [ärch-bĭsh′əp] *noun*,
the chief bishop in the Christian
church

ar-cher-y [är′chə-rē] *noun*, the
practice or art of shooting with a
bow and arrow

ar-chi-pel-a-go [är′kə-pĕl′ə-gō′]
noun, a group or chain of islands

ar-chi-tect [är′kĭ-tĕkt′] *noun*, one
who draws plans and
specifications for buildings

ar-chi-tec-ture [är′kĭ-tĕk′chər]
noun, the art and study of building
design and structure

ar-chive [är′kīv′] *noun*, a place in
which public records and historic
documents are kept

arc-tic [ärk′tĭk, är′tĭk] *adjective*,
relating to the area around the
North Pole

ar-dent [är′dnt] *adjective*,
passionate, zealous

ar-dor [är′dər] *noun*, passion, zeal,
enthusiasm, great excitement

ar-du-ous [är′jōō-əs] *adjective*,
difficult, attended with great labor
or exertion, strenuous

are [är] *verb*, the part of the *verb* **is**
used with we, you and they

ar-e-a [âr′ē-ə] *noun*, 1) a location or
vicinity 2) a surface measured by
multiplying the width times the
length

a-re-na [ə-rē′nə] *noun*, a playing
field or a stadium surrounded by
seats used for sports or
entertainment

aren't [ärnt, är′ənt] the
*contraction,*for the two words **are**
and **not**

ar-gon [är′gŏn′] *noun*, one of the
noble gases, a colorless, odorless,
inert gas

ar-gue [är′gyōō] *verb*, to fight by
using words, to disagree, to
debate, to dispute

ar-gu-ment [är′gyə-mənt] *noun*, a
disagreement, a dispute

ar-id [är′ĭd] *adjective*, dry, parched,
dusty

a-rise [ə-rīz′] *verb*, to come up, to
issue, to spring forth, to get up

a-ris-to-crat [ə-rĭs′tə-krăt′] *noun*, a
man or woman of fashion, a
member of the nobility

a-rith-me-tic [ə-rĭth′mĭ-tĭk] *noun*,
the science of numbers

Ar-i-zo-na [ăr′ĭ-zō′nə] *noun*, one of
the 50 United States, located in the
Southwest, the capital is Phoenix.
The state flower of **Arizona** is the
blossom of the saguaro cactus and
the motto is "God enriches."

ark [ärk] *noun*, a large flat-bottomed
ship

Ar-kan-sas [är′kən-sô′] *noun*, a
state in the southern part of the
United States, the capital is Little
Rock. The **Arkansas** state flower
is the apple blossom and the motto
is "The people rule."

arm [ärm] *noun,* 1) the part of the body between the shoulder and the hand, *verb,* 2) to provide with weapons, to prepare for combat

ar-ma-ments [är′mə-mənts] *noun, plural,* military forces and weapons

ar-mi-stice [är′mĭ-stĭs] *noun,* a treaty of peace, a truce

ar-mor [är′mər] *noun,* a covering of metal worn by soldiers for protection

ar-mor-y [är′mə-rē] *noun,* a military storehouse

arms [ärmz] *noun, plural,* weapons, such as bombs and guns

ar-my [är′mē] *noun,* a large number of soldiers training for war on land, ground troops

a-ro-ma [ə-rō′mə] *noun,* smell, scent, fragrance

a-round [ə-round′] *adverb,* 1) in a circle, surrounding all sides, 2) nearby 3) approximately, *preposition,* 4) on every side

a-rouse [ə-rouz′] *verb,* 1) to awaken, to animate, to coax 2) to excite, to provoke, to stimulate

ar-raign [ə-rān′] *verb,* to call to account, to bring into court to answer charges, to accuse publicly

ar-range [ə-rānj′] *verb,* to put in proper order or sequence

ar-range-ment [ə-rānj′mənt] *noun,* 1) the act of putting in an orderly condition 2) plan

ar-ray [ə-rā′] *noun,* 1) a display, an exhibition, *verb,* 2) to arrange in a display, to place, to order

ar-rest [ə-rĕst′] *noun,* 1) the act of taking someone into custody, *verb,* 2) to stop the movement or progress of 3) to seize by legal authority and charge with breaking the law

ar-ri-val [ə-rī′vəl] *noun,* the moment when a place or object is reached

ar-rive [ə-rīv′] *verb,* to reach a destination or a goal

ar-ro-gance [ăr′ə-gəns] *noun,* an overbearing sense of self-importance, excessive pride

ar-ro-gant [ăr′ə-gənt] *adjective,* having a high opinion of oneself

ar-row [ăr′ō] *noun,* 1) a pointed stick that is shot from a bow 2) a mark shaped like an arrow that shows direction

ar-se-nal [är′sə-nəl] *noun,* a collection of weapons, a storehouse of ammunition

ar-son [är′sən] *noun,* the crime of purposely setting property on fire

art [ärt] *noun,* the creation of beautiful or significant things through music, drawing, painting, sculpture, cooking, dancing, etc.

ar-ter-y [är′tə-rē] *noun,* the thick blood vessels that carry blood from the heart

ar-te-sian well [är-tē′zhən] *noun,* a well that taps ground water that is under pressure and therefore does not require a pump, so called from Artois, France

ar-thri-tis [är-thrī′tĭs] *noun,* inflammation of the joints

ar-ti-cle [är′tĭ-kəl] *noun,* 1) a particular thing 2) a section, provision, item 3) a brief written composition, as in a newspaper or magazine 4) one of the limiting articles, *a, an,* or *the*

ar-tic-u-late [är-tĭk′yə-lĭt] *adjective*, 1) effective, distinct, able to express ideas clearly, [är-tĭk′yə-lāt] *verb*, 2) to speak clearly to express an idea

ar-ti-fact [är′tə-făkt′] *noun*, something made by humans from an earlier civilization

ar-ti-fice [är′tə-fĭs] *noun*, skill, scheme, ability, trick

ar-ti-fi-cial [är′tə-fĭsh′əl] *adjective*, 1) made of or contrived by art 2) not natural, not made by nature, made by humans 3) assumed, affected

ar-t-il-ler-y [är-tĭl′ə-rē] *noun*, the mounted guns in an army, the soldiers in charge of such guns

art-ist [är′tĭst] *noun*, a person skilled in the techniques of the fine arts, such as painting, dancing, drama, etc.

as [ăz] *conjunction*, 1) when, while 2) because, *preposition*, 3) in such a way, like

ascend [ə-sĕnd′] *verb*, to climb, to go upward, to rise

as-cen-sion [ə-sĕn′shən] *noun*, the act of going up, a rising

as-cent [ə-sĕnt′] *noun*, the act of climbing up an incline, a slope

as-cer-tain [ăs′ər-tān′] *verb*, to determine, to establish

as-cet-ic [ə-sĕt′ĭk] *adjective*, self-denying, austere, disciplined

ash [ăsh] *noun*, 1) the gray powder residue left after something has burned 2) a tree of the olive family, with hard wood

a-shamed [ə-shāmd′] *adjective*, upset because you have done something that you think is silly, not good enough or wrong, embarrassed, feeling inadequate

a-shore [ə-shôr′] *adverb*, on to land

A-sia [ā′zhə] *noun*, one of the seven continents in the world, holding 57% of the population

a-side [ə-sīd′] *adverb*, 1) to or toward one side, away, *noun*, 2) departure from the main topic, 3) a whisper

ask [ăsk] *verb*, 1) to pose or speak a question, to inquire 2) to request something

a-skew [ə-skyōō′] *adjective*, out of line, crooked

a-sleep [ə-slēp′] *adjective*, sleeping, not awake

as-pect [ăs′pĕkt] *noun*, 1) appearance, look 2) part, or point of view

as-phalt [ăs′fôlt′] *noun*, a tar like material mixed with sand or gravel for highway surfaces or pavement,

as-phyx-i-a-tion [ăs-fĭk′sē-ā′-shən] *noun*, death by lack of oxygen

as-pi-ra-tion [ăs′pə-rā′shən] *noun*, an ambition, a strong desire

as-pire [ə-spīr′] *verb*, to desire, to strive, to hope for

as-pi-rin [ăs′pər-ĭn, -prĭn] *noun*, a medicine used to relieve pain, acetylsalicylic acid

as-sas-si-nate [ə-săs′ə-nāt′] *verb*, to murder a public official or other important person

as-sault [ə-sôlt′] *noun*, 1) an attack, *verb*, 2) to strike, to hit

as-sem-ble [ə-sĕm′bəl] *verb*, to gather or put together

as-sem-bly [ə-sĕm′blē] *noun*, 1) a gathering, for educational, religious, or entertainment programs of students and teachers 2) a legal body such as Congress or a legislature

as-sert [ə-sûrt′] *verb*, to declare, to state forcefully

as-sess [ə-sĕs′] *verb*, to evaluate

as-sess-ment [ə-sĕs′mənt] *noun*, an appraisal, an estimation

as-set [ăs′ĕt′] *noun*, something of value or worth

as-sign [ə-sīn′] *verb*, 1) to give out or allot 2) to delegate a task

as-sign-ment [ə-sīn′mənt] *noun*, homework, an obligation, work given to someone to accomplish

as-sim-i-late [ə-sĭm′ə-lāt′] *verb*, to take in food or knowledge, to make part of oneself

as-sist [ə-sĭst′] *verb*, to aid or help

as-sis-tance [ə-sĭs′təns] *noun*, help or aid given

as-sis-tant [ə-sĭs′tənt] *noun*, a helper, an aide, a subordinate,

as-so-ci-ate *noun*, [ə-sō′shē-ĭt] 1) a colleague or co-worker, [ə-sō′shē-āt′] *verb*, 2) to think of something in relation with something else 3) to keep company, to socialize with someone

as-so-ci-a-tion [ə-sō′sē-ā′shən,] *noun*, a group of people joined together for one purpose

as-sort-ment [ə-sôrt′mənt] *noun*, a variety of things

as-suage [ə-swāj′] *verb*, to lessen, to ease, to comfort

as-sume [ə-sōōm′] *verb*, to think something is true without proof

as-sump-tion [ə-sŭmp′shən] *noun*, something taken for granted

as-sur-ance [ə-shŏŏr′əns] *noun*, a promise, a pledge

as-sure [ə-shŏŏr′] *verb*, to tell someone firmly, to promise

as-ter-isk [ăs′tə-rĭsk′] *noun*, the sign *

as-ter-oid [ăs′tə-roid′] *noun*, small planets, most of which are located between Mars and Jupiter, that revolve around the sun

asth-ma [ăz′mə] *noun*, a respiratory disorder that causes difficulty in breathing accompanied by wheezing

a-stig-ma-tism [ə-stĭg′mə-tĭz′əm] *noun*, an eye defect that prevents proper focus

as-ton-ish [ə-stŏn′ĭsh] *verb*, to give a feeling of surprise, amaze

as-ton-ish-ment [ə-stŏn′ĭsh-mənt] *noun*, complete surprise, amazement

as-tound [ə-stound′] *verb*, to amaze, to shock, to surprise

as-tral [ăs′trəl] *adjective*, relating to the stars

a-stray [ə-strā′] *adverb*, off course, in error

as-trin-gent [ə-strĭn′jənt] *adjective*, capable of drawing tissue together

as-tro-naut [ăs′trə-nôt′] *noun*, a person who travels in space

as-trol-o-gy [ə-strŏl′ə-jē] *noun*, the study of the assumed influence of planets and stars on the course of human affairs

as-tron-o-mer [ə-strŏn′ə-mər] *noun*, a person who studies the stars and the heavens

as-tro-nom-i-cal [ăs′trə-nŏm′ĭ-kəl] *adjective*, enormously large or extensive, huge

as-tron-o-my [ə-strŏn′ə-mē] *noun*, the study of the sun, moon, stars, and the heavens

as-tute [ə-stōōt′] *adjective*, having a clever, shrewd, or cunning mind, perceptive, insightful

a-sy-lum [ə-sī′ləm] *noun*, protection from persecution

at [ăt] *preposition*, 1) showing where 2) showing when 3) showing how much

ate [āt] *verb*, the *past tense* of **eat**

a-the-ism [ā′thē-ĭz′əm] *noun*, the belief that there is no God

ath-lete [ăth′lēt′] *noun*, someone who is good at sports

ath-let-ic [ăth-lĕt′ĭk] *adjective*, strong, vigorous, having to do with sports

at-las [ăt′ləs] *noun*, a book or section of a book that has maps

at-mos-phere [ăt′mə-sfîr′] *noun*, 1) the mass of air surrounding the earth 2) the mood or feeling of a place, a tone conveyed

at-om [ăt′əm] *noun*, the smallest particle of an element

a-tom-ic [ə-tŏm′ĭk] *adjective*, tiny, infinitesimal, having to do with atoms

at-om-iz-er [ăt′ə-mī′zər] *noun*, an instrument for reducing a liquid to a fine spray

a-tri-um [ā′trē-əm] *noun*, **atria** or **atriums**, *plural*, 1) one of the chambers of the heart 2) the central court in a Roman building

a-tro-cious [ə-trō′shəs] *adjective*, very bad, outrageously cruel

a-troc-i-ty [ə-trŏs′ĭ-tē] *noun*, a brutal deed, a cruel act

a-tro-phy [ăt′rə-fē] *verb*, to stop the development of an organ, to wither from lack of use

at-tach [ə-tăch′] *verb*, 1) to connect something with something else 2) to feel affection toward someone 3) to ascribe

at-tach-ment [ə-tăch′mənt] *noun*, 1) an affection, fondness 2) an additional part for a machine

at-tack [ə-tăk′] *noun*, 1) fight, an attempt to harm someone, *verb*, 2) to assail, to try to injure someone, to assault

at-tain [ə-tān′] *verb*, to succeed in getting something done, to reach a goal

at-tempt [ə-tĕmpt′] *noun*, 1) a try, an endeavor, *verb*, 2) to try, to endeavor, to make an effort

at-tend [ə-tĕnd′] *verb*, 1) to be present at 2) to take care of 3) to pay attention to

at-tend-ance [ə-tĕn′dəns] *noun*, the act of showing up or putting in an appearance, presence

at-tend-ant [ə-tĕn′dənt] *noun*, one who accompanies or attends, as a companion, a servant

at-ten-tion [ə-tĕn′shən] *noun*, application of the mind to something, concentration

at-ten-tive [ə-tĕn′tĭv] *adjective*, careful to notice little things

at-tic [ăt′ĭk] *noun*, the top floor of a house, right under the roof

at-tire [ə-tīr′] *noun*, anything that dresses or adorns, clothing

at-ti-tude [ăt′ĭ-tōōd′] *noun*, a mood or feeling, a way of thinking

at-tor-ney [ə-tûr′nē] *noun*, one legally authorized to act for another, a lawyer

at-tract [ə-trăkt′] *verb*, 1) to draw the attention of someone or something 2) to cause someone or something to come near

at-trac-tion [ə-trăk′shən] *noun*, 1) the power to bring things together 2) a fascination that holds someone's attention

at-trac-tive [ə-trăk′tĭv] *adjective*, pleasing to look at, appealing

at-trib-ute *noun*, [ə-trăb′yōōt] 1) a distinguishing feature that belongs to someone, [ətrĭb′yōōt] *verb*, 2) to explain how one thing is associated with another

at-tri-tion [ə-trĭsh′ən] *noun*, a gradual wearing down

auc-tion [ôk′shən] *noun*, a public sale at which buyers bid on items to be sold

auc-tion-eer [ôk′shə-nîr′] *noun*, one licensed to hold a public sale at which items go to the highest bidder

au-dac-i-ty [ô-dăs′ĭ-tē] *noun*, impertinence, boldness, self-assurance, daring

au-di-ble [ô′də-bəl] *adjective*, capable of being heard

au-di-ence [ô′dē-əns] *noun*, 1) a group gathered to watch or listen to a performance 2) a formal hearing

au-di-o [ô′dē-ō′] *adjective*, relating to sound or sound reproduction

au-dit [ô′dĭt] *noun*, 1) a special examination of accounting records, *verb*, 2) to examine or investigate, to evaluate

au-di-tion [ô-dĭsh′ən] *noun*, a tryout for a performance

au-di-to-ri-um [ô′dĭ-tôr′ē-əm] *noun*, an assembly hall with a stage and seats

au-ger [ô′gər] *noun*, a tool for making holes, a drill

aug-ment [ôg-mĕnt′] *verb*, to make larger, to increase, to add on to

au-gur [ô′gər] *verb*, to foretell, to see into the future, to portend, to be an omen

Au-gust [ô′gəst] *noun*, the eighth month of the year, having 31 days

aunt [ănt, änt] *noun*, the sister of one of your parents or the wife of the brother of one parent

aus-pices [ô′spĭ-sēz′] *noun*, *plural*, 1) patronage, protection 2) omens

aus-pi-cious [ô-spĭsh′əs] *adjective*, fortunate, showing signs that promise success

aus-tere [ô-stîr′] *adjective*, 1) severe or strict in judging, harsh, rough or bitter acting, 2) very plain, simple, bare, ascetic

Aus-tra-lia [ô-strāl′yə] *noun*, one of the seven continents in the world, the only continent that is also a country containing .5% of the world's population

au-then-tic [ô-thĕn′tĭk] *adjective*,
genuine, known to be true

au-then-ti-cate [ô-thĕn′tĭ-kāt′]
verb, to prove genuine

au-thor [ô′thər] *noun*, a person
who writes books, articles, etc.

au-thor-i-ta-tive [ə-thôr′ĭ-tā′tĭv] -
adjective, reliably accurate

au-thor-i-ty [ə-thôr′ĭ-tē] *noun*, 1) a
person who runs something or
controls it 2) command, prestige,
influence, control 3) an expert

au-thor-ize [ô′thə-rīz′] *verb*, 1) to
empower 2) to make legal 3) to
give permission to act

au-to-bi-og-ra-phy
[ô′tō-bī-ŏg′rə-fē] *noun*, a story
written about the author's life

au-to-crat [ô′tə-krăt′] *noun*, a ruler
with supreme power

au-to-graph [ô′tə-grăf′] *noun*,
a person's signature

au-to-mat-ic [ô′tə-măt′ĭk]
adjective, acting mechanically
without human direction

au-to-mat-i-cal-ly [ô′tə-măt′ĭk-lē]
adverb, 1) by a machine 2)
without trying or thinking first

au-tom-a-tion [ô′tə-mā′shən]
noun, a machine that imitates the
actions of humans, a robot

au-to-mo-bile [ô′tə-mō-bēl′] *noun*,
a vehicle on wheels, powered by
an engine to transport people on
roads, a car

au-ton-o-mous [ô-tŏn′ə-məs]
adjective, self-governing, acting
independently from government

au-top-sy [ô′tŏp′sē] *noun*, the
dissection of a dead body to
determine the cause of death

au-tumn [ô′təm] *noun*, the third
season of each year, between
summer and winter, September
22-December 21, known as fall

aux-il-ia-ry [ôg-zĭl′yə-rē]
adjective, additional, serving
alongside another, supporting

a-vail-a-ble [ə-vā′lə-bəl] *adjective*,
capable of being used, accessible

av-a-lanche [ăv′ə-lănch′] *noun*, a
large overwhelming quantity of
snow, rocks, or mud that falls
from a mountain suddenly,
gaining size as it falls

av-a-rice [ăv′ə-rĭs] *noun*, greed for
money or power

a-venge [ə-vĕnj′] *verb*, to punish in
kind, to retaliate, to get even

av-e-nue [ăv′ə-nōō′] *noun*, a wide
road, often with many roads
intersecting at right angles

av-er-age [ăv′ər-ĭj] *adjective*,
1) ordinary, usual, typical, *noun*,
2) the mean value of a set of
numbers, *verb*, 3) to find the
mean

a-ver-sion [ə-vûr′zhən] *noun*, a
dislike, antipathy, opposition

a-vert [ə-vûrt′] *verb*, to avoid, to
prevent or turn away

a-vi-a-tion [ā′vē-ā′shən, ăv′ē-]
noun, air transportation

a-vi-a-tor [ā′vē-ā′tər] *noun*, an
airplane or helicopter pilot

av-id [ăv′ĭd] *adjective*, eager,
enthusiastic, excited

av-o-ca-tion [ăv′ō-kā′shən] *noun*,
a hobby

a-void [ə-void′] *verb*, to stay away
from, to evade, to shun

a-wait [ə-wāt'] *verb*, to expect, to wait, to anticipate

a-wake [ə-wāk'] *adjective*, not sleeping, alert

a-ward [ə-wôrd'] *noun*, 1) a prize or an honor to recognize exceptional service, achievement, etc., *verb*, 2) to present a certificate or plaque or trophy in recognition of an honor

a-ware [ə-wâr'] *adjective*, knowing, conscious, informed

a-way [ə-wā'] *adverb*, 1) off in a different direction 2) from one's possession

awe [ô] *noun*, a solemn wonder

aw-ful [ô'fəl] *adjective*, very bad, appalling, frightful, horrible

awk-ward [ôk'wərd] *adjective*, 1) clumsy, ungraceful 2) embarrassing

awl [ôl] *noun*, a pointed tool used to make holes in wood or leather

awn-ing [ô'nĭng] *noun*, a sunshade, a canvas covering for a porch, patio, deck, etc.

a-wry [ə-rī'] *adjective*, 1) amiss, crooked, wrong, *adverb*, 2) distorted, twisted to one side

ax or axe [ăks] *noun*, a tool with a metal blade fixed onto a handle, used for chopping

ax-i-om [ăk'sē-əm] *noun*, a self-evident truth or principle

ax-is [ăk'sĭs] *noun*, a real or imaginary line around which something rotates

ax-le [ăk'səl] *noun*, the rod on which a wheel revolves

B

ba-by [bā'bē] *noun*, an infant, a very young child or animal

bach-e-lor [băch'ə-lər] *noun*, a man who has never been married

back [băk] *adverb*, 1) to or in a place where something or someone was before 2) toward the back part, away from the front, *noun*, 3) the part of the body opposite the face, extending from the neck to the hips, *verb*, 4) to move in the opposite direction from 5) to give support to

back-ground [băk'ground'] *noun*, 1) the surroundings behind something 2) past experience, culture

back-ward [băk'wərd] *adjective*, 1) having the part designed for the back in the front 2) following tradition and resisting progress, *adverb*, 3) in reverse 4) beginning at the end

ba-con [bā'kən] *noun*, meat from the back and sides of a pig, salted and smoked

bac-te-ri-um [băk-tîr'ē-əm] *noun*, **bacteria**, *plural*, a single-celled living thing that cannot be seen without a microscope, reproducing rapidly and sometimes causing diseases

bad [băd] *adjective*, 1) not good, rotten 2) severe, unpleasant

badge [băj] *noun*, a pin or emblem worn to show authority or accomplishment

baf-fle [băf'əl] *verb*, to mix up, to confuse, to puzzle

bag [băg] *noun*, a container made of paper, cloth, plastic, or leather that has an opening at the top or in the side

bag-gage [băg′ĭj] *noun, no plural*, suitcases, bags, or trunks one takes along on a journey

bail [bāl] *noun*, 1) a bond or pledge backed with money or property, *verb*, 2) to ladle or empty out

bail-iff [bā′lĭf] *noun*, an official who keeps order in the court

bait [bāt] *noun*, 1) food used to lure or entice fish or animals, *verb*, 2) to annoy or taunt

bake [bāk] *verb*, to cook by dry heat, usually in an oven

bak-er [bā′kər] *noun*, someone who makes pastries, cakes and breads for a living

bak-er-y [bā′kə-rē] *noun*, a place where pastries, cakes, and breads are made and sold

bal-ance [băl′əns] *noun*, 1) steadiness 2) an instrument used to weigh something 3) the difference between the debits and credits of an account, *verb*, 4) to keep oneself steady 5) to make equal and stable, to compensate for

bal-co-ny [băl′kə-nē] *noun*, a porch outside of a building and above the first floor

bald [bôld] *adjective*, having no hair

bale [bāl] *noun*, 1) a large amount of materials bundled tightly together, *verb*, 2) to bundle into a package

balk [bôk] *verb*, 1) to hesitate, to refuse to act 2) to hinder

ball [bôl] *noun*, 1) a round object used in games or as a toy 2) a large party for dancing

bal-lad [băl′əd] *noun*, a poem or song that tells a story

bal-last [băl′əst] *noun*, 1) heavy material carried by a ship to balance it 2) crushed stones

bal-let [bă-lā′] *noun*, a play without speech in which the story is told through dance

bal-loon [bə-loon′] *noun*, a rubber bag that expands as it is filled with air or gas

bal-lot [băl′ət] *noun*, 1) a printed ticket used in voting to make a choice 2) the whole vote cast

balm [bäm] *noun*, 1) something that relieves pain 2) a soothing ointment

balm-y [bä′mē] *adjective*, mild, refreshing, soft and warm

bam-boo [băm-boo′] *noun*, a woody grass with hollow stems, abundant in the tropics

ban [băn] *noun*, 1) an order that does not allow something, *verb*, 2) to not allow something or to prevent it from taking place

ba-nal [bə-năl′, bā′nəl] *adjective*, ordinary, commonplace, trite

ba-nan-a [bə-năn′ə] *noun*, a long yellow tropical fruit having a tasty soft pulp

band [bănd] *noun*, 1) a group of musicians who get together to play their instruments, usually brass, percussion, and woodwinds 2) a strip of something 3) a group 4) a piece that wraps around something, *verb*, 5) to join together

band-age [băn/dĭj] *noun*, 1) a piece of cloth or adhesive strip put over a wound, *verb*, 2) to cover a wound with a cloth or adhesive strip

ban-dan-na [băn-dăn/ə] *noun*, a cotton scarf or handkerchief

ban-dit [băn/dĭt] *noun*, a robber

ban-dy [băn/dē] *verb*, to exchange, to pass to and fro

bane [bān] *noun*, the cause of ruin

bane-ful [bān/fəl] *adjective*, ruinous, having poisonous qualities, causing misery

bang [băng] *noun*, 1) a startling loud sound, *verb*, 2) to produce a loud sound by striking one thing against another

ban-ish [băn/ĭsh] *verb*, 1) to send away, to dismiss 2)2 to exile as a form of punishment

ban-is-ter [băn/ĭ-stər] *noun*, a railing that guards the edges of stairs to prevent someone from falling

ban-jo [băn/jō] *noun*, a stringed musical instrument, like a ukulele or guitar, but with a circular sound box

bank [băngk] *noun*, 1) the land along a body of water, the side of a hill 2) a commercial institution where money is kept and loaned

bank-er [băng/kər] *noun*, one who conducts the business of a bank

bank-rupt [băngk/rŭpt] *adjective*, broke, out of business

ban-ner [băn/ər] *noun*, a flag, a cloth bearing an emblem

ban-quet [băng/kwĭt] *noun*, a feast or ceremonious dinner

ban-ter [băn/tər] *noun*, 1) good-natured ridiculing or teasing 2) to speak or to address in a witty or teasing manner

bap-tism [băp/tĭz/əm] *noun*, the ceremony of initiation into Christianity

bap-tize [băp-tīz/] *verb*, to sprinkle someone with holy water and bestow a name

bar [bär] *noun*, 1) a counter where drinks are sold 2) a long solid object made of wood or metal 3) the legal profession, *verb*, 4) to exclude or block

barb [bärb] *noun*, the sharp projections from a fishhook, arrow, etc.

bar-ber [bär/bər] *noun*, a person who cuts men's hair

bare [bâr] *adjective*, 1) uncovered, naked 2) unadorned, empty

bare-ly [bâr/lē] *adverb*, almost, not, hardly, only, scarcely

bar-gain [bär/gĭn] *noun*, 1) something bought at a lower price than expected 2) an agreement or compact between two parties, *verb*, 3) to haggle for a lower price

barge [bärj] *noun*, a large boat with a flat bottom, used to carry things on a river or a canal

bar-i-um [bâr/ē-əm] *noun*, one of the elements of the alkaline earth group

bark [bärk] *noun*, 1) the outer covering of a tree trunk and branches 2) a sound made by a

dog or a brusque voice, *verb,*
3) to speak like a dog

bar-ley [bär′lē] *noun,* one of the cereal grains

barn [bärn] *noun,* a farm building where animals and harvested crops are kept

bar-na-cle [bär′nə-kəl] *noun,* a marine crustacean that attaches itself to rocks and boats

ba-rom-e-ter [bə-rŏm′ĭ-tər] *noun,* a device that measures air pressure in the atmosphere

bar-on [băr′ən] *noun,* a nobleman, an aristocrat, a tycoon

ba-roque [bə-rōk′] *adjective,* an ornate style of the 17th and 18th centuries

bar-racks [băr′əks] *noun, plural,* buildings for lodging soldiers

bar-rage [bär′ĭj] *noun,* an artillary attack covering a wide area

bar-rel [băr′əl] *noun,* 1) a large container shaped like a cylinder 2) the long metal tube forming part of a gun

bar-ren [băr′ən] *adjective,* 1) bleak, lacking in good things 2) unable to bear children, unable to support growth

bar-ri-cade [băr′ĭ-kād] *noun,* 1) an obstruction or means of defense, a barrier, *verb,* 2) to block, to fortify, to bar

bar-ri-er [băr′ē-ər] *noun,* 1) a stumbling block, a deterrent, an obstacle, something blocking the way 2) a fence or wall to mark the limits of a place

bar-ris-ter [băr′ĭ-stər] *noun,* in England, a counselor at law, a lawyer

bar-ter [bär′tər] *verb,* to trade

base [bās] *adjective,* 1) low, menial, inferior, *noun,* 2) the bottom on which something stands 3) an area designated safe, in baseball one of four sandbags

base-ball [bās′bôl′] *noun,* a game played with a bat and a ball by two teams with nine players on a side, on a field with four bases at the corners of a diamond

base-ment [bās′mənt] *noun,* storage or living space in the foundation of a building

ba-sic [bā′sĭk] *adjective,* 1) forming a starting point, fundamental 2) plain, simple

ba-sin [bā′sĭn] *noun,* 1) a low, bowl-shaped area, a depression in the land 2) a shallow sink

ba-sis [bā′sĭs] *noun,* the starting point or central idea of something, the core

bask [băsk] *verb,* to lay in the sun

bas-ket [băs′kĭt] *noun,* a container woven from reeds or twigs and used to carry things

bas-ket-ball [băs′kĭt-bôl′] *noun,* a game in which two teams of five players each compete to throw a ball through a hoop

bass [bās] *adjective,* 1) the lowest range of the male voice, as in sound, [băs] *noun,* 2) a fresh-water fish

bas-tion [băs′chən] *noun,* a fortress, a defense

bat [băt] *noun,* 1) a piece of wood used to hit a ball in a game 2) a flying mammal, *verb,* 3) to hit a ball with a piece of wood

batch [băch] *noun*, a number of things in a group

bath [băth, bäth] *noun*, 1) a container large enough to hold water to wash a body 2) the act of washing one's body

bathe [bāth] *verb*, to wash with water, usually a part of a body

bath-room [băth′rōōm] *noun*, a room with a toilet and a sink where people wash

ba-ton [bə-tŏn] *noun*, a wand, a night-stick, a rod, a stick used for conducting an orchestra

bat-tal-ion [bə-tăl′yən] *noun*, a large group of army soldiers ready for battle

bat-ter [băt′ər] *noun*, 1) the person holding the bat in baseball 2) a mixture of flour, eggs, and milk, *verb*, 3) to hit repeatedly

bat-ter-y [băt′ə-rē] *noun*, an apparatus for storing chemical energy and converting it to electrical power

bat-tle [băt′l] *noun*, 1) a fight or skirmish between people or different groups, *verb*, 2) to fight

bay [bā] *adjective*, 1) reddish-brown, *noun*, 2) part of a sea that stretches into land 3) a recess in a room 4) a tree or shrub of the laurel family, *verb*, 5) to howl, to bark at

bay-o-net [bā′ə-nĭt] *noun*, a blade on the end of a rifle

ba-zaar [bə-zär′] *noun*, a marketplace where miscellaneous articles are sold

B.C., signifying a time before the birth of Christ

be [bē] *verb*, 1) used to give information about people or things and to join words for people or things to the qualities or position they have 2) the present indicative of verb **be**

Singular	Plural
I **am**	We **are**

I am proud of you.
We are happy to see you.

You **are**   You **are**
You are what you eat.
You are the students in the class.

He/she/it **is**   They **are**
He is a gentleman, he is kind.
They are all our friends.

Past Tense

I **was**   We **were**
I was waiting for you.
We were hoping you could stay.

You **were**   You **were**
You were a true friend.
You were good children.

He/she it **was**   They **were**
It was time to go.
They were our heroes.

beach [bēch] *noun*, a shore of sand or pebbles along a lake or ocean

bea-con [bē′kən] *noun*, a lantern, a beam of light, a signal

bead [bēd] *noun*, a small ball of glass or other material, with a small hole for string or wire to pass through

beak [bēk] *noun*, the hard, pointed mouth of a bird

beak-er [bē′kər] *noun*, 1) a deep, open-mouthed, thin, glass vessel with a lip 2) a tall wide-mouthed cup

beam [bēm] *noun,* 1) a large piece of timber used to brace or support a ceiling 2) a ray, a shaft of light, *verb,* 3) to smile happily 4) to send or transmit, to shine

bean [bēn] *noun,* the seed of any bean plant, often used for food

bear [bâr] *adjective,* 1) referring to unfavorable market conditions. *noun,* 2) a large, furry mammal with four feet, *verb,* 3) to carry 4) to suffer or endure 5) to produce, to bring forth, to yield 6) to exhibit, to show, to relate

beard [bîrd] *noun,* hair on the face below the mouth

beast [bēst] *noun,* an animal, especially a savage animal

beat [bēt] *noun,* 1) a stroke or movement that is part of a rhythm, *verb,* 2) to pound, to tap 3) to conquer, to defeat

beau-ti-ful [byo͞o′tə-fəl] *adjective,* charming and delightful to the senses, very pretty, lovely

beau-ty [byo͞o′tē] *noun,* qualities pleasing to the eye or ear, charm

bea-ver [bē′vər] *noun,* an amphibious rodent with brown fur that builds dams as homes

be-cause [bǐ-kôz] *conjunction,* since, for the reason that

beck-on [bĕk′ən] *verb,* to signal, call or summon to come over by motioning silently

be-come [bǐ-kŭm′] *verb,* to change or to grow to be, to suit

bed [bĕd] *noun,* 1) a piece of furniture on which someone sleeps 2) the bottom of something 3) a garden plot

bed-lam [bĕd′ləm] *noun,* confusion, noise, uproar

bed-room [bĕd′ro͞om] *noun,* the room for sleeping in

bee [bē] *noun,* an insect with a stinger and wings that makes honey and carries pollen from flower to flower

beech [bēch] *noun,* a family of hardwood trees that includes oak and elm

beef [bēf] *noun,* the meat from cattle

bee-hive [bē′hīv′] *noun,* a house made for bees to live in

been [bǐn] the *past tense* of the *verb* **to be**

beer [bîr] *noun,* an alcoholic beverage made of grain and hops

beet [bēt] *noun,* a purplish root vegetable, used for dye and eaten like a turnip

bee-tle [bēt′l] *noun,* an insect whose outside wings make a hard, protective cover for its body

be-fore [bǐ-fôr] *adverb,* 1) happening in advance of, earlier than, *preposition,* 2) in front of, ahead of

be-fore-hand [bǐ-fôr′hănd] *adverb,* ahead of, in advance

beg [bĕg] *verb,* to ask as a favor

be-gan [bǐ-găn′] *verb, past tense* of **begin**

beg-gar [bĕg′ər] *noun,* one who asks for favors or money

be-gin [bǐ-gǐn′] *verb,* to start, to commence

be-gin-ning [bǐ-gǐn'ǐng] *noun*, the start of something, the origin

be-guile [bǐ-gīl'] *verb*, to divert or to entertain, to trick, to charm

be-gun [bǐ-gǔn'] *verb, past tense* of **begin**

be-half [bǐ-hǎf] *noun*, interest, side

be-have [bǐ-hāv'] *verb*, to act, to conduct yourself

be-hav-ior [bǐ-hāv'yər] *noun*, manner of acting or bearing oneself, conduct

be-he-moth [bǐ-hē'məth] *noun*, a huge creature

be-hind [bǐ-hīnd'] *adverb*, 1) further away from, late, *preposition*, 2) following, at the back of, remaining after

be-hoove [bǐ-hoov'] *verb*, to be fitting or proper, to require

be-ing [bē'ǐng] *noun*, 1) a living thing, *verb*, 2) *present participle of the verb* to **be**

be-la-bor [bǐ-lā'bər] *verb*, to repeat over and over

be-lat-ed [bǐ-lā'tǐd] *adjective*, too late, delayed, tardy

be-lea-guered [bǐ-lē'gərd] *adjective*, in a difficult position, besieged, attacked

bel-fry [běl'frē] *noun*, a tower where bells hang above a building

be-lie [bǐ-lī'] *verb*, to contradict, to give a false impression

be-lief [bǐ-lēf'] *noun*, faith, acceptance, conviction

be-lieve [bǐ-lēv'] *verb*, 1) to have faith or confidence 2) to think

be-lit-tle [bǐ-lǐt'l] *verb*, to tease, to make fun of

bell [běl] *noun*, a round, hollow object of metal or glass that sounds when it is struck

bel-li-cose [běl'ǐ-kōs'] *adjective*, warlike, ready to fight

bel-lig-er-ent [bə-lǐj'ər-ənt] *adjective*, hostile, pugnacious, preparing to fight, aggressive

bel-low [běl'ō] *verb*, to make a loud deep sound like a bull

bel-lows [běl'ōz] *noun, plural,* a machine that draws air through a valve and expels it through a tube by alternate expansion and contraction, used in an organ or to blow air on a fire

bel-ly [běl'ē] *noun*, stomach, gut,

be-long [bǐ-lông] *verb*, 1) to be a part of, to be a member 2) to own or have possession of

be-long-ings [bǐ-lông'ǐngs] *noun, plural,* one's personal possessions

be-lov-ed [bǐ-lǔv'ǐd] *adjective*, cherished, highly valued, adored

be-low [bǐ-lō'] *adverb*, 1) at a lower level, *preposition*, 2) at a lower place or rank

belt [bělt] *noun*, 1) a band worn around the waist,, often made of cloth or leather 2) a band or strip indicating a region or zone, *verb*, 3) to hit or smack, to clobber 4) to strap, to surround, to attach by wrapping a cord around something

bench [běnch] *noun*, 1) a long seat often wooden 2) the table at which someone works 3) a judge's seat in court

bend [bĕnd] *noun*, 1) a curve, *verb*, 2) to shape into a curve or make crooked 3) to stoop

be-neath [bĭ-nēth′] *preposition*, below, under, at a lower level than

ben-e-dic-tion [bĕn′ĭ-dĭk′shən] *noun*, a blessing

ben-e-fac-tor [bĕn′ə-făk′tər] *noun*, a gift-giver, a patron

be-nef-i-cent [bə-nĕf′ĭ-sənt] *adjective*, performing acts of kindness and charity, generous

ben-e-fi-cial [bĕn′ə-fĭsh′əl] *adjectiven*, useful, profitable

ben-e-fi-ci-ar-y [bĕn′ə-fĭsh′ē-ĕr′ē] *noun*, one who is going to receive something valuable

ben-e-fit [bĕn′ə-fĭt] *noun*, 1) an advantage, 2) a fundraiser *verb*, 3) to be helpful, to aid

be-nev-o-lence [bə-nĕv′ə-ləns] *noun*, goodwill or kindness, charity given, generosity

be-nev-o-lent [bə-nĕv′ə-lənt] *adjective*, generous, kind-hearted

be-nign [bĭ-nīn′] *adjective*, harmless, not cancerous, kind

bent [bĕnt] *past tense* of **bend**

be-quest [bĭ-kwĕst′] *noun*, the act of leaving by a written will, a legacy for the next generation

be-rate [bĭ-rāt′] *verb*, to criticize or scold vigorously

be-reave-ment [bĭ-rēv′-mĕnt] *noun,* the state of being deprived of something, sorrow, mourning

be-reft [bĭ-rĕft′] *adjective*, lacking, deprived of, doing without

ber-ry [bĕ-rē′] *noun*, a small, round fruit from a bush

ber-serk [bər-sûrk] *adjective*, frenzied with rage, crazy

be-seech [bĭ-sēch′] *verb*, to ask or entreat, to implore, to beg

be-side [bĭ-sīd′] *preposition*, next to, at the side of, adjacent

be-sides [bĭ-sīdz′] *adverb*, also, in addition to, as an extra

be-siege [bĭ-sēj′] *verb*, to surround with armed forces, to harass, to encircle, to crowd around

best [bĕst] *adjective*, finest, exceeding all others in quality

be-stow [bĭ-stō′] *verb*, to give something, to confer

bet [bĕt] *noun*, 1) an agreement to risk money on the odds of winning, *verb*, 2) to risk money on a gamble, to wager

be-tray [bĭ-trā′] *verb*, to break a trust, to reveal a secret

bet-ter [bĕt′ər] *adjective*, 1) superior, *adverb*, 2) more, larger, *verb*, 3) to improve

bet-ween [bĭ-twēn′] *adverb*, 1) showing where in relation to things or places on either side 2) showing when in relation to events before and after, *preposition*, 3) showing how things are joined 4) showing how things are divided

bev-er-age [bĕv′ər-ij] *noun*, a drink, a liquid refreshment

bev-y [bĕv′ē] *noun*, 1) a large group, 2) a group of birds

be-ware [bĭ-wâr′]*verb*, to be wary, to be careful, to be on guard of

be-wild-er-ed [bĭ-wĭl′dərd] *adjective*, confused, puzzled, perplexed

be-witch [bǐ-wǐch′] *verb* to charm, to put under a magic spell

be-yond [bē-ŏnd] *preposition*, at a distance farther away, on the other side of, past

bi-as [bī′əs] *adjective*, 1) in a slanting manner, obliquely, diagonally, *noun*, 2) inclination, tendency, *verb*, 3) to influence, to show prejudice, to sway

Bi-ble [bī′bəl] *noun*, the religious book of the Christian and Jewish faiths

bib-li-og-ra-phy [bǐb′lē-ŏg′rə-fē] *noun*, a list of books on any subject usually found at the end of a manuscript

bick-er [bǐk′ər] *verb*, to quarrel about petty things

bi-cy-cle [bī′sǐk′əl] *noun*, a two wheeled vehicle propelled by pedals

bid [bǐd] *noun*, 1) an offer to buy something, *verb*, 2) to offer a price for something 3) to ask, plea 4) to utter a greeting

bi-en-ni-al [bī-ĕn′ē-əl] *adjective*, happening every two years

big [bǐg] *adjective*, large in size, weight, importance, etc.

big-ot [bǐg′ət] *noun*, a person filled with stubborn hatred

big-ot-ry [bǐg′ə-trē] *noun*, prejudice, intolerance

bi-lin-gual [bī-lǐng′gwəl] *adjective*, capable of speaking two languages

bill [bǐl] *noun*, 1) a piece of paper stating what you owe 2) a plan for a new law 3) the beak of a bird, *verb*, 4) to send a list of charges to someone

bil-liards [bǐl′yərdz] *noun, plural*, a game similar to pool

bil-lion [bǐl′yən] *noun, adjective*, a thousand million, written 1,000,000,000

bil-low [bǐl′ō] *noun*, 1) a wave, a surge of water or smoke, *verb*, 2) to surge, to swell

bin [bǐn] *noun*, a large container with a lid, for flour, grain, etc.

bind [bīnd] *verb*, 1) to tie with rope or string 2) to constrict 3) to put under an obligation

bind-er [bīn′dər] *noun*, that which fastens or binds together, such as a notebook with large rings to hold paper

binge [bǐnj] *noun*, a spree, uncontrolled eating

bin-oc-u-lars [bə-nŏk′yə-lərz] *noun, plural*, a pair of special glasses that make things in the distance look closer

bi-o-de-grad-a-ble [bī′ō-dǐ-grā′də-bəl] *adjective*, capable of being broken down by microorganisms into simple, stable compounds such as carbon dioxide and water

bi-og-ra-phy [bī-ŏg′rə-fē] *noun*, a written history of a person's life

bi-ol-o-gy [bī-ŏl′ə-jē] *noun*, the branch of knowledge that studies all living things

birch [bûrch] *noun*, a hardwood tree known for its thin, peeling bark and yellow leaves in the fall

bird [bûrd] *noun*, any of a class of warm-blooded, two-legged, egg-laying vertebrates with feathers and wings

birth [bûrth] *noun*, the act of being born, the beginning of existence

birth-day [bûrth′dā′] *noun*, the day someone is born

bis-cuit [bĭs′kĭt] *noun*, a small soft bread

bish-op [bĭsh′əp] *noun*, a senior member of the Christian clergy

bi-son [bī′sən, -zən] *noun*, a large mammal native to North America and Europe, including the buffalo

bit [bĭt] *noun*, 1) a very small amount 2) the metal mouthpiece on a bridle used to control a horse 3) the cutting edge of a tool, *verb*, 4) *past tense* of **bite**

bite [bīt] *noun*, 1) a wound made by biting or stinging, *verb*, 2) to seize or cut with teeth

bit-ter [bĭt′ər] *adjective*, 1) having a sharp, sour taste 2) grievous, painful 3) piercingly cold

bi-zarre [bĭ-zär′] *adjective*, very strange or unusual, weird

black [blăk] *adjective*, 1) lacking color or light, the opposite of white, *noun*, 2) a Negro or person of African descent

black-mail [blăk′māl′] *noun*, 1) compliance with another person's terms, hush money, *verb*, 2) to threaten to reveal a secret unless money is paid or favors given

blad-der [blăd′ər] *noun*, a sack attached to the kidneys to hold urine

blade [blād] *noun*, 1) the flat cutting part of anything sharp 2) a long flat leaf of grass, or anything with such a shape

blame [blām] *noun*, 1)responsibility for something bad, *verb*, 2) to say that someone is the cause of something unfortunate

blanch [blănch] *verb*, 1) to bleach, to whiten, to fade 2) to cook briefly in boiling water

bland [blănd] *adjective*, mild, almost tasteless, neutral

blank [blăngk] *adjective*, 1) without writing or other marks 2) without expression

blan-ket [blăng′kĭt] *noun*, a warm cloth cover used on a bed

blas-phe-my [blăs′fə-mē] *noun*, speech or actions that are disrespectful to God or sacred things

blast [blăst] *noun*, 1) a strong gust of wind 2) an explosion, *verb*, 3) to launch into space 4) to use explosions to break something apart 4) to make a loud sound

bla-tant [blāt′nt] *adjective*, loudly offensive, very obvious

blaze [blāz] *noun*, 1) a strong fire, *verb*, 2) to burn, to burst into flame 3) to shine brightly

blaz-er [blā′zər] *noun*, a light sports jacket of wool or silk

bleach [blēch] *noun*, 1) a substance used to whiten or remove color, *verb*, 2) to make white, to remove color

bleach-ers [blē′chərs] *noun*, *plural*, seats for spectators

bleak [blēk] *adjective*, cold and unpleasant, empty

bleed [blēd] *verb*, 1) to lose blood 2) to become mixed or run (e.g., dyes in wet cloth)

blem-ish [blĕm′ĭsh] *noun,* a flaw, an imperfection, a pimple

blend [blĕnd] *noun,* 1) a thorough mixture, *verb,* 2) to mix together into one 3) to go together

bless [blĕs] *verb,* to make holy, to ask God's favor, to praise

bless-ing [blĕs′ĭng] *noun,* 1) words that thank God for His gifts 2) good fortune

blew [bloo] *verb, past tense* of **blow**

blight [blīt] *noun,* 1) a disease on plants that makes the leaves dry up, *verb,* 2) to injure, to damage, to ruin a crop

blind [blīnd] *adjective,* 1) unable to see, without the sense of sight 2) concealed, hard to see 3) oblivious, unaware, ignorant, *noun,* 4) a window covering to keep out light, *verb,* 5) to make unable to see

blink [blĭngk] *noun,* 1) the quick opening and closing of an eyelid, *verb,* 2) to open and shut the eyes quickly

bliss [blĭs] *noun,* complete joy, happiness, or delight

blis-ter [blĭs′tər] *noun,* a sack under the skin filled with water or blood, from a burn or rubbing

bliz-zard [blĭz′ərd] *noun,* a snow storm with strong winds and cold temperatures

block [blŏk] *noun,* 1) a cube, a chunk 2) the area bounded by four city streets 3) something that stands in the way and prevents movement, *verb,* 4) to hinder, clog or jam, to impede, prevent, stop, or obstruct 5) to form, shape, or press

block-ade [blŏ′kād] *noun,* the closure of an area , port, etc.

blond or blonde [blŏnd] *adjective,* a light hair color the shade of straw or wheat

blood [blŭd] *noun,* a red fluid in the veins of people and animals

blood ves-sel [blŭd vĕs′əl] *noun,* any of the tubes in the body that carry blood, veins, arteries, capillaries

bloom [bloom] *noun,* 1) a flower, *verb,* 2) to have a flower

blos-som [blŏs′əm] *noun,* 1) a flower, *verb,* 2) to bloom or open from a bud to come in to a flower

blot [blŏt] *noun,* 1) a spot or stain, *verb,* 2) to absorb a liquid with cloth or a sponge to remove it

blouse [blous] *noun,* a garment similar to a shirt covering the top of a woman's body, from the neck to the waist

blow [blō] *noun,* 1) a sudden strike with a hand or weapon, *verb,* 2) to force air into a current, to expel air from the mouth

blue [bloo] *adjective,* 1) having the color of a cloudless sky, 2) unhappy, depressed, *noun,* 3) one of the three primary colors: red, blue, yellow 3) a feeling of unhappiness, sadness

bluff [blŭf] *noun,* 1) a high, steep bank, *verb,* 2) to try to trick or fool someone 3) to pretend

blun-der [blŭn′dər] *noun,* a stupid mistake, an error

blunt [blŭnt] *adjective,* 1) not sharp 2) frank, candid, abrupt, *verb,* 3) to deaden, insensitize, dull

blur [blûr] *verb*, to make unreadable or indistinct, to obscure

blush [blŭsh] *verb*, to become red in the face from embarrassment

board [bôrd] *noun*, 1) a long flat piece of wood 2) a group of directors who act as a body 3) a piece of cardboard or wood on which a game is played, *verb*, 4) to cover with wood 5) to climb onto a vessel or vehicle

board-er [bôr′dər] *noun*, a paying guest who receives meals

boast [bōst] *verb*, to brag, to praise oneself, to show off

boat [bōt] *noun*, a small ship or vessel that floats on water

bode [bōd] *verb*, to predict, to portend, to foretell

bod-y [bŏd′ē] *noun*, 1) the form of a person or animal or object 2) a group of persons who act as a unit 3) a corpse

bog [bôg] *noun*, a swamp, a marsh

boil [boil] *noun*, 1) a painful sore under the skin, *verb*, 2) to heat to 212 degrees Fahrenheit 3) to be angered, to be enraged

bold [bōld] *adjective*, brave, assertive, forward, fearless

bolt [bōlt] *noun*, 1) a metal screw used with a nut to hold something in place, a metal bar 2) a stroke of lightning, a thunderbolt, *verb*, 3) to lock with a bar across a doorway 4) to run quickly from the scene

bomb [bŏm] *noun*, 1) a device of explosive materials, *verb*, 2) to bombard with explosives

bom-bard [bŏm-bärd] *verb*, to attack repeatedly

bond [bŏnd] *noun*, 1) a mutual feeling of trust that joins people together 2) a written promise to pay money, *verb*, 3) to join together, to unite

bond-age [bŏn′dĭj] *noun*, confinement, servitude

bone [bōn] *noun*, a hard white substance forming the skeleton of an animal

bon-fire [bŏn′fīr′] *noun*, a large controlled fire

bo-nus [bō′nəs] *noun*, a sum paid in addition to a salary

book [bŏŏk] *noun*, 1) sheets of paper bound together for reading or writing, a long work of literature, etc., in electronic form, *verb*, 2) to make reservations for a future date

book-keep-ing [bŏŏk′kē′pĭng] *noun*, a systematic record of business transactions

boo-mer-ang [bōō′mə-răng′] *noun*, an angular shaped object that returns after it is thrown

boor [bŏŏr] *noun*, a rude person, a jerk, a brash individual

boost [bōōst] *noun*, 1) a lift, a helping hand, *verb*, 2) to support, to encourage

boot [bōōt] *noun*, 1) a shoe that covers above the ankle, *verb*, 2) to kick 3) to load the operating system on a computer

booth [bōōth] *noun*, an enclosure, a cubicle, a compartment

bor-der [bôr′dər] *noun*, 1) the dividing line between two countries or territories 2) an edge or trim, *verb*, 3) to lie along the edge of a geographic boundary

bore [bôr] *noun*, 1) a tiresome person, a nuisance, *verb*, 2) to drill a hole, to penetrate 3) to make someone feel disinterested

bore-dom [bôr′dəm] *noun*, dullness, lack of interest

boring [bôr′ĭng] *adjective*, not interesting, dull, tedious

born [bôrn] *adjective*, having been given life, existing as a result of birth

bor-ough [bûr′ō] *noun*, a self-governing incorporated town

bor-row [bŏr′ō] *verb*, 1) to use a thing that does not belong to you, then return it 2) to adopt or use as one's own

bos-om [bŏŏz′əm] *adjective*, 1) relating to the closeness between friends or family, *noun*, 2) chest area 3) a woman's breast

boss [bôs] *noun*, 1) the person in charge, someone in control, the employer, *verb*, 2) to give orders in a domineering way

bot-a-nist [bŏt′n-ĭst] *noun*, one who studies plants

bot-a-ny [bŏt′n-ē] *noun*, the science of plants

both [bōth] *adjective*, *pronoun*, the two together in conjunction

both-er [bŏth′ər] *noun*, *no plural*, 1) trouble or difficulty, a nuisance, *verb*, 2) to trouble or annoy, to harass or pester

bot-tle [bŏt′l] *noun*, 1) a container with a narrow neck, usually made of glass or plastic, used to hold liquids *verb*, 2) to store in a glass container

bot-tom [bŏt′əm] *noun*, 1) the lowest part or end of something 2) the buttocks, seat

bough [bou] *noun*, a tree branch

bouil-lon [bŏŏl′yŏn′, -yən] *noun*, a broth, consommé

boul-der [bōl′dər] *noun*, a very large stone or rock

bounce [bouns] *verb*, to spring back from a surface, to jump

bound [bound] *adjective*, 1) constrained, restricted, confined 2) going to, destined for, *noun*, 3) a jump, a leap

bound-a-ry [boun′də-rē] *noun*, a real or imaginary limit, especially between two properties

boun-ti-ful [boun′tə-fəl] *adjective*, generous, plentiful, provided freely, abundant

bow [bō] *noun*, 1) a ribbon worn as a hair ornament 2) a piece of wood bent with a string, used to shoot arrows 3) a piece of wood with hairs fastened, to create vibrations when pulled across the strings of an instrument, such as a violin, [bou] 4) the front of a boat, *verb*, 5) to bend the body forward to show respect 6) to submit to another, to consent

bowl [bōl] *noun*, a round deep dish

box [bŏks] *noun*, 1) a container like a cube, constructed from wood, cardboard, metal, etc. *verb*, 2) to fight with clenched fists

boy [boi] *noun*, a male child

boy-cott [boi′kŏt′] *noun*, 1) the refusal to purchase the products of an individual, corporation, or nation as a way to bring

brace

economic pressure for social or
political change, *verb*, 2) to
refuse to deal with or trade with,
to desert, to abandon

brace [brās] *noun*, 1) a support, a
vise, 2) two like items, a pair,
verb, 3) to fortify

brack-et [brăk′ĭt] *noun*, 1) a shelf
supported against a wall 2) one
of the signs [ ] in a sentence that
encloses additional information

brack-ish [brăk′ĭsh] *adjective*, a
mixture of fresh and salt water

brag [brăg] *verb*, to praise oneself,
to sound conceited, to boast

braid [brād] *noun*, 1) a rope, twine,
verb, 2) to weave hair or rope

Braille [brāl] *noun*, a system of
writing for people who are blind
using raised dots as letters and
numbers to be read with the
fingertips

brain [brān] *noun*, 1) the mass of
nerve tissue in the heads of
people and animals, the center
of the nervous system 2) the
intellect, where we get our
thoughts and ideas

brake [brāk] *noun*, 1) a mechanical
device used to stop a bicycle,
car, train, etc., *verb*, 2) to stop
with the help of a mechanical
device

branch [brănch] *noun*, 1) a part of
a tree that extends from the trunk
2) an office that is located some
distance from the headquarters
3) a stream or river that flows
into a larger one, *verb*, 4) to
move away or divide from the
main body into branches

brand [brănd] *noun*, 1) a label
indicating the name of a product
and the manufacturer, *verb*, 2) to

make a permanent mark on an
animal to identify it

brass [brăs] *noun*, 1) a yellow
metal that is a copper and zinc
alloy 2) musical instruments,
such as a trumpet, that are made
out of metal and that give a loud
sound when blown

bra-va-do [brə-vä′dō] *noun*, an air
of defiance, fake bravery

brave [brāv] *adjective*, willing to
make a personal sacrifice

brav-er-y [brā′və-rē] *noun*,
courage, daring, boldness

brawl [brôl] *noun*, 1) a fight, an
altercation, a dispute, *verb*, 2) to
argue and wrestle or fight

breach [brēch] *noun*, the breaking
of a contract, a gap in a fence

bread [brĕd] *noun*, a food made of
flour, water, and yeast that is
baked

breadth [brĕdth] *noun*, the
distance from one side to the
other, width

break [brāk] *noun*, 1) an opening
made when something is torn or
broken, 2) a pause, a rest, a time
away from school or work, *verb*,
3) to cause to fall apart 4) to
violate, to disobey

break-fast [brĕk′fəst] *noun*, the
first meal of the day, eaten in the
morning

breast [brĕst] *noun*, 1) one of the
two parts on the front of a
woman's body that can give
milk 2) the top part of the front
of the body

breath [brĕth] *noun*, air inhaled
and exhaled in respiration

breathe [brēth] *verb*, to inhale air into the lung and then exhale

bred [brĕd] *verb, past tense and past participle* of **breed**

breed [brēd] *noun*, 1) a type or group of animals descended from a common ancestor, *verb*, 2) to reproduce, to multiply 3) to train and raise animals

breed-ing [brē/dǐng] *noun*, values a person learns, upbringing

breeze [brēz] *noun*, a gentle wind

brev-i-ty [brĕv/ǐ-tē] *noun*, shortness, ability to say something briefly, succinctly

brew [broo] *verb*, to make drinks such as tea, coffee, or beer

bribe [brīb] *noun*, 1) money given to buy cooperation, *verb*, 2) to get someone's cooperation by paying them, to pay off

brick [brǐk] *noun*, a block of baked clay used in construction

brid-al [brīd/əl] *adjective*, referring to the bride in a wedding

bride [brīd] *noun*, a woman about to be married, is in the process of being married, or who has just been married

bride-groom [brīd/groom] *noun*, a man who is going to be married, is in the process of being married, or has just been married

bridge [brǐj] *noun*, 1) an elevated structure such as a viaduct or an overpass that crosses over water or a highway 2) a card game 3) a link, a connection, *verb*, 4) to join, connect, bring together

bri-dle [brīd/l] *noun*, 1) a leather band on the head of a horse used

for control, *verb*, 2) to show anger or resentment

brief [brēf] *adjective*, 1) for a short period of time, *noun*, 2) a summary of a case for the court, *verb*, 3) to inform

bri-er [brī/ər] *noun* prickly vegetation

bri-gade [brǐ-gād/] *noun*, a large group of soldiers

bright [brīt] *adjective*, 1) giving light 2) shining, not dull 3) smart, intelligent 4) cheerful

bril-liant [brǐl/yənt] *adjective*, 1) very bright, glittering, splendid 2) very clever

brim [brǐm] *noun*, 1) the edge of a cup, glass, or bowl 2) the part of the hat that is the edge

bring [brǐng]*verb*, to carry something or to lead someone

brink [brǐngk] *noun*, the edge of a steep slope, the verge

brisk [brǐsk] *adjective*, 1) quick and active, energetic 2) curt

bris-tle [brǐs/əl] *noun*, 1) a coarse brush, *verb*, 2) to feel irritated or annoyed, to show indignation

brit-tle [brǐt/l] *adjective*, hard but easily broken or snapped

broach [brōch] *verb*, to bring up, to begin discussion of

broad [brôd] *adjective*, 1) wide, extensive 2) tolerant

broad-cast [brôd/kăst/] *noun*, 1) a program aired on television or radio, *verb*, 2) to convey a message through radio or television or other electronic media

broad-en [brôd/n] *verb*, to expand

bro-chure [brō-shoŏr′] *noun*, a pamphlet dealing with a subject of passing interest, a leaflet

broc-co-li [brŏk′ə-lē] *noun*, a plant with dense green flowers eaten as a vegetable

broil [broil] *verb*, to cook by exposing to direct, intense heat

broke [brōk] *adjective*, 1) without money, bankrupt, *verb*, 2) *past tense* of **break**

bro-ker [brō′kər] *noun*, an agent who buys and sells for others

bron-chi-tis [brŏn-kī′tĭs] *noun*, an inflammation of the lungs that causes chronic coughing

bronze [brŏnz] *noun*, a hard metal made by mixing copper and tin

brooch [brōch] *noun*, an ornamental dress-clasp, a decorative pin

brood [broōd] *noun*, 1) a group of animals born together, or the children of a family, *verb*, 2) to think deeply and sadly about something

brook [broŏk] *noun*, 1) a small river or stream, *verb*, 2) to allow

broom [broōm] *noun*, a brush with a long handle

broth [brôth] *noun*, watery soup, bouillon

broth-er [brŭth′ər] *noun*, a boy or man with the same parents as another person

brought [brôt] *verb*, *past tense* of **bring**

brow [brou] *noun*, the part of the face between the eyes and the hair, the forehead

brown [broun] *adjective*, a dark color like coffee or earth

browse [brouz] *verb*, to leaf through, to scan, to pass over

bruise [broōz] *noun*, 1) a red or blue mark left on damaged skin caused by blood vessels breaking beneath the skin, *verb*, 2) to injure in such a way that the blood vessels beneath the skin are broken

brunch [brŭnch]*noun*, a meal between breakfast and lunch

bru-nette [broō-nĕt′] *noun*, a woman with brown hair

brush [brŭsh] *noun*, 1) a device with wires or plastic bristles spread from a handle for combing, or cleaning, or painting, *verb*, 2) to clean, straighten, or paint with a brush

brusque [brŭsk] *adjective*, rough and short in manner, blunt,

bru-tal [broōt′l] *adjective*, fierce, harsh, destructive

brute [broōt] *noun*, a cruel person who acts like a wild animal

bub-ble [bŭb′əl] *noun*, 1) a sphere containing liquid or gas, *verb*, 2) to boil, to froth

buck [bŭk] *noun*, a male deer, goat, or rabbit

buck-et [bŭk′ĭt] *noun*, a container, usually with a curved handle to carry something, a pail

buck-le [bŭk′əl] *noun*, a device for uniting two loose ends of a belt or to fasten shoes, etc.

bu-col-ic [byoō-kŏl′ĭk] *adjective*, rustic, pastoral, in the country

bud [bŭd] *noun*, a sprout on a stem that becomes a flower or branch

Bud-dhism [bōō'dĭz'əm] *noun*, one of the world's major religions, practiced primarily in Asia and taught by monks

budge [bŭj] *verb*, to make something heavy move a little

budg-et [bŭj'ĭt] *noun*, a plan that indicates how money will be spent

buf-fa-lo [bŭf'ə-lō'] *noun*, a large, shaggy, wild ox

buff-er [bŭf'ər] *noun*, 1) a solution that neutralizes different substances 2) a person or thing between two opposing forces that softens the impact of their collision, *verb*, 3) to lessen

buf-fet [bə-fā'] *noun*, 1) a counter or table for refreshments, [bə-fĭt] *verb*, 2) to batter, to flap, to hit

buf-foon [bə-fōōn'] *noun*, one who clowns around

bug [bŭg] *noun*, 1) an insect that drinks juices from plants or animals 2) an error in data, *verb*, 3) to eavesdrop electronically

bug-gy [bŭg'ē] *noun*, 1) a hand-pushed carriage for babies 2) a one-horse carriage for two people

bu-gle [byōō'gəl] *noun*, a musical instrument, a horn used mainly in the military

build [bĭld] *verb*, 1) to create or construct 2) to increase

build-ing [bĭl'dĭng] *noun*, a structure with a foundation, roof, and walls

built [bĭlt] *verb*, *past tense* of **build**

bulb [bŭlb] *noun*, 1) the underground part of a plant formed by thick leaves, which separates and becomes a new plant 2) any object of this shape, such as a light bulb

bulge [bŭlj] *noun*, 1) a swelling shape, *verb*, 2) to swell outwards

bulk-head [bŭlk'hĕd'] *noun*, a partition separating the compartments of a vessel

bull [bōōl] *adjective*, 1) describing the stock market when prices are going up and the economy is strong, *noun*, 2) male animal of the ox, cow, whale, or other animals

bull-doz-er [bōōl'dō'zər] *noun*, a heavy machine that moves earth

bul-let [bōōl'ĭt] *noun*, a piece of metal fired from a gun

bul-le-tin [bōōl'ĭ-tn] *noun*, an announcement made by an organization, a newsletter

bul-lion [bōōl'yən] *noun*, a block of metal such as gold or silver

bul-ly [bōōl'ē] *noun*, 1) a person who likes to hurt or tease weaker people, *verb*, 2) to intimidate someone, to make someone feel afraid or overpowered

bul-wark [bōōl'wərk] *noun*, protection, a defensive wall

bum-ble-bee [bŭm'bəl-bē'] *noun*, a large yellow and black hairy social bee

bump [bŭmp*]* *noun*, 1) a sudden blow 2) a raised round lump due to swelling 3) an elevated place in the road or on a surface, *verb*, 4) to knock against, to strike

bun [bŭn] *noun*, 1) a small sweet roll or dinner roll 2) a hairstyle in which the hair is lifted off the neck and wrapped into a circle

bunch [bŭnch] *noun*, 1) a cluster of similar things grouped together, *verb*, 2) to gather together in a mass

bun-dle [bŭn'dl] *noun*, 1) a group of things tied together to make a package, *verb*, 2) to make into a bunch by tying things together

bu-oy [bōō'ē] *noun*, an anchored floating device used as a navigation marker

buoy-ant [boi'ənt] *adjective*, 1) having the quality of rising or floating in fluid 2) light-hearted

bur-den [bûr'dn] *noun*, 1) a heavy thought or object that is carried, *verb*, 2) to load

bu-reau [byōōr'ō] *noun*, 1) a chest of drawers 2) a satellite office for a news agency

bu-reauc-ra-cy [byōō-rŏk'rə-sē] *noun*, a system of government through agencies to which tasks and authority are delegated

bur-geon [bûr'jən] *verb*, to grow and develop rapidly

bur-glar [bûr'glər] *noun*, one who breaks into other people's property to rob them

bur-i-al [bĕr'ē-əl] *noun*, the act of putting a dead body in the ground, internment

burn [bûrn] *noun*, 1) a wound caused by fire or heat, or friction, *verb*, 2) to be destroyed by fire, heat or acid

burnt [bûrnt] *adjective*, showing damage by fire

burr [bûr] *noun*, a round seed covered with spurs or barbs

bur-ro [bûr'ō] *noun*, a donkey

bur-row [bûr'ō] *noun*, 1) a tunnel or hole dug by an animal as a den, *verb*, 2) to dig or hide in a hole

burst [bûrst] *noun*, 1) a sudden action, *verb*, 2) to break due to force from inside, to combust

bury [bĕr'ē] *verb*, to dig a hole to conceal something underground, to cover, to conceal

bus [bŭs] *noun*, a large vehicle that carries many people to a destination by a road

bush [bōōsh] *noun*, a shrub

bush-el [bōōsh'əl] *noun*, dry measure equal to 64 pints or 32 quarts

busi-ness [bĭz'nĭs] *noun*, 1) regular occupation, work, profession 2) something to be transacted 3) affairs involving money

bust [bŭst] *noun*, a sculpture of a person from the chest up

bus-y [bĭz'ē] *adjective*, 1) having a lot to do, *verb*, to work actively

but [bŭt; bət when unstressed] *adverb*, 1) only, merely, *conjunction*, 2) yet, however, *preposition*, 3) except, save 4) other than

butch-er [bōōch'ər] *noun*, a person who cuts meat for sale

but-ter [bŭt'ər] *noun*, a substance made from churning cream

but-ter-fly [bŭt'ər-flī'] *noun*, an insect with four colorful wings and a slender body

but-ton [bŭt'n] *noun*, 1) a variety of forms or materials used to fasten a dress, pants, shirt, etc. 2) a badge, a form of identification, 3) a knob pressed to operate a device, *verb,* 4) to secure with a button or snap

but-ton-hole [bŭt⁄n-hōl⁄] *noun,* the hole in a piece of clothing that a button goes through in order to fasten two sides together

but-tress [bŭt⁄rĭs] *noun,* a support projecting outwards to strengthen the walls of a building

buy [bī] *verb,* to acquire something by giving an accepted price, to purchase with money

buy-er [bī⁄ər] *noun,* a customer, one who makes a purchase

by [bī] *adverb,* 1) near, aside, past *preposition,* 2) near, beside 3) through, by way of, via 4) before 5) past

by-pro-duct [bī⁄prŏd⁄əkt] *noun,* anything produced in the process of making something else

byte [bīt] *noun,* 1) a small unit of information 2) a fixed number of bits (usually eight)

C

cab [kăb] *noun,* 1) a vehicle for hire, a taxi 2) the part of a truck or train where the driver sits

cab-bage [kăb⁄ĭj] *noun,* a vegetable with a short stem and thick green or purple overlapping leaves that form a dense head

cab-in [kăb⁄ĭn] *noun,* 1) a small wooden house 2) a room for living quarters on a ship 3) the passenger area on an airplane

cab-i-net [kăb⁄ə-nĭt] *noun,* 1) a cupboard with drawers or

shelves for keeping items 2) a group of people who advise the head of state

ca-ble [kā⁄bəl] *noun,* 1) a strong, large diameter wire or rope 2) a bundle of insulated wires that carry electrical current 3) a system delivering television signals by cable

ca-boose [kə-boōs⁄] *noun,* the last car used on a freight train, containing facilities for the crew

cache [kăsh] *noun,* 1) a hiding place for food or treasures, *verb,* 2) to hide or store something

cack-le [kăk⁄əl] *noun,* 1) a loud laugh, *verb,* 2) to laugh loudly to sound like a hen

ca-coph-o-ny [kə-kŏf⁄ə-nē] *noun,* harsh or dissonant noise, a discordant mixture of sounds

cac-tus [kăk⁄təs] *noun, plural,* **cacti or cactuses,** a prickly, succulent plant with thick stems that grows in hot, dry climates

ca-dav-er [kə-dăv⁄ər] *noun,* a dead body

ca-det [kə-dĕt⁄] *noun,* a student at a military school

caf-e-te-ri-a [kăf⁄ĭ-tîr⁄ē-ə] *noun,* a place to eat where customers select food from a serving line

caf-feine [kă-fēn] *noun,* a stimulant found especially in coffee, tea, or some sodas

cage [kāj] *noun,* a box-like enclosure with bars in which birds or animals are kept, a pen

cake [kāk] *noun,* 1) a sweet, baked food made of flour, fat, and eggs, *verb,* 2) to harden from a wet substance into a solid crust

ca-lam-i-ty [kə-lăm′ĭ-tē] *noun*, an unfortunate event, a disaster

cal-ci-um [kăl′sē-əm] *noun*, a silver-white, rather soft metal that occurs in bones, shells, etc.

cal-cu-late [kăl′kyə-lāt′] *verb*, to find the answer using arithmetic, to plan using reasoning

cal-cu-la-tion [kăl′kyə-lā′shən] *noun*, the result of numbers added together, subtracted, etc.

cal-cu-la-tor [kăl′kyə-lā′tər] *noun*, a small computer used to perform math problems

cal-cu-lus [kăl′kyə-ləs] *noun*,
1) a branch of mathematics that provides a method for describing change 2) a buildup of materials within the body, such as a gallstone

cal-en-dar [kăl′ən-dər] *noun*, a table of the days and the months of the year

calf [kăf] *noun*, 1) the newborn or young of any large mammal, such as a cow, whale, or elephant 2) part of the leg between the knee and the ankle, the back of the shin

cal-i-ber [kăl′ə-bər] *noun*, 1) the diameter of a cylinder or tube 2) a person's degree of ability

Cal-i-for-nia [kăl′ĭ-fôr′nyə] *noun*, a state on the Pacific coast of the United States, the capital is Sacramento. The state flower of **California** is the golden poppy and the motto is "Eureka!"

cal-lis-then-ics [kăl′ĭs-thĕn′ĭks] *noun, plural*, exercise to promote strength and grace

call [kôl] *noun*, 1) the act of reaching someone on the telephone or paying a visit 2) a shout or plea, *verb*, 3) to name 4) to shout 5) to ask someone to come 6) to telephone 7) to visit

cal-lig-ra-phy [kə-lĭg′rə-fē] *noun*, beautiful writing, the art of hand lettering

cal-lous [kăl′əs] *adjective*,
1) lacking feeling, hard-hearted, feeling no pity 2) thick skinned

cal-lus [kăl′əs] *noun*, a hard thickened spot (of skin)

calm [käm] *adjective*, quiet, not excited

cal-o-rie [kăl′ə-rē] *noun*, a unit used to measure the amount of energy produced

cam-el [kăm′əl] *noun*, a large animal with one or two humps on its back, used for transportation

cam-e-o [kăm′ē-ō′] *noun*, a piece of jewelry with a stone or shell on which figures are carved

cam-er-a [kăm′ər-ə] *noun*, an instrument used to take photographs or film pictures

cam-ou-flage [kăm′ə-fläzh] *noun*,
1) special clothing for people or colors in an animal that help them blend into their surroundings, *verb*, 2) an organism's ability to blend in with the environment

camp [kămp] *noun*, 1) a place with tents or cabins for temporary shelter, *verb*, 2) to live outdoors and sleep in a tent under the stars, etc.

cam-paign [kăm-pān'] *noun*,
1) activities organized to gain or
win something, *verb*, 2) to create
a connected series of operations
to achieve a desired result

cam-pus [kăm'pəs] *noun*, the
grounds surrounding a college,
school, or organization

can [kăn] *noun*, 1) a metal
container, *verb*, 2) able to, to
know how to 3) to preserve food
in a can

ca-nal [kə-năl'] *noun*, 1) an
artificial waterway designed for
navigation 2) a duct in the body

ca-nar-y [kə-nâr'ē] *noun*, a
songbird, usually yellow

can-cel [kăn'səl] *verb*, to annul, to
revoke, to end or stop

can-cel-la-tion [kăn'sə-lā'shən]
noun, a stop or end to
something, withdrawal

can-cer [kăn'sər] *noun*, a serious
illness in which abnormal cells
multiply rapidly

can-di-date [kăn'dĭ-dāt'] *noun*, one
who is being considered or who
applies for a certain job

can-dle [kăn'dl] *noun*, a cylinder of
wax with a wick embedded in it
designed to burn to give off light

can-dor [kăn'dər] *noun*, the quality
of being fair, unprejudiced, and
honest

cane [kān] *noun*, 1) a hollow stick
made from some plants 2) a stick
with a curved handle used for
support when walking

ca-nine [kā'nīn] *adjective*, relating
to dogs

can-is-ter [kăn'ĭ-stər] *noun*, a small
box or container, often of metal,
for holding tea, coffee, etc.

can-ni-bal [kăn'ə-bəl] *noun*, **a**
person who eats people or an
animal who eats one of its own
kind

can-non [kăn'ən] *noun*, a mounted
gun or piece of artillery

can-not [kăn'ŏt] unable to

ca-noe [kə-nōō'] *noun*, a narrow
light boat tapered at the ends,
moved with paddles

can-o-py [kăn'ə-pē] *noun*, a
covering from the sun, an
awning or umbrella

cant [kănt] *noun*, 1) empty talk,
deceit, 2) jargon, slang, *verb*,
3) to speak insincerely

can't [kănt] the *contraction* of the
words **can** and **not**

can-ta-loupe [kăn'tl-ōp'] *noun*, a
variety of muskmelon with an
orange-red color fruit

can-tan-ker-ous [kăn-tăng'kər-əs]
adjective, irritable, cross

can-vas [kăn'vəs] *noun*, 1) a
strong, coarse, water-repellant
cloth used to make tents, sails,
etc. 2) a piece of heavy cloth,
stretched over a frame, on which
pictures are painted

can-vass [kăn'vəs] *verb*, 1) to
examine thoroughly, scrutinize
2) to solicit votes or opinions

can-yon [kăn'yən] *noun*, a valley
with high, steep sides between
hills or mountains

cap [kăp] *noun*, 1) a soft hat 2) the
covering for a bottle or tube

ca-pa-ble [kā′pə-bəl] *noun*, able to do things well, having ability, competent or efficient

ca-pac-i-ty [kə-păs′ĭ-tē] *noun*, 1) the maximum amount of liquid a container can hold, 2) the ability or aptitude for a specified task

cape [kāp] *noun*, 1) a piece of land that goes out into the sea 2) a coat without sleeves that covers shoulders, arms, and back

cap-il-lar-y [kăp′ə-lĕr′ē] *noun*, one of the tiniest blood vessels

cap-i-tal [kăp′ĭ-tl] *adjective*, 1) first, chief, 2 punishable by death, *noun*, 3) resources, means or money 4) the city where the rules for a state or county or country are made 5) a letter that begins a sentence or a proper noun

cap-i-tal-ism [kăp′ĭ-tl-ĭz′əm] *noun*, an economic system based on profit and private ownership

cap-i-tal-ize [kăp′ĭ-tl-īz′] *verb*, 1) to finance or invest in for profit 2) to use a capital letter

Cap-i-tol [kăp′ĭ-tl] *noun*, 1) the building in which the Congress of the United States meets to create laws, **capitol** 2) the building in which a state legislature meets to create laws

ca-price [kə-prēs′] *noun*, a silly thought, a notion, whimsy

cap-size [kăp′sīz′] *verb*, to upset or overturn as of a boat

cap-sule [kăp′səl] *noun*, 1) a container with a matching top and bottom that holds medicine 2) a small spacecraft

cap-tain [kăp′tən] *noun*, the leader of a team or a company of soldiers, or the commander of a ship or aircraft

cap-tion [kăp′shən] *noun*, 1) a short title heading 2) text under an illustration

cap-tive [kăp′tĭv] *adjective*, 1) unable to escape, *noun*, 2) a prisoner

cap-ture [kăp′chər] *verb*, 1) to seize and hold as a prisoner 2) to take hold of something

car [kär] *noun*, an automobile, a form of transportation with four wheels and an engine, usually fueled by gasoline

ca-rafe [kə-răf′] *noun*, a glass bottle, a decanter

car-at [kăr′ət] *noun*, a unit of weight for precious stones

car-a-van [kăr′ə-văn′] *noun*, 1) a group of people traveling together with vehicles or animals 2) a mobile home

car-bo-hy-drate [kär′bō-hī′drāt′] *noun*, a class of foods, that supply energy to the body

car-bon [kär′bən] *noun*, a nonmetallic element, symbolized as C, the required common substance in organic chemistry

car-bo-nate [kär′bə-nāt′] *noun*, a salt of carbonic acid

car-bon di-ox-ide [kär′bən dī-ŏk′sīd] *noun*, a colorless, odorless gas that is absorbed by plants

car-bon mon-ox-ide [kär′bən mə-nŏk′sīd′] *noun*, a colorless, odorless poisonous gas

46

car-cass [kär′kəs] *noun,* the dead body of an animal or bird

car-cin-o-gen [kär-sĭn′ə-jən] *noun,* a substance that causes cancer

card [kärd] *noun,* a small, flat piece of thick, stiff paper (e.g., a playing card, a postcard, a greeting or business card)

car-di-ac [kär′dē-ăk′] *adjective,* pertaining to the heart, stimulating the heart action

car-di-gan [kär′dĭ-gən] *noun,* a sweater that buttons or opens down the front

car-di-nal [kär′dn-əl] *adjective,* 1) chief, most important, *noun,* 2) an important leader of the Roman Catholic church, appointed by the pope as one of his advisors 3) a bright red bird common in North America

care [kâr] *noun,* 1) thought or interest 2) worry, anxiety, *verb,* 3) to show concern for others 4) to look after someone and tend to his or her needs 5) to show affection or love

ca-reen [kə-rēn′] *verb,* to sway or lean over to one side

ca-reer [kə-rîr′] *noun,* a profession, a chosen pursuit

care-ful [kâr′fəl] *adjective,* cautious, watchful

care-ful-ly [kâr′fə-lē] *adverb,* cautiously, with much care

care-less [kâr′lĭs] *adjective,* neglectful, reckless

ca-ress [kə-rĕs′] *noun,* 1) a tender or loving touch, *verb,* 2) to stroke with affection, to touch in a loving way

car-et [kär′ĭt] *noun,* a mark used by writers to indicate something like a word – to be inserted

car-go [kär′gō] *noun,* the goods or freight carried by a ship, train, plane, or any vehicle

car-i-bou [kär′ə-bōō′] *noun,* a type of reindeer

car-i-ca-ture [kär′ĭ-kə-chŏŏr′] *noun,* a representation of a person or thing in which the peculiarities are exaggerated to produce a ridiculous effect

car-nage [kär′nĭj] *noun,* the killing of many people, a massacre

car-na-tion [kär-nā′shən] *noun,* a garden flower of the pink family

car-ni-val [kär′nə-vəl] *noun,* a festival with parades and dancing, a fair

car-ni-vore [kär-nĭv′ər] *adjective,* a meat-eating mammal

car-ol [kăr′əl] *noun,* a song of joy

ca-rouse [kə-rouz′] *verb,* to drink and be merry, especially with a group

carp [kärp] *noun,* 1) a kind of fish, *verb,* 2) to find fault, to criticize

car-pen-ter [kär′pən-tər] *noun,* a builder or repairer of wooden structures or objects

car-pen-try [kär′pən-trē] *noun,* the art of making things out of wood

car-pet [kär′pĭt] *noun,* a woven or felted floor covering of wool, cotton, or a synthetic, a rug

car-riage [kär′ĭj] *noun,* 1) a wheeled vehicle 2) a manner of bearing or posture

car-ri-er [kăr′ē-ər] *noun,* 1) a messenger 2) one engaged in the

business of carrying goods for
others for hire

car-rot [kăr′ət] *noun*, a plant with
an edible root of orange color
used as a vegetable

car-ry [kăr′ē] *verb*, 1) to transport
something, to convey, to move,
to haul 2) to support a weight

cart [kärt] *noun*, a small wagon
used to carry goods

car-ti-lage [kär′tl-ĭj] *noun*, elastic
animal tissue attached to bones
near the joints

car-tog-ra-pher [kär-tŏg′rə-fûr]
noun, a maker of maps or charts

car-ton [kär′tn] *noun*, a box or
container made of cardboard

car-toon [kär-tōōn′] *noun*, a
comical drawing of a person,
event, or place

car-tridge [kär′trĭj] *noun*, a case
holding something that is
dispensed mechanically

cart-wheel [kärt′hwēl′] *noun*, a
sideways flip that is done by
springing the body onto one
hand and then the other,
followed by the feet

carve [kärv] *verb*, 1) to reshape in
an artistic or decorative manner
by cutting 2) to cut meat for
serving

cas-cade [kă-skād′] *noun*, a small
waterfall, a profusion

case [kās] *noun*, 1) a container to
hold things 2) a condition, an
example of an illness 3) a
question of law decided in court
4) something that has happened,
an instance

cash [kăsh] *noun*, 1) money
consisting of dollars or loose
change, *verb*, 2) to receive bills

and coins in exchange for a
check

cash-ier [kă-shîr′] *noun*, one who
has charge of payments, etc., as
at a store

cas-ket [kăs′kĭt] *noun*, a coffin

cas-se-role [kăs′ə-rōl′] *noun*, a dish
consisting of several different
foods combined together

cas-sette [kə-sĕt′, kă-] *noun*, a
magnetic tape used for electronic
recording enclosed in a plastic
case that can fit directly into a
recorder

cast [kăst] *noun*, 1) the performers
in a play 2) a plaster dressing
used to hold surgery in place,
verb, 3) to direct a glance at
someone or something 4) to
assign a role in a play 5) to form
a shape from clay on a potter's
wheel 6) to throw or toss 7) the
act of throwing a fishing line 8)
to overshadow 9) to register a
vote 10) to discard or shed

caste [kăst] *noun*, 1) one of the
hereditary classes in Hindu
society 2) any exclusive social
class

cas-tle [kăs′əl] *noun*, 1) a fortress
or palace usually the residence
of nobility 2) a chess piece also
known as the rook

cas-u-al [kăzh′ōō-əl] *adjective*,
1) not planned or prearranged
2) informal 3) careless

cas-u-al-ty [kăzh′ōō-əl-tē] *noun*,
one injured or killed, as in a
battle

cat [kăt] *noun*, a furry animal kept
in the house as a pet or to catch
mice

cat-a-combs [kăt′ə-kōmz′] *noun*, *plural*, a burial ground of underground rooms

cat-a-log [kăt′l-ôg′] *noun*, 1) a list of names, titles, or articles arranged in order, *verb*, 2) to list names and objects with a description of each one

cat-a-lyst [kăt′l-ĭst] *noun*, an agitator or force of change

cat-a-pult [kăt′ə-pŭlt′] *noun*, 1) a device that uses tension to throw objects, a weapon, *verb*, 2) to hurl or make an object go as far as possible

cat-a-ract [kăt′ə-răkt′] *noun*, 1) a great waterfall 2) an eye abnormality, cloudiness on the lens of the eye resulting in blurry vision

ca-tas-tro-phe [kə-tăs′trə-fē] *noun*, a sudden calamity, a disaster

catch [kăch, kĕch] *noun* 1) something that has been captured 2) the metal clasp that connects a door to a door frame, *verb*, 3) to get hold of something and not let go, to grasp 4) to get someone's attention 5) to trap

cat-e-chism [kăt′ĭ-kĭz′əm] *noun*, a set of questions and answers, especially for teaching about religion

cat-e-go-ry [kăt′ĭ-gôr′ē] *noun*, division or class to which something belongs

ca-ter [kā′tər] *verb*, to provide food or personal attention, to serve up

ca-ter-pil-lar [kăt′ər-pĭl′ər] *noun*, the larva of a butterfly

ca-thar-sis [kə-thär′sĭs] *noun*, 1) purging or cleansing of any part of the body 2) a release of tension or strong feelings

ca-the-dral [kə-thē′drəl] *noun*, a very large church, the main church of a diocese

Cath-o-lic [kăth′ə-lĭk] *noun*, a member of the church that recognizes the pope as its leader

cat-tle [kăt′l] *noun*, livestock such as cows, bulls, or steer kept for meat, milk, or skins

cau-cus [kô′kəs] *noun*, a group of politicians who gather to decide a policy or select a candidate

caught [kôt] *verb*, *past tense* of **catch**

caulk [kôk] *verb*, to make watertight, to seal cracks

cause [kôz] *noun*, 1) the reason, the thing that made something happen 2) something you believe in strongly enough to take action, *verb*, 3) to bring about, to make something happen

caus-tic [kô′stĭk] *adjective*, 1) burning 2) sarcastically biting

cau-tion [kô′shən] *noun*, care and watchfulness, a warning

cau-tious [kô′shəs] *adjective*, wary, prudent, careful, watchful

cave [kāv] *noun*, a hollow place under the ground or in the side of a mountain or rock, sheltered from the elements

ca-ve-at [kā′vē-ăt′] *noun*, an indication of limitations

cav-ern [kăv′ərn] *noun*, a hollow place in a rock, a cave

cav-i-ar [kăv′ē-är′] *noun*, the prepared and salted eggs of the sturgeon or other large fish

cav-i-ty [kăv′ĭ-tē] *noun*, 1) a hollow place or a hole 2) a hole in the tooth caused by decay

cease [sēs] *verb*, to end, to stop

cease-less [sēs′lĭs] *adjective*, without end or interruption

ce-dar [sē′dər] *noun*, a large evergreen tree with reddish, fragrant wood

ceil-ing [sē′lĭng] *noun*, 1) the covering of a room 2) the top of a space 3) upper limit

cel-e-brate [sĕl′ə-brāt′] *verb*, to do certain things because of a special occasion, to rejoice

cel-e-bra-tion [sĕl′ə-brā′-shən] *noun*, a festive occasion

ce-leb-ri-ty [sə-lĕb′rĭ-tē] *noun*, fame, renown, a famous person

ce-ler-i-ty [sə-lĕr′ĭ-tē] *noun*, speed,

cel-er-y [sĕl′ə-rē] *noun*, a plant of the parsley family, whose leaf - stalks are eaten raw or cooked

ce-les-tial [sə-lĕs′chəl] *adjective*, in the stars, heavenly

cel-i-ba-cy [sĕl′ə-bə-sē] *noun*, the state of being unmarried

cell [sĕl] *noun*, 1) a small room where a prisoner is kept or where a nun or monk lives 2) a small, microscopic piece of a living organism

cel-lar [sĕl′ər] *noun*, a room under a house, partly or completely underground, a basement

cel-lu-lar [sĕl′yə-lər] *adjective*, 1) formed of cells 2) relating to a mobile telephone system

Cel-si-us [sĕl′sē-əs] *noun*, a scale on which the freezing point is 0

ce-ment [sĭ-mĕnt′] *noun*, a substance that consists of burned lime and clay, which is mixed with water and sand to make concrete

cem-e-ter-y [sĕm′ĭ-tĕr′ē] *noun*, a burial place, a graveyard

cen-sor [sĕn′sər] *noun*, 1) one who filters inappropriate material from books, movies, etc., before they are published or released *verb*, 2) to filter out information considered unsuitable

cen-sus [sĕn′səs] *noun*, an official count of a population

cent [sĕnt] *noun*, a metal coin equal to one penny or 1/100 of a dollar

cen-ten-ni-al [sĕn-tĕn′ē-əl] *adjective*, of or pertaining to a hundredth anniversary

cen-ter [sĕn′tər] *noun*, 1) the middle, a point equidistant from all sides 2) a place where people gather 3) a hub of activity

cen-ti-grade [sĕn′tĭ-grād′] *noun*, the temperature scale in which 0 degrees is the freezing point and 100 degrees is the boiling point of water

cen-ti-me-ter [sĕn′tə-mē′tər] *noun*, a measure of length somewhat less than ½ an inch, a standard unit in the metric system

cen-tral [sĕn′trəl] *adjective*, located in the middle

cen-trif-u-gal [sĕn-trĭf′yə-gəl] *adjective*, relating to forces caused by rotation directed outward from the center

cen-trip-e-tal [sĕn-trĭp′ĭ-tl] *adjective*, directed toward the center

cen-tu-ry [sĕn′chə-rē] *noun*, a period of one hundred years ce-re-al [sîr′ē-əl] *noun*, any edible grain, including oats, rye, rice

cer-e-bel-lum [sĕr′ə-bĕl′əm] *noun*, the part of the brain related to muscular movements and coordination

ce-re-bral [sĕr′ə-brəl] *adjective*, appealing to the intellect and not the emotions

cer-e-mo-ni-al [sĕr′ə-mō′nē-əl] *adjective*, following a tradition or certain rituals, formal

cer-e-mo-ny [sĕr′ə-mō′nē] *noun*, a special occasion that honors traditions or rituals

cer-tain [sûr ′tn] *adjective*, 1) sure 2) unquestionable 3) not named, but thought to be known

cer-tain-ty [sûr′tn-tē] *noun*, a state of being sure of something

cer-tif-i-cate [sər-tĭf′ĭ-kĭt] *noun*, a document verifying qualification or ability or fact

cer-ti-fy [sûr′tə-fī′] *verb*, to authorize the validity of something, to guarantee

chafe [chāf] *verb*, 1) to rub together leaving a sore 2) to annoy

chaff [chăf] *noun*, 1) a worthless or trivial thing 2) the outer coating of wheat

cha-grin [shə-grĭn′] *noun*, a feeling of embarrassment because one has failed, deep disappointment

chain [chān] *noun*, 1) links or rings joined together, *verb*, 2) to hold with a chain, to restrain

chair [châr] *noun*, furniture with four legs and a back used to seat someone

chal-ice [chăl′ĭs] *noun*, a goblet

chalk [chôk] *noun*, a soft white limestone substance used to write on a blackboard

chal-lenge [chăl′ənj] *noun*, 1) an offer to test ability or skill 2) a formal objection, *verb*, 2) to call or invite to a contest of any kind

cham-ber [chām′bər] *noun*, 1) a room 2) a space surrouded by walls 3) a compartment in a firearm that holds the ammunition

cham-pi-on [chăm′pē-ən] *noun*, the winner of a competition

cham-pi-on-ship [chăm′pē-ən-shĭp′] *noun*, a competition among people or teams to decide who is best

chance [chăns] *noun*, 1) luck, fate 2) possibility or probability 3) risk 4) a turn to do something, an opportunity 5) a coincidence

chan-de-lier [shăn′də-lîr′] *noun*, a branched lighting fixture that hangs from the ceiling in a frame

change [chānj] *noun*, 1) a transformation, the process of becoming different 2) loose coins, *verb*, 3) to make or become different 4) to transform

change-a-ble [chān′jə-bəl] *adjective*, variable, adaptable

chan-nel [chăn′əl] *noun*, 1) a narrow stream of flowing water that connects two large bodies of water, *verb*, 2) to make something, such as energy or water, flow in a certain direction

chant [chănt] *noun*, 1) words repeated in rhythm, *verb*, 2) to speak in a singing way

cha-os [kā′ŏs′] *noun*, disorder, confusion, upheaval

chap-el [chăp′əl] *noun*, a small room within a larger building set aside for religious purposes

chap-er-one [shăp′ə-rōn′] (also **chaperon**) *noun*, an older person who accompanies as a protector

chap-lain [chăp′lĭn] *noun*, a clergyman, minister priest or rabbi serving in a hospital, the armed forces, etc.

chap-ter [chăp′tər] *noun*, a division of a book

char [chär] *verb*, to burn, to scorch

char-ac-ter [kăr′ək-tər] *noun*, 1) the moral makeup of a person 2) a person in a book or movie or play 3) a symbol, sign, or written letter used in a language

char-ac-ter-is-tic [kăr′ək-tə-rĭs′tĭk] *noun*, a trait, an attribute

char-ac-ter-ize [kăr′ək-tə-rīz′] *verb*, to describe, to indicate details or traits of someone or something

char-ac-ter-i-za-tion [kăr′ək-tə-rīz′ā′-shən] *noun*, a description of someone or something

char-coal [chär′kōl′] *noun*, a black porous material made by partially burning wood

charge [chärj] *noun*, 1) an accusation 2) care or instruction given 3) the cost, expense, *verb*, 4) to request money 5) to accuse someone of doing something wrong 6) to rush or attack 7) to fill with power 8) to control

char-i-ot [chăr′ē-ət] *noun*, a horse-drawn cart

cha-ris-ma [kə-rĭz′mə] *noun*, attraction, charm, and allure, having a strong effect on others

char-i-ta-ble [chăr′ĭ-tə-bəl] *adjective*, 1) giving freely and generously 2) lenient, kind

char-i-ty [chăr′ĭ-tē] *noun*, 1) goodness, generosity, and kindness 2) an agency that provides a service to those in need, especially the poor

charm [chärm] *noun*, 1) a pleasant, courteous manner 2) a thing like a talisman or a group of words spoken to cause good luck, *verb*, 3) to please someone

charm-ing [chär′mĭng] *adjective*, pleasing, beautiful, enchanting

chart [chärt] *noun*, 1) a piece of paper or spreadsheet with information on it indicating, patterns, information, or changes, *verb*, 2) to plan a route on a map of the ocean or other large area

char-ter [chär′tər] *noun*, 1) a document establishing the creation of an entity 2) a reservation of a vehicle, ship, etc., *verb*, 3) to hire a ship, bus, plane, etc.

chase [chās] *noun*, 1) the act of running after someone, *verb*, 2) to follow someone while trying to capture them, to pursue

chasm [kăz′əm] *noun*, a deep hole

chas-sis [shăs′ē] *noun*, the under part of a car, consisting of the frame with the wheels and machinery

chaste [chāst] *adjective*, 1) pure, celibate 2) simple in style

chat [chăt] *noun*, 1) a pleasant conversation, *verb*, 2) to make conversation or small talk

chauf-feur [shō'fər] *noun*, a person employed as a driver of a car

chau-vin-ist [shō'və-nĭst] *noun*, a belief in the superiority of your own race, sex, etc.

cheap [chēp] *adjective*, low in price, inexpensive, poorly made

cheat [chēt] *verb*, to do something that is not honest, to deceive

check [chĕk] *noun*, 1) an order for money, *verb*, 2) to make sure everything is in order

check-ers [chĕk'ərz] *noun, plural*, a board game played by two people, each with twelve pieces

cheek [chēk] *noun*, 1) the fleshy skin covering the bone beneath the eye socket on both sides of the face 2) impudent speech

cheer [chîr] *noun*, 1) a shout of support 2) gladness, a joyful state of mind, *verb*, 3) to make happy 4) to encourage with shouts

cheese [chēz] *noun*, the consolidated curd of milk, used as food

chee-tah [chēNt'ə]*noun*, a swift, animal of Africa and Asia, like a leopard, with a small head, long legs, and black-spotted, tan coat

chef [shĕf] *noun*, a head cook

chem-i-cal [kĕm'ĭ-kəl] *noun*, a substance or mixture of substances used in or produced by changes in atoms or molecules

chem-ist [kĕm'ĭst] *noun*, a person who studies matter such as gases, metal, and liquids to see what they do and what they are made of

chem-is-try [kĕm'ĭ-strē] *noun*, the study of the composition, properties, and reactions of matter, particularly at the level of atoms and molecules

cher-ish [chĕr'ĭsh] *verb*, to love dearly, to adore

cher-ry [chĕr'ē] *noun*, an edible, fleshy, red fruit containing a pit

chess [chĕs] *noun*, a game of skill played on a checkered board by two players each with 16 pieces

chest [chĕst] *noun*, 1) the front of the body between the shoulders and the waist 2) a large box made of metal, wood, etc.

chew [chōō] *verb*, to grind food between the teeth

chic [shēk] *noun*, great artistic cleverness or skill, style

chick-en [chĭk'ən] *noun*, fowl kept for eggs or meat

chide [chīd] *verb*, to scold

chief [chēf] *adjective*, 1) highest in office or rank, *noun* 2) the leader of a group or organization

chif-fon [shĭ-fŏn'] *noun*, 1) a soft gauzy silk material used for dresses 2) a light airy dessert made with egg whites

child [chīld] *noun, plural* **children**, a young person, offspring

child-ish [chīl'dĭsh] *adjective*, to be selfish and inconsiderate

chil-i or chili con carne[chĭl'ē] *noun*, a dish of tomatoes, meat, and sometimes beans, flavored with hot spices

chill [chĭl] *adjective*, 1) cold, frosty, *noun*, 2) coldness, freezing, *verb*, 3) to make or become cold

chime [chīm] *verb*, to make a tinkling sound like a bell

chim-ney [chǐm/nē] *noun*, a structure by which smoke passes from a building to the outdoors

chim-pan-zee [chǐm/pǎn-zē/] *noun*, an ape native to Africa larger than a monkey, without a tail

chin [chǐn] *noun*, the part of the face below the lips

chi-na [chī/nə] *noun*, *no plural*, dishes, such as plates, cups, and saucers, made of fine clay or porcelain, used to serve a meal

chip [chǐp] *noun*, 1) a small piece of something that has broken off. 2) a cracker or a thinly sliced fried food 3) the small silicon object that enables the computer to process information, *verb*, 4) to break off small pieces from the main part

chip-munk [chǐp/mǔngk/] *noun*, a tan rodent like a small squirrel with a black stripe from its head to the tip of its tail

chirp [chûrp] *noun*, 1) a high pitched sound, *verb*, 2) to warble, to tweet like a bird

chis-el [chǐz/əl] *noun*, 1) a metal tool with a cutting edge at the end of a blade, *verb*, 2) to carve a sculpture or use a chisel as a tool 3) to swindle, to cheat

chiv-al-ry [shǐv/əl-rē] *noun*, bravery, heroism, courtesy,

chlo-ride [klôr/īd] *noun*, a compound of chlorine with another substance

chlo-rine [klôr/ēn/] *noun*, a yellow-green gas added to water supplies as a disinfectant

chlo-ro-form [klôr/ə-fôrm/] *noun*, a colorless, sweetish liquid used as an anesthetic

chlo-ro-phyll [klôr/ə-fǐl] *noun*, a green pigment in plants, essential for photosynthesis

choc-o-late [chô/kə-lǐt] *noun*, a candy made from cocoa, the roasted seeds of cacao

choice [chois] *adjective*, 1) first rate, *noun*, 2) an act of making a selection or choosing

choir [kwīr] *noun*, a band of singers, especially in church

choke [chōk] *verb*, 1) to feel suffocated because the throat is obstructed 2) to repress

chol-er [kŏl/ər] *noun*, anger

choose [chōōz] *verb*, to pick or select from a group, to make a choice

chop [chŏp] *noun*, 1) a piece of meat near the bone, *verb*, 2) to cut with a sharp blade

cho-ral [kôr/əl] *adjective*, for or relating to a chorus

chord [kôrd] *noun*, a combination of three or more tones sounded together in harmony

chore [chôr] *noun*, a job or distasteful task

cho-re-og-ra-phy [kôr/ē-ŏg/rə-fē, kōr/-] *noun*, 1) the plan of the steps and movements in dancing 2) the creation of ballets or dances

chor-tle [chôr/tl] *verb*, to make a chuckling or snorting noise

cho-rus [kôr′əs] *noun*, 1) a company of singers singing in concert 2) the part of a song that is repeated, the refrain

chow-der [chou′dər] *noun*, a thick soup or stew usually featuring fish, corn, etc.

chris-ten [krĭs′ən] *verb*, to give a name to someone who is baptized into the Christian faith

Chris-tian [krĭs′chən] *noun*, a person who believes in Jesus Christ

chromosome [krō′mə-sōm′] *noun*, a thread-like structure in the nucleus of a cell that carries the genes

chron-ic [krŏn′ĭk] *adjective*, continuing for a long time, habitual, prolonged

chron-i-cle [krŏn′ĭ-kəl] *noun*, a historical register of facts in order of their time

chron-o-log-i-cal [krŏn′ə-lŏj′ĭ-kəl] *adjective*, documented according to the order of time

chuck-le [chŭk′əl] *noun*, 1) a quick laugh or giggle, *verb*, 2) to laugh softly, in a gentle manner

chunk [chŭngk] *noun*, a thick piece of something, a block, a slab

church [chûrch] *noun*, a building in which Christians meet to worship and pray

churn [chûrn] *verb*, to move about with force, to turn violently

ci-der [sī′dər] *noun*, a drink made from pressed apples

ci-gar [sĭ-gär′] *noun*, tobacco leaves rolled together in paper for smoking

cig-a-ret-te [sĭg′ə-rĕt′] *noun*, a cylinder of finely cut tobacco rolled in paper

cin-der [sĭn′dərz] *noun*, a hot coal, an ember

cin-e-ma [sĭn′ə-mə] *noun*, 1) a building where films are shown 2) the movie business

cin-na-mon [sĭn′ə-mən] *noun*, the bark of an East Indian tree, ground into a spice

cir-cle [sûr′kəl] *noun*, 1) a closed curve in which all points are equidistant from the center, a ring 2) a group of people

cir-cuit [sûr′kĭt] *noun*, the circumference or distance around an area

cir-cuit-ous [sər-kyōō′ĭ-təs] *adjective*, roundabout, indirect, meandering, winding

cir-cu-lar [sûr′kyə-lər] *adjective*, 1) round, *noun*, 2) a leaflet, a pamphlet, a newsletter

cir-cu-late [sûr′kyə-lāt′] *verb*, to move about or around

cir-cu-la-tion [sûr′kyə-lā′shən] *noun*, 1) the act of moving around, especially of blood through the body 2) the extent or amount of distribution, dissemination

cir-cum-fer-ence [sər-kŭm′fər-əns] *noun*, the distance around a circle or circular figure

cir-cum-lo-cu-tion [sûr′kəm-lō-kyōō′shən] *noun*, an indirect or roundabout way of expressing something

cir-cum-spec-tion [sûr′kəm-spĕk′shən] *noun*, caution, care, forethought

cir-cum-stance [sûr′kəm-stăns′] *noun*, a particular incident, a state of affairs, events

cir-cum-stan-tial [sûr′kəm-stăn′shəl] *adjective*, relating to evidence that tends to prove a fact at issue by proving other basic events

cir-cum-vent [sûr′kəm-vĕnt′] *verb*, to find a way around, to evade a difficulty

cir-cus [sûr′kəs] *noun*, a traveling show usually performed by clowns and acrobats and tamed animals presented in an arena

cit-a-del [sĭt′ə-dəl] *noun*, fortress

ci-ta-tion [sī-tā′shən] *noun*, 1) a summons to appear in court, a ticket 2) a quote or reference to a document 3) honorary mention to receive an award or degree for meritorious service

cite [sīt] *verb*, 1) to quote or refer to a document 2) to recognize someone for commendable service 3) to write a ticket for violating the law

cit-i-zen [sĭt′ĭ-zən] *noun*, a person whose legal home is a certain place or nation

cit-i-zen-ship [sĭt′ĭ-zən-shĭp′] *noun*, 1) the fact of being a citizen 2)community participation

cit-y [sĭt′ē] *noun*, a large important town, a metropolis

civ-ic [sĭv′ĭk] *adjective*, pertaining to a community or city

civ-il [sĭv′əl] *adjective*, 1) polite 2) relating to a government employee who is not in the armed forces

ci-vil-ian [sĭ-vĭl′yən] *noun*, a person not in the armed forces

ci-vil-i-ty [sĭ-vĭl′ĭ-tē] *noun*, good manners, courtesy

civ-i-li-za-tion [sĭv′ə-lĭ-zā′shən] *noun*, 1)the condition of being civilized or having culture 2)people sharing their way of life and living in one place at a time, any human society

civ-i-lize [sĭv′ə-līz′] *verb*, to reclaim from a savage state

civ-il war *noun*, a war fought in a country between two different groups of the same nation

claim [klām] *noun*, 1) a statement, an assertion *verb*, 2) to say and demand possession of something by demonstrating ownership

claim-ant [klā′mənt] *noun*, a person submitting an application or making a claim

clair-voy-ant [klâr-voi′ənt] *adjective*, having foresight

clam [klăm] *noun*, a shellfish similar to an oyster

clam-or [klăm′ər] *noun*, 1) a loud steady noise, an outcry, *verb*, 2) to make a lot of noise

clan [klăn] *noun*, a group of people sharing one ancestor

clan-des-tine [klăn-dĕs′tĭn] *adjective*, secret, concealed

clang [klăng] *noun*, the sound of one piece of metal hitting another, a ringing sound

clap [klăp] *noun*, 1) a loud noise, as in thunder, *verb*, 2) to make a sound by hitting your hands together, applause

clar-i-fy [klăr′ə-fī′] *verb*, to make or become clear, to explain

clar-i-on [klăr′ē-ən] *adjective*, shrill, loud and clear

clar-i-ty [klăr′ĭ-tē] *adjective*, clearness

clash [klăsh] *noun*, 1) a fight or angry dispute 2) the sound of metal on metal, *verb*, 3) to hit or fight 4)of colors, to look awful together 5) to collide noisily

clasp [klăsp] *noun*, 1) a fastening, *verb*, 2) to hold tightly

class [klăs] *noun*, 1) a group of similar things or people 2) students meeting together for instruction, *verb*, 3) to classify

clas-sic [klăs′ĭk] *adjective*, showing excellence, exemplary

clas-si-cal [klăs′ĭ-kəl] *adjective*, 1)pertaining to ancient Greeks and Romans 2)excellent in a traditional style, esp. of music

clas-si-fi-ca-tion [klăs′ə-fĭ-kā′shən] *noun*, categorizing, grouping

clas-si-fy [klăs′ə-fī′] *verb*, to sort, to form into classes or groupings

clause [klôz] *noun*, 1) a group of words in a sentence that contains a subject and a verb 2) a single part in a contract, law, or treaty

claus-tro-pho-bi-a [klô′strə-fō′bē-ə] *noun*, a fear of being in a close space

claw [klô] *noun*, 1) the sharp, hard nails on the foot of an animal or bird, *verb*, 2) to tear or scratch with the hand or nails

clay [klā] *noun*, a common earth used for making pottery and bricks when baked

clean [klēn] *adjective*, 1) free from dirt, neat, *verb*, 2) to remove dirt and soil or impurities

clean-li-ness [klĕn′lē-nĭs] *noun*, the state of being clean, neatness of person, good hygiene

cleanse [klĕnz] *verb*, 1) to scrub, to wash, to disinfect 2) to absolve

clear [klîr] *adjective*, 1) easily understood 2) transparent 3) distinct or easy to hear, *verb*, 4) to remove items 5) to remove an obstacle, to bring into focus

clear-ance [klîr′əns] *noun*, 1) the act of removing whatever may obstruct 2) permission

clear-ly [klîr′lē] *adverb*, plainly

cleave [klēv] *verb*, 1) to cling, to adhere to 2) to separate or split

cleft [klĕft] *noun*, a space or opening made by or as if by splitting, a crack, a fissure

clem-en-cy [klĕm′ən-sē] *noun*, mildness, leniency, mercy

clench [klĕnch] *verb*, to hold tightly, to grip, to grasp

cler-gy [klûr′j*noun,* ministers of the church as a group

clerk [klûrk] *noun*, a person who does office work, a salesperson

cle-ver [klĕv′ər] *adjective*, quick at learning, smart, good at doing things, resourceful, intelligent

cli-ché [klē-shā′] *noun*, a phrase repeated often, e.g. *down and out*

click [klĭk] *verb*, 1) to make a small noise like a tick on a clock 2) to press the mouse button once

cli-ent [klī′ənt] *noun*, a customer who uses the professional help of another, a patron

cliff [klĭf] *noun*, a high, steep wall of rock or bank on a coast

cli-mac-tic [klĭ-măk′tĭk] *adjective*, relating to the highest point or climax

cli-mate [klī′mĭt] *noun*, the typical weather or atmosphere of a place year after year

cli-max [klī′măks′] *noun*, the crucial point when everything comes together, culmination

climb [klīm] *noun*, 1) the distance traveled up a hill or mountain, *verb*, 2) to go up, to ascend

clime [klīm] *noun*, region, climate

cling [klĭng] *verb*, to hold on tightly, to clutch, to grip

cling-ing [klĭng′ĭng] *adjective*, 1) devoted 2) holding fast 3) dependent

clin-ic [klĭn′ĭk] *noun*, a place that provides medical treatment

clin-ic-al [klĭn′ĭ-kəl] *adjective*, 1) related to observation and treatment of patients 2)scientific and observable

clip [klĭp] *noun*, 1) an object used to fasten things 2) a brisk pace, *verb*, 3) to cut or trim

clique [klēk] *noun*, a small group with joint interests, an exclusive set of friends, a gang

cloak [klōk] *noun*, 1) a loose piece of clothing, usually sleeveless, worn as an outer garment, *verb*, 2) to conceal

clock [klŏk] *noun*, an instrument used to measure time

clog [klôg] *noun*, 1) a blockage 2) a thick-soled shoe with an open back, *verb*, 3) to dance in the

shoes 4) to hinder or obstruct, to be blocked up

close [klōs] *adjective*, 1) near 2) alike, similar, *verb*, 3) to shut out 4) to end

clos-et [klŏz′ĭt] *noun*, a small room or space where clothes are hung and items are stored

clot [klŏt] *noun*, a thickened mass of blood tissue

cloth [klôth] *noun*, a piece of fabric made of natural or synthetic fibers, such as cotton or rayon

cloth-ing [klō′thĭng] *noun*, *no plural*, garments, apparel, things worn as clothes, articles of dress

cloud [kloud] *noun*, 1) a visible mass of water droplets floating in the sky 2) a mass of dust

cloud-y [klou′dē] *adjective*, filled with clouds, overcast

clown [kloun] *noun*, someone who is paid to make people laugh, usually wearing a costume and makeup

club [klŭb] *noun*, 1) a group of people who meet for a common purpose 2) a heavy stick

clue [kloo] *noun*, information or evidence that helps you find the answer to a puzzling question

clum-sy [klŭm′zē] *adjective*, awkward, unhandy, unwieldy

clus-ter [klŭs′tər] *noun*, 1) a clump, a bunch, a small, close group, *verb*, 2) to gather together into a small group

clutch [klŭch] *noun*, 1) the part of a machine that connects and dis-connects the power from the rest of the machine, *verb*, 2) to hold something tightly, to grip, to cling to

clut-ter [klŭt′ər] *noun*, things lying about, a mess

coach [kōch] *noun*, 1) one who trains athletes, actors, or singers 2) a part of a train or bus that carries passengers 3) a carriage drawn by horses, *verb*, 4) to assist talented people develop their capability, to train

co-ag-u-late [kō-ăg′yə-lāt′] *verb*, to form into a dense mass, solidify from a liquid, to congeal

coal [kōl] *noun*, a fossil fuel in solid form that gives off heat when burned

co-a-lesce [kō′ə-lĕs′] *verb*, to combine, to fuse, to join together

co-a-li-tion [kō′ə-lĭsh′ən] *noun*, a union of people of differing views in a single body or group

coarse [kôrs, kōrs] *adjective*, 1) rough in surface or texture 2) crude, ill-mannered

coast [kōst] *noun*, 1) the edge of land that touches the ocean, *verb*, 2) to slide or glide

coat [kōt] *noun*, a piece of clothing with sleeves, worn over everything else, a jacket

coax [kōks] *verb*, to gently persuade

cob-bler [kŏb′lər] *noun*, someone who makes and repairs shoes

cob-web [kŏb′wĕb′] *noun*, threads woven by a spider in which it catches insects

co-caine [kō-kān′] *noun*, a bitter, crystalline alkaloid used as a local anesthetic and illegally as a stimulant

cock [kŏk] *noun*, a male bird

cock-pit [kŏk′pĭt′] *noun*, the compartment in a vehicle where the driver of a race car or the pilot of an airplane sits

co-co-nut [kō′kə-nŭt′] *noun*, the fruit of a variety of palm tree

co-coon [kə-kōōn′] *noun*, the silky case insects live in during the pupa stage

cod [kŏd] *noun*, *no plural*, a family of sea fish used for food

cod-dle [kŏd′l] *verb*, to treat gently, to pamper, to spoil

code [kōd] *noun*, 1) a collection of laws 2) a system of symbols given certain meanings

co-erce [kō-ûrs′] *verb*, to persuade by force

co-er-cion [kō-ûr′zhən] *noun*, persuasion by force or threats, pressuring

cof-fee [kô′fē] *noun*, the hot beverage made from the seeds of a coffee plant, a pale brown color

cof-fin [kô′fĭn] *noun*, a box in which a dead body is placed

cog [kŏg] *noun*, the tooth projecting from a wheel rim or a bar

cog-ni-zant [kŏg′nĭ-zənt] *adjective*, conscious, aware, knowledgeable

co-her-ent [kō-hîr′ənt] *adjective*, 1) able to be understood 2) forming a connection

co-he-sion [kō-hē′zhən] *noun*, the act of sticking together

coil [koil] *noun*, 1) a wire in a continuous circling shape, *verb*, 2) to wrap up around in a ring

coin [koin] *noun*, 1) a piece of money made of metal, legally authorized by a government 2) a quantity of value, *verb*, 3) to make coins 4)to invent

co-in-cide [kō′ĭn-sīd′] *verb*, to occur at the same time, to correspond exactly

co-in-cid-ence [kō-ĭn′sĭ-dəns] *noun*, random events that happen at the same time, chance, luck

col-an-der [kŭl′ən-dər] *noun*, a bowl-shaped container that is perforated for use as a strainer

cold [kōld] *adjective*, 1) feeling no heat, not warm 2) unfriendly, *noun*, 3) a virus with symptoms of a sore throat and runny nose

col-lab-o-rate [kə-lăb′ə-rāt′] *verb*, to work together as a group

col-lab-o-ra-tion [kə-lăb′ə-rā′shən] *noun*, a project that includes ideas from two or more people working together

col-lapse [kə-lăps′] *noun*, 1) any sudden or complete breakdown, *verb*, 2) to break down suddenly 3) to fall down

col-lar [kŏl′ər] *noun*, 1) a band worn around the neck of an animal 2) the part of a shirt around the neck

col-late [kə-lāt′] *verb*, 1) to examine in order to verify a special authenticity 2) to combine and arrange in order

col-lat-er-al [kə-lăt′ər-əl]*adjective*, 1)secondary, *noun*, 2) security in the form of property for repayment of a loan

col-league [kŏl′ēg′] *noun*, an associate from work, a friend or a peer, a co-worker

col-lect [kə-lĕkt′] *verb*, 1) to accumulate, to compile, to scrape together 2) to gather, to meet, to flock, to convene

col-lec-tion [kə-lĕk′shən] *noun*, an accumulation of things of a similar nature

col-lec-tive [kə-lĕk′tĭv] *adjective*, gathered, compiled, joint

col-lege [kŏl′ĭj] *noun*, a place where people study after high school that gives degrees

col-lide [kə-līd′] *verb*, to come together with great force

col-li-sion [kə-lĭzh′ən] *noun*, the act of striking or dashing together, a crash

co-lon [kō′lən] *noun*, 1) the sign [:] which is used before a listing or examples 2) the part of the large intestine extending to the rectum

colo-nel [kûr′nəl] *noun*, the commanding officer of a regiment, below brigadier general

co-lo-ni-al [kə-lō′nē-əl] *adjective*, relating to a period in America before independence

col-o-nist [kŏl′ə-nĭst] *noun*, someone who settles a territory

col-o-ni-za-tion [kŏl′ə-nĭ-zā′shən] *noun*, the act of setting up homes and starting a community in a new place with the purpose of living there a long time

col-o-ny [kŏl′ə-nē] *noun*, a country, area, etc.under the jurisdiction of another country and occupied by settlers

col-or [kŭl′ər] *noun*, 1) any of the hues of the rainbow, including white, *verb*, 2) to paint, dye, tint, to change the hue 3) to affect

Col-o-rado [kŏl'ə-răd'ō] *noun*, one of the United States, the capital city is Denver. The state flower of Colorado is the rocky mountain columbine, and the motto is "Nothing without the divine will."

co-los-sal [kə-lŏs'əl] *adjective*, huge, gigantic, immense

colt [kōlt] *noun*, a young male horse

col-umn [kŏl'əm] *noun*, 1) a supporting pillar 2) a perpendicular set of lines of a text in a book or periodical

col-um-nist [kŏl'əm-nĭst] *noun*, a writer who is featured regularly in a newspaper, or magazine

co-ma [kō'mə] *noun*, state of being unresponsive, unconsciousness

comb [kōm] *noun*, 1) a piece of plastic, wood, or metal with teeth to smooth and adjust hair, *verb*, 2) to tidy hair with a comb

com-bat [kəm-băt'] *noun*, 1) an armed battle, *verb*, 2) to fight

com-bi-na-tion [kŏm'bə-nā'shən] *noun*, the act or result of combining, a union, a mixture

com-bine [kəm-bīn'] *verb*, to mix together, to blend, to unite

com-bus-ti-ble [kəm-bŭs'tə-bəl] *adjective*, apt to catch fire and burn, flammable

come [kŭm] *verb*, 1) to arrive, to approach 2) to happen

com-e-dy [kŏm'ĭ-dē] *noun*, a funny performance that makes the audience laugh, humor

come-ly [kŭm'lē] *adjective*, attractive, beautiful, or handsome

com-et [kŏm'ĭt] *noun*, a celestial object of a frozen mass of dust that vaporizes as it nears the sun

com-fort [kŭm'fərt] *noun*, 1) consolation in trouble, *verb*, 2) to show kindness to someone, to console

com-fort-a-ble [kŭm'fər-tə-bəl] *adjective*, relaxed, content

com-ic [kŏm'ĭk] *adjective*, funny, humorous

com-ma [kŏm'ə] *noun*, a punctuation mark (,) used to indicate pauses and to separate elements within a sentence

com-mand [kə-mănd'] *noun*, 1) an order 2) mastery, rule, *verb*, 3) to be in charge of, to order someone to do something

com-man-deer [kŏm'ən-dîr'] *verb*, to take, often for military use

com-mem-o-rate [kə-měm'ə-rāt'] *verb*, to honor, to memorialize

com-mence-ment [kə-měns'mənt] *noun*, 1) the beginning 2) the ceremony of graduation

com-mend [kə-měnd'] *verb*, to praise, to compliment, to support

com-men-su-rate [kə-měn'sər-ĭt] *adjective*, equal in extent, in proportion, corresponding

com-ment [kŏm'ĕnt] *noun*, 1) a remark or something said, *verb*, 2) to make a remark about something, to express an opinion

com-ment-ary [kŏm'ĕntrĕr'ē] *noun*, remarks or observations about something, an explanation

com-merce [kŏm'ərs] *noun*, business, the buying and selling of goods, all forms of trade

com-mer-cial [kə-mûr'shəl] *adjective*,
1) for business purposes, having
profit as an aim, *noun*, 2) an
advertisement on television or radio

com-mis-er-ate [kə-mĭz'ə-rāt']
verb, to feel or express sorrow

com-mis-sion [kə-mĭsh'ən] *noun*,
1) a committee or board that
studies an issue 2) the
percentage paid to an agent

com-mit [kə-mĭt'] *verb*, 1) to
entrust 2) to pledge 3) to act out,
to perform 4) to put into custody

com-mit-ment [kə-mĭt'mənt] *noun*, a
pledge, a promise, a responsibility

com-mit-tee [kə-mĭt'ē] *noun*, a
group appointed or formed to
consider or accomplish some
matter or business

com-mod-i-ty [kə-mŏd'ĭ-tē] *noun*,
an item that can be bought and
sold, merchandise

com-mon [kŏm'ən] *adjective*,
1) ordinary, found everywhere,
general 2) joint, shared, *noun*,
3) a public outdoor space

com-mon-wealth [kŏm'ən-wĕlth']
noun, 1) a group of independent
states in a country 2)a self-
governed nation or state

com-mo-tion [kə-mō'shən] *noun*,
noise, confusion, disruption,

com-mune [kŏm'yo͞on'] *noun*,
a living arrangement in which
everyone shares possessions,
work, etc.

com-mu-ni-ca-ble
[kə-myo͞o'nĭ-kə-bəl] *adjective*,
contagious, infectious

com-mu-ni-cate [kə-myo͞o'nĭ-kāt']
verb, 1) to give or exchange
information 2) to transmit

com-mu-ni-ca-tion
[kə-myo͞o'nĭ-kā'shən] *noun*,
1) exchange of information
between people 2) that which is
made known 3) transmission

com-mun-ion [kə'myo͞onyən]
noun, 1) the mutual sharing of
feelings and thoughts 2) a
religious fellowship among
members of a church

com-mu-nism [kŏm'yə-nĭz'əm]
noun, a political system in which
property is owned by the state

com-mu-nist [kŏm'yə-nĭst] *noun*, a
person who believes the state
should own all industry and land

com-mu-ni-ty [kə-myo͞o'nĭ-tē]
noun, a town, city, suburb, or
other place where people live
and work, a society

com-mute [kə-myo͞ot'] *verb*, 1) to
make a sentence of punishment
less severe 2) to travel, to go back
and forth to work

com-pact [kəm-păkt'] *adjective*,
1) taking up a small amount of
space, *noun*, 2) a small case
with makeup and a mirror 3) an
agreement, *verb*, 4) to press
close together

com-pan-ion [kəm-păn'yən] *noun*,
a friend or associate, one who
accompanies another

com-pa-ny [kŭm'pə-nē] *noun*,
1) an association for business or
social purposes 2) a corporation
or firm 3) guests, visitors 4) a
subdivision of a regiment

com-pa-ra-ble [kŏm'pər-ə-bəl]
adjective, similar, equivalent

com-pare [kəm-pâr'] *verb*, to look
at similarities and differences

com-par-i-son [kəm-păr′ĭ-sən] *noun*, an examination of two or more objects with the view to discovering the similarities or differences, contrast

com-pass [kŭm′pəs] *noun*, 1) an instrument using a magnetic needle that always points to the north 2) a tool used to draw a circle 3) a range, scope, or limits

com-pas-sion [kəm-păsh′ən] *noun*, sympathy for suffering, kindness

com-pat-i-ble [kəm-păt′ə-bəl] *adjective*, in harmony with something, well-suited

com-pel [kəm-pĕl′] *verb*, 1) to drive or urge with force 2) to coerce

com-pen-di-um [kəm-pĕn′dē-əm] *noun*, an abridgement, collection, summary of information

com-pen-sate [kŏm′pən-sāt′] *verb*, to make up for something, to make amends, to pay

com-pen-sa-tion [kŏm′pən-sā′shən] *noun*, an amount paid to make up for something, payment

com-pete [kəm-pēt′] *verb*, to try to win a race, contest, etc.

com-pe-tent [kŏm′pĭ-tənt] *adjective*, capable, qualified, adequate, proficient, able

com-pe-ti-tion [kŏm′pĭ-tĭsh′ən] *noun*, 1) rivalry, free market conditions 2) a contest to see who performs better, a game

com-pet-i-tor [kəm-pĕt′ĭ-tər] *noun*, a rival, one who competes

com-pile [kəm-pīl′] *verb*, to gather information

com-pla-cen-cy [kəm-plā′sən-sē] *noun*, self-satisfaction, smugness

com-plac-ent [kəm-plā′sənt] *adjective*, 1) self-satisfied, smug 2) agreeable, lazy

com-plain [kəm-plān′] *verb*, 1) to express unhappiness or dissatisfaction or resentment 2) to make a formal accusation

com-plaint [kəm-plānt′] *noun*, 1) a criticism, reproach 2) an illness

com-ple-ment [kŏm′plə-mənt] *noun*, that which fills up, completes, or balances

com-plete [kəm-plēt′] *adjective*, 1) lacking nothing, full, whole, 2) finished, *verb*, 3) to finish

com-plex [kəm-plĕks′] *adjective*, 1) complicated, puzzling 2) consisting of connected parts, *noun*, 3) a group of buildings

com-plex-ion [kəm-plĕk′shən] *noun*, 1) the color or hue of the skin of the face 2) general appearance or aspect

com-pli-ance [kəm-plī′əns] *noun*, the act of yielding to demand, consent, agreement

com-plic-ate [kŏm′plĭ-kāt′] *verb*, to confuse, to perplex, to make more difficult or complex

com-pli-ment [kŏm′plə-mənt] *noun*, 1) nice words said about someone, praise, *verb*, 2) to express admiration, to laud

com-ply [kəm-plī′] *verb*, to follow, to conform, to go along with an order or a rule

com-po-nent [kəm-pō′nənt] *noun*, an essential part, a fundamental piece, a constituent part

com-port [kəm-pôrt′] *verb*, to act in a specified way, to carry oneself

com-pose [kəm-pōz′] *verb*, 1) to write or create music, literature, etc. 2) to blend the ingredients or components of something

com-pos-ite [kəm-pŏz′ĭt] *adjective*, 1) made up of separate distinctive parts 2) relating to a combination of the Corinthian and Ionic styles of architecture

com-po-si-tion [kŏm′pə-zĭsh′ən] *noun*, 1) something written, such as a story or music 2) a creation or formation

com-post [kŏm′pōst′] *noun*, the product from the decomposition of organic materials, such as yard waste or dead plants

com-po-sure [kəm-pō′zhər] *noun*, a settled state, calmness

com-pound [kŏm-pound′] *noun*, 1) a composite, a mixture 2) a fenced-in area with one or more buildings in it, *verb*, 3) to make by mixing together 4) to increase

com-pre-hend [kŏm′prĭ-hĕnd′] *verb*, to understand

com-pre-hen-sive [kŏm′prĭ-hĕn′sĭv] *adjective*, thorough, all-inclusive

com-press [kŏm′prĕs′] *noun*, 1) a bandage, a pad, *verb*, [kŭm′prĕs] 2) to pack, to squeeze

com-prise [kəm-prīz′] *verb*, to include, consisting of

com-pro-mise [kŏm′prə-mīz′] *noun*, 1)the result of adjustments made by concessions to make a mutual agreement, *verb* 2) to adjust by making concessions

com-pul-sion [kəm-pŭl′shən] *noun*, 1) duress, urgency, duty 2) an obsession, a fixation

com-pul-so-ry [kəm-pŭl′sə-rē] *adjective*, required, mandatory

com-pute [kəm-pyo͞ot′] *verb*, to figure mathematically

com-rade [kŏm′răd′] *noun*, a faithful friend, a colleague

con-cave [kŏn-kāv′] *adjective*, sunken, as the inside of a sphere or a spoon

con-ceal [kən-sēl′] *verb*, to hide , to disguise

con-cede [kən-sēd′] *verb*, to surrender, to grant, to allow

con-ceit [kən-sēt′] *noun*, vanity, an exaggerated opinion of oneself, self-importance

con-ceive [kən-sēv′] *verb*, 1) to imagine, to take into one's mind 2) to become pregnant

con-cen-trate [kŏn′sən-trāt′] *verb*, 1) to focus all one's thoughts and efforts on 2) to bring or come together in one place to increase the strength of

con-cen-tra-tion [kŏn′sən-trā′shən] *noun*, 1) density, consistency 2) close attention, intense thought

con-cen-tric [kən-sĕn′trĭk] *adjective*, having a common center

con-cept [kŏn′sĕpt′] *noun*, an abstract idea, a thought

con-cep-tion [kən-sĕp′shən] *noun*, 1) the act of conceiving life 2) the beginning or understanding of an idea

con-cern [kən-sûrn′] *noun*, 1) anxiety 2) something that

involves a person or people,
verb, 3) to be about, to interest
4) to trouble or worry

con-cert [kŏn′sûrt′] *noun*, 1) music
played for an audience,
[kŏn′sûrt] *verb* 2) to plan or
arrange together

con-ces-sion [kən-sĕsh′ən] *noun*,
the act of yielding, a grant

con-cil-i-ate [kən-sĭl′ē-āt]*verb*, to
gain goodwill, to placate

con-cil-i-a-to-ry [kən-sĭl′ē-ə-tôr′ē]
adjective, making less angry or
hostile to overcome animosity

con-cise [kən-sīs′] *adjective*, short,
to the point, brief, succinct

con-clude [kən-klōōd′] *verb*, 1) to
form an opinion after thinking
about something 2) to finish to
bring or come to an end

con-clu-sion [kən-klōō′zhən] *noun*,
1) the end, an outcome 2) a
decision, a judgment

con-coct [kən-kŏkt′] *verb*, 1) to
prepare by combining different
ingredients 2) to devise a plan or
scheme, to invent

con-cor-dant [kən-kôr′dant]
adjective, in agreement,
harmonious

con-crete [kŏn-krēt′] *adjective*,
1) not abstract, particular, *noun*,
2) a compound mass of cement,
sand, gravel, and water used for
building

con-cus-sion [kən-kŭsh′ən] *noun*, a
head injury that is the result of a
blow or a fall, a shock

con-demn [kən-dĕm′] *verb*, 1)to
pronounce sentence against
someone 2) to disapprove of or
censure, to denounce

con-dem-na-tion
[kŏn′dĕm-nā′shən] *noun*,
criticism, blame, an objection

con-den-sa-tion [kŏn′dĕn-sā′shən]
noun, 1) the act, process, or state
of compressing or being
compressed into a smaller
enclosed space 2) the process by
which a substance changes from
its gaseous state to a liquid state
3) the liquid formed by this
process

con-dense [kən-dĕns′] *verb*, to
shorten or compress

con-de-scend [kŏn′dĭ-sĕnd′] *verb*,
to act superior to someone else

con-di-ment [kŏn′də-mənt] *noun*, a
type of relish or seasoning

con-di-tion [kən-dĭsh′ən] *noun*,
1) a stipulation or provision
2) the state in which a person or
thing exists, *verb*, 3) to prepare,
to adapt, to train, to influence

con-di-tion-ing [kən-dĭsh′ən-ing]
noun, preparation, training

con-dol-ence [kən-dō′ləns] *noun*,
an offering of sympathy, an
expression of regret

con-done [kən-dōn′] *verb*, to
pardon, to forgive, to overlook

con-du-cive [kən-dōō′sĭv]
· *adjective*, tending to promote,
helpful, beneficial

con-duct *noun*, [kən-dŭkt′]
1) behavior, [kən-dŭkt′] *verb*, 2)
to lead or guide 3) to direct

con-duc-tor [kən-dŭk′tər] *noun*,
1) someone who sells tickets on
a train 2) something that
transmits energy 3) the leader of
a musical ensemble

con-duit [kŏn′dōō-ĭt] *noun*, a
channel or passage through
which electrical wires run

cone [kōn] *noun*, 1) a cylinder that
tapers to a point at the end
2) the reproductive structures of
the conifer trees, a pine cone
3) a cylindrical wafer on which a
scoop of ice cream is placed

con-fed-er-ate [kən-fĕd′ər-ĭt] *noun*,
1) an ally, an accomplice
Condederate 2) someone who
fought for the Confederacy during
the Civil War

con-fed-er-a-tion
[kən-fĕd′ə-rā′shən] *noun*, an
alliance, a coalition

con-fer [kən-fûr′] *verb*, 1) to give
as a gift 2) to meet and discuss

con-fer-ence [kŏn′fər-əns] *noun*, a
meeting for an exchange of
ideas, a conversation with
someone to share information

con-fess [kən-fĕs′] *verb*, to
acknowledge or admit a fault

con-fes-sion [kən-fĕsh′ən] *noun*,
an admission of guilt or
wrongdoing

con-fet-ti [kən-fĕt′ē] *noun*, small
pieces of colorful paper scattered
at celebrations

con-fi-dant [kŏn′fĭ-dănt′] *noun*,
one to whom secrets are
entrusted, a friend

con-fide [kən-fīd′] *verb*, to trust, to
disclose a secret, to reveal

con-fi-dence [kŏn′fĭ-dəns] *noun*,
complete trust, a secret

con-fi-dent [kŏn′fĭ-dənt] *adjective*,
assured beyond doubt, self-
reliant, feeling certain, sure

con-fi-den-tial [kŏn′fĭ-dĕn′shəl]
adjective, secret, private, trusted

con-fine [kən-fīn′] *verb*, to
restrain, within a specific place

con-firm [kən-fûrm′] *verb*, to give
proof of something, to ratify

con-fir-ma-tion [kŏn′fər-mā′shən]
noun, 1) proof, collaboration 2) a
ceremony recognizing a member
of the church

con-fis-cate [kŏn′fĭ-skāt′] *verb*, to
seize, to take without consent

con-flict [kŏn′flĭkt′] *noun*, 1) a fight
or argument, a disagreement,
verb, 2) to disagree or clash

con-form [kən-fôrm′] *verb*, to
comply, to obey social norms

con-form-i-ty [kən-fôr′mĭ-tē]
noun, harmony, agreement

con-fuse [kən-fyōōz′] *verb*, to mix
up in the mind, to perplex

con-fu-sion [kən-fyōō′zhən] *noun*,
a state of disorder, chaos,
bewilderment

con-geal [kən-jēl′] *verb*, 1) to
change from a fluid state to a
solid state 2) to thicken

con-gen-ial [kən-jēn′yəl] *adjective*,
naturally adapted, pleasant and
sympathetic, good-natured

con-gen-i-tal [kən-jĕn′ĭ-tl]
adjective, existing at birth

con-ges-tion [kən-jĕs′shən] *noun*,
1) a gathering or accumulation
2) an overcrowded state

con-glom-er-a-tion
[kən-glŏm′ə-rā′shən] *noun*,
material sticking together

con-grat-u-la-tions
[kən-grăch′ə-lā′shənz]
noun, plural, expressions of good

wishes for a happy event or achievement

con-gre-gate [kŏng′grĭ-gāt′] *verb*, to gather together, to assemble

con-gre-ga-tion [kŏng′grĭ-gā′shən] *noun*, a gathering or assembly

con-gress [kŏng′grĭs] *noun*, 1) a meeting of a group of people **Congress** 2)the legislature of the United States consisting of the Senate and the House of Representatives

con-gru-ent [kŏng′grōō-ənt] *adjective*, in agreement, exactly alike, matching, equal

con-jec-ture [kən-jĕk′chər] *noun*, theory, an unfounded remark

con-ju-gate [kŏn′jə-gāt′] *verb*, to change the form of a verb depending on the subject and the tense, e.g. *I am, you are, he is, we are, you are, they are*

con-junc-tion [kən-jŭngk′shən] *noun*, a word that joins two other words or phrases together

con-jure [kŏn′jər] *verb*, 1) to seem to create out of thin air as if by magic 2) to entreat, to summon

con-nect [kə-nĕkt′] *verb*, to join or bring together, to link, to unite

Con-nect-i-cut [kə-nĕt′ĭ-kət] *noun*, one of the 50 United States, the capital is Hartford. The state flower of **Connecticut** is the mountain laurel, and the motto is "He who transplanted still sustains."

con-nec-tion [kə-nĕk′shən] *noun*, the act of joining, a relationship

con-nive [kə-nīv′] *verb*, to cooperate in a crime or fault, to secretly allow, to deceive

con-nois-seur [kŏn′ə-sûr′] *noun*, one who is an expert judge of art and style or taste

con-no-ta-tion [kŏn′ə-tā′shən] *noun*, suggested meaning

con-quer [kŏng′kər] *verb*, 1) to gain or acquire by force, to be victorious, to win, to defeat 2) to master, to overcome

con-quest [kŏn′kwĕst′] *noun*, a takeover, a triumph, a victory

con-science [kŏn′shəns] *noun*, a sense of moral goodness

con-sci-en-tious [kŏn′shē-ĕn′shəs] *adjective*, influenced by conscience, careful, thoughtful

con-scious [kŏn′shəs] *adjective*, aware of, awake, alert

con-scious-ly [kŏn′shəs-lē] *adverb*, after thorough consideration, with full awareness

con-se-crate [kŏn′sĭ-krāt′] *verb*, to dedicate, to declare sacred

con-sec-u-tive [kən-sĕk′yə-tĭv] *adjective*, one after another

con-sen-sus [kən-sĕn′səs] *noun*, agreement in opinion, custom, or function, the popular choice

con-sent [kən-sĕnt′] *noun*, 1) an agreement, permission, *verb*, 2) to agree, to comply

con-se-quence [kŏn′sĭ-kwĕns′] *noun*, 1) that which follows as a result, outcome 2) importance

con-se-quen-tial [kŏn′sĭ-kwĕn′shəl] *adjective*, significant, very important

con-ser-va-tion [kŏn′sûr-vā′shən] *noun*, the planned management of natural resources to prevent loss, destruction, or waste

con-serv-a-tive [kən-sûr′və-tĭv]
adjective, 1) opposed to change
or innovation 2) traditional
3) a low estimated number

con-ser-va-tor-y [kən-sûr′və-tôr′ē]
noun, 1) a small greenhouse for
growing plants 2) a college of
music, an academy

con-serve [kən-sûrv′] *verb*, to keep
from loss or waste, to preserve

con-sid-er [kən-sĭd′ər] *verb*, 1) to
think about carefully, 2) to take
into account 3) to believe

con-sid-er-a-ble [kən-sĭd′ər-ə-bəl]
adjective, important, great, large

con-sid-er-ate [kən-sĭd′ər-ĭt]
adjective, caring about a
person's feelings, courteous

con-sid-er-a-tion
[kən-sĭd′ə-rā′shən] *noun*,
1) thought and attention
2) a payment

con-sign [kən-sīn′] *verb*, 1) to ship
something to an agent in another
place, to deliver 2) to assign

con-sign-ment [kən-sīn′mənt]
noun, 1) the entrusting of
something to another's care 2) a
quantity of goods for delivery

con-sist [kən-sĭst′] *verb*, to be
made of or composed of

con-sist-ent [kən-sĭs′tənt]
adjective, sticking to the same
principles, the same throughout

con-so-la-tion [kŏn′sə-lā′shən]
noun, comfort, sympathy

con-sole [kən-sōl′] *verb*, to
comfort, to calm, to soothe

con-sol-i-date [kən-sŏl′ĭ-dāt′] *verb*,
to unite, to bring together , to
strengthen, to make solid

con-so-nant [kŏn′sə-nənt]

adjective, 1) in agreement, *noun*,
2) a letter in the alphabet other
than a vowel

con-spic-u-ous [kən-spĭk′yoo-əs]
adjective, plainly visible,
prominent, attracting attention

con-spir-a-cy [kən-spîr′ə-sē] *noun*,
a combination of people often
for an evil purpose, a secret plan

con-stant [kŏn′stənt] *adjective*,
continuous, unceasing, faithful

con-stel-la-tion [kŏn′stə-lā′shən]
noun, an arrangement of stars
that resembles a figure

con-sti-tute [kŏn′stĭ-toot′] *verb*, to
make up, to empower

con-sti-tu-tion [kŏn′stĭ-too′shən]
noun, the fundamental law of a
nation, state, or society

con-sti-tu-tion-al[kŏn′stĭtoo′shənl]
adjective, according to law

con-strain [kən-strān′] *verb*, to
force, to restrain unnaturally

con-struct [kən-strŭkt′] *verb*, to
build a structure, to erect

con-struc-tion [kən-strŭk′shən]
noun, 1) something that is built,
a structure 2) the arrangement of
words in parts of a sentence

con-struc-tive [kən-strŭk′tĭv]
adjective, helpful, useful,
productive, beneficial

con-strue [kən-stroo′] *verb*, to
interpret, to try to understand

con-sult [kən-sŭlt′] *verb*, to ask for
help looking for more
information, to confer

con-sult-ant [kən-sŭl′tənt] *noun*,
an expert hired to study data to
resolve a problem or give advice

con-sume [kən-soōm'] *verb*, 1) to eat 2) to exhaust, to expend 3) to make use of, to apply 4) to destroy

con-sum-er [kən-soō'mər] *noun*, 1)a higher level organism that gets its food from other living things 2) someone who buys products, a customer

con-sum-mate [kŏn'sə-māt'] *verb*, to bring to completion, to perfect

con-sump-tion [kən-sŭmp'shən] *noun*, 1) the use of goods 2) a disease of the lungs, such as tuberculosis 3) the eating of food

con-tact [kŏn'tăkt'] *noun*, 1) a physical touch 2) a connection through writing or speaking, *verb*, 3) to talk or write to, to touch

con-ta-gi-ous [kən-tā'jəs] *adjective*, of a disease passed from one person to another by touch or proximity

con-tain [kən-tān'] *verb*, 1) to have inside, to hold 2) to include

con-tain-er [kən-tā'nər] *noun*, anything that can hold and carry something, eg., a box, jar, basket

con-tam-i-nant [kən-tăm'ə-nənt] *noun*, a compound that pollutes, making the original substance impure, a poison, a toxin

con-tam-i-nate [kən-tăm'ə-nāt'] *verb*, to soil, to stain or corrupt by contact, to pollute, to infect

con-tam-i-na-tion [kən-tăm'ə-nā'shən] *noun*, the act of making a substance impure or unusable

con-tem-plate [kŏn'təm-plāt'] *verb*, to consider with continued attention, to think about, to ponder

con-tem-po-rar-y [kən-tĕm'pə-rĕr'ē] *adjective*, 1) of the present day, current, *noun*, 2) a person of the same age, a peer

con-tempt [kən-tĕmpt'] *noun*, a feeling that someone or something is bad

con-tempt-i-ble [kən-tĕmp'tə-bəl] *adjective*, despicable, vile

con-tent [kən-tĕnt'] *adjective*, 1) happy, satisfied, [kŏn'-tĕnt] *noun*, 2) that which is inside 3) the subject matter of a book

con-ten-tion [kən-tĕn'shən] *noun*, a struggle, an argument, a dispute

con-ten-tious [kən-tĕn'shəs] *adjective*, argumentative, quarrelsome, causing disagreement

con-test [kŏn'tĕst] *noun*, 1) a game in which there is a winner [kən-tĕst']*verb*, 2) to disagree, to object to, to challenge

con-text [kŏn'tĕkst'] *noun*, the words or actions that provide a necessary link or explanation to the meaning of a word or event

con-tig-u-ous [kən-tĭg'yoō-əs] *adjective*, adjoining, touching

con-ti-nent [kŏn'tə-nənt] *noun*, a major land area in the world unbroken by major oceans

con-tin-gent [kən-tĭn'jənt] *adjective*, conditional, relying on chance or something happening

con-tin-u-al [kən-tĭn'yoō-əl] *adjective*, happening repeatedly

con-tin-ue [kən-tĭn'yoō] *verb*, 1) to go on, to resume 2) to persevere

con-tin-u-ous [kən-tĭn'yoō-əs] *adjective*, uninterrupted

con-tor-tion [kən-tôr′shən] *noun*, something bent or twisted out of shape, a distortion

con-tour [kŏn′tŏŏr′] *noun*, the outline of a figure, body, hill, coastline, etc.

con-tra-band [kŏn′trə-bănd′] *noun*, illegal goods, smuggled materials

con-tract [kŏn′trăkt′] *noun*, 1) a written agreement between two or more persons that has the force of law, [kən′-trăkt′] *verb*, 2) to draw closer together 3) to make a binding agreement

con-trac-tion [kŏn′trăk′ shən] *noun*, 1) the shortening of a word or group of words by omitting a letter or letters and replacing them with an apostrophe, e.g. y*ou'll* 2) the act of drawing together like muscles

con-tra-dict [kŏn′trə-dĭkt′] *verb*, to say the opposite, to oppose in words, to conflict with

con-trar-y [kŏn′trĕr′ē] *adjective*, opposite, perverse, wayward

con-trast [kən-trăst′] *noun*, 1) the difference, *verb*, 2) to compare in order to show the differences between two things

con-trib-ute [kən-trĭb′yŏŏt] *verb*, to give as part of a group effort, to help in causing

con-tri-bu-tion [kŏn′trĭ-byŏŏ′shən] *noun*, an offering, a donation

con-trite [kən-trīt′] *adjective*, asking forgiveness, remorseful

con-trive [kən-trīv′] *verb*, to invent or make a clever device

con-trol [kən-trōl′] *noun*, 1) power, guidance, *verb*, 2) to manage or oversee a situation or machine

con-tro-ver-sy [kŏn′trə-vûr′sē] *noun*, a disagreement or debate

con-tu-sion [kən-tŏŏ′zhən] *noun*, a wound or bruise that does not break the skin

con-va-les-cent [kŏn′və-lĕs′ənt] *adjective*, recovering from sickness

con-vene [kən-vēn′] *verb*, to assemble, to call together

con-ven-ience [kən-vēn′yəns] *noun*, the state of being easily used or immediately available

con-ven-ient [kən-vēn′yənt] *adjective*, adapted to one's comfort or ready use, handy

con-vent [kŏn′vənt] *noun*, a home where nuns live

con-ven-tion [kən-vĕn′shən] *noun*, 1) an assembly of members of a delegation 2) a practice or custom 3) a formal agreement

con-ven-tion-al [kən-vĕn′shə-nəl] *adjective*, contemporary

con-verge [kən-vûrj′] *verb*, to come together, to assemble

con-ver-sant [kən-vûr′sənt] *adjective*, familiar with

con-ver-sa-tion [kŏn′vər-sā′shən] *noun*, an informal discourse, a chat or familiar talk

con-verse *noun*, [kən- vûrs′] 1) the contrary or opposite, [kŏn′vûrs′] *verb*, 2) to talk or exchange ideas

con-ver-sion [kən-vûr′zhən] *noun*, a change from one thing, state, or religion to another

con-vert [kən-vûrt′] *verb*, to change into something else

con-vex [kŏn′vĕks′] *adjective*, curved out like the outside of a sphere or ball or spoon

con-vey [kən-vā′] *verb*, 1) to take or transport, to carry 2) to communicate, to pass on, to impart, to give 3) to transmit

con-vict [kən-vĭkt′] *noun*, 1) a person who has been judged guilty of a crime, and sentenced *verb*, 2) to decide in court that someone has committed a crime

con-vic-tion [kən-vĭk′shən] *noun*, a strong belief, the state of being convinced, complete confidence

con-vince [kən-vĭns′] *verb*, to satisfy by proof

con-vo-lut-ed [kŏn′və-loo′tĭd] *adjective*, coiled around, intricate, complicated

con-vul-sions [kŏn′və-loo′shənz] *noun, plural,* strong and uncontrolled involuntary muscle contractions

cook [kook] *noun,* 1) someone who prepares food to eat, *verb,* 2) to prepare food for eating on the stove or in an oven, to bake

cool [kool] *adjective,* 1) moderately cold 2) calm, *verb,* 3) to lower temperature 4) to calm down

coop [koop] *noun,* a pen, a hen-house, a cage for poultry

co-op-er-ate [kō-ŏp′ə-rāt′] *verb*, to work together, to collaborate

co-op-er-a-tion [kō-ŏp′ə-rā′shən] *noun,* the process of working together toward a common goal

co-op-er-a-tive [kō-ŏp′ər-ə-tĭv] *adjective*, willing to join together to help other people

co-or-di-nate [kō-ôr′dn-āt′] *verb,* to make the parts of something work together, to harmonize

co-or-di-na-tion [kō-ôr′dn-ā′shən] *noun,* 1)the organization of separate elements working together 2) dexterity

cope [kōp] *verb,* to deal successfully with something

cop-per [kŏp′ər] *noun,* a common metal of a reddish color, a good conductor of heat and electricity

cop-y [kŏp′ē] *noun,* 1) an imitation, reproduction, *verb,* 2) to make something that is the same as something else

cop-y-right [kŏp′ē-rīt′] *noun,* the exclusive right to publish and sell the matter and form of a literary or artistic work

cor-al [kôr′əl] *noun,* 1) a pink reddish color, salmon 2) a stony substance formed from the skeletons of tiny animals that live on reefs in the ocean

cord [kôrd] *noun,* thin rope

cor-dial [kôr′jəl] *adjective,* sincere, friendly, encouraging, gracious

core [kôr] *noun,* 1) the heart, essence 2) the center of focus

cork [kôrk] *noun,* a light substance that comes from the outer bark of a tree

corn [kôrn] *noun,* 1) a sore that sometimes grows on toes when shoes are tight 2) a grain grown on a stalk as an ear (maize)

cor-ner [kôr′nər] *noun,* 1) a nook, a niche 2) where two lines, edges or streets meet, *verb,* 3) to put someone in a place they cannot escape 4) to monopolize

cor-nu-co-pi-a [kôr′nə-kō′pē-ə] *noun*, 1) a horn containing an abundantly overflowing supply of food 2) abundance, plenty

cor-ol-lary [kôr′ə-lĕr-ē] *noun*, what follows logically, the consequence or effect

cor-o-na-tion [kôr′ə-nā′shən] *noun*, a ceremony to crown a king or queen

cor-po-ra-tion [kôr′pə-rā′shən] *noun*, a business that operates as a person under the law

corps [kôr] *noun*, a troop, a main subdivision of an army

corpse [kôrps] *noun*, a dead body

cor-pu-lent [kôr′pyə-lənt] *adjective*, very fat

cor-pus-cle [kôr′pə-səl] *noun*, a minute particle of matter, a cell, a red or white blood cell

cor-ral [kə-răl′] *noun*, a pen for livestock

cor-rect [kə-rĕkt′] *adjective*, 1) without error, *verb*, 2) to point out an error 3) to make right

cor-rec-tion [kə-rĕk′shən] *noun*, a change or revision, to remove error, to make right

cor-rel-ate [kôr′ə-lāt′] *verb*, to be linked to something

cor-re-la-tion [kôr′ə-lā′shən] *noun*, a mutual relationship, a connection

cor-re-spond [kôr′ĭ-spŏnd′] *verb*, 1) to communicate by writing and receiving letters 2) to fit in with, to match, to agree

cor-re-spond-ence [kôr′ĭ-spŏn′dəns] *noun*, an exchange of letters

cor-ri-dor [kôr′ĭ-dər] *noun*, a hallway connecting rooms or apartments opening onto it

cor-rob-o-rate [kə-rŏb′ə-rāt′] *verb*, to confirm or support with facts,

cor-ro-sive [kə-rō′sĭv] *adjective*, 1) eating away gradually by chemicals 2) sarcastic

cor-ru-gat-ed [kôr′ə-gā′tĭd] *adjective*, bent into a series of alternate ridges and grooves for added stiffness

cor-rupt [kə-rŭpt′] *adjective*, 1) crooked, dishonest, *verb*, 2) to cause to become dishonest

cor-rup-tion [kə-rŭp′shən] *noun*, dishonesty, depravity

cort-ege [kôr-tĕzh′] *noun*, a funeral procession

cos-met-ic [kŏz-mĕt′ĭk] *noun*, a beauty product

cos-mic [kŏz′mĭk] *adjective*, universal, vast

cost [kôst] *noun*, 1) the price you pay when you buy something, *verb*, 2) to have as a price

cos-tume [kŏs′tōōm′] *noun*, clothes worn for a special occasion to represent a particular period in history, traditions of a country, or an assumed character

cot [kŏt] *noun*, a lightweight collapsible bed that usually folds up to a smaller size

cot-tage [kŏt′ĭj] *noun*, a small country house, a bungalow

cot-ton [kŏt′n] *noun*, 1) the white part of the cotton plant used to make cloth 2) the fabric made from this

couch [kouch] *noun*, an upholstered piece of furniture that seats several people

cough [kôf] *noun*, 1) a hacking sound made when air is expelled from the lungs, *verb*, 2) to make a sharp noise when air comes up from the lungs

could [kŏŏd] *verb past tense* of **can**

could-n't [kŏŏd'nt] the *contraction* of the words **could** and **not**

coun-cil [koun'səl] *noun*, an assembly of men and women convened for consultation

coun-sel [koun'səl] *noun*, 1) an attorney, a lawyer 2) an interchange of opinions, advice, *verb*, 3) to advise

coun-se-lor [koun'sə-lər] *noun*, someone who helps you make the best choice

count [kount] *noun*, 1) the total number added together, *verb*, 2) to add up 3) to recite numbers in the correct order 4) to list

coun-te-nance [koun'tə-nəns] *noun*, a facial expression, aspect, appearance, composure

coun-ter [koun'tər] *noun*, 1) the table between customers and workers in a business, *verb*, 2) to make an offer against another

coun-ter-act [koun'tər-ăkt'] *verb*, to act against, to neutralize, to prevent the effects of

coun-ter-clock-wise [koun'tər-klŏk'wīz'] *adjective*, in the opposite direction from the movement of the hands of a clock

coun-ter-feit [koun'tər-fĭt'] *noun*, 1) an imitation intended to deceive, *verb*, 2) to imitate or make a copy of

coun-ter-part [koun'tər-pärt'] *noun*, a thing that completes another, a mate

coun-try [kŭn'trē] *noun*, 1) the land ruled by a government, a nation 2) the land outside of a city, usually farmland or forests

coun-ty [koun'tē] *noun*, an administrative division of a state

coup [kōō] *noun*, a successful sudden attack to seize power

coupe [kōōp] *noun*, a sports car with a sloping back

cou-ple [kŭp'əl] *noun*, 1) two people or things that are usually thought of together, a pair, *verb*, 2) to fasten

cou-pon [kōō'pŏn'] *noun*, a certificate that gives a discount on a purchase, a rebate

cour-age [kûr'ĭj] *noun, no plural*, the strength to face danger when overwhelmed by fear

cou-ra-geous [kə-rā'jəs] *adjective*, brave or bold in danger

cour-i-er [kŏŏr'ē-ər] *noun*, a messenger who carries documents

course [kôrs] *noun*, 1) the path of something, the sequence of events 2) a portion of a meal 3) a series of lessons in a school

court [kôrt] *noun*, 1) a place where judges decide how people who break laws should be punished and civil cases heard 2) an open space next to a house in an enclosed area 3) the members of a royal family 4) a royal palace *verb*, 5) to date

cour-te-ous [kûr′tē-əs] *adjective*, showing good manners, polite

cour-te-sy [kûr′tĭ-sē] *noun*, politeness, civility, consideration

court-ship [kôrt′shĭp′] *noun*, going steady, a period of dating before marriage

cous-in [kŭz′ĭn] *noun*, the son or daughter of your uncle or aunt

cove [kōv] *noun*, an inlet

cov-e-nant [kŭv′ə-nənt] *noun*, 1) a legal undertaking to do or to refrain from doing some act or thing 2) a contract under seal

cov-er [kŭv′ər] *noun*, 1) something that is placed over something to protect it, *verb*, 2) to protect by placing a lid, wrapping, etc., around or on top of 3) to hide 4) to go over

co-vert [kŭv′ərt] *adjective*, concealed, hidden, or sheltered

cov-et [kŭv′ĭt] *verb*, to want to have a thing belonging to another person

cow [kou] *noun*, a grown female cattle or certain other large animals

cow-ard [kou′ərd] *noun*, someone who is easily frightened, a person who lacks courage

cow-ard-ice [kou′ər-dĭs]*noun*, lack of courage to face danger, timidity, fearfulness

cow-ard-ly [kou′ərd-lē] *adjective*, timid, afraid, scared, fearful

cow-boy [kou′boi′] *noun*, a man who rides a horse and looks after livestock on a ranch

cow-er [kou′ər] *verb*, to shrink from as if from fear, to tremble

coy-o-te [kī-ō′tē] *noun*, a North American, wolflike dog

co-zy [kō′zē] *adjective*, snug, warm

crab [krăb] *noun*, a sea animal with eight legs, a pair of pincers and a hard shell that lives in a hole

crack [krăk] *noun*, 1) a line showing where something is broken, a crevice 2) a sharp noise, such as a gunshot or thunder, *verb*, 3) to break while separating

cra-dle [krād′l] *noun*, 1) a small bed for an infant 2) the holder for a telephone, *verb*, 3) to rock or shelter an infant or comfort a crying baby

craft [krăft] *noun*, 1) something made by hand to be used as a decoration 2) a boat or plane 3) guile, slyness, skill

cram [krăm] *verb*, to fill or force in

cramp [krămp] *noun*, 1) a painful muscle spasm, *verb*, 2) to keep within narrow limits, to confine

crane [krān] *noun*, a machine designed to lift heavy loads from one place to another

cra-ni-um [krā′nē-əm] *noun*, the skull of a vertebrate animal

crank [krăngk] *noun*, a handle that is attached to a machine and that turns, causing motion

crash [krăsh] *noun*, 1) a loud noise caused by a collision or something falling, *verb*, 2) to shatter violently, scattering pieces everywhere

crass [krăs] *adjective*, grossly insensible, rude coarse

crate [krāt] *noun*, a large usually wooden box or container, a case

cra-ter [krā'tər] *noun*, a bowl-shaped cavity, a hole

crave [krāv] *verb*, to want something badly

crawl [krôl] *verb*, to move on one's hands and knees, to move slowly

cray-on [krā'ŏn'] *noun*, a small pencil of colored wax used for drawing or writing

craze [krāz] *noun*, a fad, a popular idea, a trend

cra-zy [krā'zē] *adjective*, insane, wild, daft, very foolish

creak [krēk] *verb*, to make the sound of a door that has not been oiled, a long squeak

cream [krēm] *adjective*, 1) the color yellowish white, ivory 2) a thick lotion, *noun*, 3) the fatty part of milk

crease [krēs] *noun*, the mark or line left by a fold, a wrinkle, a furrow

cre-ate [krē-āt'] *verb*, to make, to bring into being, to produce for the first time

cre-a-tion [krē-ā'shən] *noun*, the act of causing to exist, that which is produced

cre-a-tive [krē-ā'tĭv] *adjective*, having new or original ideas

cre-a-tiv-i-ty [krē-ā'tĭv-ĭ-tē] *noun*, the ability to make or invent things, originality

crea-ture [krē'chər] *noun*, an animal or insect or person

cre-den-tials [krĭ-děn'shəlz] *noun*, a document verifying a person's ability or authority, references

cred-i-ble [krěd'ə-bəl] *adjective*, 1) believable 2) reliable or trustworthy

cred-it [krěd'ĭt] *noun*, 1) a system in which merchandise is given with the understanding that it will be paid for later 2) attention and praise received for doing something

cred-o [krē'dō] *noun*, creed, a belief

cred-u-lous [krěj'ə-ləs] *adjective*, easily imposed upon, gullible

creed [krēd] *noun*, a statement of religious or ethical beliefs, principles

creek [krēk, krĭk] *noun*, a stream smaller than a river and larger than a brook, an inlet of water

creep [krēp] *verb*, to move slowly and quietly, to move furtively

cre-o-sote [krē'ə-sōt'] *noun*, an oily liquid obtained from coal tar and used as a wood preservative

cre-scen-do [krə-shěn'dō] *noun*, a musical direction used to indicate increasing loudness

cres-cent [krěs'ənt] *noun*, a curved shape like a new moon

crest [krěst] *noun*, 1) the feathers that stick up on top of a bird's head 2) the top of something

crev-ice [krěv'ĭs] *noun*, a narrow opening in a surface resulting from a split, a cleft, a gap

crew [krōō] *noun*, a group of people who work together

crib [krĭb] *noun*, 1) a bed made for an infant 2) a container for grain

crick-et [krĭk'ĭt] *noun*, 1) a ball game played with two teams of eleven players 2) a small brown insect that makes a shrill chirping noise at night

cried [krīd] *verb, past tense* of **cry**

crime [krīm] *noun*, something that is against the law, illegal acts

crim-i-nal [krĭm'ə-nəl] *adjective*, 1) illegal, wrong, *noun*, 2) one who has broken the law and is guilty of a crime

cringe [krĭnj] *verb*, to shrink back in fear, to cower in fear

crip-ple [krĭp'əl] *verb*, to disable or make lame

cri-sis [krī'sĭs] *noun, plural,* **crises** [krī'-sēz], a stressful time when something serious is happening

crisp [krĭsp] *adjective*, 1) dry, brittle, easily broken 2) firm and fresh 3) very clean and pressed

criss cross [krĭs'krôs'] *noun*, a pattern of intersecting lines

cri-te-ri-on [krī-tîr'ē-ən] *noun, plural,* **criteria**, a standard for judgment, a benchmark

crit-ic [krĭt'ĭk] *noun*, 1) a person who is paid to review a performance or art 2) one who finds faults

crit-i-cal [krĭt'ĭ-kəl] *adjective*, 1) very important, able or inclined to pass judgment 2) crucial, pivotal, key

crit-i-cism [krĭt'ĭ-sĭz'əm] *noun*, faultfinding, review

crit-i-cize [krĭt'ĭ-sīz'] *verb*, to examine as a critic, to censure

croak [krōk] *noun*, 1) a hoarse sound like that made by frogs, *verb*, 2) to make a low hoarse sound in the throat

croc-o-dile [krŏk'ə-dīl'] *noun*, a large reptile, like an alligator, that lives in tropical climates

crook-ed [krŏok'ĭd] *adjective*, 1) bent, not straightened 2) dishonest, deceitful

crop [krŏp] *noun*, food that is planted and grown in a field

cross [krôs] *adjective*, 1) irritated, angry, *noun*, 2) a shape with four arms, *verb*, 3) to go over, to extend across

crouch [krouch] *verb*, to stoop

crow [krō] *noun*, 1) any of a genus of large black birds including the raven, *verb*, 2) to make a sound like a rooster

crowd [kroud] *noun*, 1) a large gathering of people or things, *verb*, 2) to press or cram

crown [kroun] *noun*, 1) a circular head covering, often made of metal with precious stones, worn by royalty, *verb*, 2) to top, to culminate, to climax

cru-ci-al [krōo'shəl] *adjective*, important or essential as decisive in determining a doubtful crisis

cru-ci-ble [krōo'sə-bəl] *noun*, a vessel used for melting substances

cru-ci-fix-ion [krōo'sə-fĭk'shən] *noun*, the killing of someone by nailing them to a cross

crude [krōod] *adjective*, 1) roughly made 2) rude, ill-mannered

cru-el [krōo'əl] *adjective*, mean, deliberately causing pain

cru-el-ty [krōo'əl-tē] *noun*, unkindness, oppression

cruise [krōoz] *noun,* 1) a holiday on ship, *verb*, 2) to sail or drive around

crum-ble [krŭm′bəl] *verb*, to fall or break apart into small pieces

cru-sade [kroo-sād′] *noun*, 1) a campaign conducted by a band of people devoted to advancing a cause, *verb*, 2) to battle for a cause

crush [krŭsh] *verb*, to hurt or flatten by applying pressure

crust [krŭst] *noun*, a hard surface on the outside of something that often preserves what is inside, such as bread, pie, or the earth

crutch [krŭch] *noun*, a piece of wood or metal extending from under the arm to the ground, to support a person who cannot walk unaided

crux [krŭks] *noun*, the crucial point

cry [krī] *noun*, 1) a shout or call for help, *verb*, 2) to call out loudly 3) tears flowing from the eyes

crypt [krĭpt] *noun*, a vault where bodies are buried, a tomb

cryp-tic [krĭp′tĭk] *adjective*, having a hidden meaning, puzzling

crys-tal [krĭs′təl] *adjective*, 1) clear, transparent, *noun*, 2) a clear mineral 3) a high-quality clear glass

crys-tal-lize [krĭs′tə-līz′] *verb*, 1) to form crystals 2) to become clear

cub [kŭb] *noun*, a young animal of certain mammals, such as a bear, lion, or fox

cube [kyoob] *noun*, a solid shape with six equal square sides

cu-bic-le [kyoo′bĭ-kəl] *noun*, a small space for work partitioned off in a larger room

cu-cum-ber [kyoo′kŭm′bər] *noun*, a long, green-skinned fruit, pickled or eaten green as a salad

cue [kyoo] *noun*, 1) a signal or hint 2) a rod used to hit a billiard ball

cul-de-sac [kŭl′dĭ-săk′] *noun*, a small dead end off the main road

cu-li-nar-y [kyoo′lə-něr′ē] *adjective*, relating to cooking

cull [kŭl] *verb*, to select or gather, to pick out from others

cul-mi-nate [kŭl′mə-nāt′] *verb*, to reach the highest point of altitude, power, climax

cul-pa-ble [kŭl′pə-bəl] *adjective*, deserving blame, liable

cul-prit [kŭl′prĭt] *noun*, a person charged with or found guilty of a crime or misdeed

cul-ti-vate [kŭl′tə-vāt′] *verb*, 1) to improve or develop, to refine 2) to foster and promote healthy growth, as in crops, to farm

cul-tur-al [kŭl′chər-əl] *adjective*, relating to culture, the arts, good taste, etc.

cul-ture [kŭl′chər] *noun*, 1) advancement of knowledge of a civilization 2) a level of education that appreciates art and style 3) a growth of micro-organisms and bacteria

cum-ber-some [kŭm′bər-səm] *adjective*, heavy, hard to manage, unwieldy

cu-mu-la-tive [kyoom′yə-lā′tĭv] *adjective*, increasing by successive additions

cun-ning [kŭn′ĭng] *noun*, cleverness, craftiness, skill

cup [kŭp] *noun*, 1) a bowl-shaped drinking container with a handle 2) a unit of measure equal to 8 ounces

cup-board [kŭb'ərd] *noun*, a small closet or recessed shelf

cu-ra-tor [kyŏŏ-rā'tər] *noun*, one who has the care of a museum, a custodian, keeper

curb [kûrb] *noun*, 1) control, restraint 2) a ledge, a boundary, especially that along a street

cur-dle [kûr'dl] *verb*, to sour and coagulate from liquid to a solid, e.g., milk to cheese

cure [kyŏŏr] *noun*, 1) the remedy that made someone who was sick well again, *verb*, 2) to make someone who is ill, healthy, to heal

cur-few [kûr'fyŏŏ] *noun*, a set time enforced by law when people are to be off the streets

cu-ri-os-i-ty [kyŏŏr'ē-ŏs'ĭ-tē] *noun*, 1) the feeling of wanting to know about something 2) something that is strange or unusual

cu-ri-ous [kyŏŏr'ē-əs] *adjective*, 1) eager to know about all things 2) singular, unusual, odd

curl [kûrl] *noun*, 1) a ringlet or spiral shape, *verb*, 2) to make straight hair wavy and curly

cur-mudg-eon [kər-mŭj'ən] *noun*, a mean, bad-tempered person

cur-rant [kûr'ənt] *noun*, a small berry, similar to a raisin

cur-ren-cy [kûr'ən-sē] *noun*, money in circulation

cur-rent [kûr'ənt] *adjective*, 1) up to date, pertaining to the present, *noun*, 2) the powerful flow of water or electricity or air

cur-ric-u-lum [kə-rĭk'yə-ləm] *noun*, the classes that a school requires or offers

cur-ry [kûr'ē, kŭr'ē] *noun*, 1) a yellow powder containing several spices, including turmeric, used to flavor cooking, *verb*, 2) to seek favor by flattery 3) to brush or groom a horse

curse [kûrs] *noun*, 1) something said hoping harm will come to someone, *verb*, 2) to wish bad luck or injury on someone 3) to use profanity

cur-sive [kûr'sĭv] *adjective*, characteristic of handwriting in which the letters flow together

cur-tail [kər-tāl'] *verb*, to cut short, to reduce, to decrease

cur-tain [kûr'tn] *noun*, a piece of cloth hung over a window or doorway as a screen or cover

cur-tsy [kûrt'sē] *noun*, 1) a formal bow made with bent knees by a woman, *verb*, 2) to make a bow with one foot forward, as a gesture of respect

cur-va-ture [kûr'və-chŏŏr'] *noun*, a curve, a bend

curve [kûrv] *noun*, a bend or arch

curv-ed [kûrvd] *adjective*, having a line with no part straight or flat

cush-ion [kŏŏsh'ən] *noun*, a case or bag stuffed with some soft and elastic material

cus-tard [kŭs'tərd] *noun*, a pudding made of milk and eggs

cus-to-di-an [kŭ-stō'dē-ən] *noun*, a caretaker or porter, a janitor

cus-to-dy [kŭs′tə-dē] *noun*, safe-keeping under penalty or under a judge's ruling, imprisonment

cus-tom [kŭs′təm] *noun*, a tradition passed on from one generation to the next

cus-tom-ar-y [kŭs′tə-měr′ē] *adjective*, established by common usage, habitual

cus-tom-er [kŭs′tə-mər] *noun*, one who makes regular purchases from a business, a patron

cut [kŭt] *noun*, 1) a wound or injury that may cause the skin to bleed 2) an insult, a derogatory remark 3) something that has been made shorter, *verb*, 4) to break with a knife or blade

cute [kyōōt] *adjective*, lovable, adorable, delightful

cu-ti-cle [kyōō′tĭ-kəl] *noun*, the skin surrounding the fingernail

cy-cle [sī′kəl] *noun*, 1) events that happen in the same order over and over again 2) a bicycle, *verb*, 3) to move in a circuit controlled by alternating negative and positive currents

cy-clone [sī′klōn′] *noun*, a violent windstorm, sometimes called a typhoon or hurricane, depending on location and intensity

cyl-in-der [sĭl′ən-dər] *noun*, a solid spherical figure with two faces that are circles

cy-lin-dri-cal [sə-lĭn′drĭ-kəl] *adjective*, a circular or spherical shape with straight sides

cym-bal [sĭm′bəl] *noun*, a large round metal plate used as a percussion instrument

cyn-ic [sĭn′ĭk] *noun*, a doubter, a skeptic, an unbeliever

cyn-i-cism [sĭn′ĭ-sĭz′əm] *noun*, an attitude given to sneering at honesty or virtue, a belief that people are self-interested

cy-press [sī′prĭs] *noun*, an evergreen tree with scale-like needles

cyst [sĭst] *noun*, a fluid-filled pouch attached to a body part

czar [zär, tsär] *noun*, the supreme ruler of an empire, especially the ruler of Russia before 1917

D

dad [dăd] *noun*, father

daf-fo-dil [dăf′ə-dĭl] *noun*, a spring flowering bulb, yellow or white, with a trumpet-like center

dag-ger [dăg′ər] *noun*, a weapon used specifically for stabbing, a knife

dai-ly [dā′lē] *adjective*, done or occurring every day

dain-ty [dān′tē] *adjective*, delicate, fragile, small, pretty, refined

dair-y [dâr′ē] *noun*, a place where milk is produced and pasteurized

da-is [dā′ĭs] *noun*, a raised platform for honored guests

dai-sy [dā′zē] *noun*, a flower with a yellow or brown center surrounded by petals

dal-ly [dăl′ē] *verb*, to loiter, to fiddle around, to flirt

dam [dăm] *noun*, 1) a wall built across a river or lake that controls water flow, *verb*, 2) to construct a wall in a lake to retain the water and to regulate its flow

dam-age [dăm′ĭj] *noun*, 1) loss or detriment due to injury or harm, *verb*, 2) to hurt or cause harm or injury to something, to destroy

damp [dămp] *adjective*, humid, somewhat wet, moist

dance [dăns] *noun*, 1) a set of movements designed to accompany music, *verb*, 2) to move in rhythm with music, to skip or leap, to perform

dan-de-li-on [dăn′dl-ī′ən] *noun*, a bitter herb with yellow flowers, often cooked and eaten

dan-ger [dān′jər] *noun*, the possibility of harm

dan-ger-ous [dān′jər-əs] *adjective*, full of risk, perilous, hazardous, likely to harm

dan-gle [dăng′gəl] *verb*, to hang, to suspend loosely

dap-pled [dăp′əld] *adjective*, spotted with color or shade

dare [dâr] *verb*, to be brave, bold

dark [därk] *adjective*, 1) without light, not reflecting light, shadowy, *noun*, 2) a space without light

dark-ness [därk′nĕs] *noun*, no plural, a lack of light

darl-ing [där′lĭng] *adjective*, 1) a term of affection for someone who is loved, *noun*, 2) a sweetheart, the favorite

darn [därn] *verb*, to mend socks

dart [därt] *noun*, 1) a small weapon like a tiny arrow that can be thrown by hand, *verb*, 2) to move quickly or suddenly

dash [dăsh] *noun*, 1) a punctuation mark used to indicate a pause 2) a small amount, *verb*, 3) to move quickly 4) to hit, to shatter, to break, to strike

da-ta [dā′tə, dăt′ə, dä′tə] *noun*, information collected on a subject for reference

da-ta-base [dā′tə-bās′, dăt′ə-] *noun*, information arranged for computer access

date [dāt] *noun*, 1) the date, month, and year 2) a small, sweet, brown fruit grown in tropical climates, *verb*, 3) to measure, to mark 4) to court

daub [dôb] *verb*, to dab, to smear, to spread paint or another liquid

daugh-ter [dô′tər] *noun*, a human female considered with reference to her parents

daunt [dônt] *verb*, to intimidate

daunt-less [dônt′lĭs] *adjective*, bold

daw-dle [dôd′l] *verb*, to dilly dally, to waste time

dawn [dôn] *noun*, the break of day when the sun rises

day [dā] *noun*, 1) the period of 24 hours when the earth completes one rotation on its axis 2) the opposite of night, when the sun is in the sky

daze [dāz] *noun*, 1) a stupor, amazement, *verb*, 2) to cause to feel stunned

daz-zle [dăz′əl] *verb*, to awe, to impress with splendor

dead [dĕd] *adjective*, 1) not alive, inactive, *noun*, 2) referring to people who are no longer alive

dead-line [dĕd′līn′] *noun*, a set time when an assignment is to be finished, a time limit

dead-lock [dĕd′lŏk′] *noun*, a stalemate, a state in which no progress can be made

dead-ly [dĕd′lē] *adjective*, dangerous, possibly fatal, causing death, mortal

deaf [dĕf] *adjective*, 1) not able to hear 2) not listening

deal [dēl] *noun*, 1) a business agreement 2) an unspecified amount 3) a bargain, *verb*, 4) to barter, or buy and sell 5) to be concerned, to cope 6) to pass out or to distribute, i.e. playing cards

deal-er [dē′lər] *noun*, 1) a person who buys and sells things 2) in a card game, the person who holds the cards and passes them out

dear [dîr] *adjective*, 1) beloved 2) costly

dear-ly [dîr′lē] *adverb*, very much

death [dĕth] *noun*, the end of life

de-ba-cle [dĭ-bä′kəl] *noun*, a sudden downfall

de-bat-a-ble [dĭ-bā′tə-bəl] *adjective*, disputable, open to question

de-bate [dĭ-bāt′] *noun*, 1) a public discussion of a topic in which opposing points of view are presented, *verb*, 2) to argue different points of view

de-bil-i-tate [dĭ-bĭl′ĭ-tāt′] *verb*, to weaken

deb-it [dĕb′ĭt] *noun*, an entry on an account for a sum owed

de-bris [də-brē′, dā′brē′] *noun*, rubbish, especially such as results from destruction

debt [dĕt] *noun*, money owed

debt-or [dĕt′ər] *noun*, one who owes something, especially money

de-but [dā-byōō′] *noun*, 1) a beginning 2) first public appearance

dec-ade [dĕk′ād′] *noun*, a period of ten years

de-cay [dĭ-kā′] *noun*, 1) the condition of being rotten or degenerating, *verb*, 2) to rot, to decompose 3) to decline

de-ceased [dĭ-sēst′] *adjective*, dead, defunct, without life

de-ceit [dĭ-sēt′] *noun*, fraud, trickery, deception, lie

de-ceit-ful [dĭ-sēt′fəl] *adjective*, dishonest, deceptive, false

de-ceive [dĭ-sēv′] *verb*, to lead into error, to mislead, to delude, to lie to

De-cem-ber [dĭ-sĕm′bər] *noun*, the twelfth month of the year, having 31 days

de-cen-cy [dē′sən-sē] *noun*, behavior that is proper and moral

de-cent [dē′sənt] *adjective*, honorable, good, fitting, ethical

de-cep-tion [dĭ-sĕp′shən] *noun*, the act of deceiving, fraud, false representation, dishonesty

de-cide [dĭ-sīd′] *verb*, to determine, to make a choice, to resolve, to choose

de-cid-u-ous [dĭ-sĭj′ōō-əs] *adjective*, falling out at a certain stage of development (as some leaves, antlers, insect wings, or milk teeth)

dec·i·mal [dĕs'ə-məl] *adjective,* pertaining to or founded on the number ten

de·ci·pher [dĭ-sī'fər] *verb,* 1) to translate from coded characters 2) to make out or read

de·ci·sion [dĭ-sĭzh'ən] *noun,* act or result of deciding or settling, a conclusion, a resolution

de·ci·sive [dĭ-sī'sĭv] *adjective,* positive, able to decide quickly

de·ci·sive·ly [dĭ-sī'sĭv-lē] *adverb,* in a clean manner, precisely

deck [dĕk] *noun,* 1) the floor on each level of a ship 2) a pack of playing cards 3) a flat structure without a roof attached to a house

dec·la·ra·tion [dĕk'lə-rā'shən] *noun,* an announcement or statement, a proclamation

de·clare [dĭ-klâr'] *verb,* to formally announce, to state firmly and solemnly

de·cline [dĭ-klīn'] *noun,* 1) a gradual lessening of strength or numbers, *verb,* 2) to refuse 3) to steadily become less

de·com·pose [dē'kəm-pōz'] *verb,* 1) to rot or decay 2) to separate a chemical into constituent parts

de·com·po·si·tion [dē-kŏm'pə-zĭsh'ən] *noun,* the process of decay

dec·o·rate [dĕk'ə-rāt'] *verb,* to beautify, to adorn, to enhance

dec·o·ra·tion [dĕk'ə-rā'shən] *noun,* 1) an ornament 2) an award such as a ribbon or a medal

dec·o·rous [dĕk'ər-əs] *adjective,* proper, correct, polite

de·coy [dē'koi'] *noun,* something used as a lure or bait

de·crease [dĭ-krēs'] *noun,* 1) the amount by which something has been made smaller, *verb,* 2) to diminish and lessen the amount, to reduce

de·cree [dĭ-krē'] *noun,* 1) a pronouncement, a declaration, *verb,* 2) to proclaim, to order

de·crep·it [dĭ-krĕp'ĭt] *adjective,* broken down with age, feeble, worn out, dilapidated

de·cry [dĭ-krī'] *verb,* to discredit, to denounce publicly

ded·i·cate [dĕd'ĭ-kāt'] *verb,* 1) to recognize in a solemn ceremony 2) to devote oneself to something 3) to inscribe a message in the front of a book

ded·i·ca·tion [dĕd'ĭ-kā'shən] *noun,* 1) devotion to something 2) an acknowledgement of another person by an author

de·duce [dĭ-dōōs'] *verb,* to reach a conclusion by reasoning

de·duct [dĭ-dŭkt'] *verb,* to subtract, to take away

deed [dĕd] *noun,* 1) an action taken, something someone has done 2) a legal document proving that someone owns a piece of land or property

deep [dēp] *adjective,* 1) extending or reaching a long distance beneath the surface of the earth 2) intense, heart-felt, feelings

deer [dîr] *noun,* an animal with hooves that eats grass and leaves; the males have antlers

de·face [dĭ-fās'] *verb,* to mar, to vandalize, to destroy the appearance of

def-a-ma-tion [děf′ə-mā′shən] *noun*, harm to a person's good reputation, slander, libel

de-fault [dĭ-fôlt′] *noun*, 1)failure to fulfill an obligation 2) a computer setting that is used if the user does not make another choice

de-feat [dĭ-fēt′] *noun*, 1) a loss to be overcome, *verb*, 2) to beat, to conquer, to cause to fail

de-fect [dē′fĕkt′] *noun*, 1) a fault, a failing, a drawback, *verb*, 2) to desert your country or cause

de-fec-tive [dĭ-fĕk′tĭv] *adjective*, faulty, broken, imperfect

de-fend [dĭ-fĕnd′] *verb*, to fight to protect something, to guard

de-fend-ant [dĭ-fĕn′dənt] *noun*, a person required to make an answer in a lawsuit or a criminal case

de-fense [dĭ-fĕns′] *noun*, 1) protection from harm 2) justification for an action 3) protection of the goal in sports

de-fen-sive [dĭ-fĕn′sĭv] *adjective*, guarding, protective

de-fer [dĭ-fûr′] *verb*, 1) to put off, to postpone 2) to submit respectfully

de-fer-ence [děf′ər-əns] *noun*, a yielding of judgment with respect to another, courtesy

de-fi-ance [dĭ-fī′əns] *noun*, a state of open opposition, a challenge

de-fi-ant [dĭ-fī′ənt] *adjective*, opposing or resisting power or authority, disobedient

def-i-cit [děf′ĭ-sĭt] *noun*, an amount that falls short of a goal or perfect balance

de-fine [dĭ-fīn′] *verb*, 1) to determine the boundaries of something 2) to give the meaning of

def-i-nite [děf′ə-nĭt] *adjective*, fixed, having certain limits, precise, clearly defined

def-i-nite-ly [děf′ə-nĭt-lē] *adverb*, precisely, clearly stated, certainly

def-i-ni-tion [děf′ə-nĭsh′ən] *noun*, an explanation of the meaning of a word or term

de-fin-i-tive [dĭ-fĭn′ĭ-tĭv] *adjective*, final, conclusive, decisive

de-flate [dĭ-flāt′] *verb*, 1) to let the air out 2) to dishearten, to discourage

de-flect [dĭ-flĕkt′] *verb*, 1) to turn aside 2) to cause something to change direction

de-form-i-ty [dĭ-fôr′mĭ-tē] *noun*, a lack of proper form or symmetry, distortion

de-fraud [dĭ-frôd′] *verb*, to deprive someone of a right or property through deceit, to swindle

de-fray [dĭ-frā′] *verb*, to meet the cost of something, to pay

de-frost [dē-frôst′] *verb*, to melt, to thaw, to remove ice by melting

deft [dĕft] *adjective*, able, skillful,

de-funct [dĭ-fŭngkt′] *adjective*, ended, dead, no longer existing

de-fy [dĭ-fī′] *verb*, to challenge a stronger force, to disobey

de-gen-er-ate [dĭ-jĕn′ər-āt′] *verb*, to become worse physically, mentally or morally, to decay

de-grade [dĭ-grād′] *verb*, to lower someone's reputation or character, to treat disrespectfully

de-gree [dǐ-grē′] *noun*, 1) a unit for measuring temperature or angles 2) a grade or rank conferred by colleges or un graduates or other scholars 3) a measured portion determined on a scale 4) a proportion

de-i-fy [dē′ə-fī′] *verb*, to idolize or worship as a god

de-jec-tion [dǐ-jĕk′shən] *noun*, sadness, depression, low spirits

Del-a-ware [dĕl′ə-wâr′] *noun*, a state on the east coast of the United States; the capital is Dover. The state flower of **Delaware** is the peach blossom and the motto is "Liberty and Independence."

de-lay [dǐ-lā′] *noun*, 1) a period of waiting, *verb*, 2) to postpone, to make something take longer

de-lec-ta-ble [dǐ-lĕk′tə-bəl] *adjective*, delicious

del-e-gate [dĕl′ǐ-gāt′] *noun*, 1) one sent and empowered to act for another, a deputy, *verb*, 2) to entrust a duty or task to another, to assign

de-lete [dǐ-lēt′] *verb*, to erase, to mark for omission, to remove

de-lib-er-ate [dǐ-lǐb′ər-ǐt] *adjective*, 1) planned or done on purpose, *verb*, [dǐ-lǐb′ər-āt] 2) to think carefully in or to make up one's mind, to consider reasons for and against

de-lib-er-ate-ly [dǐ-lǐb′ər-ǐt-lē] *adverb*, after mature consideration, consciously, intentionally, on purpose

del-i-ca-tes-sen [dĕl′ǐ-kə-tĕs′ən] *noun*, a shop where meat, cheese, and salads are sold

del-i-ca-cy [dĕl′ǐ-kə-sē] *noun*, 1) good taste, tact 2) choice food

de-li-cious [dǐ-lǐsh′əs] *adjective*, giving pleasure to the senses, especially taste

de-light [dǐ-līt′] *noun*, 1) a joy, *verb*, 2) to please, to cause joy or happiness

de-light-ful [dǐ-līt′fəl] *adjective*, pleasing, causing pleasure and satisfaction

de-lin-quent [dǐ-lǐng′kwənt] *adjective*, 1) failing to do what is required 2) past due, *noun*, 3) a child who persistently breaks the law

de-lir-i-ous [dǐ-lîr′ē-əs] *adjective*, wandering in mind, light-headed

de-liv-er [dǐ-lǐv′ər] *verb*, 1) to carry or take to a person to whom something is addressed 2) to assist in the birth of a baby 3) to utter, to speak 4) to rescue or set free

de-liv-er-y [dǐ-lǐv′ə-rē] *noun*, the act of delivering goods, a letter, etc. 2) goods that have been brought to be handed over

del-ta [dĕl′tə] *noun*, a fan-shaped area of land where a river splits into channels at its mouth

de-lude [dǐ-lōōd′] *verb*, to deceive, to fool, to mislead

de-lu-sion [dǐ-lōō′zhən] *noun*, 1) a mirage, a fantasy 2) a mistake, a misconception, a false belief

delve [dĕlv] *verb*, to examine, to probe, to look through, to search

dem-a-gogue [dĕm′ə-gôg′] *noun*, a person who wins support by appealing to popular feelings and prejudices especi

de-mand [dǐ-mănd′] *noun*,
1) a strong request, *verb*, 2) to
ask for something very strongly,
to insist or require, to claim

de-mean [dǐ-mēn′] *verb*, to
humiliate, to lower

de-mean-or [dǐ-mē′nər] *noun*, a
person's posture or conduct,
behavior, attitude

de-mise [dǐ-mīz′] *noun*, the death
of a person, the end of
something, a failure

de-moc-ra-cy [dǐ-mŏk′rə-sē] *noun*,
a form of government in which
people exercise power by
electing representatives

Dem-o-crat [děm′ə-krăt′] *noun*, a
person who advocates
democracy, one who believes in
government in which all people
have a vote

dem-o-crat-ic [děm′ə-krăt′ ĭk]
adjective, 1) favoring equality,
considerate of humanity
2) representative

de-mol-ish [dǐ-mŏl′ĭsh] *verb*, to
destroy, to ruin, to take down

dem-o-li-tion [děm′ə-lĭsh′ən]
noun, destruction

dem-on-strate [děm′ən-strāt′]
verb, to establish beyond doubt,
to show

dem-on-stra-tion
[děm′ən-strā′shən] *noun*, 1) a
presentation of evidence, proof
2) an exhibit, a display 3) a
peaceful march, a protest

de-mor-al-ize [dǐ-môr′ə-līz′] *verb*,
1) to corrupt, to destroy the
morals of someone 2) to
discourage 3) to confuse

de-mur [dǐ-mûr′] *noun*,
1) hesitation, objection, refusal,

verb, 2) to make an objection, to
delay

de-mure [dǐ-myŏŏr′] *adjective*,
quietly modest, reserved

den [děn] *noun*, 1) a place in which
a wild animal lives, a lair 2) a
quiet, private room

den-i-grate [děn′ĭ-grāt′] *verb*, to
ridicule, to belittle, to defame

den-im [děn′ĭm] *noun*, a heavy
cotton fabric, usually blue, used
to make clothing such as jeans

de-nom-i-na-tion
[dǐ-nŏm′ə-nā′shən] *noun*,
1) classification, identification,
2) a branch of a religion 3) the
value of a banknote, stamp, etc.

de-nom-i-na-tor [dǐ-nŏm′ə-nā′tər]
noun, the number base or the
quantity below the line of a
fraction

de-nounce [dǐ-nouns′] *verb*, to
attack as deserving of
punishment or censure

dense [děns] *adjective*, compact,
closely packed together

den-si-ty [děn′sǐ-tē] *noun*, 1) mass
per unit of volume 2) the number
of people in a specified area

dent [děnt] *noun*, 1) an indentation,
a nick, *verb*, 2) to make a gouge

den-tal [děn′tl] *adjective*, referring
to teeth or dentistry

de-nun-ci-a-tion
[dǐ-nŭn′sē-ā′shən] *noun*, a public
accusation, condemnation

de-ny [dǐ-nī′] *verb*, to declare
something untrue

de-part [dǐ-pärt′] *verb*, to leave, to
go away from 2) deviate, to
withdraw 3) to die

de-part-ment [dĭ-pärt′mənt] *noun,* a separate division of a government or a business

de-par-ture [dĭ-pär′chər] *noun,* the act of leaving a place or the subject

de-pend [dĭ-pĕnd′]*verb,* to be determined, to be a result of 2) to need, to trust, to rely on

de-pend-a-ble [dĭ-pĕnd′ā′bəl] *adjective,* reliable

de-pend-ant or de-pend-ent [dĭ-pĕn′dənt] *noun,* a person supported by another

de-pend-ent [dĭ-pĕn′dənt] *adjective,* relying on something else for support, contingent

de-pict [dĭ-pĭkt′] *verb,* to portray

de-plete [dĭ-plēt′] *verb,* to use up

de-plor-able [dĭ-plôr′ə-bəl] *adjective,* shockingly bad, vile, horrible, unfortunate

de-plore [dĭ-plôr′] *verb,* to feel or express disapproval

de-ploy [dĭ-ploi′] *verb,* to move troops to the battle line to make it stronger, to position strategically

de-port [dĭ-pôrt′] *verb,* to force someone to leave a country

de-pose [dĭ-pōz′] *verb,* 1)to remove from office or power 2) to testify under oath

de-pos-it [dĭ-pŏz′ĭt] *noun,* 1) money placed in a bank for safekeeping 2) money to hold something until the full price is paid 3) sediment that has settled on the bottom, *verb,* 4) to put aside for safekeeping

de-po-si-tion [dĕp′ə-zĭsh′ən] *noun,* testimony under oath

de-pot [dē′pō] *noun,* a railroad or bus station 2) a warehouse

de-praved [dĭ-prāvd′] *adjective,* morally corrupt

de-pre-ci-ate [dĭ-prē′shē-āt′] *verb,* to diminish in value

de-pre-ci-a-tion [dĭ-prē′shē-ā′shən] *noun,* a decrease in value

dep-re-da-tion [dĕp′rĭ-dā′shən] *noun,* stealing, pillage, plundering, destruction

de-press [dĭ-prĕs′] *verb,* 1) to make someone feel sad and despondent 2) to hold down

de-pres-sion [dĭ-prĕsh′ən] *noun,* 1) a feeling of sadness 2) a mental illness characterized by hopelessness and despair 3)a low place or hole or basin 4) a major slump in the economy, a long recession

de-prive [dĭ-prīv′] *verb,* to deny, to keep from having, to prevent from enjoying something

depth [dĕpth] *noun,* 1) wisdom, intellect 2)the distance from the top downward

de-ranged [dĭ-rānjd′] *adjective,* insane, mad, crazy

der-by [dûr′bē] *noun,* 1) a contest or race, a horserace 2) a round hat with a narrow brim

der-e-lict [dĕr′ə-lĭkt′] *adjective,* 1) abandoned 2) failing in one's duty, *noun* 3) a vagrant

de-ride [dĭ-rīd′] *verb,* to scoff at

de-ri-sion [dĭ-rĭzh′ən] *noun,* ridicule, scorn, mockery

de-riv-a-tive [dĭ-rĭv′ə-tĭv] *noun,* something derived from another source

de-rive [dĭ-rīv′] *verb*, to obtain or issue from a source

de-rog-a-to-ry [dĭ-rŏg′ə-tôr′ē] *adjective*, negative, mean, detracting, disparaging

der-rick [dĕr′ĭk] *noun*, 1) a tall tower that fits over an oil well, that supports drilling machinery 2) a large hoisting crane

de-scend [dĭ-sĕnd′] *verb*, to go or move down, to fall, to drop

de-scend-ant [dĭ-sĕn′dənt] *noun*, a person descended from a particular ancestor, such as a child or a grandchild

de-scent [dĭ-sĕnt′] *noun*, a change from higher to lower, a downward movement

de-scribe [dĭ-skrīb′] *verb*, 1) to set forth in words, to tell about, to recount 2) to mark out, to draw

de-scrip-tion [dĭ-skrĭp′shən] *noun*, act or result of representing by words, a narration

des-e-crate [dĕs′ĭ-krāt′] *verb*, to destroy something sacred or of religious significance

des-ert [dĕz′ərt] *noun*, 1) a dry region that is sandy and without trees, [dĭ-zûrt′] *verb*, 2) to leave, to leave the armed forces without permission, to abandon

de-ser-tion [dĭ-zûr′shən] *noun*, 1) abandonment 2)the act of leaving service in the armed forces without permission

de-serve [dĭ-zûrv′] *verb*, to merit or be worthy of, to earn by service

de sign [dĭ-zīn′] *noun*, 1) a plan, 2-) a pattern, *verb*, 3) to conceive, to invent 4) to create a plan for something, to scheme

des-ig-nate [dĕz′ĭg-nāt′] *verb*, 1) to point out, to indicate 2) to give a name 3) to appoint

de-sign-er [dĭ-zī′nər] *noun*, a person who creates plans for clothes, buildings, products, etc.

de-sire [dĭ-zīr′] *noun*, 1) a want, wish, craving, *verb*, 2) to long for, to set your heart on

desk [dĕsk] *noun*, a work table usually with drawers for paper, pencils, etc.

des-o-late [dĕs′ə-lĭt] *adjective*, deserted, forsaken, comfortless, dismal, abandoned

des-o-la-tion [dĕs′ə-lā′shən] *noun*, 1) emptiness, extinction 2) extreme sadness

de-spair [dĭ-spâr′] *noun*, 1) the state of being without hope, *verb*, 2) to have no hope or optimism

des-per-ate [dĕs′pər-ĭt] *adjective*, hopeless, downcast, frantic, reckless because of despair

des-per-a-tion [dĕs′pə-rā′shən] *noun*, a great need, an anxious feeling out of hopelessness

de-spise [dĭ-spīz′] *verb*, to look down upon with contempt, to consider unworthy of respect

de-spite [dĭ-spīt′] *preposition*, 1)in spite of, notwithstanding, *noun* 2) malice, contemptuous disregard

de-spoil [dĭ-spoil′] *verb*, to plunder

de-spond-ent [dĭ-spŏn′dənt] *adjective*, discouraged, without hope

des-pot-ic [dĭ-spŏt′ĭk] *adjective*, 1)possessing unlimited power 2) tyrannical

des-pot-ism [dĕs′pə-tĭz′əm] *noun*, tyranny, dictatorship, repression

des-sert [dĭ-zûrt′] *noun*, usually sweet, the last course of a meal

des-ti-na-tion [dĕs′tə-nā′shən] *noun*, the place someone is going, a goal, the end of a journey

des-ti-ny [dĕs′tə-nē] *noun*, fate, a condition predetermined by divine will, providence

des-ti-tute [dĕs′tĭ-tōōt′] *adjective*, without means of existence, extremely poor, penniless

de-stroy [dĭ-stroi′] *verb*, to put an end to, to ruin or annihilate

de-struc-tion [dĭ-strŭk′shən] *noun*, the act of tearing down, causing harm or damage

de-struc-tive [dĭ-strŭk′tĭv] *adjective*, harmful, ruinous, causing damage

de-tach [dĭ-tăch′] *verb*, to separate, to remove, to disconnect, to undo

de-tail [dĭ-tāl′] *noun*, a small part of a larger whole, an item

de-tain [dĭ-tān′] *verb*, 1) to restrain, to confine, to hold back, 2) to delay, to hinder, to impede

de-tect [dĭ-tĕkt′] *verb*, to discover the presence of, to find

de-tec-tive [dĭ-tĕk′tĭv] *noun*, 1) a special policeman who is trained to investigate crimes 2) a person whose job it is to obtain information for clients

de-ter-gent [dĭ-tûr′jənt] *noun*, a chemical substance like soap used to wash clothes or dishes

de-te-ri-o-rate [dĭ-tîr′ē-ə-rāt′] *verb*, to grow worse, to rot, to decay

de-te-ri-o-ra-tion [dĭ-tîr′ē-ə-rā′shən] *noun*, a process of getting worse

de-ter-mi-na-tion [dĭ-tûr′mə-nā′shən] *noun*, a firm purpose, resolve, willpower

de-ter-mine [dĭ-tûr′mĭn] *verb*, to come to a decision, to realize

de-test [dĭ-tĕst′] *verb*, to hate

de-tour [dē′tōōr′] *noun*, a temporary way around a blockage in the road

de-tract [dĭ-trăkt′] *verb*, to belittle, to take away from

det-ri-men-tal [dĕt′rə-mĕn′tl] *adjective*, harmful, injurious

dev-as-tate [dĕv′ə-stāt′] *verb*, 1) to lay waste, to destroy 2) to cause someone sorrow

de-vel-op [dĭ-vĕl′əp] *verb*, unfold gradually, to evolve, to mature

de-vel-op-ment [dĭ-vĕl′əp-mənt] *noun*, 1) expansion, growth 2) a new piece of information

de-vi-ate [dē′vē-āt′] *verb*, to turn away from an accepted course of action or standard, to stray

de-vice [dĭ-vīs′] *noun*, 1) an instrument used for a particular purpose 2) a scheme, a trick

dev-il [dĕv′əl] *noun*, 1) an evil spirit, thought to cause destruction and bad things 2) a wicked or mischievous person

de-vi-ous [dē′vē-əs] *adjective*, crafty, dishonest, gone astray

de-vise [dĭ-vīz′] *verb*, to contrive, to invent, to plan, to create

de-void [dĭ-void′] *adjective*, empty, entirely without, lacking

de-vote [dĭ-vōt′] *verb*, to dedicate , to give entirely, to use for a specific purpose

de-vo-tion [dĭ-vō′shən] *noun*, 1) dedication, affection, love 2) religious worship

de-vour [dĭ-vour′] *verb*, to consume greedily, to eat

de-vout [dĭ-vout′] *adjective*, sincere, dedicated, having religious feeling

dew-drop [dōō′drŏp′] *noun*, drops of water that form on anything exposed to air overnight

dex-ter-i-ty [dĕk-stĕr′ĭ-tē] *noun*, the ability to operate skillfully by hand, adroitness

di-a-be-tes [dī′ə-bē′tĭs] *noun*, a metabolic disorder in which one is very thirsty, produces excessive urine, and is unable to produce or use sufficient insulin

di-a-bol-ic-al [dī′ə-bŏl′ĭ-kəl] *adjective*, evil, devilish

di-ag-no-sis [dī′əg-nō′sĭs] *noun*, an identification of a disease based on signs or symptoms

di-ag-o-nal [dī-ăg′ə-nəl] *adjective*, a line extending from one corner of a polygon to another corner, that is not adjacent

di-a-gram [dī′ə-grăm′] *noun*, 1) a figure, or plan drawn to show how something works, *verb*, 2) to represent by a drawing

di-al [dī′əl] *noun*, a round face on a machine, often with numbers on it, that sets the instrument to perform a specific task 2) the face of a clock, watch, etc.3) to make a telephone call

di-a-lect [dī′ə-lĕkt′] *noun*, a form of speech characterized by local peculiarities

di-a-logue [dī′ə-lôg′] *noun*, 1) a conversation between two or more people, especially in a play or narrative 2) a discussion

di-am-e-ter [dī-ăm′ĭ-tər] *noun*, any straight line passing from side to side, through the center of a figure or body

dia-mond [dī′ə-mənd] *noun*, 1) a hard clear stone that is very precious 2) a plane shape with four equal sides with two acute angles and two obtuse angles 3) a baseball field

di-a-phragm [dī′ə-frăm′] *noun*, the muscle for breathing located between the lungs and the stomach

di-ar-rhe-a [dī′ə-rē′ə] *noun*, a purging or looseness of the bowels

di-a-ry [dī′ə-rē] *noun*, a journal in which a person makes daily entries of observations and personal experiences

di-a-tribe [dī′ə-trīb′] *noun*, a tirade, a scolding, a forceful and bitter verbal attack against someone or something

dice, [dīs] *noun, plural* 1) a small square cube with a different number of dots on each side ranging from 1-6, often used in games of chance, 2) *verb*, to cut into small cubes

dichotomy

di-chot-o-my [dī-kŏt′ə-mē] *noun,*
a division into two parts

dic-tate [dĭk′tāt′] *verb,* 1) to speak
into a recording device or so that
someone else can write or type
what is said 2) to impose, to
decree, to command

dic-ta-tor [dĭk′tā′tər] *noun,* an
absolute ruler, a tyrant

dic-tion [dĭk′shən] *noun,*
enunciation of words

dic-tion-ar-y [dĭk′shə-něr′ē] *noun,*
a word list, usually with
definitions, pronunciations, etc.

did [dĭd] *past tense* of **do**

did-n't [dĭd′nt] the *contraction* of
the words **did** and **not**

die [dī] *verb,* 1) to stop living or
existing 2) to lose strength, to
fade away

die-sel [dē′zəl, -səl] *noun,* 1) an
engine that burns oil instead of
gasoline 2)the petroleum fuel
used in a diesel engine

di-et [dī′ĭt] *noun,* 1) the food
someone eats, *verb,* 2) to reduce
the intake of food

dif-fer [dĭf′ər] *verb,* to be unlike, to
vary, to disagree

dif-fer-ence [dĭf′ər-əns] *noun,*
1) contrast, unlikeness
2) disagreement, dissension
3) the answer in subtraction

dif-fer-ent [dĭf′ər-ənt] *adjective,*
1) not alike 2) not the same as
the rest, strange 3) separate

dif-fer-ent-ial [dĭf′ə-rěn′shəl]
adjective, 1) showing or making
a difference, *noun* 2) a gear that
allows two wheels to rotate at
different speeds

dif-fi-cult [dĭf′ĭ-kŭlt′] *adjective,*
hard to do, not easy, hard to
manage or please, tough

dif-fi-cul-ty [dĭf′ĭ-kŭl′tē] *noun,* a
hardship, a problem

dif-fuse *adjective,* [dĭ-fyoō′ s′]
1) not concentrated, [dĭ-fyoōz′]
verb, 2) to spread or circulate 3)
to cause to flow on all sides

dif-fu-sion ən] *noun,* the process of
spreading in all directions like
gas

dig [dĭg] *verb,* 1) to unearth dirt
with tools or a machine to make
a hole 2) to search, to probe

di-gest [dī-jěst′]*noun,* 1) a
condensed literary work, article,
etc. *verb,* 2) to convert food into
an absorbable form 3) to think
over and arrange

di-ges-tion [dī-jěs′chən] *noun,* the
process by which food is
converted into a source of energy
that can be easily assimilated by
the body

di-ges-tive tract *noun,* the
alimentary canal where food is
processed and broken down into
sugars for energy and wastes are
eliminated

dig-it [dĭj′ĭt] *noun,* 1) a finger or
toe 2) any number 0 through 9

dig-ni-fy [dĭg′nə-fī] *verb,* to give
honor to

dig-ni-tar-y [dĭg′nĭ-těr′ē] *noun,*
1) a person who is well-known
and respected 2) a person
holding high rank or position

dig-ni-ty [dĭg′nĭ-tē] *noun,* 1) an
office or rank 2) nobleness of
manner, aspect, or style 3) the
quality of being respected and
respecting oneself

di-gres-sion [dī-grěsh′ən, dĭ-]
noun, an act or instance of
wandering away from the
subject temporarily

dike [dīk] *noun*, a dam or wall that holds back water

di-lap-i-dat-ed [dǐ-lăp′ǐ-dā′tǐd] *adjective*, falling into ruin, decaying, in disrepair

di-late [dī-lāt′] *verb*, to expand, to enlarge or become wider

dil-a-to-ry [dǐl′ə-tôr′ē] *adjective*, delaying, wasting time

di-lem-ma [dǐ-lěm′ə] *noun*, a case in which a person must make a difficult choice, a quandary

dil-i-gence [dǐl′ə-jəns] *noun*, careful attention and application to work, a constant effort to accomplish something

dil-i-gent [dǐl′ə-jənt] *adjective*, careful, tireless in work

di-lute [dī-lōōt′] *verb*, to make thinner or weaker by mixing in something else

dim [dǐm] *adjective*, 1) poorly lit, 2) becoming less bright or distinct

dime [dīm] *noun*, a coin worth ten cents in the United States

di-men-sion [dǐ-měn′shən] *noun*, size in a particular direction such as length or width, scope, extent

di-min-ish [dǐ-mǐn′ǐsh] *verb*, to make or grow less, to reduce

dim-i-nu-tion [dǐm′ə-nōō′shən] *noun*, a lessening, a reduction in size or duration

dim-ple [dǐm′pəl] *noun*, a small dent in a surface

dine [dīn] *verb*, to eat supper

din-gy [dǐn′jē] *adjective*, dirty, soiled, dull and drab, shabby

din-ner [dǐn′ər] *noun*, the main meal of the day served in the evening

di-no-saur [dī′nə-sôr′] *noun*, extinct gigantic reptiles of the Mesozoic era that were either herbivores, carnivores, or omnivores

dip [dǐp] *noun*, 1) a decline 2) a plunge, a soaking, an immersion 3) a mixture into which foods are dunked, *verb*, 4) to put something into a liquid and then take it out again 5) to slope

diph-thong [dǐf′thông′] *noun*, a combination of two vowels forming a compound sound

di-plo-ma [dǐ-plō′mə] *noun*, a document under seal attesting a degree conferred on a person

di-plo-ma-cy [dǐ-plō′mə-sē] *noun*, the business of conducting international negotiations

dip-lo-mat [dǐp′lə-măt′] *noun*, 1) an ambassador 2) a tactful person

dire [dīr] *adjective*, disastrous, serious, threatening

di-rect [dǐ-rěkt′, dī-] *adjective*, 1) straight to something without stopping, *verb*, 2) to aim 3) to guide, to control, to manage

di-rec-tion [dǐ-rěk′shən] *noun*, 1) the way in which someone is going or pointing 2) **di-rec-tions** instructions explaining how to do something

di-rect-ly [dǐ-rěkt′lē] *adverb*, 1) at once, immediately 2) in a forthright manner

di-rec-to-ry [dǐ-rěk′tə-rē] *noun*, 1) a list of people and their addresses 2) a computer file listing other files

dirge [dûrj] *noun*, sorrowful music, a lament for someone who has died

dir-i-gi-ble [dĭr'ə-jə-bəl] *noun*, an airship, a blimp

dirt [dûrt] *noun*, loose soil, something which causes filth

dirt-y [dûr'tē] *adjective*, 1) not clean, soiled 2) obscene

dis-a-bil-i-ty [dĭs'ə-bĭl'ĭ-tē] *noun*, a physical or mental incapacity, an inability to do something

dis-a-ble [dĭs-ā'bəl] *verb*, to impair the activity of something, to make incapable

dis-ad-van-tage [dĭs'əd-văn'tĭj] *noun*, something that makes things more difficult, a detriment

dis-a-gree [dĭs'ə-grē'] *verb*, to be of a different opinion, to differ

dis-a-gree-a-ble [dĭs'ə-grē'ə-bəl] *adjective*, unpleasant, irritating, obnoxious, bad-tempered

dis-a-gree-ment [dĭs'ə-grē'mənt] *noun*, an argument, a dispute

dis-ap-pear [dĭs'ə-pîr'] *verb*, to vanish, to go away or become hidden, to fade away

dis-ap-point [dĭs'ə-point'] *verb*, to frustrate the hopes of someone

dis-ap-point-ment [dĭs'ə-point'mənt] *noun*, failure, frustration, a feeling of being let down

dis-ap-prove [dĭs'ə-proōv'] *verb*, to object, to have a bad opinion of

dis-arm [dĭs-ärm'] *verb*, 1)to take weapons away from someone, to subdue 2) to win over

dis-as-ter [dĭ-zăs'tər] *noun*, something very bad that happens, a catastrophe

dis-be-lief [dĭs'bĭ-lēf'] *noun*, doubt, skepticism

dis-burse [dĭs-bûrs'] *verb*, to pay out money

dis-burse-ment [dĭs-bûrs'mənt] *noun*, 1) the act of paying out money 2) money paid out

dis-card [dĭ-skärd'] *verb*, to shed, to eliminate,to throw away

dis-cern [dĭ-sûrn'] *verb*, to distinguish, to perceive

dis-charge [dĭs-chärj'] *noun*, 1) something that is sent out from its source, *verb*, 2) to unload 3) to send away, to dismiss from duty or a job

dis-ci-ple [dĭ-sī'pəl] *noun*, a follower, an apostle

dis-ci-pline [dĭs'ə-plĭn] *noun*, 1) strict training to teach self-control 2) an advanced area of knowledge *verb*, 3) to instruct, to prepare 4) to punish

dis-close [dĭ-sklōz'] *verb*, to reveal, to make known, to uncover

dis-com-fort [dĭs-kŭm'fərt] *noun*, 1) annoyance, embarrassment 2) ache

dis-con-nect [dĭs'kə-nĕkt'] *verb*, to cut off, to detach, to sever

dis-con-tent [dĭs'kən-tĕnt'] *noun*, dissatisfaction, restlessness, unhappiness

dis-con-tin-ue [dĭs'kən-tĭn'yoō] *verb*, to cease, to stop

dis-cord [dĭs'kôrd'] *noun*, a conflict, opposition, differences

dis-count [dĭs'kount'] *noun*, 1) a reduction in the price of something , *verb,* 2) to disregard or disbelieve someone

dis-cour-age [dǐ-skûr'ǐj] *verb,* to dishearten, to deter

dis-course [dǐs'kôrs'] *noun,* a talk, a long written or verbal discussion

dis-cov-er [dǐ-skǔv'ər] *verb,* 1) to make known the existence of something 2) to find out through study or observation

dis-cov-er-y [dǐ-skǔv'ə-rē] *noun,* something seen or learned for the first time

dis-cred-it [dǐs-krěd'ǐt] *verb,* to destroy confidence in, to cause to disbelieve

dis-creet [dǐ-skrēt'] *adjective,* prudent, careful, tactful, unobtrusive

dis-crep-an-cy [dǐ-skrěp'ən-sē] *noun,* inconsistency between facts or figures, failure to match

dis-cre-tion [dǐ-skrěsh'ən] *noun,* discernment, wise conduct and management, freedom to decide something, the act of being discreet

dis-crim-i-nate [dǐ-skrǐm'ə-nāt'] *verb,* to make a difference or distinction, to treat differently

dis-crim-i-na-tion [dǐ-skrǐm'ə-nā'shən] *noun, no plural,* 1) the ability to make fine distinctions 2) treatment based on differences, prejudice

dis-cuss [dǐ-skǔs'] *verb,* to talk about, to exchange ideas

dis-cus-sion [dǐ-skǔsh'ən] *noun,* the exchange of ideas, a debate

dis-dain [dǐs-dān'] *noun,* scorn or contempt

dis-ease [dǐ-zēz'] *noun,* 1) any mental or physical disorder 2) any quality or social condition considered harmful

dis-en-gage [dǐs'ěn-gāj'] *verb,* to release, to detach, to become free

dis-fig-ure [dǐs-fǐg'yər] *verb,* to deform, to injure, to spoil

dis-grace [dǐs-grās'] *noun,* 1) something to feel ashamed of *verb,* 2) to shame, to discredit

dis-grace-ful [dǐs-grās'fəl] *adjective,* causing shame

dis-grunt-led [dǐs-grǔn'tld] *adjective,* resentful, annoyed, discontented, angry

dis-guise [dǐs-gīz'] *noun,* 1) things worn to change the appearance, *verb,* 2) to change the appearance of someone or something, to cover up

dis-gust [dǐs-gǔst'] *noun,* 1) a strong feeling of dislike, revulsion, *verb,* 2) to cause someone a strong feeling of dislike or offense

dish [dǐsh] *noun,* 1) a container used at a meal to serve food 2) food served

dis-hon-est [dǐs-ŏn'ǐst] *adjective,* deceitful, lying, corrupt

disk [dǐsk] *noun,* any flat round object, a circular plate

dis-like [dǐs-līk'] *noun,* 1) distaste, hostility *verb,* 2)to detest, to hate

dis-mal [dǐz'məl] *adjective,* dark or gloomy, dreary, depressing

dis-man-tle [dǐs-măn'tl] *verb,* to take apart, to break down to basic parts to see how something is made

dis-may [dĭs-mā′] *noun*, 1) an uneasy feeling of alarm, *verb*, 2) to feel alarm and distress

dis-miss [dĭs-mĭs′] *verb*, to send away, to cause or permit to go

dis-obed-i-ent [dĭs′ə-bē′dē-ənt] *adjective*, refusing to obey

dis-o-bey [dĭs′ə-bā′] *verb*, not to do what you are told, to resist

dis-or-der [dĭs-ôr′dər] *noun*, 1) sickness, ailment 2) confusion, chaos

dis-or-gan-ized [dĭs-ôr′gə-nīzd′] *adjective*, not properly planned

dis-par-age [dĭ-spăr′ĭj] *verb*, to belittle, to criticize

dis-pa-rate [dĭs′pər-ĭt] *adjective*, very different in kind, containing unrelated elements

dis-par-i-ty [dĭ-spăr′ĭ-tē] *noun*, a noticeable difference, inequality

dis-patch [dĭ-spăch′] *noun*, 1) a message 2) promptness, *verb*, 3) to send off to a destination

dis-pel [dĭ-spĕl′] *verb*, to drive or clear away

dis-pense [dĭ-spĕns′] *verb*, to distribute, to give out medicine

dis-perse [dĭ-spûrs′] *verb*, to scatter, to distribute in different directions, to disseminate

dis-per-sion [dĭ-spûr′zhən] *noun*, scattering, diffusion, distribution

dis-place [dĭs-plās′] *verb*, 1) to rearrange, to move around 2) to force people from their homes 3) to take the place of

dis-play [dĭ-splā′] *noun*, 1) a show, an exhibit, *verb*, 2) to show or exhibit something, to present

dis-pose [dĭ-spōz′] *verb*, 1) to get rid of 2) to adjust, to settle 3) to

place or arrange 4) to influence in favor of

dis-po-si-tion [dĭs′pə-zĭsh′ən] *noun*, 1) nature, personality, makeup 2) arrangement

dis-pro-por-tion-ate [dĭs′prə-pôr′shə-nĭt] *adjective*, relatively too large or too small, uneven, out of proportion

dis-prove [dĭs-prōōv′] *verb*, to refute, to prove false

dis-pute [dĭ-spyōōt′] *noun*, 1) an argument, a strong difference of opinion, *verb*, 2) to call into question, to debate

dis-qual-i-fy [dĭs-kwŏl′ə-fī′] *verb*, to invalidate, to judge ineligible

dis-re-gard [dĭs′rĭ-gärd′] *noun*, 1) indifference, disrespect, neglect, *verb*, 2) to fail to notice

dis-re-spect-ful [dĭs′rĭ-spĕkt′fəl] *adjective*, rude, lacking respect

dis-rupt [dĭs-rŭpt′] *verb*, to interrupt, to disturb

dis-sat-is-fac-tion [dĭs-săt′ĭs-făk′shən] *noun*, discontent, uneasiness

dis-sat-is-fied [dĭs-săt′ĭs-fīd′] *adjective*, displeased, fed up, disgruntled, unhappy

dis-sect [dĭ-sĕkt′] *verb*, 1) to divide into separate parts 2) to analyze

dis-sec-tion [dĭ-sĕk′shən] *noun*, analysis, the act of cutting apart in order to examine internal structure

dis-sem-i-nate [dĭ-sĕm′ə-nāt′] *verb*, to scatter, to spread around

dis-sem-i-na-tion [dĭ-sĕm′ə-nā′shən] *noun*, a scattering or spreading around, diffusion

dis-sen-sion [dĭ-sĕn′shən] *noun*, a disagreement causing strife

dis-sent [dĭ-sĕnt′] *noun*, disagreement, a quarrel

dis-sim-i-lar [dĭ-sĭm′ə-lər] *adjective*, not alike, different

dis-si-pate [dĭs′ə-pāt′] *verb*, 1) to lessen, to diminish, to scatter 2) to fritter away

dis-solve [dĭ-zŏlv′] *verb*, 1) to make a solid disappear into a liquid solution 2) to break up an assembly, to end an agreement

dis-so-nance [dĭs′ə-nəns] *noun*, discord, noise, harsh sounds

dis-suade [dĭ-swād′] *verb*, to discourage by persuasion, to deter

dis-tance [dĭs′təns] *noun*, 1) the space between two points, an interval 2) a place far away

dis-tant [dĭs′tənt] *adjective*, 1) far 2) cool, reserved in manner

dis-tend [dĭ-stĕnd′] *verb*, to expand, to bloat, to stretch

dis-tinct [dĭ-stĭngkt′] *adjective*, 1) distinguished by nature or station 2) individual, unique 3) well-defined, very clear

dis-tinc-tion [dĭ-stĭngk′shən] *noun*, 1) notable difference as in a feature 2) excellence, recognition of an accomplishment

dis-tin-guish [dĭ-stĭng′gwĭsh] *verb*, 1) to stand out, to be different 2) to recognize as different

dis-tort [dĭ-stôrt′] *verb*, to twist out of shape, to bend, to falsify

dis-tract [dĭ-străkt′] *verb*, to take one's attention from something

dis-trac-tion [dĭ-străk′shən] *noun*, 1) mental distress 2) something that distracts or amuses

dis-traught [dĭ-strôt′] *adjective*, very worried, disturbed, overcome with anxiety, upset

dis-tress [dĭ-strĕs′] *noun*, 1) a feeling of worry, sadness or difficulty, *verb*, 2) to make someone sad or worried

dis-trib-ute [dĭ-strĭb′yōōt] *verb*, 1) to allot or divide among several 2) to spread out over an area, to give out

dis-tri-bu-tion [dĭs′trə-byōō′shən] *noun*, the passing out of things, circulation

dis-trict [dĭs′trĭkt] *noun*, 1) a division of territory 2) a defined portion of a state, county, or city

dis-trust [dĭs-trŭst′] *noun*, 1) suspicion, doubt, *verb*, 2) to lack confidence or trust in

dis-turb [dĭ-stûrb′] *verb*, to bother or interrupt, to make anxious

ditch [dĭch] *noun*, 1) a long narrow channel, a shallow waterway *verb*, 2) to discard

dive [dīv] *noun*, 1) a downward plunge, *verb*, 2) to plunge head first into water 3) to move downward, to drop sharply

div-er [dī′vər] *noun*, 1) a person who dives into water 2) a person who works underwater

di-verge [dĭ-vûrj′] *verb*, to go off in different directions from the same starting point

di-verse [dĭ-vûrs′] *adjective*, various, many and different

di-ver-sion [dĭ-vûr′zhən] *noun*, amusement, play, distraction

di-ver-si-ty [dĭ-vûr′sĭ-tē] *noun*, variety, a wide range

divert

di-vert [dĭ-vûrt′] *verb*, to distract, to draw aside, to entertain, to change the course of

di-vest [dĭ-věst′] *verb*, to strip, to take away from, to get rid of

di-vide [dĭ-vīd′] *verb*, 1) to calculate how many times one number can go into another 2) to separate 3) to share or distribute

div-i-dend [dĭv′ĭ-děnd′] *noun*, 1) the share of profits earned by any policy or company 2) a number to be divided by another number 3) a benefit from an action

di-vine [dĭ-vīn′] *adjective*, of or relating to God, holy, sacred

di-vis-i-ble [dĭ-vĭz′ə-bəl] *adjective*, capable of being divided or separated

di-vi-sion [dĭ-vĭzh′ən] *noun*, 1) the act or result of separating anything into parts 2) a difference in opinion or feeling 3) an operation on two numbers that results in a quotient 4) a military group 5) a section of a company

di-vorce [dĭ-vôrs′] *noun*, 1) a legal end of a marriage, *verb*, 2) to arrange by law for a husband and wife to separate and end their marriage

di-vulge [dĭ-vŭlj′] *verb*, to reveal

do [dōō] *verb*, 1) to act, to produce 2) to travel 3) to be enough 4) to give 5) used with another verb to ask a question

doc-ile [dŏs′əl] *adjective*, easy to control, gentle, submissive

dock [dŏk] *noun*, 1) a pier where ships load and unload cargo, *verb*, 2) to tie a ship up at a port or wharf or boat landing 3) to deduct from someone's wages

doc-tor [dŏk′tər] *noun*, a person trained and licensed to practice medicine

doc-trine [dŏk′trĭn] *noun*, a tenet, a principle of faith or religion

doc-u-ment [dŏk′yə-mənt] *noun*, 1) an original or official paper 2) any writing that conveys information, *verb*, 3) to write down or put on paper 4) to provide information as proof

dodge [dŏj] *verb*, to avoid something by moving out of the way, to evade, to escape

doe [dō] *noun*, a female deer

does [dŭz] *verb*, the part of the verb **do** used with he, she and it

does-n't [dŭz′ənt] the *contraction* of the words **does** and **not**

dog [dôg] *noun*, a domesticated mammal four legs that eats meat

dog-ma [dôg′mə] *noun*, 1)opinion or beliefs widely held but not based on facts 2) doctrine

dol-drums [dōl′drəmz′] *noun*, 1) listlessness, an inactive period, depression 2) an ocean region near the equator with calm waters and little wind

dol-lar [dŏl′ər] *noun*, 1) currency used in the United States and Canada, valued at 100 cents 2) the basic unit of currency used in many countries

dol-phin [dŏl′fĭn] *noun*, 1) any of various small cetaceans with the snout in the shape of a beak and the neck vertebrae partially fused like a whale 2) any of various fish

do-main [dō-mān′] *noun,* specialty, area ruled over, jurisdiction, field

dome [dōm] *noun,* a roof that resembles a half circle

do-mes-tic [də-mĕs′tĭk] *adjective,* found in the home or in one's home land

dom-i-nant [dŏm′ə-nənt] *adjective,* governing, controlling, bossy

dom-i-nate [dŏm′ə-nāt′] *verb,* to have control over someone

dom-i-no [dŏm′ə-nō′] *noun,* a game played with uniform blocks with one side divided into two halves, each half showing any number from 0 to 6

do-nate [dō′nāt′] *verb,* to make a contribution, to bestow, to give

do-na-tion [dō-nā′shən] *noun,* a gift of money or goods given to a charitable organization

done [dŭn] *adjective,* 1) finished or complete 2) cooked, *verb,* 3) the *past tense* of **do**

don-key [dŏng′kē] *noun,* an animal like a small horse with long ears

do-nor [dō′nər] *noun,* a person who gives money or something of value

don't [dōnt] the *contraction* of the words **do** and **not**

doom [do͞om] *noun,* 1) a grim fate, *verb,* 2) to make certain that something fails or is destroyed

door [dôr] *noun,* the moveable piece of wood or metal standing at an entrance, a portal

door-way [dôr′wā′] *noun,* the opening for an entrance to a building or a room

dor-mant [dôr′mənt] *adjective,* sleeping, inactive, inert

dor-mi-to-ry [dôr′mĭ-tôr′ē] *noun,* a building containing rooms for sleeping, a residence hall 2) a large room with many beds

dor-sal [dôr′səl] *adjective,* of or on the back of an animal

dose [dōs] *noun,* the amount of medicine that is to be taken at one time to be effective

dot [dŏt] *noun,* a very small round spot or mark, a point, a fleck

dou-ble [dŭb′əl] *adjective,* 1) twice as much, *noun,* 2) a stand in or look alike 3) a two-base hit in baseball, *verb,* 4) to make twice as much, to fold in two

doubt [dout] *noun,* 1) a question, a feeling of uncertainty, mistrust, *verb,* 2) to question, to wonder 3) to hesitate, to ponder

doubt-ful [dout′fəl] *adjective,* 1) questionable, unlikely 2) feeling uncertain

dough [dō] *noun,* a mixture of mostly flour and a liquid to be baked to make bread or cake

douse [dous] *verb,* to drench, to saturate, to put out a light

dove [dŭv] *noun,* 1) one of many of a small type of pigeon, *verb,* [dōv] 2) *past tense* of **dive**

down [doun] *adverb,* 1) toward the ground, *noun,* 2) soft feathers, *preposition,* 3) in or to a lower place

down-stairs [doun′stârz′] *adverb,* 1) on or to a lower floor, *noun,* 2) a lower floor of a building

downtown [doun′toun′] *noun,* the main business area of a city or town

down-ward [doun'wərd] *adverb*, descending from a higher to a lower level, moving toward the ground

doze [dōz] *verb*, to take a nap, to sleep for a brief time, to sleep lightly

doz-en [dŭz'ən] *noun*, twelve

Dr. the abbreviation of doctor

drab [drăb] *adjective*, dull in color, dreary, dingy, not interesting

draft [drăft] *noun*, 1) the first unedited copy of a manuscript 2) an order for payment of money 3) a current of air 4) forced military service

drag [drăg] *verb*, to pull along with effort, to haul

drag-on [drăg'ən] *noun*, a mythical creature that breathes fire

drain [drān] *noun*, 1) a pipe used to transport water into a sewer, *verb*, 2) to relieve the pressure of fluid in a wound 3) to become dry as water flows away 4) to make weak

dra-ma [drä'mə] *noun*, 1) a story that can be performed on stage 2) excitement

dra-mat-ic [drə-măt'ĭk] *adjective*, theatrical, exciting, stirring

dra-mat-i-cal-ly [drə-măt'ĭk-lē] *adverb*, in a sudden or alarming way, impressively

drank [drăngk] *past tense* of **drink**

drape [drāp] *noun*, 1) a heavy curtain, *verb*, 2) to cover with a piece of cloth

dra-per-y [drä'pə-rē] *noun*, a heavy curtain or fabric designed to cover a window

dras-tic [drăs'tĭk] *adjective*, forceful, severe, extreme

draw [drô] *noun*, 1) a tie score, *verb*, 2) to get, to take, to understand 3) to pull along 4) to make a picture with a writing instrument 5) to choose at random 6) to formulate, to prepare 7) to suck

draw-bridge [drô'brĭj'] *noun*, a bridge that can be raised or turned to allow boats and ships to pass

drawl [drôl] *noun*, a manner of speaking that stretches out the sound of a word or vowels

drawn [drôn] *adjective*, thin, gaunt

dread [drĕd] *noun*, 1) fear, horror, terror, *verb*, 2) to anticipate with anxiety, to fear greatly

dream [drēm] *noun*, 1) images seen while you sleep 2) desires, goals, *verb*, 3) to picture something with your imagination 4) to see images while sleeping

drear-y [drîr'ē] *adjective*, gloomy, depressing

dredge [drĕj] *verb*, 1) to remove something from deep water 2) to cover food with sugar, flour, etc.

drench [drĕnch] *verb*, to make completely wet, to soak

dress [drĕs] *noun*, 1) a piece of clothing that covers the bust, waist and thighs 2) a general term for clothing or attire, *verb*, 3) to put clothes on 4) to adorn

dress-er [drĕs'ər] *noun*, 1) a chest of drawers, a bureau 2) a person who helps another to dress 3) a person who dresses a certain way

drew [drōo] *past tense* of **draw**

drift [drĭft] *noun*, 1) the general meaning 2) a pile of snow, leaves, etc. *verb*, 3) to float

drill [drĭl] *noun*, 1) a tool made of hard material used to make holes in something 2) a practice, an exercise, *verb*, 3) to make a hole in something with a special machine 4) to be trained

drink [drĭngk] *noun*, 1) liquid refreshment, a beverage, *verb*, 2) to consume liquid through the mouth, to swallow, to imbibe

drip [drĭp] *verb*, to fall in drops

drive [drīv] *noun*, 1) a short journey or trip made in a vehicle, *verb*, 2) to steer and control a moving vehicle 3) to force to go, to push through 4) to make, to compel, to urge

driv-er [drī'vər] *noun*, 1)the person steering and controlling a moving vehicle 2) a golf club for hitting long shots

droll [drōl] *adjective*, odd, strange and amusing

drone [drōn] *noun*, 1) a male bee with no stinger that mates with the queen bee, *verb*, 2) to talk dully, to buzz or murmur like a bee

drop [drŏp] *noun*, 1) a small amount of a liquid, *verb*, 2) to let something fall 3) to decrease

dross [drŏs] *noun*, waste, impurity

drought [drout] *noun*, a long period without rain

drown [droun] *verb*, to suffocate by immersion under water

drow-sy [drou'zē] *adjective*, sleepy, sluggish

drudg-er-y [drŭj'ə-rē] *noun*, dull routine work

drug [drŭg] *noun*, 1) a substance that changes the body's chemistry, medicine 2)a narcotic

drug-gist [drŭg'ĭst] *noun*, a pharmacist, one who is licensed to sell drugs

drum [drŭm] *noun*, 1) a percussion instrument consisting of a hollow cylinder with a taut covering 2) a cylindrical metal container, *verb*, 3) to make music or beat on a drum

drunk [drŭngk] *adjective*, showing the effect of too much alcohol, losing control of one's movement or speech because of alcohol

dry [drī] *adjective*, 1) without moisture or water, *verb*, 2) to expel or remove moisture

dry-er [drī'ər] *noun*, a machine that adds heat and tumbles clothes to evaporate and remove moisture

dual [dōo'əl] *adjective*, having two purposes or parts

duch-ess [dŭch'ĭs] *noun*, the wife or widow of a duke

duck [dŭk] *noun*, 1) a bird that swims and is hunted for its eggs and meat, *verb*, 2) to crouch or lower one's head to avoid something, to dodge

duct [dŭkt] *noun*, a tube or channel, a ventilation shaft

due [dōo] *adjective*, 1) owed, unpaid 2) expected, appropriate, *noun*, 3) a charge or fee for membership

duel [dōo'əl] *noun*, 1) a fight or competition, *verb*, 2) to fight

du-et [dōō-ĕt′] *noun*, a song or a piece of music for two people

duke [dōōk] *noun*, the title of a man who is a high-ranking nobleman

dull [dŭl] *adjective*, 1) not sharp, blunt 2) boring, slow, dim

dumb [dŭm] *adjective*, 1) unable to speak, mute, silent 2) unintelligent, stupid

dump [dŭmp] *noun*, 1) a public place where garbage is collected and usually buried, *verb*, 2) to leave, to drop or throw away

dune [dōōn] *noun*, a rounded hill of sand heaped up by the wind

dun-geon [dŭn′jən] *noun*, a close, dark prison, an underground cell

dupe [dōōp] *verb*, to fool, to trick

du-pli-cate [dōō′plĭ-kĭt] *adjective*, 1) alike, twin, *noun*, 2) a copy, a reproduction, [dōō′pl ĭ-kāt′]*verb*, 3) to reproduce, to remake, to do again

du-ra-ble [dōōr′ə-bəl] *adjective*, able to endure, lasting

du-ra-tion [dōō-rā′shən] *noun*, the length of time something continues or exists

dur-ing [dōōr′ĭng] *preposition*, in the course of a period of time, throughout the course of

dusk [dŭsk] *noun*, evening, the time just after the sun has set, twilight

dust [dŭst] *noun*, 1) fine particles or powder of matter, *verb*, 2) to remove the powder by cleaning or wiping

du-ty [dōō′tē] *noun*, 1) an obligation or a commitment 2) the responsibilities of one's

job 3) a tax on goods, especially imports and exports

dwarf [dwôrf] *noun*, 1) an unusually small person, *verb*, 2) to make something look small by comparison

dwell [dwĕl] *verb*, 1) to inhabit, to live in 2) to emphasize, to think about for a long time, to ponder

dwell-ing [dwĕl′ĭng] *noun*, a home to live in, a residence, an abode

dwin-dle [dwĭn′dl] *verb*, to reduce

dye [dī] *noun*, 1) a substance used to color cloth, hair, etc. *verb*, 2) fixing colors permanently in the fibers of materials, to change the color

dy-na-mic [dī-năm′ĭk] *adjective*, relating to the forces producing motion, forceful, energetic

dy-na-mite [dī′nə-mīt′] *noun*, an explosive of nitroglycerin absorbed in porous matter

dy-nas-ty [dī′nə-stē] *noun*, a series of rulers from the same family

dys-func-tion-al [dĭs-fŭngk′shən-əl] *adjective*, functioning abnormally

E

each [ēch] *adjective*, every, one of two or more things, all

ea-ger [ē′gər] *adjective*, very willing to do something, enthusiastic

ea-gle [ē′gəl] *noun*, a very large keen-sighted bird of prey

ear [îr] *noun*, 1) the organ, one on each side of the head, used to hear 2) the sleeve in a cereal plant used to hold seeds or flowers

ear-ly [ûr′lē] *adjective*, 1) near the beginning of a time period, *adverb*, 2) before the set time

earn [ûrn] *verb*, 1) to get something through work, to achieve, to gain money 2) to achieve by one's own efforts

ear-nest [ûr′nĭst] *adjective*, fervent, serious, sincere

ear-ring [îr′rĭng, îr′ĭng] *noun*, an ornament worn on the earlobe

Earth [ûrth] *proper noun*, 1) the name of the planet on which we live, our world, , 2) **earth** *common noun*, soil, dirt, ground

earth-quake [ûrth′kwāk′] *noun*, a shaking movement of the earth caused by underground movement

ease [ēz] *noun*, 1) relaxation, relief, *verb*, 2) to move carefully 3) to make less painful or difficult

ea-sel [ē′zəl] *noun*, a tripod frame used to support an artist's canvas

eas-i-ly [ē′zə-lē] *adverb*, without difficulty, effortlessly

east [ēst] *noun*, one of the four points of a compass, pointing right of north, where the sun rises

east-ern [ē′stərn] *adjective*, 1) belonging to or characteristic of the east 2) Asian

eas-y [ē′zē] *adjective*, 1) effortless, not difficult 2) relaxed, comfortable 3) free from pain or worry 4) not strict

eat [ēt] *verb*, 1) to put food in the mouth, chewing it and swallowing it 2) to corrode

eaves [ēvz] *noun*, *plural*, the lower edges of a roof that overhang a building

ebb [ĕb] *noun*, 1) the receding of the tide, *verb*, 2) to fall back

eb-on-y [ĕb′ə-nē] *adjective*, 1) black, *noun*, 2) a hard, heavy and durable wood 3) a tropical Asian tree

ec-cen-tric [ĭk-sĕn′trĭk] *adjective*, 1) off-center from the regular or normal, *noun*, 2) an odd person

ec-cle-si-as-tic [ĭ-klē′zē-ăs′tĭk] *adjective*, pertaining to the Christian church or clergy

ech-o [ĕk′ō] *noun*, 1) a series of reflected sound waves that repeat as they bounce back from an object, repeating the sound *verb*, 2) to reverberate, to reflect a sound back

e-clipse [ĭ-klĭps′] *noun*, 1) a period of time when the light from one celestial object is blocked another, *verb*, 2) to overshadow and cause a loss of light

e-col-o-gy [ĭ-kŏl′ə-jē] *noun*, the study of how plants and animals interact with the environment

e-co-nom-ic [ĕk′ə-nŏm′ĭk] *adjective*, related to business and the production of goods

e-co-nom-i-cal [ĕk′ə-nŏm′ĭ-kəl] *adjective*, affordable, inexpensive

e-co-nom-ics [ĕk′ə-nŏm′ĭks] *noun*, the study of the way people secure goods and services and the necessities of life

e-con-o-my [ĭ-kŏn′ə-mē] *noun*, 1) the careful or thrifty management of resources 2) a system for the management of resources, money, and jobs

ec-o-sys-tem [ĕk′ō-sĭs′təm] *noun*, living things that work together and their environment

ec-sta-sy [ĕk′stə-sē] *noun*, intense delight, bliss

ec-ze-ma [ĕk′sə-mə] *noun*, a rash, inflammatory disease of the skin

edge [ĕj] *noun*, 1) the segment where two surfaces meet 2) the rim or brink of something 3) the sharp blade of a cutting instrument such as a knife 4) the point farthest from the middle of a surface 5) an advantage, *verb*, 6) to take small, cautious steps 7) to put a border on something

ed-i-ble [ĕd′ə-bəl] *adjective*, fit to be eaten as food

ed-i-fice [ĕd′ə-fĭs] *noun*, a large, imposing building or structure

ed-i-fy [ĕd′ə-fī′] *verb*, to educate, to instruct, to guide spiritually

ed-it [ĕd′ĭt] *verb*, to revise and correct, to prepare something for publication, to cut a part of

e-di-tion [ĭ-dĭsh′ən] *noun*, an issue of a book, newspaper or magazine

ed-i-tor [ĕd′ĭ-tər] *noun*, one who reads and revises books or newspapers before they are published

ed-u-cate [ĕj′ə-kāt′] *verb*, to teach people, to provide knowledge

ed-u-ca-tion [ĕj′ə-kā′shən] *noun*, teaching and learning, acquired knowledge

eel [ēl] *noun*, a long fish that looks like a snake that lives in freshwater and the sea

ee-rie [îr′ē] *adjective*, spooky, strange, causing dread

ef-fect [ĭ-fĕkt′] *noun*, a result, consequence, outcome

ef-fec-tive [ĭ-fĕk′tĭv] *adjective*, having a positive result, helpful

ef-fer-ves-cence [ĕf′ər-vĕs′sĭns] *noun*, 1) the process of gas escaping in innumerable small bubbles 2) irrepressible enthusiasm

ef-fi-ca-cious [ĕf′ĭ-kā′shəs] *adjective*, producing a desired result, effective, efficient

ef-fi-cien-cy [ĭ-fĭsh′ən-sē] *noun*, productivity with little or no wasted effort

ef-fi-cient [ĭ-fĭsh′ənt] *adjective*, working well with no waste of money or effort, capable

ef-fi-gy [ĕf′ə-jē] *noun*, a likeness in the form of a dummy, an image of a hated person usually hung

ef-fort [ĕf′ərt] *noun*, an attempt, an action, strenuous exertion

ef-fu-sion [ĭ-fyōō′zhən] *noun*, a pouring forth of liquid, light, etc.

e.g. for example

egg [ĕg] *noun*, 1) a shell covered fetus of a baby bird, fish or insect 2) an ovum, a female reproductive cell

e-go [ē′gō, ĕg′ō] *noun*, a person's self-importance, self-esteem

e-go-tist [ē′gə-tĭst] *noun*, one who is excessively interested in herself or himself

eight [āt] *noun*, the number 8, one plus seven

eight-een [ā-tēn′] *noun*, the number 18, ten plus eight

eight-eenth [ā-tēnth′] *noun*, *adjective*, the number eighteen in order, 18th

eighth [ātth] *noun, adjective,* the number eight in order, one of eight equal parts

eight-i-eth [ā'tē-ĭth] *noun,* the number 80 in order, one of eighty equal parts

eight-y [ā'tē] *adjective, noun,* the number 80, eight times ten

ei-ther [ē'thər, ī'thər] *adjective, pronoun,* one or the other of two

e-ject [ĭ-jĕkt'] *verb,* to exit suddenly and forcefully, to expel

e-lab-o-rate [ĭ-lăb'ər-ĭt] *adjective,* 1) made with great care, carefully planned, complicated, [ĭ-lă-bə-rāt']*verb,* 2) to explain in detail

e-lapse [ĭ-lăps'] *verb,* to pass by

e-las-tic [ĭ-lăs'tĭk] *adjective,* 1) able to return to an original size and shape after having been stretched completely, *noun,* 2) fabric with fine strings of rubber woven in it

e-la-tion [ĭ-lā' shən] *noun,* excitement, joy

el-bow [ĕl'bō'] *noun,* the joint in the arm that allows it to bend in the middle

eld-er [ĕl'dər] *adjective,* 1)older, more aged, *noun,* 2) one who is older than others 3) an influential older person

e-lect [ĭ-lĕkt'] *verb,* to choose by vote, to decide a course of action or representative

e-lec-tion [ĭ-lĕk'shən] *noun,* the process of making a choice by voting

e-lec-tor-ate [ĭ-lĕk'tər-ĭt] *noun,* the people qualified to vote

e-lec-tric [ĭ-lĕk'trĭk] *adjective,* relating to or powered by electricity

e-lec-tri-cian [ĭ-lĕk-trĭsh'ən] *noun,* one who is licensed to install and repair electrical equipment

e-lec-tric-i-ty [ĭ-lĕk-trĭs'ĭ-tē] *noun,* a form of energy resulting from the activity of electrons and protons

e-lec-tro-cute [ĭ-lĕk'trə-kyōōt']*verb,* to kill by electric shock

e-lec-trode [ĭ-lĕk'trōd'] *noun,* a conductor by which an electric unit enters or leaves a region or object

e-lec-tron [ĭ-lĕk'trŏn'] *noun,* a particle smaller than an atom and having a negative electric charge

e-lec-tron-ic [ĭ-lĕk'trŏnĭk] *adjective,* operating by transistors, microchips, etc. that control an electric current

el-e-gant [ĕl'ĭ-gənt] *adjective,* lovely, gorgeous, refined

el-e-ment [ĕl'ə-mənt] *noun,* 1) a basic substance of which the universe is composed, *plural,* 2) the forces that constitute the weather

el-e-men-ta-ry [ĕl'ə-mĕn'tə-rē] *adjective,* of or related to the first principles or basic facts of a subject

el-e-phant [ĕl'ə-fənt] *noun,* a huge, herbivore mammal that lives in Africa and India, weighs 3-7 tons, stands 8-13 feet high, has thick skin, two tusks and a long nose called a trunk

el-e-vate [ĕl'ə-vāt'] *verb,* to raise to a higher level, to lift up

el-e-va-tion [ĕl′ə-vā′shən] *noun*, the altitude, the height of something from a reference point such as sea level

el-e-va-tor [ĕl′ə-vā′tər] *noun*, a machine with hoisting equipment for conveying persons, goods, etc. to or from different levels

e-lev-en [ĭ-lĕv′ən] *noun*, the number 11, one plus ten

e-lev-enth [ĭ-lĕv′ənth] *noun*, the number 11 in order, 11th

elf [ĕlf] *noun*, an imaginary small person with pointed ears who makes mischief

elic-it [ĭ-lĭs′ĭt] *verb*, to draw forth, to evoke a response

el-i-gi-ble [ĕl′ĭ-jə-bəl] *adjective*, qualified to be chosen

e-lim-i-nate [ĭ-lĭm′ə-nāt′] *verb*, to get rid of, to exclude from consideration, to leave out

e-lite [ĭ-lēt′] *adjective*, choice, select, superior, considered best

elk [ĕlk] *noun*, an animal similar to a moose, a large deer

elm [ĕlm] *noun*, a tall hardwood shade tree

e-lope [ĭ-lōp′] *verb*, to run away to marry secretly

el-o-quence [ĕl′ə-kwəns] *noun*, persuasive use of language

else [ĕls] *adverb*, 1) otherwise, instead of 2) more, in addition

else-where [ĕls′hwâr′] *adverb*, in some other place

e-lude [ĭ-lo͞od′] *verb*, to get away from, to avoid, to escape

e-lu-sive [ĭ-lo͞o′sĭv] *adjective*, hard to grasp or catch, hard to remember

em-a-nate [ĕm′ə-nāt′] *verb*, to flow out, to radiate, to come out

e-man-ci-pate [ĭ-măn′sə-pāt′] *verb*, to set free from restrictions or slavery

e-man-ci-pa-tion [ĭ-măn′sə-pā′shən] *noun*, the act or condition of being freed from oppression or slavery

em-bar-go [ĕm-bär′gō] *noun*, a law that prevents a country from trading with another

em-bark [ĕm-bärk′] *verb*, 1) to board an airplane or boat 2) to begin an undertaking

em-bar-rass [ĕm-băr′əs] *verb*, to make ill at ease or self-conscious

em-bar-rass-ment [ĕm-băr′əs-mənt] *noun*, a feeling of self-consciousness, distress or shame

em-bas-sy [ĕm′bə-sē] *noun*, the building in which people work to represent their own country in another country

em-bed [ĕm-bĕd′] *verb*, to implant into something, to fix firmly

em-bel-lish [ĕm-bĕl′ĭsh] *verb*, to adorn, to make beautiful by adding decoration

em-bez-zle [ĕm-bĕz′əl] *verb*, to steal money from one's company or from savings accounts entrusted to one

em-blem [ĕm′bləm] *noun*, a badge or symbol of something

em-bod-y [ĕm-bŏd′ē] *verb*, 1) to include as a part of a whole 2) to represent

em-brace [ĕm-brās′] *verb*, 1) to hold closely in one's arms, to hug 2) to accept something, to include 3) to take up seriously

em-broi-der [ĕm-broi'dər] *verb*, 1) to sew ornamental patterns on fabric 2) to embellish, to add false details

em-bry-o [ĕm'brē-ō'] *noun*, an early stage of development of an animal or plant organism

em-bry-on-ic [ĕm'brē-ŏn'ĭk] *adjective*, in an early stage of development of an organism

em-er-ald [ĕm'ər-əld] *noun*, a precious stone of rich, bright green color, a variety of beryl

e-merge [ĭ-mûrj'] *verb*, to come out or become visible, to appear

e-mer-gen-cy [ĭ-mûr'jən-sē] *noun*, an unexpected event that calls for immediate action, a crisis

em-i-grant [ĕm'ĭ-grənt] *noun*, a person leaving one country to live in another

em-i-grate [ĕm'ĭ-grāt'] *verb*, to leave one country to go and live in another

em-i-nent [ĕm'ə-nənt] *adjective*, high, lofty, noted, famous

e-mis-sion [ĭ-mĭsh'ən] *noun*, a substance given off into the air

e-mo-tion [ĭ-mō'shən] *noun*, feelings, passion, excitement

e-mo-tion-al [ĭ-mō'shə-nəl] *adjective*, excitable, showing emotions more than usual, fervent

em-pa-thize [ĕm'pə-thīz'] *verb*, to relate to the feelings of others

em-pa-thy [ĕm'pə-thē] *noun*, the ability to share the feelings of another person

em-per-or [ĕm'pər-ər] *noun*, the male ruler of a country or empire

em-pha-sis [ĕm'fə-sĭs] *noun*, importance or stress given to something

em-pha-size [ĕm'fə-sīz'] *verb*, to call to someone's attention, to bring out clearly, to stress

em-pire [ĕm'pīr'] *noun*, a group of nations or states united under a single sovereign power

em-pir-i-cal [ĕm-pîr'ĭ-kəl] *adjective*, based on observation and experience rather than theory

em-ploy [ĕm-ploi'] *verb*, to put into use, to engage, to hire for work

em-ploy-ee [ĕm-ploi'ē] *noun*, one who works for another for wages

em-ploy-er [ĕm-ploi'ər] *noun*, a person or business that employs or hires one or more persons

em-ploy-ment [ĕm-ploi'mənt] *noun*, a job, an occupation

em-pow-er [ĕm-pou'ər] *verb*, to authorize, to enable

emp-ty [ĕmp'tē] *adjective*, 1) having nothing inside, without content or meaning, *verb*, 2) to remove the contents completely, to make vacant, to unload

em-u-late [ĕm'yə-lāt'] *verb*, to follow or copy in the hope of equaling

en-a-ble [ĕ-nā'bəl] *verb*, to make possible, to empower

en-act [ĕn-ăkt'] *verb*, 1) to make into law 2) to act, to perform

e-nam-el [ĭ-năm'əl] *noun*, 1) a smooth glossy surface finish 2) a hard glassy colored substance fused to metal, glass or pottery 3) the outer covering of the teeth

en-chant [ĕn-chănt'] *verb*, 1) to put a spell on 2) to captivate, to delight

en-chant-ment [ĕn-chănt'mənt] *noun*, 1) a magical spell, 2) a fascination, appeal, charm

en-clave [ĕn'klāv'] *noun*, territory enclosed in a foreign land

en-close [ĕn-klōz'] *verb*, to put something inside of something else, to shut in on all sides

en-clo-sure [ĕn-klōz'hər] *noun*, something that surrounds on all sides

en-com-pass [ĕn-kŭm'pəs] *verb*, 1) to enclose in a circle, to surround 2) to include as a part of

en-core [ŏn'kôr'] *noun*, an additional performance given in response to calls from the audience, as by applause

en-coun-ter [ĕn-koun'tər] *noun*, 1) a casual meeting 2) a skirmish, *verb*, 3) to meet by chance 4) to confront in battle

en-cour-age [ĕn-kûr'ĭj] *verb*, to give praise or hope to someone, to urge

en-cour-age-ment [ĕn-kûr'ĭj-mənt, -kŭr'-] *noun*, support, assurance

en-croach-ment [ĕn-krōch'mənt] *noun*, the act of overstepping boundaries or someone's rights

en-cy-clo-pe-di-a [ĕn-sī'klə-pē'dē-ə] *noun*, a comprehensive summary of knowledge on many subjects or a specialilzed subject written in a set of volumes

end [ĕnd] *noun*, 1) the farthest point or edge of anything 2) completion, finish 3) the aim, reason, design, *verb*, 4) to finish

en-dan-ger [ĕn-dān'jər] *verb*, to put in danger, to hazard

en-deav-or [ĕn-dĕv'ər] *noun*, 1) an attempt, a serious effort, *verb*, 2) to try, to make an earnest effort, to strive

end-less [ĕnd'lĭs] *adjective*, without end, infinite, ceaseless

en-dorse [ĕn-dôrs'] *verb*, 1) to write on the back of a check to cash it or give it to another person 2) to sanction, to declare approval of

en-dow [ĕn-dou'] *verb*, 1) to provide or bestow income or property 2) to give a quality to

en-dow-ment [ĕn-dou'mənt] *noun*, giving of money to provide a regular income

en-dur-ance [ĕn-dŏŏr'əns] *noun*, the ability to survive, the will to persevere

en-dure [ĕn-dŏŏr'] *verb*, to bear, to put up with, to tolerate, to suffer

en-e-my [ĕn'ə-mē] *noun*, a hostile person or group or country, a foe

en-er-gize [ĕn'ər-jīz'] *verb*, to make active, to invigorate, to give energy to

en-er-gy [ĕn'ər-jē] *noun*, 1) the capacity for performing work 2) power that makes machines work

en-fold [ĕn-fōld'] *verb*, to envelope, to enclose

en-force [ĕn-fôrs'] *verb*, to impose by force, to require compliance

en-gage [ĕn-gāj'] *verb*, 1) to put in gear 2) to fight 3) to hire 4) to become involved 5) to be busy or occupied 6) to promise

en-gage-ment [ĕn-gāj′mənt] *noun*,
1) an encounter, a military action
2) a promise by two people to
marry 3) an appointment

en-gen-der [ĕn-jĕn′dər] *verb*, to
cause, to give rise to

en-gine [ĕn′jĭn] *noun*, 1) a machine
that converts energy into motion
2) a locomotive 3) a source of
power

en-gi-neer [ĕn′jə-nîr′] *noun*, 1) one
who designs machines 2) one
who drives an engine, *verb*, 3) to
bring about an event

Eng-lish [ĭng′glĭsh] *adjective*,
1) the language of the people of
Britain, America, Canada,
Australia, and other countries
2) relating to or belonging to the
people of England

en-grave [ĕn-grāv′] *verb*, 1) to cut
into a surface 2) to leave an
impression

en-gulf [ĕn-gŭlf′] *verb*, to cover
completely, to close over

en-hance [ĕn-hăns′] *verb*, to make
better, to increase the value or
quality of something

e-nig-ma [ĭ-nĭg′mə] *noun*,
something hard to explain, a
puzzle, a mysterious person

en-joy [ĕn-joi′] *verb*, to take
pleasure in

en-joy-ment [ĕn-joi′mənt] *noun*,
delight, satisfaction, happiness,
pleasure

en-large [ĕn-lärj′] *verb*, to increase,

en-light-en [ĕn-līt′n] *verb*, to
educate, to inform, to give
spiritual insight

en-list [ĕn-lĭst′] *verb*, to sign up, to
enroll in the armed forces

en-mi-ty [ĕn′mĭ-tē] *noun*, hatred

e-nor-mous [ĭ-nôr′məs] *adjective*,
monstrous, huge, immense

e-nough [ĭ-nŭf′] *adjective*, 1) as
much as is needed, ample,
adverb, 2) to an adequate or
sufficient degree, *noun*,
3) the required amount

en-rage [ĕn-rāj′] *verb*, to anger, to
inflame, to make furious

en-rich [ĕn-rĭch′] *verb*, to improve,
to make rich, to enhance

en-roll [ĕn-rōl′] *verb*, to register in
a list or as a student in a school,
to become a member

en-roll-ment [ĕn-rōl′mənt] *noun*,
the total number registered

en-sem-ble [ŏn-sŏm′bəl] *noun*, the
whole, all the parts taken
together as a group

en-sue [ĕn-sōō′] *verb*, to make sure
or certain, to follow up

en-sure [ĕn-shōōr′] *verb*, to
guarantee, to make sure of, to
insure

en-ter [ĕn′tər] *verb*, to go into, to
become involved in

en-ter-prise [ĕn′tər-prīz′] *noun*, a
bold undertaking, a project or
business activity, a venture

en-ter-tain [ĕn′tər-tān′] *verb*, 1) to
hold the interest of the people
you are talking to or performing
for, 2) to amuse, to delight
3) to have in mind

en-ter-tain-ment [ĕn′tər-tān′mənt]
noun, a performance that tries to
interest an audience

en-thrall [ĕn-thrôl′] *verb*, to
fascinate, to mesmerize

en-thu-si-asm [ĕn-thōō′zē-ăz′əm]
noun, eager interest, excitement

en-thu-si-as-tic [ĕn-thoo′zē-ăs′tĭk]
adjective, showing a passionate
and devoted interest in a belief
or idea

en-tice [ĕn-tīs′] *verb*, to lure, to
attract, to tempt, to persuade

en-tire [ĕn-tīr′] *adjective*, whole,
complete, with no parts missing

en-ti-tle [ĕn-tīt′l] *verb*, 1) to give as
a right 2) to give a title to

en-ti-ty [ĕn′tĭ-tē] *noun*, a being, an
individual, an existence

en-trance [ĕn′trəns] *noun*, 1) a
means of entry or access 2) the
act of coming in

en-tree [ŏn′trā] *noun*, the main dish
of a meal

en-tre-pre-neur [ŏn′trə-prə-nûr′]
noun, a businessman, one who
starts a business and assumes
financial risk for it

en-trust [ĕn-trŭst′] *verb*, to
confide, to give to for
safekeeping

en-try [ĕn′trē] *noun*, 1) entrance, a
way in 2) an item in a log

e-nun-ci-ate [ĭ-nŭn′sē-āt′] *verb*, to
pronounce, to state clearly

en-vel-op [ĕn-vĕl′əp] *verb*, to
cover, to enclose, to surround

en-vel-ope [ĕn′və-lōp′] *noun*, a
folded paper cover like a pocket
for a letter

en-vi-ous [ĕn′vē-əs] *adjective*,
jealous, full of envy

en-vi-ron-ment [ĕn-vī′rən-mənt]
noun, the surroundings or place
in which something lives

en-vy [ĕn′vē] *noun*, 1) a feeling of
anger or bitterness because
someone has more of something,
or a better life, *verb*, 2) to want

something someone has, to be
jealous

e-on [ē′ŏn′, ē′ən] *noun*, a billion
years, a long time

e-phem-er-al [ĭ-fĕm′ər-əl]
adjective, short-lived, fleeting

ep-ic [ĕp′ĭk] *noun*, a long poem
about a hero and his deeds

ep-i-dem-ic [ĕp′ĭ-dĕm′ĭk]
adjective, 1) affecting many in
the community, widespread,
noun, 2) a contagious disease
infecting many among the
population

ep-i-der-mis [ĕp′ĭ-dûr′mĭs] *noun*,
the outer layer of the skin

ep-i-gram [ĕp′ĭ-grăm′] *noun*, a
pithy phrase, a witty saying

ep-i-lep-sy [ĕp′ə-lĕp′sē] *noun*, a
disorder of the nervous system
accompanied by convulsions and
loss of consiousness

ep-i-logue [ĕp′ə-lôg′] *noun*, a short
conclusion added to the end of a
book, play, etc.

ep-i-sode [ĕp′ĭ-sōd′] *noun*, 1) a
distinctive occurrence 2) a
separate incident in a longer
story or poem

ep-i-taph [ĕp′ĭ-tăf′] *noun*, an
inscription on a monument in
memory of a dead person who is
buried there

e-pit-o-me [ĭ-pĭt′ə-mē] *noun*, a
typical or perfect example of a
group or type

ep-och [ĕp′ək] *noun*, 1) a time
period characterized by a
distinctive development 2) a date
marking the beginning of a new
period of history 3) a division of
geological time

e-qual [ē′kwəl] *adjective*, 1) being the same as 2) alike, *noun*, 3) something valued as the same a symbol = that shows both sides have the same value, *verb*, 5) to be as good as someone or something else

e-qual-i-ty [ĭ-kwŏl′ĭ-tē] *noun*, the state of being the same as

e-qual-ize [ē′kwə-līz′] *verb*, to make even, to balance

e-qual-ly [ē′kwə-lē] *adverb*, in an equal way, to an equal degree

e-qua-tion [ĭ-kwā′shən] *noun*, 1) the act or process of considering or making equal 2) a statement that the values of two mathematical expressions are equal (=)

e-qua-tor [ĭ-kwā′tər] *noun*, the imaginary band circling the middle of the earth, at an equal distance from the North and South Poles

e-ques-tri-an [ĭ-kwĕs′trē-ən] *adjective,* 1) relating to horseback riding, *noun,* 2) a rider on horseback

e-qui-lib-ri-um [ē′kwə-lĭb′rē-əm] *noun*, a state of balance between opposing forces

e-qui-lat-er-al tri-angle [ē′kwə-lăt′ər-əl trī′ăng′gəl] *noun*, a triangle with 60 degree angles and three equal sides

e-qui-nox [ē′kwə-nŏks′] *noun*, either of two times in the year when night and day are of equal length: March 21; October 21

e-quip [ĭ-kwĭp′] *verb*, to provide what is needed, to outfit

e-quip-ment [ĭ-kwĭp′mənt] *noun*, tools, supplies, etc., needed for a job or a special activity

eq-ui-ty [ĕk′wĭ-tē] *noun*, 1) the value of property or stock after subtracting liens against it 2) just, impartial, fairness

e-quiv-a-lent [ĭ-kwĭv′ə-lənt] *noun*, 1) equal in value or worth 2) similar in force, measure, meaning or effect, identical

e-quiv-o-cate [ĭ-kwĭv′ə-kāt′] *verb*, to use deliberately evasive language

e-ra [îr′ə, ĕr′ə] *noun*, a distinct period of time, or history

e-rad-i-cate [ĭ-răd′ĭ-kāt′] *verb*, to destroy completely, to get rid of

e-rase [ĭ-rās′] *verb*, to rub out, to remove all traces of

e-rect [ĭ-rĕkt′] *adjective*, 1) standing straight, upright, *verb*, 2) to build or construct

er-mine [ûr′mĭn] *noun*, a small weasel with white fur and black-tipped tail in winter

e-rode [ĭ-rōd′] *verb*, 1) to wear away gradually 2) to destroy slowly

e-ro-sion [ĭ-rō′zhən] *noun*, the process of wearing down, breaking up, and carrying off land, soil, and rock, by wind and water

err [ûr, ĕr] *verb*, to be mistaken

er-rand [ĕr′ənd] *noun*, a short trip to accomplish a task

er-rat-ic [ĭ-răt′ĭk] *adjective*, irregular, inconsistent

er-ro-ne-ous [ĭ-rō′nē-əs] *adjective*, false, incorrect

er-ror [ĕr/ər] *noun*, 1) a belief in what is untrue 2) an act involving a departure from truth and accuracy, a mistake

er-satz [er/säts] *adjective*, 1) made or used as a substitute 2) not real or genuine

er-u-dite [ĕr/yə-dīt] *adjective*, learned, well-educated, scholarly

e-rupt [ĭ-rŭpt/] *verb*, 1) to burst out suddenly, to explode 2) to express an emotion suddenly and forcefully

es-ca-la-tor [ĕs/kə-lā/tər] *noun*, moving stairs attached to a circulating belt

es-cape [ĭ-skāp/] *noun*, 1) a means to get away from danger or unpleasantness, *verb*, 2) to free oneself

es-chew [ĕs-choo/] *verb*, to avoid, to keep away from, to evade

es-cort [ĕs/kôrt/] *noun*, 1) a guide, an attendant, *verb*, 2) to accompany someone, to go with them as protection or an honor

es-crow [ĕs/krō/] *noun*, money, a bond or a deed held by a third person until a specified condition is met

Es-ki-mo [ĕs/kə-mō/] *noun*, a member of a people living in Russia, Alaska, Canada, and Greenland, the Inuit

e-soph-a-gus [ĭ-sŏf/ə-gəs] *noun*, the tube that leads from the pharynx to the stomach

es-o-ter-ic [ĕs/ə-tĕr/ĭk] *adjective*, understood only by a chosen few

es-pe-cial-ly [ĕ-spĕsh/ə-lē] *adverb*, particularly, to a great extent

es-pi-o-nage [ĕs/pē-ə-näzh/] *noun*, of spying, the practice of spying

es-prit de corps [ĕ-sprē/ də kôr/] *noun*, the spirit of the group

es-say [ĕs/ā/, ĕ-sā/] *noun*, 1) a literary composition expressing personal observations, *verb*, 2) to try out, to test, to attempt

es-sence [ĕs/əns] *noun*, 1) the real character or nature of something 2) perfume

es-sen-tial [ĭ-sĕn/shəl] *adjective*, 1) indispensable 2) of or pertaining to the essential nature, *noun*, 3) a necessity, the basic elements

es-tab-lish [ĭ-stăb/lĭsh] *verb*, 1) to make stable or firm, to settle or set up, *verb*, 2)to prove to be true

es-tab-lish-ment [ĭ-stăb/lĭsh-mənt] *noun*, 1) a place of business or residence 2) an organization

es-tate [ĭ-stāt/] *noun*, 1) a property 2) property left at someone's death

es-teem [ĭ-stēm/] *noun*, 1) respect, honor, *verb*, 2) to regard favorably

es-ti-mate [ĕs/tə-mĭt/] *noun*, 1) an educated guess, an approximation, [ĕs/tə-māt/]*verb*, 2) to calculate the approximate value or amount of something 3) to give an approximate rather than an exact answer, to guess

et cet-er-a [ĕt sĕt/ər-ə] *abbr.* **etc.**, and so on

etch [ĕch] *verb*, to engrave by biting out with an acid

e-ter-nal [ĭ-tûr/nəl] *adjective*, endless, infinite, forever

e-ter-ni-ty [ĭ-tûr/nĭ-tē] *noun*, forever

eth-i-cal [ĕth/ĭ-kəl] *adjective*, having or relating to morals

eth-ics [ĕth/ĭks] *noun*, *plural*, rules of moral principles governing a group

eth-nic [ĕth′nĭk] *adjective*, relating to different races, ancestry, or culture

eth-nol-o-gy [ĕth-nŏl′ə-jē] *noun*, the study of different races and their characteristics

et-i-quette [ĕt′ĭ-kĕt′] *noun*, good manners, the rules for polite behavior

et-y-mol-o-gy [ĕt′ə-mŏl′ə-jē] *noun*, the study of the origin and derivation of words

eu-gen-ics [yōō-jĕn′ĭks]*noun*, the study of genetic traits by controlling breeding

eu-lo-gy [yōō′lə-jē] *noun*, a speech or written tribute lauding a deceased person

eu-phe-mism [yōō′fə-mĭz′əm] *noun*, a mild expression to replace an offensive remark

eu-re-ka [yōō-rē′kə] *exclamation*, an expression of triumph concerning a discovery

Eu-rope [yōōr′əp] *noun*, one of the seven continents, the second smalles continent

eu-tha-na-sia [yōō′thə-nā′zhə] *noun*, mercy killing

e-vac-u-ate [ĭ-văk′yōō-āt′] *verb*, to abandon, to empty out

e-vade [ĭ-vād′] *verb*, to avoid, to escape by cleverness

e-val-u-ate [ĭ-văl′yōō-āt′] *verb*, to measure the value, to appraise

e-vap-o-rate [ĭ-văp′ə-rāt′] *verb*, 1) to turn from solid or liquid into vapor 2) to lose moisture, to dry up 3) to vanish

e-vap-o-ra-tion [ĭ-văp′ə-rā′shən] *noun*, the process in which water disappears from a surface as it becomes vapor, the loss of water into the air

e-va-sive [ĭ-vā′sĭv] *adjective*, 1) avoiding something, elusive 2) intentionally not answering

eve [ēv] *noun*, the night before

e-ven [ē′vən] *adjective*, 1) level, flat, smooth 2) able to be divided by two 3) equal, *adverb*, 4) more than expected 5) indeed 6) exactly

eve-ning [ēv′nĭng] *noun*, the time between the end of the afternoon and bedtime, dusk

e-ven-ly [ē′vən-lē] *adverb*, in an equal way, smoothly

e-vent [ĭ-vĕnt′] *noun*, something that takes place, an activity

e-ven-tu-al-ly [ĭ-vĕn′chōō-ə-lē] *adverb*, at long last, after the passing of some time

ev-er [ĕv′ər] *adverb*, 1) always, at all times 2) at any time

ev-er-green [ĕv′ər-grēn′] *noun*, a plant that keeps its leaves all year long, including holly, rhododendrons, pine trees, and others

eve-ry [ĕv′rē] *adjective*, each, all possible

eve-ry-bod-y [ĕv′rē-bŏd′ē] *pronoun*, every person

eve-ry-day [ĕv′rē-dā′] *adjective*, ordinary, commonplace, normal

eve-ry-one [ĕv′rē-wŭn′] *pronoun*, each person, everybody

eve-ry-thing [ĕv′rē-thĭng′]*pronoun*, all together, all things

eve-ry-where [ĕv′rē-hwâr′] *adverb*, in every place

ev-i-dence [ĕv′ĭ-dəns] *noun*, 1) one or more facts or items 2) testimony 3) the basis on which one believes something to be true

ev-i-dent [ĕv′ĭ-dənt] *adjective*, clear, apparent, obvious

e-vil [ē′vəl] *adjective*, very bad, corrupt, immoral, wicked

e-voke [ĭ-vōk′] *verb*, 1) to call forth, 2) to bring to mind

ev-o-lu-tion [ĕv′ə-lōō′shən] *noun*, the natural process of growth and change, development

e-volve [ĭ-vŏlv′] *verb*, to come into being, to develop gradually

ex-ac-er-bate [ĭg-zăs′ər-bāt′] *verb*, to make worse

ex-act [ĭg-zăkt′] *adjective*, precise, correct, completely accurate

ex-ag-ger-ate [ĭg-zăj′ə-rāt′] *verb*, to enlarge beyond the bounds of truth, to overstate

ex-alt [ĭg-zôlt′] *verb*, to praise, to elevate, to raise in rank

ex-am-i-na-tion [ĭg-zăm′ə-nā′shən] *noun*, scrutiny, inquiry, a test

ex-am-ine [ĭg-zăm′ĭn] *verb*, 1) to inspect carefully, to look at every point 2) to scrutinize 3) to question

ex-am-ple [ĭg-zăm′pəl] *noun*, 1) a model, a sample of what others are like 2) a person punished as a warning to others

ex-as-per-ate [ĭg-zăs′pə-rāt′] *verb*, to irritate, to provoke, to enrage

ex-ceed [ĭk-sēd′] *verb*,1) to pass beyond the measure of something, 2) to surpass

ex-cel [ĭk-sĕl′] *verb*, to be better than others at something, to do well

ex-cel-lent [ĕk′sə-lənt] *adjective*, superior, very good

ex-cel-si-or[ĕk′sə-l′sē′ər] *adjective*, higher, always upward

ex-cept [ĭk-sĕpt′] *preposition*, 1) apart from, not including, *verb*, 2) to exclude

ex-cep-tion [ĭk-sĕp′shən] *noun*, 1) a circumstance not conforming to the general rule 2) an omission

ex-cep-tion-al [ĭk-sĕp′shə-nəl] *adjective*, superior, unusually good

ex-cerpt [ĕk′sûrpt′] *noun*, section that has been removed from a longer text

ex-cess [ĭk-sĕs′] *adjective*, 1) extra, more than expected, *noun*, 2) an amount that is more than enough 3) immoderate behaivor

ex-change [ĭks-chānj′] *noun*, 1) the process of settling accounts or trading items between parties, *verb*, 2) to change something for something else, to replace, to trade

ex-cise [ĕk′sīz′]*noun*, a tax levied upon specific articles and services within a country

ex-cite [ĭk-sīt′] *verb*, to be energized or to have strong feeling

ex-cite-ment [ĭk-sīt′mənt] *noun*, 1) ado, commotion 2) a thrill

ex-claim [ĭk-sklām′] *verb*, to speak suddenly and with strong feeling

ex-cla-ma-tion mark [ĕk′sklə-mā′shən märk] *noun*,

the sign ! used to show surprise, humor, or strong feeling

ex-clude [ĭk-sklo͞od′] *verb*, to keep out

ex-clu-sive [ĭk-sklo͞o′sĭv] *adjective*, restricted to particular group of people

ex-cru-ci-at-ing [ĭk skro͞o′shē-ā′tĭng] *adjective*, very painful, agonizing

ex-cur-sion [ĭk-skûr′zhən] *noun*, a journey chiefly for recreation, a brief tour, an outing

ex-cuse [ĭk′skyo͞os] *noun*, 1) a reason, a defense, [ĭk-skyo͞oz′] *verb*, 2) to free, to allow an interruption 3) to give a reason for a fault

ex-e-cute [ĕk′sĭ-kyo͞ot′] *verb*, 1) to kill someone legally as punishment for a crime 2) to take action

ex-e-cu-tion [ĕk′sĭ-kyo͞o′shən] *noun*, 1) accomplishment, implementation 2) the act of putting to death a condemned person

ex-ec-u-tive [ĭg-zĕk′yə-tĭv] *noun*, 1) a business person responsible for making decisions, a manager 2) one of the three branches of the United States government

ex-em-pla-ry [ĭg-zĕm′plə-rē] *adjective*, commendable, serving as a desirable model

ex-em-pli-fy [ĭg-zĕm′plə-fī′] *verb*, to show or illustrate by example

ex-empt [ĭg-zĕmpt′] *verb*, to excuse from an obligation or rule, to make immune

ex-er-cise [ĕk′sər-sīz′] *noun*, 1) an activity used to train the body,

verb, 2) to train the body by using one's muscles

ex-ert [ĭg-zûrt′] *verb*, 1) to make an effort 2) to bring to bear

ex-er-tion [ĭg-zûr′shən] *noun*, hard work, a strong effort

ex-hale [ĕks-hāl′] *verb*, to breathe out, to blow, to emit

ex-haust [ĭg-zôst′] *verb*, 1) to be thorough covering all points 2) to use up 3) the waste fumes from an engine

ex-haus-tion [ĭg-zôs′chən] *noun*, fatique, tiredness

ex-haus-tive [ĭg-zô′stĭv] *adjective*, complete, thorough, attending to every detail, comprehensive

ex-hib-it [ĭg-zĭb′ĭt] *noun*, 1) a display of a collection, *verb*, 2) to display

ex-hi-bi-tion [ĕk′sə-bĭsh′ən] *noun*, a public display of art or other items

ex-hil-a-ra-tion [ĭg-zĭl′ə-rā′shən] *noun*, a feeling of excitement and joy

ex-i-gen-cy [ĕk′sə-jən-sē] *noun*, a pressing necessity, a case demanding immediate action

ex-ile [ĕg′zīl′] *noun*, 1) one who is not allowed to live in his or her own country as a form of punishment, *verb*, 2) to be forced out of a place and not allowed to return

ex-ist [ĭg-zĭst′] *verb*, 1) to be, to live, to be present, to occur

ex-ist-ence [ĭg-zĭs′təns] *noun*, 1) state of being actual, life 2) reality 3) all that which lives

ex-it [ĕg′zĭt] *noun*, 1) a way to go out, the door leading out of a building 2) the ramp leading off a major highway, *verb*, 3) to leave, to go out, to depart

ex-o-dus [ĕk'sə-dəs] *noun*, mass departure of people, migration

ex-o-skel-e-ton [ĕk'sō-skĕl'ĭ-tn] *noun*, an outer structure that provides protection to an insect, shellfish, turtle, etc.

ex-ot-ic [ĭg-zŏt'ĭk] *adjective*, strange, interesting, or unusual

ex-pand [ĭk-spănd'] *verb*, to grow or make larger, to extend

ex-panse [ĭk-spăns'] *noun*, a large open space, an area of land

ex-pa-tri-ate [ĕk-spā'trē-āt'] *noun*, someone who left his native land

ex-pect [ĭk-spĕkt'] *verb*, to wait for something that is supposed to happen, to anticipate

ex-pec-ta-tion [ĕk'spĕk-tā'shən] *noun*, anticipation, calculation

ex-pe-di-en-cy [ĭk-spē'dē-ən-sē] *noun*, that which is practical

ex-pe-di-tion [ĕk'spĭ-dĭsh'ən] *noun*, a journey or excursion for a specific purpose, a trip

ex-pe-di-tious [ĕk'spĭ-dĭsh'əs] *adjective*, efficient and speedy

ex-pel [ĭk-spĕl'] *verb*, to drive out

ex-pend-i-ture [ĭk-spĕn'də-chər] *noun*, a laying out, as of money or labor, the cost

ex-pense [ĭk-spĕns'] *noun*, 1) cost, payment 2) detriment, sacrifice

ex-pen-sive [ĭk-spĕn'sĭv] *adjective*, costing a lot of money

ex-pe-ri-ence [ĭk-spîr'ē-əns] *noun*, 1) an encounter that provokes a reaction 2) knowledge gained by observation or trial, *verb*, 3) to live, to feel by participating

ex-per-i-ment [ĭk-spĕr'ə-mənt] *noun*, 1) a test done to see if something is valid or true, *verb*, 2) to carry out a plan in order to test a prediction

ex-pert [ĕk'spûrt'] *noun*, a very knowledgeable person in his or her particular field, an authority

ex-per-tise [ĕk'spûr-tēz'] *noun*, specialized knowledge or skill

ex-pi-ra-tion [ĕk'spə-rā'shən] *noun*, 1) a coming to a close 2) death, the end

ex-pire [ĭk-spīr'] *verb*, 1) to end, to cease to exist 2) to breath out

ex-plain [ĭk-splān'] *verb*, to clarify or to give a reason, to account for

ex-pla-na-tion [ĕk'splə-nā'shən] *noun*, the act of interpreting an action or giving a description

ex-ple-tive [ĕk'splĭ-tĭv] *noun*, a curse word, an obscenity

ex-plic-it [ĭk-splĭs'ĭt] *adjective*, plain, definite, expressed clearly

ex-plode [ĭk-splōd'] *verb*, 1) to release energy with a loud noise as something is destroyed by bursting outward 2) to increase suddenly

ex-ploit [ĕk'sploit'] *noun*, 1) a deed or act, especially one of renown, *verb*, 2) to make use of for one's own profit

ex-plo-ra-tion [ĕk'splə-rā'shən] *noun*, a search in order to discover, an investigation

ex-plore [ĭk-splôr'] *verb*, 1) to look into closely, to examine or investigate 2) to go into new or unknown places to find new things and learn about them

ex-plo-sion [ĭk-splō'zhən] *noun*, a blast, a bomb bursting

ex-plo-sive [ĭk-splō′sĭv] *adjective*, flammable, combustible

ex-port [ĭk-spôrt′] *noun*, 1) something sold abroad as part of international trade, *verb*, 2) merchandise conveyed from one country to another

ex-pose [ĭk-spōz′] *verb* 1) to make something easy to see 2) to reveal, to make known 3) to leave unprotected

ex-po-si-tion [ĕk′spə-zĭsh′ən] *noun*, a statement of intent, a public exhibition or display

ex-po-sure [ĭk-spō′zhər] *noun*, not sheltered from the elements such as cold, sun, rain, wind, etc.

ex-press [ĭk-sprĕs′] *adjective*, 1) the fastest means available, *verb*, 2) to indicate, to show

ex-pres-sion [ĭk-sprĕsh′ən] *noun*, 1) the look on someone's face, a facial gesture 2) a remark, a cliché 3) a way of showing feelings or emotion through actions or words

ex-pul-sion [ĭk-spŭl′shən] *noun*, a driving or forcing out

ex-punge [ĭk-spŭnj′] *verb*, to cancel, to remove

ex-quis-ite [ĕk′skwĭ-zĭt] *adjective*, 1) carefully crafted or executed, 2) delicately beautiful

ex-tend [ĭk-stĕnd′] *verb*, 1) to stretch out, to lengthen 2) to offer

ex-ten-sion [ĭk-stĕn′shən] *noun*, a part added on

ex-ten-sive [ĭk-stĕn′sĭv] *adjective*, having wide reach, broad

ex-tent [ĭk-stĕnt′] *noun*, the area covered or affected by something, the amount

ex-ten-u-ate [ĭk-stĕn′yōō-āt′] *adjective*, out of reach, beyond your grasp or control

ex-te-ri-or [ĭk-stîr′ē-ər] *noun*, 1) external, outward 2) on the surface or appearance

ex-ter-mi-nate [ĭk-stûr′mə-nāt′] *verb*, to drive out, to destroy completely, to kill

ex-ter-nal [ĭk-stûr′nəl] *adjective*, 1) on or relating to the outside of the subject 2) the outer part

ex-tinct [ĭk-stĭngkt′] *adjective*, no longer existing or living

ex-tin-guish [ĭk-stĭng′gwĭsh] *verb*, to put out as a fire or a light

ex-tort [ĭk-stôrt′] *verb*, to get money by making threats and by intimidation or coercion

ex-tor-tion [ĭk-stôr′shən] *noun*, demanding money by making threats, blackmail

ex-tra [ĕk′strə] *adjective*, 1) a surplus, more than needed, *adverb*, 2) in addition

ex-tract [ĭk-străkt′] *verb*, 1) to take out 2) to distill or remove

ex-tra-di-tion [ĕk′strə-dĭsh′ən] *noun*, the surrender of a prisoner by another authority

ex-tra-ne-ous [ĭk-strā′nē-əs] *adjective*, not essential, foreign

ex-traor-di-nar-y [ĭk-strôr′dn-ĕr′ē, ĕk′strə-ôr′-] *adjective*, unusual, rare, exceptional, uncommon

ex-tra-ter-res-tri-al [ĕkstrətə′ restrēəl] *adjective*, of or from outside the earth's atmosphere

ex-trav-a-gant [ĭk-străv′ə-gənt] *adjective*, wasteful, exceeding reasonable limits, spending too much, very expensive

ex-treme [ĭk-strēm/] *adjective*, 1) to the highest or a very high degree 2) the utmost limit or degree, radical 3) final, last

ex-trem-i-ty [ĭk-strĕm/ĭ-tē] *noun*, 1) the end or the boundary 2) an appendage such as a hand or foot

ex-tri-cate [ĕk/strĭ-kāt/] *verb*, to clear away, to free, to untangle

ex-trin-sic [ĭk-strĭn/sĭk] *adjective*, external, from outside

ex-u-ber-ant [ĭg-zōō/bər-ənt] *adjective*, joyful, high spirits

ex-ude [ĭg-zōōd/] *verb*, to discharge, to ooze, to give forth

ex-ul-ta-tion [ĕk/səl-tā/shən] *noun*, joy, celebration, showing delight

eye [ī] *noun*, 1) the organ located on the head used to see 2) the tiny hole at the end of a needle

eye-lash [ī/lăsh/] *noun*, one of the hairs growing on the eyelid

eye-lid [ī/lĭd/] *noun*, the skin which covers the eye

F

fa-ble [fā/bəl] *noun*, a fictitious short story with a moral in which animals talk

fab-ric [făb/rĭk] *noun*, 1) any cloth that is woven or knit from fibers 2) make up, substance

fab-ri-cate [făb/rĭ-kāt/] *verb*, 1) to build, to construct 2) to lie

fab-u-lous [făb/yə-ləs] *adjective*, marvelous, wonderful, amazing

fa-cade [fə-säd/] *noun*, the decorated entrance of a building

face [fās] *noun*, 1) the front of the head, with the eyes, nose and mouth 2) the front of something 3) a flat surface of a space figure, *verb*, 4) to stand in front of or turn to confront

fac-et [făs/ĭt] *noun*, 1) one of the polished plane surfaces of a precious stone 2) an aspect of a subject, a side, a feature

fa-ce-tious [fə-sē/shəs] *adjective*, joking, sportive, kidding around, not serious, flippant, glib

fac-ile [făs/əl] *adjective*, easy

fa-cil-i-tate [fə-sĭl/ĭ-tāt/] *verb*, to make easier, to aid, to help

fac-sim-i-le [făk-sĭm/ə-lē] *noun*, an exact copy or likeness of anything, a reproduction

fact [făkt] *noun*, an indisputable piece of information, something that is true, a certainty

fac-tion [făk/shən] *noun*, a dissenting party, an inner circle, a clique, a group within a group

fac-tious [făk/shəs] *adjective*, broken into groups

fac-tor [făk/tər] *noun*, 1) a condition that causes a result 2) the numbers multiplied or divided to give a product

fac-to-ry [făk/tə-rē] *noun*, a building where products are manufactured

fac-ul-ty [făk/əl-tē] *noun*, 1) the professors in an institution of higher learning 2) a physical or mental ability, talent, capacity

fad [făd] *noun*, temporary fashion or style, the "in" thing

fade [fād] *verb*, to lose light or color, to become dull or dim

Fahr-en-heit [făr′ən-hīt′] *adjective*, of or relating to the temperature scale in which the freezing point of water is 32 degrees and the boiling point of water is 212 degrees under normal atmospheric pressure

fail [fāl] *verb*, to not accomplish what you set out to

fail-ure [fāl′yər] *noun*, lack of success, a debacle

faint [fānt] *adjective*, 1) hard to see, dim 2) inaudible, indistinct, soft, *verb*, 3) to feel weak or dizzy, to collapse unconscious

fair [fâr] *adjective*, 1) treating everyone equally, not favoring one more than another, 2) so-so, mediocre 3) pale, light-skinned complexion, *noun*, 4) a gathering for buying and selling goods

fair-y [fâr′ē] *noun*, an imaginary person with magical powers

faith [fāth] *noun*, 1) a belief in something that is not seen, relying on trust 2) religion

faith-ful [fāth′fəl] *adjective*, loyal, trustworthy, full of faith

fake [fāk] *noun*, 1) forgery, imitation, *verb*, 2) to pretend, to falsify 3) to counterfeit

fall [fôl] *noun*, 1) the season of autumn, *verb*, 2) to come down, to tumble 3) to lose power

fal-lacy [făl′ə-sē] *noun*, an error in reasoning, an erroneous idea

fal-li-ble [făl′ə-bəl] *adjective*, liable to err, vulnerable

fall line *noun*, a place where the height of the land drops

suddenly and is usually marked by many waterfalls and rapids

false [fôls] *adjective*, 1) not true 2) artificial, not real

false-hood [fôls′hŏŏd′] *noun*, a lie

fal-ter [fôl′tər] *verb*, to hesitate

fame [fām] *noun*, *no plural*, wide recognition, to become a household name, celebrity

fa-mil-iar [fə-mĭl′yər] *adjective*, to have some knowledge of something or someone

fam-i-ly [făm′ə-lē] *noun*, 1) a parent or parents and children 2) all of a person's relatives

fam-ine [făm′ĭn] *noun*, 1) general scarcity of food 2) extreme scarcity of something

fam-ish-ed [făm′ĭshd] *adjective*, extremely hungry

fa-mous [fā′məs] *adjective*, well known, celebrated, noted

fan [făn] *noun*, 1) any device designed to circulate air 2) an ardent follower or supporter, *verb*, 3) to move air, to cool with a fan 4) to spread out

fa-nat-ic [fə-năt′ĭk] *adjective*, 1)carrying an interest or enthusiasm to extremes, *noun*, 2) a person with a very strong interest in something

fan-cy [făn′sē] *adjective*, elaborate, unusually decorated, not plain

fang [făng] *noun*, a long sharp tooth, the incisor

fan-tas-tic [făn-tăs′tĭk] *adjective*, imaginary, fanciful, unreal

fan-ta-sy [făn′tə-sē] *noun*, a daydream, an imaginary situation, make believe

far

far [fär] *adjective*, 1) at a great
distance, not near or close by,
adverb, 2) exceedingly 3) a
certain point

fare [fâr] *noun*, 1) money paid for a
trip by bus or train for example
2) food and drink *verb* 3) to get
along well

fare-well [fâr-wĕl'] *noun*, goodbye,
adieu, parting

farm [färm] *noun*, buildings or
land in the country where people
grow food as cash crops or raise
animals to sell

farm-er [fär'mər] *noun*, a person
who owns and or cultivates
crops on a portion of land

far-ther [fär'thər] *preposition*, to
be far away, in a remote place

fas-ci-nate [făs'ə-nāt'] *verb*, to
attract and hold interest, to
captivate, to excite

fas-ci-na-tion [făs'ə-nā'shən] *noun*,
personal attraction, infatuation

fash-ion [făsh'ən] *noun*, 1) clothing
or articles that are in style, in
vogue, *verb*, 2) to shape or form

fast [făst] *adjective*, 1) quick, rapid
2) fixed in place, cannot move,
verb, 3) to go for an extended
period of time without eating

fas-tid-i-ous [făst'ĭd'ē-əs]*adjective*,
hard to please, very critical

fat [făt] *adjective*, 1) with a wide
round shape 2) thick, *noun*, 3) an
oily substance from cooked meat

fa-tal [fāt'l] *adjective*, in a manner
that results in death, lethal

fate [fāt] *noun*, an invisible hand
that seems to cause certain
things to happen over which
people have no control, destiny

fa-ther [fä'thər] *noun*, the male
parent

fa-ther-in-law [fä'thər-ĭn-lô']
noun, the father of your wife or
husband

fath-om [făth'əm] *verb*, to
understand, to comprehend

fa-tigue [fə-tēg'] *noun*, 1) the
condition or being very tired or
exhausted, *verb*, 2) to become or
make tired

fau-cet [fô'sĭt] *noun*, a fixture for
drawing liquid from a pipe and
regulating the flow

fault [fôlt] *noun*, 1) mistake, failure
to perform a duty 2) a fracture in
the earth's surface causing a
displacement 3) a defect

fa-vor [fā'vər] *noun*, 1) an act of
kindness, *verb*, 2) to prefer, to
patronize, to fancy, to like

fa-vor-ite [fā'vər-ĭt] *adjective*,
something preferred above
others, liked the best

fawn [fôn] *noun*, a young deer less
than a year old

fear [fîr] *noun*, 1) expecting harm,
verb, 2) to dread or be afraid of

fear-ful [fîr'fəl] *adjective*, afraid,
timid, frightened, scared

fea-si-ble [fē'zə-bəl] *adjective*,
capable of being done, practical,
possible, achievable

feast [fēst] *noun*, 1) an elaborate
meal, a banquet, *verb*, 2) to eat
large amounts of food and drink

feat [fēt] *noun*, an accomplishment,
a remarkable achievement

feath-er [fĕth'ər] *noun*, a soft thing
which covers birds, like a
toothpick covered with fine hairs

fea-ture [fē′chər] *noun*, 1) a distinctive aspect on a person, a characteristic 2) an article in the newspaper

Feb-ru-ar-y [fĕb′rōō-ĕr′ē] *noun*, the second month in the year, having 28 days but 29 every four years on the leap year

fed [fĕd] *past tense* of **feed**

fed-er-al [fĕd′ər-əl] *adjective*, belonging or pertaining to a state formed by the consolidation of several states

fed-er-a-tion [fĕd′ə-rā′shən] *noun*, an alliance, an association

fee [fē] *noun*, money charged for something, the cost or expense

fee-ble [fē′bəl] *adjective*, weak, frail, unsteady, infirm

feed [fēd] *noun*, 1) food for animals, *verb*, 2) to give someone food, to nourish

feel [fēl] *verb*, 1) to perceive in a way other than your five senses, to sense with emotions 2) to acknowledge with the sense of touch 3) to form an opinion

feign [fān] *verb*, to pretend

feist-y [fī′stē] *adjective*, very active or spirited, exuberant

fe-lic-i-ty [fĭ-lĭs′ĭ-tē] *adjective*, the state of being happy

fell [fĕl] *adjective*, 1) cruel, deadly, *verb*, 2) *past tense* of **fall**

fel-low [fĕl′ō] *noun*, 1) a man 2) a companion, a comrade

fel-on [fĕl′ən] *noun*, a person convicted of a serious crime

fel-o-ny [fĕl′ə-nē] *noun*, any offense that is punishable by confinement in prison

felt [fĕlt] *noun*, 1) a soft synthetic fabric without a nap 2) the *past tense* of **feel**

fe-male [fē′māl′] *adjective*, 1) referring to a woman, feminine, *noun*, 2) attributes of a woman and characteristics

fem-i-nine [fĕm′ə-nĭn] *adjective*, of or pertaining to the female sex

fence [fĕns] *noun*, 1) a partition made of wood or wire 2) a person who receives stolen goods, *verb*, 3) to put in an enclosure 4) to duel with a sword

fend-er [fĕn′dər] *noun*, the strip of metal over the wheels of a car, bicycle, or other vehicle to protect against mud or water

fer-ment [fər-mĕnt′] *verb*, to ripen, to acidify with bacteria

fern [fûrn] *noun*, a bright green plant that does not have flowers, and grows in shady places

fe-ro-cious [fə-rō′shəs] *adjective*, savage, fierce, cruel

fer-ret [fĕr′ĭt] *noun*, 1) a small rodent like a weasel, *verb*, 2) to drive or hunt out of hiding

fer-ry [fĕr′ē] *noun*, a boat used to transport people or goods from one side to the other

fer-tile [fûr′tl] *adjective*, fruitful, able to produce abundantly

fer-ti-lize [fûr′tl-īz′] *verb*, to make ready for planting by providing proper amounts of nitrogen, potash, oxygen, etc.

fer-vent [fûr′vənt] *adjective*, hot, showing intense feeling

fes-ter [fĕs′tər] *verb*, to become worse due to infection or anger

fes-ti-val [fĕs′tə-vəl] *noun,* 1) a big party that takes place on a holiday or at another special time 2) a program of cultural events 3) a carnival

fetch [fĕch] *verb,* 1) to go after something and bring it back, to retrieve 2) to bring in

fet-ish [fĕt′ĭsh] *noun,* 1) a quirky habit based on a belief in magic 2) a compulsion

feud [fyo͞od] *noun,* 1) a long bitter quarrel, especially between two families, verb, 2) to fight like enemies, to quarrel

fe-ver [fē′vər] *noun,* when the body temperature rises above 98.6 degrees the body is trying to fight off bacteria and infection

few [fyo͞o] *adjective,* three or more, not many, hardly any

fi-an-cé [fē′än-sā′, fē-än′sā′] *noun,* a man engaged to be married

fi-an-cée [fē′än-sā′] *noun,* a woman engaged to be married

fi-as-co [fē-ăs′kō] *noun,* a situation that is a total failure, an upheaval

fi-ber [fī′bər] *noun,* 1) thread-like structures combined with others to create tissue 2) a filament

fick-le [fĭk′əl] *adjective,* moody, flighty, liable to change, inconsistent, not loyal

fic-tion [fĭk′shən] *noun,* that which is not true or based in fact, make-believe

fic-ti-tious [fĭk-tĭsh′əs] *adjective,* imaginary, unreal, false

fid-dle [fĭd′l] *noun,* 1) another word for a violin, *verb,* 2) to tinker with something

fid-dler [fĭd′l-ər] *noun,* a person who plays a hand-held stringed instrument

fi-del-i-ty [fĭ-dĕl′ĭ-tē, fī-] *noun,* faithfulness, loyalty, honesty

field [fēld] *noun,* 1) land put to special use for sports or farming 2) a sphere or range of activities, *verb,* 3) to receive a ball in a game and pass it to another player

fiend [fēnd] *noun,* a person who is wicked, cruel, or malicious

fierce [fîrs] *adjective,* furious, violent or aggressive

fier-y [fīr′ē] *adjective,* burning, heated, impassioned

fif-teen [fĭf-tēn′] *adjective, noun,* the number 15, ten plus five

fif-teenth [fĭf-tēnth′] *adjective, noun,* number 15 in order, 15th

fifth [fĭfth] *adjective, noun,* number five in order, written 5th

fif-ti-eth [fĭf′tē-ĭth] *adjective,* the ordinal of fifty, written 50th

fif-ty [fĭf′tē] *adjective, noun,* the number 50, 5 times 10

fig [fĭg] *noun,* a small fruit grown in warm climates, full of seeds

fight [fīt] *noun,* 1) the use of the body or weapons against someone, *verb,* 2) to engage in a physical struggle 3) to quarrel 4) to struggle in any way

fig-ment [fĭg′mənt] *noun,* an imaginary thing

fig-ur-a-tive [fĭg′yər-ə-tĭv] *adjective,* not literal, metaphorical

fig-ure [fĭg′yər] *noun,* 1) the shape or outline of something 2) numbers or digits in an equation or used as measurements, *verb*, 3) to calculate numbers 4) to try to simplify something that is hard to understand

fig-ure-head [fĭg′yər-hĕd′] *noun*, 1) a carved figure set at the front of a sailing ship 2) a leader in name only who has no power or authority

fil-a-ment [fĭl′ə-mənt] *noun*, a slender thread-like structure

filch [fĭlch] *verb*, to steal

file [fĭl] *noun*, 1) a drawer for papers 2) a metal tool with a rough edge for making things smooth 3) a line of people 4) a stored collection of data, *verb*, 5) to organize papers or other items into a system 6) to make a surface smooth through friction with a tool 7) to walk in a straight and orderly line 8) to register

fil-i-al [fĭl′ē-əl] *adjective*, referring to the duty of a son or daughter

fill [fĭl] *verb*, 1) to occupy with as much as possible 2) to make full

fil-let [fĭl′ĭt] *noun*, 1) a boneless piece of meat or fish, *verb*, 2) to remove bones from

film [fĭlm] *noun*, 1) a solid layer that floats on liquid 2) a sensitized coating which receives photographic impressions 3) a movie shown in a theater or on television, *verb*, 4) to photograph something on film 5) to make a movie using a camera

filth-y [fĭl′thē] *adjective*, 1) very dirty, nasty, squalid 2) obscene

fil-tra-tion [fĭl-trā′shən] *noun*, purification, processing

fin [fĭn] *noun*, part of a fish that sticks out, may be fan-shaped, used for steering or balance

fi-nal [fī′nəl] *adjective*, the last

fi-na-le [fə-năl′ē] *noun*, the last part of a show or a musical composition, the culmination

fi-nal-ly [fī′nə-lē] *adverb*, at last, reaching the end, ultimately, eventually, concluding

fi-nance [fə-năns′] *noun*, 1) the management of money, *verb*, 2) to use money to pay for something through a loan

find [fĭnd] *verb*, to uncover or see something after a search

fine [fīn] *adjective*, 1) pleasant, nice, refined, *noun*, 2) a penalty, *verb*, 3) to punish someone by making them pay money

fin-esse [fə-nĕs′] *noun*, 1) a delicate skill, dexterity 2) tact

fin-ger [fĭng′gər] *noun*, 1) one of five digits on a hand, *verb*, 2) to handle, to touch or feel

fin-ger-nail [fĭng′gər-nāl′] *noun*, the claw or talon on the end of a finger or foot

fin-ick-y [fĭn′ĭ-kē] *adjective*, very fussy, hard to please, picky

fin-ish [fĭn′ĭsh] *noun*, 1) a surface appearance, *verb*, 2) to end or complete 3) to use up

fi-nite [fī′nīt′] *adjective*, 1) limited in number 2) having boundaries

fir [fûr] *noun*, an evergreen tree

fire [fīr] *noun*, 1) animation, excitement, inspiration 2) things that are burning, *verb*, 3) to discharge or dismiss from a job

firm [fûrm] *adjective*, 1) solid, hard, *noun*, 2) a company managing a business

firm-ly [fûrm′lē] *adverb*, solidly, resolutely, unwaveringly

first [fûrst] *adjective*, 1) the most important 2) initial, beginning

first aid [fûrst'ād'] *noun*, the emergency help given someone who has been hurt

fish [fĭsh] *noun*, 1) any animal that lives in the sea, seafood, *verb;* 2) to try to catch a fish or get something from someone

fis-sure [fĭsh'ər] *noun*, a crack, a narrow groove, a cleft

fist [fĭst] *noun*, the hand with fingers closed tightly together

fit [fĭt] *adjective*, 1) healthy, active, vibrant 2) good enough, *verb*, 3) to be able to wear the right size 4) to be in harmony

five [fĭv] *adjective*, *noun*, the number 5, one plus four

fix [fĭks] *noun*, 1) a dilemma, a predicament, *verb*, 2) to repair 3) to set, to arrange, to put in place 4) to focus on

fix-ture [fĭks'chər] *noun*, that which is attached to something permanently, apparatus

flac-cid [flăk'sĭd, flăs'ĭd] *adjective*, flabby, hanging loosely

flag [flăg] *noun*, 1) cloth with a special pattern on it, used as the sign of a country, club, etc., *verb*, 2) to wave to someone as a signal to stop 3) to droop

flag-rant [flā'grənt] *adjective*, plainly wicked, unashamed

flail [flāl] *verb*, to move wildly as if beating something, to thrash

flair [flâr] *noun*, an aptitude or talent for doing something well

flake [flāk] *noun*, 1) a small sliver of something, *verb*, 2) to peel off in shavings or tiny bits

flam-boy-ant [flăm-boi'ənt] *adjective*, showy, flashy

flame [flām] *noun*, burning gas seen in a fire

flam-ma-ble [flăm'ə-bəl] *adjective*, capable of igniting easily and burning quickly

flank [flăngk] *noun*, a side, the lateral edge, on either side

flan-nel [flăn'əl] *noun*, a soft woolen cloth of loose texture

flap [flăp] *noun*, 1) the covering of an opening, hanging loose, *verb*, 2) to wave to and fro

flare [flâr] *noun*, 1) a torch or brilliant light, *verb*, 2) to shine, to burn brightly 3) to spread out like a fan, to expand outward

flash [flăsh] *noun*, 1) a split second, a gleam, an instant, *verb*, 2) to show a bright light

flash-back [flăsh'băk] *noun*, an interruption in the continuity of a story, play, etc. by the presentation of an earlier episode

flash-light [flăsh'līt'] *noun*, a hand held light operated by batteries

flat [flăt] *adjective*, a level, horizontal surface, smooth

flat-ter-y [flăt'ə-rē] *noun*, no *plural*, excessive compliments

flaunt [flônt] *verb*, to boast, to wave under one's nose

fla-vor [flā'vər] *noun*, 1) the seasoning of food, the taste of something, *verb*, 2) to add something to make food taste better 3) to savor

flaw [flô] *noun*, a defect, a weak spot, an imperfection

flax [flăks] *noun*, a slender plant with blue flowers whose stalks are used to make thread

flay [flā] *verb*, to whip, to beat with a strap or stick, to hit

flea [flē] *noun*, a jumping insect the size of a pinhead that sucks blood from people and animals

fled [flĕd] *past tense* of **flee**

flee [flē] *noun*, to run away

fleece [flēs] *noun*, 1) the wool on sheep, *verb*, 2) to shake someone down for money 3) to swindle

fleet [flēt] *noun*, a group of ships sailing together, or vehicles, or aircraft under one command

fleet-ing [flē′tĭng] *adjective*, swift in motion, passing quickly

flex [flĕks] *verb*, to bend

flex-i-ble [flĕk′sə-bəl] *adjective*, 1) able to bend easily 2) willing to change a course of action, easily adaptable

flick-er [flĭk′ər] *verb*, 1) to change unsteadily from bright to dim light 2) a brief sensation

flight [flīt] *noun*, 1)the act of flying 2) an airplane trip

flim-sy [flĭm′zē] *adjective*, 1) weak and easily broken 2) ineffectual, not well thought out

flinch [flĭnch] *verb*, to move back suddenly in fear, to make a nervous movement

flint [flĭnt] *noun*, stone, slate

flip [flĭp] *adjective*, 1) sarcastic, kidding, joking 2) a somersault in the air, *verb*, 3) to turn suddenly or swiftly in the air

flip-pant [flĭp′ənt] *adjective*, glib, sarcastic, disrespectful

flirt [flûrt] *verb*, to tease affectionately

float [flōt] *noun*, 1) a portable display in a parade, *verb*, 2) to be supported by liquid or gas

flock [flŏk] *noun*, 1) a company of birds, animals, or people 2) to gather, to congregate, to huddle

flood [flŭd] *noun*, 1) water that stays on land that is below sea level, *verb*, 2) when water overflows or invades a dry area

floor [flôr] *noun*, 1) the part of the room you walk on 2) a level of a building, *verb*, 3) to knock down

flo-ral [flôr′əl] *adjective*, decorated with flowers

Flor-i-da [flôr′ĭ-də] *noun*, on of the 50 United States, located in the Southeast, the capital is Tallahassee. The **Florida** state flower is the orange blossom, the motto is "In God we trust."

floss [flôs] *noun*, 1) a soft silky substance found in the husks of some plants 2) a thin silk thread used for embroidery 3) a thread covered with wax used to clean between the teeth, *verb*, 4) to run thread through the teeth to remove food and tarter

flo-til-la [flō-tĭl′ə] *noun*, a small fleet of ships

floun-der [floun′dər] *noun*, 1) any member of the flatfish family, *verb*, 2) to flail about

flour [flour] *noun*, the finely ground meal of wheat or other cereal plants like oats, rice, corn

flour-ish [flûr′ĭsh] *noun*, 1) a handwritten decoration, *verb*, 2) to prosper, to grow well

flout [flout] *verb*, to scoff at, to ridicule, to disobey a law

flow [flō] *noun, no plural,* 1) a current, a steady stream, *verb,* 2) the movement of gases or fluid

flow-er [flou'ər] *noun,* the part of a plant that bears the seeds, the blossom where fruit develops

flu [flōō] *noun,* an illness characterized by fever, chills and coughing

fluc-tu-ate [flŭk'chōō-āt'] *verb,* 1) to move back and forth like a wave, 2) to vary in degree or value

fluc-tu-a-tion [flŭk'chōō-ā' shən] *noun,* 1) wavering 2) the change of the level or degree of something

flu-ent [flōō'ənt] *adjective,* spoken smoothly and easily

flu-id [flōō'ĭd] *adjective,* 1) not fixed or settled, able to flow, *noun,* 2) a liquid that flows

fluo-res-cent [flōō-rĕs'ənt] *adjective,* absorption of light from another source

flur-ry [flûr'ē] *noun,* a brief excitement, quick movement

flush [flŭsh] *adjective,* 1) even, *noun,* 2) in poker, five cards of the same suit, *verb,* 3) to turn red in the face 4) to wash out

flust-er [flŭs'tər] *verb,* to confuse, to embarrass, to agitate

flute [flōōt] *noun,* a musical instrument like a pipe with keys to control the flow of air that can make different sounds

flut-ter [flŭt'ər] *verb,* to flap, to move wings hurriedly

flux [flŭks] *noun,* a flowing series of continuous changes

fly [flī] *noun,* 1) a small flying insect, *verb,* 2) to move through the air 3) to move very fast

foam [fōm] *noun,* froth formed on the surface of liquids by agitation, a mass of small bubbles

fo-cal [fō'kəl] *adjective,* central, midway, of or at a focus

fo-cus [fō'kəs] *noun,* 1) a central point, *verb,* 2) to concentrate, to pay attention to something

foe [fō] *noun,* an enemy, an adversary, an opponent

fog [fôg] *noun,* a cloud of fine water drops of vapor found close to the ground or sea

foil [foil] *noun,* 1) a paper-like sheet of metal, *verb,* 2) to throw off someone's plans

fo-li-age [fōlē'ĭj] *noun,* the leaves of trees and other plants

fold [fōld] *noun,* 1) a part of something that has been wrapped or enclosed *verb,* 2) to double or bend over, to envelope 3) to withdraw or quit

fold-er [fōl'dər] *noun,* a cardboard cover to protect papers and keep them together

folk [fōk] *noun,* people

fol-low [fŏl'ō] *verb,* 1) to go after, to pursue 2) to come after or behind 3) to pay close attention

fol-ly [fŏl'ē] *noun,* foolishness

fond [fŏnd] *adjective,* to have feelings of affection

fon-dle [fŏn'dl] *adverb,* to caress, to stroke lovingly

food [fōōd] *noun,* a source of nourishment, what you eat

fool [fōōl] *noun,* 1) a silly person, *verb,* 2) to trick or deceive

fool-ish [fōō'lĭsh] *adjective,* crazy, silly, senseless, ridiculous

foot [fŏŏt] *noun, plural,* **feet,** 1) the part of the leg that touches the ground 2) a measure of length equal to 12 inches 3) any base that resembles a foot

foot-ball [fŏŏt'bôl'] *noun,* 1) a game in which two teams of eleven players try to score points by passing a ball to each other in a period of time 2) an oval shaped inflated ball

for [fôr, fər when unstressed] *conjunction,* 1) because, *preposition,* 2) being as 3) to be given or used by 4) at a certain price 5) to be going toward 6) to show the meaning of as in an example

for-age [fôr'ĭj] *verb,* to look for food or supplies

for-ay [fôr'ā'] *noun,* a raid, an attempt at something unfamiliar

for-bear [fôr-bâr'] *verb,* to hold back, to wait, to refrain from

for-bear-ance [fôr-bâr'əns] *adjective,* the act of refraining from anything, self-restraint

for-bid [fər-bĭd'] *verb,* to prohibit, to order someone not to do something

force [fôrs, fōrs] *noun,* 1) power 2) a group of people trained in the same manner, *verb,* 3) to cause to happen with conviction

fore-bod-ing [fôr-bō'dĭng] *noun,* a warning or sign that something bad or evil will happen

fore-cast [fôr'kăst'] *noun,* 1) a prediction that something will happen, *verb,* 2) to anticipate, to figure out and say what will happen before it takes place

fore-close [fôr-klōz'] *verb,* to take away land from a person who owes money on it

for-eign [fôr'ĭn] *adjective,* belonging to another country

for-eign-er [fôr'ə-nər] *noun,* someone from another country

fore-man [fôr'mən] *noun,* 1) the overseer of a set of workmen 2) the spokesman of a jury

fore-most [fôr'mōst'] *adjective,* first in importance, time or place

fo-ren-sic [fə-rĕn'sĭk] *adjective,* information that is a suitable argument in court

fore-see-a-ble [fôr-sē'ə-bəl] *adjective,* predictable, able to be seen in the future

fore-sight [fôr'sīt'] *noun,* the ability to foresee future happenings or needs

for-est [fôr'ĭst] *noun,* a large place where trees grow together

fore-stall [fôr-stôl'] *verb,* to keep safe by taking action first

fore-tell [fôr-tĕl'] *verb,* to predict, to make a prophecy, to forecast

for-ev-er [fôr-ĕv'ər] *adverb,* until the end of time, always

for-feit [fôr'fĭt] *verb,* to lose the right, to surrender, to give up

forge [fôrj] *verb,* 1) to move ahead or progress with difficulty 2) to mold metal with heat and then hammering it into shapes 3) to invent or create something 4) to counterfeit with intent to defraud

for-ger-y [fôr'jə-rē] *noun,* the making of a false or altered document for the purpose of fraud, counterfeit

for-get [fər-gĕt′] *verb*, 1) to fail to recall or remember 2) to neglect

for-give [fər-gĭv′] *verb*, to accept an apology, to get rid of a grudge, to cease to feel angry

for-got [fər-gŏt′] *past tense* of **forget**

for-got-ten [fər-gŏt′n] *adjective*, left behind

fork [fôrk] *noun*, 1) a utensil with prongs on the end used to stab food 2) a place in a road where it separates in different directions

for-lorn [fər-lôrn′] *adjective*, sad and unhappy, lonely

form [fôrm] *noun*, 1) the shape of something 2) a document with questions that need to be answered, *verb*, 3) to shape or create, to develop, to mold

for-mal [fôr′məl] *adjective*, following the customs of an occasion, ceremonious

for-mal-i-ty [fôr-măl′ĭ-tē] *noun*, adherence to established rules of etiquette and convention

for-ma-tion [fôr-mā′shən] *noun*, 1) a creation 2) an arrangement

form-er [fôr′mər] *adjective*, the one mentioned first of two

for-mi-da-ble [fôr′mĭ-də-bəl] *adjective*, very large, alarming

for-mu-la [fôr′myə-lə] *noun*, 1) substances mixed together in specific amounts to create something 2) a mathematical statement

for-mu-late [fôr′myə-lāt′] *verb*, to give form to, to express precisely in a few words

fort [fôrt] *noun*, a place for protecting soldiers

forte [fôrt] *noun*, a strong point or special talent or ability

for-ti-eth [fôr′tē-ĭth] *noun*, the ordinal of forty, 40th

for-ti-fy [fôr′tə-fī′] *verb*, 1) to make stronger or more secure 2) to strengthen against attack 3) to empower, to invigorate

for-ti-tude [fôr′tĭ-tood′] *noun*, courage, strength of mind

for-tress [fôr′trĭs] *noun*, a building with strong walls made to be defended against attack, a fort

for-tu-nate [fôr′chə-nĭt] *adjective*, lucky, favorable, advantageous

for-tune [fôr′chən] *noun*, 1) whatever good or bad happens to people, luck 2) a large amount of money, wealth, riches

for-ty [fôr′tē] *noun*, the number 40, four times ten

fo-rum [fôr′əm] *noun*, a public meeting place and market square

for-ward [fôr′wərd] *adjective*, 1) near or at the front part, ahead 2) onward 3) bold, confident

fos-sil [fŏs′əl] *noun*, the impression in a rock of the petrified remains of an organism or animal

fos-ter [fô′stər] *verb*, to help, to raise, to encourage

fought [fôt] *past tense* of **fight**

foul [foul] *adjective*, 1) dirty, filthy, squalid, *noun*, 2) a ball hit outside the first or third base line

found [found] *verb*, 1) to establish, to lay a foundation 2) *past tense* of **find**

foun-da-tion [foun-dā′shən] *noun*, 1) the base of a building 2) the principles of a program or agency 3) a charitable institution

found-er [foun′dər] *noun*, 1) the author or prime mover, *verb*, 2) to take on water, to sink

found-ry [foun′drē] *noun*, a plant refining metal or glass, a factory

foun-tain [foun′tən] *noun*, water spraying into the air from a pipe

four [fôr] *adjective*, *noun*, the number 4, one plus three

four-teen [fôr-tēn′] *noun*, 4+10=14

four-teenth [fôr-tēnth′] *adjective*, *noun*, number 14 in order, 14th

fourth [fôrth] *adjective*, *noun*, the ordinal number after third, one of four equal parts, 4th

fowl [foul] *noun*, a bird eaten as food or kept for its eggs

fox [fŏks] *noun*, a wild animal the size of a dog with a pointed muzzle and bushy tail

foy-er [foi′ər] *noun*, the entry way in a hall, a hotel lobby

frac-tion [frăk′shən] *noun*, 1) a piece of something 2) a number that names part of a group, not a whole number

frac-ture [frăk′chər] *noun*, 1) a break, a fissure, *verb*, 2) to break

frag-ile [frăj′əl, -īl′] *adjective*, easily broken, delicate

frag-ment [frăg′mənt] *noun*, a piece broken off, a particle

fra-grance [frā′grəns] *noun*, having a sweet smell, perfume, aroma

frail [frāl] *adjective*, weak, fragile, delicate, sickly, infirm, ill

frame [frām] *noun*, 1) the structure that supports something 2) the outline of something encasing something, *verb*, 3) to enclose in a frame 4) to make someone appear guilty of a crime by arranging false evidence

fran-chise [frăn′chīz′] *noun*, a special right or privilege granted by a government to do business

frank [frăngk] *adjective*, candid, honest in expressing your thoughts

fran-tic [frăn′tĭk] *adjective*, wild

fra-ter-ni-ty [frə-tûr′nĭ-tē] *noun*, a fellowship of men in a college

fraud [frôd] *noun*, 1) an imposter, a fake 2) criminal deception

fraud-u-lent [frô′jə-lənt] *adjective*, tricky, deceitful, dishonest

fray [frā] *noun*, 1) a conflict, a commotion, *verb*, 2) to unravel

freak [frēk] *noun*, odd, a strange event or person, out of the ordinary, an aberration

freck-le [frĕk′əl] a small, brownish spot on the skin

free [frē] *adjective*, 1) able to do as you please, unrestrained 2) something that doesn't cost any money 3) available, *verb*, 4) to release something from captivity, to turn loose

free-dom [frē′dəm] *noun*, liberty, independence, being free

freeze [frēz] *verb*, to become chilled by cold, to change to ice

freez-er [frē′zər] *noun*, an appliance that preserves food by keeping it frozen

freight [frāt] *noun*, transportation of products in bulk, cargo

freight-er [frā′tər] *noun*, a ship or aircraft laden with cargo

fren-zy [frĕn′zē] *noun*, craziness, wild excitement, fury

fre-quen-cy [frē′kwən-sē] *noun,* a common occurrence, returning often or repeatedly

fre-quent [frē′kwənt] *adjective,* 1) happening often, repeated, many times, *verb,* 2) to go to a place often for visits

fresh [frĕsh] *adjective,* new, unused, arrived recently

fresh-man [frĕsh′mən] *noun,* a person in his first year of high school or college

fret [frĕt] *verb,* to fuss, to fume, to feel anxious, to worry

fric-tion [frĭk′shən] *noun,* 1) the force that resists movement between two things that are in contact with each other 2) an argument caused by differences of opinion, rivalry

Fri-day [frī′dē, -dā′]*noun,* the sixth day of the week

friend [frĕnd] *noun,* a person who knows and likes another

friend-ship [frĕnd- shĭp] *noun,* mutual respect, companionship

fright [frīt] *noun,* sudden fear, alarm, horror, a shock

fright-en [frīt′n] *verb,* to scare or alarm, to fill with fear

frig-id [frĭj′ĭd] *adjective,* very cold

frill [frĭl] *noun,* a doodad, bells and whistles, an unnecessary extra feature or luxury

fringe [frĭnj] *noun,* 1) an edge made of short lengths of thread, used to decorate clothes, curtains, etc. 2) an outside edge

frisk-y [frĭs′kē] *adjective,* playful, active, lively, bouncy

frit-ter [frĭt′ər] *verb,* to waste

friv-o-lous [frĭv′ə-ləs] *adjective,* 1) of little weight or importance 2) given to trifling, silly

frog [frôg] *noun,* 1) a jumping amphibian that can swim in water or live on land 2) a tool designed to sit in the bottom of the bowl or vase to hold flower stems in place for Ikebana

frol-ic [frŏl′ĭk] *verb,* merry making, to play happily about

from [frŭm] *preposition,* 1) used to show a starting point 2) used to show a point of separation 3) used to show material source or cause, given by

front [frŭnt] *adjective,* 1) first, ahead of the others, *noun,* 2) the face or the part of something that faces forward 3) the facade

fron-tier [frŭn-tîr′] *noun,* 1) the line between two countries 2) the outer limits of a settled part of a country 3) the outer limits of knowledge

frost [frôst] *noun, no plural,* the frozen water that covers the surface of everything outdoors when the temperature goes below freezing, 32 degrees

froth [frôth] *noun,* 1) fine bubbles, foam, effervescence, *verb,* 2) to cause to foam

frown [froun] *noun,* 1) a stern look, *verb,* 2) to scowl or look unhappy, to show disapproval

froze [frōz] *past tense* of **freeze**

fro-zen [frō′zən] *adjective,* the temperature cooled to the point that liquid turns to solid

fru-gal [frōō′gəl] *adjective,* careful management of resources, stingy

fruit [frōot] *noun*, 1) an edible product of a flower, bearing seeds 2) the results, the outcome

fruit-ful [frōot′fəl] *adjective*, successful, productive

fru-i-tion [frōo-ĭsh′ən] *noun*, fulfillment, realization

frus-trate [frŭs′trāt′] *verb*, to prevent from attaining a purpose

fry [frī] *verb*, to cook in hot oil

fudge [fŭj] *noun*, a soft candy usually made with chocolate

fuel [fyōo′əl] *noun*, something that gives off heat when it is burned

fu-gi-tive [fyōo′jĭ-tĭv] *noun*, one who flees from pursuit

ful-fill [fŏol-fĭl′] *verb*, 1) to satisfy a contract 2) to complete

full [fŏol] *adjective*, 1) leaving no empty space, holding as much as possible, *adverb*, 2) entirely

full-ness [fŏol′nĭs] *noun*, the state of being full or complete

fumes [fyōomz] *noun*, *plural*, gases

fu-mi-gate [fyōo′mĭ-gāt′] *verb*, to apply smoke or vapor as a means of disinfecting or killing bugs

fun [fŭn] *noun*, *no plural*, light-hearted, amusement

func-tion [fŭngk′shən] *noun*, 1) the natural and proper action of anything 2) a service, duty, purpose 3) how something works

fund [fŭnd] *noun*, 1) a sum of money collected to help a special purpose, *verb*, 2) to provide money to support a cause

fun-da-men-tal [fŭn′də-měn′tl] *adjective*, 1) of first importance, essential 2) elementary

fu-ner-al [fyōo′nər-əl] *noun*, a ceremony honoring the life of someone who died

fun-gus [fŭng′gəs] *noun*, a plant that lacks chlorophyll, leaves, and a flower, i.e., mushrooms, mold, yeast

fun-nel [fŭn′əl] *noun*, an open cone wide at the top with a smaller end to pour liquids from one container to another

fun-ny [fŭn′ē] *adjective*, 1) amusing, entertaining, to make someone laugh 2) strange, unusual, odd

fur [fûr] *noun*, a soft hair covering on some animals, the pelt

fu-ri-ous [fyŏor′ē-əs] *adjective*, 1) very angry 2) very fast, strong or wild, intense

fur-nace [fûr′nĭs] *noun*, 1) an enclosed place in which heat is produced by the combustion of fuel 2) a large structure containing a very hot fire

fur-nish [fûr′nĭsh] *verb*, to supply, to stock, or provide, to give

fur-ni-ture [fûr′nĭ-chər] *noun*, no plural, the articles in a home that make it more comfortable, such as beds, chairs, tables, etc.

fu-ror [fyŏor′ôr′] *noun*, frenzy, a state of great excitement

fur-ther [fûr′thər] *adjective*, at a greater distance, beyond

fur-tive [fûr tĭv] adjective, done in a sneaky way, hoping to be unnoticed

fu-ry [fyŏor′ē] *noun*, 1) great anger 2) wild or uncontrolled force

fur-ry [fûr′ē] *adjective*, covered with hair, like fur

129

fuse [fyo͞oz] *noun*, 1) tinder, kindling, a wick, *verb*, 2) to combine, to blend, to mix

fu-sion [fyo͞o′zhən] *noun*, the process of joining two or more things together as one

fuss [fŭs] *noun*, 1) complaint, bother, commotion, *verb*, 2) to behave in an excited, worried way, to be overly emotional

fu-tile [fyo͞ot′l, fyo͞o′tĭl′] *adjective*, ineffective, fruitless, pointless

fu-ture [fyo͞o′chər] *adjective*, 1) coming after the present, *noun*, 2) a time that has not yet arrived

G

gadg-et [găj′ĭt] *noun*, a mechanical device or tool, a thingamajig

gag [găg] *noun*, 1) something used to keep people from talking, *verb*, 2) to restrain someone from speaking 3) to choke

gai-e-ty [gā′ĭ-tē] *noun*, fun, merriment, cheerfulness

gain [gān] *noun*, 1) an increase, *verb*, 2) to win, to acquire

gait [gāt] *noun*, a manner of walking, skipping or running

gal-ax-y [găl′ək-sē] *noun*, a group of billions of stars held together by mutual gravitation

gale [gāl] *noun*, a strong wind

gall [gôl] *noun*, 1) bitterness, nerve, *verb*, 2) to annoy, to anger, to goad, to infuriate, to chafe

gal-lant [găl′ənt] *adjective*, brave, bold, daring, chivalrous

gal-le-on [găl′ē-ən] *noun*, a large sailing ship of earlier times

gal-ler-y [găl′ə-rē] *noun*, 1) a long, narrow, room-like corridor or passageway 2) a room for the exhibition of works of art

gal-ley [găl′ē] *noun*, 1) an oblong tray to hold type which has been set 2) the lower part of a ship

gal-lon [găl′ən] *noun*, a unit of liquid measure equal to 4 quarts or 96 ounces

gal-lop [găl′əp] *verb*, to trot, to run like a horse

gal-lows [găl′ōz] *noun*, a public place where criminals are hung

gal-va-nize [găl′və-nīz′] *verb*, to stimulate with shock, to stir up

gam-ble [găm′bəl] *verb*, to try to win money by betting

gam-bler [găm′blər] *noun*, a risk taker, a bettor

game [gām] *noun*, a form of entertainment played with rules that tests skill and knowledge

gam-ut [găm′ət] *noun*, the entire range from beginning to end

gan-der [găn′dər] *noun*, a rooster

gang [găng] *noun*, an organized group of people who intimidate and harass

gang-plank [găng′plăngk′] *noun*, a temporary board or ramp used to board or leave a ship

gan-grene [găng′grēn′] *noun*, the death of a limb such as a leg due to infection

gap [găp] *noun*, a hole, an opening, the distance between two places

ga-rage [gə-räzh′] *noun*, 1) a place for housing automobiles 2) a place where automobiles or buses are repaired

gar-bage [gär′bĭj] *noun*, another word for solid waste, especially household waste, trash

gar-den [gär′dn] *noun*, 1) a plot of land where flowers or vegetables grow, *verb*, 2) to look after the plants by watering and pruning

gar-den-er [gärd′nər] *noun*, one who makes and tends a garden

gar-gle [gär′gəl] *verb*, to rinse the throat with a liquid kept in motion by air forced through it from the lungs

gar-goyle [gär′goil′] *noun*, figures of demons carved as a roof spout

gar-ish [gâr′ĭsh, găr′-] *adjective*, in bad taste, gaudy, showy

gar-lic [gär′lĭk] *noun*, a plant like an onion with a strong taste and smell, used to season food

gar-ment [gär′mənt] *noun*, a piece of clothing

gar-ner [gär′nər] *verb*, to gather up, to accumulate, to amass

gar-net [gär′nĭt] *noun*, a precious stone of a deep red color

gar-nish [gär′nĭsh] *noun*, 1) a decoration for food, *verb*, 2) to decorate or adorn 3) to take from someone a little at a time by order of the court to pay a debt

gar-ri-son [găr′ĭ-sən] *noun*, troops stationed in a fort or fortified town, a military post

gas [găs] *noun*, 1) a state of matter in which a substance like air is capable of infinitely expanding, has no fixed form or volume and takes the shape of its container 2) the short word for gasoline

gas-e-ous [găs′ē-əs, găsh′əs] *adjective*, in vapor form

gas-ket [găs′kĭt] *noun*, a piece of rubber sealing a joint between metal surfaces

gas-o-line [găs′ə-lēn′] *noun*, petroleum or diesel motor fuel

gasp [găsp] *noun*, 1) a short breath, *verb*, 2) to pant with a short, excited breath 3) to wheeze

gas-tron-o-my [gă-strŏn′ə-mē] *noun*, the science of preparing and serving good food

gate [gāt] *noun*, a doorway which closes an opening in a wall or fence with a hinged door

gath-er [găth′ər] *verb*, 1) to bring together or accumulate, to harvest 2) to infer from what someone has said

gauche [gōsh] *adjective*, clumsy, lacking social grace, awkward

gaud-y [gô′dē] *adjective*, showy in a tasteless way, ostentatious

gauge [gāj] *noun*, 1) an instrument used to find the exact measurement, *verb*, 2) to measure or estimate

gaunt [gônt] *adjective*, thin, lean

gauze [gôz] *noun*, 1) a cotton bandage 2) a thin fabric

gaze [gāz] *verb*, to stare, to look at steadily and intently, to gawk

gaz-et-teer [gaezə′tir] *noun*, a geographical dictionary

gear [gîr] *noun*, 1) a toothed wheel that passes motion and power along 2) equipment, supplies

gel-a-tin [jĕl′ə-tn] *noun*, a tasteless, transparent, substance, obtained from connective animal tissue such as skin, hooves, or horns

gem [jĕm] *noun*, a precious stone used as an ornament

gen-der [jĕn′dər] *noun*, a set of categories applied to nouns as masculine or feminine

ge-ne-al-o-gy [jē′nē-ŏl′ə-jē] *noun*, a record of family history

gen-er-al [jĕn′ər-əl] *adjective*, 1) of or from the whole 2) not particular or definite 3) usual or customary, common, lacking detail, *noun*, 2) the title of the commander in an army

Gen-er-al As-sem-bly *noun*, 1) the law-making body in the United States 2) the assembly of the representatives of the United Nations

gen-er-al-i-ty [jĕn′ə-răl′ĭ-tē] *noun*, a vague statement, a theory

gen-er-al-ize [jĕn′ər-ə-līz′] *verb*, to make a broad statement

gen-er-al-ly [jĕn′ər-ə-lē] *adverb*, usually, as a rule, normally

gen-er-ate [jĕn′ə-rāt′] *verb*, to make or create, to produce

gen-er-a-tion [jĕn′ə-rā′shən] *noun*, 1) the average time interval between the birth of parents and the birth of their offspring 2) all of the people born at the same time 3) the act or process of producing something

gen-er-a-tor [jĕn′ə-rā′tər] *noun*, a machine by which mechanical energy is changed into electrical energy

gen-er-os-i-ty [jĕn′ə-rŏs′ĭ-tē] *noun*, given freely, unselfishness

gen-er-ous [jĕn′ər-əs] *adjective*, liberal, open-handed, abundant

gen-er-ous-ly [jĕn′ər-əs-lē] *adverb*, plentifully, unselfishly

ge-ni-al [jēn′yəl] *adjective*, kind, cheerful, gracious friendly

gen-ius [jēn′yəs] *noun*, extraordinary mental superiority

gen-re [zhän′rə] *noun*, a category, art or music characterized by a particular style, class

gen-til-i-ty [jĕn-tĭl′ĭ-tē] *noun*, men or women who are born to money, well-bred

gen-tle [jĕn′tl] *adjective*, 1) kind, courteous, amiable 2) soft and mild 3) not steep, moderate

gen-tle-man [jĕn′tl-mən] *noun*, a well-mannered man

gent-ly [jĕnt′lē] *adverb*, carefully

gen-u-flect [jĕn′yə-flĕkt′] *verb*, to bend one knee and bow in worship or reverence

gen-u-ine [jĕn′yōō-ĭn] *adjective*, the real thing, not false

gen-u-ine-ly [jĕn′yōō-ĭn-lē] *adverb*, truly, really

ge-og-ra-phy [jē-ŏg′rə-fē] *noun*, the science that describes the surface of the earth, and its division into continents

ge-ol-o-gist [jē-ŏl′ə-jĭst] *noun*, a person who studies the structure of the earth, its physical changes and the causes producing these to form a hypothesis

ge-ol-o-gy [jē-ŏl′ə-jē] *noun*, the science that studies the history and structure of the earth, its physical changes, and the causes producing these changes

ge-om-e-try [jē-ŏm′ĭ-trē] *noun*, the branch of mathematics that studies the relations, properties, and measurement of solids, surfaces, lines, and angles

Geor-gia [jôr′jə] *noun*, one of the 50 United States located in the Southeast, the capital city is Atlanta. The state flower of **Georgia** is the cherokee rose and the motto is: "Wisdom, justice, and moderation."

ge-ra-ni-um [jə-rā′nē-əm] *noun*, a flower with pink, red, or white blooms and velvety leaves

germ [jûrm] *noun*, a microorganism that causes disease

ger-mi-nate [jûr′mə-nāt′] *verb*, to cause to grow or develop

ges-ta-tion [jĕ-stā′shən] *noun*, the period of time a new life is in the womb until it is born, pregnancy

ges-tic-u-late [jĕ-stĭk′yə-lāt′] *verb*, to make a motion, to gesture

ges-ture [jĕs′chər] *noun*, 1) any action of the hand or face 2) something done to show one's feelings, *verb*, 2) to make a movement of the arm or hand, to signal

get [gĕt] *verb*, 1) to take, have or buy, to acquire 2) to become

gey-ser [gī′zər] *noun*, a natural hot spring that throws out a spray of steam and water occasionally

ghet-to [gĕt- tō] *noun*, any section of a city in which many members of a minority group live, or to which they are restricted by discrimination

ghost [gōst] *adjective*, the appearance of a dead person, an apparition haunting the living

gi-ant [jī′ənt] *adjective*, 1) very large, huge, *noun*, 2) a legendary person or animal who is a very, very large size

gift [gĭft] *noun*, 1) a present 2) a person's inborn ability to do something well, talent

gi-gan-tic [jī-găn′tĭk] *adjective*, very big, large, huge, titanic

gig-gle [gĭg′əl] *verb*, to laugh in a silly, undignified way

gill [gĭl] *noun*, respiratory organs in fish that separate dissolved oxygen from water

gi-raffe [jə-răf′] *noun*, a tall African animal with a very long neck and very long legs and large brown spots on its coat

gird-er [gûr′dər] *noun*, iron or steel beams to span an opening or carry weight of a building

girl [gûrl] *noun*, a female child

gist [jĭst] *noun*, the main point

give [gĭv] *verb*, 1) to present, to donate, to handover 2) to impart something 3) to provide

giv-en [gĭv′ən] *adjective*, 1) stated, typical 2) habitually inclined

gla-cier [glā′shər] *noun*, a body of ice, formed in a region of perpetual snow, moving slowly down a mountain slope or valley

glad [glăd] *adjective*, 1) feeling pleasure or joy 2) very willing

glad-i-o-lus [glăd′ē-ō′ləs] *noun*, *plural*, **gladioli**, a native bulb from Africa of the iris family, that has sword-shaped leaves stems of brightly colored flowers

glad-ly [glăd′lē] *adverb*, happily, willingly, joyfully, thrilled

glam-or [glăm′ər] *noun*, beauty, attraction, alluring charm

glance [glăns] *noun*, 1) a quick or a brief look, *verb*, 2) to look quickly or briefly, to glimpse

gland [glănd] *noun*, a vital part of a living organism that secretes a substance

glare [glâr] *noun*, 1) a bright light reflecting shine or a gleam 2) a frown or scowl, *verb*, 3) to stare disapprovingly, to glower

glass [glăs] *noun, no plural*, 1) a hard clear substance that is easily shattered, used for windows, *plural*, **glasses**, 2) a drinking container 3) specially cut lenses made of plastic or glass held in a frame to adjust vision so that a person can see better, spectacles

glaze [glāz] *noun*, 1) a shiny, glossy surface, *verb*, 2) to cover with a thin shiny surface

gleam [glēm] *noun*, 1) a brief flash of light, *verb*, 2) to shine brightly, to glisten, to glitter

glean [glēn] *verb*, to gather leftovers, to collect

glee [glē] *noun*, joy, merriment

glib [glĭb] *adjective*, flippant, to speak freely, sarcastic

glide [glīd] *verb*, to move very smoothly, effortlessly

glid-er [glī′dər] *noun*, an aircraft that flies without an engine

glimpse [glĭmps] *noun*, 1) a brief look at something, *verb*, 2) to get a quick look at something

glit-ter [glĭt′ər] *noun*, 1) something that sparkles or twinkles, *verb*, 2) to sparkle or twinkle as a reflection of light, to shimmer

gloat [glōt] *verb*, to brag, to boast

globe [glōb] *noun*, 1) the round replica of the Earth marked with countries, continents, oceans 2) anything round like a ball

gloom [glōōm] *noun*, 1) darkness 2) a feeling of sadness, dejection

gloom-y [glōō′mē] *adjective*, 1) dark, shadowy 2) despondent, dejected, disheartened

glo-ri-fy [glôr′ə-fī′] *verb*, to exalt, to acclaim, to worship

glo-ri-ous [glôr′ē-əs] *adjective*, exhibiting qualities that deserve or receive glory or praise

glory [glôr′ē] *noun*, praise given to someone who has accomplished something extraordinary

glos-sa-ry [glô′sə-rē] *noun*, a list of specialized words used in the text with definitions

gloss-y [glô′sē] *adjective*, smooth and shiny, gleaming bright

glove [glŭv] *noun*, a covering for the hand with separate sections for the fingers and the thumb

glow [glō] *noun*, 1) gentle radiance, light and warmth, *verb*, 2) to radiate light or heat

glu-cose [glōō′kōs′] *noun*, sugar created in the body by processing starch

glue [glōō] *noun*, 1) a substance used to make things stick together 2) to fasten with an adhesive, to attach closely

glut-ton [glŭt′n] *noun*, someone who is greedy for food, a pig

glyc-er-in [glĭs′ər-ĭn] *noun*, a softening agent for skin

gnarled [närld] *adjective*, twisted in a knotted form

gnat [năt] *noun*, a very small flying insect which bites or sucks

gnaw [nô] *verb*, to bite so as to wear away persistently

go [gō] *noun*, 1) a try, an effort, *verb*, 2) to move along 3) to depart 4) to proceed

goad [gōd] *verb*, to use some object to make an animal move

goal [gōl] *noun*, 1) a personal level of achievement 2) the cage or line at the end of the field which the opposite team tries to penetrate 3) a score when the ball goes into the end zone or cage 4) an objective

goat [gōt] *noun*, a small, horned farm animal that is raised for its milk and fur

gob-ble [gŏb/əl] *verb*, to eat fast

gob-lin [gŏb/lĭn] *noun*, in folklore, an ugly, grotesque, evil creature

god [gŏd] *noun*, a being to whom people pray and has control of the forces in the world

God [gŏd] *proper noun*, the supreme being, the master of the universe

god-dess [gŏd/ĭs] *noun*, a female form of deity

goes [gōz] *present tense* of **go** used in the singular, with *he, she* or *it*

gog-gles [gŏg/əlz] *noun*, large spectacles for protecting the eyes

gold [gōld] *adjective*, 1) bright yellow color, *noun*, 2) the precious metal

golf [gŏlf] *noun*, a game played by two or more people in which a small ball is hit into 18 holes arranged on a large piece of land called a course

gone [gôn] *past tense* of **go,**

gong [gông] *noun*, a large piece of metal hung up and hit to make a loud noise

good [gŏŏd] *adjective*, 1) right, not wrong, the opposite of bad 2) appropriate, suitable, useful 3) well-behaved 4) nice, pleasant, *noun, no plural*, 5) what is virtuous and kind

good-bye [gŏŏd-bī/] *interjection*, an expression used to acknowledge parting

good-ness [gŏŏd/nĭs] *noun*, generosity, kindness, strength

goods [gŏŏdz] *noun*, merchandise, things made by people

good-will [gŏŏd wĭl] *noun*, the value of kindness in business and relationships

goose [gŏŏs] *noun, plural*, **geese**, a water bird like a duck but larger and having a longer neck

gore [gôr] *noun*, blood and guts

gorge [gôrj] *noun*, to stuff yourself

gor-geous [gôr/jəs] *adjective*, strikingly beautiful

go-ril-la [gə-rĭl/ə] *noun*, a very large animal similar to a monkey, the largest ape

gos-pel [gŏs/pəl] *noun*, the word of God according to the Bible

gos-sa-mer [gŏs/ə-mər] *adjective*, sheer, like cobwebs

gos-sip [gŏs/əp] *noun*, 1) rumors about people that are unkind or untrue 2) a person who makes false remarks about others, *verb*, 3) to talk about other people

got [gŏt] *past tense* of **get**

gouge [gouj] *noun*, 1) a chisel with a trough-like blade 2) a groove or hole, *verb*, 3) to cut or tear out

gourd [gôrd] *noun*, a large fruit similar to squash, its shell is often made into a container

gour-met [gŏor-mā′] *adjective*, the finest food and drink

gov-ern [gŭv′ərn] *verb*, to lead or control by authority

gov-ern-ment [gŭv′ərn-mənt] *noun*, the offices, agencies, and people who control a nation, state, or city by making laws and seeing that they are followed

gov-er-nor [gŭv′ər-nər] *noun*, 1) the elected leader who controls a state or country 2) an attachment to an engine for controlling its speed

gown [goun] *noun*, 1) a dress worn by a woman that reaches to the floor 2) a covering over the body so that a doctor can examine you without your clothes on

grab [grăb] *verb*, to seize, to clutch, to snatch suddenly

grace [grās] *noun*, 1) elegance, refinement, charm 2) kindness, 3) holiness, devotion, love 4) mercy, pardon, 5) a blessing, giving thanks, *verb*, 6) to beautify, to enhance, to adorn

grace-ful [grās′fəl] *adjective*, having beauty of movement

grace-ful-ly [grās′fə-lē′] *adverb*, gently, calmly, smoothly

gra-cious [grā′shəs] *adjective*, kindly, pleasing, courteous

grade [grād] *noun*, 1) a rating of evaluation or class, *verb*, 2) to rate in a group, according to size, quantity or aptitude

grad-u-al [grăj′ōo-əl] *adjective*, slow progress, step by step

grad-u-al-ly [grăj′ōo-ə-lē] *adverb*, progressively, slowly

grad-u-ate [grăj′ōo-āt′] *noun*, 1) someone who has received a diploma to document that he has completed a required course of study 2) a cup or cylinder marked for measuring liquid, *verb*, 3) to get one's degree by finishing school

grad-u-a-tion [grăj′ōo-ā′shən] *noun*, a ceremony to award diplomas to graduates

graf-fi-to [grə-fē′tō] *noun*, *plural*, **graffiti**, words written or painted in public places to deface a building or surface

graft [grăft] *verb*, 1) a bud or a slit of a tree inserted into another tree to grow 2) a piece of transplanted living skin or tissue 3) use of one's position to make dishonest gains

grain [grān] *noun*, 1) a very small piece of something, a particle 2) seed from a cereal plant such as wheat, corn or rice 3) the design or pattern of wood

gram [grăm] *noun*, the metric unit of weight used to measure small objects

gram-mar [grăm′ər] *noun*, *no plural*, rules that govern the correct use of language

grand [grănd] *adjective*, very large and fine, impressive in size

grand-child [grănd′chīld′] *noun*, *plural* **grandchildren**, the child of someone's son or daughter

grand-daugh-ter [grăn′dô′tər] *noun*, the daughter of a person's son or daughter

gran-deur [grăn′jər] *adjective,* magnificent, impressive greatness

grand-fa-ther [grănd′fä′thər] *noun,* the father of one of your parents

grand-moth-er [grănd′mŭth′ər] *noun,* the mother of one of your parents

grand-son [grănd′sŭn′] *noun,* the father of a person's mother or father

gran-ite [grăn′ĭt] *noun,* a hard igneous rock, consisting of feldspar and quartz used in monuments or buildings

grant [grănt] *noun,* 1) money donated by the government or a charitable foundation, *verb,* 2) to allow, to confer, to give

gran-u-late [grăn′yə-lāt′] *verb,* to process a dense solid into grains

grape [grāp] *noun,* a small, round edible, juicy fruit that grows in clusters on a vine

grape-fruit [grāp′frōōt′] *noun,* a bitter-tasting citrus fruit

graph [grăf] *noun,* 1) a picture indicating measurements to show change 2) a drawing used to show information

graph-ic [grăf′ĭk] *adjective,* 1) pertaining to the arts of painting and drawing 2) clearly and vividly described

graph-ite [grăf′īt′] *noun,* native carbon in the form of crystals

grap-ple [grăp′əl] *verb,* to grab and struggle, to seize in a firm grip

grasp [grăsp] *noun,* 1) a clasp, held in the hand, *verb,* 2) to hold or seize 3) to understand or learn, to comprehend, to take in

grass [grăs] *noun,* 1) a fine ground cover with thin leaves that animals eat 2) as a lawn

grass-hop-per [grăs′hŏp′ər] *noun,* an insect that lives in the grass with strong back legs for jumping and wings for flying

grate [grāt] *noun,* 1) a metal frame with wires laid in the shape of a grid, *verb,* 2) to cut or shave into small pieces, to shred by rubbing on a jagged surface

grate-ful [grāt′fəl] *adjective,* thankful, appreciative

grat-i-fy [grăt′ə-fī′] *verb,* to satisfy, to please, to delight, to indulge

grat-i-tude [grăt′ĭ-tōōd′] *noun, no plural,* a feeling of thankfulness

gra-tu-i-tous [grə-tōō′ĭ-təs] *adjective,* given freely or without charge or recompense

gra-tu-i-ty [grə-tōō′ĭ-tē] *noun,* a tip

grave [grāv] *adjective,* 1) serious, *noun,* 2) a hole in the ground where a dead person is buried

grav-el [grăv′əl] *noun,* a mixture of pebbles and rock fragments

grav-i-ty [grăv′ĭ-tē] *noun,* 1) the force that draws everything to the earth's center 2) solemnity

gra-vy [grā′vē] *noun,* a sauce made with meat drippings

gray [grā] *adjective,* a mixture of white and black

graze [grāz] *verb,* 1) to eat grass or vegetation 2) to rub against something and scraping off the surface 3) to eat small meals often during the day

grease [grēs] *noun,* 1) a soft animal fat, any oily matter, *verb,* 2) to lubricate or make slippery with oils, to coat with grease

great [grāt] *adjective*, 1) large in size, quantity, duration 2) eminent, remarkable

great-er [grā'tər] *adjective*, more than something in comparison to it, bigger, larger, better

great-est [grā'tĭst] *adjective*, the most, superior, the best

greed [grēd] *noun*, *no plural*, the feeling that you want more than you need, desire for wealth

green [grēn] *adjective*, 1) a color made by combining yellow and blue, *noun*, 2) a plot of grass

green-house [grēn'hous'] *noun*, a house made of glass or transparent plastic used to grow plants in a controlled environment, year round

greet [grēt] *verb*, to welcome

greet-ing [grē'tĭng] *noun*, good wishes, a friendly expression

gre-gar-i-ous [grĭ-gâr'ē-əs] *adjective*, very social

grew [grōō] *past tense* of **grow**

grey [grā] see **gray**, *adjective*, a mixture of black and white

grid [grĭd] *noun*, 1) grate, a lead plate with perforations 2) a network of horizontal and vertical lines used to locate a particular point on a map

grid-dle [grĭd'l] *noun*, a flat square pan used for cooking waffles

grief [grēf] *noun*, very deep sorrow, sadness

griev-ance [grē'vəns] *noun*, cause of complaint, a protest

grieve [grēv] *verb*, to be upset about something lost or done, to be filled with sadness

grill [grĭl] *noun*, 1) a cooking unit fueled by a flame with a metal rack used for broiling food 2) a system of bars forming a lattice, *verb*, 3) to broil food 4) to question intensely

grim [grĭm] *adjective*, dreadful, ghastly, stern, unyielding

grin [grĭn] *noun*, 1) a big smile, *verb*, 2) to smile broadly

grind [grīnd] *verb*, to crush something so hard that it becomes powder

grip [grĭp] *noun*, 1) a hold, a grasp, *verb*, 2) to hold or clench something tightly

gris-ly [grĭz'lē] *adjective*, ghastly, horrible, gruesome, shocking

grist [grĭst] *noun*, corn

grit [grĭt] *noun*, 1) courage, fortitude, bravery 2) sand, gravel

grits [grĭts] *noun*, *plural*, coarsely ground hominy

griz-zly [grĭz'lē] *noun*, a big bear

groan [grōn] *noun*, 1) a moan, a complaint, a cry of distress, *verb*, 2) to emit a low cry in disapproval or pain

gro-cer [grō'sər] *noun*, someone who sells food and sundries

gro-cer-y [grō'sə-rē] *noun*, food and household items

groom [grōōm] *noun*, 1) the husband to be 2) a stable boy, *verb*, 3) to make oneself presentable, neat and trim 4) to train for a career

groove [gro͞ov] *noun*, 1) a channel or furrow cut into something, *verb*, 2) to move to a rhythm

grope [grōp] *verb*, to feel your way in the dark

gross [grōs] *adjective*, 1) bulky, coarse, unrefined, *noun*, 2) twelve dozen

gro-tesque [grō-těsk′] *adjective*, distorted, abnormal, strange-looking in shape, bizarre

ground [ground] *noun, no plural*, 1) the surface of the earth, *verb*, 2) past tense of **grind**

ground-wa-ter [ground′wô′tər] *noun*, water beneath the earth's surface that supplies wells and springs

group [gro͞op] *noun*, 1) people or things classed together because of similar qualities 2) people who share the same needs and interests

grove [grōv] *noun*, a group of trees

grov-el [grŏv′əl] *verb*, to crawl or creep, to beg, to cringe

grow [grō] *verb*, 1) to become larger, to increase in size or maturity 2) to change and become 3) to sprout, to germinate, to develop

growl [groul] *noun*, 1) a low angry or unfriendly noise coming from the throat like a dog, *verb*, 2) to make such a sound

grown [grōn] *adjective*, to reach maturity or full growth

growth [grōth] *noun, no plural*, 1) development 2) a tumor or other form of swelling

grub [grŭb] *noun*, 1) larva, a maggot, *verb*, 2) to dig, to uproot

grudge [grŭj] *noun*, hatred, spite

gruel-ing [gro͞o′ə-lǐng] *adjective*, exhausting, very difficult

grue-some [gro͞o′səm] *adjective*, ghastly, frightening, horrible

grum-ble [grŭm′bəl] *verb*, to complain, to grouse, to mutter

grunt [grŭnt] *verb*, to make a guttural sound, to snort like a pig

guar-an-tee [găr′ən-tē′] *noun*, 1) a pledge, *verb*, 2) to honor a promise

guard [gärd] *noun*, 1) a person or thing which forms security or a defense, *verb*, 2) to watch over, to prevent an escape

guard-i-an [gär′dē-ən] *noun*, someone who takes care of another or their property

guer-ril-la [gə-rǐl′ə] *noun*, 1) a revolutionary 2) an ape

guess [gěs] *noun*, 1) a conjecture, *verb*, 2) to imagine, to think or believe 3) to give an answer without really knowing

guest [gěst] *noun*, 1) a person invited to stay with someone else, a visitor 2) a customer

guid-ance [gīd′ns] *noun, no plural*, help, the act or result of guiding

guide [gīd] *noun*, 1) someone or something that shows the way to find something, *verb*, 2) to show the way or lead 3) to counsel

guile [gīl] *noun*, the ability to trick others, crafty, cunning, deceit

guilt [gǐlt] *noun, no plural*, knowing you have done wrong, accepting liability and blame for a wrongdoing

guilt-y [gǐl′tē] *adjective*, 1) legally charged with a crime 2) full of shame, feeling remorse

guin-ea [gǐn′ē] *noun*, Italian money

guise [gīz] *noun*, general, external appearance, manner, pretense

gui-tar [gǐ-tär′] *noun*, a musical instrument with six strings, a fretted neck, and a pear-shaped sound box

gulf [gŭlf] *noun*, 1) part of a sea partially surrounded by land, larger and deeper than a bay 2) a large empty space, or chasm

gul-li-ble [gŭl′ə-bəl] *adjective*, easily tricked or cheated

gul-ly [gŭl′ē] *noun*, a small gulch

gulp [gŭlp] *noun*, 1) a mouthful, *verb*, 2) to swallow quickly 3) to choke or gasp nervously

gum [gŭm] *noun*, 1) the tissue in your mouth above the teeth to protect the roots of each tooth 2) a sticky substance used to hold things together, like glue 3) a soft substance, flavored like candy that can be chewed but it does not dissolve in the mouth

gun [gŭn] *noun*, a weapon consisting of a metal tube used to shoot bullets under pressure

gust [gŭst] *noun*, a sudden rush of wind or strong blast of air

gut [gŭt] *noun*, a stomach, the belly

gut-ter [gŭt′ər] *noun*, drainage ditch, drainpipe, the lower ground or channel along the side of the road

gym-na-si-um [jǐm-nā′zē-əm] *noun*, a place where athletic exercises are performed

gym-nas-tics [jǐm-năs′tǐks] *noun*, *plural*, exercises that develop and train the body and the muscles

gyp-sy [jǐp′sē] *noun*, a person who belongs to a wandering group of people that came from India to Europe, 4,000 years ago, and now live all over the world

H

hab-it [hăb′ǐt] *noun*, a tendency to do something as part of a routine

hab-i-tat [hăb′ǐ-tăt′] *noun*, the natural environment in which an animal or plant lives

hab-i-ta-tion [hăb′ǐ-tā′shən] *noun*, home, abode, dwelling

hab-it-u-al [hə-bǐch′ōō-əl] *adjective*, customary regular, according to habit

hack-les [hăk′əlz] *noun*, hairs on the back and neck of a dog

hack-neyed [hăk′nēd] *adjective*, common, dull, worn-out

had [hăd] *past tense* of **have**

hag-gle [hăg′əl] *verb*, to argue about price, to bargain

hai-ku [hī′kōō] *noun*, a form of poetry consisting of 3 lines of 5, 7, and 5 syllables each

hail [hāl] *noun*, 1) frozen rain drops, *verb*, 2) to shout with enthusiasm, to call out in a greeting, to welcome

hair [hâr] *noun*, a strand of filament that grows out of the skin of animals

hal-cy-on [hăl′sē-ən] *adjective*, calm, peaceful, happy

hale [hāl] *adjective,* 1) healthy, strong, *verb,* 2) to haul, to draw

half [hăf] *noun,* 1) one of two equal parts of a whole 2) partial

half-dol-lar [hăf′dŏl′ər] *noun,* a coin equal to fifty cents

half-way [hăf′wā′] *adjective,* midway between two points

hal-i-but [hăl′ə-bət] *noun,* the largest species of marine flatfish

hall [hôl] *noun,* 1) the corridor in a building 2) a large room for entertaining 3) a building at a college or university

hal-low [hăl′ō] *verb,* to bless or make holy or sacred

hal-lu-ci-na-tion [hə-lōō′sə-nā′shən] *noun,* something that is seen or heard but is not actually happening, a delusion, a vision

halt [hôlt] *verb,* to cause to stop

halt-er [hôl′tər] *noun,* 1) a rope for a horse, a rein 2) a woman's top tied behind the neck across the back 3) a hangman's noose

halve [hăv] *verb,* to divide in two

ham [hăm] *noun,* the meat from a pig's leg, preserved with salt or smoke 2) a comedian

ham-burg-er [hăm′bûr′gər] *noun,* ground beef served as a patty on a sandwich or alone

ham-mer [hăm′ər] *noun,* 1) an instrument used for driving nails, *verb,* 2) to hit or pound with a hammer or mallet, to strike

ham-mock [hăm′ək] *noun,* a bed of canvas cord hanging between two supports

ham-per [hăm′pər] *noun,* 1) a basket for dirty clothes, *verb,* 2) to obstruct, to hinder

ham-ster [hăm′stər]*noun,* a rodent similar to a rat, with large cheek pouches often kept as a pet

hand [hănd] *noun,* 1) the part of the arm used to hold something, *verb,* 2) to deliver or pass along

hand-i-cap [hăn′dē-kăp′] *noun,* an impediment, a physical defect

hand-ker-chief [hăng′kər-chĭf] *noun,* a cloth carried for wiping hands, the face or nose

han-dle [hăn′dl] *noun,* 1) the part of a tool or instrument held in the hand, *verb,* 2) to touch, feel, or examine with the hand 3) to control, manage or deal with

han-dle-bar [hăn′dl-bär′] *noun,* the part of a bicycle used to steer when you ride it

hand-shake [hănd′shāk′] *noun,* a greeting made by shaking hands

hand-some [hăn′səm] *adjective,* good-looking, attractive, manly

hand-writ-ing [hănd′rī′tĭng] *noun,* penmanship, writing done with a pen usually in cursive

hand-y [hăn′dē] *adjective,* convenient, easy to use

hang [hăng] *verb,* 1) to fasten so that something can swing freely, to suspend 2) to suspend from a rope until dead 3) to linger, to wait 4) to be contingent

hang-ar [hăng′ər] *noun,* a building for storing aircraft

hang-er [hăng′ər] *noun,* a device on which something hangs

hap [hăp] *noun,* chance, luck

hap-haz-ard [hăp-hăz′ərd] *adjective,* random, by chance

hap-less [hăp′lĭs] *adjective,* unfortunate, unlucky

hap-pen [hăp/ən] *verb*, 1) to occur by chance, 2) to come to pass

hap-pi-ly [hăp/ə-lē] *adverb*, good-natured, graciously, kindly

hap-pi-ness [hăp/ē-nĭs] *noun*, conscious enjoyment of good fortune, contentment

hap-py [hăp/ē] *adjective*, content, delighted or pleased

ha-rangue [hə-răng/] *noun*, a loud address to a multitude, a noisy, ranting speech

ha-rass [hăr/əs] *verb*, to trouble by repeated attacks, to annoy

har-bor [här/bər] *noun*, 1) a port where ships or boats can dock safely, *verb*, 2) to hide, to protect, or conceal

hard [härd] *adjective*, 1) difficult to understand 2) firm, solid, impenetrable 3) difficult, fatiguing, challenging, *adverb*, 4) intensely, diligently

hard drive [hard-drīv] *noun*, the memory on a computer

hard-en [här/dn] *verb*, 1) to make solid 2) to become unfeeling

hard-ly [härd/lē] *adverb*, barely, almost never, scarcely

hard-ship [härd/shĭp/] *adjective*, suffering, extreme privation

hard-ware [härd/wâr/] *noun*, 1) the pieces of equipment that make up a computer 2) the items such as nuts and bolts needed to put something together

hare [hâr] *noun*, an animal similar to a rabbit, that is larger, unlike a rabbit, it does not burrow and its young are born covered with fur

harm [härm] *noun*, 1) injury, damage, *verb*, 2) to hurt or injure

harm-ful [härm/fəl] *adjective*, something that could cause damage or injury

harm-less [härm/lĭs] *adjective*, causing no harm or damage

har-mon-i-ca [här-mŏn/ĭ-kə] *noun*, a hand-held rectangular musical instrument played by exhaling and inhaling through a row of metal reeds

har-mo-ni-ous [här-mō/nē-əs] *adjective*, symmetrical, congruous, in agreement

har-mo-nize [här/mə-nīz/] *verb*, to sing in harmony, to cooperate

har-mo-ny [här/mə-nē] *noun*, 1) in tune 2) agreement, accord

har-ness [här/nĭs] *noun*, the working gear of a horse

harp [härp] *noun*, 1) a large stringed instrument, played with fingers, *verb*, 2) to nag

har-poon [här-pōōn/] *noun*, 1) a barbed spear, like a missile, *verb*, 2) to stab with a harpoon

har-row [hăr/ō] *noun*, 1) a tractor accessory used to turn over the soil, *verb*, 2) to cultivate

harsh [härsh] *adjective*, 1) hard to bear, severe, cruel 2) inharmonious, jarring, dissonant

har-vest [här/vĭst] *noun*, 1) the season's crop, the amount gathered, *verb*, 2) to gather or pick a crop, to reap, to gain

has [hăz] the part of the *verb* **have** used with *he*, *she*, and *it*

haste [hāst] *noun*, hurry

hast-i-ly [hāst/ĭ-lē] *adverb*, hurriedly, quickly, fast

hast-y [hā/stē] *adjective*, done in a hurry, quickly, swiftly

hat [hăt] *noun*, a clothing accessory used to cover the head

hatch [hăch] *noun*, 1) a small doorway or opening in a wall or a floor, *verb*, 2) to emerge from an egg when born

hatch-et [hăch/ĭt] *noun*, a small ax with a short handle

hate [hāt] *verb*, to dislike, to detest

hate-ful [hāt/fəl] *adjective*, full of hate, feeling a strong dislike

ha-tred [hā/trĭd] *noun*, a strong feeling of dislike, hostility

haugh-ty [hô/tē] *adjective*, snobbish, proud, arrogant

haul [hôl] *verb*, to pull or draw with force, to drag

haunt [hônt] *noun*, 1) a deserted place, *verb*, 2) to intrude upon continually, to annoy

have [hăv] *verb*, 1) to hold possession of or keep 2) a word used to indicate the *past tense* in a description 3) need to, must

ha-ven [hā/vən] *noun*, a safe place

hav-oc [hăv/ək] *noun*, widespread destruction of life and property, devastation, confusion

Ha-waii [hə-wä/ē] *noun*, one of the 50 United States located in the Pacific ocean, the capital city is Honolulu. The state flower of **Hawaii** is the red hibiscus, and the motto is "The life of the land is preserved in righteousness."

hawk [hôk] *noun*, 1) a large bird of prey that kills birds and small animals for food, *verb*, 2) to peddle, to sell on the street

hay [hā] *noun*, dry grass eaten by farm animals such as cows, goats, horses

haz-ard [hăz/ərd] *noun*, a danger

haz-ard-ous [hăz/ər-dəs] *adjective*, dangerous, risky

haze [hāz] *noun*, *no plural*, widely dispersed dust particles in the air that cloud the view

ha-zel [hā/zəl] *adjective*, a color of gray, blue, and brown

he [hē] *pronoun*, *plural*, **they**, the male person or animal, who is the subject of the sentence

head [hĕd] *noun*, 1) the boney structure at the top of humans and animals that contains the brain, the face, the ears, eyes, mouth, nose 2) the seat of reason 3) the leader 4) the top of something, *verb*, 5) to move in the direction of something 6) to lead, to be the chief of

head-ache [hĕd/āk/] *noun*, 1) a dispute, a nuisance 2) pain in the head behind the eyes, a migraine

head-ing [hĕd/ĭng] *noun*, the title or caption at the top of a piece of writing

head-line [hĕd/līn/] *noun*, 1) a line of type displayed conspicuously at the top of a page or column of a newspaper, etc.

head-quar-ters [hĕd/kwôr/tərz] *noun*, the center of operations from which orders are issued

heal [hēl] *verb*, to cure, to treat an illness, to remedy, to repair

health [hĕlth] *noun*, 1) the condition of the body or mind free from sickness or disease

health-y [hĕl/thē] *adjective*, 1) having a sound mind and body, strong, vibrant, robust 2) wholesome, nutritious

heap [hēp] *noun*, 1) a pile of things, *verb*, 2) to put into a large pile, to stack

hear [hîr] *verb*, 1) to take in sounds 2) to listen 3) to receive news

heard [hûrd] *past tense* of **hear**

hear-ing [hîr′ĭng] *noun*, an opportunity to be heard before a judge or peers

hearse [hûrs] *noun*, a car used to carry a coffin to the cemetery

heart [härt] *noun*, 1) the hollow muscular organ that pumps blood to the arteries and receives blood from the veins 2) the center of someone's feelings and spirit

hearth [härth] *noun*, 1) the bottom of a furnace where metal that is melted into a liquid, collects 2) a fireplace or fireside

heat [hēt] *noun, no plural*, 1) the feeling of warmth or something hot caused by friction, *verb*, 2) to raise the temperature to become hot, to make warmer

heat-er [hē′tər] *noun*, an appliance that warms a room

heath-en [hē′thən] *noun*, an atheist, someone who has no god

heave [hēv] *verb*, to lift or pull something of great weight

heav-en [hěv′ən] *noun*, 1) the home of God, where the saved go to live after death 2) a state of supreme happiness or bliss

heav-en-ly [hěv′ən-lē] *adjective*, divine, very nice or pleasant

heav-i-er [hěv′ē-ər] *adjective*, more weight

heav-y [hěv′ē] *adjective*, 1) a lot of weight 2) burdensome

heck-ler [hěk′əl- ər] *noun*, a person who shouts and bothers a public speaker by asking impertinent questions

hec-tic [hěk′tĭk] *adjective*, unsettled, confused, frenzied

hedge [hěj] *noun*, a dense row of shrubs or bushes to make a wall or border forming a boundary

heed [hēd] *verb*, to notice, to pay careful attention to

heel [hēl] *noun*, 1) the back part of a foot, below the ankle 2) the back, bottom part of a shoe 3) an unpleasant person, *verb*, 4) to follow obediently or closely

heif-er [hěf′ər] *noun*, a young cow

height [hīt] *noun*, distance upwards, how tall something is

hei-nous [hā′nəs] *adjective*, hateful, odious, flagrant

heir [âr] *noun*, one who inherits, or has the right to inherit, property after the death of its owner

heir-ess [âr′ĭs] *noun*, a woman who has inherited a fortune

heir-loom [âr′lōōm′] *noun*, a family possession that is given to a new generation

held [hěld] *past tense* of **hold**

hel-i-cop-ter [hěl′ĭ-kŏp′tər] *noun*, a flying machine propelled by action of screws and propeller blades rotating on a vertical axis without supporting wings

he-li-um [hē′lē-əm] *noun*, an inert, gaseous element occurring principally in the atmosphere of the sun and stars

hell [hĕl] *noun*, a place where Satan lives, and where the wicked go when they die

hel-lo [hĕ-lō'] a greeting

helm [hĕlm] *noun*, 1) the wheel or tiller by which a ship is steered 2) a position of control

hel-met [hĕl'mĭt] *noun*, a protective head covering

help [hĕlp] *noun*, 1) assistance, support, guidance, *verb*, 2) to do something for someone, to assist

help-ing [hĕl'pĭng] *adjective*, 1) willing to assist, *noun*, 2) a portion of food, a serving

help-less [hĕlp'lĭs] *adjective*, unable to help oneself

help-ful [hĕlp'fəl] *adjective*, ready to give help, useful

hem [hĕm] *noun*, 1) the edge of a garment that has been sewn to keep it from fraying and to hang on the body at the correct length, *verb*, 2) to sew the bottom of a garment 3) to confine, to enclose

hem-i-sphere [hĕm'ĭ-sfîr'] *noun*, one of the halves of the Earth

hem-or-rhage [hĕm'ər-ĭj] *noun*, any discharge of blood from the blood vessels, heavy bleeding

hen [hĕn] *noun*, a female bird

her [hər, ər; hûr when stressed] *pronoun*, belonging to a female

her-ald [hĕr'əld] *noun*, 1) a bearer of news, *verb*, 2) to announce publicly, to proclaim

herb [ûrb] *noun*, a plant used for medicine or adding flavor to food or aromatherapy

her-biv-o-rous [hûr-bĭv'ər-əs] *adjective*, plant or grain-eating

herd [hûrd] *noun*, 1) a group of animals eating, traveling, or living together, *verb*, 2) to control or steer a group of animals 3) to congregate

here [hîr] *adverb*, referring to at this place or going to this place

he-red-i-tar-y [hə-rĕd'ĭ-tĕr'ē] *adjective*, an inherited trait passed on through genes

he-red-i-ty [hə-rĕd'ĭ-tē] *noun*, inherited characteristics or traits, from parents to offspring

her-e-sy [hĕr'ĭ-sē] *noun*, nonconformity, dissenting view

her-e-tic [hĕr'ĭ-tĭk] *noun*, a nonbeliever, a skeptic

her-it-age [hĕr'ĭ-tĭj] *noun*, rights and or possessions handed down from ancestors, traditions

her-mit [hûr'mĭt] *noun*, a recluse

her-mit-age [hûr'mĭ-tĭj] *noun*, home of one who lives alone

he-ro [hîr'ō] *noun*, a person of great strength or courage

her-o-ine [hĕr'ō-ĭn] *noun*, a woman admired for her brave deeds

her-o-ism [hĕr'ō-ĭz'əm] *noun*, courage, boldness, bravery

her-on [hĕr'ən] *noun*, a large bird that lives in the wetlands

her-ring [hĕr'ĭng] *noun*, a small fish abundant in the ocean and occasionally in fresh water

hers [hûrz] *pronoun*, something belonging to a woman or girl

her-self [hûr-sĕlf'] *pronoun*, *plural*, **themselves**, the reflexive form of **she**, belonging to her

hes-i-tate [hĕz'ĭ-tāt'] *verb*, to act slowly, as if in doubt, to be uncertain because of fear

hesitation

hes-i-ta-tion [hĕz′ĭ-tā′shən] *noun*, doubt, uncertainty, skepticism

hew [hyoō] *verb*, to cut to pieces

hex-a-gon [hĕk′sə-gŏn′] *noun*, a plane figure having six sides

hi-a-tus [hī-ā′təs] *noun*, a gap, an interval in time, a pause

hi-ber-nate [hī′bər-nāt′] *verb*, to sleep during the winter

hic-cup [hĭk′əp] *noun*, a small belch

hid-den [hĭd′n] *adjective*, concealed from sight

hide [hīd] *noun, no plural*, 1) the skin of an animal, *verb*, 2) to put out of sight or keep a secret

hid-e-ous [hĭd′ē-əs] *adjective*, horribly ugly, shocking

hi-er-ar-chy [hī′ə-rär′kē] *noun*, a pecking order, ranking

hi-er-o-glyph-ics [hī′ər-ə-glĭf′ĭks] *noun, plural*, characters in the picture writing of the ancient Egyptians

high [hī] *adjective*, 1) how tall something is from the ground 2) expensive, above average 3) a shrill pitch 4) elated, happy

high-land [hī′lənd] *noun*, land that is high up in the hills

high-ness [hī′nĭs] *noun*, a title of a member of the royal family

high-way [hī′wā′] *noun*, the main public road that usually connects cities and towns

hi-jack [hī′jăk′] *verb*, to force the driver of a vehicle to go somewhere, to commandeer

hike [hīk] *noun*, 1) a walk, a journey, a trek, *verb*, 2) to go on an extended walk

hi-lar-i-ous [hĭ-lâr′ē-əs] *adjective*, very funny, boisterously merry

hill [hĭl] *noun*, a rise in land making the ground higher than the earth's surface

him [hĭm] *pronoun*, a man or boy

him-self [hĭm-sĕlf′] *pronoun*, the subject mentioned later in the sentence, *plural*, **themselves**

hind [hīnd] *adjective*, situated in the rear, back, posterior

hind-er [hĭn′dər] *verb*, to make it more difficult for someone to do something, to obstruct

hind-rance [hĭn′drəns] *noun*, something that slows you down, an impediment

Hin-du [hĭn′doō] *noun*, 1) a native of India 2) a religion in the culture of India that embraces ancient philosophy and traditions

hinge [hĭnj] *noun*, 1) a joint on which a door or gate turns or swings, *verb*, 2) to hang on or attach to something

hint [hĭnt] *noun*, 1) a suggestion, a clue 2) a slight trace

hip [hĭp] *noun*, the part of your body below the stomach where your legs are connected to the rest of your body

hip-po-pot-a-mus [hĭp′ə-pŏt′ə-məs] *noun*, a beast with thick skin that measures 4-5 feet high, 12 feet long, and weighs 4 tons that lives in Africa

hire [hīr] *verb*, to pay someone to do work or perform services

his [hĭz] *pronoun*, belonging to a man or a boy, the possessive case of **he**

hiss [hĭs] *noun*, 1) a sound made by forcing air through the teeth, *verb*, 2) to make a sound like a defensive cat

his-tol-o-gy [hĭ-stŏl′ə-jē] *noun*, the science which treats of the minute structure of animal and vegetable tissues

his-to-ri-an [hĭ-stôr′ē-ən] *noun*, an authority or author of past events in history

his-tor-ic [hĭ-stôr′ĭk] *adjective*, something embodying people or things of the past

his-tor-ic-al [hĭ-stôr′ĭ-kəl] *adjective*, information or articles belonging to the past

his-to-ry [hĭs′tə-rē] *noun*, the story and knowledge of the past

hit [hĭt] *noun*, 1) a blow 2) when the ball comes in contact with the bat 3) a smash, a wow, a success, *verb*, 4) to bring something down hard onto something else, to smack

hitch [hĭch] *verb*, to tie something to something else, to attach

hive [hīv] *noun*, 1) any place busy with activity 2) a variety of allergic reactions marked by itching welts or a rash

hoard [hôrd] *noun*, 1) a large amount of something, *verb*, 2) to collect and save, to accumulate, to set aside and hide away

hoarse [hôrs] *adjective*, sounding husky and rough or harsh

hoax [hōks] *noun*, a practical joke, a deceitful trick, a prank

hob-by [hŏb′ē] *noun*, a favorite activity that holds someone's interest that one likes to do

hock-ey [hŏk′ē] *noun*, a game played on ice or grass by two teams of several players who use curved sticks to hit a puck or a ball into a net or goal

hoe [hō] *noun*, 1) a tool used to lift and loosen the earth, *verb*, 2) to turn the soil over with a hoe

hog [hôg, hŏg] *noun*, a large pig

hoist [hoist] *verb*, to lift up, especially with a pulley

hold [hōld] *noun*, 1) the part of the ship that holds cargo, *verb*, 2) to grasp 3) to contain 4) to host an event 5) to restrain, to keep back 6) to balance something

hole [hōl] *noun*, an empty space in something, a gap, a cavity

hol-i-day [hŏl′ĭ-dā′] *noun*, 1) a period of time that involves relaxation, not work 2) a day on which a particular event is celebrated

hol-low [hŏl′ō] *adjective*, 1) not solid, an empty space inside 2) feeling unworthy, small, *noun*, 3) a small valley

hol-ly [hŏl′ē] *noun*, an evergreen, with bright red berries and prickly and glossy leaves

hol-o-caust [hŏl′ə-kôst′] *noun*, great or total destruction by fire, extermination, genocide

ho-ly [hō′lē] *adjective*, of God or the gods, divine, sacred

hom-age [hŏm′ĭj] *noun*, anything done to pay tribute and respect to a person publicly

home [hōm] *noun*, a place where someone lives, a residence

home-ly [hōm′lē] *adjective*, unattractive, plain looking

homeopath

ho-me-o-path [hō′mē -ə-păth′] *noun*, one who combats disease with remedies producing a similar complaint on a healthy person

home run [hōm rŭn′] *noun*, a run scored on a hit which enables the batter to touch all four bases

home-stead [hōm′stĕd′] *verb*, to make a place one's home

home-work [hōm′wûrk′] *noun*, material from school to be completed at home

hom-i-cide [hŏm′ĭ-sīd′] *noun*, the killing of one human being by another

hom-i-ly [hŏm′ə-lē] *noun*, a sermon, a moral lesson

ho-mo-ge-neous [hō′mə-jē′nē-əs] *adjective*, 1) of the same kind or nature 2) consisting of similar parts throughout

ho-mog-e-nize [hə-mŏj′ə-nīz′] *verb*, to reduce particles in liquids such as milk or paint to the same size

hom-o-phone [hŏm′ə-fōn′] *noun*, a word that sounds the same as another, but is spelled differently, and has a different meaning,e.g. *see* and *sea*

hone [hōn] *verb*, to sharpen

hon-est [ŏn′ĭst] *adjective*, truthful, not deceitful, trustworthy

hon-est-ly [ŏn′ĭst-lē] *adverb*, truthfully, openly, candidly

hon-es-ty [ŏn′ĭ-stē] *noun*, telling the truth, integrity, fairness, truthfulness, sincerity

hon-ey [hŭn′ē] *noun*, a syrup made by bees with treacle gathered from flowers

hon-ey-comb [hŭn′ē-kōm′] *noun*, six-sided wax cells made by bees to store honey or eggs

hon-ey-moon [hŭn′ē-mōōn′] *noun*, a holiday taken by a couple who have just been married

hon-or [ŏn′ər] *noun*, 1) fame or a rank of high esteem, *verb*, 2) to hold in high respect 3) to keep an agreement

hon-or-a-ble [ŏn′ər-ə-bəl] *adjective*, respectable

hood [hŏŏd] *noun*, 1) a covering for the head attached to a jacket or a robe 2) an engine cover

hoof [hŏŏf] *noun*, *plural,* **hooves**, the horny, hard covering on the foot of a horse, cow, or goat

hook [hŏŏk] *noun*, 1) a bent piece of metal or plastic used to catch something, *verb*, 2) to clasp, to hang or fasten with a hook

hoop [hŏŏp] *noun*, a circular band such as a hoola hoop or a basketball hoop

hop [hŏp] *noun*, 1) a short jump, *verb*, 2) to move on one foot 3) to jump with both feet together to move along like a bird or rabbit

hope [hōp] *noun*, 1) a feeling of confidence, expectation *verb*, 2) to look forward to something believing that it will happen

horde [hôrd] *noun*, crowd, a mob, a large multitude, a swarm

ho-ri-zon [hə-rī′zən] *noun*, where the earth appears to intersect the sky, the skyline

hor-i-zon-tal [hôr′ĭ-zŏn′tl] *adjective*, 1) parallel to the horizon 2) flat, level

horn [hôrn] *noun*, 1) one of two hard growths growing out from the heads of some animals such as deer, elk, etc. 2) the device on a car or bicycle used to warn people 3) a musical wind instrument in the brass family with a set of keys to regulate the flow of air

hor-net [hôr′nĭt] *noun*, a bee similar to a wasp

hor-o-scope [hôr′ə-skōp′] *noun*, an astrological prediction

hor-ri-ble [hôr′ə-bəl] *adjective*, shocking, hideous, terrible

hor-rid [hôr′ĭd] *adjective*, vile, disgusting, vulgar, frightful

hor-ri-fy [hôr′ə-fī′] *verb*, to frighten, to terrify, to petrify

hor-ror [hôr′ər] *noun*, great fear and shock caused by something terrible, a feeling of terror

horse [hôrs] *noun*, an animal with long legs that eats grass and can pull a cart or carry people

horse-back [hôrs′băk′] *noun*, to ride on the back of a horse

horse-pow-er [hôrs′pou′ər] *noun*, a unit of power, 33,000 foot pounds of work per minute

horse-shoe [hôrs′shoo′] *noun*, a strip of iron conformed to the rim of a horse's hoof

hor-ti-cul-ture [hôr′tĭ-kŭl′chər] *noun*, the study of growing fruits, vegetables, flowers

hose [hōz] *noun*, 1) a rubber tube used to transfer liquid, *verb*, 2) to water with a hose

hos-pi-tal [hŏs′pĭ-tl] *noun*, a place that provides medical and surgical care for the sick and injured

hos-pi-tal-i-ty [hŏs′pĭ-tăl′ĭ-tē] *noun*, *no plural*, a warm welcome or reception to visitors

host [hōst] *noun*, 1) a person who entertains guests 2) an organism harboring a parasite 3) the communion wafer, representing the bread of the last supper, *verb*, 4) to receive guests, to entertain 5) to serve as a master of ceremonies

hos-tage [hŏs′tĭj] *noun*, a person or thing taken prisoner for ransom

host-ess [hō′stĭs] *noun*, the woman of the house, the one who entertains the guests

hos-til-i-ty [hŏ-stĭl′ĭ-tē] *noun*, unfriendliness, antagonism, showing ill will, rancor

hot [hŏt] *adjective*, 1) a very high temperature 2) a very strong, burning taste, spicy

ho-tel [hō-tĕl′] *noun*, a large building that offers lodging and food to paying customers, etc.

hound [hound] *noun*, a breed of dog used for hunting or racing

hour [our] *noun*, 1)sixty minutes, a measure of time, 1/24th of a day 2) a particular time of day

house [hous] *noun*, 1) a building or part of a building where people live or dwell 2) a residence

house-hold [hous′hōld′] *noun*, all the people who live in a house together as a unit

House of Representatives *noun*, the lower house of the legislature of the United States

house-wife [hous′wīf′] *noun*, the spouse who maintains the house for the family

hov-el [hŭv′əl] *noun*, a shack

hov-er [hŭv′ər] *verb*, to stay in one place floating, flying, or fluttering in the air

hov-er-craft [hŭv′ər-krăft′] *noun*, a sort of boat that travels over land or water by floating on air pushed out by its engines

how [hou] *adverb*, 1) used in questions about time, amount, or size 2) used to ask about health 3) used to show surprise or pleasure 4) used to show the way something is done

how-ev-er [hou-ev′ər] *adverb*, nonetheless, despite, though, yet, after all, in whatever manner

howl [houl] *verb*, 1) to make a long wailing cry like a wolf, 2) to moan loudly in pain

hub [hŭb] *noun*, 1) the center of activity 2) the center position of a wheel or propeller

hud-dle [hŭd′l] *verb*, to gather together, to cluster

hue [hyōō] *noun*, a shade of a color

hug [hŭg] *noun*, 1) a close embrace with arms around the body, *verb*, 2) to put arms around someone, to hold them closely, to embrace

huge [hyōōj] *adjective*, very large

hulk [hŭlk] *noun*, a bulky body, a big clumsy person or thing

hull [hŭl] *noun*, 1) the body of a ship 2) a shell, a husk, a case

hum [hŭm] *noun*, 1) to make a low, buzzing sound like a bee, *verb*, 2) to sing a melody to yourself with lips closed

hu-man [hyōō′mən] *noun*, pertaining to mankind, a person

hu-mane [hyōō-mān′] *adjective*, kind, compassionate, loving

hu-man-i-ty [hyōō-măn′ĭ-tē] *noun*, mankind, people, the human race

hum-ble [hŭm′bəl] *adjective*, 1) modest, not proud, 2) poor, plain, small 3) respectful, courteous, *verb*, 4) to bring down to defeat, to humiliate

hu-mid-i-ty [hyōō-mĭd′ĭ-tē] *noun*, moisture, warm, damp air

hu-mil-i-ate [hyōō-mĭl′ē-āt′] *verb*, to treat in a way that takes away a person's pride or self-respect

hu-mil-i-a-tion [hyōō-mĭl′ē-ā′shən] *noun*, embarrassment, shame

hu-mil-i-ty [hyōō-mĭl′ĭ-tē] *noun*, the state of being modest, meek

hu-mor [hyōō′mər] *noun*, *no plural*, 1) being able to make others laugh, *verb*, 2) to indulge

hu-mor-ous [hyōō′mər-əs] *adjective*, full of or characterized by humor, funny, comical

hump [hŭmp] *noun*, a round lump

hu-mus [hyōō′məs] *noun*, organic material consisting of decayed vegetable matter that provides nutrients for plants

hunch [hŭnch] *noun*, 1) a premonition or suspicion, *verb*, 2) to sit or stand with the back bent or arched

hun-dred [hŭn′drĭd] *noun*, the number 100, ten times ten

hun-dreth [hŭn′drĭdth] *noun*, 1) the ordinal number after 99th 2) the number two digits to the right of the decimal point

hung [hŭng] *past tense* of **hang**

hun-ger [hŭng′gər] *noun*,
1) wanting food, craving, *verb*,
2) to feel a strong desire for
something 3) to yearn

hun-gry [hŭng′grē] *adjective*, to
desire something like food

hunt [hŭnt] *verb*, to seek out to
capture for food or sport, 2) to
search for

hur-dle [hûr′dl] *noun*, 1) a barrier,
an obstacle to overcome, *verb*,
2) to jump over, to vault

hurl [hûrl] *verb*, to throw hard

hur-ri-cane [hûr′ĭ-kān′] *noun*, a
severe storm or cyclone that
develops in tropical areas

hur-ry [hûr′ē] *noun*, 1) confusion,
verb, 2) to move quickly, to
hasten, to rush, to be quick

hurt [hûrt] *verb*, 1) to injure, to
inflict pain or damage 2) to
offend 3) to ache, to throb

hur-tle [hûr′tl] *verb*, to move at
great speed, to rush headlong

hus-band [hŭz′bənd] *noun*, the
male spouse in a marriage

hus-band-ry [hŭz′bən-drē] *noun*,
home management, careful
attention to spending money

hush [hŭsh] *noun*, 1) quiet, calm,
silence, *verb*, 2) to muffle, to
make silent, to quiet down

hus-tle [hŭs′əl] *verb*, 1) to hurry,
move, or do quickly 2) to trick
someone in business

hut [hŭt] *noun*, a small, usually
wooden building, a shack

hy-brid [hī′brĭd] *noun*, two species
fertilized to create a new breed

hy-drant [hī′drənt] *noun*, a pipe
located at a curb with a valve for
fire engines to connect a hose to
a source of water to fight fire

hy-drau-lic [hī-drô′lĭk] *noun*,
operated or moved by means of
water under pressure

hy-dro-gen [hī′drə-jən] *noun*, a gas
that is tasteless, odorless, and
inflammable used in rockets

hy-dro-pho-bi-a [hī′drə-fō′bē-ə]
noun, 1) fear of water 2) a
symptom of rabies

hy-dro-plane [hī′drə-plān′] *noun*,
1) a boat which glides on the
surface of water, *verb*, 2) to lose
control when a vehicle does not
have traction and loses the
ability to stop

hy-e-na [hī-ē′nə] *noun*, a large,
carnivorous wild dog that lives
in Africa and Australia

hy-giene [hī′jēn′] *noun*, practices
that keep people clean and
healthy, cleanliness

hymn [hĭm] *noun*, a religious song

hy-per-bo-le [hī-pûr′bə-lē] *noun*,
an expression used as a figure of
speech, *i.e., I would give him the
shirt off my back.*

hy-phen [hī′fən] *noun*, the mark -,
used to separate syllables, as at
the end of a line e.g. *composition,* or to join the parts of
compound words e.g.
self-confidence, self-reliant

hyp-no-tize [hĭp′nə-tīz′] *verb*, to
put in a trance in which the
subject is susceptible to
suggestion, to mesmerize

hy-po-chon-dri-ac
[hī′pə-kŏn′drē-ăk′] *noun*, a
person always worrying about
the state of their health

hy-poc-ri-sy [hĭ-pŏk′rĭ-sē] *adjective*, the act or practice of feigning to be what one is not, especially the false assumption of virtue or religion

hyp-o-crite [hĭp′ə-krĭt′] *noun*, someone who says one thing and does another, a fraud

hy-poth-e-sis [hī-pŏth′ĭ-sĭs] *noun*, an educated guess

hy-po-thet-i-cal [hī′pə-thĕt′ĭ-kəl] *adjective*, an assumption based on theory or conjecture

hys-ter-i-cal [hĭ-stĕr′ĭ-kəl] *adjective*, excitable, nervous

I

I [ī] *pronoun*, *plural*, **we**, first person singular, the individual speaking

ice [īs] *noun*, 1) frozen water, *verb*, 2) to put frosting on a cake

ice-berg [īs′bûrg′] *noun*, a large mass of ice floating in the water

ice cream [īs′krēm′] *noun*, cream, milk, flavoring, and eggs mixed together in a pot of ice and salt to make frozen cream

i-ch-thy-ol-o-gy [ĭk′thē-ŏl′ə-jē] *noun*, the study of fish

i-cing [ī′sĭng] *noun*, frosting

i-ci-cle [ī′sĭ-kəl] *noun*, a piece of ice in the form of a spike made by water dripping and freezing

i-con [ī′kŏn′] *noun*, 1) a religious image 2) a symbol that represents something

i-cy [ī′sē] *adjective*, 1) very cold, freezing, chilly 2) slippery

I'd [īd] the *contraction* of the words: **I** and **would**

Ida-ho [ī′də-hō′] *noun*, one of the 50 United States located in the Northwest, the capital city is Boise. The state flower of **Idaho** is the syringa, and the motto is "May she endure forever."

i-de-a [ī-dē′ə] *noun*, 1) a concept, a thought, an impression 2) a belief, a judgment, a view, an opinion 3) a goal or intention

i-de-al [ī-dē′əl] *adjective*, 1) perfect, ultimate, imaginary, *noun*, 2) an image of something in its perfect form, a model

i-den-ti-cal [ī-dĕn′tĭ-kəl] *adjective*, the very same in every way

i-den-ti-fi-ca-tion [ī-dĕn′tə-fĭ-kā′shən] *noun*, the means to verify who someone is

i-den-ti-fy [ī-dĕn′tə-fī′] *verb*, 1) to classify or name 2) to equate

i-den-ti-ty [ī-dĕn′tĭ-tē] *noun*, who someone is, individuality

i-de-ol-o-gy [ī′dē-ŏl′ə-jē] *noun*, beliefs, opinions, political ideas

id-i-om [ĭd′ē-əm] *noun*, a group of words which when used together have a special meaning, i.e., *raining cats and dogs*

id-i-o-syn-cra-sy [ĭd′ē-ō-sĭng′krə-sē] *noun*, a peculiar habit, a quirk ·

id-i-ot [ī′ē-ət] *noun*, a nitwit, jerk

i-dle [īd′l] *adjective*, not busy, unoccupied, inactive, lazy

i-dol [īd′l] *noun*, a figure that people worship or honor

i.e. an abbreviation, for example...

if [ĭf] *conjunction*, 1) on condition that 2) whether

ig-loo [ĭg′lo͞o] *noun*, a home made of ice and snow used by Eskimos

ig-ne-ous [ĭg′nē-əs] *adjective*, produced by fire, volcanic

ig-nite [ĭg-nīt′] *verb*, 1) to set on fire, to burn 2) to inspire

ig-no-ble [ĭg-nō′bəl] *adjective*, unworthy, of low character

ig-no-rance [ĭg′nər-əns] *noun*, *no plural*, lack of knowledge

ig-no-rant [ĭg′nər-ənt] *adjective*, not knowing something

ig-nore [ĭg-nôr′] *verb*, to take no notice of, to pretend something is not there, to disregard

ill [ĭl] *adjective*, feeling unhealthy or badly, uneasy, not well

I'll [ĭl] the *contraction* of the words **I** and **will**

il-le-gal [ĭ-lē′gəl] *adjective*, against the law, prohibited, criminal

il-leg-i-ble [ĭ-lĕj′ə-bəl] *adjective*, so poorly written that it is unreadable

il-le-git-i-mate [ĭl′ĭ-jĭt′ə-mĭt] *adjective*, unlawful, illegal

il-lic-it [ĭ-lĭs′ĭt] *adverb*, not according to law, not permitted or allowed, forbidden

il-lim-it-a-ble [ĭ-lĭm′ĭ-tə-bəl] *adjective*, infinite, vast, limitless

Il-li-nois [ĭl′ə-noi′] *noun*, one of the 50 United States located in the Midwest, the capital is Springfield. The state flower of **Illinois** is the meadow violet, and the motto is "State sovereignty, national union."

il-lit-er-ate [ĭ-lĭt′ər-ĭt] *adjective*, unable to read and write

il-log-i-c-al [ĭ-lŏj′ĭ-kəl] *adjective*, not observing the rules of correct reasoning, unreasonable

il-lu-mi-nate [ĭ-lo͞o′mə-nāt′] *verb*, 1) to fill with light 2) to make understandable, to clarify

il-lu-sion [ĭ-lo͞o′zhən] *noun*, a fantasy, a fallacy, a delusion

il-lu-sive [ĭ-lo͞o′sĭv] *adjective*, deceptive, false, evasive

il-lus-trate [ĭl′ə-strāt′] *verb*, 1) to explain by examples or verbal images 2) to provide with pictures or designs, to show

il-lus-tra-tion [ĭl′ə-strā′shən] *noun*, 1) an explanation 2) a diagram that provides a design or pictures

il-lus-tri-ous [ĭ-lŭs′trē-əs] *adjective*, distinguished, well known, acclaimed, celebrated

I'm [īm] the *contraction* of the words, **I** and **am**

im-age [ĭm′ĭj] *noun*, 1) a picture in the mind, or in a mirror 2) a figure made of stone, wood, etc.

im-age-ry [ĭ-măj′ĕr′ē] *noun*, 1) mental images 2) descriptions and figures of speech

im-ag-i-nar-y [ĭ-măj′ə-nĕr′ē] *adjective*, unreal, fanciful, existing only in the mind

im-ag-i-na-tion [ĭ-măj′ə-nā′shən] *noun*, fantasy, dreams

im-ag-ine [ĭ-măj′ĭn] *verb*, 1) to develop and idea in your mind or mental picture 2) to conceive, to suppose

im-bue [ĭm-byo͞o′] *verb*, 1) to teach, to inspire 2) to saturate with moisture or color

im-i-tate [ĭm/ĭ-tāt/] *verb*, to do
something the same way as
someone else, to emulate

im-i-ta-tion [ĭm/ĭ-tā/shən]
adjective, 1) artificial, synthetic,
counterfeit, *noun*, 2) a copy of
something, a fake, a replica

im-mac-u-late [ĭ-măk/yə-lĭt]
adjective, without stain or
blemish, spotlessly clean

im-ma-te-ri-al [ĭm/ə-tîr/ē-əl]
adjective, not applicable,
irrelevant, not important

im-ma-ture [ĭm/ə-tyŏŏr/]
adjective, 1) not grown up
2)using poor judgment, childish

im-meas-ur-a-ble
[ĭ-mĕzh/ər-ə-bəl] *adjective*, vast,
limitless, endless, infinite

im-me-di-ate [ĭ-mē/dē-ĭt]
adjective, right away

im-me-di-ate-ly [ĭ-mē/dē-ĭt-lē]
adverb, at once, without interval
of time or delay, now

im-mense [ĭ-mĕns/] *adjective*,
huge, very large, enormous

im-men-si-ty [ĭ-mĕn/sĭ-tē] *noun*,
enormity, endlessness

im-mi-grant [ĭm/ĭ-grənt] *noun*, a
settler from another country

im-mi-gra-tion [ĭm/ĭ-grā/shən]
noun, a journey or voyage to
another place

im-mi-grate [ĭm/ĭ-grāt/] *verb*, to go
to a country of which one is not
a native to live as a resident

im-mi-nent [ĭm/ə-nənt] *adjective*,
impending, near at hand, likely
to occur at any moment

im-mo-bil-i-ty [ĭ-mō-bĭl/-ĭ-tē]
noun, the state of being unable to
move, motionless

im-mortal [ĭ-môr/tl] *adjective*,
undying, everlasting, perpetual

im-mor-tal-i-ty [ĭm/ôr-tăl/ĭ-tē]
noun, eternal life, unending fame

im-mune [ĭ-myoōn/] *adjective*,
1) exempt from an obligation
2) not affected by disease

im-mu-ni-ty [ĭ-myōō/nĭ-tē] *noun*,
freedom from natural or usual
liability

im-mu-nize [ĭm/yə-nīz/] *verb*, to
protect the body from incurable
diseases by injecting an inactive
form of the virus or bacteria

im-mu-ni-za-tion
[ĭm/yə-nĭ-zā/shən] *noun*, an
injection that protects the body
from a virus or disease

im-pact [ĭm/păkt/] *noun*, 1) the
striking of one object by another
2) a forceful impression, a
strong effect

im-pair [ĭm-pâr/] *verb*, to weaken,
to diminish in value, make worse

im-pale [ĭm-pāl/] *verb*, to pierce

im-part [ĭm-pärt/] *verb*, to tell, to
reveal, to make known, to give

im-par-tial [ĭm-pär/shəl] *adjective*,
fair, just, not favoring one more
than another, not biased

im-pas-sa-ble [ĭm-păs/ə-bəl]
adjective, a place that cannot be
passed or traversed

im-passe [ĭm/păs/] *noun*, an
inescapable situation

im-pa-tience [ĭm-pā/shəns] *noun*,
no plural, anticipation, anxious
expectancy, feeling anxious

im-pa-tiens[ĭm-pā′shəns] *noun*, a flower with white or red flowers that bloom in summer

im-pa-tient [ĭm-pā′shənt] *adjective*, not wanting to wait

im-peach [ĭm-pēch′] *verb*, to charge with a crime while in office, to discredit

im-pec-ca-ble [ĭm-pĕk′ə-bəl] *adjective*, faultless, perfect

im-pede [ĭm-pēd′] *verb*, to hinder or obstruct, to slow action

im-ped-i-ment [ĭm-pĕd′ə-mənt] *noun*, hindrance, obstacle

im-pel [ĭm-pĕl′] *verb*, to push, to motivate, to drive forward

im-pend-ing [ĭm-pĕn′dĭng] *adjective*, nearing, approaching

im-per-a-tive [ĭm-pĕr′ə-tĭv] *adjective*, 1) expressive of command 2) binding, obligatory

im-per-fect [ĭm-pûr′fĭkt] *adjective*, flawed, defective, faulty

im-per-fec-tion [ĭm′pər-fĕk′shən] *noun*, 1) a flaw, a defect 2) a failing, a shortcoming, a fault

im-pe-ri-al [ĭm-pîr′ē-əl] *adjective*, relating to an empire and its ruler

im-per-il [ĭm-pĕr′əl] *verb*, to put in danger or peril

im-pe-ri-ous [ĭm-pîr′ē-əs] *adjective*, bossy, domineering

im-per-me-a-ble [ĭm-pûr′mē-ə-bəl] *adjective*, unable to pass through something, impervious

im-per-son-al [ĭm-pûr′sə-nəl] *adjective*, detached, withdrawn

im-per-son-ate [ĭm-pûr′sə-nāt′] *verb*, to pretend to be someone by assuming their appearance

im-per-ti-nent [ĭm-pûr′tn-ənt] *adjective*, 1) rude, insolent, pert 2) irrelevant

im-per-vi-ous [ĭm-pûr′vē-əs] *adjective*, 1) impenetrable, not admitting entrance or passage through 2) unaffected

im-pet-u-ous [ĭm-pĕch′ōō-əs] *adjective*, impulsive, rash

im-pe-tus [ĭm′pĭ-təs] *noun*, a driving force, motive, incentive

im-plau-si-ble [ĭm-plô′zə-bəl] *adjective*, unlikely, unbelievable

im-ple-ment [ĭm′plə-mənt] *noun*, 1) a tool, a device, *verb*, 2) to complete, to accomplish, to make good on an idea

im-pli-ca-tion [ĭm′plĭ-kā′shən] *noun*, something that is implied, hinted or suggested

im-plic-it [ĭm-plĭs′ĭt] *adjective*, 1) implied, unsaid, understood 2) trusting without reserve

im-plore [ĭm′plôr] *verb*, to plead with or beg for with much feeling

im-ply [ĭm-plī′] *verb*, to suggest a meaning not spoken, to hint

im-po-lite [ĭm′pə-līt′] *adjective*, rude, discourteous, disrespectful

im-port [ĭm-pôrt′] *noun*, 1) merchandise brought into another country 2) the significance, the meaning, *verb*, 3) to bring goods into another country 4) to signify

im-por-tance [ĭm-pôr′tns] *noun, no plural*, of great significance or consequence, prominence

im-por-tant [ĭm-pôr′tnt] *adjective*, significant, having a great value

im-por-tu-nate [ĭm-pôr′chə-nĭt] *adjective*, urging, demanding

im-pose [ĭm-pōz′] *verb*, 1) to take unfair advantage of 2) to force on others

im-pos-si-ble [ĭm-pŏs′ə-bəl] *adjective*, unrealizable, unattainable, hopeless

im-pos-tor [ĭm-pŏs′tər] *noun*, one who practices deception, a cheat

im-po-tent [ĭm′pə-tənt] *adjective*, weak, ineffective, powerless

im-prac-ti-cal [ĭm-prăk′tĭ-kəl] *adjective*, not easily done, infeasible, not useful

im-pre-cate [ĭm′prĭ-kāt′] *verb*, to hope evil will happen, to curse

im-preg-na-ble [ĭm-prĕg′nə-bəl] *adjective*, invulnerable, unbeatable, irrefutable

im-press [ĭm-prĕs′] *verb*, to affect someone's feelings or mind in a positive way

im-pres-sion [ĭm-prĕsh′ən] *noun*, 1) a sensation, a feeling 2) an imprint on the mind, an effect

im-pres-sive [ĭm-prĕs′ĭv] *adjective*, touching, stirring, convincing

im-print [ĭm-prĭnt′] *noun*, 1) a deep impression left by pressure, *verb*, 2) to leave a mark by applying pressure

im-pris-on [ĭm-prĭz′ən] *verb*, to hold someone in jail

im-prob-a-ble [ĭm-prŏb′ə-bəl] *adjective*, unlikely to happen

im-prop-er [ĭm-prŏp′ər] *adjective*, something that is considered rude or inappropriate

im-pro-pri-e-ty [ĭm′prə-prī′ĭ-tē] *noun*, an inappropriate expression or act

im-prove [ĭm-proōv′] *verb*, to make better, to uplift, to refine

im-prove-ment [ĭm-proōv′mənt] *noun*, an act, a state, or result of improving or bettering

im-pro-vise [ĭm′prə-vīz′] *verb*, 1) to make do with whatever is at hand 2) to perform without preparation at a moment's notice

im-pru-dent [ĭm-proōd′nt] *adjective*, injudicious, indiscreet

im-pu-dent [ĭm′pyə-dənt] *adjective*, shameless, bold

im-pulse [ĭm′pŭls′] *noun*, a sudden desire to do something, a whim

im-pul-sive [ĭm-pŭl′sĭv] *adjective*, spontaneous, unexpected

im-pu-ni-ty [ĭm-pyoō′nĭ-tē] *noun*, freedom from punishment

im-pu-ri-ty [ĭm-pyoōr′ĭ-tē] *noun*, something mixed with something else that is usually not as good, contamination

im-pute [ĭm-pyoōt′] *verb*, to credit, to attribute, to ascribe

in [ĭn] *adjective*, 1) being inside, *preposition*, 2) showing where 3) at or inside of something 4) during, before the end 5) wearing 6) at hand or on hand 7) near

in-a-bil-i-ty [ĭn′ə-bĭl′ĭ-tē] *adjective*, not able

in-ac-ces-si-ble [ĭn′ăk-sĕs′ə-bəl] *adjective*, 1) out of reach, unattainable 2) hard to contact

in-ac-cu-ra-cy [ĭn-ăk′yər-ə-sē] *noun*, inexactness, the state of being incorrect, an error

in-ad-e-quate [ĭn-ăd′ĭ-kwĭt] *adjective*, not sufficient, deficient, not enough

in-ad-ver-tent-ly [ĭn′əd-vûr′tnt-lē] *adverb*, not purposely, unintentionally, accidentally

in-al-ien-a-ble [ĭn-āl′yə-nə-bəl] *adjective*, not to be taken away

in-an-i-mate [ĭn-ăn′ə-mĭt] *adjective*, lifeless, dull

in-ar-tic-u-late [ĭn′är-tĭk′yə-lĭt] *adjective,* lacking the ability to express oneself in speech

in-au-gu-rate [ĭn-ô′gyə-rāt′] *verb*, 1) to commence or enter upon, to begin 2) to install into office in a formal manner

in-can-des-cent [ĭn′kən-dĕs′ənt] *adjective*, glowing or luminous with intense heat or brightness

in-can-ta-tion [ĭn′kăn-tā′shən] *noun*, singing or chanting of magic spells

in-ca-pa-ble [ĭn-kā′pə-bəl] *adjective,* unable, powerless

in-ca-pac-i-tate [ĭn′kə-păs′ĭ-tāt′] *verb*, to disable

in-car-cer-a-tion [ĭn-kär′sə-rā′shən] *noun*, imprisonment

in-car-nate [ĭn-kär′nĭt] *adjective*, in the flesh, in human form

in-car-na-tion [ĭn′kär-nā′shən] *noun*, the act of assuming a human body after death

in-cen-di-ar-y [ĭn-sĕn′dē-ĕr′ē] *noun*, 1) causing something to burn 2) tending to inflame passion, a political agitator

in-cense [ĭn-sĕns′] *noun*, 1) scent, aroma, fragrance, *verb*, 2) anger

in-cen-tive [ĭn-sĕn′tĭv] *noun*, encouragement, stimulus

in-ces-sant [ĭn-sĕs′ənt] *adjective*, continuing without interruption

in-ces-sant-ly [ĭn-sĕs′ənt-lē] *adverb*, without stopping, continual, not ceasing

inch [ĭnch] *noun*, a measure of length, 1/12 of a foot

in-ci-dent [ĭn′sĭ-dənt] *noun*, a happening, an event, a casual occurrence, an episode

in-ci-den-tal-ly [ĭn′sĭ-dĕn′tl-ē] *adverb*, casually, by chance

in-cin-er-a-tor [ĭn-sĭn′ə-rā′tər] *noun*, a container or facility where garbage is burned

in-ci-sion [ĭn-sĭzh′ən] *noun*, a cut or slit into tissue, a gash

in-cite [ĭn-sīt′] *verb*, to stir up, to stimulate to action, to provoke

in-cite-ment [ĭn-sīt′mĕnt] *noun*, a stimulus, a catalyst

in-clem-ent [ĭn-klĕm′ənt] *adjective*, stormy, unkind

in-cli-na-tion [ĭn′klə-nā′shən] *noun*, a preference, a tendency

in-cline [ĭn-klīn′] *verb*, 1) to lean, to slant 2) likely to, to tend to

in-clude [ĭn-klōōd′] *verb*, 1) to have as part of, to comprise, to contain 2) to count or think of someone or something as a part of a group, to involve

in-clu-sive [ĭn-klōō′sĭv] *adjective*, not leaving anyone out

in-cog-ni-to [ĭn′kŏg-nē′tō] *adjective*, in disguise, a secret identity

in-co-her-ent [ĭn′kō-hîr′ənt]
adjective, incomprehensible,
lacking meaningful connection

in-come [ĭn′kŭm′] *noun*, the money
a person earns from work or
investments, salary

in-com-par-able
[ĭn-kŏm′pər-ə-bəl] *adjective*,
excellent, unequaled by
comparison, unrivaled,

in-com-pat-i-ble
[ĭn′kəm-păt′ə-bəl] *adjective*, not
easy to get along with

in-com-pe-tent [ĭn-kŏm′pĭ-tənt]
adjective, unfit, clumsy

in-com-plete [ĭn′kəm-plēt′]
adjective, unfinished, under
construction, lacking

in-con-ceiv-a-ble
[ĭn′kən-sē′və-bəl] *adjective*,
unimaginable, incredible, hard to
believe, unthinkable

in-con-gru-ous [ĭn-kŏng′grōō-əs]
adjective, not fitting, absurd

in-con-se-quen-tial
[ĭn-kŏn′sĭ-kwĕn′shəl] *adjective*,
of little importance or
consequence

in-con-ven-ience [ĭn′kən-vēn′yəns]
adjective, bothersome,
troublesome, bad timing

in-con-ven-ient [ĭn′kən-vēn′yənt]
adjective, untimely, awkward

in-cor-po-rate [ĭn-kôr′pə-rāt′]
verb, 1) to unite into one body
2) to form into a corporation

in-cor-rect [ĭn′kə-rĕkt′] *adjective*,
not right in facts, wrong

in-cor-rect-ly [ĭn′kə-rĕkt′-lē]
adverb, mistakenly, erroneously

in-crease [ĭn-krēs′] *noun*, 1) the
amount by which something gets

larger , *verb*, 2) to become
greater in size or quantity

in-cred-i-ble [ĭn-krĕd′ə-bəl]
adjective, surpassing belief,
unlikely, unbelievable

in-cred-u-lous [ĭn-krĕj′ə-ləs]
adjective, shocking, surprising,
full of disbelief

in-cre-ment [ĭn′krə-mənt, ĭng′-]
noun, an increase, addition

in-crim-i-nate [ĭn-krĭm′ə-nāt′]
verb, to accuse or charge with a
crime or fault

in-crim-i-nat-ing
[ĭn-krĭm′ə-nā′tĭng] *adjective*,
showing proof of guilt

in-cu-bate [ĭn′kyə-bāt′] *verb*, to
apply enough heat or warmth to
make something hatch

in-cum-bent [ĭn-kŭm′bənt]
adjective, 1) required, obligatory,
noun, 2) an officeholder

in-cur [ĭn-kûr′] *verb*, to bring
something unpleasant upon
oneself

in-cur-a-ble [ĭn-kyōōr′ə-bəl]
adjective, irreparable, incapable
of being cured, terminally ill

in-cur-sion [ĭn-kûr′zhən] *noun*,
temporary invasion

in-debt-ed [ĭn-dĕt′ĭd] *adjective*,
under obligation to repay money

in-deed [ĭn-dēd′] *adverb*, really,
truly, in fact, certainly

in-def-i-nite [ĭn-dĕf′ə-nĭt]
adjective, uncertain, inexact

in-def-i-nite-ly [ĭn-dĕf′ə-nĭt-lē]
adverb, no set time frame

in-del-i-ble [ĭn-dĕl′ə-bəl] *adjective*,
something that cannot be
removed or blotted out,
permanent

in-dem-ni-ty [ĭn-dĕm′nĭ-tē] *noun*, protection or exemption from loss or damage, security

in-dent [ĭn-dĕnt′] *verb*, 1) to set lines in from the margin 2) to form notches from the edge

in-den-ture [ĭn-dĕn′chər] *verb*, the written work agreement of a servant to a master

in-de-pend-ence [ĭn′dĭ-pĕn′dəns] *noun, no plural*, the state of acting alone or separately

in-de-pend-ent [ĭn′dĭ-pĕn′dənt] *adjective*, free, not relying on others, without bias

in-de-pend-ent-ly [ĭn′dĭ-pĕn′dənt-lē] *adverb*, to work alone, self-reliant, self-directed, autonomously

in-de-struct-i-ble [ĭn′dĭ-strŭk′tə-bəl] *adjective*, incapable of being destroyed

in-dex [ĭn′dĕks′] *noun*, a table for finding reference to topics, names, etc.

In-di-an [ĭn′dē-ən] *noun*, a native American

In-di-ana [ĭn′dē-ăn′ə] *noun*, one of the 50 United States located in the Midwest, the capital is Indianapolis. The state flower of **Indiana** is the peony, and the state motto is "The crossroads of America."

in-di-cate [ĭn′dĭ-kāt′] *verb*, to show or describe, to point out

in-di-ca-tion [ĭn′dĭ-kā′shən] *noun*, something that shows a trait

in-di-ca-tor [ĭn′dĭ-kā′tər] *noun*, 1) something that points to a trait 2) an instrument for automatically showing the pressure of the working fluid in an engine

in-dict [ĭn-dīt′] *verb*, to formally charge with a crime

in-dict-ment [ĭn-dīt′mənt] *noun*, a formal accusation charging someone with a crime

in-dif-fer-ent [ĭn-dĭf′ər-ənt] *adjective*, mediocre, unresponsive, unconcerned

in-dig-e-nous [ĭn-dĭj′ə-nəs] *adjective*, native to an area

in-di-gent [ĭn′dĭ-jənt] *adjective*, poor, homeless, destitute

in-di-gest-i-ble [ĭn′dĭ-jĕs′tə-bəl] *adjective*, something that cannot be swallowed or eaten

in-di-ges-tion [ĭn′dĭ-jĕs′chən] *noun*, a stomach ache

in-dig-nant [ĭn-dĭg′nənt] *adjective*, angry because of something that is not right, resentful

in-dig-na-tion [ĭn′dĭg-nā′shən] *noun*, anger, displeasure, rage

in-dig-ni-ty [ĭn-dĭg′nĭ-tē] *noun*, insulting or abusive treatment

in-di-go [ĭn′dĭ-gō′] *noun*, a deep blue-violet dye made from plants

in-di-rect [ĭn′dĭ-rĕkt′] *adjective*, in a roundabout way, circuitous

in-di-rect-ly [ĭn′dĭ-rĕkt′lē] *adverb*, inadvertently, not intentionally

in-dis-creet [ĭn′dĭ-skrēt′] *adjective*, lacking prudence or discretion, unwise, not careful, imprudent

in-dis-pen-sa-ble [ĭn′dĭ-spĕn′sə-bəl] *adjective*, absolutely necessary, essential

in-dis-put-a-ble [ĭn′dĭ-spyo͞o′tə-bəl] *adjective*, sure, undeniable, certain

in-di-vid-u-al [ĭn′də-vĭj′ōō-əl], *adjective,* 1) unique, special *noun* 2) a person, an entity, one

in-di-vid-u-al-ly [ĭn′də-vĭj′ōō-əl-lē] *adverb,* separately, one by one, distinctly

in-di-vis-i-ble [ĭn′də- vĭz′ə-bəl] *adjective,* 1) that cannot be divided 2) cannot be divided without leaving a remainder

in-do-lent [ĭn′də-lənt] *adjective,* lazy, inactive, slothful

in-dom-i-ta-ble [ĭn-dŏm′ĭ-tə-bəl] *adjective,* unconquerable, invincible, unyielding

in-door [ĭn′dôr′] *adjective,* located or used inside of a building

in-duce [ĭn-dōōs′] *verb,* to persuade, to influence

in-duce-ment [ĭn-dōōs′mənt] *noun,* any motive that leads one to act

in-duc-tive [ĭn-dŭk′tĭv] *adjective,* going from specific to general

in-dulge [ĭn-dŭlj′] *verb,* to allow, to give way to, to foster

in-dul-gence [ĭn-dŭl′jəns] *noun,* a giving way to one's desires

in-dus-tri-al [ĭn-dŭs′trē-əl] *adjective,* commercial, related to economy or industry

in-dus-tri-ous [ĭn-dŭs′trē-əs] *adjective,* hard-working

in-dus-try [ĭn′də-strē] *noun,* 1) hard work, being active 2) center of commerce, enterprise, business activity

in-el-i-gi-ble [ĭn-ĕl′ĭ-jə-bəl] *adjective,* not qualified to be chosen for an office

in-ept [ĭn-ĕpt′] *adjective,* out of place, incapable of performing a task, incompetent, unskilled

in-eq-ui-ty [ĭn-ĕk′wĭ-tē] *noun,* unfairness, not equal, bias

in-ert [ĭn-ûrt′] *adjective,* without power, inactive

in-er-tia [ĭ-nûr′shə] *noun,* 1) a state of matter by which it retains its state of rest, inactivity 2) acted upon by an external force

in-ev-i-ta-ble [ĭn-ĕv′ĭ-tə-bəl] *adjective,* not to be evaded or shunned, unavoidable

in-fal-li-ble [ĭn-făl′ə-bəl] *adjective,* unfailing, reliable, certain

in-fa-mous [ĭn′fə-məs] *adjective,* notoriously bad, wicked

in-fan-cy [ĭn′fən-sē] *adjective,* the first part of life, early childhood

in-fant [ĭn′fənt] *noun,* a very young child in the first stage of life, a newborn, a baby

in-fan-try [ĭn′fən-trē] *noun,* the ground forces of the army

in-fat-u-a-tion [ĭ-făch′ōō-ā′shən] *adjective,* the state of having very strong love or admiration for someone, an obsession

in-fect [ĭn-fĕkt′] *verb,* to share a virus or infection with others

in-fec-tion [ĭn-fĕk′shən] *noun,* any disease caused by germs

in-fec-tious [ĭn-fĕk′shəs] *adjective,* capable of being spread or communicated, contagious

in-fer [ĭn-fûr′] *verb,* to arrive at a conclusion, to deduce, to guess

in-fer-ence [ĭn′fər-əns] *noun,* the act of drawing a conclusion from certain premises, a guess

in-fe-ri-or [ĭn-fîr′ē-ər] *adjective,* 1) lower 2) of less importance 3) inequality, subordinate

in-fer-nal [ĭn-fûr′nəl] *adjective*, referring to hell, diabolical

in-fest [ĭn-fĕst′] *verb*, to overrun in a troublesome manner

in-fil-tra-tion [ĭn′fĭl-trā′shən] *noun*, 1) the act of penetrating the pores of a substance 2) passing or joining gradually

in-fi-nite [ĭn′fə-nĭt] *adjective*, unending, there is no end

in-fin-i-tes-i-mal [ĭn′fĭn-ĭ-tĕs′ə-məl] *adjective*, immeasurably small

in-fin-i-ty [ĭn-fĭn′ĭ-tē] *noun*, the symbol ~, to continue indefinitely

in-firm [ĭn-fûrm′] *adjective*, weak, sick, in poor health, ill, not well

in-fir-ma-ry [ĭn-fûr′mə-rē] *noun*, a small hospital, a first-aid tent

in-fir-mi-ty [ĭn-fûr′mĭ-tē] *noun*, weakness or ailment

in-flam-ma-ble [ĭn-flăm′ə-bəl] *adjective*, explosive, volatile

in-flam-ma-tion [ĭn′flə-mā′shən] *noun*, swelling, redness

in-flate [ĭn-flāt′] *verb*, to fill with air, to enlarge, to expand

in-fla-tion [ĭn-flā′shən] *noun*, ever higher price levels

in-flict [ĭn-flĭkt′] *verb*, to force, to impose, to deal as a blow

in-flu-ence [ĭn′flōo-əns] *noun*, 1) power, authority or control 2) the gradual or unseen operation of some cause, *verb*, 3) to act upon 4) to persuade

in-flu-en-tial [ĭn′flōo-ĕn′shəl] *adjective*, important, able to change people's thoughts on something, compelling

in-flu-en-za [ĭn′flōo-ĕn′zə] *noun*, no plural, the flu, an epidemic characterized by fever, headaches and fatigue

in-flux [ĭn′flŭks′] *noun*, flowing into or coming in

in-form [ĭn-fôrm′] *verb*, 1) to tell, to notify, to advise 2) to teach

in-for-mal [ĭn-fôr′məl] *adjective*, casual, not dressy or formal

in-form-ant [ĭn-fôr′mənt] *noun*, someone who gives information

in-for-ma-tion [ĭn′fər-mā′shən] *noun*, facts, data, the things you need to know, knowledge

in-frac-tion [ĭn-frăk′shən] *noun*, a violation, a breach of trust

in-fringe-ment [ĭn-frĭnj′mənt] *adjective*, an act that goes further than what is right or fair

in-fu-ri-ate [ĭn-fyŏor′ē-āt′] *verb*, to make someone angry, furious

in-fuse [ĭn-fyōoz′] *verb*, 1) to instill a principle or quality 2) to steep in water or other fluid without boiling for the purpose of extracting useful qualities

in-fu-sion [ĭn-fyōo′zhən] *noun*, the act of introducing, spreading or dispersion of properties

in-ge-nu-i-ty [ĭn′jə-nōo′ĭ-tē] *noun*, skill in discovering, inventing or planning

in-gest [ĭn-jĕst′] *verb*, to take in food or liquids gradually

in-grat-i-tude [ĭn-grăt′ĭ-tōod′] *adjective*, unthankfulness

in-gre-di-ent [ĭn-grē′dē-ənt] *noun*, 1) a component part of any mixture 2) things that are mixed together to make something

in-hab-it [ĭn-hăb′ĭt] *verb*, to live someplace, to make a place a home, to live or dwell in

in-hab-it-ant [ĭn-hăb′ĭ-tənt] *noun*, an animal or person who lives at a location, a resident

in-hale [ĭn-hāl′] *verb*, to take a deep breath, to breathe in

in-her-ent [ĭn-hîr′ənt] *adjective*, part of the nature of a person or thing

in-her-it [ĭn-hĕr′ĭt] *verb*, to receive something, usually from a relative by will or succession

in-her-it-ance [ĭn-hĕr′ĭ-təns] *noun*, the estate, heritage, legacy

in-hib-it [ĭn-hĭb′ĭt] *verb*, 1) to intimidate, to make someone hold back in fear 2) to restrain

in-hi-bi-tion [ĭn′hə-bĭsh′ən] *noun*, feeling painfully self-conscious

in-iq-ui-ty [ĭ-nĭk′wĭ-tē] *noun*, a gross injustice, wickedness

in-i-tial [ĭ-nĭsh′əl] *adjective*, 1) first, *noun*, 2) the first letter of a name, *verb*, 3) to sign with one's initials

in-i-tial-ly [ĭ-nĭsh′ə-lē] *adverb*, at the beginning, starting with

in-i-ti-ate [ĭ-nĭsh′ē-āt′] *verb*, to introduce, to begin or start something, to originate

in-i-ti-a-tion [ĭ-nĭsh′ē-ā′shən] *noun*, an induction, an inaugural

in-i-t-ia-tive [ĭ-nĭsh′ə-tĭv] *noun*, 1) an act that begins 2) to do something because it needs to be done, an introductory step

in-ject [ĭn-jĕkt′] *verb*, 1) to introduce, to insert 2) to give someone a shot 3) to force something into

in-jec-tion [ĭn-jĕk′shən] *noun*, an insertion of medicine through a needle into a vein, a shot

in-jure [ĭn′jər] *verb*, to cause harm of any kind, to wound

in-ju-ri-ous [ĭn-jŏŏr′ē-əs] *adjective*, hurtful, harmful

in-ju-ry [ĭn′jə-rē] *noun*, 1) a wound, harm to the body 2) an offense, harm done

in-jus-tice [ĭn-jŭs′tĭs] *noun*, violation of the rights of another, an unfair or unjust act

ink [ĭngk] *noun*, a colored liquid used with a pen for writing

in-land [ĭn′lənd] *adjective*, away from the shore or water

in-law [ĭn′lô′] *noun*, used after a word to mean a person related through marriage

in-let [ĭn′lĕt′] *noun*, a channel of water extending into the land from the river

in-mate [ĭn′māt′] *noun*, a prisoner or resident of a mental hospital

inn [ĭn] *noun*, a small hotel that serves meals, a tavern

in-nate [ĭ-nāt′] *adjective*, instinct, inherited, natural behavior

in-ner [ĭn′ər] *adjective*, 1) further in, or in the middle, 2) spiritual

in-ning [ĭn′ĭng] *noun*, the period in a baseball game for both teams to get three outs

in-no-cence [ĭn′ə-səns] *noun*, *no plural*, 1) freedom from guilt, 2) simplicity, naive

in-no-cent [ĭn′ə-sənt] *adjective*, 1) not guilty of a crime, blameless 2) pure, harmless

in-no-va-tion [ĭn′ə-vā′shən] *noun*, making changes, modernization

in-no-va-tive [ĭn′ə-vā′tĭv] *adjective*, the introduction of something new, change

in-nu-en-do [ĭn′yōō-ĕn′dō] *noun*, a suggestion, a hint, an insinuation

in-oc-u-late [ĭ-nŏk′yə-lāt′] *verb*, to inject an animal or person with a virus to prevent an infection

in-op-por-tune [ĭn-ŏp′ər-tōōn′] *adjective*, poorly timed

in-or-di-nate [ĭn-ôr′dn-ĭt] *adjective*, excessive, extravagant

in-or-gan-ic [ĭn′ôr-găn′ĭk] *adjective*, matter that does not contain carbon atoms in its main structure

in-put [ĭn′pŏŏt′] *noun*, anything put in, feedback, data entry

in-quest [ĭn′kwĕst′] *noun*, judicial inquiry or examination

in-quire [ĭn-kwīr′] *verb*, to ask about, to investigate

in-quir-y [ĭn-kwīr′ē, ĭng′-] *noun*, investigation, study, research

in-qui-si-tion [ĭn′kwĭ-zĭsh′ən, ĭng′] *noun*, formal questioning

in-quis-i-tive [ĭn-kwĭz′ĭ-tĭv] *adjective*, curious, apt to ask questions, given to research

in-sane [ĭn-sān′] *adjective*, crazy, psychotic, mad, deranged

in-sa-tia-ble [ĭn-sā′shə-bəl] *adjective*, incapable of being satisfied or appeased

in-scrip-tion [ĭn-skrĭp′shən] *noun*, an engraved message

in-scru-ta-ble [ĭn-skrōō′tə-bəl] *adjective*, unexplainable, mysterious

in-sect [ĭn′sĕkt′] *noun*, a bug with six legs and two pairs of wings

in-sec-ti-cide [ĭn-sĕk′tĭ-sīd′] *noun*, a poison used to kill bugs

in-sen-si-ble [ĭn-sĕn′sə-bəl] *adjective*, not aware, unconscious, unable to feel

in-sep-a-ra-ble [ĭn-sĕp′ər-ə-bəl] *adjective*, incapable of being separated or disjoined

in-sert [ĭn-sûrt′] *noun*, 1) an extra piece sewn or put n place, *verb*, 2) to put something into something, to inject, to set in place

in-side [ĭn-sīd′] *adjective*, 1) internal, interior, *noun*, 2) the portion that is in the middle of something, *preposition*, 3) something contained in something else, lying within

in-sid-i-ous [ĭn-sĭd′ē-əs] *adjective*, evil, sly, deceitful, beguiling

in-sight [ĭn′sīt′] *noun*, understanding, perceptiveness

in-sig-ni-a [ĭn-sĭg′nē-ə] *noun*, an emblem, a symbol, a badge

in-sig-nif-i-cance [ĭn′sĭg-nĭf′ĭ-kəns] *noun*, lack of importance, irrelevance

in-sig-nif-i-cant [ĭn′sĭg-nĭf′ĭ-kənt] *adjective*, unimportant, trivial

in-sin-cere [ĭn′sĭn-sîr′] *adjective*, untrue, false, disingenuous

in-sin-u-ate [ĭn-sĭn′yōō-āt′] *verb*, to introduce artfully, to suggest, to imply, to hint slyly

in-sip-id [ĭn-sĭp′ĭd] *adjective*, uninteresting, dull, banal

in-sist [ĭn-sĭst′] *verb*, 1) to say firmly, to demand, to speak with emphasis 2) to assert or demand persistently, to reiterate

in-so-lence [ĭn'sə-ləns] *noun*, arrogance, rudeness, impudence

in-so-lent [ĭn'sə-lənt] *adjective*, rude, insulting, disrespectful

in-sol-u-ble [ĭn-sŏl'yə-bəl] *adjective*, incapable of being dissolved

in-som-ni-a [ĭn-sŏm'nē-ə] *noun*, the inability to sleep

in-spect [ĭn-spĕkt'] *verb*, to examine carefully and critically, to scrutinize, to look over

in-spec-tion [ĭn-spĕk'shən] *noun*, a careful examination

in-spec-tor [ĭn-spĕk'tər] *noun*, someone who investigates

in-spi-ra-tion [ĭn'spə-rā'shən] *noun*, something that stimulates imagination and goodwill

in-spire [ĭn-spīr'] *verb*, to stimulate to think and to act, to influence

in-sta-bil-i-ty [ĭn'stə-bĭl'ĭ-tē] *noun*, lack of stability, unsteadiness

in-stall [ĭn-stôl'] *verb*, 1) to place in possession of an office, rank, or order 2) to put in place

in-stal-la-tion [ĭn'stə-lā'shən] *noun*, hooking up, placement

in-stall-ment [ĭn-stôl'mənt] *noun*, one of a number of parts, an affordable payment

in-stance [ĭn'stəns] *noun*, an example, a case in point

in-stant [ĭn'stənt] *adjective*, 1) happening or done at once, *noun*, 2) a moment, a very short period of time

in-stan-ta-ne-ous [ĭn'stən-tā'nē-əs] *adjective*, done in an instant

in-stant-ly [ĭn'stənt-lē] *adverb*, at once, immediately

in-stead [ĭn-stĕd'] *adverb*, in place of someone or something, a substitute, replacement

in-step [ĭn'stĕp'] *noun*, the arched middle portion of the human foot or of a shoe

in-sti-gate [ĭn'stĭ-gāt'] *verb*, to urge, to start, to provoke

in-still [ĭn-stĭl'] *verb*, 1) to teach, to educate, to inform 2) to saturate, to infuse, to permeate

in-stinct [ĭn'stĭngkt'] *noun*, a natural impulse that makes animals know how to take care of themselves, innate aptitude

in-stinc-tive-ly [ĭn-stĭngk'tĭv-lē] *adverb*, inborn, natural habits

in-sti-tute [ĭn'stĭ-tōōt'] *noun*, 1) an organization devoted to research and study, *verb*, 2) to form or establish an organization

in-sti-tu-tion [ĭn'stĭ-tōō'shən] *noun*, 1) a building used to serve a group of people 2) a commitment to a way of life and society's rules or customs

in-struct [ĭn-strŭkt'] *verb*, to teach, to show someone how to do something, to direct

in-struc-tion [ĭn-strŭk'shən] *noun*, teaching, direction, a training manual, knowledge imparted

in-struc-tor [ĭn-strŭk'tər] *noun*, a teacher or mentor

in-stru-ment [ĭn'strə-mənt] *noun*, 1) a device, a mechanism, a tool 2) a device, such as a trumpet, piano, or drum, used to make musical sounds 3) a means

in-stru-men-tal [ĭn′strə-mĕn′tl] *adjective*, helpful, acting to get something done

in-suf-fer-a-ble [ĭn-sŭf′ər-ə-bəl] *adjective*, painful, not to be endured, agonizing, intolerable

in-suf-fi-cient [ĭn′sə-fĭsh′ənt] *adjective*, not enough

in-su-late [ĭn′sə-lāt′] *verb*, to cover, to wrap, to protect

in-su-la-tion [ĭn′sə-lā′shən] *noun*, a material that prevents passage of heat, electricity, or sound

in-sult [ĭn-sŭlt′] *noun*, 1) an unkind or rude remark, *verb*, 2) to treat with abuse

in-sur-ance [ĭn-shŏŏr′əns] *noun*, *no plural*, money paid to an agency that keeps it as an investment to be returned to pay the cost of an accident, property damage, death, etc.

in-sure [ĭn-shŏŏr′] *verb*, to guarantee, to protect

in-sur-gent [ĭn-sûr′jənt] *noun*, a person who rises up against the law or leadership

in-sur-rec-tion [ĭn′sə-rĕk′shən] *noun*, an uprising, a rebellion

in-tan-gi-ble [ĭn-tăn′jə-bəl] *adjective*, something that cannot be touched, like an idea

in-te-ger [ĭn′tĭ-jər] *noun*, a whole number, an intact unit

in-te-grate [ĭn′tĭ-grāt′] *verb*, to make into a whole, to combine into one unit, to merge

in-teg-ri-ty [ĭn-tĕg′rĭ-tē] *noun*, honesty and virtue

in-tel-lect [ĭn′tl-ĕkt′] *noun*, the power to understand, the mind

in-tel-lec-tu-al [ĭn′tl-ĕk′chŏŏ-əl] *adjective*, smart, intelligent, brainy, able to reason

in-tel-li-gence [ĭn-tĕl′ə-jəns] *noun*, *no plural*, 1) the faculty of understanding 2) information communicated, reasoning

in-tel-li-gent [ĭn-tĕl′ə-jənt] *adjective*, very smart, clever

in-tel-li-gent-ly [ĭn-tĕl′ə-jənt-lē] *adverb*, sensibly, skillfully

in-tel-li-gi-ble [ĭn-tĕl′ĭ-jə-bəl] *adjective*, capable of being understood

in-tend [ĭn-tĕnd′] *verb*, 1) to plan to do something 2) to signify

in-tense [ĭn-tĕns′] *adjective*, a strong feeling, earnest

in-ten-si-fy [ĭn-tĕn′sə-fī′] *verb*, to make greater or more intense

in-ten-si-ty [ĭn-tĕn′sĭ-tē] *noun*, great concentration of energy

in-ten-sive [ĭn-tĕn′sĭv] *adjective*, thorough, involving special effort

in-tent [ĭn-tĕnt′] *noun*, 1) purpose 2) meaning

in-ten-tion [ĭn-tĕn′shən] *noun*, aim, a plan, a purpose, a meaning

in-ten-tion-al-ly [ĭn-tĕn′shə-nəl-lē] *adverb*, to do something on purpose, deliberately

in-tent-ly [ĭn-tĕnt′lē] *adverb*, strongly, purposefully

in-ter [ĭn-tûr′] *verb*, to bury

in-ter-act [ĭn′tər-ăkt′] *verb*, to relate mutually to, to exchange

in-ter-cede [ĭn′tər-sēd′] *verb*, to mediate, to act on one's behalf

in-ter-cept [ĭn′tər-sĕpt′] *verb*, to stop or seize something before it reaches its intended destination

in-ter-est [ĭn/trĭst] *noun*, 1) a concern or pleasure from learning something 2) title or share in a thing 3) a rate percent of money paid for the use of money, *verb*, 4) to involve or gain the attention of someone

in-ter-est-ing [ĭn/trĭ-stĭng] *adjective*, able to hold the attention or curiosity of someone

in-ter-face [ĭn/tər-fās/] *noun*, 1) a surface forming a common boundary between adjacent areas 2) in computer science the software or hardware connecting one drive or system to another

in-ter-fere [ĭn/tər-fîr/] *verb*, to be in opposition, to meddle

in-ter-fer-ence [ĭn/tər-fîr/əns] *noun*, obstruction, interrupting

in-ter-im [ĭn/tər-ĭm] *noun*, 1) in the meantime 2) temporary

in-te-ri-or [ĭn-tîr/ē-ər] *adjective*, 1)having to do with the inside part of something, inside *noun*, 2) the inside part of something

in-ter-lude [ĭn/tər-lōōd/] *noun*, a pause, a lull, a recess

in-ter-me-di-ate [ĭn/tər-mē/dē-ĭt] *adjective*, in the middle

in-ter-ment [ĭn-tûr/mənt] *noun*, the burial ceremony

in-ter-mi-na-ble [ĭn-tûr/mə-nə-bəl] *adjective*, endless, prolonged

in-ter-mis-sion [ĭn/tər-mĭsh/ən] *noun*, a break or recess

in-ter-mit-tent [ĭn/tər-mĭt/nt] *adjective*, coming and going at intervals, beginning again

in-tern [ĭn/tûrn/] *noun*, 1) a doctor's apprentice, *verb*, 2) to imprison, to confine

in-ter-nal [ĭn-tûr/nəl] *adjective*, 1) inside of something, inner 2) referring to any function inside the body, in word

in-ter-na-tion-al [ĭn/tər-năsh/ə-nəl] *adjective*, in nations all over the world, universal, global

in-ter-ne-cine [ĭn/tər-nĕs/ēn/] *adjective*, mutually destructive

In-ter-net [ĭn/tûr-nĕt] *noun*, the link to other computers, connected by a server

in-ter-pret [ĭn-tûr/prĭt] *verb*, to translate, to define, to explain

in-ter-pre-ta-tion [ĭn-tûr/prĭ-tā/shən] *noun*, an explanation of someone's art work, a translation

in-ter-pret-er [ĭn-tûr/prĭ-tər] *noun*, 1) one who explains or expounds 2) a translator

in-ter-ro-gate [ĭn-tĕr/ə-gāt/] *verb*, to ask questions of someone

in-ter-rupt [ĭn/tə-rŭpt/] *verb*, to stop something from continuing, to disturb, to hinder

in-ter-sect [ĭn/tər-sĕkt/] *verb*, when two lines meet to form angles

in-ter-sec-tion [ĭn/tər-sĕk/shən] *noun*, 1) a figure formed by two lines 2) a place where two or more roads meet

in-ter-state [ĭn/tər-stāt/] *adjective*, pertaining to commerce between the states

in-ter-val [ĭn/tər-vəl] *noun*, the space of time between any two points or events, a break

in-ter-vene [ĭn/tər-vēn/] *verb*, 1) to come or be between 2) to occur between points of time or events

in·ter·view [ĭn′tər-vyoō′] *noun*, a meeting in which people exchange information

in·ti·ma·cy [ĭn′tə-mə-sē] *noun*, close familiarity or association, very personal

in·ti·mate [ĭn′tə-mĭt] *adjective*, familiar, close, dear, private

in·tim·i·date [ĭn-tĭm′ĭ-dāt′] *verb*, to make someone afraid, to threaten someone, to scare

in·to [ĭn′toō] *preposition*, to go toward the middle of something

in·tol·er·a·ble [ĭn-tŏl′ər-ə-bəl] *adjective*, unbearable, unendurable, insufferable

in·tol·er·ance [ĭn-tŏl′ər-əns] *noun*, prejudice, bias, bigoted

in·to·na·tion [ĭn′tə-nā′shən] *noun*, a tone of voice, speech pattern, inflection, melody of pitch

in·tox·i·cate [ĭn-tŏk′sĭ-kāt′] *verb*, 1) to enliven, to excite, to elate 2) to feel drugged or drunk

in·trac·ta·ble [ĭn-trăk′tə-bəl] *adjective*, unruly, refractory

in·tran·si·tive [ĭn-trăn′sĭ-tĭv] *adjective*, a verb in a sentence that does not need a direct object to complete its meaning

in·trep·id [ĭn-trĕp′ĭd] *adjective*, fearless, dauntless

in·tri·cate [ĭn′trĭ-kĭt] *adjective*, complicated, involved, complex

in·tri·cate·ly [ĭn′trĭ-kĭt-lē] *adverb*, in a complex or involved manner

in·trigue [ĭn′trēg′] *noun*, 1) a conspiracy, a strategy, a plan, *verb*, 2) to be drawn into, to fascinate, to arouse curiosity

in·trin·sic [ĭn-trĭn′zĭk] *adjective*, basic and essential to what something is

in·tro·duce [ĭn′trə-doōs′] *verb*, 1) to bring into notice 2) to make known by formal announcement 3) to bring into use, to lead in

in·tro·duc·tion [ĭn′trə-dŭk′shən] *noun*, 1) a piece of writing at the beginning of a book that explains something about the story 2)) the act of formally making persons known to each other

in·tro·vert [ĭn′trə-vûrt′] *noun*, a loner, someone who feels self-conscious, a shy person

in·trude [ĭn-troōd′] *verb*, to trespass, to enter uninvited

in·tru·sion [ĭn-troō′zhən] *noun*, the act of forcing in without right or welcome or permission

in·tu·i·tion [ĭn′toō-ĭsh′ən] *noun*, instinctive knowledge or feeling

in·un·date [ĭn′ŭn-dāt′] *verb*, to overflow, to flood, to overwhelm

in·ure [ĭn-yoōr′] *verb*, to accustom, to harden by use or exposure

in·vade [ĭn-vād′] *verb*, to enter by force in order to take over

in·va·lid [ĭn-văl′ĭd] *adjective*, 1) null and void, insupportable, [ĭn-val′ĭ-d] *noun*, 2) a person who is feeble, weak, frail, sickly

in·val·i·date [ĭn-văl′ĭ-dāt′] *verb*, to deprive of legal force

in·var·i·ab·ly [ĭn-vâr′ē-ə-blē] *adverb*, without fail, predictably

in·va·sion [ĭn-vā′zhən] *noun*, an attack, a raid

in-vent [ĭn-vĕnt′] *verb*, to create or design a new product

in-ven-tion [ĭn-vĕn′shən] *noun*, a design or creation of an idea

in-ven-tor [ĭn-vĕn′tər] *noun*, one who finds out or devises a new product or device

in-ven-to-ry [ĭn′vən-tôr′ē] *noun*, an itemized list of stock on hand with their estimated worth

in-verse [ĭn-vûrs′] *adjective*, the opposite, reverse in direction

in-vert [ĭn-vûrt′] *verb*, to overturn

in-ver-te-brate [ĭn-vûr′tə-brĭt] *noun*, animals without a backbone or spinal column, e.g. *a worm*

in-vest [ĭn-vĕst′] *verb*, to empower, to qualify, to devote time

in-ves-ti-gate [ĭn-vĕs′tĭ-gāt′] *verb*, to examine into, to inquire

in-ves-ti-ga-tion [ĭn-vĕs′tĭ-gā′shən] *noun*, an inquiry into a matter, a thorough exploration or inspection, an examination

in-vest-ment [ĭn-vĕst′mənt] *noun*, money used to create a source of income or profit

in-ves-tor [ĭn-vĕs′tər] *noun*, one who makes an investment or spends money on something with a view of obtaining income or profit

in-vet-er-ate [ĭn-vĕt′ər-ĭt] *adjective*, deep-rooted, habitual

in-vig-o-rate [ĭn-vĭg′ə-rāt′] *verb*, to fill with life and energy

in-vin-ci-ble [ĭn-vĭn′sə-bəl] *adjective*, irresistible, unyielding

in-vis-i-ble [ĭn-vĭz′ə-bəl] *adjective*, something that cannot be seen

in-vi-ta-tion [ĭn′vĭ-tā′shən] *noun*, a request asking for someone to attend a gathering

in-vite [ĭn-vīt′] *verb*, to ask someone to do something or come somewhere

in-voke [ĭn-vōk′] *verb*, to call upon, to ask for, to cause

in-vol-un-tar-y [ĭn-vŏl′ən-tĕr′ē] *adjective*, without will or choice, done unwillingly

in-volve [ĭn-vŏlv′] *verb*, to take part in, to make a part of

in-vul-ner-a-ble [ĭn-vŭl′nər-ə-bəl] *adjective*, incapable of injury

in-ward [ĭn′wərd] *adjective*, internal, inner, center

in-ward-ly [ĭn′wərd-lē] *adverb*, 1) toward the middle, halfway 2) internal, privately

i-o-dine [ī′ə-dīn′] *noun*, a nonmetallic element isolated as a crystalline solid

i-o-ta [ī-ō′tə] *noun*, the very smallest quantity or degree, a particle

Io-wa [ī′ə-wə] *noun*, one of the 50 United States located in the Midwest, the capital city is Des Moines. The state flower of **Iowa** is the wild rose and the state motto is "Our liberties we prize and our rights we will maintain."

i-rate [ī-rāt′] *adjective*, angry

ir-i-des-cent [ĭr′ĭ-dĕs′ənt] *adjective*, the rainbow-like play of colors, shimmering

irk-some [ûrk′səm] *adjective*, repetitious, tedious, annoying

i-ron [ī′ərn] *noun*, 1) a gray metal 2) a heated device used to smooth the wrinkles from clothes 3) an element, *verb*, 4) to press with a heated iron to remove wrinkles on clothes

i-ron-ic [ĭ-rŏn′ĭk] *adjective*, what appears to be false or contradictory, but in fact is true

i-ro-ny [ĭ′rə-nē, ĭ′ər-] *noun*, the outcome of events contrary to what was expected

ir-rad-i-ate [ĭ-rā′dē-āt′] *verb*, 1) to illuminate, to enlighten 2) to expose to ultraviolet rays

ir-ra-tion-al [ĭ-răsh′ə-nəl] *adjective*, absurd, unreasonable,

ir-rec-on-cil-a-ble [ĭ-rĕk′ən-sī′lə-bəl] *adjective*, not able to be resolved by compromise, unfriendly

ir-reg-u-lar [ĭ-rĕg′yə-lər] *adjective*,1) not conforming to rule 2) erratic, not uniform

ir-rel-e-vant [ĭ-rĕl′ə-vənt] *adjective*, not applicable or pertinent, not relevant

ir-rep-a-ra-ble [ĭ-rĕp′ər-ə-bəl] *adjective*, permanently damaged

ir-re-proach-a-ble [ĭr′ĭ-prō′chə-bəl] *adjective*, blameless, above reproach

ir-re-sist-i-ble [ĭr′ĭ-zĭs′tə-bəl] *adjective*, tempting

ir-re-triev-a-ble [ĭr′ĭ-trē′və-bəl] *adjective*, lost, gone forever

ir-rev-er-ent [ĭ-rĕv′ər-ənt] *adjective*, lacking proper respect

ir-rev-o-ca-ble [ĭ-rĕv′ə-kə-bəl] *adjective*, fixed, constant

ir-ri-gate [ĭr′ĭ-gāt′] *verb*, to supply with water by causing a stream to flow through, as in channels

ir-ri-tate [ĭr′ĭ-tāt′] *verb*, 1) to annoy, to excite to anger, to bother 2) to make skin sore, red or swollen

ir-ri-ta-tion [ĭr′ĭ-tā′shən] *noun*, 1) something that makes a person mildly angry 2) an allergic reaction, an irritant

is [ĭz] the part of the *verb* to **be** that we use with *he*, *she* and *it*

Is-lam [ĭs-läm′] *noun*, Muslim religion founded in Arabia in the 7th century based on the teaching of Muhammed

is-land [ĭ′lənd] *noun*, a body of land completely surrounded by water

isle [īl] *noun*, a small island

is-n't [ĭz′ənt] the *contraction* of the words **is** and **not**

i-so-late [ĭ′sə-lāt′] *verb*, 1)to separate and set apart, to place alone 2) to cut off from others

iso-la-tion [ĭ′sə-lā′shən] *noun*, solitude, detachment

i-sos-ce-les tri-an-gle [ĭ-sŏs′ə-lēz′ trī′ăng′gəl] *noun*, a triangle with two equal sides

is-sue [ĭsh′ōō] *noun*, 1) a subject, a topic 2) the condition or action of being made available, *verb*, 3) to give, to send, or come out

isth-mus [ĭs′məs] *noun*, a neck of land joining two larger portions of land bordered by water

it [ĭt] *pronoun, plural*, **they**, 1) the subject of the sentence 2) used about the weather, time, and dates, and in other phrases

i-tal-ic [ĭ-tăl′ĭk] *noun*, type in which the letters slant

itch [ĭch] *noun*, 1) a tickling feeling in the skin that makes one want to scratch, *verb*, 2) to scratch and rub a sore because it is irritating

i-tem [ī′təm] *noun*, a point, a news article, a single thing in a list

i-tem-ize [ī′tə-mīz′] *verb*, to list or state by particulars

itin-er-ant [ī-tĭn′ər-ənt] *adjective*, traveling from place to place

itin-er-ar-y [ī-tĭn′ə-rĕr′ē] *noun*, the detailed plan for a journey

its [ĭts] of **it**, belonging to **it**, the possessive of the word **it**

it's [ĭts] the *contraction* of the words**:** **it** and **is**

it-self [ĭt-sĕlf′] *plural*, **themselves**, referring to the subject in the sentence

I've [īv] the *contraction* of the words **I** and **have**

i-vo-ry [ī′və-rē, īv′rē] *noun*, hard, white substance taken from the tusks of elephants

i-vy [ī′vē] *noun*, a leafy vine

J

jack-al [jăk′əl] *noun*, a wild animal like a dog that eats meat

jack-et [jăk′ĭt] *noun*, 1) a covering worn over clothing, similar to a coat, cut below the waist 2) a covering put over something

jade [jād] *noun*, a stone of a green color, but sometimes whitish, capable of a fine polish

jad-ed [jā′dĭd] *adjective*, tired, weary from overwork

jag-uar [jăg′wär′] *noun*, a wild cat with a spotted coat that lives in South America

jail [jāl] *noun*, a prison

jam [jăm] *noun*, *no plural*, 1) a sweet spread, made of boiled fruit and sugar 2) when traffic is stopped because no one can move 3) a predicament, a spot, *verb*, 4) to pack tightly together, to compress, to press or push

jan-i-tor [jăn′ĭ-tər] *noun*, one who takes care of the repairs and cleaning of a public building

Jan-u-ary [jăn′yōō-ĕr′ē] *noun*, the first month of the year, having 31 days

jar [jär] *noun*, a container like a bottle with a wide opening

jar-gon [jär′gən] *noun*, language used by a particular group, special terminology

jaun-dice [jôn′dĭs] *noun*, a blood condition that makes the skin look yellow

jaunt [jônt] *noun*, a short trip

jave-lin [jăv′lĭn] *noun*, a spear thrown by hand for distance as in an athletic event

jaw [jô] *noun*, the bony part of the face in which the teeth are set

jazz [jăz] *noun*, a style of music using unusual tone effects on brass instruments improvised by southern blacks in the 1900's

jeal-ous [jĕl′əs] *adjective*, to be unhappy because you want what someone else has, envious

jeal-ous-y [jĕl′ə-sē] *noun*, suspicious fear or watchfulness, resentment of someone's success

jeans [jēnz] *noun*, *plural*, pants made of denim fabric

jeer [jîr] *verb*, to make fun of someone and laugh in their face, to mock, to scorn

jel-ly [jĕl′ē] *noun, no plural,* 1) any substance between liquid and solid 2) a sweet spread made of fruit and pectin

jel-ly-fish [jĕl′ē-físh′] *noun*, a soft gelatinous sea creature that looks like a squishy blob

jeop-ard-ize [jĕp′ər-dīz′] *verb*, to expose to danger or even death

jerk [jûrk] *noun*, 1) a quick pull or twist movement, *verb*, 2) to pull, to push or to twist suddenly

jer-sey [jûr′zē] *noun*, clothing usually made of cotton with elastic that covers the top of the body like a shirt

jest [jĕst] *verb*, to joke, to jeer

jet [jĕt] *noun*, 1) an aircraft propelled through air by an engine, which releases a stream of hot air behind itself as it travels 2) a stream of gas, air, or liquid that spurts from a hole

jet-ti-son [jĕt′ĭ-sən] *verb*, to throw overboard, to discard

jet-ty [jĕt′ē] *noun*, a kind of wall built out into water for protection against the waves

Jew [jōō] *noun*, a member of the Jewish religion

jew-el [jōō′əl] *noun*, a precious stone used as an ornament, a gem of great value

jew-el-er [jōō′ə-lər] *noun*, one who makes, or deals in jewels, gems and precious stones, etc.

jew-el-ry [jōō′əl-rē] *noun, no plural*, ornaments like rings, earrings, necklaces made with precious or semiprecious stones, gems and metals

jilt [jĭlt] *verb*, to break up a romantic interest

jin-gle [jĭng′gəl] *verb*, 1) to make a tingling sound like the sound of bells, *noun*, 2) a catchy verse

job [jŏb] *noun*, 1) a task or responsibility 2) work done for payment 3) a position or duty

jog [jŏg] *verb*, 1) to run for exercise 2) to jolt, to bump, to shake 3) to stir into activity

join [join] *verb*, 1) to connect, to bring together, to meet 2) to become a member

joint [joint] *adjective*, 1) an endeavor involving two or more people, *noun*, 2) the part of the body where bones connect 3) the place where two things are joined or connected 4) a poor quality restaurant or night club

joke [jōk] *noun*, 1) a funny story or funny phrase spoken to amuse people, *verb*, 2) to tell funny stories or say things to make people laugh, to fool around

jolt [jōlt] *noun*, 1) a sudden and unexpected movement, *verb*, 2) to cause a sudden movement

joule [jōōl, joul] *noun*, the measurement of force or energy

jour-nal [jûr′nəl] *noun*, a book that records daily thoughts or transactions, a diary

jour-nal-ism [jûr′nə-lĭz′əm] *noun, no plural*, the job of writing for a publication or broadcasting news

jour-nal-ist [jûr′nə-lĭst] *noun*, a professional writer for a newspaper or magazine

jour-ney [jûr′nē] *noun*, the passage from one place to another, a trip

jo-vi-al [jō′vē-əl] *adjective*, joking in a friendly manner, light-hearted, joyous humor

joy [joi] *noun*, *no plural*, great happiness, delight, elation

joy-ful [joi′fəl] *adjective*, full of joy, very glad, happy

Jr. the abbreviation of the word **junior** when referring to a son who has his father's name

ju-bi-lant [jōō′bə-lənt] *adjective*, thrilled, rejoicing, great joy

Ju-da-ism [jōō′dē-ĭz′əm] *noun*, the religion of people descended from the Israelites in the Bible

judge [jŭj] *noun*, 1) one with legal authority who applies the rules of law in a court 2) the person designated to decide the winner in a contest, *verb*, 3) to make a decision, to form an opinion

judg-ment [jŭj′mənt] *noun*, 1) a decision or opinion 2) intelligence, understanding

ju-di-cial [jōō-dĭsh′əl] *adjective*, providing or relating to justice or a fair decision, just, legal

ju-di-cious [jōō-dĭsh′əs] *adjective*, sound in judgment, wise, discreet, sagacious, fair

ju-do [jōō′dō] *noun*, *no plural*, a form of martial arts that uses the body as a weapon, and bans throws and blows

jug [jŭg] *noun*, a container with a handle for holding liquids

jug-ger-naut [jŭg′ər-nôt′] *noun*, an overpowering or crushing force

jug-gle [jŭg′əl] *verb*, to throw several things into the air and keep them moving by throwing and catching them as a trick

jug-u-lar [jŭg′yə-lər] *noun*, one of the large veins returning the blood from the head

juice [jōōs] *noun*, the natural fluid that comes from fruit, vegetables or cooked meat

Ju-ly [jōō-lī′] *noun*, the seventh month of the year, having 31 days

jump [jŭmp] *noun*, 1) a spring or leap, *verb*, 2) to lift the feet off the ground into the air, to leap 3) to rise suddenly

jump-er [jŭm′pər] *noun*, a sleeveless dress worn over a blouse

junc-tion [jŭngk′shən] *noun*, a place where roads or lines of railways meet and cross

June [jōōn] *noun*, the sixth month of the year, having 30 days

jun-gle [jŭng′gəl] *noun*, a thick growth of tropical bushes, vines, trees, etc., extending over a large area

jun-ior [jōōn′yər] *adjective*, 1) a student in his third year of a four-year course 2) the son named after his father

junk [jŭngk] *noun*, stuff regarded as unwanted or useless

jun-ket [jŭng′kĭt] *noun*, a trip, a short pleasure excursion

ju-ris-dic-tion [jŏŏr′ĭs-dĭk′shən] *noun*, the legal authority of a court, to apply the law

ju-ror [jŏŏr′ər, -ôr′] *noun*, one of a group of peers chosen to judge someone accused of a crime

ju-ry [jŏŏr′ē] *noun*, a group of people chosen to decide if a person is guilty or innocent of a crime in a court of law

just [jŭst] *adjective*, 1) fair and right 2) normal, *adverb*, 3) to the amount needed, but no more 4) a very short time ago, by a short time 5) only 6) used to compare two things

jus-tice [jŭs′tĭs] *noun, no plural*, fairness, equity, impartiality

jus-ti-fy [jŭs′tə-fī′] *verb*, 1) to show or prove to be right 2) to make even or true, as lines of type by proper spacing

ju-ve-nile [jŏŏ′və-nīl′] *adjective*, 1) young, youthful, *noun*, 2) a youth, anyone under the legal adult age of 18

K

ka-lei-do-scope [kə-lī′də-skōp′] *noun*, an optical instrument exhibiting an endless variety of colored forms

kan-ga-roo [kăng′gə-rōō′] *noun*, a marsupial, an animal that eats only plants, lives in Australia, jumps around on its large back legs

Kan-sas [kăn′zəz] *noun*, one of the 50 United States, located in the Midwest, the capital city is Topeka. The state flower of **Kansas** is the sunflower, and the motto is "To the stars through difficulties."

kar-at [kăr′ət] *noun*, the unit measure of the purity of gold

kay-ak [kī′ăk′] *noun*, a canoe that holds one person

keel [kēl] *noun*, the bottom of the boat, the underside

keen [kēn] *adjective*, 1) 1) having a sharp edge 2) mentally aware, quick to understand 3) showing a stong interest, eager

keep [kēp] *verb*, 1) to hold something 2) to store something, to stock it 3) to make someone stay someplace 4) to prevent someone from doing something 5) to continue on

ken-nel [kĕn′əl] *noun*, a place to keep and care for dogs

Ken-tucky [kən-tŭk′ē] *noun*, one of the 50 United States, located in the South, the capital is Frankfort. The state flower of **Kentucky** is the goldenrod, and the state motto is "United We Stand, Divided We Fall."

kept [kĕpt] *past tense* of **keep**

ker-chief [kûr′chĭf] *noun*, a woman's scarf worn as a covering for the head

ker-nel [kûr′nəl] *noun*, a grain or seed, the edible part of a nut

ker-o-sene [kĕr′ə-sēn′] *noun*, thin oil used to ignite a fire

ketch-up [kĕch′ŭp] *noun*, a thick sauce made of tomatoes, flavored with onion, salt, sugar, and spice

ket-tle [kĕt′l] *noun*, a large metal pot with a lid and a handle and a spout

key [kē] *noun*, 1) a metal instrument used for locking and unlocking things 2) a lever on a musical instrument that affects the sound 3) the piece of information needed to make something understood

key-board [kē′bôrd′] *noun*, a common input device

khak-i [kăk′ē] *noun*, a tan or brownish cotton cloth

kick [kĭk] *noun*, 1) an impulsive
move with the foot, *verb*,
2) to hit something with the foot,
to move the foot suddenly

kid [kĭd] *noun*, 1) a young goat 2) a
child, *verb*, 3) to tease or joke .

kid-nap [kĭd′năp′] *verb*, to take
someone against their will

kid-nap-per [kĭd′nă-pər] *noun*,
someone who takes a person
against their will

kid-ney [kĭd′nē] *noun*, one of two
parts inside the body which
remove waste liquid from the
blood and excretes uric acid

kill [kĭl] *verb*, to make someone die

kill-er [kĭl′ər] *noun*, a person who
murders or takes the life from
another

kil-o-gram [kĭl′ə-grăm′] *noun*, a
unit of weight equal to 1,000
grams

kil-o-me-ter [kĭ-lŏm′ĭ-tər] *noun*, a
distance equal to 1,000 meters,
or 3,281feet

kil-o-watt [kĭl′ə-wŏt′] *noun*, a unit
of power equal to 1,000 watts

kin [kĭn] *noun*, *no plural*, family
members, one's relatives

kind [kīnd] *adjective*, 1) nice,
good, helpful, willing to please,
noun, 2) a sort or particular one

kin-der-gar-ten [kĭn′dər-gär′tn]
noun, a preschool for children
before the first grade

kin-dle [kĭn′dl] *verb*, 1) to set fire,
to ignite 2) to arouse, to inspire

kind-ness [kīnd′nĭs] *noun*, *no
plural*, goodness, compassion

kin-dred [kĭn′drĭd] *adjective*,
1) similar in nature, comparable,
alike 2) related by family

ki-net-ic [kĭ-nĕt′ĭk] *adjective*, the
changes of motion produced by
forces, the force of motion

king [kĭng] *noun*, a male ruler of a
country, especially one who
comes from a family of rulers

king-dom [kĭng′dəm] *noun*, the
lands owned by a monarchy, an
empire, an independent realm

kin-ship [kĭn′shĭp′] *noun*, a
relationship or connection
between family members

kiss [kĭs] *noun*, 1) a slight touch
with the lips, *verb*, 2) to touch
with the lips as a sign of
affection or love

kit [kĭt] *noun*, a set of instruments
needed for doing something or
going somewhere

kitch-en [kĭch′ən] *noun*, the room
where food is prepared and
cooked and eaten

kite [kīt] *noun*, a light frame
covered with fabric, plastic or
paper, flown in the air at the end
of a long string

kit-ten [kĭt′n] *noun*, a baby cat

knap-sack [năp′săk′] *noun*, a
supply bag of canvas or leather
with shoulder straps, worn on
the back

knave [nāv] *noun*, an unscrupulous,
dishonest person, a rascal

knead [nēd] *verb*, to manipulate by
pressing and stretching to mix
and remove air, to massage

knee [nē] *noun*, the joint between
the thigh and the lower leg
connecting the femur and tibia

kneel [nēl] *verb*, to stand on your knees, to bend down so that your calf is laying on the ground

knew [nōō] *past tense* of **know**

knife [nīf] *noun, plural, knives,* a cutting instrument consisting of a sharp blade fastened to a handle

knight [nīt] *noun*, 1) an armed soldier in the Middle Ages 2) a chess piece in the shape of a horse's head 3) an honorary title in Britain

knit [nĭt] *verb*, to join wool into a cloth using long needles

knob [nŏb] *noun*, a handle in the shape of a round lump

knock [nŏk] *noun*, 1) a noise made when something is hit *verb*, 2) to hit or strike with the fist 4) to make a noise by hitting on the surface

knoll [nōl] *noun*, a small round hill

knot [nŏt] *noun*, 1) one or more threads tied together, *verb*, 2) to tie something securely with rope or cord so that it cannot come untied

know [nō] *verb*, 1) to understand clearly, to learn 2) to be skilled in 3) to be acquainted with someone

knowl-edge [nŏl′ĭj] *noun*, something learned and remembered, gained by experience

know-ledge-a-ble [nŏl′ĭ-jə-bəl] *adjective*, familiar with, learned

known [nōn] past participle of **know**

knuck-le [nŭk′əl] *noun*, one of the joints in the finger or toe

Ko-ran [kə-răn′, -rän′, kô-, kō-] *noun*, the holy book of Islam containing the revelations of Muhammed

L

la-bel [lā′bəl] *noun*, 1) a slip of paper indicating contents, ownership, etc. *verb*, 2) to affix a tag or sticker on something naming what it is

la-bor [lā′bər] *noun*, 1) work 2) the pain a woman feels birthing a baby, *verb*, 3) to work hard

lab-o-ra-to-ry [lăb′rə-tôr′ē] *noun*, a place devoted to experiments in natural science

la-bo-ri-ous [lə-bôr′ē-əs] *adjective*, hardworking, tiresome, tedious

lab-y-rinth [lăb′ə-rĭnth′] *noun*, a series of intricate passageways, a maze, an inexplicable difficulty

lace [lās] *noun*, 1) a string used to tie a shoe 2) frilly threadwork used as edging or as an embroidery design, *verb*, 3) to thread through holes with a string or cord

lac-er-a-tion [lăs′ə-rā′shən] *noun*, a cut, a tear made with a knife

lack [lăk] *noun*, 1) not enough, a shortage, *verb* 2) to be without

lack-a-dai-si-cal [lăk′ə-dā′zĭ-kəl] *adjective*, half-hearted, lazy, indifferent, listless

la-con-ic [lə-kŏn′ĭk] *adjective*, brief and to the point

lac-quer [lăk′ər] *noun*, a liquid that hardens into a clear tough film

lac-tic acid [lăk′tĭk-ăs′ĭd] *noun*, a colorless, syrupy liquid, occurring in sour milk

lad [lăd] *noun*, a boy

lad-der [lăd′ər] *noun*, a device used for climbing designed with two side pieces joined together with shorter pieces called rungs that form steps

lad-en [lād′n] *adjective*, heavily loaded, full of cargo

la-dle [lād′l] *noun*, a cup-shaped spoon with a long handle, used for serving or dipping

la-dy [lā′dē] *noun*, 1) a polite and considerate woman 2) in Britain, a title for the wife or daughter of a Lord

lag [lăg] *verb*, to move at a slower pace to stay behind the others

la-goon [lə-gōōn′] *noun*, a shallow body of water near a sea, or pond-like body of water

laid [lād] *past tense* of lay

lair [lâr] *noun*, a den, a hole, a hideout for a wild animal

la-i-ty [lā′ĭ-tē] *noun*, someone not connected to the clergy, a layman practicing religion

lake [lāk] *noun*, a body of water with land all around

lamb [lăm] *noun*, a baby sheep

lame [lām] *adjective*, limping or disabled in a hand or joint

la-ment [lə-mĕnt′] *verb*, to mourn, to express grief or regret

lam-i-nat-ed [lăm′ə-nā′tĭd] *adjective*, arranged in layers of plastic one upon the other

lamp [lămp] *noun*, a device used to project artificial light

lam-poon [lăm-pōōn′] *noun*, a cartoon or satire in print

lance [lăns] *noun*, 1) a spear, a harpoon, a javelin, *verb*, 2) to puncture 3) to cut into with a surgical knife

land [lănd] *noun, no plural*, 1) the dry part of the earth, not covered by water 2) a country, region, area, *verb*, 3) to arrive on the ground from the air or water

land-fill [lănd′fĭl′] *noun*, a large outdoor site where solid waste is covered by soil

land-lord [lănd′lôrd′] *noun*, a person who owns a building which he lets others use or live in, in return for money

land-mark [lănd′märk′] *noun*, 1) an achievement, a turning point, benchmark 2) a distinctive building or geographical marker like a bend in the river

land-scape [lănd′skāp′] *noun*, a view of an area with its natural surroundings

lane [lān] *noun*, a short road

lan-guage [lăng′gwĭj] *noun*, 1) any means of conveying or communicating ideas 2) human speech 3) dialect, jargon, vocabulary used by a group

lan-guish [lăng′gwĭsh] *verb*, to lose strength, to weaken

lan-guor [lăng′gər] *noun*, a feeling of depression, nervous exhaustion, weakness of mind or body

lank [lăngk] *adjective*, 1)thin, lean 2) hanging straight or limp

lan-tern [lăn′tərn] *noun*, a portable lamp, with a protective case for lights, carried with a handle often used outdoors for light

lap [lăp] *noun*, 1) the seat created by the legs and chest when sitting 2) the distance once around a track 3) a place of rest, *verb*, 4) to drink water with a tongue, like an animal

lapel [lə-pĕl'] *noun*, the flat hanging appendage on a jacket

lapse [lăps] *noun*, 1) an interval of time in which something stops and then starts again 2) termination of policy because of non-payment of premium when due 3) a slip or error

lar-ce-ny [lär'sə-nē] *noun*, taking and carrying away of things, stealing, robbery

lard [lärd] *noun*, grease, fat

large [lärj] *adjective*, greater than average in size, number, etc., immense, big

large-ly [lärj'lē] *adverb*, mostly

lar-ger [lär'jər] *adjective*, bigger

lar-gess [lär-zhĕs'] *noun*, the generous giving of gifts

lar-va [lär'və] *noun, plural, larvae or larvas*, the second stage of an insect that goes through ⌐complete metamorphosis

lar-yn-gi-tis [lăr'ən-jī'tĭs] *noun*, infection of the larynx or upper end of the windpipe

lar-ynx [lăr'ĭngks] *noun*, the voice organ in the upper throat

la-ser [lā'zər] *noun*, a narrow beam of high-energy light that is all exactly the same color

lash [lăsh] *noun*, 1) a whip, a cane, *verb*, 2) to hit hard 3) to secure something in place with a rope

las-so [lăs'ō] *noun*, 1) a rope with a loop at the end used for catching cattle, *verb*, 2) to catch by throwing the noose of a rope around the neck or torso

last [lăst] *adjective*, 1) the end, final 2) an instance when something happens 3) to come after all others 4) to be a part of for a long time, to endure, *adverb*, 5) to stay in good condition, to be preserved 6) most recently

last-ing [lăs'tĭng] *adjective*, the length of time something continues, enduring

latch [lăch] *noun*, 1) a small bolt used to fasten a door, *verb*, 2) to fasten something shut

late [lāt] *adjective*, 1) after the time agreed on 2) near the end of a day, year, etc. 3) a missed opportunity 4) deceased

late-ly [lāt'lē] *adverb*, recently, a short time ago, not long since

la-tent [lāt'nt] *adjective*, hidden, present but not visible

lat-er [lāt'ər] *adverb*, after a certain amount of time, subsequently

lat-er-al [lăt'ər-əl] *adjective*, coming from the side

lat-est [lā'tĭst] *adjective*, most recent, newest, popular

lath-er [lăth'ər] *noun, no plural*, the bubbles created by soap

lat-i-tude [lăt'ĭ-tōōd'] *noun, no plural*, 1) vertical lines on a map that indicate north and south 2) freedom to act and to choose

lat-ter [lăt'ər] *adjective*, the second of two things, the last mentioned

laud [lôd] *verb*, to praise, to commend

laugh [lăf] *verb*, to make a sound showing something is funny, to express happiness

laugh-ter [lăf′tər] *noun, no plural*, a giggle, mirth, a chuckle

launch [lônch] *noun*, 1) a small boat propelled by an engine, *verb*, 2) to send off, to put a boat into water or send a space ship into orbit 3) to plunge boldly into action

laun-dry [lôn′drē] *noun*, dirty clothes washed together

lau-rel [lôr′əl] *noun*, an evergreen shrub with pink flowers

la-va [lä′və] *noun*, very hot melted rock that bursts out of a volcano

lav-a-to-ry [lăv′ə-tôr′ē] *noun*, a room with a toilet and a sink

lav-en-der [lăv′ən-dər] *noun*, a fragrant plant with purple flowers, classified as an herb

lav-ish [lăv′ĭsh] *adjective*, 1) extravagant, excessive, 2) giving in great amounts, *verb*, 3) to give generously

law [lô] *noun*, a written rule of conduct made and enforced by the government

law-mak-er [lô′mā′kər] *noun*, a person in government who is part of the legislature

lawn [lôn] *noun*, a piece of ground where grass is grown and is kept short in front of a building

law-yer [lô′yər] *noun*, a professional who practices law, an attorney, barrister

lax-a-tive [lăk′sə-tĭv] *noun*, a medicine or herb that induces a bowel movement

lay [lā] *verb*, 1) to place something in a horizontal position 2) when an adult female produces eggs 3) to remain, to rest

lay-er [lā′ər] *noun*, a covering that is set between two levels

la-zy [lā′zē] *adjective*, disinterested in work, slow-moving, indolent

lead [lĕd] *noun*, 1) a heavy, metallic element, having a bright luster 2) the part of a pencil used for writing, [lēd] *verb*, 3) to guide, to show someone the way

lead-er [lē′dər] *noun*, the chief, the person in charge, the ruler

lead-er-ship [lē′dər-shĭp′] *noun*, the quality of those who take charge or show the way

leaf [lēf] *noun, plural, leaves*, 1) a green part of a stem that grows off a branch of a plant 2) a sheet of paper

leaf-let [lē′flĭt] *noun*, a brochure or a small sheet of printed matter

league [lēg] *noun*, 1) an association or alliance with other individuals 2) sports teams organized to compete against each other 3) three nautical miles

leak [lēk] *noun*, 1) a crack or hole through which liquid, gas or light can ooze, *verb*, 2) to let something escape through an unintended opening such as a crack or hole

lean [lēn] *adjective*, 1) thin, without fat, *verb*, 2) to bend or incline toward 3) to rest on something for support to keep from falling, to recline

leap [lēp] *noun*, 1) a jump, *verb*, 2) to jump or spring over a hurdle or through space

leap year *noun*, a year, once every four years, in which February has 29 days instead of 28

learn [lûrn] *verb*, 1) to acquire knowledge or skill through study or experience 2) to find out, to commit to memory

learn-ing [lûr'nǐng] *noun*, knowledge, education

leash [lēsh] *noun*, a restraining device in the form of a rope or cord, chain or strap

least [lēst] *adjective*, the smallest amount, degree or size

leath-er [lĕth'ər] *noun*, skin of a dead animal prepared for use

leave [lēv] *noun*, 1) permission to be absent, *verb*, 2) to go away from, to depart, to exit 3) to allow something to remain untouched 4) to bequeath

lech-er-ous [lĕch'ər-əs] *adjective*, impure in thought and act, lustful, perverted

lec-tern [lĕk'tərn] *noun*, a podium for public speaking

lec-ture [lĕk'chər] *noun*, 1) a speech on any subject, *verb*, 2) to speak, to talk, to teach

ledge [lĕj] *noun*, a narrow shelf, such as at the bottom of a window, or a narrow, flat piece of rock, on which you can stand

ledg-er [lĕj'ər] *noun*, a book of accounts listing names and debits and credits

left [lĕft] *adjective*, 1) the side of a person or thing that is to the west when facing north, the opposite

of the right side, *verb*, 2) the *past tense* of **leave**

leg [lĕg] *noun*, 1) the body part attached to the foot or paw, used for walking 2) one of at least three pieces on a piece of furniture, used to make it stand

leg-a-cy [lĕg'ə-sē] *noun*, a gift of personal property left in a will

le-gal [lē'gəl] *noun*, based upon or in accordance with law

leg-end [lĕj'ənd] *noun*, 1) a story about someone that has no factual basis 2) a description or key accompanying a map or picture 3) an admirable person

leg-er-de-main [lĕj'ər-də-mān'] *noun*, slight of hand, magic

leg-i-ble [lĕj'ə-bəl] *adjective*, capable of being read with ease

le-gion [lē'jən] *noun*, a large group of soldiers, a multitude of people

leg-is-la-ture [lĕj'ĭ-slā'chər] *noun*, persons in a state elected by the people, having power to make, repeal or change laws

le-git-i-mate [lə-jĭt'ə-mĭt] *adjective*, 1) lawful, conforming to accepted standards 2) genuine

leg-ume [leg'yōōm] *noun*, a plant of the pea family grown as a crop

lei-sure [lē'zhər] *noun*, *no plural*, free time from the demand of work or duty, spare time

lem-ming [lĕm'ĭng] *noun*, a small rat-like animal known for its mass migration into the sea

lem-on [lĕm'ən] *noun*, a yellow citrus fruit with a very sour taste, grown in tropical climates

lem-on-ade [lĕm′ə-nād′] *noun*, a beverage of sweetened lemon juice and water

lend [lĕnd] *verb*, 1) to let someone use something for a while, until they return it 2) to offer help

length [lĕngkth] *noun*, 1) the distance from end to end 2) the amount of time

length-en [lĕngk′thən-] *verb*, to make longer, drawn out

le-ni-ent [lē′nē-ənt] *adjective*, mild, merciful, not strict

lens [lĕnz] *noun*, 1) a piece of curved glass or other transparent material by which light rays meet to form an image 2) a part of the eye that focuses light rays to form an image on the retina

leop-ard [lĕp′ərd] *noun*, one of the big cats with a spotted coat, that weighs 100-175 pounds, is seven feet long and lives in Africa

le-sion [lē′zhən] *noun*, a wound, a sore, diseased tissue

less [lĕs] *adjective*, a smaller amount, a reduction

less-en [lĕs′ən] *verb*, to make smaller, to become less

les-son [lĕs′ən] *noun*, something that must be learned or studied

let [lĕt] *verb*, 1) to allow, to permit, to grant 2) to rent, to lease

le-thal [lē′thəl] *adjective*, deadly

le-thar-gy [lĕth′ər-jē] *noun*, fatigue, without energy, feeling tired, drowsy, sluggish

let's [lĕts] the *contraction* of the words **let** and **us**

let-ter [lĕt′ər] *noun*, 1) a message in writing, often sent through the mail 2) one of the characters of the alphabet

let-tuce [lĕt′əs] *noun*, a plant having succulent leaves that are used in salads

lev-ee [lĕv′ē] *noun*, an embankment, dike, dam

lev-el [lĕv′əl] *adjective*, 1) flat, with no higher or lower places, *noun*, 2) a place or position of a particular height, *verb*, 3) to make a surface flat or even

lev-er [lĕv′ər] *noun*, 1) a bar used to exert pressure or sustain weight 2) a means to an end

lev-i-ty [lĕv′ĭ-tē] *noun*, lightness of mind, high spirits, happiness

le-vy [lĕv′ē] *verb*, to put a judgment on property to collect money, to impose a tax

lewd [lood] *adjective*, obscene, indecent, lecherous, lustful

lex-i-cog-ra-pher [lĕk′sĭ-kŏg′rə-fər] *noun*, a person who writes dictionaries

lex-i-con [lĕk′sĭ-kŏn′] *noun*, a dictionary, a word list

li-a-bil-i-ty [lī′ə-bĭl′ĭ-tē] *noun*, 1) a responsibility, 2) a monetary obligation, a debt

li-a-ble [lī′ə-bəl] *adjective*, 1) legally responsible 2) likely, prone, inclined, apt

li-ai-son [lē′ā-zŏn′] *noun*, cooperation that facilitates a close working relationship between people or organizations

li-ar [lī′ər] *noun*, someone who does not tell the truth

li-bel [lī′bəl] *noun*, 1) a false statement made about someone

lib-er-al [lĭb′ər-əl] *adjective*,
1) progressive reform
2) generous, ample, abundant

lib-er-ate [lĭb′ə-rāt′] *verb*, to free
from constraints, to release

lib-er-a-tion [lĭb′ə-rā′shən] *noun*,
freeing, emancipation

lib-er-ty [lĭb′ər-tē] *noun*, freedom,
independence from foreign rule

li-bi-do [lĭ-bē′dō] *noun*, emotional
urges behind human activity

li-brar-i-an [lī-brâr′ē-ən] *noun*,
one who has charge or care of
the materials in a library

li-brar-y [lī′brĕr′ē] *noun*, 1) a place
where books are kept for reading
and research 2) a room or
building where books and
documents are preserved for
future generations

lib-ret-to [lĭ-brĕt′ō] *noun*, the text
of an opera or other dramatic
musical work

li-cense [lī′səns] *noun*, 1) authority
given to do any act 2) excess of
liberty, *verb*, 3) to authorize

li-cen-tious [lī-sĕn′shəs] *adjective*,
unprincipled, unrestrained

li-chen [lī′kən] *noun*, a fungus that
grows like algae on rocks and
tree bark

lick [lĭk] *noun*, 1) a stroke of the
tongue over something *verb*,
2) to touch with the tongue 3) to
defeat

lic-o-rice [lĭk′ər-ĭs] *noun*, a dried
root, or an extract used in candy

lid [lĭd] *noun*, a cover for a pot or
pan, or some other container

lie [lī] *noun*, 1) the intentional
statement of an untruth, *verb*,
2) to put oneself in a reclining
position 3) to say something that
is not true, to fib

lien [lēn] *noun*, a legal claim upon
real or personal property

lieu [lōō] *preposition*, in place, as
in the phrase "in lieu of"

lieu-ten-ant [lōō-tĕn′ənt] *noun*,
1) a substitute for another in
performance of any duty 2) a
commissioned officer in the
military below captain

life [līf] *noun*, 1) the ability of
living organisms to grow and
reproduce 2) the period between
birth and death

lift [lĭft] *noun*, 1) a free ride in a car
or other form of transportation 2)
the means by which something is
raised, *verb*, 3) to pick up, to
raise, to elevate 4) to go up, to
ascend

lig-a-ment [lĭg′ə-mənt] *noun*, a
tough band of fibrous tissue
connecting bones, or to support
an organ in place in the body

light [līt] *adjective*, 1) buoyant, not
heavy 2) carefree, *noun*, no
plural, 3) the opposite of
darkness, *verb*, 4) to ignite a fire
5) to illuminate, to brighten

light-ning [līt′nĭng] *noun*, no
plural, flashing of light by
electricity discharged from one
cloud to another during a storm

like [līk] *adjective*, 1) similar to,
equal to, *preposition*,
2) resembling, typical of, *verb*,
3) to enjoy, to find agreeable

like-ly [līk′lē] *adjective*,
1) expected, probable, suitable,
adverb, 2) probably, certainly

like-ness [līk′nǐs] *noun*,
1) similarity, resemblance, 2) a
picture of a person, a portrait

like-wise [līk′wīz′] *adverb*, in the
same way, also, similarly

li-lac [lī′lək] *noun*, a shrub in the
olive family that has fragrant
white or purple flowers

lil-li-pu-tian [lǐl′ə-pyōō′shən]
adjective, extremely small

lil-y [lǐl′ē] *noun*, a plant with
trumpet-like flowers and thick
tubular roots

limb [lǐm] *noun*, 1) a part of the
body such as an arm or leg or
wing 2) the large branch of a
tree

lim-ber [lǐm′bər] *adjective*,
flexible, elastic, easy to bend

lim-bo [lǐm′bō] *noun*, 1) a place
near heaven or hell where certain
souls are kept 2) a West Indian
dance 3) a state of oblivion

lime [līm] *noun*, a green citrus
fruit, similar to a lemon, grown
on trees in warm climates

lim-it [lǐm′ǐt] *noun*, 1) that which
terminates or confines 2) the full
extent, *verb*, 3) to set
boundaries, to restrict

lim-i-ta-tion [lǐm′ǐ-tā′shən] *noun*,
shortcomings, restriction

lim-ou-sine [lǐm′ə-zēn′] *noun*, a
long automobile with many seats
and a permanent top

limp [lǐmp] *adjective*, 1) without
stiffness, not firm, *noun*, 2) the
way you walk when one leg is
hurt, *verb*, 3) to walk carefully
without putting too much
pressure on the leg or foot

lim-pid [lǐm′pǐd] *adjective*, crystal
clear, transparent

line [līn] *noun*, 1) the distance
between 2 points 2) people or
things arranged in a row 3) a
business or vocation 4) a streak
made with a pencil and ruler 5) a
collection of points along a straight
path that goes on and on in
opposite directions 6) a boundary
marker 7) dialogue in performance,
verb, 8) to put a layer between the
container and the product 9) to
collect in a row, to watch or wait
for something 10) to draw a thin
mark

lin-en [lǐn′ən] *noun*, a thread or
cloth made of flax

lin-er [lī′nər] *noun*, a first class
passenger ship or airplane

lin-ger [lǐng′gər] *verb*, 1) to stay on
longer than expected, to dawdle
2) to persist

lin-ge-rie [län′zhə-rā′] *noun*, lacey,
silk or cotton underwear worn by
women, undergarments

lin-guis-tic [lǐng-gwǐs′tǐk]
adjective, pertaining to language

lin-i-ment [lǐn′ə-mənt] *noun*, a
liquid applied to soothe the skin

lin-ing [lī′nǐng] *noun*, a fold, an
overlay that forms a covering

link [lǐngk] *noun*, 1) a connection,
a bond, a tie, *verb*, 2) to be
joined together, to unite

li-no-le-um [lǐ-nō′lē-əm] *noun*, a
washable floor covering having
a base of solidified oil on a
canvas foundation

lint [lǐnt] *noun*, dirt, dust, fuzz

li-on [lī′ən] *noun*, one of the big
cats that lives in Africa

lip [lĭp] *noun*, one of the soft red rims round the mouth

liq-uid [lĭk′wĭd] *adjective*, 1) flowing like water, *noun*, 2) fluid, not solid or gas

liq-ui-date [lĭk′wĭ-dāt′] *verb*, to sell possessions for cash

liq-uor [lĭk′ər] *noun*, any liquid substance, an alcoholic beverage

lisp [lĭsp] *noun*, a speech impediment making it difficult to make an **S** sound

list [lĭst] *noun*, 1) names of different things written down one after another, *verb*, 2) to order things by writing them down in a sequence

lis-ten [lĭs′ən] *verb*, to pay attention to what someone is saying, to heed

list-less [lĭst′lĭs] *adjective*, lacking spirit or energy, languid, tired

lit [lĭt] *past tense* of **light**

lit-a-ny [lĭt′n-ē] *noun*, a prayer in the form of a religious song alternating with the congregation

li-ter [lē′tər] *noun*, a unit in the metric system used to measure liquid equal to 1.057 quarts

lit-er-ac-y [lĭt′ə-r′ə-sē] , *noun* the ability to listen, speak, read, write, view, represent, compute, and solve problems at levels of proficiency necessary to function in the family, in the community, and on the job

li-ter-ate:*adjective,* able to read and write

lit-er-al-ly [lĭt′ər-ə-lē] *adverb*, word for word, as stated, verbatim

lit-er-a-ture [lĭt′ər-ə-chŏŏr′] *noun*,

no *plural*, 1) the study of writing and books 2) printed material

lithe [līth] *adjective*, pliable, bendable, limber, supple

lith-i-um [lĭth′ē-əm] *noun*, a soft, silver-white metallic element of the alkali group

lit-i-gant [lĭt′ĭ-gənt] *noun*, a person who wants to sue another

lit-i-ga-tion [lĭt′ĭ-gā′ shən] *noun*, the subject of a lawsuit, any matter before the court or a judge

lit-mus [lĭt′məs] *noun*, a coloring matter obtained from lichens, that is violet-blue, and turns red by an acid, and is restored to blue by an alkali

lit-ter [lĭt′ər] *noun*, 1) newborn baby animals, offspring 2) trash, small pieces of garbage thoughtlessly discarded, *verb*, 3) to throw trash on the ground, not in a garbage can

lit-tle [lĭt′l] *adjective*, 1) a small amount or size 2) a brief period of time

live [līv, lĭv] *adjective*, 1) performed unrehearsed, broadcasted directly 2) full of energy, *verb*, 3) to be, to exist 4) to reside in, to inhabit 5) to be active and to satisfy an ideal

live-li-hood [līv′lē hŏŏd] *noun*, the means of supporting oneself

live-ly [līv′lē] *adverb*, full of energy, very active, full of life

liv-er [lĭv′ər] *noun*, an organ inside the body which cleans the blood

live-stock [līv′stŏk′] *noun*, animals raised on a farm or ranch

liv-id [lĭv′ĭd] *adjective*, 1) angry 2) lead colored, black and blue

liv-ing [lĭv′ĭng] *adjective*, 1) alive, *noun*, 2) a manner of existence

liz-ard [lĭz′ərd] *noun*, a cold blooded reptile with four short legs and a scaly body

lla-ma [lä′mə] *noun*, a South American ruminant animal, related to the camel and raised for its fleecy wool

load [lōd] *noun*, 1) something carried by a person, vehicle or animal 2) a burden, *verb*, 3) to put cargo or materials on a truck or vehicle 4) to fill a gun with ammunition 5) to burden

loaf [lōf] *noun*, 1) the whole amount of bread before it is sliced, *verb*, 2) to take it easy, to idle away time, to waste time

loan [lōn] *noun*, 1) a thing, especially money, lent to another person, *verb*, 2) to let someone borrow something, to lend

loathe [lōth] *verb*, to detest, to feel intense dislike for, to abhor

lob-by [lŏb′ē] *noun*, 1) an entrance way, a foyer, *verb*, 2) to influence, to pressure, to sway

lob-ster [lŏb′stər] *noun*, an edible sea animal with a shell, a tail, and ten legs

lo-cal [lō′kəl] *adjective*, regional, in a confined area or place

lo-cal-i-ty [lō-kăl′ĭ-tē] *noun*, a position, a situation, a place

lo-cate [lō′kāt′] *verb*, to find, to search out, to come across

lo-ca-tion [lō-kā′shən] *noun*, where something is, a certain place

lock [lŏk] *noun*, 1) a device for fastening things like doors that can only be opened or closed with a key or secret code 2) a strand of hair, *verb*, 3) to close and make secure 4) to fasten with a lock

lock-er [lŏk′ər] *noun*, a box often with a lock, for keeping things

lo-co-mo-tive [lō′kə-mō′tĭv] *noun*, a railroad engine that pulls trains

lo-cust [lō′kəst] *noun*, an insect like a grasshopper that travels in swarms and eats plants

lode [lōd] *noun*, vein-like deposit of mineral ore

lodge [lŏj] *noun*, 1) a place to stay where you pay for the service, *verb*, 2) to pay to stay someplace, like a motel or inn 3) to become embedded in something

loft [lôft] *noun*, an upper room, a storage area, an attic

loft-y [lôf′tē] *adjective*, very high

log [lôg, lŏg] *noun*, 1) a piece of wood that was part of the trunk or limb of a tree 2) a book of records, a register of a trip

log-ic [lŏj′ĭk] *noun*, the art of correct reasoning, especially of inference, sound judgment

log-i-cal [lŏj′ĭ-kəl] *adjective*, in a way that is orderly and makes sense, reasonable

lo-go [lō′gō′] *noun*, a slogan or symbol that represents a name

loi-ter [loi′tər] *verb*, to hang around, to linger aimlessly, to proceed slowly, to waste time

loll [lŏl] *verb*, to lounge about

lone [lōn] *adjective*, single, one, standing apart, isolated

lone-li-ness [lōn'lē-nĕs] *noun*, feeling alone, solitude

lone-ly [lōn'lē] *adjective*, 1) a sad, depressing feeling because one is alone 2) desolate, remote

long [lông] *adjective*, 1) measuring a distance from one end to another 2) farther or taller than the others 3) an extended period or time, *adverb*, 4) a time in the distant past 5) conditionally, *verb*, 6) to want something badly, to pine, to yearn

lon-gev-i-ty [lŏn-jĕv'ĭ-tē] *noun*, to live the duration of a long life

long-ing [lông'ĭng] *verb*, desiring, wanting, yearning, craving

lon-gi-tude [lŏń'jĭ-tōōd'] *noun*, *no plural,* imaginary lines shown on maps that go from east to west

look [lōōk] *noun*, 1) a glance, a gaze 2) appearance, *verb*, 3) to stare, or glance at 4) to seem or appear 5) to expect, to await

loom [lōōm] *noun*, 1) a machine used to weave cloth from yarn, *verb*, 2) to hover over 3) likely to will happen in the future

loop [lōōp] *noun*, a ring made by a rope or string crossing itself

loop-hole [lōōp'hōl'] *noun*, a way of getting around a law or legal agreement, a means of escape

loose [lōōs] *adjective*, 1) not fastened tightly or securely 2) free, not confined or shut in

loos-en [lōō'sən] *verb*, to become unfastened, to make less tight

loot [lōōt] *noun*, 1) money or spoils, *verb*, 2) to steal, to rob, to pillage and plunder

lope [lōp] *verb*, to run with long, slow steps, to gallop slowly

lop-sid-ed [lŏp'sī'dĭd] *adjective*, hanging over to one side, uneven

lo-qua-cious[lōkwā'shəs]*adjective*, talkative, chatty, fond of talking

lord [lôrd] *noun*, 1) a person having great power or authority, a master or ruler 2) the title for a judge, bishop, or nobleman

lore [lôr] *noun*, a lesson, a teaching

lose [lōōz] *verb*, 1) to fail to win 2) to misplace something

loss [lôs] *noun*, 1) damage, injury, ruin 2) deprivation

lost [lôst] *adjective*, 1) confused, bewildered, disoriented 2) wasted 3) the *past tense* of **lose**

lot [lŏt] *noun*, 1) a piece of land or property 2) a large quantity of something 3) a kind or sort

lo-tion [lō'shən] *noun*, a liquid put on the skin to add moisture and make it soft or clean

lot-tery [lŏt'ə-rē] *noun*, a game of gambling in which a prize is given to the person with the matching digits drawn from a pool of numbers

lo-tus [lō'təs] *noun*, a water plant with white, yellow, blue or pink flowers, a water lily

loud [loud] *adjective*, 1) noisy, making or having a loud sound 2) offensively bright colors

Lou-i-si-ana [lōō-ē'zē-ăn'ə] *noun*, one of the 50 United States located in the South, the capital is Baton Rouge. The state flower of **Louisiana** is the flower of the magnolia tree, and the motto is "Union, justice, confidence."

lounge [lounj] *noun*, 1) a couch with little or no back 2) a room in a bar where people relax and listen to music, *verb*, 3) to rest or recline comfortably

louse [lous] *noun, plural,* **lice**, a small insect without wings that lives on the skin of animals, birds, and people

lous-y [lou′zē] *adjective*, bad

lov-a-ble [lŭv′ə-bəl] *adjective*, able to be loved, warm, deep feeling

love [lŭv] *noun*, 1) a very strong warm feeling or deep concern for someone, commitment 2) darling, sweetheart, *verb*, 3) to feel passion, or a strong affection for someone or something

love-ly [lŭv′lē] *adjective*, beautiful, having pleasing qualities

lov-ing [lŭv′ĭng] *adjective*, showing affection or fondness

low [lō] *adjective*, 1) close to the ground, not very high 2) quiet, not very loud 3) coarse, mean 4) inferior quality

low-er [lou′ər] *adjective*, 1) inferior 2) less 3) under, *verb*, 4) to make something closer to the ground 5) to diminish the volume of sound 6) to demean, to debase in estimation

loy-al [loi′əl] *adjective*, true and faithful to a person

loy-al-ty [loi′əl-tē] *adjective*, allegiance, faithfulness

lu-bri-cant [loo′brĭ-kənt] *noun*, grease or gear oil

lu-bri-cate [loo′brĭ-kāt′] *verb*, to make smooth or slippery

lu-cent [loo′sənt] *adjective*, glowing with light, shining

lu-cid [loo′sĭd] *adjective*, 1) bright, 2) easily understood, clear

luck [lŭk] *noun*, 1) something good or bad that happens by chance or accident 2) good fortune

luck-y [lŭk′ē] *adjective*, fortunate

lu-cra-tive [loo′krə-tĭv] *adjective*, profitable, money making

lu-cre [loo′kər] *noun*, money

lu-di-crous [loo′dĭ-krəs] *adjective*, funny, ridiculous, absurd

lug-gage [lŭg′ĭj] *noun, no plural*, bags, suitcases, trunks and traveling accessories, baggage

luke-warm [look′wôrm′] *adjective*, not very warm, but not cold, room temperature, tepid

lull [lŭl] *noun*, 1) a quiet interval, a pause, *verb*, 2) to soothe, to calm

lull-a-by [lŭl′ə-bī′] *noun*, a soft song that puts someone to sleep

lum-ba-go [lŭm-bā′gō] *noun*, rheumatic pain in the loins and small of the back

lum-ber [lŭm′bər] *noun*, 1) logs or timber cut into planks or boards, *verb*, 2) to move along slowly and heavily, to plod

lu-mi-nous [loo′mə-nəs] *adjective*, 1) well lit, bright, radiating light 2) glowing in the dark

lump [lŭmp] *noun*, 1) a swelling on the body that becomes a mass 2) a hard form without a special shape or size, *verb*, 3) to put together in a pile

lu-nar [lōō′nər] *adjective*, having to do with the moon

lu-na-tic [lōō′nə-tĭk] *adjective*, 1) crazy, mad, psychotic, *noun*, 2) an insane person

lunch [lŭnch] *noun*, the meal you eat in the middle of the day

lunch-eon [lŭn′chən] *noun*, a midday meal enjoyed with others

lung [lŭng] *noun*, one of the two sac-like organs inside the chest with which we breathe

lunge [lŭnj] *verb*, to leap, to charge at someone suddenly

lu-pine [lōō′pən] *noun*, a plant related to peas and beans with tall spikes of flowers

lure [lōōr] *noun*, 1) something appealing, *verb*, 2) to entice, to bait, to attract, to tempt

lu-rid [lōōr′ĭd] *adjective*, horrible, sensational, shocking, gruesome

lurk [lûrk] *verb*, to wait in hiding, to watch someone without their knowledge, to go furtively

lus-cious [lŭsh′əs] *adjective*, appealing to taste or smell

lust [lŭst] *noun*, 1) a strong feeling of wanting something that would be selfish 2) sexual appetite

lus-ter [lŭs′tər] *noun*, shine, brightness, sheen or gloss

lux-u-ri-ous [lŭg-zhŏŏr′ē-əs] *adjective*, fine and expensive, very nice, sumptuous

lux-u-ry [lŭg′zhə-rē] *noun*, an item that adds to pleasure and comfort

lynch [lĭnch] *verb*, to hang someone in an act of mob violence

lyr-ic [lĭr′ĭk] *noun*, a poem intended to be a song

M

ma-ca-bre [mə-kä′brə] *adjective*, horrible, gruesome, ghastly

mac-a-ro-ni [măk′ə-rō′nē] *noun*, a flour paste dried in long slender tubes, pasta

ma-chet-e [mə-shĕt′ē] *noun*, a long, curved knife used for cutting tall vegetation

mach-i-na-tion [măk′ə-nā′shən] *noun*, a scheme, a plot, or plan

ma-chine [mə-shēn′] *noun*, a device made to consume energy to produce another form of energy to do some kind of work

ma-chin-er-y [mə-shē′nə-rē] *noun*, *no plural*, equipment, devices

mack-er-el [măk′ər-əl] *noun*, a fish found traveling in schools in the North Atlantic

mad [măd] *adjective*, 1) insane, crazy, out of your right mind, reckless 2) angry, enraged

mad-am [măd′əm] *noun*, a respectful way of speaking to or writing to a woman

made [mād] *past tense* of **make**

mad-ri-gal [măd′rĭ-gəl] *noun*, a folk song or ballad of the 16th and 17th century

mael-strom [māl′strəm] *noun*, a powerful whirlpool

maes-tro [mīs′trō] *noun*, an eminent composer, a master

mag-a-zine [măg′ə-zēn′] *noun*, a pamphlet or news summary published periodically

mag-ic [măj′ĭk] *noun, no plural,* 1) the art or pretended art of controlling forces through the use of secret charms 2) clever tricks done to outsmart people, using sleight of hand

mag-i-cal [măj′ĭ-kəl] *adjective*, enchanting, marvelous

ma-gi-cian [mə-jĭsh′ən] *noun*, one who uses tricks to do things that seem impossible

mag-is-trate [măj′ĭ-strāt′] *noun*, a public civil officer charged with administering the law, a justice of the peace

mag-nan-i-mous [măg-năn′ə-məs] *adjective*, great of mind, generous and forgiving

mag-nate [măg′nāt′] *noun*, a person of prominence and influence, a tycoon

mag-ne-si-um [măg-nē′zē-əm] *noun*, a ductile silver-white metallic element

mag-net [măg′nĭt] *noun*, 1) a combination of metals that have a force that attract metals like iron 2) something that attracts

mag-net-ic [măg-nĕt′ĭk] *adjective*, 1) possessing the properties of the magnet 2) exerting a moral attractive force or charm

mag-nif-i-cence [măg-nĭf′ĭ-səns] *adjective*, grandeur, splendor

mag-nif-i-cent [măg-nĭf′ĭ-sənt] *adjective*, wonderful, impressive

mag-ni-fy [măg′nə-fī′] *verb*, to increase the size of what you are looking at, to enlarge

mag-ni-fy-ing glass [măg′nə-fī′ĭng glăs] *noun*, a lens that enlarges something small so that it is easier to see

mag-ni-tude [măg′nĭ-tōōd′] *noun*, great in size, or extent

ma-hog-a-ny [mə-hŏg′ə-nē] *noun*, a hard, reddish wood from tropical American trees

maid [mād] *noun*, a female servant

maid-en name [mād′n-nām] *noun*, a woman's last name before she is married

mail [māl] *noun*, letters and packages sent through and delivered by the postal service

maim [mām] *verb*, to injure so that part of the body is useless

main [mān] *adjective*, chief, most important, the center piece

Maine [mān] *noun*, one of the 50 United States located in New England, the capital is Augusta. The state flower of **Maine** is the eastern white pine cone and tassel, and the motto is "Direct or guide."

main-spring [mān′sprĭng′] *noun*, the principal spring in a mechanism, as in a watch

main-stay [mān′stā′] *noun*, 1) pillar, support 2) strength

main-tain [mān-tān′] *verb*, 1) to hold or keep in any particular condition, to preserve 2) to support, to insist

main-te-nance [mān′tə-nəns] *noun,* *no plural,* support, sustenance, upkeep, preservation

maize [māz] *adjective,* 1) pale yellow, *noun,* 2) corn

ma-jes-ti-cal-ly [mə-jĕs′tĭk-lē] *adverb,* with grandeur and stately dignity, regal

maj-es-ty [măj′ĭ-stē] *noun,* the title of a sovereign power, grandeur

ma-jor [mā′jər] *adjective,* 1) chief, most important, the largest, *noun,* 2) an officer in the military between Lieutenant Colonel and General

ma-jor-i-ty [mə-jôr′ĭ-tē] *noun,* the greater number, more than half

make [māk] *verb,* 1) to create or produce 2) to force 3) to earn or win 4) to appoint or name

mal-aise [mă-lāz′] *noun,* uneasiness, distress, fatigue

mal-a-prop-ism [măl′ə-prŏp-ĭz′əm] *noun,* comic misuse of a word, *i.e., a verbal agreement isn't worth the paper it is written on*

ma-lar-i-a [mə-lâr′ē-ə] *noun,* a disease produced by the bite of a mosquito causing a fever

male [māl] *adjective,* 1) belonging to men and boys, *noun,* 2) a grown boy, masculine, manly

ma-lev-o-lent [mə-lĕv′ə-lənt] *adjective,* wishing evil or harm

mal-ice [măl′ĭs] *noun,* a desire to inflict bad feelings on another

ma-lign [mə-līn′] *verb,* to say bad things about someone

ma-lig-nant [mə-lĭg′nənt] *adjective,* tending or threatening to produce death as a tumor

mall [môl] *noun,* a public walk, a marketplace, a shopping center

mal-le-a-ble [măl′ē-ə-bəl] *adjective,* 1) capable of being extended or shaped by beating with a hammer 2) easy to influence

mal-let [măl′ĭt] *noun,* a stick, a club, a hammer-like tool

mal-nu-tri-tion [măl′nōō-trĭsh′ən] *noun, no plural,* undernourishment caused by poor diet

mam-mal [măm′əl] *noun,* any warm-blooded vertebrate that nurses its young

mam-moth [măm′əth] *adjective,* very large, gigantic, huge

man [măn] *noun, plural,* **men,** 1) a full grown male person 2) speaking of mankind in general *verb,* 3) to supply with people

man-age [măn′ĭj] *verb,* 1) to succeed in getting something done, to reach a goal 2) to control or have power over something 3) to function

man-age-a-ble [măn′-ĭ-jə-bəl] *adjective,* governable, submitting to control

man-age-ment [măn′ĭj-mənt] *noun,* people who manage any enterprise, an administration

man-ag-er [măn′ĭ-jər] *noun,* a person who looks after and directs the activities of a business, a supervisor

man-date [măn′dāt′] *noun,* an order, a command

man-da-to-ry [măn′də-tôr′ē] *adjective,* required, imperative

man-drel [măn′drəl] *noun,* an axis inserted to support something

189

mane [mān] *noun*, the long hair on the back of the neck of an animal, such as a horse or lion

ma-neu-ver [mə-nōō′vər] *noun*, 1) a military movement 2) a scheme or manipulation, *verb*, 3) to move in a skillful way

mange [mānj] *noun*, a contagious skin disease of animals marked by itching and hair loss

man-go [măng′gō] *noun*, a juicy fruit with a large seed that grows on a tree in tropical climates

ma-ni-ac [mā′nē-ăk′] *noun*, a madman, an insane person

man-i-cure [măn′ĭ-kyŏŏr′] *noun*, a grooming of hands and fingernails

man-i-fest [măn′ə-fĕst′] *adjective*, 1) something obvious or clear, *noun*, 2) an invoice of a ship's, or truck's, or plane's cargo, *verb*, 3) to show, to display, to reveal

man-i-fes-to [măn′ə-fĕs′tō] *noun*, a statement of policy and plans

man-i-fold [măn′ə-fōld′] *adjective*, having many and various kinds or features

ma-nip-u-late [mə-nĭp′yə-lāt′] *verb*, 1) to treat or work with the hands 2) to control the action of something by management

man-kind [măn′kīnd′] *noun*, *no plural*, all human beings

man-ner [măn′ər] *noun*, 1) the way in which something is done or happens, prevailing customs *plural*, 2) ways of behaving in social situations

man-or [măn′ər] *noun*, a large house, a mansion,

man-sion [măn′shən] *noun*, a large, impressive house, a castle

man-tel [măn′tl] *noun*, 1) the shelf above a fireplace 2)the earth's interior layer between the crust and the core

man-u-al [măn′yōō-əl] *adjective*, 1) done by hand, *noun*, 2) an instruction guide

man-u-fac-ture [măn′yə-făk′chər] *verb*, to assemble parts into a product in a factory

ma-nure [mə-nŏŏr′] *noun*, livestock excrement

man-u-script [măn′yə-skrĭpt′] *noun*, a copy of a work intended for publication

man-y [měn′ē] *adjective*, containing a large number of something

map [măp] *noun*, 1) a representation of the physical features of the earth, *verb*, 2) to plan, to chart, to outline

ma-ple [mā′pəl] *noun*, a hardwood tree that produces sweet sap, boiled into syrup

mar [mär] *verb*, to damage, to hurt, to disfigure, to impair, to injure

mar-ble [mär′bəl] *noun*, *no plural*, 1) a hard stone that polishes well, used in buildings 2) a small glass or stone ball used in a game

March [märch] *noun*, the third month of the year, having 31 days

march [märch] *noun*, 1) the distance of a walk using regular steps 2) a piece of music to which soldiers walk, *verb*, 3) to walk with measured steps, to advance in this manner

mare [mâr] *noun*, a female horse

mar-ga-rine [mär'jər-ĭn] *noun*, *no plural*, a butter substitute made from vegetable oils

mar-gin [mär'jĭn] *noun*, 1) the border of empty space around the text on paper 2) a deposit of a portion of the value of stocks or bonds

mar-gin-al [mär'jə-nəl] *adjective*, borderline, passable

mar-i-gold [mär'ĭ-gōld'] *noun*, a yellow or orange flower that is a member of the daisy family

ma-rine [mə-rēn'] *noun*, having to do with the sea

mar-i-on-ette [mär'ē-ə-nĕt'] *noun*, a puppet manipulated by strings

mar-i-time [mär'ĭ-tīm'] *adjective*, bordering on the sea, nautical

mark [märk] *noun*, 1) a spot or a scratch, imprint 2) a point or the total of points indicating how one has scored on an examination or in a class 3) a distinguishing feature, *verb*, 4) to indicate a line or boundary 5) to leave a spot or write something 6) to distinguish

mar-ket [mär'kĭt] *noun*, 1) a store, an outlet, a shop 2) supply and demand, commodity market, *verb*, 3) to develop ways to sell a product by making it attractive

mar-ma-lade [mär'mə-lād'] *noun*, a preserve or jam made of the pulp and rind of fruit

ma-roon [mə-rōōn'] *verb*, to leave someone isolated

mar-riage [mär'ĭj] *noun*, a wedding ceremony, the state of being married

mar-row [mär'ō] *noun*, soft tissue filling in cavities of bones

mar-ry [mär'ē] *verb*, to take someone as a husband or wife

marsh [märsh] *noun*, a low, wet place where the ground is damp and swampy, a bog

mar-shal [mär'shəl] *noun*, 1) the master of ceremonies of a parade or an event 2) an officer of justice similar to a sheriff, *verb*, 3) to manage, to direct

mar-su-pi-al [mär-sōō'pē-əl] *noun*, animals that nurse their offspring in a pouch

mar-tial [mär'shəl] *adjective*, pertaining to military affairs, war or battle, inclined to war

mar-tyr [mär'tər] *noun*, one who suffers persecution, torture or death for a cause or beliefs

mar-vel [mär'vəl] *noun*, 1) something that is remarkable or exciting, *verb*, 2) to be filled with wonder or astonishment

mar-vel-ous [mär'və-ləs] *adjective*, astonishing, causing wonder

Mary-land [mĕr'ə-lənd] *noun*, one of the 50 United States located on the East Coast, the capital is Annapolis. The state flower of **Maryland** is the black-eyed susan and the motto is "Manly deeds, womanly words."

mas-cot [măs'kŏt'] *noun*, an animal or person that represents a school, team, or other group

mas-cu-line [măs'kyə-lĭn] *adjective*, of or pertaining to the male sex, manly

mash [măsh] *verb*, to make into a pulpy mass or mush

mask [măsk] *noun*, 1) a covering that hides a face or its expressions *verb*, 2) to disguise or hide, to cover, to conceal

ma-son [mā′sən] *noun*, a person
who builds with brick, stone, etc.

mas-quer-ade [măs′kə-rād′] *noun*,
1) a party at which people wear
masks and sometimes costumes,
verb, 2) to dress in costume, to
wear a disguise, to conceal

mass [măs] *noun*, 1) a quantity or
amount of something with no
particular shape or number
2) the quantity of matter that a
body contains as measured by
the force of gravity on it
3) a large gathering of people
4) in the Catholic church the
celebration of the Eucharist

Mas-sa-chu-setts [măs′ə-chōō′sĭts]
noun, one of the 50 United
States, located on the East
Coast, the capital is Boston. The
state flower of **Massachusetts**
is the mayflower, and the motto
is "By the sword we seek peace,
but peace only under liberty."

mas-sa-cre [măs′ə-kər] *noun*,
1) the killing of many
defenseless people, *verb*, 2) to
murder a large number of people

mas-sage [mə-säzh′] *noun*, 1) a
rubdown, kneading of the body
with the hands, *verb*, 2) to rub to
stimulate circulation, to caress

mas-sive [măs′ĭv] *adjective*, heavy,
weighty, consisting of a large
amount, immense, huge

mast [măst] *noun*, a tall pole that
holds up a ship's sail

mas-ter [măs′tər] *noun*, 1) an
accomplished artist, a teacher,
one in control 2) the title of
address in front of a boy's name,

verb 3) to accomplish a difficult
task

mas-ter-piece [măs′tər-pēs′] *noun*,
a fine example of skill or
excellence

mat [măt] *noun*, 1) a floor covering
made of straw, rubber, vinyl,
etc. 2) a tangled hair mass

match [măch] *noun*, 1) a slender
piece of wood or cardboard
tipped with a flammable mixture
2) a sports contest, 3) a person
or thing equal to another, *verb*,
4) to sort similar objects, to pair
up

mate [māt] *noun*, 1) an associate,
one of a male and female pair of
animals, birds, etc., *verb*, 3) to
bring together a male and
female animal to reproduce

ma-te-ri-al [mə-tîr′ē-əl] *adjective*,
1) pertaining to or composed of
matter 2) of consequence,
substantial, *noun* 3) data 4) cloth,
the fabric something is made of
5) possessions, real things not
spiritual things

ma-te-ri-al-ize [mə-tîr′ē-ə-līz′]
verb, to take form, to emerge

ma-ter-nal [mə-tûr′nəl] *adjective*,
motherly, relating to a mother

ma-ter-ni-ty [mə-tûr′nĭ-tē] *noun*,
motherhood, the time during
pregnancy, or for a mother to
care for a newborn infant

math-e-mat-ics [măth′ə-măt′ĭks]
noun, *plural*, the study of
numbers, arithmetic

ma-tin-ee [măt′n-ā′] *noun*, an
afternoon theater performance

ma-tri-arch [mā′trē-ärk′] *noun*, the
woman who rules a family or
social group, clan or tribe

mat-ri-mo-ny [măt′rə-mō′nē]
noun, marriage, wedlock

ma-trix [mā′trĭks] noun, 1) an
environment from which
something develops or originates
2) a mold or die

mat-ter [măt′ər] noun, no plural,
1) the substance of which
something is made 2) a situation
or affair verb, 3) to be of
importance, to signify

mat-tress [măt′rĭs] noun, a stuffed
cushion to sleep on

ma-ture [mə-tyo͝or′] adjective,
fully grown or developed, adult

ma-tu-ri-ty [mə-tyo͝or′ĭ-tē] noun,
adulthood, full development

maud-lin [môd′lĭn] adjective,
tearfully sentimental

maul [môl] verb, to handle
roughly, to lacerate

mau-so-le-um [mô′sə-lē′əm] noun,
a stately tomb, an above ground
structure for burials

mav-er-ick [măv′ər-ĭk] noun, a
rebel, a nonconformist

max-im [măk′sĭm] noun, a
proverb, wise words

max-i-mum [măk′sə-məm]
adjective, 1) greatest attainable,
most, noun, 2) the largest
amount possible

May [mā] noun, the fifth month of
the year, having 31 days

may [mā] verb, 1) used to show
that something is possible 2) to
be allowed or permitted to 3)
showing a hope that something
will happen

may-be [mā′bē] adverb, perhaps,
possibly

may-hem [mā′hĕm′] noun,
commotion, disturbance

may-on-naise [mā′ə-nāz′] noun, a
dressing for salad or sandwiches,
usually made from eggs and oil

may-or [mā′ər, mâr] noun, the
chief magistrate and leader of a
city or town

me [mē] pronoun, the form of "I"
used as an object, used by a
speaker to refer to himself or
herself

mead-ow [mĕd′ō] noun, a field of
grass or flowers, grassland

mea-ger [mē′gər] adjective, small
in amount, scant

meal [mēl] noun, food served and
eaten, the occasion for eating

mean [mēn] adjective, 1) unkind,
cruel, uncaring 2) the middle,
verb, 3) to be the same as, to
have as a definition 4) to intend
to do something 5) to denote

me-an-der [mē-ăn′dər] verb, to
wander around, to follow a path
with twists and turns

mean-ing [mē′nĭng] noun, 1) the
definition of a word 2) the
significance of an action , signs
or symbols

means [mēnz] noun, plural,
resources that help us to do
what we want to do, wealth

meant [mĕnt]verb, past tense of
mean

mean-while [mēn′hwīl′] adverb,
at the same time

mea-sles [mē′zəlz] noun, plural, a
contagious disease marked by
distinct red circular spots,
accompanied by a fever

meas-ure [mĕzh/ər] *noun*, 1) a standard or test 2) dimension, size, capacity 3) step, action, proceeding, maneuver, *verb*, 4) to take measurements, to gauge, to scale, to calibrate

meas-ure-ment [mĕzh/ər-mənt] *noun*, the size, weight, distance, mass, etc. of something

meat [mēt] *noun*, the parts of an animal's body used as food

me-chan-ic [mĭ-kăn/ĭk] *noun*, 1) one who repairs cars or other machines, 2) *plural,* **mechanics**, the inner workings or things, the study of how machines work

mech-an-ism [mĕk/ə-nĭz/əm] *noun*, 1) the parts of a machine taken collectively 2)any system that works like a machine

med-al [mĕd/l] *noun*, a small, award, often embossed, given for achievement

med-dle [mĕd/l] *verb*, to interfere

me-di-a [mē/dē-ə] *plural*, *noun*, see **medium**

me-di-an [mē/dē-ən] *adjective*, 1) halfway, central, *noun*, 2) the middle, center, mid-point

me-di-ate [mē/dē-āt/] *verb*, to settle a dispute as an impartial third party

med-i-cal [mĕd/ĭ-kəl] *adjective*, healing, therapeutic

me-dic-i-nal [mĭ-dĭs/ə-nəl] *adjective*, having properties that cure disease or sickness

med-i-cine [mĕd/ĭ-sĭn] *noun*, 1) the study and treatment of illness 2) a remedy to treat disease and restore good health

me-di-e-val [mē/dē-ē/vəl] *adjective*, characteristic of the Middle Ages from about the fifth to the fifteenth centuries

me-di-oc-ri-ty [mē/dē-ŏk/rĭ-tē] *noun*, the average, commonplace, ordinary

med-i-tate [mĕd/ĭ-tāt/] *verb*, to think deeply

med-i-ta-tion [mĕd/ĭ-tā/shən] *noun*, deep, solemn reflection

me-di-um [mē/dē-əm] *adjective*, 1) sized between large and small, *noun*, 2) conditions, the environment 3) a means to communicate with the dead *plural*, **media,** 4) a network of communication such as television, radio, newspapers , etc. that reaches the public

med-ley [mĕd/lē] *noun*, a mixture

meek [mēk] *adjective*, humble, gentle, patient, quiet

meet [mēt] *verb*, to come face to face, to approach, to encounter

meet-ing [mē/tĭng] *noun*, 1) a gathering to discuss an issue or idea 2) point of contact

meg-a-phone [mĕg/ə-fōn/] *noun*, a cone or electric device that amplifies the sound of a voice

mel-an-chol-y [mĕl/ən-kŏl/ē] *adjective*, 1) filled with sorrow, very sad, *noun*, 2) a feeling of sadness characterized by depression

mel-low [mĕl/ō] *adjective*, 1) good-natured, relaxed, *verb*, 2) to soften with maturity

mel-o-dy [mĕl/ə-dē] *noun*, a harmonious tune, music

mel-on [mĕl′ən] *noun*, a large juicy fruit growing on vines

melt [mĕlt] *verb*, to change to a liquid state by applying heat

mem-ber [mĕm′bər] *noun*, 1) one of the limbs of the body, such as a leg, árm, hand, etc. 2) a part of a group, a component 3) one that belongs to a certain group

mem-ber-ship [mĕm′bər-shĭp′] *noun*, the state of belonging to a certain group

mem-brane [mĕm′brān′] *noun*, a thin piece or layer of animal or vegetable tissue that serves to cover separate cells, organs, etc.

me-men-to [mə-mĕn′tō] *noun*, a token as a reminder, a souvenir

mem-oir [mĕm′wär′, -wôr′] *noun*, an autobiography

mem-o-ra-ble [mĕm′ər-ə-bəl] *adjective*, worthy of remembrance, remarkable

mem-o-ran-dum [mĕm′ə-răn′dəm] *noun*, a note made as a reminder, a written message, a memo

me-mo-ri-al [mə-môr′ē-əl] *noun*, a monument, a marker, a statue

mem-o-rize [mĕm′ə-rīz′] *verb*, to commit to memory, to learn by heart, to remember exactly

mem-o-ry [mĕm′ə-rē] *noun*, something a person remembers, the ability to remember

men-ace [mĕn′ĭs] *noun*, a danger

me-nag-er-ie [mə-năj′ə-rē] *noun*, a varied group or collection of animals, persons, or things that are strange, odd, or startling

mend [mĕnd] *verb*, 1) to repair or fix, to sew a tear, or patch a hole 2) to heal, to improve, to recover

from illness 3) to set right a dispute

me-ni-al [mē′nē-əl] *adjective*, suitable for servants, low

men-in-gi-tis [mĕn′ĭn-jī′tĭs] *noun*, an infection of the three membranes that envelop the brain and spinal cord, that could be fatal

men-tal [mĕn′tl] *adjective*, of or existing in the mind

men-tal-ly [mĕn′tl-lē] *adverb*, in or using the mind, intellectually

men-tion [mĕn′shən] *noun*, 1) a reference, a notice, *verb*, 2) to remark, to refer to briefly

men-tor [mĕn′tôr′] *noun*, a trusted teacher, a wise counselor

men-u [mĕn′yōō] *noun*, 1) a list indicating the choice of meals at a restaurant 2) a list of options in a computer program

mer-chan-dise [mûr′chən-dīz′] *noun*, 1) commodities, wares, goods, *verb*, 2) to sell, to promote, to market

mer-chant [mûr′chənt] *noun*, a person who buys and sells goods

mer-ci-ful [mûr′sĭ-fəl] *adjective*, compassionate, kind-hearted

mer-ci-less [mûr′sĭ-lĭs] *adjective*, cruel, unkind, showing no compassion, inhumane

mer-cu-ry [mûr′kyŏŏrē] *noun, no plural,* a heavy, silver-white metallic chemical element, liquid at ordinary temperatures

mer-cy [mûr′s *noun*, the act of sparing someone punishment shown to an offender or enemy

mere [mîr] *adjective*, not more than what is specified, only

mere-ly [mîr'lē] *adverb*, simply, hardly, barely

merge [mûrj] *verb*, to combine into one, to blend gradually

me-rid-i-an [mə-rĭd'ē-ən] *noun*, an imaginary great circle on the surface of the earth, passing through the poles and any given place on the earth's surface

mer-it [mĕr'ĭt] *noun*, 1) worth, good qualities, *verb*, 2) to deserve

mer-maid [mûr'mād'] *noun*, a mythical creature that lives in the water, having the head and torso of a woman and the tail of a fish

mer-ry [mĕr'ē] *adjective*, happy, full of laughter, joyful

me-sa [mā'sə] *noun*, a flat-topped hill with steep sides, common in dry areas

mesh [mĕsh] *noun*, 1) a net-like material of cords or wires that interlock with spaces between them, like a screen, *verb*, 2) to blend, to intertwine

mes-mer-ize [mĕz'mə-rīz'] *verb*, to hypnotize, to spellbind

mess [mĕs] *noun*, 1) many things mixed up, a jumble, *verb*, 2) to make something dirty or untidy 3) to make a muddle of

mes-sage [mĕs'ĭj] *noun*, 1) a letter or note 2) a communication transmitted from one person to another 3) a central theme

mes-sen-ger [mĕs'ən-jər] *noun*, one who does an errand, a carrier

mes-sy [mĕs'ē] *adjective*, untidy

met [mĕt] *past tense* of **meet**

me-tab-o-lism [mĭ-tăb'ə-lĭz'əm] *noun*, the chemical and physical changes in living cells that process energy in the body

met-al [mĕt'l] *noun*, 1) a chemical element such as silver or gold, or any combination of metals, such as brass, copper, or nickel

met-al-lic [mə-tăl'ĭk] *adjective*, resembling, pertaining to or consisting of metal

meta-mor-phic [mĕt'ə-môr'fĭk] *adjective*, changed in form

met-a-mor-pho-sis [mĕt'ə-môr'fə-sĭs] *noun*, a change from one form of development or shape into another

met-a-phor [mĕt'ə-fôr'] *noun*, a figure of speech in which one thing is spoken of in terms of another, *i.e., the road was a ribbon of moonlight...*

met-a-phys-ics [mĕt'ə-fĭz'ĭks] *noun*, speculative philosophy

me-te-or [mē'tē-ər'] *noun*, a fragment of solid matter that enters the earth's atmosphere and burns, leaving a bright streak in the sky

me-te-or-ite [mē'tē-ə-rīt'] *noun*, the metallic or stony remains of a body that has entered the earth's atmosphere

me-te-or-ol-o-gist [mē'tē-ə-rŏl'ə-jĭst] *noun*, a person who studies the weather

me-ter [mē'tər] *noun*, 1) a machine used for measuring 2) a measure of length equal to 100 centimeters or approximately 39 inches 3) the rhythm in a poem

meth-od [mĕth′əd] *noun*, a process or system used to do something

me-thod-i-cal [mə-thŏd′ĭ-kəl] *adjective*, systematic, orderly

Me-tho-dist [mə-thŏdĭst] *noun*, a member of the Protestant Christian denomination that developed from the teachings of John and Charles Wesley

me-tic-u-lous [mĭ-tĭk′yə-ləs] *adjective*, extremely careful

met-ric sys-tem *noun*, a system that measures length in centimeters, meters, and kilometers; capacity in liters, mass in grams and kilograms; temperature in degrees Celsius

me-trop-o-lis [mĭ-trŏp′ə-lĭs] *noun*, the chief city of a country, state or region, an urban center

met-tle [mĕt′l] *noun*, courage, spirit, fortitude, character

Mich-i-gan [mĭsh′ĭ-gən] *noun*, one of the 50 United States, located in the North, the capital is Lansing. The state flower of **Michigan** is the apple blossom and the motto is "If you seek a pleasant peninsula, look about you."

mi-cro-cosm [mī′krə-kŏz′əm] *noun*, a small world

mi-cro-or-gan-ism [mī′krō-ôr′gə-nĭz′əm] *noun*, an animal , bacterium, plant, or virus that can only be seen with a microscope

mi-cro-phone [mī′krə-fōn′] *noun*, a device that converts sounds into electrical energy signals that can then be amplified

mi-cro-scope [mī′krə-skōp′] *noun*, an optical instrument with a lens

that makes it possible to see things too small to be seen with the naked eye

mi-cro-scop-ic [mī′krə-skŏp′ĭk] *adjective*, too small to be seen with a naked eye

mid [mĭd] *adjective*, halfway

mid-dle [mĭd′l] *adjective*, 1) halfway between two points, median, central, *noun*, 2) the center, the point equally distant from two sides

mid-get [mĭj′ĭt] *noun*, a small person who is fully mature

mid-night [mĭd′nīt′] *noun*, 12 o'clock at night

midst [mĭdst, mĭtst] *noun*, the middle, the central point

might [mīt] *noun*, no plural, 1) strength or force, *verb*, 2) *past tense* of **may**

might-y [mī′tē] *adjective*, strong, powerful, important, great

mi-grant [mī′grənt] *adjective*, one who travels from place to place in search of work

mi-grate [mī′grāt′] *verb*, 1) to move from one land to settle in another 2) to make a journey each year from one place to another at the same time of year

mi-gra-tion [mī-grā′shən] *noun*, movement to leave one area to live in another

mild [mīld] *adjective*, 1) gentle in feeling 2) not severe or extreme

mile [mīl] *noun*, a measure of length equal to 5,280 feet, 1,760 yards, or 1.6 kilometers

mile-age [mī′lĭj] *noun*, 1) an allowance for the cost per mile traveled 2) the total amount of miles traveled in a given time

mile-stone [mīl′stōn′] *noun*, a turning point, a great achievement or significant event

mil-i-tant [mĭl′ĭ-tənt] *adjective*, 1) warlike, combative, *noun*, 2) a revolutionary, a violent objector, a terrorist

mil-i-tar-y [mĭl′ĭ-tĕr′ē] *noun*, the armed forces of a country

milk [mĭlk] *noun*, 1) the liquid produced by a female mammal to feed her young, *verb*, 2) to force milk from a female mammal

mill [mĭl] *noun*, a building or group of buildings in which resources such as lumber, cotton, corn and steel, are processed

mil-len-ni-um [mə-lĕn′ē-əm] *noun*, a span of one thousand years

mil-li-liter [mĭl′ə-lē′tər] *noun*, a liquid measure equal to 1/1000 of a liter, or less than .04 fluid ounces

mil-li-me-ter [mĭl′ə-mē′tər] *noun*, a measure of length, 1/1000 of a meter, or about .04 inches

mil-lion [mĭl′yən] *noun*, ten times one hundred thousand, 1,000,000

mil-lion-aire [mĭl′yə-nâr′] *noun*, a person whose property and assets total $1,000,000

mime [mīm] *noun*, 1) a performer who only uses motion and facial expression, but no voice, to communicate, *verb*, 2) to use actions instead of speech to communicate

mim-e-o-graph [mĭm′ē-ə-grăf′] *noun*, a stenciling copying device fed by an ink drum

mim-ic [mĭm′ĭk] *verb*, to copy or repeat what someone does or says, to imitate playfully

mim-ic-ry [mĭm′ĭ-krē] *noun*, an imitation, an impersonation

min-a-ret [mĭn′ə-rĕt′] *noun*, a lofty slender tower attached to a mosque

mince [mĭns] *verb*, 1) to cut into very small pieces 2) to moderate or restrain words

mind [mīnd] *noun*, 1) thoughts, a person's reason or way of feeling, *verb*, 2) to watch over, to pay attention to, to obey

mine [mīn] *noun*, 1) a large hole or tunnel deep in the ground made to reach and remove metals or other natural resources from the earth, *pronoun*, 2) something that belongs to the person who is speaking, *verb*, 3) digging into land to remove metal ore or other valuable resources

min-er-al [mĭn′ər-əl] *noun*, any inorganic substance occurring naturally in the earth

min-gle [mĭng′gəl] *verb*, to join or mix together, to blend

min-i-a-ture [mĭn′ē-ə-chŏŏr′] *adjective*, 1) very small, done on a small scale, *noun*, 2) a very small painting, especially a portrait

min-i-mum [mĭn′ə-məm] *adjective*, 1) smallest, *noun*,

2) the least quantity possible or allowable in a given case

min-is-ter [mĭn′ĭ-stər] *noun*,

1) the head of a government department in some countries 2) a representative to a foreign country ranking under an ambassador 3) a Christian member of the clergy, *verb*, 4) to give help to someone, to care for, to serve, to attend

min-is-try [mĭn′ĭ-strē] *noun*, 1) a department of government headed by a minister 2) the work of the clergy 3) the act of serving

Min-ne-so-ta [mĭn′ĭ-sō′tə] *noun*, one of the 50 United States located in the North, the capital is St. Paul. The state flower of **Minnesota**, is the pink and white lady slipper and the motto is,"The star of the north."

min-now [mĭn′ō] *noun*, a small fish

mi-nor [mī′nər] *adjective*,

1) smaller, not very important *noun*, 2) a person younger than the legal age

mi-nor-i-ty [mə-nôr′ĭ-tē] *noun*, a number, part or amount forming less than half of a whole

mint [mĭnt] *noun*, 1) a large amount of money 2) any of the plants of the mint family, used to flavor food, gum, etc. 3) a candy

mi-nus [mī′nəs] *preposition*, less

min-ute [mĭn′ĭt] *adjective*, 1) very small, *noun*, 2) a period of time equal to sixty seconds

mi-nu-ti-a [mĭ-nōō′shē-ə] *noun*, *plural*, **minutiae**, very small, petty details, trifling matters

mir-a-cle [mĭr′ə-kəl] *noun*, an occurrence that is unusual and goes beyond the laws of nature

mi-rac-u-lous [mĭ-răk′yə-ləs] *adjective*, supernatural, awesome, incredible

mi-rage [mĭ-räzh′] *noun*, an unreal reflection, an optical illusion

mire [mīr] *noun*, 1) a bog, a swamp, *verb*, 2) to immerse in swampy ground, to entangle

mir-ror [mĭr′ər] *noun*, 1) a looking glass in which one can see reflections 2) something that reflects

mirth [mûrth] *noun*, laughter, glee

mis-be-have [mĭs′bĭ-hāv′] *verb*, to behave badly, to be disruptive

mis-cel-la-ne-ous [mĭs′ə-lā′nē-əs] *adjective*, consisting of several different kinds, mixed, various

mis-chief [mĭs′chĭf] *noun*, an annoying action on the part of a person, havoc, harm or damage

mis-chie-vous [mĭs′chə-vəs] *adjective*, causing petty injury or annoyance to others

mis-con-cep-tion [mĭs′kən-sĕp′shən] *noun*, a misunderstanding, a mistake

mis-con-duct [mĭs-kŏn′dŭkt] *noun*, wrongdoing, improper behavior

mis-con-strue [mĭs′kən-strōō′] *verb*, to misunderstand

mis-cre-ant [mĭs′krē-ənt] *noun*, an evil person, a lawbreaker

mis-de-mean-or [mĭs′dĭ-mē′nər] *noun*, a crime less than a felony, any minor misdeed

mi-ser [mī′zər] *noun*, a tightwad, one who hoards money mis-er-a-ble [mĭz'ər-ə-bəl] *adjective*, unhappy, causing misery

mis-er-y [mĭz'ə-rē] *noun*, great unhappiness, or distress

mis-for-tune [mĭs-fôr'chən] *noun*, bad luck, something bad that happens, an unlucky event

mis-giv-ing [mĭs-gĭv'ĭng] *noun*, a feeling of worry, doubt about a future event, apprehension

mis-hap [mĭs'hăp'] *noun*, an unfortunate accident

mis-in-ter-pret [mĭs'ĭn-tûr'prĭt] *verb*, to confuse, to mistake

mis-judge [mĭs-jŭj'] *verb*, to mistake, to underestimate

mis-lead [mĭs-lēd'] *verb*, to lead astray, to deceive, to lie

mis-lead-ing [mĭs-lē'dĭng] *adjective*, deceptive, vague, unclear, not accurate

mis-no-mer [mĭs-nō'mər] *noun*, the wrong name, an incorrect identification

mis-place [mĭs-plās'] *verb*, to lose temporarily, to mislay

Miss [mĭs] *noun*, the title before the name of an unmarried woman

miss [mĭs] *noun*, 1) a failure, an error, a slip, *verb*, 2) to fail to make the most of an opportunity or moment 3) to notice someone's absence, to feel sad someone is gone 4) to avoid, to fail to hit, to escape 5) to omit

mis-sile [mĭs'əl] *noun*, a weapon capable of being hurled

mis-sion [mĭsh'ən] *noun*, a special service, task or duty

mis-sion-ar-y [mĭsh'ə-nĕr'ē] *noun*, one whose work is to teach others about his religion

Mis-sis-sip-pi [mĭs'ĭ-sĭp'ē] *noun*, one of the 50 United States, located in the South, the capital is Jackson. The state flower of **Mississippi** is the magnolia blossom, and the motto is "By valor and arms."

mis-sive [mĭs'ĭv] *noun*, a letter

Mis-sou-ri [mĭ-zoor'ē] *noun*, one of the 50 Unieted States, located in the Midwest, the capital is Jefferson City. The state flower of **Missouri** is the hawthorn, and the motto is:"Let the welfare of the people be the supreme law."

mis-spell [mĭs-spĕl'] *verb*, to spell incorrectly

mist [mĭst] *noun*, a thin cloud of fine droplets of water vapor or fog near the ground

mis-take [mĭ-stāk'] *noun*, an error, the wrong answer or action

Mis-ter [mĭs'tər] *noun*, a title for a man, abbreviated, 'Mr.'

mis-tle-toe [mĭs'əl-tō'] *noun*, a plant that lives off another, with evergreen leaves and white berries used at Christmas for decoration

mis-tress [mĭs'trĭs] *noun*, a woman who has control over others

mis-trust [mĭs-trŭst'] *noun*, 1) suspicion, uncertainty, doubt, lack of confidence, *verb*, 2) to doubt, to question, to challenge

mist-y [mĭs'tē] *adjective*, hazy, damp, and foggy, consisting of a mass of fine droplets of water vapor in the atmosphere

mis-un-der-stand [mĭs'-ŭn-dər-stănd'] *verb*, to misconstrue, to mistake

mite [mīt] *noun*, 1) a small amount 2) a small, usually parasitic arachnid, related to the tick

mi-ter [mī'tər] *verb*, to bevel the ends for the purpose of matching together, as a picture frame

mitt [mĭt] *noun*, a baseball glove with padding to protect the hand

mit-ten [mĭt'n] *noun*, a glove with a section for covering the thumb and a larger section to cover all four fingers

mix [mĭks] *verb*, to combine different things to make one

mix-ture [mĭks'chər] *noun*, a combination of different substances

moan [mōn] *verb*, to make a sound of pain or suffering, to complain

mob [mŏb] *noun*, a crowd, a horde

mo-bile [mō'bəl, *adjective* 1) moveable, portable, [mō'-bīl'] *noun*, 2) objects attached by a wire that move airily

mo-bi-lize [mō'bə-līz'] *verb*, to put into action, to move

moc-ca-sin [mŏk'ə-sĭn] *noun*, a heelless shoe of deerskin or other soft leather

mock [mŏk] *adjective*, 1) not real, pretended, 2) *verb*, to make fun of, to treat with ridicule

mode [mōd] *noun*, 1) manner 2) fashion, style

mod-el [mŏd'l] *noun*, 1) a person who sets a good example 2) a version of something that can be studied, a copy, 3) someone who wears clothes for

advertisement, *verb*, 3) to make a copy of something 4) to wear clothes as part of an exhibit

mod-er-a-tion [mŏd'ər-ā'shən] *noun*, restraint, a happy medium

mod-ern [mŏd'ərn] *adjective*, representative of the current trends and fashions

mod-est [mŏd'ĭst] *adjective*, 1) humble, decent 2) simple

mod-es-ty [mŏd'ĭ-stē] *noun, no plural*, humility, decency

mod-i-cum [mŏd'ĭ-kəm] *noun*, a moderate or small amount

mod-i-fi-ca-tion [mŏd'ə-fĭ-kā'shən] *noun*, a slight change in form, an alteration

mod-i-fy [mŏd'ə-fī'] *verb*, to change, to adjust, to alter

mod-u-late [mŏj'ə-lāt'] *verb*, to adjust the sound

mo-gul [mō'gəl] *noun*, a powerful person, especially in business

moist [moist] *adjective*, a little wet, damp, humid, soggy

mois-ture [mois'chər] *noun, no plural*, small drops of water, wetness caused by water

mo-lar [mō'lər] *noun*, one of several back teeth used for chewing

mo-las-ses [mə-lăs'ĭz] *noun*, the thick brown syrup drained from sugar in the refining process

mold [mōld] *noun*, 1) a cast for shapes into which a substance is poured 2) a furry substance that grows on clothing or food if left damp and away from the sun, it is a kind of small fungus, *verb*, 3)

to shape something into a form
or a mold

mold-ing [mōl′dǐng] *noun*, a plane
or curved narrow surface, used
for ornamentation

mole [mōl] *noun*, 1) a small
insectivore that makes and lives
in holes underground 2) a small
round brown mark on the skin

mol-e-cule [mŏl′ǐ-kyool′] *noun*,
1) a unit of matter consisting of
two or more atoms combined
2) a particle

mo-lest [mə-lĕst′] *verb*, 1) to touch
without permission 2) to annoy

molt [mōlt] *verb*, to shed the outer
skin, feathers or exoskeleton

mol-ten [mōl′tən] *adjective*, made
liquid by great heat, melted

mo-ment [mō′mənt] *noun*, a very
brief period of time, an instant

mo-men-tar-y [mō′mən-tĕr′ē]
adjective, fleeting, passing

mo-men-tous [mō-mĕn′təs]
adjective, very important

mo-men-tum [mō-mĕn′təm] *noun*,
the force or speed of movement

mon-arch [mŏn′ərk, -ärk′] *noun*, a
king or queen 2) an orange and
black butterfly

mon-ar-chy [mŏn′ər-kē] *noun*, a
government headed by one
person, a king or a queen

mon-as-ter-y [mŏn′ə-stĕr′ē] *noun*,
a residence in which monks live

Mon-day [mŭn′dē, -dā′] *noun*, the
second day of the week

mon-e-tar-y [mŏn′ǐ-tĕr′ē]
adjective, of or pertaining to
money or currency, pecuniary

mon-ey [mŭn′ē] *noun*, currency
and coins issued by a
government to use in exchange
for goods or services

mon-i-tor [mŏn′ǐ-tər] *noun*, 1) a
pupil or student given authority
2) a video screen attached to a
computer, *verb*, 3) to keep watch
over, to supervise, to check

monk [mŭngk] *noun*, a religious
man who lives with other men
who devote their lives to prayer
and religion, a member of a
religious order

mon-key [mŭng′kē] *noun*, a
primate that usually has a long
tail and lives in trees

mon-o-gram [mŏn′ə-grăm′] *noun*,
initials consisting of two or more
letters interwoven, usually
written, embroidered, or
engraved

mon-o-logue [mŏn′ə-lôg′] *noun*, a
long speech, a soliloquy

mo-nop-o-lize [mə-nŏp′ə-līz′]
verb, to have exclusive
possession of something

mo-nop-o-ly [mə-nŏp′ə-lē] *noun*,
exclusive control of the supply
of any commodity

mon-o-the-ism [mŏn′ə-thē-ĭz′əm]
noun, belief in one God

mon-o-tone [mŏn′ə-tōn′] *noun*, a
voice that never changes in pitch

mo-not-o-nous [mə-nŏt′n-əs]
adjective, 1) unvarying in pitch
2) repetitiously dull, being the
same all the time

mon-soon [mŏn-soon′] *noun*,
heavy rains and strong winds in
southern Asia

mon-ster [mŏn′stər] *noun*, 1) an animal or person with a strange or unusual shape 2) an imaginary and usually frightening creature

Mon-tana [mŏn-tăn′ə] *noun*, one of the 50 United States located in the Northwest, the capital is Helena. The state flower of **Montana** is the bitteroot, and the motto is "Gold and silver."

month [mŭnth] *noun*, a period of 30 days, four weeks, or 1/12 of the year

mon-u-ment [mŏn′yə-mənt] *noun*, a statue or building erected as a tribute to someone who has died

mon-u-men-tal [mŏn′yə-měn′tl] *adjective*, massive, enormous, exceptionally great

mood [mo͞od] *noun*, the way a person feels, state of mind

moon [mo͞on] *noun*, the large body in the sky that shines at night, a satellite of a planet

moose [mo͞os] *noun*, a large North American and Eurasian deer

moot [mo͞ot] *adjective*, questionable, debatable

mop [mŏp] *noun*, 1) a tool with a long handle and a sponge or fabric on the bottom used for cleaning floors, *verb*, 2) to clean the floor, usually with soap and water or to remove spilled liquids

mor-al [môr′əl] *adjective*, ethical, honest, concerned with right conduct, virtuous, upright

mo-rale [mə-răl′] *noun*, spirit, confidence, resolve,

mo-ral-i-ty [mə-răl′ĭ-tē] *noun*, virtue, righteousness, ethics

mor-al-ly [môr′ə-lē] *adverb*, in accordance with ethical duty, righteously, respectfully

mor-a-to-ri-um [môr′ə-tôr′ē-əm] *noun*, 1) a suspension, an interval 2) a legal delay of payment

mor-bid [môr′bĭd] *adjective*, depressing, having to do with disease, gruesome

more [môr] *adjective*, 1) larger in amount or number, *adverb*, 2) again, in addition

mo-res [môr′āz′] *noun, plural*, the customs of a society, the code of acceptable conduct

morgue [môrg] *noun*, a place where dead bodies go to be identified before burial

Mor-mon [môr mŭn] *noun*, a member of the Church of Jesus Christ of Latter-day Saints founded in the U.S. in 1830 by Joseph Smith

morn-ing [môr′nĭng] *noun*, the time from when the sun rises until noon or the time from midnight to noon

mo-rose [mə-rōs′] *adjective*, sad, dejected, gloomy or sullen

mor-phine [môr′fēn′] *noun*, a narcotic derived from opium

morse code [môrs kōd] *noun, no plural*, a way of sending messages using flashing lights or a pattern of sounds

mor-sel [môr′səl] *noun*, a little piece of food, a crumb

mor-tal [môr′tl] *adjective*, 1) destructive to life, fatal 2) human and therefore able to die

mor-tal-i-ty [môr-tăl′ĭ-tē] *noun*, the condition of being mortal

mor-tar [môr′tər] *noun*, 1) a mixture made of cement, lime, sand, and water, used to hold bricks or stone together 2) a short cannon used to fire shells at a high angle 3) a bowl in which substances are crushed to a powder with a pestle

mort-gage [môr′gĭj] *noun*, a legal agreement regarding property between a borrower and a lender

mor-ti-cian [môr-tĭsh′ən] *noun*, an undertaker, a funeral director

mor-ti-fy [môr′tə-fī′] *verb*, to shame, to belittle, to humiliate

mor-tu-ar-y [môr′chōō-ĕr′ē] *noun*, a place where dead bodies are kept until burial or cremation

mo-sa-ic [mō-zā′ĭk] *noun*, a surface decoration made by inlaying small pieces of variously colored material such as tile, marble, or glass

Mos-lem [mŏz′ləm] *noun*, *adjective*, see Muslim

mosque [mŏsk] *noun*, a holy building where Muslims worship

mos-qui-to [mə-skē′tō] *noun*, an insect capable of puncturing the skin of humans and other animals and sucking blood

moss [môs, mŏs] *noun*, a bright green plant that grows flat on wet ground and stones

most [mōst] *adjective*, 1) greatest in amount or number, *adverb*, 2) very, *noun*, 3) the largest amount or number

mote [mōt] *noun*, a small speck

moth [môth] *noun*, an insect with four wings, like a butterfly that flies at night

moth-er [mŭth′ər] *noun*, the female parent

moth-er-in-law [mŭth′ər-ĭn-lô′] *noun*, the mother of one's spouse

mo-tion [mō′shən] *noun*, the action or process of moving

mo-tion-less [mō′shən-lĭs] *adjective*, not moving

mo-ti-vate [mō′tə-vāt′] *verb*, to provide the inner drive that causes one to act

mo-ti-va-tion [mō′tə-vā′shən] *noun*, the feeling that moves one to act

mo-tive [mō′tĭv] *noun*, the reason for doing something, incentive

mo-tor [mō′tər] *noun*, a compact engine that makes things move or work

mo-tor-boat [mō′tər-bōt′] *noun*, a small boat with an engine

mo-tor-cy-cle [mō′tər-sī′kəl] *noun*, a two-wheeled vehicle without a top, moved by a motor

mot-tled [mŏt′ld] *adjective*, spotted with different colors

mot-to [mŏt′ō] *noun*, a saying or catch-phrase that expresses a belief, a guiding principle

mound [mound] *noun*, 1) a heap of earth or a small hill, a knoll 2) any small pile

mount [mount] *noun*, 1) a mountain named after someone, *verb*, 2) to rise 3) to get on 4) to ascend 5) to prepare by putting in place

moun-tain [moun'tən] *noun*, a large hill or raised part of land with steep sides that rises from the earth's surface

mourn [môrn] *verb*, to feel sadness at a loss or death of someone

mourn-ing [môr'nĭng] *noun*, *no plural*, a period of grief to honor someone who died

mouse [mous] *noun*, *plural*, **mice**, 1) a small rodent, similar to a rat 2) a hand-held device that guides the cursor or pointer on a computer

mouth [mouth] *noun*, 1) the opening through which all animals consume food 2) an entry

move [mōōv] *verb*, 1) to change position or cause something to change position 2) to go to live in a new place 3) to affect, to arouse, or influence 3) to budge, to change opionion, to go on

move-ment [mōōv'mənt] *noun*, 1) an inclination, a tendency toward change 2) action, transit, change

mov-ie [mōō'vē] *noun*, a film, a motion picture

mov-ing [mōō'vĭng] *adjective*, touching, emotional

mow [mō] *verb*, to cut grass

Mr. *noun*, a title put before a man's name

Mrs. *noun*, a title put before a married woman's name

Ms. *noun*, a title put before a woman's name

much [mŭch] *adjective*, 1) of a large amount, great. *adverb*, 2) often, to a great degree *noun*, 3) a large amount or a lot of

mucus [myōō'kəs] *noun*, spit, of or relating to mucus, a shiny substance coating the inside of the body cavities

mud [mŭd] *noun*, wet soft earth

mud-dy [mŭd'ē] *adjective*, 1) murky, dirty 2) not clear or pure

muf-fin [mŭf'ĭn] *noun*, a quick bread made from batter and baked in a cup-shaped pan

muf-fle [mŭf'əl] *verb*, to cover or suppress a sound, to tone down

muf-fler [mŭf'lər] *noun*, 1) any of various devices to deaden the noise of escaping gases or vapors 2) a scarf worn around the neck

mug [mŭg] *noun*, 1) a cup with a handle, *verb*, 2) to assault someone, usually to rob them

mug-gy [mŭg'ē] *adjective*, warm and very damp, humid

mulch [mŭlch] *noun*, a protective layer of decomposing organic matter

mule [myōōl] *noun*, an animal whose parents were a female horse and a male donkey

mul-ti-form [mŭl'tə-fôrm'] *adjective*, having many shapes or forms

mul-ti-ple [mŭl'tə-pəl] *adjective*, 1) many 2) having many parts

mul-ti-pli-ca-tion [mŭl'tə-plĭ-kā'shən] *noun*, *no plural*, the process of finding the number or quantity by repeated addition of a specified number

mul-ti-ply [mŭl'tə-plī'] *verb*, to increase by a number of times

mul-ti-tude [mŭl'tĭ-tōōd'] *noun*, a crowd, a large gathering

mum-my [mŭm′ē] *noun*, a dead body preserved with chemicals and wrapped in cloth

mumps [mŭmps] *noun*, *plural*, an illness that causes fever and swelling in the neck and throat

mun-dane [mŭn-dān′] *adjective*, commonplace, worldly as opposed to spiritual

mu-nic-i-pal [myōō-nĭs′ə-pəl] *adjective*, having a local self-government, as in a city or town

mu-ral [myōor′əl] *noun*, a picture painted directly on a wall

mur-der [mûr′dər] *noun*, 1) the act of killing someone, either after first planning to do so or during another crime, such as a robbery, *verb*, 2) to kill a person intentionally

mur-der-er [mûr′dər-ər] *noun*, a person who intends to kill someone and does so

mur-mur [mûr′mər] *verb*, to speak very softly, to whisper

mus-cle [mŭs′əl] *noun*, an organ whose special function is to produce movement

muse [myōoz] *noun*, 1) one's inner voice as a source of creativity, **Muse**, 2) one of the nine Greek goddesses, responsible for art, music, and literature, *verb*, 3) to ponder, to meditate, to think, to reflect

mu-se-um [myōo-zē′əm] *noun*, a building that exhibits a collection of things of interest

mush-room [mŭsh′rōom′] *noun*, a plant that is not green and is a fungus, it usually has a stem with a cap on it

mu-sic [myōo′zĭk] *noun*, the art or science of harmonic sounds

mu-si-cian [myōo-zĭsh′ən] *noun*, one who plays a musical instrument and performs

mus-ket [mŭs′kĭt] *noun*, a gun with a long barrel, used by soldiers before rifles were invented

musk-rat [mŭs′krăt′] *noun*, a rodent that lives in or near water

Mus-lim [mŭz′ləm] *noun*, a follower of the religion that believes in Allah as the one god and the teachings of Muhammed as written in the Koran

must [mŭst] *verb*, 1) used with another verb to show what is necessary or what has to be done 2) showing what is sure or likely

mus-tache [mŭs′tăsh′] *noun*, the hair covering an upper lip

mus-tang [mŭs′tăng′] *noun*, a wild horse of the American plains

mus-tard [mŭs′tərd] *noun*, 1) a plant with yellow flowers and a seed in pods 2) powder or sauce made of ground mustard seed

mu-ta-ble [myōo′tə-bəl] *adjective*, 1) changing in form 2) fickle

mute [myōot] *adjective*, voiceless, speechless, unable to speak

mu-ti-late [myōot′l-āt′] *verb*, to cut off or remove an essential part

mu-ti-nous [myōot′n-əs] *adjective*, unruly, rebellious, insurgent

mu-ti-ny [myōot′n-ē] *noun*, a revolt, a rebellion, an uprising

mu-tual [myōo′chōo-əl] *adjective*, having a common interest

muz-zle [mŭz′əl] *noun*, 1) a fastening on the mouth of an animal to prevent it from biting or eating 2) the open end of a gun from which the bullet comes out when the gun is fired, *verb*, 3) to gag, to silence, to hush, to restrain speech and expression

my [mī] *adjective*, belonging to the person speaking

my-op-ic [mī-ŏp′ĭk] *adjective*, 1) nearsighted 2) self-centered, small minede

myr-i-ad [mĭr′ē-əd] *noun*, a very large number

my-self [mī-sĕlf′] *pronoun*, the same person as the one speaking

mys-ter-y [mĭs′tə-rē] *noun*, something not explained or beyond human comprehension

mys-ti-cal [mĭs′tĭ-kəl] *adjective*, beyond understanding, spiritual

mys-ti-fy [mĭs′tə-fī′] *verb*, to confuse, to puzzle, to bewilder

myth [mĭth] *noun*, 1) a legendary story used to explain nature or religion and often featuring heroes or supernatural beings

my-thol-o-gy [mĭ-thŏl′ə-jē] *noun*, the study of stories and legends

N

nag [năg] *verb*, to pester, to annoy, to bother, to find faults

nail [nāl] *noun*, 1) a piece of pointed metal to be put into wood with a hammer 2) the horny tip on the ends of fingers and toes, *verb*, 3) to fasten with a hammer and nail

na-ive [nä-ēv′] *adjective*, unsophisticated, innocent

na-ked [nā′kĭd] *adjective*, without clothes, uncovered, nude

name [nām] *noun*, 1) a word given to someone or something for identification, *verb*, 2) to decide what someone or something will be called, to specify

name-ly [nām′lē] *adverb*, that is

name-sake [nām′sāk′] *noun*, one having the same name as another one, named after another

nap [năp] *noun*, 1) a short rest 2) a textured surface on fabric

nap-kin [năp′kĭn] *noun*, a piece of cloth or paper used at a meal to keep one's clothes, hands, and mouth clean while eating

nar-cot-ic [när-kŏt′ĭk] *noun*, a drug that relieves pain, blunts the senses and produces sleep

nar-rate [năr′āt′] *verb*, to make known, to tell a story, to recount

nar-ra-tive [năr′ə-tĭv] *noun*, a story, a history, a recital

nar-ra-tor [năr′āt′ ər] *noun*, a person who relates a story

nar-row [năr′ō] *adjective*, limited in width, breadth, or scope

na-sal [nā′zəl] *adjective*, associated with the nose

nas-cent [năs′ənt] *adjective*, coming into existence, the beginning

na-tion [nā′shən] *noun*, a group of people living in a particular territory under the same government, a federation

na-tion-al [năsh′ə-nəl] *adjective*, of or pertaining to a country or territory

na-tion-al-i-ty [năsh′ə-năl′ĭ-tē] *noun*, the identification of a person based on the country where he or she was born or holds citizenship

na-tive [nā′tĭv] *adjective*, 1) belonging to the place where a person is born, indigenous, *noun*, 2) a person born and raised in a certain place

nat-u-ral [năch′ər-əl] *adjective*, 1) produced by nature, not man-made 2) inborn, an innate ability

nat-u-ral-ly [năch′ər-ə-lē] *adverb*, as one would expect

na-ture [nā′chər] *noun*, *no plural*, 1) that which is not man-made, the physical world 2) traits characteristic of someone, disposition, personality

nau-se-a [nô′zē-ə] *noun*, 1) a stomach sickness accompanied by a desire to vomit 2) disgust

nau-se-ate [nô′zē-āt′] *verb*, to cause to become sick, to fill with disgust, causing a sick feeling

nau-ti-cal [nô′tĭ-kəl] *adjective*, having to do with the sea

na-val [nā′vəl] *adjective*, seafaring, nautical, relating to the navy

na-vel [nā′vəl] *noun*, the belly button, where the umbilical cord was attached before birth

nav-i-gate [năv′ĭ-gāt′] *verb*, to control in which direction a vehicle will go on a route

nav-i-ga-tion [năv′ĭ-gā′shən] *noun*, *no plural*, the ability to travel through water or plan and follow a specific route

nav-i-ga-tor [năv′ĭ-gā′tər] *noun*, one who directs and controls the course of a vehicle

na-vy [nā′vē] *noun*, the officers and personnel of warships

near [nîr] *adverb*, 1) a short distance away, *preposition*, 2) close to

near-by [nîr′bī′] *adverb*, close at hand, not far away

near-ly [nîr′lē] *adverb*, almost

near-sight-ed [nîr′sī′tĭd] *adjective*, able to see only things close by

neat [nēt] *adjective*, clean and orderly, well arranged

Ne-bras-ka [nə-brăs′kə] *noun*, one of the 50 United States, centrally located west of the Missouri River, the capital is Lincoln. The state flower of **Nebraska** is the goldenrod, and the motto is "Equality before the law."

nec-es-sar-y [něs′ĭ-sĕr′ē] *adjective*, needing to be done, essential

ne-ces-si-tate [nə-sĕs′ĭ-tāt′] *verb*, to demand, to require

ne-ces-si-ty [nə-sĕs′ĭ-tē] *noun*, 1) something indispensable or necessary 2) an urgent matter

neck [něk] *noun*, 1) the part of the body connecting the head and the torso 2) a narrow connecting part, as of a bottle

neck-lace [něk′lĭs] *noun*, jewelry worn around the neck

nec-tar [něk′tər] *noun*, a sweet liquid made by flowers

need [nēd] *noun*, 1) a lack, *verb*, 2) to lack something that is necessary or essential 3) must

nee-dle [nēd′l] *noun*, an instrument for sewing, made of steel, sharp at one end, with an eyehole for thread at the other end

need-y [nē′dē] *adjective*, poor, penniless, impoverished

neg-a-tive [nĕg′ə-tĭv] *adjective*, 1) expressing denial, refusal or resistance, not positive, *noun*, 2) an image on developed film

ne-glect [nĭ-glĕkt′] *noun, no plural*, 1) disregard, carelessness, lack of care or attention, *verb*, 2) to not look after something, letting it deteriorate, to ignore

neg-li-gence [nĕg′lĭ-jəns] *noun*, failure to give the care the occasion demands

neg-li-gi-ble [nĕg′lĭ-jə-bəl] *adjective*, very small, insignificant

ne-go-ti-a-ble [nĭ-gō′shə-bəl] *adjective*, 1) transferable or able to be assigned to another person 2) able to be compromised about, open to discussion

ne-go-ti-ate [nĭ-gō′shē-āt′] *verb*, to settle, to work out, to deal or bargain with others, to compromise

Ne-gro [nē′grō] *noun*, a member of the human species having black or brown skin color

neigh-bor [nā′bər] *noun*, a person who lives near another

neigh-bor-hood [nā′bər-hŏod′] *noun*, a small part of a community shared by a group of people who live near each other

nei-ther [nē′thər] *adjective*, *pronoun*, 1) not the one nor the other, *conjunction*, 2) not either

ne-on [nē′ŏn′] *noun*, an inert gaseous element often used in display lights

neph-ew [nĕf′yoo] *noun*, the son of a brother or a sister

nep-o-tism [nĕp′ə-tĭz′əm] *noun*, favoritism to a relative in a business situation

nerve [nûrv] *noun*, a thread in the body that carries feelings and messages to and from the brain

nerv-ous [nûr′vəs] *adjective*, very worried and a little scared

nest [nĕst] *noun*, a temporary home built by an animal or insect

nes-tle [nĕs′əl] *verb*, to be very close to someone else in a comfortable way

net [nĕt] *noun* 1) a fabric made of tying threads together in a uniform design to form a mesh 2) remaining income after deducting taxes and expenses

net-tle [nĕt′l] *noun*, 1) a weed with small thorns, *verb*, 2) to annoy, to bother, to irritate, to vex

neu-rot-ic [noo-rŏt′ĭk] *adjective*, suffering from a mental disorder characterized by anxiety and worry and phobias

neu-ter [noo′tər] *verb*, to make sterile, to spay or castrate

neu-tral [noo′trəl] *adjective*, 1) neither positive nor negative 2) not on either side during a war 3) in the middle 4) a position in which gears are not engaged

neu-tron [noo′trŏn′] *noun*, an uncharged particle in an atomic nucleus

Ne-va-da [nə-văd/ə] *noun*, one of the 50 United States, located in the West, the capital is Carson City. The state flower of **Nevada** is the sagebrush, and the motto is "All for our country."

nev-er [něv/ər] *adverb*, not at any time, absolutely not

nev-er-the-less [něv/ər-thə-lěs/] *adverb*, notwithstanding, in spite of that, yet, however

new [nōō] *adjective*, 1) not having been seen or used before 2) additional

New Hampshire [nōō hămp/shər] *noun*, one of the 50 United States located in New England, the capital is Concord. The state flower of **New Hampshire** is the purple lilac, the motto is "Live free or die."

New Jersey [nōō, jûr/zē] *noun*, one of the 50 United States located in the East, the capital is Trenton. The state flower of **New Jersey** is the purple violet and the motto is "Liberty and prosperity."

New Mexico [nōō měk/sĭ-kō/] *noun*, one of the 50 United States, located in the Southwest, the capital is Santa Fe. The state flower of **New Mexico** is the yucca and the motto is "It grows as it goes."

news [nōōz] *noun, plural*, a report of current events, things that happened recently

news-pa-per [nōōz/pā/pər] *noun*, a publication that appears daily or weekly, containing recent information

New York [nōō yôrk] *noun*, one of the 50 United States located in the Northeast, the capital is Albany. The state flower of **New York** is the rose and the motto is "Excelsior", which expresses the idea of still higher, ever upward.

next [někst] *adverb*, 1) in the nearest position, without anything between 2) immediately following

nib-ble [nĭb/əl] *verb*, to eat small bites of something

nice [nīs] *adjective*, 1) kind, good 2) pleasant, socially agreeable

niche [nĭch] *noun*, 1) a small, suitable place 2) the position of a particular population in an ecological community

nick-el [nĭk/əl] *noun*, 1) five cents, equal to five pennies 2) a hard, silvery metallic element of the iron group

nick-name [nĭk/nām/] *noun*, a name given to someone which is not his real name

nic-o-tine [nĭk/ə-tēn/] *noun*, a toxic alkaloid, the addictive property of tobacco

niece [nēs] *noun*, the daughter of one's brother or sister

nig-gard-ly [nĭg/ərd-lē] *adjective*, meanly stingy, meager

night [nīt] *noun*, the time of day after the sun goes down

night-mare [nīt/mâr/] *noun*, a terrifying dream or event

nine [nīn] *adjective, noun*, the number 9, eight plus one

nine-teen [nīn-tēn′] *noun*, nine plus ten, written 19

nine-teenth [nīn-tēnth′]*adjective*, the number 19 in order, 19th

nine-ti-eth [nīn′tē-ĭth] *adjective*, the number ninety in order, 90th

nine-ty [nīn′tē] *noun*, written 90, 9 X 10

ninth [nīnth] *noun, adjective*, number 9 in order, 9th

nip-ple [nĭp′əl] *noun*, 1) the tip of the breast where the milk ducts discharge 2) the rubber cap on a baby bottle

nir-va-na [nîr-vä′nə] *noun*, in Buddhist teachings, the ideal state, freedom from pain and worry, perfect bliss

ni-tro-gen [nī′trə-jən] *noun*, a gas necessary for life that is colorless, tasteless and odorless

no [nō] *adjective*, 1) not any, *adverb*, 2) a word we use to answer a question, or indicate disagreement

no-bil-i-ty [nō-bĭl′ĭ-tē] *adjective*, a member of the royal circle

no-ble [nō′bəl] *adjective*, 1) aristocratic, born to wealth 2) unselfish, of good character

no-bod-y [nō′bŏd′ē] *pronoun*, no one, a person of no importance

noc-tur-nal [nŏk-tûr′nəl] *adjective*, active or functioning at night

nod [nŏd] *noun*, 1) an inclination of the head, *verb*, 2) to tip the head slightly to acknowledge something

noise [noiz] *noun*, 1) a loud harsh sound, 2) sound of any kind

no-mad [nō′măd′] *noun*, a person who travels about with a tribe and has no address or home

nom-i-nate [nŏm′ə-nāt′] *verb*, to name for an office or place

nom-i-na-tion [nŏm′ə-nā′shən] *noun*, to submit a name for an award or appointment

nom-i-nee [nŏm′ə-nē′] *noun*, a person selected or appointed to run for a position

non-cha-lant [nŏn′shə-länt′] *adjective*, showing a jaunty coolness, aloof, unconcerned

none [nŭn] *adjective*, not any, nothing, no one, not one

non-ex-ist-ent [nŏn′ĭg-zĭs′tənt] *adjective*, not real

non-fic-tion [nŏn-fĭk′shən] *noun*, a true story

non-sense [nŏn′sĕns′] *noun*, folly, silliness, absurdity, meaningless

noon [nōōn] *noun*, midday, twelve o'clock, daytime

nor [nôr; nər when unstressed] *conjunction*, a word used between two choices after neither

nor-mal [nôr′məl] *adjective*, not unusual, common, every day

nor-mal-ly [nôr′mə-lē] *adverb*, generally, ordinarily, frequently

north [nôrth] *adjective*, 1) facing or coming from the north, *adverb*, 2) to or toward the north *noun*, 3) the direction to the left of one facing east, the compass point opposite to south, **North**, 4) regions or countries north of a point that is mentioned or understood

North America [nôrth-ə-mĕr′ĭ-kə]
noun, one of the seven continents
containing 7.9% of the world's
population

North Carolina [nôrth kăr′ə-lī′nə]
noun, one of the 50 United States
located in the Southeast, the
capital is Raleigh. The state flower
of **North Carolina** is the
dogwood, the state motto is"To be
rather than to seem."

North Dakota [nôrth də-kō′tə]
noun, a state located in the
Northwest of the United States,
the capital is Bismark. The state
flower of **North Dakota** is the
wild prairie rose, and the state
motto is "Liberty and union,
now and forever, one and
inseparable."

north-east [nôrth-ēst′] *noun,* the
point between north and east on
a compass

north-west [nôrth-wĕst′] *noun,* the
point between north and west on
the compass

nose [nōz] *noun,* 1) the part of the
face that contains the nostrils
and the organs of smell 2) the
front of a plane, rocket, etc.

nose-gay [nōz′gā′] *noun,* a small
hand-held fragrant bouquet

nos-tal-gia [nŏ-stăl′jə] *noun,*
homesickness, a sentimental
longing for something in the past

nos-tril [nŏs′trəl] *noun,* either of
the external openings of the nose

not [nŏt] *adverb,* a word that forms
a contradiction in a sentence

no-ta-ble [nō′tə-bəl] *adjective,*
remarkable, worthy of notice

no-ta-ry [nō′tə-rē] *noun,* an officer
who witnesses and verifies
commercial papers and is
authorized to take affidavits

no-to-ri-ous [nō-tôr′ē-əs]
adjective, widely or commonly
known, usually unfavorable

not-with-stand-ing
[nŏt′wĭth-stăn′dĭng] despite,
although, nevertheless

no-ta-tion [nō-tā′shən] *noun,* notes
or marks to indicate something

notch [nŏch] *noun,* 1) a nick, a
dent, *verb,* 2) to make a notch

note [nōt] *noun,* 1) an observation
stuck in the mind 2) a bill, IOU,
paper money 3) a single sound
of music on the scale 4) a brief
written message, *verb,* 5) to
make an observation and commit
it to memory 6) to mention

noth-ing [nŭth′ĭng] *adjective,* not
anything, zero, insignificant

no-tice [nō′tĭs] *noun,* 1) a written
warning indicating that
something has happened or will
happen, *verb,* 2) to observe, to
become aware of

no-tice-a-ble [nō′tĭ-sə-bəl]
adjective, capable of being
observed, conspicuous

no-ti-fi-ca-tion [nō′tə-fĭ-kā′shən]
noun, to inform someone of
something, to give notice

no-ti-fy [nō′tə-fī′] *verb,* to let
someone know, to inform

no-tion [nō′shən] *noun,* a general or
vague idea, a thought, a whim

no-to-ri-e-ty [nō′tə-rī′ĭ-tē] *noun,*
fame, renown, celebrity status

noun [*noun*] *noun*, a word that refers to a person, place, or thing

nour-ish [nûr′ĭsh] *verb*, 1) to feed or foster the growth of something 2) to keep healthy, to nurture, to strengthen

nour-ish-ment [nûr′ĭsh-mənt] *noun*, food that strengthens the body and helps it grow

nov-el [nŏv′əl] *adjective*, 1) new, unusual, *noun*, 2) a work of fiction or romance

nov-el-ist [nŏv′ə-lĭst] *noun*, a person who writes fictional stories

nov-el-ty [nŏv′əl-tē] *noun*, something new

No-vem-ber [nō-vĕm′bər] *noun*, the eleventh month of the year, having 30 days

nov-ice [nŏv′ĭs] *noun*, 1) a beginner 2) a person admitted to a religious order before taking the final vows

now [nou] *adverb*, at the present time, immediately

no-where [nō′hwâr′] *adverb*, 1) not anywhere, *noun*, 2) a place that does not exist

nox-ious [nŏk′shəs] *adjective*, harmful, deadly fumes

noz-zle [nŏz′əl] *noun*, a short outlet or pipe as of a hose, a spout

nu-ance [nōō′äns′] *noun*, a shade or trace of differences in meaning, or color, or tone

nu-cle-ar [nōō′klē-ər] *adjective*, using the very great power made by splitting an atom or joining atoms in nuclear fission

nu-cle-us [nōō′klē-əs] *noun*, 1) a central mass of an atom about which matter is concentrated 2) the seed of the cell is the

positively charged central region of an atom

nude [nōōd] *adjective*, naked, bare

nudge [nŭj] *noun*, 1) a gentle push, *verb*, 2) to push someone lightly

nug-get [nŭg′ĭt] *noun*, a small lump, especially of natural gold

nui-sance [nōō′səns] *noun*, anything which annoys or gives trouble, a disturbance

nul-li-fy [nŭl′ə-fī′] *adjective*, to render invalid or void

numb [nŭm] *adjective*, 1) insensitive from excessive cold 2) unable to feel pain

num-ber [nŭm′bər] *noun*, 1) a symbol representing a quantity 2) abundance, *verb*, 3) to identify with a number 4) to amount to

nu-mer-al [nōō′mər-əl] *noun*, a symbol used to represent a number

nu-mer-ous [nōō′mər-əs] *adjective*, very many, myriad, several

nun [nŭn] *noun*, a woman who gives her life to serving God

nup-tial [nŭp′shəl] *adjective*, marriage vows, a wedding

nurse [nûrs] *noun*, 1) a person who takes care of the sick and dying, *verb*, 2) to look after and attend to the needs of the sick

nurs-er-y [nûr′sə-rē] *noun*, 1) a child's room or playroom 2) a greenhouse for young plants

nur-ture [nûr′chər] *verb*, to care for, to feed and protect

nut [nŭt] *noun*, 1) the edible kernel of a seed 2) a small piece of metal with a hole in it, used to hold a bolt in place

nut-meg [nŭt′mĕg′] *noun*, the aromatic seed of an East Indian tree used as a spice

nu-tri-ent [nōō′trē-ənt] *noun*, vitamins and minerals derived from food, proteins

nu-tri-tion [nōō-trĭsh′ən] *noun*, a healthy diet, that nourishes the body

nu-tri-tious [nōō-trĭsh′əs] *adjective*, wholesome, healthy

ny-lon [nī′lŏn′] *noun*, a strong man-made elastic thread

nymph [nĭmf] *noun*, 1) the young of an insect that has not fully developed the structural proportions and size of an adult 2) a fairy

O

oaf [ōf] *noun*, a clumsy person

oak [ōk] *noun*, a tree of hard wood bearing the acorn as a fruit

oar [ôr, ōr] *noun*, a paddle with a flat blade at the end, used to row or push a boat

o-a-sis [ō-ā′sĭs] *noun*, a fertile spot in a desert having a spring

oat [ōt] *noun*, a member of the cereal family having edible seeds such as rice, wheat or corn

oath [ōth] *noun*, a promise, a commitment, a solemn appeal

o-be-di-ence [ō-bē′dē-əns] *noun*, *no plural*, compliance with authority, submission

o-be-di-ent [ō-bē′dē-ənt] *adjective*, willing to do what one is told to do

ob-e-lisk [ŏb′ə-lĭsk] *noun*, a tall 4-sided column tapering and ending in a pyramid apex

o-bese [ō-bēs′] *adjective*, very fat

o-bey [ō-bā′] *verb*, to follow or carry out an order or law

ob-fus-cate [ŏb′fə-skāt′] *verb*, to confuse, to muddle, to obscure

o-bit-u-ar-y [ō-bĭch′ōō-ĕr′ē] *noun*, an announcement of someone's death often with a short biography

ob-ject [ŏb′jĭkt] *noun*, 1) a thing, *verb*, 2) to oppose, to disagree

ob-jec-tion [əb-jĕk′shən] *noun*, a statement, a complaint

ob-jec-tive [əb-jĕk′tĭv] *adjective*, 1) not influenced by emotions, fair, *noun*, 2) a purpose or goal

ob-jur-gate [ŏb′jər-gāt′] *verb*, to scold, to rebuke severely

ob-li-ga-tion [ŏb′lĭ-gā′shən] *noun*, 1) the binding power of a promise 2) a debt of gratitude

ob-lig-a-to-ry [ə-blĭg′ə-tôr′ē] *adjective*, necessary, binding in law or conscience, mandatory

o-blige [ə-blīj′] *verb*, 1) to put under obligation, to accommodate 2) to do a favor for, to help, to assist

o-blique [ō-blēk′] *adjective*, 1) sloping or slanting 2) indirect or evasive, not explicit

ob-lit-er-ate [ə-blĭt′ə-rāt′] *verb*, to erase or blot out, to efface

ob-liv-i-on [ə-blĭv′ē-ən] *noun*, being utterly forgotten

ob-liv-i-ous [ə-blĭv′ē-əs] *adjective*, forgetful, lost in thought

ob-long [ŏb′lông′] *adjective*, a flat shape with four straight sides and four equal angles, that is longer than it is wide

ob-nox-ious [ŏb-nŏk/shəs]
adjective, annoying, offensive

ob-scure [ŏb-skyo͝or/] *adjective*,
1) unclear, vague, unknown
2) not easily seen or heard
3) dark, hidden

ob-scu-ri-ty [ŏb-skyo͝or/ĭ-tē] *noun*,
oblivion, no where

ob-se-qui-ous [ŏb-sē/kwē-əs]
adjective, submissive, fawning

ob-ser-vance [əb-zûr/vəns] *noun*,
1) noticing with attention 2)
compliance as a duty or custom

ob-ser-va-tion [ŏb/zər-vā/shən]
noun, the noting and recording
of facts and events

ob-serv-a-to-ry [əb-zûr/və-tôr/ē]
noun, a building equipped with
instruments for observing the
heavenly bodies, such as the
stars, moon, etc.

ob-serve [əb-zûrv/] *verb*, 1) to see
or notice 2) to comment 3) to
mark an event or day

ob-ses-sion [əb-sĕsh/ən, ŏb-] *noun*,
a fixed idea, continued brooding

ob-so-lete [ŏb/sə-lēt/] *adjective*, no
longer in use, outdated

ob-sta-cle [ŏb/stə-kəl] *noun*,
something that stands in the
way, an obstruction

ob-ste-tri-cian [ŏb/stĭ-trĭsh/ən]
noun, a physician specializing in
the delivery of babies

ob-sti-nate [ŏb/stə-nĭt] *adjective*,
not yielding to reason, stubborn

ob-struct [əb-strŭkt/] *verb*, to get
in the way of something or stop
it completely, to hinder

ob-struc-tion [əb-strŭk/shən] *noun*,
a barrier, an interference

ob-tain [əb-tān/] *verb*, to acquire or
win through effort or request

ob-tain-a-ble [əb-tān/ə-bəl]
adjective, capable of being
acquired or won

ob-trude [ŏb-tro͞od/] *verb*, 1) to get
in on, to meddle, 2) to stick out

ob-tuse [ŏb-to͞os/] *adjective*, an
angle greater than 90 degrees

ob-vi-ous [ŏb/vē-əs] *adjective*,
easily seen or understood,
evident, apparent to everyone

ob-vi-ous-ly [ŏb/vē-əs-lē] *adverb*,
apparently, clearly, evidently

oc-ca-sion [ə-kā/zhən] *noun*, 1) an
event, a happening, an important
time 2) a chance, an opportunity

oc-cas-ion-al-ly [ə-kā/zhə-nə-lē]
adverb, once in a while

oc-cult [ə-kŭlt/] *adjective*, the
mysterious, secret, supernatural

oc-cu-pant [ŏk/yə-pənt] *noun*, the
inhabitant, a resident, a tenant

oc-cu-pa-tion [ŏk/yə-pā/shən]
noun, 1) a job, a way of using
time, *no plural*, 2) being in a
certain place or space

oc-cu-py [ŏk/yə-pī/] *verb*, 1) to
make or hold possession of
something 2) to live in a place

oc-cur [ə-kûr/] *verb*, 1) to happen
2) to come to mind, to appear

oc-cur-rence [ə-kûr/əns] *noun*,
something that happens

o-cean [ō/shən] *noun*, a body of
salt water covering three fifths of
the earth

o-cea-nog-ra-phy [ō/shə-nŏg/rə-fē]
noun, the study of life in the sea

o'clock [ə-klŏk/] *adverb*, according to the clock

Oc-to-ber [ŏk-tō/bər] *noun*, the tenth month of the year having 31 days

oc-to-pus [ŏk/tə-pəs] *noun*, a sea creature that has eight long limbs

oc-u-list [ŏk/yə-lĭst] *noun*, a doctor who treats the eyes

odd [ŏd] *adjective*, 1) any number that cannot be evenly divided by two 2) unusual, very different

odds [ŏdz] *noun*, *plural*, uncertain advantages, doubtful chances

odi-ous [ō/dē-əs] *adjective*, hateful, repulsive, repugnant

odi-um [ō/dē-əm] *noun*, repugnance, intense hatred

o-dom-e-ter [ō-dŏm/ĭ-tər] *noun*, a device in a vehicle used to measure distance traveled

o-dor [ō/dər] *noun*, a smell

o-dor-ous [ō/dər-əs] *adjective*, having a strong smell

of [ŭv] *preposition*, 1) belonging to 2) from among 3) made from 4) about 5) in relation to

off [ôf] *adverb*, 1) away from 2) not on or not working, *preposition*, 3) at a distance

of-fend [ə-fĕnd/] *verb*, to hurt someone's feelings, to insult

of-fense [ə-fĕns/] *noun*, a misdeed, an insult, a sense of insult or injury, an act of aggression

of-fen-sive [ə-fĕn/sĭv] *adjective*, 1) insulting, in poor taste, *noun*, 2) the position of an attack

of-fer [ô/fər] *noun*, 1) a proposal, a suggestion, *verb*, 2) to present to be accepted or refused

of-fice [ô/fĭs] *noun*, 1) a place in which business or professional work is done 2) a position that requires certain duties and tasks

of-fi-cer [ô/fĭ-sər] *noun*, a person lawfully invested with a position of trust or authority

of-fi-cial [ə-fĭsh/əl] *adjective*, 1) having the right or permission to do something, *noun*, 2) a person who is in charge of something 3) of or pertaining to the holding of an office

of-fi-ci-ate [ə-fĭsh/ē-āt/] *verb*, to act as an officer in performing a duty such as a minister

off-spring [ôf/sprĭng/] *noun*, descendants, children, progeny

of-ten [ô/fən] *adverb*, many times, frequently, repeatedly

o-ha-na [ōhŏna] *noun*, family, no one left behind

Ohio [ō-hī/ō] *noun*, one of the 50 United States located in the Midwest region, the capital is Columbus. The state flower of **Ohio** is the scarlet carnation and the motto is "With God all things are possible."

ohm [ōm] *noun*, the unit of electrical resistance

oil [oil] *noun*, 1) any liquid substance that does not dissolve in water 2) a nutrient derived from a pressed nut 3) a dark, thick mineral liquid, found deep in the ground 4) a substance used to burn in a lantern or lamp post, *verb*, 5) to lubricate with grease or oil

oint-ment [oint'mənt] *noun*, a lubricant put on the skin, containing medicine

Okla-ho-ma [ō'klə-hō'mə] *noun*, one of the 50 United States located in the Southwest, the capital is Oklahoma City. The state flower of **Oklahoma** is the mistletoe, and the motto is "Labor conquers all things."

old [ōld] *adjective*, 1) not young, having lived a long time 2) the word we use to show our age 3) not new 4) something that has lasted over time, antique

ol-fac-to-ry [ŏl-făk'tə-rē] *adjective*, referring to the nose and the sense of smell

ol-i-gar-chy [ŏl'ĭ-gär'kē] *noun*, a government run by a few leaders

ol-ive [ŏl'ĭv] *noun*, the fruit of an olive tree eaten as a relish

om-i-nous [ŏm'ə-nəs] *adjective*, looking or sounding as if something bad will happen, portending evil or harm

o-mis-sion [ō-mĭsh'ən] *noun*, failure to do something, something that is left out

o-mit [ō-mĭt'] *verb*, to leave something out, to fail to include

om-e-lette [ŏm'ə-lĭt] *noun*, eggs beaten together and cooked in hot fat in a flat pan

om-nip-o-tent [ŏm-nĭp'ə-tənt] *adjective*, having power over all

om-ni-pres-ent [ŏm'nĭ-prĕz'ənt] *adjective*, universally present at the same time, everywhere

om-nis-cient [ŏm-nĭsh'ənt] *adjective*, all-knowing

om-ni-vore [ŏm'nə-vôr'] *noun*, an animal that eats both plants and animals

on [ŏn] *adverb*, 1) to be precise 2) a location 3) to show time or date 4) about 5) to continue, *preposition*, 6) atop

once [wŭns] *adverb*, 1) one time 2) a long time ago

one [wŭn] *adjective*, 1) the number 1 2) the same, unified 3) act as the same, *noun*, 4) a single thing 5) any person 6) a unit

one-self [wŭn-sĕlf'] *pronoun*, the same person who is the subject of the sentence

on-ion [ŭn'yən] *noun*, a garden vegetable having an edible bulb with pungent taste and odor

on-ly [ōn'lē] *adjective*, 1) sole, no one else, nothing more, 2) but, *adverb*, 3) merely, just

on-o-mat-o-poe-ia [ŏn'ə-măt'ə-pē'ə] *noun*, a term used to describe words that actually sound like the noises they depict such as *boom*

on-slaught [ŏn'slôt'] *noun*, a vicious assault, a massacre

on-to [ŏn'tōō'] *preposition*, to a place, to a position on

o-nus [ō'nəs] *noun*, 1) a burden 2) a responsibility, blame

on-ward [ŏn'wərd] *adverb*, moving toward a point ahead, forward

ooze [ōōz] *verb*, to flow out slowly

o-pal [ō'pəl] *noun*, a precious stone of milky hue, with a play of iridescent colors

o-paque [ō-pāk′] *adjective*, not reflecting or giving out light, not transparent; dull, dark

o-pen [ō′pən] *adjective*, 1) not shut or covered 2) ready for business 3) not surrounded by other things 4) unbiased, free thinking, *verb*, 5) to allow entrance 6) to start, to unfold 7) to remove the cover or door 8) to undo, to untie

o-pe-ra [ŏp′ər-ə] *noun*, a dramatic presentation set to music

op-er-ate [ŏp′ə-rāt′] *verb*, to make something work or function

op-er-a-tion [ŏp′ə-rā′shən] *noun*, 1) any methodical action 2) a plan put into action 3) surgery

op-er-a-tor [ŏp′ə-rā′tər] *noun*, one who operates equipment or works as a manager

o-pi-ate [ō′pē-ĭt] *noun*, a drug which causes rest or sleep, a narcotic or sedative

o-pin-ion [ə-pĭn′yən] *noun*, a belief stronger than an impression, a point of view, a conclusion

o-pos-sum [ə-pŏs′əm] *noun*, a rodent that sleeps upside down hanging from a tree during the day, and travels at night

op-po-nent [ə-pō′nənt] *noun*, a member of the other team, an antagonist, an adversary

op-por-tune [ŏp′ər-tōōn′] *adjective*, timely, well chosen

op-por-tun-ist [ŏp′ər-tōō′nĭst] *noun*, an individual who takes advantage of a situation and ignores ethics to achieve a goal

op-por-tu-ni-ty [ŏp′ər-tōō′nĭ-tē] *noun*, a fit or convenient time, occasion, a good chance

op-pose [ə-pōz′] *verb*, to go against, to defend, to combat, to object, to resist, to fight

op-po-site [ŏp′ə-zĭt] *adjective*, 1) facing, set over against 2) one that is contrary to another

op-po-si-tion [ŏp′ə-zĭsh′ən] *noun*, against, hostile or contrary action, a negative response

op-press [ə-prĕs′] *verb*, to overpower, to subdue, to treat harshly, to hold down

op-pres-sion [ə-prĕsh′ən] *noun*, hardship, cruelty, persecution

op-pres-sive [ə-prĕs′ĭv] *adjective*, 1) unreasonably burdensome 2) tyrannical, cruel, unfair

op-tic [ŏp′tĭk] *adjective*, pertaining to the eye, light and vision

op-ti-cal [ŏp′tĭ-kəl] *adjective*, visual, seeing

op-ti-cian [ŏp-tĭsh′ən] *noun*, a person who makes glasses, a dealer in optical goods

op-ti-mal [ŏp′tə-məl] *adjective*, most favorable condition

op-ti-mist [ŏp′tə-mĭst] *noun*, one who looks on the bright side of things, positive thinking

op-ti-mis-tic [ŏp′tə-mĭs-tĭk] *adjective*, having a positive outlook, upbeat, hopeful

op-tion [ŏp′shən] *noun*, 1) a choice 2) a stock available at a certain time at a stated price

op-tom-e-trist [ŏp-tŏm′ĭ-trĭst] *noun*, one who examines eyes and fits glasses to help a person see better

op-u-lence [ŏp′yə-ləns] *adjective*, having property, wealthy, rich, affluent, luxurious

o-pus [ō′pəs] *noun*, a great creative literary or musical work

or [ôr;] *conjunction*, used to connect words when given a choice

o-ral [ôr′əl] *adjective*, 1) spoken information 2) of the mouth

or-ange [ôr′ĭnj] *adjective*, 1) a color made when red and yellow are mixed together, *noun*, 2) a sweet, juicy fruit grown on trees in tropical climates

or-a-tor [ôr′ə-tər] *noun*, a public speaker of great eloquence

or-a-to-ri-o [ôr′ə-tôr′ē-ō′] *noun*, a dramatic poem set to music

or-a-to-ry [ôr′ə-tôr′ē] *noun*, a moving or powerful speech

or-bit [ôr′bĭt] *noun*, 1) the course an object follows in space around another, *verb*, 2) to travel through space in a cycle

or-chard [ôr′chərd] *noun*, a grove where fruit trees grow for food

or-ches-tra [ôr′kĭ-strə] *noun*, 1) a band of performers on various instruments 2) the lower floor in a theater for instruments

or-chid [ôr′kĭd] *noun*, an exotic tropical flower with three petals

or-dain [ôr-dān′] *verb*, to appoint, to install, to elect, to decree

or-deal [ôr-dēl′] *noun*, an extremely stressful situation

or-der [ôr′dər] *noun*, 1) a careful arrangement 2) a special system used to organize information 3) grouping, placement 4) a request telling someone to do something, *verb*, 5) to arrange carefully 6) to issue a command, to instruct

or-di-nal num-ber [ôr′dn-əl-nŭm′bər] *noun*, a number expressing degree or order in a series such as 1ˢᵗ, 2ⁿᵈ,

or-di-nance [ôr′dn-əns] *noun*, 1) a local law, an edict or decree 2) a prescribed practice or usage

or-di-nar-i-ly [ôr′dn-âr′ə-lē] *adverb*, usually, generally

or-di-nar-y [ôr′dn-ĕr′ē] *adjective*, 1) according to custom or established order 2) regular, commonplace, normal

ore [ôr, ōr] *noun*, a kind of rock in which metal is found

Or-e-gon [ôr′ĭ-gən] *noun*, one of the 50 United States in the Northwest, the capital is Salem. The state flower of **Oregon** is the Oregon grape, and the motto is "The Union."

or-gan [ôr′gən] *noun*, 1) a musical instrument similar to a piano, with long pipes through which air travels through to make the sound 2) a part of the body that serves a specific function

or-gan-ic [ôr-găn′ĭk] *adjective*, grown naturally without pesticides or fertilizers

or-gan-ism [ôr′gə-nĭz′əm] *noun*, any individual life form

or-gan-i-za-tion [ôr′gə-nĭ-zā′shən] *noun*, an association, a group of people working together for a common purpose

or-gan-ize [ôr′gə-nīz′] *verb*, 1) to plan, to arrange and implement in an orderly way 2) to establish or construct a plan or a scheme

o-ri-en-tal [ôr′ē-ĕn′tl] *adjective*, pertaining to the Orient or East Asia

o-ri-en-ta-tion [ôr'ē-ĕn-tā'shən]
noun, the act of getting your
bearings, an introduction

or-i-fice [ôr'ə-fĭs] *noun*, a
mouthlike opening, a slit, any
hole in a body

or-i-gin [ôr'ə-jĭn] *noun*, the first
use or the beginning

o-rig-i-nal [ə-rĭj'ə-nəl] *adjective*,
the first of its kind, new and
different, inventive

o-rig-i-nal-i-ty [ə-rĭj'ə-năl'ĭ-tē]
noun, creativeness, innovation

o-rig-i-nate [ə-rĭj'ə-nāt'] *verb*, 1) to
bring into existence, to initiate
2) to produce as new

or-na-ment [ôr'nə-mənt] *noun*, a
decoration, beautification

or-na-men-tal [ôr'nə-mĕn'tl]
adjective, decorative, adorned,
beautiful, embellished

or-nate [ôr-nāt'] *adjective*,
excessively decorated, adorned

or-ni-thol-o-gist [ôr'nə-thŏl'ə-jĭst]
noun, one who studies birds

or-phan [ôr'fən] *noun*, a child
whose parents are dead

or-phan-age [ôr'fə-nĭj] *noun*, a
home for children who have no
family

or-tho-dox [ôr'thə-dŏks']
adjective, accepted, traditional
doctrine, very conservative

or-thog-ra-phy [ôr-thŏg'rə-fē]
noun, correct spelling

os-cil-late [ŏs'ə-lāt'] *verb*, 1) to
swing backward and forward, to
vibrate 2) varying above or
below a mean value

os-si-fy [ŏs'ə-fī'] *verb*, 1) to change
or harden cartilage into bone
2) to set into a repeating pattern

os-ten-si-ble [ŏ-stĕn'sə-bəl]
adjective, shown, professed,
apparent, pretended

os-ten-ta-tious [ŏs'tĕn-tā'shəs]
adjective, pretentious,
conspicuous, showiness as an
attempt to attract attention

os-tra-cize [ŏs'trə-sīz'] *verb*, to
banish, to cast out from social
favor or fellowship

os-trich [ŏs'trĭch] *noun*, a very
large bird, with long legs, that is
black and white, and cannot fly

oth-er [ŭth'ər] *adjective*, 1) not the
same, a different one, *adverb*,
2) differently, *pronoun*,
3) someone or something not
mentioned specifically

oth-er-wise [ŭth'ər-wīz'] *adverb*,
1) if not 2) except for that
3) of a different kind

ought [ôt] *verb*, should

ounce [ouns] *noun*, 1) a weight
measurement equal to 28.35
grams 2) a tiny bit

our [our] *adjective*, belonging to us

our-selves [our-sĕlvz'] *pronoun*,
referring to the subjects in a
sentence, we or us

oust [oust] *verb*, to dismiss, to kick
out, to expel, to force out

out [out] *adverb*, 1) not in or
inside, away from 2) absent,
away 3) not shining or burning
4) to bring to a conclusion
5) excluded, omitted

out-cast [out'kăst'] *noun*, a
displaced person, an exile

out-come [out′kŭm′] *noun*, a possible result as in an experiment, a final product

out-doors [out-dôrz′, -dōrz′] *adjective*, not inside a building, located outside in the open air

out-doors-man [out-dôrz′mən, -dōrz′-] *noun*, a person who enjoys nature and outdoor activities

out-er [ou′tər] *adjective*, on the outside or edge of something

out-fit [out′fĭt′] *noun*, 1) clothing used for a particular purpose, *verb*, 2) to provide clothes or equipment

out-grow [out-grō′] *verb*, to change as one develops

out-growth [out′grōth′] *noun*, development, product

out-ing [ou′tĭng] *noun*, a short trip

out-let [out′lĕt′, -lĭt] *noun*, 1) an opening, 2) manufacturer

out-line [out′līn′] *noun*, 1) a line showing the shape of something 2) the plan or format for a composition, *verb*, 3) to give the main points of

out-live [out-lĭv′] *verb*, to outlast, to live or last longer than

out-rage [out′rāj′] *noun*, 1) anger caused by injury or insult 2) anything that causes resentment or anger, a wicked or brutal act or remark *verb*, 2) to fill with anger of resentment

out-side [out-sīd′] *adverb,* 1) on or to the exterior surface, *noun*, 2) the outer part or surface

out-stand-ing [out-stăn′dĭng] *adjective,* 1) very good, excellent 2) not paid or settled

o-val [ō′vəl] *adjective*, a round flat shape like an egg

ov-en [ŭv′ən] *noun*, an electric appliance like a sealed box used to bake food

o-ver [ō′vər] *adjective*, 1) in control of 2) finished, *adverb*, 3) from start to finish again 4) unused, extra 5) to go beyond the top, *preposition*, 6) covering 7) across, from one side to the other 8) in every part

o-ver-all [ō′vər-ôl′] *adjective*, including all things, as a whole

o-ver-alls [ō′vər-ôlz′] *noun*, a kind of loose trousers with a bib

o-ver-board [ō′vər-bôrd′] *adverb*, over the side of a boat into the water

o-ver-cast [ō′vər-kăst′] *adjective*, cloudy, sunless, gloomy

o-ver-coat [ō′vər-kōt′] *noun*, a coat worn over the other clothing

o-ver-come [ō′vər-kŭm′] *verb*, to beat, to conquer, to lick

o-ver-due [ō′vər-dōō′] *adjective*, delinquent, late, past due

o-ver-es-ti-mate [ō′vər-ĕs′tə-māt′] *verb*, to calculate over the actual amount

o-ver-flow [ō′vər-flō′] *verb*, 1) to pour over the edge of a container when filled 2) to flood

o-ver-haul [ō′vər-hôl′] *verb*, to restore, to repair, to rebuild

o-ver-head [ō′vər-hĕd′] *adjective*, 1) above our heads, in the sky, *noun, no plural*, 2) the fixed costs to maintain something

o-ver-lap [ō′vər-lăp′] *verb*, 1) to rest on top of or over something

and cover part of it 2) to
partially coincide

o-ver-look [ō′vər-lŏŏk′] *verb*, 1) to
fail to notice 2) to excuse

o-ver-night [ō′vər-nīt′] *adjective*,
1) from one day to the next,
adverb, 2) during the night

o-ver-seas [ō′vər-sēz′] *adjective*,
across the ocean, abroad

o-ver-seer [ō′vər-sē′ər] *noun*, one
who watches over an area or
institution, a supervisor

o-ver-sight [ō′vər-sīt′] *noun*, an
error, a blunder, a failure

o-vert [ō-vûrt′] *adjective*, open to
view, not concealed

o-ver-take [ō′vər-tāk′] *verb*, to
chase and catch up to

o-ver-ture [ō′vər-chŏŏr′] *noun*, a
proposal, an introduction

o-ver-whelm [ō′vər-hwĕlm′] *verb*,
1) to overpower in mind and
feeling 2) to engulf, to inundate

owe [ō] *verb*, 1) to have to give or
pay 2) to feel grateful to
someone for something

owl [oul] *noun*, a large bird that
lives in the forest, it flies at night
and eats small animals

own [ōn] *adjective*, 1) of or
belonging to oneself or itself,
verb, 2) to have or possess

own-er [ō′nər] *noun*, the person
who has the right to something

own-er-ship [ō′nər-shĭp′] *noun*, a
right of possession, a lawful
claim or title

ox [ŏks] *noun, plural*, **oxen**,
a full-grown male of domestic
cattle used for farm work

ox-i-dize [ŏk′sĭ-dīz′] *verb*, to
combine with oxygen

ox-y-gen [ŏk′sĭ-jən] *noun*, a
colorless, tasteless, odorless,
chemically active gas, the part of
air that animals, plants and
people need to stay alive

oys-ter [oi′stər] *noun*, an edible
shellfish, a bivalve mollusk

o-zone [ō′zōn′] *noun*, a faintly blue
gas obtained by the silent
discharge of electricity in air

P

pace [pās] *noun*, 1) a steady step or
speed that is maintained, *verb*,
2) to walk back and forth

pach-y-derm [păk′ĭ-dûrm′] *noun*, a
thick-skinned animal

pac-i-fist [pə-sĭf′ĭ-st] *noun*,
someone who looks for peaceful
means, opposed to force

pac-i-fy [păs′ə-fī′] *verb*, to
appease, to calm, to soothe

pack [păk] *noun*, 1) a bundle or a
collection of things 2) a group of
wild animals that hunt together,
verb, 3) to bundle or place a
group of things into a container

pack-age [păk′ĭj] *noun*, a box or
bundle containing one or more
objects

pact [păkt] *noun*, an agreement, a
contract, a treaty, a bargain

pad [păd] *noun*, 1) a soft material
used to protect a wound 2) a
number of sheets of paper stuck
together at one edge

pad-dle [păd′l] *noun*, 1) an ore or
long stick used to row a boat,

verb, 2) to spank, to whack on the bottom 3) to row a boat 4) to move the hands and feet in shallow water

pad-dock [păd′ək] *noun*, a field or enclosure where horses are kept

pad-dy [păd′ē] *noun*, a field for growing rice

pad-lock [păd′lŏk′] *noun*, a portable lock, jointed at one end

page [pāj] *noun*, 1) one side of a piece of paper in a book 2) a person who delivers messages *verb*, 2) to summon or call indirectly through an intercom or paging system

pag-eant [păj′ənt] *noun*, an exhibition, a show, a parade

paid [pād] *verb*, the *past tense* of **pay**

pail [pāl] *noun*, a bucket or container with a handle

pain [pān] *noun*, physical suffering from injury or illness, distress

pain-ful [pān′fəl] *adjective*, a feeling of hurt, aching

paint [pănt] *noun*, 1) a liquid in a variety of colors that is used to cover a surface to protect or decorate it, *verb*, 2) to coat or color with paint 3) to convey an image by creating it using paints

paint-er [pān′tər] *noun*, a person who paints pictures or buildings

paint-ing [pān′tĭng] *noun*, completed pictures done with paint, a representation

pair [pâr] *noun*, 1) two like things put together as a match 2) an instrument with two parts joined together, e.g. *scissors*, *verb*, 3) to separate into groups of two

pa-ja-mas [pə-jä′mə] *noun, plural*, loose fitting clothes worn to bed

pal [păl] *noun*, a friend, chum

pal-ace [păl′ĭs] *noun*, a beautiful home of a wealthy person

pal-at-a-ble [păl′ə-tə-bəl] *adjective*, 1) tasty 2) acceptable to the mind, pleasing

pa-la-tial [pə-lā′shəl] *adjective*, suitable for a palace, impressively spacious

pale [pāl] *adjective*, 1) light in color, faded, *noun*, 2) the area enclosed by a boundary

pal-ette [păl′ĭt] *noun*, a board on which a painter mixes paints

pal-i-sade [păl′ĭ-sād′] *noun*, a partition formed as a barrier

pal-lid: [păl′id] *adjective,* pale

palm [päm] *noun*, 1) a tree with a long trunk without branches and large leaves at the top 2) the wide part inside the hand

pal-pa-ble [păl′pə-bəl] *adjective*, 1) capable of being touched or felt, obvious 2) tangible

pal-pi-tate [păl′pĭ-tāt′] *verb*, to throb, to pound with emotion or exertion, to quiver, to shake

pal-try [pôl′trē] *adjective*, insignificant, petty, trifling

pam-per [păm′pər] *verb*, to coddle, to indulge, to baby, to spoil

pam-phlet [păm′flĭt] *noun*, a book of a few sheets of printed matter

pan [păn] *noun*, a round metal pot for cooking things over heat

pan-a-ce-a [păn′ə-sē′ə] *noun*, a solution to all problems or sickness, a cure-all

pan-cre-as [păng′krē-əs] *noun*, a large gland under and behind the stomach that secretes insulin to the intestine to help digest food

pan-da [păn′də] *noun*, a large black and white animal like a bear restricted to China

pan-de-mo-ni-um [păn′də-mō′nē-əm] *noun*, a wild tumult, an uproar, confusion

pan-der [păn′dər] *verb*, to cater to the low desires of others

pane [pān] *noun*, a piece of glass used in windows or doors

pan-el [păn′əl] *noun*, 1) a sunken compartment with raised margins in a ceiling 2) a complete jury 3) a group assembled to judge a contest or conduct a public discussion

pan-ic [păn′ĭk] *noun*, 1) a sudden fear which can spread quickly, *verb*, 2) to feel frightened or alarmed, filled with terror

pan-sy [păn′zē] *noun*, a flower that blooms through the winter

pant [pănt] *verb*, to breathe quickly

pan-ther [păn′thər] *noun*, one of the large wild cats, a cougar

pan-to-mime [păn′tə-mīm′] *noun*, a play in which actors use gestures without speech

pan-try [păn′trē] *noun*, a small room where food is stored

pants [pănts] *noun, plural*, trousers

pa-pa [pä′pə] *noun*, a father, a dad

pa-per [pā′pər] *noun*, 1) sheets of thin material used for writing, wrapping, etc. 2) a newspaper 3) paper with writing or printing on it verifying identity

pap-ri-ka [pă-prē′kə] *noun*, a Turkish red pepper

pa-py-rus [pə-pī′rəs] *noun*, a reed plant that grows in the Nile Valley once used as paper

par [pär] *noun*, average, standard, the norm, equality in value

par-a-ble [păr′ə-bəl] *noun*, a short, simple story teaching a lesson

par-a-chute [păr′ə-shōōt′] *noun*, 1) a light device made of silk or nylon, designed in an umbrella shape, used to retard the free fall from an aircraft, *verb*, 2) to eject from an aircraft by jumping out equipped with a parachute used to slow something's fall to the ground from a great height

pa-rade [pə-rād′] *noun*, 1) a number of people walking or marching together, a public procession, *verb*, 2) to walk or march with a group of people

par-a-digm [păr′ə-dīm′] *noun*, a model, an example, a pattern

par-a-dise [păr′ə-dīs′] *noun*, a place of complete happiness or beauty, like heaven

par-a-dox [păr′ə-dŏks′] *noun*, a statement that contradicts itself, but is in fact true

par-af-fin [păr′ə-fĭn] *noun*, a white wax used to make candles and seal preserves

par-a-gon [păr′ə-gŏn′] *noun*, a model of perfection

par-a-graph [păr′ə-grăf′] *noun*, a subdivision in writing, beginning with an indent on a new line

par-a-keet [păr′ə-kēt′] *noun*, a small blue or green domestic song bird

par-al-lel [păr′ə-lĕl′] *adjective*,
1) lying in the same direction and
always the same distance apart,
never intersecting 2)similar

par-al-lel-o-gram
[păr′ə-lĕl′ə-grăm′] *noun*, a four
sided plane figure with opposite
sides equal and parallel

pa-ral-y-sis [pə-răl′ĭ-sĭs] *adjective*,
loss of sensation and motion of
body parts, a helpless state

par-a-lyze [păr′ə-līz′] *verb*, to
destroy the energy of something,
to stop all movement or feeling

pa-ram-e-ter [pə-răm′ĭ-tər] *noun*,
the limit, a set standard

par-a-mount [păr′ə-mount′]
adjective, most important

par-a-noi-a [păr′ə-noi′ə] *noun*,
insanity marked by delusions of
persecution or glory

par-a-phrase [păr′ə-frāz′] *verb*, to
restate a passage in one's own
words for clarity

par-a-site [păr′ə-sīt′] *noun*, animal
or plant living off another, using
it as its only source of food

par-cel [păr′səl] *noun*, 1) a package
wrapped in paper, for mailing or
carrying, *verb*, 2) to divide into
portions to hand out

parch [pärch] *verb*, to dry in the
sun, to dehydrate, to scorch

parch-ment [pärch′mənt] *noun*, the
skin of a goat or sheep prepared
for writing

par-don [pär′dn] *noun*, *no plural*,
1) forgiveness, *verb*, 2) to
excuse, to forgive, to absolve

par-don-a-ble [pär′dn-ə-bəl]
adjective, excusable, forgivable

pare [pâr] *verb*, 1) to peel, to cut
off the outer edge, 2) to reduce

par-ent [pâr′ənt] *noun*, 1) the
father or mother 2) the source

pa-ren-the-sis [pə-rĕn′thĭ-sĭs]
noun, one of the curved lines
which enclose an aside ( )

par-ish [păr′ĭsh] *noun*, an area
served by one church

park [pärk] *noun*, 1) a place in
town designated for recreation,
rest, and beauty, *verb*, 2) to put a
car or vehicle in place

par-ka [pär′kə] *noun*, a heavy
winter coat with a hood

par-ley [pär′lē] *noun*, a conference
between two opponents, a
discussion to settle a dispute

par-lia-ment [pär′lə-mənt] *noun*, an
assembly in Great Britain similar
to the United States Congress

par-lor [pär′lər] *noun*, a room that
is usually used for talking or
entertaining, a living room

pa-ro-chi-al [pə-rō′kē-əl]
adjective, of or pertaining to a
parish, a local area

par-o-dy [păr′ə-dē] *noun*, a
humorous imitation, satire

pa-role [pə-rōl′] *noun*, an early
conditional release from prison,
free on probation

par-rot [păr′ət] *noun*, a brightly
colored bird with a short curved
beak that can mimic speech

par-si-mo-ny [pär′sə-mō′nē] *noun*,
selfishness, stinginess

pars-ley [pär′slē] *noun*, an herb
with flat or curled leaves used to
flavor soups, etc., or to garnish
food

par-snip [pär′snĭp] *noun*, a fleshy white root, in the carrot group

part [pärt] *noun*, 1) some of a thing or things 2) a share in an activity 3) a character in a play or film, *verb*, 4) to separate, to leave from 5) to break apart

par-tial-ly [pär′shə-lē] *adverb*, partly, somewhat, slightly

par-ti-al-i-ty [pär′shē-ăl′ĭ-tē] *adjective*, biased, inclined to favor one side

par-tic-i-pate [pär-tĭs′ə-pāt′] *verb*, to have a share in common with others, to take part, to join in

par-tic-i-pa-tion [pär-tĭs′ə-pā′shən] *noun*, the act of getting involved with others

par-ti-ci-ple [pär′tĭ-sĭp′əl] *noun*, one of two forms of a verb forming the past or future tense

par-ti-cle [pär′tĭ-kəl] *noun*, the smallest form of matter

par-tic-u-lar [pər-tĭk′yə-lər] *adjective*, relating to a part, individual, precise, specific

par-tic-u-lar-ly [pər-tĭk′yə-lər-lē] *adverb*, specifically, in detail

par-ti-san [pär′tĭ-zən] *adjective*, an adherent to a party or faction

par-ti-tion [pär-tĭsh′ən] *noun*, 1) a division, a dividing wall, *verb*, 2) to divide, to separate

part-ly [pärt′lē] *adverb*, to some extent, partially, somewhat

part-ner [pärt′nər] *noun*, 1) an associate in business 2) a companion in dancing or sports

par-ty [pär′tē] *noun*, 1) a meeting of friends to enjoy themselves 2) a group of people who have the same interests or goals, *verb*, 3) to celebrate

pass [păs] *noun*, 1) a high mountain road 2) a paper allowing you to go somewhere or have something 3) a forward gesture, *verb*, 4) to give something to someone else 5) to be allowed to advance to the next level

pas-sage [păs′ĭj] *noun*, 1) an excerpt from a chapter, a clause or quotation 2) the act or process of passing as through time or from place to place, a journey 3) a path 4) a part of a written work or a piece of music

pass-é [pă-sā′] *adjective*, behind the times, old fashioned

pas-sen-ger [păs′ən-jər] *noun*, a traveler in a vehicle such as a car, boat, bus, etc.

pas-sion [păsh′ən] *noun*, a strong feeling or desire, enthusiasm

pas-sion-ate [păsh′ə-nĭt] *adjective*, ardent in feeling or desire

pas-sive [păs′ĭv] *adjective*, to be unresponsive, not active

pass-port [păs′pôrt′] *noun*, an official permission issued to a person allowing travel out of the country and return, a document of identification

past [păst] *adjective*, 1) referring to time and events in history, *noun, no plural*, 2) time gone by, *preposition,* 3) to or on the further side of 4) beyond in time

pas-ta [päs′tə] *noun*, noodles made from flour, water, salt, and eggs

paste [pāst] *noun*, 1) a sticky substance that glues things together, *verb*, 2) to put in place, for example with an adhesive

pas-tel [păs-stĕl′] *noun*, a sketch or drawing of a soft color or hue

pas-teur-ize [păs′chə-rīz′] *verb*, to subject fluids to a high temperature (131 degrees Celsius, 158 degrees Fahrenheit) to prevent the growth of bacteria

pas-time [păs′tīm′] *noun*, something that you do to amuse yourself or to relax, like a hobby

pas-tor [păs′tər] *noun*, a reverend, the clergyman of a church

pas-to-ral [păs′tər-əl] *adjective*, rural, in the country, rustic

pas-try [pā′strē] *noun*, sweet baked foods, such as cakes or pies

pas-ture [păs′chər] *noun*, grassland for grazing livestock

pat [păt] *noun*, 1) a light touch with an open hand, a gentle tap, *verb*, 2) to touch lightly with a hand

patch [păch] *noun*, 1) a small piece of cloth used to mend a tear, *verb*, 2) to put a piece of material on a surface to repair a hole or strengthen a worn area

pat-ent [păt′nt] *adjective*, 1) obvious, plain, *noun*, 2) the right given to an inventor by the government, to exclusively produce a product for a number of years

pa-ter-nal [pə-tûr′nəl] *adjective*, fatherly, kind, devoted

path [păth] *noun*, a track worn by people or animals walking on it

pa-thet-ic [pə-thĕt′ĭk] *adjective*, causing pity or grief, full of pathos and sympathy

pa-thol-o-gy [pă-thŏl′ə-jē] *noun*, the science of treating disease, their natural causes, results, etc.

pa-thos [pā′thŏs′] *noun*, human or animal experience that cause feelings of pity, compassion

pa-tience [pā′shəns] *noun*, *no plural*, the act of waiting calmly for someone or something

pa-tient [pā′shənt] *adjective*, 1) able to bear quietly or wait for something calmly, *noun*, 2) a person under medical treatment

pat-i-o [păt′ē-ō′] *noun*, a paved outdoor space that is used for eating, cooking or relaxing

pa-tri-arch [pā′trē-ärk′] *noun*, 1) father and ruler of a family or tribe 2) a venerable old man

pa-tri-ot [pā′trē-ət] *noun*, one who loves and defends his country

pa-tri-ot-ic [pā′trē-ŏt′ĭk] *adjective*, public-spirited, flag-waving

pa-tri-ot-ism [pā′trē-ə-tĭz′əm] *adjective*, love of one's country

pa-trol [pə-trōl′] *noun*, 1) a small group of soldiers or police officers, *verb*, 2) to follow a route regularly looking for criminal activity

pa-tron [pā′trən] *noun*, 1) someone who provides financial support to a cause 2) a customer

pa-tron-ize [pā′trə-nīz′] *verb*, 1) to act as a supporter 2) to treat with condescension, to look down on

pat-tern [păt′ərn] *noun*, 1) anything used as a guide or model for making things 2) a repeated sequence 3) to make by following a prototype or model

227

pau-per [pô′pər] *noun*, destitute, a very poor person, a beggar

pause [pôz] *noun*, 1) a break in action of speech, *verb*, 2) to stop briefly, to delay action or speech

pave [pāv] *verb*, 1) to cover the surface with asphalt bricks or cement 2) to prepare the way

pave-ment [pāv′mənt] *noun*, highway surface, asphalt

paw [pô] *noun*, the foot of a four-legged animal that has claws

pawn [pôn] *noun*, 1) a victim 2) a chess piece, *verb*, 3) to sell

pay [pā] *noun*, 1) the compensation received for work, *verb*, 2) to give someone money for goods and services

pay-ment [pā′mənt] *noun*, compensation, installment

pay-roll [pā′rōl′] *noun*, the money used to pay workers

pea [pē] *noun*, a seed from a pod bearing vine that can be eaten

peace [pēs] *noun*, 1) a period of harmony among nations when there is no war 2) a calm ordered condition,

peach [pēch] *noun*, *plural*, **peaches** 1)a juicy yellow-orange fruit with downy skin, from an orchard tree that has pink flowers 2) a yellowish-pink color

pea-cock [pē′kŏk′] *noun*, a bird with a large brightly colored tail

peak [pēk] *noun*, 1) the pointed top of a mountain or ridge 2) the point of greatest development

peal [pēl] *noun*, 1) a loud ringing of bells *verb*, 2) to resound

pea-nut [pē′nŭt′] *noun*, a legume that bears edible pods that taste like nuts

pear [pâr] *noun*, a juicy yellow, brown or green fruit from an orchard tree

pearl [pûrl] *noun*, a precious white substance like a bead found inside an oyster, used in jewelry

peas-ant [pĕz′ənt] *noun*, a person who makes a living from working the soil, especially in poorer countries

peb-ble [pĕb′əl] *noun*, a small stone worn by erosion

pe-can [pĭ-kän′] *noun*, the edible kernel nut from a hickory tree grown in the south

peck [pĕk] *noun*, 1) ¼ of a bushel, *verb*, 2) to cut or lift with the beak

pec-to-ral [pĕk′tər-əl] *adjective*, pertaining to the chest

pe-cu-liar [pĭ-kyōōl′yər] *adjective*, oddly different from the usual, strange, distinctive, particular

pe-cu-ni-ar-y [pĭ-kyōō′nē-ĕr′ē] *adjective*, pertaining to or consisting of money

ped-a-gogue [pĕd′ə-gŏg′] *noun*, a narrow-minded teacher

ped-al [pĕd′l] *noun*, 1) a lever acted on by the foot, *verb*, 2) to push with the feet when riding a bicycle in order to get the bicycle to move

ped-dle [pĕd′l] *verb*, to sell on the street or door to door

ped-es-tal [pĕd′ĭ-stəl] *noun*, a base or support for a column

pe-des-tri-an [pə-děs′trē-ən] *noun*, a person who walks

pe-di-a-tri-cian [pē′dē-ə-trǐsh′ən] *noun*, a doctor who is an expert in children's diseases

ped-i-gree [pěd′ǐ-grē′] *noun*, a register of a line of ancestors, descent, ancestry, lineage

peek [pēk] *noun*, 1) a glance, *verb*, 2) to look at, to catch sight of

peel [pēl] *noun, no plural*, 1) the outside covering of a fruit or vegetable, *verb*, 2) to cut the outside covering off of a fruit or vegetable to eat the food inside

peer [pîr] *noun*, 1) someone your own age or someone with similar interests, an equal, *verb*, 2) to take a closer look

peg [pěg] *noun*, a wooden or metal object used as a hook when put on a wall or as a fastening

pe-jo-ra-tive [pǐ-jôr′ə-tǐv] *adjective*, a deteriorating effect on the meaning of a word

pel-i-can [pěl′ǐ-kän′] *noun*, a large water bird with webbed feet and an expandable pouch in the lower beak for holding fish

pelt [pělt] *noun*, 1) the furry skin of an animal 2) to strike over and over with repeated blows

pen [pěn] *noun*, 1) an instrument for writing using ink 2) an enclosure for animals

pe-nal-ize [pē′nə-līz′] *verb*, to scold, to punish, to chastise

pen-al-ty [pěn′əl-tē] *noun*, the suffering or fine imposed as a punishment for a violation

pen-chant [pěn′chənt] *noun*, a strong mental leaning or attraction, a decided taste

pen-cil [pěn′səl] *noun*, a writing instrument with a gray substance in the middle that marks paper

pend-ant [pěn′dənt] *noun*, a hanging ornament or piece of jewelry, like a necklace

pend-ent [pěn′dənt] *adjective*, hanging or suspended

pend-ing [pěn′dǐng] *adjective*, 1) about to happen, imminent, *preposition*, 2) until 3) during

pen-du-lum [pěn′jə-ləm] *noun*, a weight which swings from side to side under the combined action of gravity and momentum

pen-e-trate [pěn′ǐ-trāt′] *verb*, 1) to enter into, 2) to affect deeply

pen-guin [pěng′gwǐn] *noun*, a large flightless sea bird of Antarctica that has flipper-like wings

pen-in-su-la [pə-nǐn′syə-lə] *noun*, a piece of land extending from the mainland, surrounded by water on three sides

pen-i-ten-tia-ry [pěn′ǐ-těn′shə-rē] *noun*, a federal prison

pen-nant [pěn′ənt] *noun*, a flag or banner with an insignia

pen-ni-less [pěn′ē-lǐs] *adjective*, without any money, destitute

Penn-syl-va-nia [pěn′səl-vān′yə] *noun*, one of the 50 United States located in the Northeast, the capital is Harrisburg. The state flower of **Pennsylvania** is the mountain laurel and the motto is "Virtue, liberty, and independence."

pen-ny [pěn′ē] *noun*, a copper coin worth one cent

pen-sion [pĕn′shən] *noun*, an allowance of money given to someone regularly starting at retirement

pen-sive [pĕn′sĭv] *adjective*, a deep thinker, thoughtful with a hint of sadness, reflective

pen-ta-gon [pĕn′tə-gŏn′] *noun*, a shape with five equal sides

pent-house [pĕnt′hous′] *noun*, an apartment on the top floor of a building

pe-on [pē′ŏn′] *noun*, an unskilled laborer, a menial worker

peo-ple [pē′pəl] *noun*, *plural* of **person**, 1) human beings, men, women, and children 2) a nation

pep-per [pĕp′ər] *noun*, *no plural*, 1) a powder made from seeds of some plants and used to flavor food 2) the fruit of pepper plants, which can be used in cooking or eaten raw in salads

pep-per-mint [pĕp′ər-mĭnt′] *noun*, 1) oil from an herb used to give a taste of mint 2) a candy that tastes like mint

per [pûr] *preposition*, for or in each, according to

per-ceive [pər-sēv′] *verb*, to comprehend, to obtain knowledge through the senses

per-cent [pər-sĕnt′] *noun*, a number in proportion to 100

per-cent-age [pər-sĕn′tĭj] *adjective*, allowance or commission on a hundred

per-cep-ti-ble [pər-sĕp′tə-bəl] *adjective*, capable of being perceived, discernible

per-cep-tion [pər-sĕp′shən] *noun*, viewpoint, observation

perch [pûrch] *noun*, 1) a place for a bird to sit, *verb*, 2) to sit on a narrow branch or stick

per-co-late [pûr′kə-lāt′] *verb*, to pass or ooze through, to trickle through, to filter

per-cus-sion [pər-kŭsh′ən] *noun*, the group of musical instruments, such as a drum, whose sound is produced by striking or hitting

per-emp-to-ry [pə-rĕmp′tə-rē] *adjective*, closed to further discussion or action

per-en-ni-al [pə-rĕn′ē-əl] *adjective*, 1) lasting through the year 2) never failing

per-fect [pûr′fĭkt] *adjective*, 1) beyond improvement, having nothing wrong, *verb*, 2) to improve, to make better

per-fec-tion [pər-fĕk′shən] *noun*, the state of being without fault the highest degree of excellence

per-fect-ly [pûr′fĭkt-lē] *adverb*, completely, ideally, flawlessly

per-fo-rate [pûr′fə-rāt′] *verb*, to make a small hole, to prick

per-form [pər-fôrm′] *verb*, 1) to act in a play or a musical event 2) to do, to carry out a task

per-for-mance [pər-fôr′məns] *noun*, a show or act presented before an audience

per-form-er [pər-fôrm′ər] *noun*, one who entertains before an audience

per-fume [pûr′fyōōm′] *noun*, *no plural*, liquid that has a sweet smell, a fragrant oil 2) a delightful odor

per-func-to-ry [pər-fŭngk′tə-rē] *adjective*, done merely as a duty with little interest or care

per-haps [pər-hăps′] *adverb*, by chance, possibly, maybe

per-il [pĕr′əl] *noun*, a danger, a grave risk, a hazard

pe-rim-e-ter [pə-rĭm′ĭ-tər] *noun*, the measurement of the distance around a two-dimensional figure

pe-ri-od [pĭr′ē-əd] *noun*, 1) an interval of time having a specific length or character 2) a punctuation mark used at the end of a sentence 3) a session in school

pe-ri-od-i-cal [pĭr′ē-ŏd′ĭ-kəl] *noun*, a publication appearing with a fixed interval between issues

pe-riph-er-al [pə-rĭf′ər-əl] *adjective*, having to do with, or situated on the outside

pe-riph-er-y [pə-rĭf′ə-rē] *noun*, the edge, usually of a round surface

per-i-scope [pĕr′ĭ-skōp′] *noun*, an optical instrument that allows observation of objects from a position not in a direct line of sight, used in submarines

per-ish [pĕr′ĭsh] *verb*, to die

per-ish-a-ble [pĕr′ĭ-shə-bəl] *adjective*, likely to spoil, something that rots in air, it has to be refrigerated to make it last

per-ju-ry [pûr′jə-rē] *noun*, false testimony under oath

per-ma-nent [pûr′mə-nənt] *adjective*, meant to last without changing, lasting, durable

per-ma-nent-ly [pûr′mə-nənt-lē] *adverb*, lasting indefinitely

per-me-a-ble [pûr′mē-ə-bəl] *adjective*, 1) capable of receiving fluids or transmitting magnetic effects 2) allowing liquids to pass through

per-me-ate [pûr′mē-āt′] *verb*, to pass through the pores of, to spread throughout, to pervade

per-mis-sion [pər-mĭsh′ən] *noun*, formal consent, authorization

per-mit [pər-mĭt′] *noun*, 1) a written notice that allows you to do something, *verb*, 2) to allow

per-ni-cious [pər-nĭsh′əs] *adjective*, destructive, ruinous, causing insidious harm

per-pen-dic-u-lar [pûr′pən-dĭk′yə-lər] *adjective*, 1) perfectly upright 2) at right angles to a horizontal plane

per-pe-trate [pûr′pĭ-trāt′] *verb*, to do or to perform, to carry through, to commit

per-pet-u-al [pər-pĕch′ōō-əl] *adjective*, never ceasing, continuing forever, endless

per-pe-tu-ate [pər-pĕch′ōō-āt′] *verb*, to continue, indefinitely

per-plex [pər-plĕks′] *verb*, to embarrass, to bewilder, to cause to doubt, to puzzle, to baffle

per-plex-i-ty [pər-plĕk′sĭ-tē] *noun*, the quality or state of being puzzled, bewilderment

per-se-cute [pûr′sĭ-kyōōt′] *verb*, to bother, to oppress, to punish

per-se-cu-tion [pûr′sĭ-kyōō′shən] *noun*, the act of persistently injuring, harassing or annoying

per-se-ver-ance [pûr′sə-vîr′əns] *noun*, the will to keep working until the job is done, persistence

per-se-vere [pûr′sə-vîr′] *verb*, to work to accomplish a goal despite difficulty

per-sist [pər-sĭst′] *verb*, to keep doing something, to persevere, to keep trying

per-sist-ence [pər-sĭs′təns] *noun*, the act of continuing to do something, not giving up

per-son [pûr′sən] *noun*, **people**, *plural*, , a human being, such as a man, woman or child, an unnamed individual

per-son-a-ble [pûr′sə-nə-bəl] *adjective*, good-natured, agreeable, charming, attractive

per-son-al [pûr′sə-nəl] *adjective*, of or concerning a particular person, concerning a person's private life, confidential

per-son-al-i-ty [pûr′sə-năl′ĭ-tē] *noun*, distinctive personal character, individuality

per-son-al-ly [pûr′sə-nə-lē] *adverb*, 1) from one's own viewpoint 2) in person

per-son-i-fi-ca-tion [pər-sŏn′ə-fĭ-kā′shən] *noun*, 1) to think of or represent as a person 2) an embodiment or example of someone

per-son-nel [pûr′sə-nĕl′] *noun*, the staff of an organization

per-spec-tive [pər-spĕk′tĭv] *noun*, as one sees it, a point of view

per-spi-ra-tion [pûr′spə-rā′shən] *noun*, sweat, a salty water fluid secreted from the sweat glands

per-spire [pər-spīr′] *verb*, to sweat

per-suade [pər-swād′] *verb*, to influence or gain over by argument or advice

per-sua-sive [pər-swā′sĭv] *adjective*, an influential argument

pert [pûrt] *adjective*, bold, flippant, forward, impertinent, saucy

per-tain [pər-tān′] *verb*, to relate, to be connected as a part

per-ti-nent [pûr′tn-ənt] *adjective*, belonging or relating to the subject at hand, relevant

per-turb [pər-tûrb′] *verb*, to trouble, or disturb, to agitate

pe-ruse [pə-rōōz′] *verb*, to read

per-vade [pər-vā′d] *verb*, to pass through, to permeate

per-va-sive [pər-vā′sĭv] *adjective*, to become spread throughout all parts, universal, permeating

per-ver-sion [pər-vûr′zhən] *noun*, turning from right to wrong

per-vert [pər-vûrt′] *verb*, to make contrary or obstinate remarks

pes-ky [pĕs′kē] *adjective*, annoying, being like a pest

pes-si-mist [pĕs′ə-mĭst] *noun*, one who looks on the dark side of things and expects the worst

pes-si-mism [pĕs′ə-mĭz′əm] *adjective*, belief that life is basically bad or evil

pest [pĕst] *noun*, an annoying and destructive insect or person

pes-ti-cide [pĕs′tĭ-sīd′] *noun*, any substance designed to kill living organisms, such as insects, plants, fungi and rodents

pes-ti-lence [pĕs′tə-ləns] *noun*, any deadly contagious epidemic of a disease or virus

pet [pĕt] *noun*, 1) an animal you look after and keep in your house, *verb*, 2) to stroke

pet-al [pĕt′l] *noun*, one of the parts of the corolla of a flower that are usually colorful

pe-tite [pə-tēt′] *adjective*, small, little, a woman or girl of small size

pe-ti-tion [pə-tĭsh′ən] *noun*, 1) a formal request accompanied by signatures as an endorsement, *verb*, 2) to request change by making a written formal request

pet-ri-fy [pĕt′rə-fī′] *verb*, to turn to stone, to harden, to deaden

pet-ro-le-um [pə-trō′lē-əm] *noun*, mineral oil, a dark brown or green inflammable liquid

pet-ty [pĕt′ē] *adjective*, a small matter of little importance, insignificant, trivial

pew [pyōō] *noun*, one of a number of fixed benches, like a seat, with backs in a church

pew-ter [pyōō′tər] *noun*, an alloy consisting mainly of tin and other metals

phan-tom [făn′təm] *noun*, an apparition, a ghost, a vision

phar-ma-cy [fär′mə-sē] *noun*, a place where medicines are dispensed, a drug store

phase [fāz] *noun*, a stage in a process of development

pheas-ant [fĕz′ənt] *noun*, a game bird with long tail feathers that lives in the woods

phe-nom-e-non [fĭ-nŏm′ə-nŏn′] *noun*, *plural*, **phenomena**, a marvel, an event, a happening

phil-an-throp-ic [fĭl′ən-thrŏp′ĭk] *adjective*, love for mankind, benevolent, generous

phi-lol-o-gist [fĭ-lŏl′ə-jĭst] *noun*, the study of languages, their structure and origin

phi-los-o-pher [fĭ-lŏs′ə-fər] *noun*, a wise person, a reflective thinker, a sage

phi-los-o-phy [fĭ-lŏs′ə-fē] *noun*, the study of moral and mental sciences, metaphysics

pho-bi-a [fō′bē-ə] *noun*, dislike, an irrational fear of something

phone [fōn] *noun*, the short term for telephone

pho-net-ic [fə-nĕt′ĭk] *adjective*, the sound of letters in a word that create speech

pho-no-graph [fō′nə-grăf′] *noun*, a record player

phos-pho-res-cence [fŏs′fə-rĕs′əns] *noun*, any bright and luminous radiating light

phos-pho-rus [fŏs′fər-əs] *noun*, a nonmetallic element used in matches

pho-to-graph [fō′tə-grăf′] *noun*, 1) a picture produced using film and a camera, *verb*, 2) to take a picture with a camera

pho-to-graph-ic [fō′tə-grăf′ĭk] *adjective*, the process of photography

pho-to-syn-the-sis [fō′tō-sĭn′thĭ-sĭs] *verb*, the process by which chlorophyll-containing cells in green plants use light as an energy source to synthesize carbohydrates from carbon dioxide and water

phrase [frāz] *noun*, 1) a part of a sentence 2) an expression, a saying, *verb*, 3) to express in words or a particular way

phys-i-cal [fĭz/ĭ-kəl] *adjective*, of or pertaining to nature or the human body

phy-si-cian [fĭ-zĭsh/ən] *noun*, a doctor of medicine

phys-ics [fĭz/ĭks] *noun*, the science that deals with matter and energy such as light, motion, sound, heat, electricity, or force, and the laws that govern them

phys-i-ol-o-gy [fĭz/ē-ŏl/ə-jē] *noun*, that part of biology which studies living organisms

phy-sique [fĭ-zēk/] *noun*, the development and bodily structure or appearance of a person, the frame, figure

pi-an-ist [pē-ăn/ĭst] *noun*, a skilled performer on the piano

pi-a-no [pē-ăn/ō] *noun*, a musical instrument played by hitting its keys on a keyboard with fingers, which hit felt-covered hammers which strike metal strings

pick [pĭk] *noun*, 1) a choice or selection 2) a tool used to break the earth, *verb*, 3) to choose 4) to hold with your fingers

pick-et [pĭk/ĭt] *noun*, 1) a stake, a peg, *verb*, 2) to strike, to boycott

pick-le [pĭk/əl] *noun*, 1) any food which has been preserved in brine or in vinegar 2) an awkward situation

pic-nic [pĭk/nĭk] *noun*, a pleasure trip with a meal eaten in the open air

pic-to-graph [pĭk/tə-grăf/] *noun*, a rudimentary diagram or symbol used to represent an idea as the primitive writing of stone tablets and cave drawings

pic-ture [pĭk/chər] *noun*, 1) visual respremensation such as a drawing, painting, photograph, etc., *verb*, 2) to imagine in your mind, to visualize

pic-tur-esque [pĭk/chə-rĕsk/] *adjective*, forming a pleasing picture, graphic, quaint

pie [pī] *noun*, a dish made with fruit, meat or vegetables, surrounded by a pastry crust on the bottom and sometimes on top

piece [pēs] *noun*, 1) a fragment or part separated from the whole, *verb*, 2) to put together, to repair

pier [pîr] *noun*, a wharf or dock extending into the water from the land used as a place to moor ships

pierce [pîrs] *verb*, 1) to pass or break through 2) to make a hole through

pierc-ing [pîrsĭng] *adjective*, very loud and shrill

pig [pĭg] *noun*, any swine raised for pork and bacon

pi-geon [pĭj/ən] *noun*, a plump bird with a small head

pig-ment [pĭg/mənt] *noun*, the color of something, a hue

pile [pīl] *noun*, 1) a heap of things laying one on another 2) the nap of a fabric 3) a post in a pier that goes into the soil beneath the water, *verb*, 4) to amass, to gather together in a heap, to accumulate, to stack

pil-grim [pĭl/grəm] *noun*, a person who journeys to pray at a holy place as an act of religious devotion

pil-grim-age [pĭl/grə-mĭj] *noun*, a journey to a holy place

pill [pĭl] *noun*, a small tablet or capsule of medicine that can be easily swallowed

pil-lage [pĭl′ĭj] *verb*, to strip of money, ransack, rob, destroy

pil-lar [pĭl′ər] *noun*, 1) a strong post 2) a column, a vertical support or structure

pil-low [pĭl′ō] *noun*, a cloth case filled with feathers or other soft material put under the head during sleep

pil-low-case [pĭl′ō-kās′] *noun*, the cloth bag put over a pillow to keep it clean

pi-lot [pī′lət] *noun*, someone who is qualified to guide or navigate a ship or a plane

pin [pĭn] *noun*, 1) a slender piece of metal or wood, sharp on one end round on the other, used to join and fasten things together, *verb*, 2) to fasten with a sharp instrument 3) to hold in a spot

pin-cers [pĭn′sərz] *noun*, an instrument or an appendage having two grasping jaws working on a pivot

pinch [pĭnch] *noun*, 1) a very small amount, *verb*, 2) to squeeze between the finger and thumb 3) to make something feel tight

pine [pīn] *noun*, 1) an evergreen tree with leaves that look like needles, *verb*, 2) to want something very badly

pine-ap-ple [pīn′ăp′əl] *noun*, 1) the fruit of a tropical plant, resembling the shape of a pinecone 2) a symbol of hospitality

pin-ion [pĭn′yən] *noun*, a cogwheel with a small number of teeth, designed to interlock its gear with a larger wheel

pink [pĭngk] *adjective*, 1) a pastel color of red and white *noun*, 2) the color made by mixing red and white

pin-na-cle [pĭn′ə-kəl] *noun*, 1) a small turret above the rest of the building 2) a lofty peak

pint [pīnt] *noun*, a liquid measurement equal to 2 cups or 16 fluid ounces

pi-o-neer [pī′ə-nîr′] *noun*, one of the first to explore an area or field of study, an innovator

pi-ous [pī′əs] *adjective*, devout

pipe [pīp] *noun*, 1) a tube, a cylinder used to convey liquid or gas 2) a device with a bowl at the end of a short straw used to smoke tobacco 3) a musical instrument through which air is blown, *verb*, 4) to make a high pitched sound

pi-quant [pē′kənt] *adjective*, 1) pleasantly tart-tasting, spicy 2) provocative

pique [pēk] *noun*, slight anger or resentment, wounded pride

pi-rate [pī′rĭt] *noun*, a person who robs ships at sea

pis-til [pĭs′təl] *noun*, the part of a flower that produces seeds

pis-tol [pĭs′təl] *noun*, a small gun like a revolver, a firearm

pis-ton [pĭs′tən] *noun*, a metal disk which moves up and down in a cylinder exerting pressure

pit [pǐt] *noun*, 1) a deep hole in the ground 2) the seed of a fruit

pitch [pǐch] *noun*, 1) a gummy substance used for sealing roads and caulking 2) a ball thrown or tossed 3) the tone of a voice or a sound, *verb*, 4) to put in place or set up 5) to toss or throw a ball 6) when a boat leans to an angle while traveling in the water

pitch-er [pǐch'ər] *noun*, 1) a container with a lip and a handle to pour liquid 2) the person who throws the ball to the batter in a baseball game

pitch-fork [pǐch'fôrk'] *noun*, a fork with a long handle used to lift and toss hay

pit-fall [pǐt'fôl'] *noun*, a trap, a snare or hazard not easily avoided, a manhole

pith-y [pǐth'ē] *adjective*, concise, short and to the point

pit-i-ful [pǐt'ǐ-fəl] *adjective*, something that causes sympathy

pit-tance [pǐt'ns] *noun*, a small amount, next to nothing

pit-y [pǐt'ē] *noun*, 1) the sadness felt when someone else is hurt or in trouble, *verb*, 2) to feel sorry for someone, to feel sympathy

piv-ot [pǐv'ət] *noun*, a fixed pin on which something turns

piz-za [pēt'sə] *noun*, a baked flat crust covered with cheese, tomato sauce, etc.

pla-cate [plā'kāt'] *verb*, to pacify, to satisfy, to please someone

place [plās] *noun*, 1) a designated area or a particular space, *verb*, 2) to put in a particular spot 3) to identify by recalling

plac-id [plăs'ǐd] *adjective*, calm, peaceful, tranquil, untroubled

pla-gia-rism [plā'jə-rǐz'əm] *noun*, the act of copying someone's work and claiming it as your own

plague [plāg] *noun*, 1) anything troublesome 2) an infectious disease, *verb*, 3) to annoy

plaid [plăd] *adjective*, a pattern on cloth with stripes of different colors that cross each other

plain [plān] *adjective*, 1) open to view, clear, easy to understand, 2) simple, *noun*, 3) a stretch of gently rolling land with few trees

plain-ly [plān'lē] *adverb*, clearly

plain-tiff [plān'tǐf] *noun*, one who commences a legal action or suit

plan [plăn] *noun*, 1) a drawing made to scale of a new building or a project 2) a scheme indicating how to accomplish something, *verb*, 3) to design, to scheme or devise

plane [plān] *noun*, 1) a hand tool used to smooth the surface of wood 2) the short term for airplane 3) any flat or level surface

plan-et [plăn'ǐt] *noun*, a large mass like the earth that revolves around the sun

plank [plăngk] *noun*, a long, flat, thin piece of wood

plank-ton [plăngk'tən] *noun*, plant and animal organisms, generally microscopic, that float and or drift in great numbers in fresh or salt water

plant [plănt] *noun*, 1) a living thing that is not a mineral or animal 2) a factory, a work place, *verb*, 3) to put into the ground to grow

plan-ta-tion [plăn-tā′shən] *noun*, a large estate or farm cultivated by workers living on it

plaque [plăk] *noun*, 1) a marker, a tablet with an inscription 2) tarter calcified on the teeth

plas-ma [plăz′mə] *noun*, the fourth state of matter, composed of broken up atoms

plas-tic [plăs′tĭk] *adjective*, 1) referring to any pliable petroleum based product, *noun*, 2) any of a group of substances made chemically and molded by heat to form, fibers, bottles, etc.

plate [plāt] *noun*, a shallow dish from which food is eaten

pla-teau [plă-tō′] *noun*, 1) an elevated plane 2) inactive period

plat-form [plăt′fôrm′] *noun*, 1) a part of a station where you get on and off trains 2) a raised stage or dais so the audience can see the speaker or performers 3) beliefs, principles

plat-i-tude [plăt′ĭ-tōōd′] *noun*, a commonplace statement

pla-ton-ic [plə-tŏn′ĭk] *adjective*, a friendly relationship

pla-toon [plə-tōōn′] *noun*, a military unit of troops

plat-ter [plăt′ər] *noun*, 1) a large serving of food 2) a large shallow plate for serving food

plau-dits [plô′dĭts] *noun*, *plural*, enthusiastic approval, applause

plau-si-ble [plô′zə-bəl] *adjective*, apparently right, seeming to be reasonable, credible

play [plā] *noun*, 1) the performance of a story on the stage, *verb*, 2) to amuse or entertain 3) to

take part in a game 4) to perform on a musical instrument

plea [plē] *noun*, 1) an appeal, an urgent request 2) a defense

plead [plēd] *verb*, 1) to ask for something that is felt to be very important, to appeal earnestly 2) to respond to a charge by a court of law

pleas-ant [plĕz′ənt] *adjective*, 1) agreeable, amiable, friendly 2) fair, mild, comfortable

pleas-ant-ly [plĕz′ənt-lē] *adverb*, agreeably, politely, kindly

please [plēz] *noun*, 1) a word added to a request to make it sound polite, *verb*, 2) to make someone happy 3) to wish

pleased [plēzd] *adjective*, glad

plea-sur-ably [plĕzh′ər-ə-bəl] *adverb*, capable of affording satisfaction, pleasant

pleas-ure [plĕzh′ər] *noun*, enjoyment or satisfaction

pledge [plĕj] *noun*, 1) a promise, a guarantee, *verb*, 2) to take an oath, to bind by a promise

plen-ty [plĕn′tē] *adjective*, enough, all that is needed

pleth-o-ra [plĕth′ər-ə] *noun*, a large or excessive amount of something, an abundance

pli-ant [plī′ənt] *adjective*, bendable

pli-ers [plī′ərz] *noun*, a small pincers with long jaws, used for bending metal rods or wire, or holding small objects

plod [plŏd] *verb*, to walk heavily, to trudge, to work steadily

plot [plŏt] *noun*, 1) a piece of land 2) a secret plan, usually to commit a crime 3) the story of a book, film, etc. *verb*, 4) to plan a secret activity, to conspire

plow [plou] *noun*, 1) a farm tool used to overturn earth for planting *verb*, 2) to turn over the soil to prepare the earth for planting 3) to move forcefully

pluck [plŭk] *verb*, to pull off or pull out 2) to grasp or grab

plug [plŭg] *noun*, 1) a stopper used to keep water from draining out of a basin 2) a device put in a wall socket to conduct electricity, *verb*, 3) to put an electric cord into a socket 4) to put a stopper into a drain hole, to fill a hole 5) to persevere

plum [plŭm] *noun*, a sweet juicy red fruit with a pit as a seed

plumb-er [plŭm′ər] *noun*, a tradesman who fits, and repairs gas and water pipes

plumb-ing [plŭm′ĭng] *noun*, *no plural*, all the water pipes, containers, etc. put in a building so that there can be running water and drainage

plume [plo͞om] *noun*, a large or conspicuous feather

plum-met [plŭm′ĭt] *verb*, to fall straight down quickly

plump [plŭmp] *adjective*, a little fat, rounded in form

plunge [plŭnj] *noun*, 1) a sudden dive or fall, *verb*, 2) to fall quickly from a great height 3) to throw oneself into

plung-er [plŭn′jər] *noun*, 1) a rubber suction cup on a handle, used to clear drains 2) a piston-like part that acts with a thrusting movement in a pump

plu-ral [plo͝or′əl] *adjective*, of or involving more than one

plus [plŭs] *preposition*, in addition to, increased by

ply-wood [plī′wo͝od′] *noun*, sheets of wood arranged in thin layers where the grain is in opposite directions to give it strength

p.m. *adjective*, post meridian, the afternoon, the period between noon and midnight

pneu-mo-nia [no͝o-mōn′yə] *noun*, infection of the lungs caused by bacteria or viruses

poach [pōch] *verb*, 1) to hunt or fish illegally 2) to cook a raw egg in boiling water

pock-et [pŏk′ĭt] *noun*, an envelope made by sewing a piece of cloth into clothing to hold things

pod [pŏd] *noun*, a long, slender part of a vine plant in which the seeds grow, like a pea or bean

po-di-um [pō′dē-əm] *noun*, a pedestal, a raised platform

po-em [pō′əm] *noun*, a composition, usually in verse, with regular rhythm and sounds that express images in powerful or beautiful language

po-et [pō′ĭt] *noun*, one who writes verse in a specific form

po-et-ic [pō-ĕt′ĭk] *adjective*, pertaining to poetry, imaginative

po-et-ry [pō′ĭ-trē] *noun*, *no plural*, words written in verse

poign-ant [poin′yənt] *adjective*, touching, piercing, sharp, keen, affecting the emotions

point [point] *noun*, 1) the tip of something, usually sharp 2) the purpose of a verbal illustration 3) the number of goals for a team 4) at a particular time 5) the location of an ordered pair of numbers, *verb*, 6) to indicate

point-less [pointlĕs] *adjective*, meaningless, senseless

poise [poiz] *noun*, 1) composure, self-assurance, confidence, *verb*, 2) to balance, to keep steady

poi-son [poi'zən] *noun*, 1) any substance dangerous to life and health, *verb*, 2) to kill with toxic chemicals 3) to ruin

poi-son-ous [poi'zə-nəs] *adjective*, deadly, toxic, noxious

poke [pōk] *verb*, to push something pointed into something, to prod

po-lar [pō'lər] *adjective*, 1) of or near the North or South Poles 2) at opposite ends

pole [pōl] *noun*, 1) a round piece of wood, metal or plastic,etc. a rod 2) one end of the earth or at the end of the axis of a sphere

po-lice [pə-lēs'] *noun, no plural*, 1) a department of government that maintains order and enforces the law 2) members of that department

pol-i-cy [pŏl'ĭ-sē] *noun*, 1) a course of action adopted by an individual or group 2) an insurance contract

pol-ish [pŏl'ĭsh] *noun*, 1) a substance such as oil or cleanser used to make a surface shine when rubbed with a cloth, *verb*, 3) rubbing something to make it shine or glossy

po-lite [pə-līt'] *adjective*, showing good manners, courteous

po-lit-i-cal [pə-lĭt'ĭ-kəl] *adjective*, of or pertaining to the conduct of government or politics

pol-i-ti-cian [pŏl'ĭ-tĭsh'ən] *noun*, a person who runs for public office

pol-i-tics [pŏl'ĭ-tĭks] *noun*, the conduct of government

pol-i-ty [pŏl'ĭ-tē] *noun*, form of government of a nation or a state

poll [pōl] *noun*, 1) a survey, *verb*, 2) to interview, to canvass

pol-len [pŏl'ən] *noun*, a fine yellow dust on the anthers of seed bearing flowers, which serves as the male agent in reproduction

pol-li-nate [pŏl'ə-nāt'] *verb*, to fertilize a flower so that it will reproduce itself by conveying pollen to the stigma

pol-lute [pə-lōōt'] *verb*, to contaminate, to make dirty or unusable, to make foul

pol-lu-tion [pə-lōō'shən] *noun*, substances in the air, in water and on land that contaminate the earth

pol-y-gon [pŏl'ē-gŏn'] *noun*, a many sided plane or figure

pomp-ous [pŏm'pəs] *adjective*, arrogant, showing off

pon-cho [pŏn'chō] *noun*, a sleeveless cover for the upper body, a waterproof cloak

pond [pŏnd] *noun*, a small body of water, smaller than a lake

pon-der [pŏn'dər] *verb*, to think about something, to contemplate, to consider carefully

po-ny [pō'nē] *noun*, a small horse

pool [pōōl] *noun*, 1) any amount of still liquid, a basin 2) a collection of things 3) billiards 4) to gather or combine resources for mutual benefit

poor [pŏŏr] *adjective*, 1) not having much money 2) needing kindness or help 3) not good

pop [pŏp] *noun, no plural*, 1) a sudden noise made when air is released 2) part of the popular culture of the 1960s, *verb*, 3) to make a sudden, sharp, explosive sound

pope [pōp] *noun*, the leader of the Roman Catholic Church

pop-py [pŏp′ē] *noun*, a red flower that has seeds that have a narcotic effect

pop-u-lar [pŏp′yə-lər] *adjective*, pleasing to people in general

pop-u-lar-i-ty [pŏp′yə-lăr′ĭ-tē] *noun, no plural*, a measurement of how happy people are with something

pop-u-late [pŏp′yə-lāt′] *verb*, to occupy, to reside in

pop-u-la-tion [pŏp′yə-lā′shən] *noun*, the count of people or organisms who live in an area

pop-u-lous [pŏp′yə-ləs] *adjective*, crowded with people

por-ce-lain [pôr′sə-lĭn] *noun*, a delicate form of china, made with a special clay

porch [pôrch] *noun*, a covered platform in front of a doorway

por-cu-pine [pôr′kyə-pīn′] *noun*, a small animal that has long spikes all over its body for protection

pore [pôr] *noun*, a small hole in the skin for perspiration

pork [pôrk] *noun, no plural*, the meat from a pig used as food

po-rous [pôr′əs] *adjective*, a rough surface, full of holes or texture

por-ridge [pôr′ĭj] *noun*, food made by boiling grain in water or milk until it is very soft, i.e., oatmeal

port [pôrt] *noun*, 1) a harbor or community where ships and boats dock 2) the left handed side of a ship when facing forward 3) a sweet red wine 4) an opening in a ship for cargo

port-a-ble [pôr′tə-bəl] *adjective*, easily carried by hand

por-tal [pôr′tl] *noun*, an entrance, a large doorway, a gate

por-tend [pôr-tĕnd′] *verb*, to foretell, to predict, to forecast

por-tent [pôr′tĕnt′] *noun*, a sign, an omen, forewarning of a threat

por-tent-ous [pôr-tĕn′təs] *adjective*, ominous, serious

por-ter [pôr′tər] *noun*, a person hired to carry luggage in a hotel or a train station or airport

port-fo-li-o [pôrt-fō′lē-ō′] *noun*, a portable case holding papers, prints, drawings, etc.

por-ti-co [pôr′tĭ-kō′] *noun*, a colonnade at the entrance of a building

por-tion [pôr′shən] *noun*, a part of a whole, a segment, a share

port-ly [pôrt′lē] *adjective*, overweight, heavy set, fat

por-trait [pôr′trĭt] *noun*, a painting or photograph of someone

por-tray [pôr-trā′] *verb*, to describe, to represent

pose [pōz] *noun*, 1) a stance or posture, *verb*, 2) to model, to stand 3) to ask a question

po-si-tion [pə-zĭsh'ən] *noun,* 1) a
posture, an attitude 2) a job

pos-i-tive [pŏz'ĭ-tĭv] *adjective,*
1) the affirmative, the opposite
of negative 2) confident attitude

pos-sess [pə-zĕs'] *verb,* to have as
property, to own, to control

pos-ses-sion [pə-zĕsh'ən] *noun,*
that which one owns, property

pos-si-bil-i-ty [pŏs'ə-bĭl'ĭ-tē] *noun,*
likelihood, probability, chance

pos-si-ble [pŏs'ə-bəl] *adjective,*
what may happen or exist

post [pōst] *noun,* 1) a piece of wood
or metal placed in the ground as a
support 2) a place where a person
is stationed, a job or responsibility
3) sending mail through the post
office, *verb,* 4) to make known by
putting notices or flyers in public
places 5) to station at a place

post-age [pō'stĭj] *noun, no plural,*
the amount of money paid for
something sent through the mail

post-card [pōst'kärd'] *noun,* a
small note card with a written
message sent through the mail

post-er [pō'stər] *noun,* a large
advertisement usually hung on a
wall in a public place

pos-ter-i-ty [pŏ-stĕr'ĭ-tē] *noun,* the
future generation, descendents

post-hu-mous [pŏs'chə-məs]
adjective, occurring after death

post-pone [pōst-pōn'] *verb,* to put
off, to defer to a later time

post-script [pōst'skrĭpt'] *noun,* 1) a
note added to a signed letter
2) an addition to a book

pos-tu-late [pŏs'chə-lāt'] *noun,*
1) a self-evident truth, *verb,* 2) to
presume, theorize, speculate

pos-ture [pŏs'chər] *noun,* a stance,
an unnatural attitude, position

pot [pŏt] *noun,* a container, usually
round made for cooking

pot-ash [pŏt'ăsh'] *noun,* wood
ashes, potassium hydrochloride

po-tas-si-um [pə-tăs'ē-əm] *noun,*
1) a soft, white metallic element
of the alkali group, 2) Vitamin K

po-ta-to [pə-tā'tō] *noun,* an
underground starchy vegetable

po-tent [pōt'nt] *adjective,*
powerful, effective, mighty

po-ten-tial [pə-tĕn'shəl] *noun,*
the capability someone has to
accomplish something

po-tion [pō'shən] *noun,* a dose of a
liquid with magical powers

pot-pour-ri [pō'pŏo-rē'] *noun,* any
miscellaneous grouping

pot-ter-y [pŏt'ə-rē] *noun, no
plural,* ceramic dishes and pots
made of baked clay

pouch [pouch] *noun,* 1) a bag,
purse 2) a sack on a marsupial
for their young

poul-tice [pōl'tĭs] *noun,* a compress
used to heal a bruise or sprain

poul-try [pōl'trē] *noun,* any
domestic fowl used as food

pounce [pouns] *verb,* to jump on
something, to seize eagerly

pound [pound] *noun,* 1) a form of
money in Britain and some other
countries 2) a measure of weight
equal to 2 cups, 16 oz. 3) a place
to keep stray animals

verb, 4) to crush something by striking it over and over

pour [pôr] *verb*, to flow or cause to flow, as in making a stream

pout [pout] *verb*, to make a long face, to sulk, to mope

pov-er-ty [pŏv′ər-tē] *noun*, the state of being poor, destitute, or without money or resources

pow-der [pou′dər] *noun*, *no plural*, fine grains of matter, like dust

pow-er [pou′ər] *noun*, the ability to do something, strength or force

pow-er-ful [pou′ər-fəl] *adjective*, strong, forceful, mighty

prac-ti-cal [prăk′tĭ-kəl] *adjective*, 1) derived from actual use and experience, virtual 2) given to action rather than to speculation

prac-ti-cal-ly [prăk′tĭk-lē] *adverb*, almost, nearly

prac-tice [prăk′tĭs] *noun*, 1) an exercise 2) an habitual action 3) the work of a profession, *verb*, 4) to perform over and over to learn a skill 5) to do something as a principle of living 6) to work at a profession

prag-mat-ic [prăg-măt′ĭk] *adjective*, practical, matter of fact, using common sense

prai-r-ie [prâr′ē] *noun*, a meadow of grassland with no trees

praise [prāz] *noun*, 1) applause, approval, admiration, *verb*, 2) to say nice things about someone, to applaud, to compliment

prance [prăns] *verb*, to frolic, to dance about in a lively manner

prank [prăngk] *noun*, a playful trick, a joke, a caper

prate [prāt] *verb*, to speak foolishly, to boast idly

pray [prā] *verb*, to talk to God or a god, often asking for something or expressing gratitude

pray-er [prâr] *noun*, words spoken aloud or silently to God

preach [prēch] *verb*, to talk to people about how they should live a better life

preach-er [prē′chər] *noun*, a person who talks about living life according to the words of the Bible, a minister

pre-am-ble [prē′ăm′bəl, prē-ăm′-] *noun*, an introduction or preface

pre-car-i-ous [prĭ-kâr′ē-əs] *adjective*, depending on the will of another, uncertain

pre-cau-tion [prĭ-kô′shən] *noun*, something that is done beforehand to guard against harm, danger, mistakes, or accidents

pre-cede [prĭ-sēd′] *adjective*, to go before, to introduce or preface

prec-e-dent [prĕs′ĭ-dənt] *noun*, 1) an authoritative example 2) preceding in time or rank serving as an example

pre-cept [prē′sĕpt′] *noun*, a principle of conduct

pre-cinct [prē′sĭngkt′] *noun*, a district with certain boundaries

pre-cious [prĕsh′əs] *adjective*, 1) of great value, much loved by someone 2) costly, expensive

prec-i-pice [prĕs′ə-pĭs] *noun*, a very high and steep cliff

pre-cip-i-tate [prĭ-sĭp′ĭ-tāt′] *adjective*, 1) headlong, rash, *noun*, 2) a solid formed in a solvent in which it will not dissolve and settles as particles, *verb*, 3) to condense from vapor and fall to the earth's surface like snow or rain

pre-cip-i-ta-tion [prǐ-sǐp′ǐ-tā′shən] *noun*, water that falls as rain or snow from the atmosphere

pre-cip-i-tious [prǐ-sǐp′ǐ- tious] *adjective*, 1) very steep 2) hasty, done without careful thought

pre-cise [prǐ-sīs′] *adjective*, exact, accurate, clearly expressed

pre-ci-sion [prǐ-sǐzh′ən] *adjective*, accuracy, exactness

pre-clude [prǐ-klōōd′] *verb*, to prevent from happening, to hinder, to make impossible

pre-co-cious [prǐ-kō′shəs] *adjective*, showing skills at an earlier age than usual

pre-cur-sor [prǐ-kûr′sər] *noun*, forerunner, predecessor

pred-a-tor [prěd′ə-tər, -tôr′] *noun*, an animal that eats other animals

pred-e-ces-sor [prěd′ǐ-sěs′ər] *noun*, one that comes before another in business or sequence

pre-dic-a-ment [prǐ-dǐk′ə-mənt] *noun*, a stressful position, dilemma, or situation

pre-dict [prǐ-dǐkt′] *verb*, to make a reasonable statement about what might happen, to foretell

pre-dic-tion [prǐ-dǐk′shən] *noun*, foretelling the future, prophecy

pre-di-lec-tion [prěd′l-ěk′shən] *noun*, an inclination toward something, preference

pre-dom-i-nance [prǐ-dŏm′ə-nəns] *noun*, power over someone

pre-em-i-nent [prē-ěm′ə-nənt] *noun*, distinction above others, outstanding, superior

pref-ace [prěf′ĭs] *noun*, an explanation to the reader at the beginning of a book

pre-fer [prǐ-fûr′] *verb*, to like one thing better than another

pref-er-a-ble [prěf′ər-ə-bəl] *adjective*, a better choice

pref-er-ence [prěf′ər-əns] *noun*, one thing that is liked more than another, inclination

pre-fix [prē′fǐks′] *noun*, letters added at the front of a word to alter the meaning

preg-nant [prěg′nənt] *adjective*, having a child or offspring developing in the body

pre-his-tor-ic [prē′hǐ-stôr′ǐk] *adjective*, a time prior to recorded history

prej-u-dice [prěj′ə-dǐs] *noun*, a strong feeling against something

prel-ude [prěl′yōod′] *noun*, the introduction, forerunner

pre-ma-ture [prē′mə-tyōor′] *adjective*, too early, undeveloped

pre-mier [prǐ-mîr′] *adjective*, a head of government in many nations, such as Russia

pre-miere [prǐ-mîr′] *noun*, the first public showing or display

pre-mi-um [prē′mē-əm] *noun*, 1) a bonus given as an inducement to purchase products 2) the amount usually paid in installments by a policy holder for coverage under a contract

premonition

pre-mo-ni-tion [prē′mə-nĭsh′ən]
noun, a dream or image in which
one sees what is to come

prep-a-ra-tion [prĕp′ə-rā′shən]
noun, the act of doing something
beforehand to get ready for
something

pre-pare [prĭ-pâr′] *verb*, to make
or get ready for something

pre-pon-der-ance
[prĭ-pŏn′dər-əns] *adjective*,
superiority of weight, influence,
overwhelming power

prep-o-si-tion [prĕp′ə-zĭsh′ən]
noun, a word used before a noun
or pronoun to indicate where or
to express connections and
relationships

pre-pos-ter-ous [prĭ-pŏs′tər-əs]
adjective, absurd, ridiculous

pre-req-ui-site [prē-rĕk′wĭ-zĭt]
noun, an essential condition,
required beforehand

pre-rog-a-tive [prĭ-rŏg′ə-tĭv] *noun*,
an exclusive or peculiar right or
privilege of a certain rank

pres-age [prĕs′ĭj] *verb*, to foretell

pre-scribe [prĭ-skrīb′] *verb*, to give
directions to guide someone

pre-scrip-tion [prĭ-skrĭp′shən]
noun, a written direction for
preparation of a medicine

pres-ence [prĕz′əns] *noun*, the act
or state of being present

pre-sent [prĕz′ənt] *adjective*,
1) not past or future, now 2) in
attendance, being in a certain
place *noun*, 3) the present time,
right now 4) a gift, *verb*, 5) to
show, to perform 6) to introduce
one person to another 7) to give
as a gift

pres-en-ta-tion [prĕz′ən-tā′shən]
noun, exhibition, demonstration,
display or lecture

pre-ser-va-tion [prĕ-zûr-vā′shən]
noun, protection from harm,
danger, or rot

pre-serve [prĭ-zûrv′] *noun*, 1) an
area for the protection of wildlife
and natural resources, *verb*, 2) to
keep something in its original
form, to protect

pre-serves [prĭ-zûrvz′] *noun*
plural, fruits preserved in syrup

pre-side [prĭ-zīd′] *verb*, to control,
to lead, to manage, to oversee

pres-i-dent [prĕz′ĭ-dənt] *noun*,
1) the elected leader of the
United States government 2) the
head of a university, college or
corporation

press [prĕs] *noun*, 1) the newspaper
business or media generated
news stories, *verb*, 2) to push on
steadily with pressure 3) trying
to get someone to do something
4) pushing something to cause
an effect 5) to iron out the
wrinkles in clothing

pres-sure [prĕsh′ər] *noun*, the
action of a force against an
opposing force

pres-tige [prĕ-stēzh′] *noun*,
influence derived from past
success or reputation

pre-sume [prĭ-zōōm′] *verb*, to
assume, to conclude, to suppose

pre-sump-tion [prĭ-zŭmp′shən]
noun, an assumption

pre-sup-pose [prē′sə-pōz′] *verb*, to
assume, to consider beforehand

pre-tend [prĭ-tĕnd′] *verb*, to fake,
to make believe, to imitate

pre-tense [prē'tĕns'] *noun*, the act of pretending to be or have something you are not

pre-ten-sion [prĭ-tĕn'shən] *adjective*, when one assumes an air of superiority

pre-text [prē'tĕkst'] *noun*, a false reason to justify an action

pret-ty [prĭt'ē] *adjective*, 1) attractive, pleasing to the eye, *adverb*, 2) close to, quite, fairly

pre-vail [prĭ-vāl'] *verb*, to command, to control, to win

prev-a-lent [prĕv'ə-lənt] *adjective*, widespread, generally accepted

pre-vent [prĭ-vĕnt'] *verb*, to keep something from happening

pre-ven-tion [prĭ-vĕn'shən] *noun*, that which hinders or obstructs

pre-view [prē'vyo͞o'] *noun*, 1) a look at something before it is reproduced, *verb*, 2) to see in advance

pre-vi-ous [prē'vē-əs] *adjective*, existing or occurring earlier, prior, preceding

pre-vi-ous-ly [prē'vē-əs-lē] *adverb*, formerly, at one time, before

prey [prā] *noun*, any animal that serves as food for another animal

price [prīs] *noun*, the cost of something, what you have to pay

prick [prĭk] *verb*, to make a small hole with something sharp

pride [prīd] *noun*, *no plural*, the feeling of doing your personal best, self-respect

priest [prēst] *noun*, a clergyman of the Catholic Church

prim [prĭm] *adjective*, very precise and formal, exceedingly proper

pri-ma-ry [prī'mĕr'ē] *adjective*, 1) pertaining to elementary education or schools 2) first

prime [prīm] *adjective*, 1) best, choice, excellent, *verb*, 2) to prepare for operation, to make ready

prime min-is-ter [prīm-mĭn'ĭ-stər] *noun*, the head of government in the parliamentary system

prim-i-tive [prĭm'ĭ-tĭv] *adjective*, characterized by the manner of an early time, crude

prince [prĭns] *noun*, 1) the son of a king or queen 2) the ruler of a small country or state

prin-cess [prĭn'sĭs] *noun*, 1) the daughter of a king or queen 2) the wife of a prince

prin-ci-pal [prĭn'sə-pəl] *noun*, 1) occupying the first place or rank, most important 2) the person in charge of a school

prin-ci-ple [prĭn'sə-pəl] *noun*, 1) a source or origin 2) a fundamental truth or doctrine

print [prĭnt] *noun*, 1) the size and style of lettering in a book or poster, *verb*, 2) to press words and pictures on paper or cloth by machine 3) to write

print-er [prĭn'tər] *noun*, a device connected to a computer to make paper copies of a document

pri-or [prī'ər] *adjective*, earlier, before, preceding in time

pri-or-i-ty [prī-ôr'ĭ-tē] *noun*, most important

prism [prĭz'əm] *noun*, 1) a three dimensional object with all sides equal 2) a transparent solid that refracts light

prison

pris-on [prĭz′ən] *noun*, a place where criminals are kept while they are punished

pris-on-er [prĭz′ə-nər] *noun*, a person who is guilty of a crime and must serve a sentence of time away from society, living among other criminals

pris-tine [prĭs′tēn′] *adjective*, 1) part of earlier times, primitive 2) unspoiled, spotless

pri-va-cy [prī′və-sē] *noun*, isolation, seclusion, solitude

pri-vate [prī′vĭt] *adjective*, 1) confidential, personal, secret, *noun*, 2) an enlisted soldier

pri-va-tion [prī-vā′shən] *noun*, hardship, want, lack of comfort

priv-i-lege [prĭv′ə-lĭj] *noun*, a peculiar benefit, favor, or advantage of a group

prize [prīz] *noun*, 1) a reward for winning a contest, *verb*, 2) to cherish, to hold dear

prob-a-bil-i-ty [prŏb′ə-bĭl′ĭ-tē] *adjective*, the chance an event will occur, likelihood

prob-a-ble [prŏb′ə-bəl] *adjective*, likely to occur, plausible

prob-a-bly [prŏb′ə-blē] *adverb*, very likely to prove true

pro-bate [prō′bāt′] *noun*, proof before an officer of the county that a will is valid

pro-ba-tion [prō-bā′shən] *noun*, a trial period, an experiment

probe [prōb] *verb*, to explore with a pointed object or tool

prob-lem [prŏb′ləm] *noun*, 1) a dilemma, something that needs to be solved or worked out 2) a question on a test

pro-ce-dure [prə-sē′jər] *noun*, a manner of proceeding in any action, a process, conduct

pro-ceed [prō-sēd′] *verb*, to go onward or forward, to advance

proc-ess [prŏs′ĕs′] *noun*, 1) a method of operation 2) to change by a special treatment

pro-ces-sion [prə-sĕsh′ən] *noun*, people following one another as part of a ceremony

pro-claim [prō-klām′] *verb*, to announce officially, to declare

proc-la-ma-tion [prŏk′lə-mā′shən] *noun*, an announcement

pro-cliv-i-ty [prō-klĭv′ĭ-tē] *noun*, an inclination, a natural tendency

pro-cras-ti-nate [prō-krăs′tə-nāt′] *verb*, to postpone, to put off doing something, to delay

pro-cras-ti-na-tion [prō-krăs′tə-nā′shən] *noun*, hesitation, delaying, tarrying

prod [prŏd] *verb*, 1) to poke, to stir up, to jab 2) to urge, to nag

prod-i-gal [prŏd′ĭ-gəl] *adjective*, one who is reckless with money

pro-di-gious [prə-dĭj′əs] *adjective*, marvelous, enormous, huge

prod-i-gy [prŏd′ə-jē] *noun*, a highly gifted child, a marvel

pro-duce [prə-dōōs′] *noun*, 1) fruits of the harvest, *verb*, 2) to create, to bring forth, to provide 3) to present, to display, to exhibit 4) to cause, to make

pro-duc-er [prə-dōō′sər] *noun*, someone in charge of making a movie or film

246

prod-uct [prŏd'əkt] *noun*,
1) something that has an economic
value such as refined natural
resources or a man-made material
2) the outcome of an endeavor
3) the result of multiplying two
numbers together

pro-duc-tion [prə-dŭk'shən] *noun*,
1) creation, construction 2) that
which is the result of effort

pro-fane [prō-fān'] *adjective*, not
sacred, irreverent, secular

pro-fan-i-ty [prō-făn'ĭ-tē] *noun*,
cursing, swearing, expletive

pro-fess [prə-fĕs'] *verb*, to lay
claim to, to affirm, to declare

pro-fes-sion [prə-fĕsh'ən] *noun*, an
employment which needs
specialized study and training

pro-fes-sion-al [prə-fĕsh'ə-nəl]
adjective, 1) engaged in an
activity as a paid job 2) highly
competent

pro-fes-sor [prə-fĕs'ər] *noun*, a
teacher of the highest rank in a
university or college

prof-fer [prŏf'ər] *verb*, to offer, to
give, to present, to submit

pro-fi-cient [prə-fĭsh'ənt]
adjective, advanced in any
occupation or study, skillful

pro-file [prō'fīl'] *noun*, a drawing
or other representation of a view

prof-it [prŏf'ĭt] *noun*, 1) a
monetary gain, *verb*, 2) to be of
advantage, to gain, to benefit

prof-li-gate [prŏf'lĭ-gĭt] *adjective*,
1) wasteful 2) licentious

pro-found [prə-found'] *adjective*,
1) intense, intellectual 2) very
deep, endless, bottomless

pro-fuse [prə-fyōōs'] *adjective*,
existing in large amounts

pro-fu-sion [prə-fyōō'zhən] *noun*,
plenty, abundance

prog-e-ny [prŏj'ə-nē] *noun*,
children, offspring

prog-no-sis [prŏg-nō'sĭs] *noun*,
foretelling the course and
termination of a disease

prog-nos-ti-cate [prŏg-nŏs'tĭ-kāt']
verb, to predict, to plan for the
future, to foretell

pro-gram [prō'grăm'] *noun*, 1) a
plan of action 2) a written
outline of the order of events in a
public exercise presented as a
leaflet 3) a set of instructions
that tells a computer to do a
specific job 4) a planned
activity, verb 5) to use create a
set of instructions for a computer

pro-gress [prŏg'rĕs'] *noun*, *no
plural*, 1) a moving toward a
goal, development, *verb*, 2) to go
forward, 3) to advance to a
higher stage, to improve

pro-gres-sion [prə-grĕsh'ən] *noun*,
the act of moving forward

pro-gres-sive [prə-grĕs'ĭv]
adjective, favoring reform,
forward thinking

pro-hib-it [prō-hĭb'ĭt] *verb*, to
prevent, to forbid, to hinder

pro-hi-bi-tion [prō'ə-bĭsh'ən]
noun, a law forbidding the sale
of alcoholic liquors

proj-ect [prŏj'ĕkt'] *noun*, 1) an
activity that requires planning
and materials, *verb*, [prō-jĕkt']
2) to cause an image to be shown
on a screen 3) to stick out, to
protrude 4) to estimate

247

pro-jec-tile [prə-jĕk′təl] *noun*, an object propelled through the air

pro-jec-tion [prə-jĕk′shən] *noun*, 1) a bulge, something sticking out 2) a forecast, a prediction

pro-le-tar-i-at [prō′lĭ-târ′ē-ĭt] *noun*, a member of the working class

pro-lif-ic [prə-lĭf′ĭk] *adjective*, abundantly fruitful, plentiful

pro-logue [prō′lôg′] *noun*, an introduction to a play or a story

pro-long [prə-lông′] *verb*, to lengthen, to extend

prom-e-nade [prŏm′ə-nād′] *noun*, 1) a walk in a public place, *verb*, 2) to walk arm in arm

prom-i-nent [prŏm′ə-nənt] *adjective*, important, noticable

prom-ise [prŏm′ĭs] *noun*, 1) a declaration, binding one to do or not to do a specific act, *verb*, 2) to engage to do, to pledge

prom-is-so-ry [prŏm′ĭ-sôr′ē] *adjective*, containing or implying a promise, an informal contract such as an I.O.U. note

pro-mote [prə-mōt′] *verb*, to further, to encourage, to advance

pro-mo-tion [prə-mō′shən] *noun*, advancement in rank, improvement, support

prompt [prŏmpt] *adjective*, 1) without delay, without too much time passing, *verb*, 2) to cause to act, to urge

prompt-ly [prŏmpt′lē] *adverb*, instantly, quickly, without delay

prone [prōn] *adjective*, 1) inclined to, apt 2) lying face down

prong [prông] *noun*, a sharp projecting part, a spike

pro-noun [prō′noun′] *noun*, a word like **he**, **she**, **it**, **they**, used instead of using a noun again

pro-nounce [prə-nouns′] *verb*, 1) to assert, to declare, to proclaim 2) to speak emphasizing proper sounds and accents, to enunciate

pro-nun-ci-a-tion [prə-nŭn′sē-ā′shən] *noun*, the act of saying words with the proper sound and accent

proof [prōof] *noun*, *no plural*, facts which prove something

prop [prŏp] *noun*, 1) an accessory, *verb*, 2) to support, to reinforce 3) to encourage

prop-a-gan-da [prŏp′ə-găn′də] *noun*, an effort to spread an idea

prop-a-gate [prŏp′ə-gāt′] *verb*, to multiply, to spread around

pro-pel [prə-pĕl′] *verb*, to impel , to cause to move or continue in motion, to push forward

pro-pel-ler [prə-pĕl′ər] *noun*, blades turned by a motor to move a boat or airplane through water or air

pro-pen-si-ty [prə-pĕn′sĭ-tē] *noun*, a natural inclination, a tendency

prop-er [prŏp′ər] *adjective*, fitting, appropriate, respectable

prop-er noun [prŏp′ər noun] a particular person, place or thing, the first letters is capitalized

prop-er-ly [prŏp′ər-lē] *adverb*, correctly, rightly, absolutely

prop-er-ty [prŏp′ər-tē] *noun*, land, buildings, cars, boats, and other things people own

prop-er-ty tax [prŏp′ər-tē-tăks] *noun*, a certain amount of money paid as a tax on the land and buildings, and cars and boats a person owns

proph-e-sy [prŏf'ĭ-sī'] *noun*, 1) a prediction made after receiving a sign or a vision, *verb*, 2) to predict, to foretell, to foresee

proph-et [prŏf'ĭt] *noun*, 1) a person who predicts what is going to happen in the future 2) a person who claims to be selected by God to lead

pro-phy-lac-tic [prō'fə-lăk'tĭk] *noun*, a medicine that prevents disease, a preventive

pro-pi-tious [prə-pĭsh'əs] *adjective*, favorable conditions

pro-por-tion [prə-pôr'shən] *noun*, the relation of one portion to another in size, the ratio

pro-pos-al [prə-pō'zəl] *noun*, a formal suggestion, an offer

pro-pose [prə-pōz'] *verb*, to offer for consideration, to put forward

prop-o-si-tion [prŏp'ə-zĭsh'ən] *noun*, a plan, a scheme

pro-pri-e-tor [prə-prī'ĭ-tər] *noun*, an owner, one who has legal right to a business

pro-pri-e-ty [prə-prī'ĭ-tē] *noun*, established standards of proper behavior, appropriateness

pro-pul-sion [prə-pŭl'shən] *noun*, driving forward, thrust

prose [prōz] *noun*, ordinary language, not poetry or verse

pros-e-cute [prŏs'ĭ-kyōōt'] *verb*, to enforce the law by legal process, to seek justice for a crime

pros-pect [prŏs'pĕkt'] *noun*, 1) an expectation, a possibility, odds

2) a view, an outlook, *verb*, 3) to explore, to search

pros-pec-tus [prə-spĕk'təs] *noun*, a summary of a plan, an outline

pros-per [prŏs'pər] *verb*, to do well, to become rich, to succeed

pros-per-i-ty [prŏ-spĕr'ĭ-tē] *noun*, material well-being, success

pros-per-ous [prŏs'pər-əs] *adjective*, doing well

pros-the-sis [prŏs-thē'sĭs] *noun*, an artificial device to replace a missing part of the body

pros-trate [prŏs'trāt'] *adjective*, 1) lying down *verb*, 2) to stretch out full on the ground

pro-tect [prə-tĕkt'] *verb*, to guard or defend, to keep from harm

pro-tec-tion [prə-tĕk'shən] *noun*, preservation from loss, injury, or annoyance, safe keeping

pro-té-gé [prō'tə-zhā'] *noun*, one under the care and protection of another, often learning a craft under the guidance of a more experienced person

pro-tein [prō'tēn'] *noun*, a nutrient found in amino acids essential to the growth and repair of animal tissue found in eggs, meat, etc.

pro-test [prə-tĕst'] *noun*, 1) a complaint or formal disagreement, *verb*, 2) to disagree strongly, to object

Prot-es-tant [prŏt'ĭ-stənt] *noun*, *adjective*, a person belonging to a Christian church

pro-to-col [prō'tə-kôl'] *noun*, decorum, formalities, proper manners, a set of rules

pro-ton [prō′tŏn′] *noun*, a particle of matter, a part of an atom

pro-to-type [prō′tə-tīp′] *noun*, original work used as a model by others, an example

pro-trac-tor [prō-trăk′tər-] *noun*, a device for measuring angles on a plane or on paper

pro-trude [prō-trōōd′] *verb*, to stick out, to cause to jut out

proud [proud] *adjective*, a feeling of satisfaction over something one owns, is, or does

proud-ly [proud′lē] *adverb*, feeling a sense of accomplishment after doing your personal best

prove [prōōv] *verb*, 1) to show that something is true with evidence and tests 2) to turn out

prov-e-nance [prŏv′ə-nəns] *noun*, place or source of origin

pro-verb [prŏv′ûrb′] *noun*, a short saying that speaks the truth

pro-vide [prə-vīd′] *verb*, 1) to look out for in advance 2) to furnish

prov-i-dence [prŏv′ĭ-dəns] *noun*, divine direction, foresight

prov-ince [prŏv′ĭns] *noun*, part of a country, with its own government

pro-vin-cial [prə-vĭn′shəl] *adjective*, limited to a small area, parochial

pro-vi-sion [prə-vĭzh′ən] *noun*, requirement, a formal stipulation

pro-voke [prə-vōk′] *verb*, 1) to make someone angry, to annoy, 2) to incite to action

prowl [proul] *verb*, to sneak, to rove about stealthily

prox-im-i-ty [prŏk-sĭm′ĭ-tē] *noun*, nearness, neighborhood, vicinity

prox-y [prŏk′sē] *noun*, 1) a person authorized to act for another 2) a document giving such consent

pru-dent [prōōd′nt] *adjective*, cautious, sagacious, advisory

prune [prōōn] *noun*, 1) a dried plum, *verb*, 2) to cut off branches of a plant

pry [prī] *verb*, 1) to lift off or open by pushing with leverage 2) to snoop, to spy, to search

psalm [säm] *noun*, a sacred song or poem used to praise God

pseu-do-nym [sōōd′n-ĭm′] *noun*, a fictitious name, a pen name

psy-che [sī′kē] *noun*, 1) the soul or spirit 2) the mind's force

psy-chic [sī′k·ĭk] *adjective*, 1) apprently sensitive to supernatural forces 2) a person who predicts the future

psy-chi-a-trist [sĭ-kī′ə-trĭst] *noun*, a doctor who analyzes and treats mental problems

psy-cho [sī′kē′ō]*noun*, the mind or mental processes

psy-chol-o-gy [sī-kŏl′ə-jē] *noun*, the study of mental states, the mind and its processes

psy-cho-sis [sī-kō′sĭs] *noun*, a major mental disorder in which the personality is very seriously disorganized and one's sense of reality is usually altered

pto-maine [tō′mān′] *noun*, an alkaloid from decomposing animals that is usually poisonous

pub-lic [pŭb′lĭk] *adjective*, 1) open to everyone, *noun*, 2) the people constituting a community

pub-li-ca-tion [pŭb′lĭ-kā′shən] *noun*, published material

pub-lic-i-ty [pŭ-blĭs/ĭ-tē] *noun*, public notice and attention

pub-lish [pŭb/lĭsh] *verb*, to print and sell a manuscript

pub-lish-er [pŭb/lĭ-shər] *noun*, one who creates and offers for sale books, magazines, or newspapers

pud-ding [poŏd/ĭng] *noun*, a custard made of milk, sugar and eggs boiled together

pud-dle [pŭd/l] *noun*, a small pool of water on the ground

puff [pŭf] *noun*, 1) a quick burst of air, smoke, etc. *verb*, 2) to make short quick breaths of air

pu-is-sant [pwĭs/ənt] *adjective*, powerful, strong, potent

pul-chri-tude [pŭl/krĭ-toōd/] *noun*, beauty, loveliness, charm

pull [poŏl] *noun*, 1) a force, a power, strength, *verb*, 2) to move something toward oneself through grasping and drawing with force 3) to put on

pul-ley [poŏl/ē] *noun*, a wheel used to transmit power by means of a band, rope, or chain

pul-mo-nar-y [poŏl/mə-nĕr/ē] *adjective*, affecting the lungs

pulp [pŭlp] *noun*, 1) a soft, moist, sticky mass of fibers made up of wood, straw, etc. and used to make paper and paperboard 2) the soft moist part of fruit that is left after the seeds and peels are removed

pul-pit [poŏl/pĭt] *noun*, an elevated desk or platform in a church for a preacher or orator

pul-sate [pŭl/sāt/] *verb*, to throb

pulse [pŭls] *noun*, a heart beat

pul-ver-ize [pŭl/və-rīz/] *verb*, to reduce to a fine powder or dust

pum-mel [pŭm/əl] *verb*, to beat

pump [pŭmp] *noun*, 1) a machine for making liquid or gas move by putting air into something or to extract water or other liquid from the ground using a special lever, *verb*, 2) to draw up using up and down action

pump-kin [pŭmp/kĭn] *noun*, a large orange gourd-like fruit, used in cooking

punch [pŭnch] *noun*, 1) a hit aimed squarely with a fist 2) a fruit drink, *verb*, 3) to hit someone very hard with a fist

punc-tu-al [pŭngk/choō-əl] *adjective*, on time

punc-tu-al-i-ty [pŭngk/choō-ăl/ĭ-tē] *adverb*, being prompt, making a point of being on time

punc-tu-ate [pŭngk/choō-āt/] *verb*, to add proper signs and marks of grammar to writing

punc-tu-a-tion [pŭngk/choō-ā/shən] *noun*, *no plural*, signs like „ : , ? and ! used in writing so that the reader emphasizes certain ideas expressed on paper

punc-ture [pŭngk/chər] *noun*, 1) perforation with something pointed, *verb*, 2) to penetrate, to pierce, to make a hole

pun-dit [pŭn/dĭt] *noun*, a critic, a commentator, an expert

pun-gent [pŭn/jənt] *adjective*, powerful or strong odor or flavor

pun-ish [pŭn/ĭsh] *verb*, to discipline, to reprove, to correct

pun-ish-ment [pŭn′ĭsh-mənt] *noun*, 1) a penalty 2) rough or injurious treatment inflicted for an offense

pu-ny [pyo͞o′nē] *adjective*, insignificant, tiny, weak

pu-pa [pyo͞o′pə] *noun*, the inactive stage of development of an insect before reaching the adult, often in a cocoon or a cell

pu-pil [pyo͞o′pəl] *noun*, 1) a boy or girl being taught by a teacher 2) a black dot, the expanding and contracting opening in the iris of the eye, in the middle of the eye that receives light

pup-pet [pŭp′ĭt] *noun*, a small doll that looks like a person or an animal that is moved by wires or with hands on a small stage

pup-py [pəpē′] *noun*, a young dog

pur-chase [pûr′chĭs] *noun*, 1) something that has been paid for, an acquisition, *verb*, 2) to acquire for a price, to buy

pure [pyo͞or] *adjective*, without anything mixed into it, clean, unpolluted, spotless

pur-ga-to-ry [pûr′gə-tôr′ē] *noun*, 1) a place where a sinner makes amends 2) limbo

purge [pûrj] *verb*, 1) to clean by removing impurities 2) to remove all criminal charges from public record

pu-ri-fy [pyo͞or′ə-fī′] *verb*, to make clean, to free from imperfection

pu-ri-ty [pyo͞or′ĭ-tē] *noun*, cleanliness, pureness, innocence

pur-loin [pər-loin′] *verb*, to steal

pur-ple [pûr′pəl] *adjective*, 1) the color of violets, *noun*, 2) a color made by mixing red and blue pigments

pur-pose [pûr′pəs] *noun*, the reason for which something exists or has been done

purse [pûrs] *noun*, 1) a small hand bag to hold money and personal items 2) prize money from a race

pur-sue [pər-so͞o′] *verb*, to follow with a view to overtake, to persecute, to capture

pur-suit [pər-so͞ot′] *noun*, an aim, an objective, a search

pur-vey-or [pər-vā′ər] *noun*, someone who provides food

push [po͝osh] *noun*, 1) a shove, a rigorous effort, *verb*, 2) to press or lean against, so as to move

put [po͝ot] *verb*, 1) to move, to place 2) to impose, to assign

pu-trid [pyo͞o′trĭd] *adjective*, foul, rotten, decayed, disgusting

put-ty [pŭt′ē] *noun*, an adhesive, glue, compound to seal something

puz-zle [pŭz′əl] *noun*, 1) a picture cut into many pieces to be put back together 2) a game designed to make it difficult for you to finish, *verb*, 3) to exercise one's mind 4) to perplex

pyg-my [pĭg′mē] *noun*, a dwarf, a very small person in Africa

pyr-a-mid [pĭr′ə-mĭd] *noun*, 1) a solid shape with a square base and pointed top, whose faces are triangles with a common corner 2) huge monuments in the desert of Egypt, built as burial vaults for ancient Egyptian kings

py-ro-ma-ni-ac [pī′rō-mā′nē-ăk′] *noun*, a person who likes to set fires and watch them burn

Q

quack [kwăk] *noun*, 1) an imposter, a fake, *verb*, 2) to make noises like a duck

quad-ri-lat-er-al [kwŏd′rə-lăt′ər-əl] *noun*, a four-sided polygon

quad-ru-ped [kwŏd′rə-pĕd′] *noun*, a four-footed animal

quad-ru-ple [kwŏ-drōō′pəl] *verb*, to multiply by four

quaff [kwŏf] *verb*, to drink with enthusiasm

quag-mire [kwăg′mīr′] *noun*, a bog, a marsh, muddy soil

quail [kwāl] *noun*, 1) a game bird that lives in the woods, *verb*, 2) to cower in fear

quaint [kwānt] *adjective*, pleasing in an unusual way, peculiar, odd

quake [kwāk] *verb*, to shake, to shudder, to tremble, to quiver

qual-i-fi-ca-tion [kwŏl′ə-fĭ-kā′shən] *noun*, special training or knowledge

qual-i-fy [kwŏl′ə-fī′] *verb*, 1) to meet the set criteria 2) to make less harsh or strict

qual-i-ty [kwŏl′ĭ-tē] *noun,* 1) a characteristic that distinguishes one person or thing from another 2) a degree of excellence

qualm [kwäm] *noun*, misgiving, remorse, uneasiness

quan-ti-ty [kwŏn′tĭ-tē] *noun*, an amount of something

quar-an-tine [kwôr′ən-tēn′] *noun*, 1) separation of people with a contagious disease, *verb*, 2) to be separated from society while suffering from an infectious disease in order to prevent the disease from spreading

quar-rel [kwôr′əl] *noun*, 1) an angry dispute, *verb*, 2) to argue or disagree, to fight with words

quar-ry [kwôr′ē] *noun*, 1) a deep pit where stone is cut out of the gound to use for buildings 2) prey, an animal that is being hunted

quart [kwôrt] *noun*, a liquid measurement equal to 32 ounces, 1.13 liters, ¼ of a gallon, 2 pints

quar-ter [kwôr′tər] *noun*, 1) a coin worth 25 cents 2) one of four equal parts, one fourth

quar-ters [kwôr′tərz] *noun*, *plural*, a place where people live, especially if they live where they work

quar-tet [kwôr-tĕt′] *noun*, a group of musicians or singers, also, a piece of music for four instruments or voices

quartz [kwôrts] *noun*, a mineral compound of silica

queen [kwēn] *noun*, 1) the wife of the king 2) any woman who rules a country born to that title, a female monarch 4) any woman who is very important

queer [kwîr] *adjective*, odd, different in a strange way

quell [kwĕl] *verb*, to put down, to quiet, to suppress, to pacify

quench [kwĕnch] *verb*, 1) to satisfy one's thirst or appetite 2) to extinguish, to put out

que-ry [kwîr′ē] *noun*, 1) a question, *verb*, 2) to doubt or question, to interrogate

quest [kwĕst] *noun*, a search, a journey, an exploration

ques-tion [kwĕs′chən] *noun*, 1) an inquiry, *verb*, 2) to ask, to inquire 3) to doubt, to quiz

ques-tion mark [kwĕs′chən-märk] *noun*, the sign ? used at the end of a sentence which asks a question

ques-tion-naire [kwĕs′chə-nâr′] *noun*, a survey submitted to obtain information, a printed set of questions

queue [kyo͞o] *noun*, a line of people waiting for something

quib-ble [kwĭb′əl] *verb*, to equivocate, to play with words

quick [kwĭk] *adjective*, very fast,

quick-en [kwĭk′ən] *verb*, to hurry, to rush, to hasten, to accelerate

quick-ly [kwĭk′lē] *adverb*, in a hurry, fast, promptly

qui-et [kwī′ĭt] *adjective*, 1) making little or no sound, not moving , still, *noun*, 2) silence

qui-et-ly [kwī′ĭt- lē] *adverb*, calmly, peacefully, silently

quill [kwĭl] *noun*, 1) a large feather from a bird's tail or wing 2) a sharp spine of a porcupine

quilt [kwĭlt] *noun*, a blanket made by sewing small pieces of fabric together in a design

quince [kwĭns] *noun*, a bitter fruit resembling a large yellow apple

quin-tes-sence [kwĭn-tĕs′əns] *noun*, the purest and highest essence of something

quip [kwĭp] *noun*, a taunting remark, a witty remark

quit [kwĭt] *verb*, to give up, to surrender, to depart, to leave

quite [kwīt] *adverb*, completely, entirely, actually, really

quiv-er [kwĭv′ər] *noun*, 1) a case for holding arrows 2) a trembling, *verb*, 2) to shake a little, to tremble nervously

quix-ot-ic [kwĭk-sŏt′ĭk] *adjective*, romantically idealistic

quiz [kwĭz] *noun*, 1) a small test, *verb*, 2) to ask a few questions

quo-rum [kwôr′əm] *noun*, the number of members of any body legally necessary to transact business

quo-ta [kwō′tə] *noun*, the amount, quantity, proportion

quo-ta-tion [kwō-tā′shən] *noun*, 1) words spoken or written lifted from their context 2) the naming or publishing of the current prices of stocks, bonds, etc., the price named

quote [kwōt] *verb*, to say or write something that has been said before by another person

quo-tient [kwō′shənt] *noun*, the product from the division of one number by another

R

rab-bi [răb′ī] *noun*, the leader or teacher of the Jewish religion

rab-bit [răb′ĭt] *noun*, a small furry animal with long ears and long back legs that burrows holes and lives underground

rab-ies [rā′bēz] *noun*, disease caused by organisms called a virus that attacks the nervous system

rac-coon [ră-kōōn'] *noun*, a large black and white nocturnal rodent that lives in trees

race [rās] *noun*, 1) a competitive event, a contest 2) a part of humanity, an ethnic background, *verb*, 3) to run in a dash or compete in a contest

ra-cial [rā'shəl] *adjective*, pertaining to ethnic differences

rac-ism [rā'sĭz'əm] *noun*, narrow-mindedness, intolerance, bigotry

rack [răk] *noun*, 1) a frame on which things are hung or kept, *verb*, 2) to cause pain

rack-et [răk'ĭt] *noun*, 1) a light bat with a netted hoop 2) a loud or confused noise

ra-dar [rā'där] *noun*, *no plural*, the ability to find the position of something using radio waves

ra-di-ant [rā'dē-ənt] *adjective*, shining, luminous, bright

ra-di-ate [rā'dē-āt'] *verb*, to give off energy or rays of light

ra-di-a-tor [rā'dē-ā'tər] *noun*, a device used to cool a liquid

rad-i-cal [răd'ĭ-kəl] *adjective*, unconventional, odd

ra-di-o [rā'dē-ō] *noun*, 1) the use of electromagnetic waves to carry messages without the use of wires, *verb*, 2) to send or transmit messages in this manner

ra-di-o-act-ive waste [rā'dē-ōăk'tĭvwāst] *noun*, waste left over from creating nuclear power or atomic energy which gives off radiant energy in rays or particles by the disintegration of the atomic nuclei such as found in radium and uranium

ra-di-um [rā'dē-əm] *noun*, a metallic element found in minute quantities, capable of spontaneously emitting rays

ra-di-us [rā'dē-əs] *noun*, the distance from the center of a circle to its perimeter

raft [răft] *noun*, large pieces of wood joined to make a flat floating surface

raft-er [răf'tər] *noun*, a crossbeam

rag [răg] *noun*, 1) an old torn garment 2) a piece of cloth used to clean, polish or dust

rage [rāj] *noun*, fierce anger that continues with great force

raid [rād] *noun*, 1) a surprise attack, *verb*, 2) to invade, to attack, to assault

rail [rāl] *noun*, 1) a bar extending horizontally between two posts as in a fence or railroad ties, *verb*, 2) to scold, to rant and rave

rail-ing [rā'lĭng] *noun*, a fence or partition to keep people or animals from straying into places they should not go

rail-road [rāl'rōd'] *noun*, a road or track built with parallel steel rails and used by trains

rain [rān] *noun*, 1) part of a weather pattern when water droplets fall from the sky *verb*, 2) to fall as water in drops from the sky 3) to fall like rain

rain-bow [rān'bō'] *noun*, an arc-shaped spectrum of colors seen in the sky, caused by sunlight refracted by raindrops

rain-coat [rān′kōt′] *noun*, a coat that protects a person from getting wet

rain-fall [rān′fôl′] *noun*, the amount of water falling within a given time or area

raise [rāz] *noun*, 1) an increase in salary, *verb*, 2) to lift up, to elevate 3) to grow or cultivate

rai-sin [rā′zĭn] *noun*, a dried grape

rake [rāk] *noun*, 1) a long-handled tool with teeth used to gather leaves on the ground, *verb*, 2) to use a tool to gather fallen leaves or to smooth soil

ral-ly [răl′ē] *noun*, 1) a mass meeting, an assembly, a gathering, *verb*, 2) to restore, to recover, to renew 3) to counter attack

ram [răm] *noun*, a male sheep

ram-ble [răm′bəl] *verb*, 1) to wander in a leisurely manner 2) to chatter, to babble

ram-i-fi-ca-tion [răm′ə-fĭ-kā′shən] *noun*, 1) branching out, a diversion 2) a complicated outcome of a statement or plan

ramp [rămp] *noun*, a slanted walk or roadway that connects a lower to a higher place

ram-page [răm′pāj′] *noun*, a rage, violent behavior, a tantrum

ramp-ant [răm′pənt] *adjective*, unruly, furious, unrestrained

ram-part [răm′pärt′, -pərt] *noun*, a defensive mound of earth

ran [răn] *past tense* of **run**

ranch [rănch] *noun*, a rural estate where livestock are raised

ran-cid [răn′sĭd] *adjective*, rotten, an unpleasant smell or taste

ran-cor [răng′kər] *noun*, bitterness, hatred, malice, ill will

ran-dom [răn′dəm] *adjective*, without order or logic

range [rānj] *noun*, 1) a line of mountains or hills 2) an extensive variety of different things 3) the distance something can travel on its own

rang-er [rān′jər] *noun*, an enforcement agent assigned to patrol a certain region

rank [răngk] *adjective*, 1) bad smell, *noun*, 2) a class thought of as higher or lower than other groups, *verb*, 3) to classify in a group 4) to arrange in a row

ran-kle [răng′kəl] *verb*, to make someone annoyed and mad

ran-sack [răn′săk′] *verb*, to search a house thoroughly

ran-som [răn′səm] *noun*, the release of a person in return for payment

rant [rănt] *verb*, to talk wildly, to speak bombastically

rap [răp] *verb*, 1) to knock, to tap, to thump 2) to talk, to chat

rap-id [răp′ĭd] *adjective*, very fast, quick, swift, often, speedy

rap-id-ly [răp′ĭd-lē] *adverb*, quickly, hurriedly, swiftly

rap-ids [răp′ĭdz] *noun*, *plural*, a place in the river where the river descends creating swift currents producing white water

rap-ture [răp′chər] *noun*, joy, delight, bliss, exhilaration

rare [râr] *adjective*, unusual, uncommon, hard to come by

rare-ly [râr′lē] *adverb*, once in a great while, very seldom

ras-cal [răs′kəl] *noun*, a deceitful person, a mischievous child

rash [răsh] *adjective*, 1) acting quickly without thinking about the results, reckless, *noun*, 2) a patch of red spots on the skin, indicating an allergy

rasp-ber-ry [răz′bĕr′ē] *noun*, a red or purple berry that grows on a bush

rat [răt] *noun*, 1) a small rodent, larger than a mouse, that lives on grain 2) an informer

rate [rāt] *noun*, 1) a relative amount 2) the speed of something, *verb*, 3) to evaluate, to rank, to grade, to consider

rath-er [răth′ər, rä′thər] *adjective*, preferable, instead, somewhat

rat-i-fy [răt′ə-fī′] *verb*, to approve formally, to endorse, to confirm

ra-tio [rā′shē-ō′] *noun*, the relation between quantity, degree or rate between one thing and another

rati-oci-na-tion [răsh′ē-ŏs′ə-nā′shən] *noun*, reasoning logically, the process of exact thinking

ra-tion [răsh′ən, rā′shən] *noun*, 1) a fixed amount of something that is given or allowed, *verb*, 2) to limit the amount of resources to each person or group

ra-tion-al [răsh′ə-nəl] *adjective*, reasonable, intelligent, sensible

ra-tion-al-i-za-tion [răsh′ə-nə-lĭ-zā′shən] *noun*, bringing into conformity with reason, logical thinking

ra-tion-al-ize [răsh′ə-nə-līz′] *verb*, to explain away, to make excuses, to justify

rat-tle [răt′l] *noun*, 1) a toy with beads inside that makes a noise when shaken, *verb*, 2) to shake, to clatter, to move noisily

rau-cous [rô′kəs] *adjective*, rough in sound, harsh, strident

rav-age [(răv′ĭj] *verb*, to plunder, to destroy or wreck, to ruin

rave [rāv] *verb*, to speak enthusiastically about something

rav-en-ous [răv′ə-nəs] *adjective*, extremely hungry

ra-vine [rə-vēn′] *noun*, a long, deep ditch or valley in the earth with steep sides, a gorge

raw [rô] *adjective*, 1) uncooked, bloody 2) something in its natural, unadulterated state 3) cold and damp

ray [rā] *noun*, 1) a thin beacon of light 2) part of a line that has an endpoint and goes on and on in one direction 3) a trace, hint

ray-on [rā′ŏn] *noun*, a fine cloth that looks like glossy silk

raze [rāz] *verb*, to level to the ground, to destroy completely

ra-zor [rā′zər] *noun*, a keen edged cutting instrument especially used for shaving

reach [rēch] *noun*, *no plural*, 1) the distance that can be attained 2) grasp, *verb*, 3) to stretch out to touch or take something 4) to get to a place, to arrive at

re-act [rē-ăkt′] *verb*, to act because of something that has happened

re-ac-tion [rē-ăk′shən] *noun*, a direct response

re-ac-tion-ar-y [rē-ăk′shə-nĕr′ē] *adjective*, someone who is against progress

read [rēd] *verb*, to look at words and understand them

read-i-ly [rĕd′ə-lē] *adverb*, easily, willingly, without hesitating

read-i-ness [rĕd′ē-nĭs] *adjective*, willingness, eagerness, ease

re-ad-just [rē′ə-jŭst′] *verb*, to adapt, to fine tune

read-y [rĕd′ē] *adjective*, 1) willing, able, prepared 2) at hand

re-al [rē′əl, rēl] *adjective*, factual, actually existing, true

re-al-ism [rē′ə-lĭz′əm] *noun*, a philosophy that regards external objects as the most fundamentally real things, and perceptions or ideas as secondary

re-al-ist [rē′ə-lĭst] *noun*, 1) someone with a practical outlook 2) an attempt to make art and literature resemble life

re-al-i-ty [rē-ăl′ĭ-tē] *noun*, fact, truth, real things, actuality

re-al-i-za-tion [rē′ə-lĭ-zā′shən] *noun*, a perception, an awareness

re-al-ize [rē′ə-līz′] *verb*, 1) to understand, to make real, to become aware of 2) to achieve

re-al-ly [rē′ə-lē′] *adverb*, truly, very, genuinely, indeed

realm [rĕlm] *noun*, region, sphere, domain or province, kingdom

ream [rēm] *noun*, in the paper business, 500 sheets of paper

reap [rēp] *verb*, to gather the harvest by cutting

rear [rîr] *adjective*, 1) at the back, behind, *noun*, 2) the back part, *verb*, 3) to raise children or livestock until they grow up

rea-son [rē′zən] *noun*, 1) the answer or explanation given as part of a belief 2) a cause for acting, thinking, or feeling a special way, *verb*, 3)) to think things through to present an opinion, to conclude, to infer

rea-son-a-ble [rē′zə-nə-bəl] *adjective*, governed by reason, not excessive, logical

rea-son-a-bly [rē′zə-nə-blē] *adverb*, adequately, fairly, sufficiently, logically

rea-son-ing [rē′zə-nĭng] *noun*, the thought process, logic

re-as-sure [rē′ə-shŏŏr′] *verb*, to help feel safe and comfortable

re-as-sur-ance [rē′ə-shŏŏr′əns] *noun*, restoring confidence

re-bate [rē′bāt′] *noun*, a deduction offered on a purchase in the form of a refund

re-bel [rĕb′əl] *noun*, 1) someone who fights against the leadership of a government, *verb*, 2) to defy any authority, to revolt

re-bel-lion [rĭ-bĕl′yən] *noun*, a revolt, resistance, mutiny

re-bel-lious [rĭ-bĕl′yəs] *adjective*, someone who resists the law, defying authority

re-bound [rē′bound′] *verb*, 1) to bounce back, to move like a boomerang 2) to recover

re-buff [rǐ-bǔf′] *noun,* 1) a sharp rejection, a snub, *verb,* 2) to drive back or repel 3) to refuse bluntly, to reject, to snub

re-build [rē-bǐld′] *verb,* to repair, to put in working order

re-but-tal [rǐ-bǔt′l] *noun,* an argument introduced by the other side in a debate

re-cal-ci-trant [rǐ-kǎl′sǐ-trənt] *adjective,* obstinately stubborn

re-call [rǐ-kôl′] *verb,* 1) to summon or call back, 2) to remember

re-cant [rǐ-kǎnt′] *verb,* to withdraw a previous statement

re-ca-pit-u-late [rē′kə-pǐch′ə-lāt′] *verb,* to repeat the principal points in a program

re-cede [rǐ-sēd′] *verb,* to move back, to retreat, to withdraw

re-ceipt [rǐ-sēt′] *noun,* a written acknowledgment that something was received

re-ceive [rǐ-sēv′] *verb,* to take in, to come into possession of, accept

re-cent [rē′sənt] *adjective,* something that happened a little while ago, prior to the present

re-cent-ly [rē′sənt-lē] *adverb,* a short while ago

re-cep-ta-cle [rǐ-sěp′tə-kəl] *noun,* 1) a container 2) a contact device in an electrical outlet

re-cep-tion [rǐ-sěp′shən] *noun,* 1) a greeting, a welcome 2) a social gathering 3) receiving television or radio wave frequencies

re-cess [rē′sěs′] *noun,* 1) a short intermission 2) a space formed by indentation, a niche

re-ces-sion [rǐ-sěsh′ən] *noun,* an economic slow down

characterized by high unemployment

re-cid-i-vism [rǐ-sǐd′ə-vǐz′əm] *noun,* habitual return to crime

rec-i-pe [rěs′ə-pē′] *noun,* a list of ingredients and directions for preparing something

re-cip-i-ent [rǐ-sǐp′ē-ənt] *noun,* the person who accepts something

re-cip-ro-cal [rǐ-sǐp′rə-kəl] *adjective,* mutual, exchangeable, interacting, given in return

re-cip-ro-cate [rǐ-sǐp′rə-kāt′] *verb,* to return the favor for something done or given, to respond in kind

re-cit-al [rǐ-sīt′l] *noun,* a program of music or dance before an audience

re-cite [rǐ-sīt′] *verb,* to repeat from memory, to narrate in detail

reck-less [rěk′lǐs] *adjective,* careless and dangerous

reck-on [rěk′ən] *verb,* to come to terms with, to settle matters

re-claim [rǐ-klām′] *verb,* to bring back, to restore, to recover

re-cline [rǐ-klīn′] *verb,* to lean back

rec-luse [rěk′lōōs′] *noun,* a hermit

rec-og-ni-tion [rěk′əg-nǐsh′ən] *noun,* 1) acknowledgment of something done or given 2) acknowledgment of acquaintance

rec-og-nize [rěk′əg-nīz′] *verb,* 1) to acknowledge formally 2) to identify as previously seen or known 3) to greet, to accept

re-coil [rǐ-koil′] *verb,* to retreat, or drawback, to shrink back

rec-ol-lect [rěk′ə-lěkt′] *verb,* to call to mind, to remember

rec-ol-lec-tion [rĕk′ə-lĕk′shən] *noun*, something remembered

re-com-mend [rĕk′ə-mĕnd′] *verb*, to present favorably, to urge or suggest, to advise

re-com-men-da-tion [rĕk′ə-mĕn-dā′shən] *noun*, a suggestion for what is most suitable

rec-om-pense [rĕk′əm-pĕns′] *noun*, 1) compensation, payment, *verb*, 2) to pay for service received

rec-on-cil-able [rĕk′ən-sī′lə-bəl, rĕk′ən-sī′-] *adjective*, capable of being restored to friendship

re-con-cile [rĕk′ən-sīl′] *verb*, 1) to restore to friendship 2) to settle a quarrel 3) to be resigned to accept things as they are

rec-on-dite [rĕk′ən-dīt′] *adjective*, hard to understand, profound, hidden from view, abstruse

re-con-nais-sance [rĭ-kŏn′ə-səns] *noun*, a survey of the enemy by soldiers, reconnoitering

re-con-struct [rē′kən-strŭkt′] *verb*, to put something together or make it again, to rebuild

re-cord [rĭ-kôrd′,rĕk′ərd] *noun*, 1) a written account of what happened 2) a plastic disk on which sounds are recorded, *verb*, 3) to write down something that has happened 4) to register on a disk in a permanent form

re-cord-er [rĭ-kôr′dər] *noun*, 1) an office worker, a secretary 2) a wooden or plastic flute played like a whistle

re-count [rĭ-kount′] *verb*, 1) to tell a story, to narrate 2) to count again

re-course [rē′kôrs′] *noun*, resorting to help when in trouble

re-cov-er [rĭ-kŭv′ər] *verb*, 1) to get back to a normal state, to get well, to recuperate 2) to get back what was lost or stolen

re-cov-er-y [rĭ-kŭv′ə-rē] *noun*, a return to good health

rec-re-a-tion [rĕk′rē-ā′shən] *noun*, sports or play as a form of enjoyable relaxation

re-crim-i-na-tion [rĭ-krĭm′ə-nā′shən] *noun*, an accusation in response to another, a countercharge

re-cruit [rĭ-krōōt′] *noun*, 1) a new member who agrees to join a group, *verb*, 2) to enlist, to attract new members

rec-tan-gle [rĕk′tăng′gəl] *noun*, a flat shape with four straight sides and four right angles, the opposite sides of which are parallel

rec-ti-fy [rĕk′tə-fī′] *verb*, to correct, to make better

rec-ti-tude [rĕk′tĭ-tōōd′] *noun*, uprightness, moral virtue

re-cu-per-ate [rĭ-kōō′pə-rāt′] *verb*, to recover, to restore to health

re-cur [rĭ-kûr′] *verb*, to return again and again as an event

re-cur-rent [rĭ-kûr′ənt] *adjective*, returning repeatedly or coming again to mind

re-cy-cle [rē-sī′kəl] *verb*, to process materials so they can be made into new products

red [rĕd] *adjective*, 1) crimson, cherry, ruby, *noun*, 2) one of the three primary colors: blue, yellow and red

re-deem [rĭ-dēm′] *verb*, 1) to recover, 2) to buy back 3) to exchange 4) to fulfill

red-o-lent [rĕd′l-ənt] *adjective*, 1) fragrant, a pleasant odor 2) strongly reminiscent

re-dress [rĭ-drĕs′] *verb*, to set right, to make amends for, to remedy

re-duce [rĭ-dōōs′] *verb*, to diminish, to make smaller or use less

re-duc-tion [rĭ-dŭk′shən] *noun*, 1) the act of making less 2) the amount by which something is diminished

re-dun-dant [rĭ-dŭn′dənt] *adjective*, superfluous, excessively wordy, repetitious

reed [rēd] *noun*, 1) a small, thin, flat piece of wood, metal, or plastic used in the mouthpiece of some musical instruments, such as the clarinet 2) a tall sturdy grass that grows in the water

reef [rēf] *noun*, a ridge of sand, rocks, or coral, off shore but close to the water's surface

reek [rēk] *verb*, to give off an odor

reel [rēl] *noun*, 1) a spool that turns, winding or unwinding a fishing line 2) a Scottish dance *verb*, 3) to feel happy, elated with excitement

re-enact [rē′ĕn-ăkt′] *verb*, to perform as if for the first time

re-fer [rĭ-fûr′] *verb*, 1)to recommend someone go to see someone for help 2) to use a resource for help

ref-er-ee [rĕf′ə-rē′] *noun*, a sports official with final authority for conducting a game

ref-er-ence [rĕf′ər-əns] *noun*, 1) a specific direction of the attention 2) a written statement of the qualifications of another 3) a resource such as a, dictionary, encyclopedia, thesaurus

re-fine [rĭ- fīnd] *verb*, to reduce to a fine, unmixed, or pure state by removing all unwanted matter

re-fined [rĭ-fīn′d] *adjective*, 1) in a pure state 2) having good manners and good taste

re-fin-er-y [rĭ-fī′nə-rē] *noun*, a factory where resources like oil or sugar are made ready for use

re-flect [rĭ-flĕkt′] *verb*, 1) to throw or cast back the sun's rays 2) to think, to ponder, to meditate

re-flec-tion [rĭ-flĕk′shən] *noun*, 1) an image bounced back from a shiny surface 2) an object seen in a mirror 3) serious thought, thinking back on something

re-flec-tor [rĭ-flĕk′tər] *noun*, a polished surface that reflects light, heat or sound

re-flex [rē′flĕks′] *adjective*, mechanical, unthinking, habitual

re-form [rĭ-fôrm′] *noun*, 1) a change, an improvement, *verb*, 2) to correct, to revise, to renew

re-form-a-to-ry [rĭ-fôr′mə-tôr′ē] *noun*, a jail or prison

re-frac-tion [rĭ-frăk′shən] *noun*, the bending of a ray of light

re-frain [rĭ-frān′] *noun*, 1) a chorus, a verse, *verb*, 2) to abstain, to keep oneself from doing something

re-fresh [rĭ-frĕsh′] *verb*, to revive with rest or food, to renew

re-fresh-ment [rĭ-frĕsh′mənt]
noun, food and drink

re-frig-er-a-tor [rĭ-frĭj′ə-rā′tər]
noun, an appliance that preserves
food in cool temperatures

ref-uge [rĕf′yŏōj] *noun*, a safe
place, a place to hide

ref-u-gee [rĕf′yŏō-jē′] *noun*, an
exile, someone forced to leave
his country

re-fund [rĭ-fŭnd′] *noun*,
1) reimbursement, repayment,
verb, 2) to give back, to
reimburse, to repay

re-fur-bish [rē-fûr′bĭsh] *verb*, to
repair and make useful

re-fus-al [rĭ-fyŏō′zəl] *noun*, a
denial, a refusal

ref-use [rĭ-fyŏōz′] *noun*, 1) a
general term for solid waste
materials, also called garbage or
trash, *verb*, 2) to deny, not to
allow or agree, to decline to do

re-fute [rĭ-fyŏōt′] *verb*, to prove
false, to disprove, to rebut

re-gain [rĭ- gān] *verb,* to get back

re-gal [rē′gəl] *adjective*, royal,
majestic, stately, splendid

re-gale [rĭ-gāl′] *verb*, to entertain

re-gard [rĭ-gärd′] *noun*, *plural*,
1) respect, concern, *verb*, 2) to
think of or see 3) to relate to

re-gard-ing [rĭ-gär′dĭng]
preposition, about, concerning

re-gard-less [rĭ-gärd′lĭs] *adverb*,
without concern for problems or
objections, despite, although

re-gat-ta [rĭ-gä′tə] *noun*, a boat or
yacht race

re-gen-er-ate [rĭ-jĕn′ə-rāt′] *verb*, to
renew, to reconstitute

re-gen-er-a-tion [rĭ-jĕn′ə-rā′shən]
noun, a spiritual rebirth

re-gime [rā-zhēm′] *noun*, character
of government or of a prevailing
social system

reg-i-men [rĕj′ə-mən] *noun*, a
systematic plan usually to
improve health

reg-i-ment [rĕj′ə-mənt] *noun*, 1) an
infantry unit 2) to systematize

re-gion [rē′jən] *noun*, an indefinite
area, a territory, a district

reg-is-ter [rĕj′ĭ-stər] *noun*, 1) an
entry in a book or record, *verb*,
2) to enter one's name on the
list, catalogue, record

reg-is-trar [rĕj′ĭ-strär′] *noun*, a
keeper of records

reg-is-tra-tion [rĕj′ĭ-strā′shən]
noun, enrollment

re-gret [rĭ-grĕt′] *noun*, 1) an
apology, a feeling of remorse,
verb, 2) to feel sadness for doing
something wrong

re-gret-ta-ble [rĭ-grĕt′ə-bəl]
adjective, unfortunate, sad

reg-u-lar [rĕg′yə-lər] *adjective*,
habitual, customary, routine

reg-u-lar-i-ty [rĕg′yə-lăr′ĭ-tē]
noun, *no plural*, uniformity,
constancy, on a regular basis

reg-u-late [rĕg′yə-lāt′] *verb*, to
control or direct by a rule

reg-u-la-tion [rĕg′yə-lā′shən]
noun, a rule of conduct, a law

re-gur-gi-tate [rē-gûr′jĭ-tāt′] *verb*,
to spit out food that has been
swallowed, to vomit

re-ha-bil-i-tate [rē′hə-bĭl′ĭ-tāt′]
verb, to restore to proper
condition, i.e., good health

re-hears-al [rǐ-hûr'səl] *noun*, a practice performance

re-hearse [rǐ-hûrs'] *verb*, to practice in preparation for a performance, to try out

reign [rān] *noun*, 1) the period of time when a king or queen rules, *verb*, 2) to rule or govern

re-im-burse [rē'ǐm-bûrs'] *verb*, to make restoration, to repay

rein [rān] *noun*, 1) a strap of a bridle for governing a horse or other animal, *verb*, 2) to pull back or control, to check

rein-deer [rān'dîr'] *noun*, a large deer of arctic regions used to pull a cart or sled

re-in-force [rē'ǐn-fôrs'] *verb*, to strengthen, to stiffen, to fortify

re-it-er-ate [rē-ǐt'ə-rāt'] *verb*, to repeat, to say or do again

re-ject [rǐ-jěkt'] *verb*, to refuse to accept or use

re-joice [rǐ-jois'] *verb*, to celebrate, to be joyful, to delight

re-ju-ve-nate [rǐ-jōō'və-nāt'] *verb*, to make more lively or youthful

re-lapse [rǐ-lǎps'] *noun*, 1) a set back 2) to return to a former state, to regress, to revert

re-late [rǐ-lāt'] *verb*, to tell, to connect in thought and meaning

re-la-tion [rǐ-lā'shən] *noun*, 1) a member of the same family 2) an association or friendship

re-la-tion-ship [rǐ-lā'shən-shǐp'] *noun*, 1) the association between things, the affect one thing has on another 2) kinship

rel-a-tive [rěl'ə-tǐv] *adjective*, 1) in relation to or compared to, *noun*,

2) a person connected by blood or marriage, kin

re-lax [rǐ-lǎks'] *verb*, 1) to rest, to be at ease 2) to make less rigid

re-lax-a-tion [rē'lǎk-sā'shən] *noun*, *no plural*, a time of rest or ease, leisure, recreation

re-lay [rē'lā] *verb*, 1) to send, to give out, to beam 2) to convey

re-lease [rǐ-lēs'] *noun*, 1) freedom from confinement, *verb*, 2) to let go, to set free, to liberate, to untie 3) to relieve

rel-e-gate [rěl'ǐ-gāt'] *verb*, to banish, to consign to an inferior position, place or condition

re-lent [rǐ-lěnt'] *verb*, to become less strict, to become more forgiving

rel-e-van-cy [rěl'ə-vəns-ē] *noun*, reference to the case at hand

re-li-a-ble [rǐ-lī'ə-bəl] *adjective*, dependable, trustworthy

re-li-ance [rǐ-lī'əns] *adjective*, confidence, something dependent on something else

rel-ic [rěl'ǐk] *noun*, that which remains or is left, anything valued as a memento

re-lief [rǐ-lēf'] *noun*, *no plural*, 1) assistance, aid, help 2) comfort, ease, cheer 3) the contour of the front of a building

re-lieve [rǐ-lēv'] *verb*, to free from worry, to alleviate, to ease

re-lig-ion [rǐ-lǐj'ən] *noun*, possessing beliefs concerning the nature and purpose of the universe and the supernatural

re-li-gious [rǐ-lǐj'əs] *adjective*, 1) possessing pious beliefs in a God or gods 2) dedicated, devout

re-lin-quish [rĭ-lĭng′kwĭsh] *verb*, to abandon, to leave alone

rel-ish [rĕl′ĭsh] *noun*, 1) a condiment made of vegetables and herbs 2) great enjoyment, *verb*, 3) to savor, to appreciate, to like, to enjoy, to delight in

re-luc-tance [rĭ-lŭk′təns] *noun*, unwillingness or aversion marked by hesitation

re-luc-tant [rĭ-lŭk′tənt] *adjective*, unwilling to participate

re-ly [rĭ-lī′] *verb*, to depend confidently, to trust

re-main [rĭ-mān′] *verb*, to stay

re-main-der [rĭ-mān′dər] *noun*, 1) the fraction left over after a number has been divided 2) what is left over, remnant, residue

re-mains [rĭ-mānz′] *noun*, *plural*, parts which are left behind exposed to air, a corpse

re-make [rē-māk′] *noun*, something that has been redone or given a different form

re-mark [rĭ-märk′] *noun*, 1) something spoken, *verb*, 2) to take notice of, to observe

re-mark-a-ble [rĭ-märʹkə-bəl] *adjective*, uncommon, extraordinary, unusual

re-mark-a-bly [rĭ-märʹkə-blē] *adverb*, notably, especially

re-me-di-al [rĭ-mēʹdē-əl] *adjective*, intended to improve poor skills

rem-e-dy [rĕmʹĭ-dē] *noun*, 1) a cure 2) a solution to the problem

re-mem-ber [rĭ-mĕmʹbər] *verb*, to keep in your mind, to not forget

re-mem-brance [rĭ-mĕmʹbrəns] *noun*, a recollection, a memory

re-mind [rĭ-mīnd′] *verb*, to help someone remember

rem-i-nisce [rĕmʹə-nĭs′] *verb*, to think back or talk about past experiences, to recollect

rem-i-nis-cence [rĕmʹə-nĭsʹəns] *noun*, the act of recalling the past, recollection, memory

rem-i-nis-cent [rĕmʹə-nĭsʹənt] *adjective*, suggestive, remindful

re-miss [rĭ-mĭs′] *adjective*, negligent, careless, neglectful

re-mit [rĭ-mĭt′] *verb*, to send money usually as a payment

re-mit-tance [rĭ-mĭt′ns] *noun*, the sending of money, bills, etc, money transmitted

rem-nant [rĕmʹnənt] *noun*, something left over

re-mon-strate [rĭ-mŏnʹstrāt′] *verb*, to plead in protest, to argue repeatedly in opposition

re-morse [rĭ-môrs′] *noun*, deep regret for wrongdoing

re-mote [rĭ-mōt′] *adjective*, far away, a great distance from everyone, slight, aloof

re-mov-al [rĭ-mōōʹvəl] *noun*, to take something away

re-move [rĭ-mōōv′] *verb*, to take and move somewhere else

re-mu-ner-a-tion [rĭ-myōōʹnə-rāʹshən] *noun*, compensation, reward

ren-ais-sance [rĕnʹĭ-säns′] *noun*, a rebirth, revival, renewal

rend [rĕnd] *verb*, 1) to split, to tear apart with violence 2) to disturb

rend-er [rĕnʹdər] *verb*, to cause to become, to provide, to perform

ren-dez-vous [rän'dā-vōo'] *noun*, a
meeting place, an appointment

ren-di-tion [rĕn-dĭsh'ən] *noun*,
the artistic interpretation of a song
or dance and how it is performed

ren-e-gade [rĕn'ĭ-gād'] *noun*, a
person who deserts a cause to
join another, an outlaw

re-new [rĭ-nōo'] *verb*, 1) to bring
up to date 2) to start again

re-new-al [rĭ-nōo'əl] *noun*, a new
start, recurrence, a revival

re-nounce [rĭ-*nouns'*] *verb*, to
abandon, to discontinue, to
disown, to repudiate

ren-o-vate [rĕn'ə-vāt'] *verb*, to
make repairs, to redecorate

re-nown [rĭ-*noun'*] *adjective*, fame,
widespread recognition

rent [rĕnt] *noun*, 1) money paid to
use property, *verb*, 2) to pay
someone to use something that
they own, to lease

re-pair [rĭ-pâr'] *noun*, 1) the result
of renewing or reconditioning
something, *verb*, 2) to fix or
mend, to make new again

re-par-a-tion [rĕp'ə-rā'shən] *noun*,
compensation demanded by a
victorious nation from a defeated
nation, amends

rep-ar-tee [rĕp'ər-tē',] *noun*, a
clever reply

re-pay [rĭ-pā'] *verb*, to give
someone money owed to them

re-peal [rĭ-pēl'] *noun*, 1) retraction,
withdrawal, *verb*, 2) to cancel

re-peat [rĭ-pēt'] *verb*, to cause to
happen again, to duplicate

re-peat-ed-ly [rĭ-pē'tĭd-lē] *adverb*,
said or done again and again

re-pel [rĭ-pĕl'] *verb*, to drive back,
to oppose, to ward off

re-pel-lent [rĭ-pĕl'ənt] *adjective*,
offensive, disgusting, repugnant

re-pent [rĭ-pĕnt'] *verb*, to express
regret, to feel contrite

re-pent-ance [rĭ-pĕn'təns] *noun*,
sorrow for what one has done or
omitted to do, regret

re-per-cus-sion [rē'pər-kŭsh'ən,
rĕp'ər-] *noun*, the effect of
something said or done

rep-er-toire [rĕp'ər-twär'] *noun*, a
list of musical scores which a
company or a person has
thoroughly rehearsed and is
prepared to perform

rep-e-ti-tion [rĕp'ĭ-tĭsh'ən] *noun*,
doing or saying something over
and over

re-place [rĭ-plās'] *verb*, 1) to take
the place of 2) to make good

re-place-ment [rĭ-plās'mənt] *noun*,
a person or thing that takes the
place of another, a substitute

re-plen-ish [rĭ-plĕn'ĭsh] *verb*, to fill
again, to supply anew

re-plete [rĭ-plēt'] *adjective*, filled
to capacity, abundantly supplied

rep-li-ca [rĕp'lĭ-kə] *noun*, a copy

re-ply [rĭ-plī'] *noun*, 1) an answer,
a response, *verb*, 2) to give an
answer, to reply

re-port [rĭ-pôrt'] *noun*, 1) an oral
or written account containing
information in an organized
form, *verb*, 2) to give an account
of something

re-port-er [rĭ-pôr'tər] *noun*, 1) a
person who reports legal
proceedings or legislative

debates 2) a person who gathers information and writes reports for a newspaper, magazine, etc.

re-pose [rĭ-pōz′] *noun*, 1) a state of calm *verb*, 2) to be in a state of rest or relaxation

re-pos-i-to-ry [rĭ-pŏz′ĭ-tôr′ē] *noun*, a storehouse, a vault where things are kept

rep-re-hen-si-ble [rĕp′rĭ-hĕn′sə-bəl] *verb*, deserving blame or censure, rebuke, wicked, deceitful

rep-re-sent [rĕp′rĭ-zĕnt′] *verb*, 1) to portray, to stand for something 2) to act or speak for someone or something

rep-re-sen-ta-tion [rĕp′rĭ-zĕn-tā′shən] *noun*, something that expresses a point of view or represents something else, a portrayal

rep-re-sen-ta-tive [rĕp′rĭ-zĕn′tə-tĭv] *adjective*, 1) typically characteristic, *noun*, 2) one acting in the place of another

re-press [rĭ-prĕs′] *verb*, to check, to overpower, to keep down

re-prieve [rĭ-prēv′] *noun*, to postpone an execution

rep-ri-mand [rĕp′rə-mănd′] *verb*, to censure, to scold

re-pris-al [rĭ-prī′zəl] *noun*, retaliation, an act short of war by which a nation seeks to redress a wrong committed against it by another nation

re-proach [rĭ-prōch′] *noun*, 1) blame, censure, *verb*, 2) to blame someone, to criticize

re-pro-duce [rē′prə-doōs′] *verb*, 1) to produce offspring or create

babies 2) to make a copy of something, to duplicate

re-prove [rĭ-proōv′] *verb*, to reprimand someone for doing something wrong, to correct someone, to rebuke, to chide

rep-tile [rĕp′tĭl] *noun*, cold-blooded, egg laying vertebrate, such as a lizard or snake

re-pub-lic [rĭ-pŭb′lĭk] *noun*, government in which people elect their representatives

re-pub-li-can [rĭ-pŭb′lĭ-kən] *noun*, a person who advocates a republican government, one who believes in government by elected by representatives

Re-pub-li-can Par-ty *noun*, A U.S. political party that developed in the 1850s from those who opposed slavery and that elected Abraham Lincoln as the first Republican president

re-pu-di-ate [rĭ-pyoō′dē-āt′] *verb*, to disown, to renounce, to reject

re-pug-nant [rĭ-pŭg′nənt] *adjective*, disgusting, vulgar, offensive, objectionable

re-pulse [rĭ-pŭls′] *verb*, to offend

re-pul-sion [rĭ-pŭl′shən] *noun*, a feeling of aversion or disgust

rep-u-ta-tion [rĕp′yə-tā′shən] *noun*, what people generally think about a person or thing

re-quest [rĭ-kwĕst′] *noun*, 1) something that is asked for, *verb*, 2) to ask for something

re-quire [rĭ-kwīr′] *verb*, to have need of, to insist or compel

re-quire-ment [rĭ-kwīr′mənt] *noun*, a condition that must be met to satisfy a need

req-ui-site [rĕk′wĭ-zĭt] *noun*, a demand, something required

req-ui-si-tion [rĕk′wĭ-zĭsh′ən] *noun*, an official written request for something

re-quite [rĭ-kwīt′] *verb*, to repay, to seek revenge, to get even

re-scind [rĭ-sĭnd′] *verb*, to cut off or remove, to cancel or abolish

res-cue [rĕs′kyōo] *noun*, 1) help or aid offered to save someone, *verb*, 2) to aid or save from danger or confinement

re-search [rĭ-sûrch′] *noun*, *no plural*, 1) a careful study conducted to learn and discover something new, *verb*, 2) to investigate or study something, to make a careful inquiry

re-sem-blance [rĭ-zĕm′bləns] *noun*, similarity, likeness

re-sem-ble [rĭ-zĕm′bəl] *verb*, to have similar qualities and likeness, to be like

re-sent [rĭ-zĕnt′] *verb*, to feel angry with someone because they were unfair, to feel indignant

re-sent-ment [rĭ-zĕnt′mənt] *noun*, exasperation, ill will, anger

res-er-va-tion [rĕz′ər-vā′shən] *noun*, 1) a commitment to hold a space for someone 2) hesitation, qualm 3) land the government gave Indians to live on

re-serve [rĭ-zûrv′] *noun*, 1) restraint, *verb*, 2) to hold something for someone

res-er-voir [rĕz′ər-vwär′] *noun*, 1) a place where a large supply of anything is built up over time 2) a body of water stored for use

re-side [rĭ-zīd′] *verb*, to live, to inhabit, to remain, to dwell in

res-i-dence [rĕz′ĭ-dəns] *noun*, living or dwelling in a place for some time, a home

res-i-dent [rĕz′ĭ-dənt] *noun*, someone who resides in a place

res-i-den-tial [rĕz′ĭ-dĕn′shəl] *adjective*, where people live

re-sid-u-al [rĭ-zĭj′ōo-əl] *adjective*, effects remaining after the principal action

res-i-due [rĕz′ĭ-dōo′] *noun*, the remainder of something

re-sign [rĭ-zīn′] *verb*, 1) to relinquish, to withdraw from an office or position 2) to calmly accept an unpleasant outcome

res-ig-na-tion [rĕz′ĭg-nā′shən] *noun*, *no plural*, 1) reluctant acceptance of something 2) a formal statement to leave a job

re-signed [rĭ-zīnd′] *adjective*, unresisting, patiently submissive

re-sil-ient [rĭ-zĭl′yənt] *adjective*, the ability to return to the same size and condition after excessive stress and strain

res-in [rĕz′ĭn] *noun*, in plastics manufacturing, the different compounds used to create the different forms of plastic

re-sist [rĭ-zĭst′] *verb*, to oppose, to refuse to comply, to withstand

re-sist-ance [rĭ-zĭs′təns] *noun*, the act of resisting or opposing, any opposing force

res-o-lute [rĕz′ə-lōot′] *adjective*, determined, purposeful, earnest

res-o-lu-tion [rĕz′ə-lōo′shən] *noun*, a firm decision, a course of action decided on

re-solve [rĭ-zŏlv'] *noun,*
1) determination, conviction,
verb, 2) to decide to take action
3) to explain, to untangle

res-o-nant [rĕz'ə-nənt] *adjective,*
echoing, resounding, vibrant,
deep in sound

re-sort [rĭ-zôrt'] *noun,* 1) a
luxurious place visited for rest
and relaxation, *verb,* 2) to turn to
for help or support

re-source [rē'sôrs'] *noun,* 1) a
source of help or supply 2) a
supply or form of wealth

re-spect [rĭ-spĕkt'] *noun,* 1) an
aspect 2) consideration for
someone, *verb,* 3) to have a good
opinion of someone, to look up
to, to hold in esteem

re-spect-a-ble [rĭ-spĕk'tə-bəl]
adjective, honorable, well
thought of, worthy of respect

re-spect-ful [rĭ-spĕkt'fəl] *adjective,*
polite, well-mannered, civil

re-spect-ful-ly [rĭ-spĕkt'fə-lē]
adverb, in a civil manner,
courteously, politely

re-spec-tive [rĭ-spĕk'tĭv] *adjective,*
in relation to one another

re-spec-tive-ly [rĭ-spĕk'tĭv-lē]
adverb, for each separately in
precisely the order given

res-pi-ra-tion [rĕs'pə-rā'shən]
noun, the emission of vapor,
exhaling, breathing

res-pite [rĕs'pĭt] *verb,*
postponement or delay

re-splend-ent [rĭ-splĕn'dənt]
adjective, brilliant, lustrous

re-spond [rĭ-spŏnd'] *verb,* to
answer, to act in return

re-spond-ent [rĭ-spŏn'dənt] *noun,*
one who answers actions in a
civil case, the defendant

re-sponse [rĭ-spŏns'] *noun,* an
answer, a reaction, something
said or done in reply

re-spon-si-bil-i-ty
[rĭ-spŏn'sə-bĭl'ĭ-tē] *noun,*
trustworthiness, dependability

re-spon-si-ble [rĭ-spŏn'sə-bəl]
adjective, 1) the willingness to
respond appropriately
2) trustworthy, reliable

rest [rĕst] *noun,* 1) a quiet time for
relaxation 2) those remaining or
left behind, *verb,* 3) to relax and
feel at ease 4) to lean or put
something on something else

res-tau-rant [rĕs'tər-ənt] *noun,* a
public eating establishment

res-ti-tu-tion [rĕs'tĭ-tōō'shən]
noun, an agreement as terms of a
settlement to pay for loss or
damage

rest-less [rĕst'lĭs] *adjective,* not
relaxed, eager to do something
else, uneasy, fitful, anxious

re-store [rĭ-stôr'] *verb,* 1) to revive
2) to bring back to a former
condition, to reinstate 3) to give
back, to return

re-strain [rĭ-strān'] *verb,* 1) to hold
back with force 2) to limit

re-straint [rĭ-strānt'] *noun,* a
control, restriction, a check

re-strict [rĭ-strĭkt'] *verb,* to
confine, to keep within limits

re-stric-tive [rĭ-strĭk'tĭv] *adjective,*
confining, limiting, inhibiting,
uncomfortable

re-sult [rĭ-zŭlt′] *noun*, 1) the product or consequence of an action, the outcome, *verb*, 2) to have been the cause of something, to end up

re-su-me [′rez-ə-mā] *noun*, 1) a summary of personal or work history [rĭ-zoom′] *verb*, 2) to start again after stopping for a period of time

res-ur-rec-tion [rĕz′ə-rĕk′shən] *noun*, 1) the act of rising from the dead 2) renewal, revival

re-sus-ci-tate [rĭ-sŭs′ĭ-tāt′] *verb*, to revive, especially from apparent death, to restore to consciousness

re-tail [rē′tāl′] *verb*, to sell goods directly to the consumer

re-tain [rĭ-tān′] *verb*, 1) to keep in place or hold 2) to have

re-tal-i-a-tion [rĭ-tăl′ē-ā′shən] *noun*, to repay like for like, especially evil for evil

re-tard [rĭ-tärd′] *verb*, to delay the progress of, to hinder

re-ten-tion [rĭ-tĕn′shən] *noun*, 1) holding something 2) having a good memory, retaining

ret-i-cence [rĕt′ĭ-səns] *noun*, not revealing your thoughts or feelings openly

ret-i-na [rĕt′n-ə] *noun*, the light-sensitive colored circle of an eye

re-tire [rĭ-tīr′] *verb*, 1) to withdraw to a place of privacy 2) to remove from active service

re-tire-ment [rĭ-tīr′mənt] *noun*, the period at the end of a career when a person stops working to relax and enjoy their savings

re-tort [rĭ-tôrt′] *verb*, a response

re-tract [rĭ-trăkt′] *verb*, 1) to draw back as claws or fangs 2) to disavow, to recant, to disclaim

re-treat [rĭ-trēt′] *noun*, 1) a place to rest and relax, a place of safety *verb*, 2) to turn around and go back, to withdraw

re-trench [rĭ-trĕnch′] *verb*, to cut down, to economize, to reduce

ret-ri-bu-tion [rĕt′rə-byoo′shən] *noun*, vengeance, compensation, punishment for offenses

re-trieve [rĭ-trēv′] *verb*, 1) to get and bring back 2) to recover

ret-ro-ac-tive [rĕt′rō-ăk′tĭv] *adjective*, that which takes effect from a time in the past

ret-ro-grade [rĕt′rə-grād′] *verb*, going or inclined to go backward

ret-ro-spect [rĕt′rə-spĕkt′] *noun*, looking back on things past

re-turn [rĭ-tûrn′] *noun*, 1) to go to a place and come back from it 2) the income from an investment, *verb*, 3) to give or put something back 4) to go back to the same place 5) to reply

re-use [rē-yooz′] *verb*, to use again, to recycle

re-veal [rĭ-vēl′] *verb*, 1) to make known, to tell, to disclose, to admit 2) to bring into view

re-veil-le [rĕv′əl lē]*noun*, a signal on a bugle, drum, etc. early in the morning to wake soldiers

rev-e-la-tion [rĕv′ə-lā′shən] *noun*, a sign from heaven, a disclosure

rev-el-ry [rĕv′əl-rē] *noun*, boisterous merrymaking

re-venge [rĭ-vĕnj′] *noun*, 1) a form of getting even, retribution, *verb*, 2) to administer punishment

rev-e-nue [rĕv'ə-nōō] *noun*, 1) the return from an investment 2) an item of income 3) the taxes collected by a government

re-ver-ber-ate [rĭ-vûr'bə-rāt'] *verb*, to echo, to resound

re-vere [rĭ-vîr'] *verb*, to regard with respect, to admire, to look upon with awe, to honor

rev-er-ence [rĕv'ər-əns] *adjective*, honor or respect given to someone because of position

rev-er-end [rĕv'ər-ənd] *noun*, the title of the leader of a church

rev-er-ie [rĕv'ə-rē] *noun*, a daydream, a musing

re-verse [rĭ-vûrs'] *adjective*, 1) opposite, backward, *noun*, 2) a lever that makes a machine go backward, *verb*, 3) to turn around 4) to evoke or annul

re-vert [rĭ-vûrt'] *verb*, to return to a former habit, practice or belief

re-view [rĭ-vyōō'] *noun*, 1) an examination or inspection 2) a critical essay 3) a periodical, *verb*, 4) to go over or examine critically 5) to look back upon

re-vile [rĭ-vīl'] *verb*, to denounce using abusive language

re-vise [rĭ-vīz'] *verb*, to review and make changes in order to bring up to date, to correct, to improve

re-vi-sion [rĭ-vĭzh'ən] *noun*, the changed version of writing, or work, or doctrine

re-vive [rĭ-vīv'] *verb*, to bring back to life or to regain strength

re-volt [rĭ-vōlt'] *noun*, 1) a planned attack on a government or its leaders, *verb*, 2) to fight as a mass of rebels against leaders

3) to offend someone by making them feel ill or disgusted

rev-o-lu-tion [rĕv'ə-lōō'shən] *noun*, 1) the motion of a body about a center or axis 2) the overthrow of a government or system by those who are governed, usually by force, a rebellion 3) a radical change

rev-o-lu-tion-ar-y [rĕv'ə-lōō'shə-nĕr'ē] *noun*, an activist who promotes change

re-volve [rĭ-vŏlv'] *verb*, 1) to orbit the way the Earth moves slowly around the sun 2) to rotate 3) to recur in cycles

re-volv-er [rĭ-vŏl'vər] *noun*, a firearm with a cylinder of several chambers to be discharged repeatedly

re-vul-sion [rĭ-vŭl'shən] *noun*, a sickening feeling, a negative reaction

re-ward [rĭ-wôrd'] *noun*, 1) something given to praise good work, kindness or bravery, *verb*, 2) to give a prize in appreciation of good work

rhap-so-dize [răp'sə-dīz'] *verb*, to speak or write enthusiastically

rhap-so-dy [răp'sə-dē] *noun*, delight, happiness, enthusiasm

rhet-o-ric [rĕt'ər-ĭk] *noun*, the art of using language effectively

rheu-ma-tism [rōō'mə-tĭz'əm] *noun*, a painful disease of the muscles and joints, accompanied by swelling and stiffness

rhi-noc-er-os [rī-nŏs'ər-əs] *noun*, a large wild animal with tough skin and two large horns on its nose, which lives in Africa

Rhode Island [rōd-ī′lənd] *noun*, one of 50 United States located on the East Coast, the capital is Providence. The state flower of **Rhode Island** is the violet and the motto is "Hope."

rhom-bus [rŏm′bəs] *noun*, a form with four equal sides in the shape of a diamond

rhu-barb [rōo′bärb′] *noun*, acid leafstalks of a coarse herb, used for sauce or pie

rhyme [rīm] *noun*, 1) correspondence of sounds in words, *verb*, 2) to end the line of a verse with the same sound

rhythm [rĭth′əm] *noun*, 1) repetition of a beat played throughout a musical piece 2) the recurrence of stress or a sound at regular intervals

rib [rĭb] *noun*, one of many narrow bones surrounding the chest

rib-ald [rĭb′əld] *adjective*, wanton, indecent, offensive, vulgar

rib-bon [rĭb′ən] *noun*, a narrow fabric usually of silk, used to trim a dress or a present

rice [rīs] *noun*, a grain in the cereal family from a grass-like plant grown in warm climates

rich [rĭch] *adjective*, 1) wealthy, having many resources 2) plentiful, abundant

rich-es [rĭch′ĭz] *noun*, *plural*, treasures, things worth a lot of money, valuable possessions

rid [rĭd] *verb*, to dispose of

rid-dance [rĭd′ns] *noun*, a cleaning up or out, relief or deliverance

rid-dle [rĭd′l] *noun*, 1) a clever question with an unexpected answer, a puzzling thing, *verb*, 2) to pierce with many holes

ride [rīd] *verb*, to travel on an animal or in a vehicle to go somewhere

rid-er [rī′dər] *noun*, 1) modification of a law, by adding a clause to legislation 2) a passenger on a journey

ridge [rĭj] *noun*, a long narrow raised part of the hill, a crest

rid-i-cule [rĭd′ĭ-kyōol′] *noun*, 1) taunts, jeers, *verb*, 2) to sneer at, to mock, to make fun of

ri-dic-u-lous [rĭ-dĭk′yə-ləs] *adjective*, unworthy of serious consideration, absurd

rife [rīf] *adjective*, prevalent, common or frequent in occurrence, widespread

ri-fle [rī′fəl] *noun*, 1) a firearm with a long barrel, *verb*, 2) to search hurriedly through

rift [rĭft] *noun*, an opening, a break

rig [rĭg] *noun*, 1) heavy equipment, 2) a vehicle used to haul large shipments, *verb*, 3) to equip

rig-ging [rĭg′ĭng] *noun*, the ropes used to raise and hold the sails of a ship

right [rīt] *adjective*, 1) of or located to the opposite of left 2) what is fair and good 3) correct, *adverb*, 4) correctly 5) straight to, without stopping, *noun*, 6) a freedom allowed by law

right triangle [rīt-trī′ăng′gəl] *noun*, a triangle that has one right angle in it, the opposite side is the hypotenuse

right-eous [rī′chəs] *adjective*, just, virtuous, acting in a moral way

rigid

rig-id [rĭj′ĭd] *adjective*, hard, fixed, immovable, not flexible

rig-or [rĭg′ər] *noun*, severity

rig-or-ous [rĭg′ər-əs] *adjective*, strict, severe discipline

rim [rĭm] *noun*, the often-curved edge of something, a border

rind [rīnd] *noun*, the tough outer skin of fruit or cheese that protects it from air

ring [rĭng] *noun*, 1) small circular band worn on the finger 2) a circular object with a vacant center 3) an area where fights are held 4) a small group 5) the sound created by a bell, *verb*, 6) to make a sound like a bell

rink [rĭngk] *noun*, a playing field, a ring, a smooth floor

rinse [rĭns] *verb*, to wash lightly, to cleanse with water after washing

ri-ot [rī′ət] *noun*, 1) unrestrained fighting, vandalism, *verb*, 2) to fight in an angry crowd

ri-ot-ous [rī′ət-əs] *adjective*, unrestrained, tumultuous

rip [rĭp] *verb*, to tear away

ripe [rīp] *adjective*, completely mature, ready to be eaten, aged

rip-en [rī′pən] *verb*, to grow to maturity or when ready to eat

rip-ple [rĭp′əl] *noun*, 1) a little wave, *verb*, 2) to cause little waves of sound or movement

rise [rīz] *noun*, 1) an increase, *verb*, 2) to stand up 3) to move upward 4) to move in a positive direction 5) to get up out of bed

risk [rĭsk] *noun*, 1) a sense or chance of danger involved with doing something, *verb*, 2) to take a chance of injury or loss

rite [rīt] *noun*, a formal ceremony, a ritual, a custom

rit-u-al [rĭch′ōō-əl] *noun*, a set action or series of actions

ri-val [rī′vəl] *noun*, a competitor

ri-val-ry [rī′vəl-rē] *noun*, a contention, a contest, jealousy

riv-er [rĭv′ər] *noun*, a large natural stream of fresh water that flows into the ocean

riv-et [rĭv′ĭt] *noun*, 1) a metal pin for passing through holes in two or more pieces to hold them together, *verb*, 2) to hold attention firmly, to engross

roach [rōch] *noun*, a cockroach or small insect that eats food

road [rōd] *noun*, a route used for vehicles to travel, an avenue or thoroughfare, a street

roam [rōm] *verb*, to wander about, to travel aimlessly

roar [rôr, rōr] *noun*, 1) a deep angry sound, a loud growl or snarl, *verb*, 2) to growl in a loud voice 3) to laugh loudly

roast [rōst] *noun*, 1) a piece of meat that has been cooked over fire or will be, *verb*, 2) to cook without water over a fire or in an oven, to expose to great heat

rob [rŏb] *verb*, to deprive, to steal from someone, to defraud ·

rob-ber [rŏb′ər] *noun*, a thief, someone who steals

robe [rōb] *noun*, a piece of clothing that covers most of the body worn for lounging or relaxing

rob-in [rŏb′ĭn] *noun*, a brown song bird with a red breast found in North America

ro-bot [rō′bət] *noun*, a programmed machine designed to do the work of a person

ro-bust [rō-bŭst′] *adjective*, vigorous, strong, healthy

rock [rŏk] *noun*, 1) a hard, natural material of mineral origin, a stone 2) the mineral matter that makes up a large portion of the earth's crust *verb*, 3) to move back and forth or from side to side

rock-et [rŏk′ĭt] *noun*, 1) a missile, a spacecraft, *verb*, 2) to shoot into space 3) to move swiftly

rod [rŏd] *noun*, a thin pole

rode [rōd] *past tense* of **ride**

ro-dent [rōd′nt] *noun*, a small furry four-legged animal, like a squirrel, mouse or rat

ro-de-o [rō′dē-ō′] *noun*, a contest for people like cowhands to show their skill

rogue [rōg] *noun*, a scoundrel

role [rōl] *noun*, a part played by an actor, a characterization

roll [rōl] *noun*, 1) a long, drawn out noise 2) a small rounded portion of bread, *verb*, 3) to move along by turning over and over 4) to make something flat by pressing it with a roller

ro-man nu-mer-als [rō-män′noō′mər-əlz] *noun*, *plural*, the number symbols used by Romans 2,500 years ago

ro-mance [rō-mǎns′] *noun*, 1) the state of being in love 2) a story about love between people, *verb*, 3) to court romantically

ro-man-tic [rō-mǎn′tĭk] *adjective*, 1) not based in fact, fanciful 2) thoughts of love and adventure

roof [roōf] *noun*, 1) the external cover of a building 2) the top of the mouth

rook-ie [roōk′ē] *noun*, a beginner

room [roōm] *noun*, 1) one of the parts of a house separated by walls and doors 2) space

roost [roōst] *noun*, 1) a perch, *verb*, 2) to sleep or rest on a perch

roost-er [roō′stər] *noun*, a domestic male fowl, a cock

root [roōt] *noun*, 1) the part of the plant that grows in the ground, it's purpose is to hold it in the earth, to absorb moisture and to store nourishment, *verb*, 2) to dig up with the nose or snout 3) to cheer for a team

rope [rōp] *noun*, a heavy cord

rose [rōz] *noun*, 1) a shrub with a beautiful sweet smelling flower, *verb*, 2) the *past tense* of **rise**

ros-ter [rŏs′tər] *noun*, a list

ros-trum [rŏs′trəm] *noun*, a stage for public speaking, a pulpit

rot [rŏt] *verb*, to decompose, to decay gradually, to spoil

ro-ta-ry [rō′tə-rē] *noun*, rotating parts turning on an axis

ro-tate [rō′tāt] *verb*, to turn around a center or axis, to revolve

ro-ta-tion [rō-tā′shən] *noun*, 1) a revolution, turning in a full circle 2) the growing of different crops in the same place usually in regular order

rote [rōt] *noun*, learning through repetition and memorization

rot-ten [rŏt′n] *adjective*, no good

ro-tun-da [rō-tŭn′də] *noun*, a round building or rooms

rough [rŭf] *adjective*, 1) not smooth, uneven, difficult 2) not calm or gentle 3) unfinished, crude, coarse to the touch

rough-ly [rŭf-lē] *adverb*, approximately

round [round] *adjective*, 1) in the shape of a circle or a ball, circular, *noun*, 2) a circle, an orb, a globe 3) a course, a cycle, a series, *verb*, 4) to turn a bend or corner 5) to express a number to the nearest whole number

round-a-bout [round′ə-bout′] *adjective*, 1) not direct or straightforward, *noun*, 2) a traffic circle

rouse [rouz] *verb*, to stimulate, to spur, to wake up, to excite

rout [rout] noun1) a disorganized retreat from an attack, *verb*, 2) to drive out, to defeat decisively

route [rōot, rout] *noun*, a road for traveling ffrom one place to another

rou-tine [rōo-tēn′] *adjective*, 1) habitual, 2) unoriginal, *noun*, 3) a regular course or procedure

row [rō] *noun*, 1) an arrangement set in a line 2) a quarrel or fight, *verb*, 3) to propel with oars

roy-al [roi′əl] *adjective*, 1) of a king or queen 2) fit for a king or queen

roy-al-ty [roi′əl-tē] *noun*, 1) a member of the monarchy 2) a payment to the owner for the use of copyright material

rub [rŭb] *verb*, 1) to create friction by moving something back and forth 2) to massage

rub-ber [rŭb′ər] *noun*, no plural, a mix of chemicals to form a pliable substance

rub-bish [rŭb′ĭsh] *noun*, no plural, refuse, garbage, trash

rub-ble [rŭb′əl] *noun*, pieces or fragments of large objects

ru-by [rōo′bē] *noun*, a precious stone of deep red

rud-der [rŭd′ər] *noun*, a steering mechanism at the back of a boat

rud-dy [rŭd′ē] *adjective*, reddish, healthy-looking

rude [rōod] *adjective*, not polite, unkind, discourteous behavior

ru-di-men-ta-ry [rōo′də-mĕn′tə-rē] *adjective*, the first undeveloped state, unrefined, imperfect

ruf-fi-an [rŭf′ē-ən] *noun*, a person who is rough and dirty

ruf-fle [rŭf′əl] *noun*, 1) trimming, frill, *verb*, 2) to make uneasy

rug [rŭg] *noun*, a floor covering made of woven fibers or wool

rug-ged [rŭg′ĭd] *adjective*, 1) rough and wild 2) full of rocks with a jagged surface

ruin [rōo′ĭn] *noun*, 1) destruction, damage, *verb*, 2) to destroy

ru-in-ous [rōo′ə-nəs] *adjective*, destructive, harmful

rule [rōol] *noun*, 1) a law, a guide for conduct or procedure, *verb*, 2) to have power and control over someone 3) to decree

rul-er [roo'lər] *noun*, 1) someone who governs a body of people 2) an instrument used to measure and draw straight lines

rum-ble [rŭm'bəl] *noun*, 1) a loud sound, like earth moving, *verb*, 2) to make a continuous loud, low noise, like thunder

ru-mi-nate [roo'mə-nāt'] *verb*, 1) to chew the cud 2) to ponder, to think about, to meditate

rum-mage [rŭm'ĭj] *noun*, 1) odds and ends, miscellany, *verb*, 2) to look for, to rifle through

ru-mor [roo'mər] *noun*, gossip, common talk, hearsay

run [rŭn] *noun*, 1) the distance traveled, a journey 2) a score in a baseball game 3) movement that is quicker than walking, *verb*, 4) to move quickly or swiftly 5) to work or make work 6) to go over 7) to escape, to retreat 8) to ooze or pour out

rung [rŭng] *noun*, 1) a rod on a ladder that is a step, *verb*, 2) *past participle* of **ring**

run-ner [rŭn'ər] *noun*, 1) a long ski on the bottom of a sled used on snow and ice 2) a person who runs errands 3) a carpet or decorative cover placed on a walk way

rup-ture [rŭp'chər] *noun*, 1) a fracture, a breach, *verb*, 2) to break, to fracture, to split

ru-ral [roor'əl] *adjective*, having to do with, in, or like farmland, country people, or life in the country, rustic

ruse [roos] *noun*, a trick, gimmick

rush [rŭsh] *noun*, *no plural*, 1) rapid movement, haste 2) reeds that grow near the water, *verb*, 3) to move quickly or fast as in a hurry 4) to charge, to attack

rust [rŭst] *noun*, *no plural*, 1) a corrosive red-brown substance that forms on iron when it has been exposed to water and oxygen, *verb*, 2) to become covered with the corrosive element 3) to deteriorate

rus-tic [rŭs'tĭk] *adjective*, referring to country people, rural

rus-tle [rŭs'əl] *verb*, to make a soft rubbing sound, to crackle

rut [rŭt] *noun*, a deep narrow groove in the ground

ruth-less [rooth'lĭs] *adjective*, cruel, harsh, merciless

rye [rī] *noun*, a grass with seeds that are made into flour

S

Sab-bath [săb'əth] *noun*, a holy day, a day of rest

sack [săk] *noun*, a large bag made of woven material strong enough to carry things

sa-cred [sā'krĭd] *adjective*, holy, worshipped, religious

sac-ri-fice [săk'rə-fīs'] *noun*, 1) an offering, the surrender of anything, *verb*, 2) to give up something, to forfeit

sac-ro-sanct [săk'rō-săngkt'] *adjective*, most sacred, holy

sad [săd] *adjective*, unhappy, sorrowful, affected by grief

sad-dle [săd′l] *noun*, 1) a seat made of leather that fits over the back of a horse, *verb*, 2) to burden

sa-dis-tic [sə-dĭs′tĭk] *adjective*, pleasure in being cruel

sa-fa-ri [sə-fär′ē] *noun*, a journey into the jungles and plains of Africa, to look at wild animals

safe [sāf] *adjective*, 1) not in danger, protected, secure, *noun*, 2) a vault, a chest, a repository

safe-ty [sāf′tē] *noun*, a way of preventing damage to workers or a machine, protection

sag [săg] *verb*, 1) to hang down, to droop 2) to decline in value

sa-ga [sä′gə] *noun*, any legend, a long drawn out story

sa-ga-cious [sə-gā′shəs] *adjective*, shrewd, wise, knowledgeable

sage [sāj] *noun*, a wise man

said [sĕd] *past tense* of **say**

sail [sāl] *noun*, 1) a large cloth used to catch the wind and move a boat, *verb*, 2) to travel on water 3) to navigate a ship equipped with sails 4) to glide

sail-or [sā′lər] *noun*, a seaman, someone who works on a ship

saint [sānt] *noun*, a person who has lived a religious life and has been recognized by a group of religious leaders for good work

sake [sāk] *noun*, used with **for**, to show purpose or reason

sal-ad [săl′əd] *noun*, a preparation of vegetables, fruit, fish, or meat, dressed with vinegar, oil, etc.

sal-a-ry [săl′ə-rē] *noun*, fixed wages for a year, quarter, or month, for services

sale [sāl] *noun*, 1) the exchange of goods for money 2) when merchandise is sold at a reduced price 3) an auction

sales-man [sālz′mən] *noun*, one whose occupation is to sell goods or merchandise

sales tax [sālz-tăks] *noun*, a tax people pay for purchases

sa-li-ent [sā′lē-ənt] *adjective*, standing out, conspicuous, striking, noticeable, obvious

sa-line [sā′lēn′] *adjective*, salty

sa-li-va [sə-lī′və] *noun*, a fluid secreted in the mouth to help digest food, spit

salm-on [săm′ən] *noun*, a species of fresh-water fish

sa-loon [sə-loon′] *noun*, a bar or tavern, a large public room

salt [sôlt] *noun*, a white crystal compound of chlorine and sodium found in sea water, used to flavor food and preserve meat

sa-lu-bri-ous [sə-loo′brē-əs] *adjective*, promoting health

sal-u-ta-tion [săl′yə-tā′shən] *noun*, a greeting, something uttered

sal-u-tar-y [săl′yə-tĕr′ē] *adjective*, beneficial, wholesome

sa-lute [sə-loot′] *noun*, 1) a sign of respect for a superior officer *verb*, 2) to hold up the right hand to the forehead

sal-vage [săl′vĭj] *noun*, 1) property saved from destruction, *verb*, 2) to save, to recycle, to recover, to rescue

sal-va-tion [săl-vā′shən] *noun*, saved from harm or loss, deliverance from evil

salve [săv] *noun*, a medicinal
ointment, a lotion, a balm

same [sām] *adjective*, 1) having the
same identifying characteristics,
identical 2) not different

sam-ple [săm′pəl] *noun*, 1) a part
of anything shown as quality, a
specimen, *verb*, 2) to try or test

san-a-to-ri-um [săn′ə-tôr′ē-əm]
noun, a place where chronically
ill patients receive the care they
need until they recover

sanc-ti-fy [săngk′tə-fī′] *verb*, to
bless, to make holy, to anoint

sanc-tion [săngk′shən] *noun*,
1) coercive measures directed
against a nation that has violated
international law, *verb*, 2) to
approve, to support, to confirm

sanc-tu-ar-y [săngk′chōō-ĕr′ē]
noun, church, a place of refuge

sand [sănd] *noun*, fine grains made
of rocks usually found near the
sea or in deserts

san-dal [săn′dl] *noun*, a kind of
shoe consisting of a sole
strapped to the foot

sand-bar [sănd′ bär] *noun*, a ridge
of sand formed in a river or
along a shore by the action of
currents or tides

sand-wich [sănd′wĭch, săn′-] *noun*,
slices of bread with something
between them such as meat,
cheese or jelly

sane [sān] *adjective*, reasonable,
sensible, sound in mind

sang [săng] *past tense* of **sing**

san-i-tar-y [săn′ĭ-tĕr′ē] *adjective*,
very clean, antiseptic

san-i-ta-tion [săn′ĭ-tā′shən] *noun*,
the job of keeping things clean

san-i-ty [săn′ĭ-tē] *noun*, a healthy
outlook, a state of being sane

sank [săngk] *verb*, *past tense* of
sink

sap [săp] *noun*, 1) the fluid in a
plant that gives nourishment,
verb, 2) to take strength from
something, to weaken gradually

sapi-ent [sā′pē-ənt] *adjective*, wise,
shrewd, showing great wisdom

sap-ling [săp′lĭng] *noun*, a young
tree, a sprout of a tree

sap-phire [săf′īr′] *noun*, a precious
gemstone of a blue color

sar-casm [sär′kăz′əm] *noun*,
scornful remarks, ridicule

sar-cas-tic [sär-kăs′tĭk] *adjective*,
taunting, satirical, scornful

sar-coph-a-gus [sär-kŏf′ə-gəs]
noun, a coffin, a casket

sar-dine [sär-dēn′] *noun*, a small
herring preserved in olive oil

sash [săsh] *noun*, a wide ribbon
worn around the waist or over
the shoulder

sat-el-lite [săt′l-īt′] *noun*, 1) a
small, heavenly body orbiting
around a planet 2) an artificial
object launched to orbit the earth
or other celestial bodies

sa-ti-ate [sā′shē-āt′] *verb*, to satisfy
fully, to supply to excess

sat-ire [săt′īr′] *noun*, a form of
writing that makes fun of habits,
ideas or customs

sat-is-fac-tion [săt′ĭs-făk′shən]
noun, the feeling of having what
you need and want

sat-is-fac-to-ry [săt′ĭs-făk′tə-rē]
adjective, sufficient, fulfilling all
requirements, adequate

satisfy

sat-is-fy [săt′ĭs-fī′] *verb*, 1) to be enough or good enough, to meet a need 2) to make sure

sat-u-rate [săch′ə-rāt′] *verb*, to become thoroughly soaked

Sat-ur-day [săt′ər-dē′]*noun*, the seventh day of the week

sauce [sôs] *noun*, a liquid of a variety of ingredients eaten with food to improve its taste

sauc-er [sô′sər] *noun*, a small plate put under a cup to catch the drips

saun-ter [sôn′tər] *verb*, to stroll, to walk slowly, to meander

sau-sage [sô′sĭj] *noun*, minced and seasoned meat, commonly enclosed in an edible casing

sav-age [săv′ĭj] *adjective*, wild, untamed, uncivilized

sa-van-nah [sə-văn′ə] *noun*, a grassy plain that has very few trees in a tropical climate

sa-vant [să-vänt′] *noun*, a scholar, a learned person, a sage

save [sāv] *verb*, 1) to rescue from harm or danger 2) to set aside for future use, to store

sav-ings [sā′vĭngz] *noun, plural, no singular*, money set aside to use in the future, reserve funds

sav-ior [sāv′yər] *noun*, someone who saves others from danger

sa-vor [sā′vər] *noun*, 1) a taste or aroma, *verb*, 2) to taste or enjoy a distinctive flavor, smell or quality, to appreciate

saw [sô] *noun*, 1) a tool with a jagged blade and handle used to cut wood, *verb*, 2) *past tense* of **see** 3) to cut with a serrated blade or saw

say [sā] *verb*, to speak something

say-ing [sā′ĭng] *noun*, a wise statement that is full of truth like a proverb or aphorism

scab [skăb] *noun*, 1) a hard covering of coagulated blood on a wound 2) a worker who stays on the job while others go on strike

scaf-fold [skăf′əld] *noun*, 1) a temporary platform built to hold laborers while working on a building 2) the gallows

scald [skôld] *verb*, 1) to injure or burn with hot liquid 2) to heat to just below the boiling point

scale [skāl] *noun*, 1) a balance to measure weight 2) a range, degree, or progression 3) a protective crust *verb*, 4) to adjust to a standard of measure 5) to climb or ascend

sca-lene tri-an-gle [skā′lēn′ trī′ăng′gəl] *noun*, a triangle with unequal sides

scal-lop [skăl′lŏp]*noun*, 1) a kind of mollusk with two deeply grooved, curved shells, that swims by rapidly snapping its shells together 2) any of a series of curves forming an ornamental edge on cloth, lace, etc.

scalp [skălp] *noun*, 1) the skin and hair of the head, *verb*, 2) to remove the hair from someone

scam-per [skăm′pər] *verb*, to scurry, to run quickly

scan [skăn] *verb*, to look over, to review, to examine closely

scan-dal [skăn′dl] *noun*, an incident which offends conscience or moral feelings

scape-goat [skāp′gōt′] *noun,* someone who bears the blame for others

scar [skär] *noun,* 1) a mark left where a wound has been, *verb,* 2) to make a deep cut or to cause deep unforgettable pain

scar-ab [skăr′əb] *noun,* a large beetle with a dark shell

scarce [skârs] *adjective,* hard to find or come by, not plentiful

scarce-ly [skârs′lē] *adverb,* with difficulty, barely, hardly

scare [skâr] *noun,* 1) a sudden fright, *verb,* 2) to make someone afraid, to frighten, to terrify

scarf [skärf] *noun, plural, scarves,* a triangular or rectangular piece of cloth worn around the head, neck, or shoulders

scat-ter [skăt′ər] *verb,* to throw things everywhere, to disperse

scav-en-ger [skăv′ən-jər] *noun,* collector of garbage, an animal that devours refuse

scene [sēn] *noun,* 1) a setting, a view 2) a specific place 3) a shocking incident, a fight

scen-er-y [sē′nə-rē] *noun, no plural,* the setting of a place or landscape, the panorama

sce-nic [sē′nĭk] *adjective,* full of natural splendors, breathtaking

scent [sĕnt] *noun,* a smell that characterizes things

sched-ule [skĕj′ool] *noun,* 1) a written formal list or inventory, *verb,* 2) to arrange tasks to fit into a specific time frame

scheme [skēm] *noun,* 1) a plan, purpose, arrangement, *verb,* 2) to make secret plans, to plot

schol-ar [skŏl′ər] *noun,* a person who studies a particular subject at great length, a student

schol-ar-ship [skŏl′ər-shĭp′] *noun,* money granted to a worthy student to pay for their education

scho-las-tic [skə-lăs′tĭk] *noun,* pertaining to a school or education

school [skool] *noun,* 1) a place of instruction 2) a style, manner, method 3) a company of fish

schoon-er [skoo′nər] *noun,* a sailing ship with fore and aft rigging

sci-ence [sī′əns] *noun,* classified knowledge of the physical world

sci-en-tif-ic [sī′ən-tĭf′ĭk] *adjective,* in conformity to the principles of the physical world

sci-en-tist [sī′ən-tĭst] *noun,* a person who studies information about natural phenomena

scis-sors [sĭz′ərz] *noun,* a tool with two blades and handles, pivoted together that is used for cutting

scoff [skŏf] *verb,* to ridicule or make fun of, to deride, to jeer

scold [skōld] *verb,* to angrily tell someone they did something wrong, to reprimand

scoop [skoop] *noun,* 1) a large spoonful, *verb,* 2) to take some from the whole thing with a spoon or the hands

scoot [skoot] *verb,* to move quickly

scope [skōp] *noun,* 1) a range of one's mind 2) opportunity to function, capacity

scorch [skôrch] *verb,* to burn lightly leaving a brown stain

score [skôr] *noun*, 1) the points you get on a test or in a game 2) the reason, the purpose 3) a copy of a musical composition showing all parts for instruments and voices 4) a period of twenty years, *verb*, 5) to make points in a game 6) to achieve success

scorn [skôrn] *noun*, 1) disrespect, disdain, hate, *verb*, 2) to act like someone is worthless

scor-pi-on [skôr′pē-ən] *noun*, an arachnid that kills with its poisonous tail

scoun-drel [skoun′drəl] *noun*, a villain, a rascal, a mean person

scour [skour] *verb*, 1) to search an area thoroughly 2) to clean and polish by rubbing

scout [skout] *noun*, a person sent out ahead to obtain information

scowl [skoul] *noun*, 1) an angry, disgusted expression on the face, *verb*, 2) to make an angry expression showing disapproval

scram-ble [skrăm′bəl] *verb*, to move quickly on hands and knees, to hurry along

scrap [skrăp] *noun*, waste with some value, particularly material left over from construction or manufacturing suitable for reprocessing

scrap-book [skrăp′bŏŏk′] *noun*, a blank book filled with mementos, cards and souvenirs

scrape [skrāp] *noun* 1) a predicament, *verb*, 2) to take something off by rubbing it with a sharp edge 3) to make a grating sound

scratch [skrăch] *noun*, 1) a mark or wound made with something

pointed, *verb*, 2) to make marks with something pointed 3) to remove a layer by rubbing

scream [skrēm] *noun*, 1) a loud, shrill cry made in pain or fear, *verb*, 2) to make a sharp cry

screech [skrēch] *noun*, 1) a loud high-pitched noise, *verb*, 2) to make a harsh shrill noise

screen [skrēn] *noun*, 1) a portable covered framework in the nature of a partition 2) a grating of fine wire 3) protection, *verb*, 4) to eliminate applicants

screw [skrōō] *noun*, 1) a cylinder, grooved in an advancing spiral on its surface, *verb*, 2) to turn around and around

scrib-ble [skrĭb′əl] *verb*, to write or draw in an unintelligible manner

scrim-mage [skrĭm′ĭj] *noun*, a football or soccer practice

script [skrĭpt] *noun*, 1) a form of handwriting that connects the letters in a word 2) written words to be spoken from a text

scrip-ture [skrĭp′chər] *noun*, any sacred writing or book

scroll [skrōl] *noun*, 1) a rod with a roll of paper attached, *verb*, 2) to move a cursor smoothly, vertically or sideways, to review data on a computer screen

scrub [skrŭb] *verb*, to rub with a hard brush to clean off a spot

scru-pu-lous [skrōō′pyə-ləs] *adjective*, careful, cautious, exact, punctilious, precise

scru-ti-nize [skrōōt′n-īz′] *verb*, to examine closely and critically

scru-ti-ny [skrōōt′n-ē] *noun*, close examination, minute inspection

sculpt [skŭlpt] *verb*, to make or shape a statue

sculp-tor [skŭlp/tər] *noun*, one who carves or cuts wood or stone into statues

sculp-ture [skŭlp/chər] *noun*, works of art made from stone, clay or metal, a statue

scythe [sīth] *noun*, a long, curved-blade instrument for cutting grass by hand

sea [sē] *noun*, part of an ocean that is partially surrounded by land

sea-gull [sē/gŭl/] *noun*, a bird that lives near the ocean and scavenges for food

seal [sēl] *noun*, 1) an emblem affixed to a document to prove authenticity 2) a mammal with sleek skin, and limbs in the form of flippers, that lives in the water and on land, *verb*, 3) to close tightly so that something cannot be opened

seam [sēm] *noun*, 1) the stitches joining two pieces of cloth together 2) a fissure

search [sûrch] *noun*, 1) a careful investigation, a hunt, *verb*, 2) to look for someone or something

sea-son [sē/zən] *noun*, 1) a special time of year devoted to a certain activity 2) one of the four divisions of the year: fall, winter, spring, summer, *verb*, 3) to flavor or add zest to food

seat [sēt] *noun*, 1) a place to sit or a cushion to sit on 2) a location

se-cede [sǐ-sēd/] *verb*, to withdraw from association or fellowship

se-ces-sion [sǐ-sĕsh/ən] *noun*, withdrawal

se-clu-sion [sǐ-kloo/zhən] *noun*, 1) hiding, isolation 2) privacy

sec-ond [sĕk/ənd] *adjective*, 1) coming directly after the first, *noun*, 2) a very short period of time, a moment, *verb*, 3) to endorse, to support a motion

se-cre-cy [sē/krǐ-sē] *noun*, keeping things quiet without the knowledge of others

se-cret [sē/krǐt] *adjective*, 1) kept from the knowledge of most people, *noun*, 2) something known only to oneself or a few

sec-re-tar-y [sĕk/rǐ-tĕr/ē] *noun*, 1) a person who writes letters, files documents 2) a government officer who is a member of the President's Cabinet

se-crete [sǐ-krēt/] *verb*, to produce a liquid discharge

se-cre-tion [sǐ-krē/shən] *noun*, a fluid emitted from a gland

sec-tion [sĕk/shən] *noun*, a piece of the whole, a portion, a part

sec-tor [sĕk/tər, -tôr/] *noun*, region, area, zone, a distinct part

sec-u-lar [sĕk/yə-lər] *adjective*, worldly, not pertaining to church matters, temporal, earthly

se-cure [sǐ-kyoor/] *adjective*, 1) safe 2) strong and fixed firmly, *verb*, 3) to assure

se-cu-ri-ty [sǐ-kyoor/ǐ-tē] *noun*, 1) safety, assurance, freedom from danger 2) stocks and bonds

se-date [sǐ-dāt/] *adjective*, dignified, composed, calm

sed-a-tive [sĕd/ə-tǐv] *noun*, a tranquilizer, a narcotic

sed-en-tar-y [sĕd′n-tĕr′ē]
adjective, accustomed to sitting
most of the day

sed-i-ment [sĕd′ə-mənt] *noun*, the
solid matter that settles to the
bottom in a liquid

se-di-tion [sĭ-dĭsh′ən] *noun*,
resistance to authority,
insubordination

sed-ul-ous-ly [sĕj′ə-ləs-lē]
adjective, diligently, loyally

see [sē] *verb*, 1) to perceive or
acknowledge with the eye 2) to
understand, to comprehend 3) to
go and look 4) to meet 5) to
think about something and to act
if necessary

seed [sēd] *noun*, a small grain from
which a plant grows

seek [sēk] *verb*, to look for

seem [sēm] *verb*, to appear to be
true or probable

seen [sēn] past perfect of **see**

seep [sēp] *verb*, a liquid flowing
slowly or leaking through

seg-ment [sĕg′mənt] *noun*, any part
which separates from the whole

seg-re-ga-tion [sĕg′rĭ-gā′shən]
noun, the act of setting groups
apart, separation, racial
discrimination

seis-mic [sīz′mĭk] *adjective*,
pertaining to an earthquake

seize [sēz] *verb*, 1) to grasp
suddenly, to take possession of
by force

sel-dom [sĕl′dəm] *adjective*, rarely,
not often, infrequently

se-lect [sĭ-lĕkt′] *adjective*, 1) first
rate, *verb*, 2) to choose, to pick

se-lec-tion [sĭ-lĕk′shən] *noun*, a
collection of things chosen

self [sĕlf] *noun*, your person, what
you are, individuality

self-ish [sĕl′fĭsh] *adjective*, to think
only of oneself and not others

self-ish-ness [sĕl′fĭsh- nĭs] *noun*,
pettiness, being small-minded

sell [sĕl] *verb*, 1) to offer in
exchange for money 2) to deal in

sem-blance [sĕm′bləns] *noun*,
likeness, resemblance, similarity

se-mes-ter [sə-mĕs′tər] *noun*,
either of two terms into which
the period of instruction is
divided in an academic year

sem-i-cir-cle [sĕm′ĭ-sûr′kəl] *noun*,
the shape of half a circle

sem-i-co-lon [sĕm′ĭ-kō′lən] *noun*, a
mark of punctuation (;) used to
separate two independent clauses
when there is no conjunction, as
*When you make a mistake, admit
it; learn from it and don't repeat
it. Bear Bryant*

sen-ate [sĕn′ĭt] *noun*, one of the
groups that constitutes the
legislative government

sen-a-tor [sĕn′ə-tər] *noun*, an
elected representative who
serves in the Senate

send [sĕnd] *verb*, to cause
something or someone to go
somewhere, to dispatch

se-nil-i-ty [sĭ-nĭl′ĭ-tē] *noun*, feeble
mindedness of old age

sen-ior [sēn′yər] *adjective*,
1) older, *noun*, 2) a student in the
final year of a four year course

sen-sa-tion [sĕn-sā′shən] *noun*,
1) a feeling 2) excited interest

sense [sĕns] *noun*, 1) reason or understanding 2) a reasonable meaning 3) a feeling, *verb*, 4) to recognize, to detect

sense-less [sĕns'lĭs] *adjective*, stupid, unconscious

sen-si-bil-i-ty [sĕn'sə-bĭl'ĭ-tē] *noun*, awareness, understanding

sen-si-ble [sĕn'sə-bəl] *adjective*, reasonable, possessing good sense, smart, perceptive

sen-si-tive [sĕn'sĭ-tĭv] *adjective*, quick to notice or feel, easily affected by slight change

sen-su-ous [sĕn'shŏō-əs] *adjective*, exuding sexuality, appealing

sen-tence [sĕn'təns] *noun*, 1) a combination of words which express a thought, beginning with a capital letter, ending with a period 2) the judgment of a court, *verb*, 3) to pass judgment on, to inflict punishment

sen-ti-ment [sĕn'tə-mənt] *noun*, feelings, thoughts, emotions

sen-ti-men-tal [sĕn'tə-mĕn'tl] *adjective*, expressing feelings of love, pity, etc. to excess

sen-ti-nel [sĕn'tə-nəl] *noun*, a soldier set to guard an army from surprise, a sentry

sen-try [sĕn'trē] *noun*, a lookout, guard, watchman, a soldier

sep-a-rate [sĕp'ə-rāt'] *adjective*, 1) not together, not joined, *verb*, 2) to divide, to disconnect, to keep apart

sep-a-ra-tion [sĕp'ə-rā'shən] *noun*, time apart from each other

Sep-tem-ber [sĕp-tĕm'bər] *noun*, the ninth month of the year, having 30 days

sep-tic [sĕp'tĭk] *adjective*, decaying, putrid or toxic, rotten

sep-ul-cher [sĕp'əl-kər] *noun*, a tomb, a burial place

se-quel [sē'kwəl] *noun*, the continuation of a story

se-quence [sē'kwəns] *noun*, a succession, a following or coming after in a series

se-ques-ter [sĭ-kwĕs'tər] *verb*, to go into isolation, to remove, to seclude, to set apart

sere-nade [sĕr'ə-nād'] *verb*, to court, to play music under a window to charm a sweetheart

ser-en-dip-i-tous [sĕr'ən-dĭp'ĭ-t əs] *adjective*, fortunate discoveries made by accident

se-rene [sə-rēn'] *adjective*, calm, tranquil, placid, clear, peaceful

se-ren-i-ty [sə-rĕn'ĭ-tē] *noun*, tranquility, peace

ser-geant [sär'jənt] *noun*, a noncommissioned officer ranking next above a corporal

se-ries [sîr'ēz] *noun*, a number of things connected in a sequence

se-ri-ous [sîr'ē-əs] *adjective*, 1) grave in manner or disposition, earnest, solemn, sincere 2) weighty

se-ri-ous-ly [sîr'ē-əs-lē] *adverb*, thoughtfully, sincerely

ser-mon [sûr'mən] *noun*, a talk given by a religious leader

ser-pent [sûr'pənt] *noun*, a snake

ser-pen-tine [sûr'pən-tēn'] *adjective*, winding, twisting

ser-rat-ed [sĕr'ā'tĭd] *adjective*, having a saw-toothed or jagged edge

se-rum [sîr′əm] *noun*, the watery protein of an animal fluid

serv-ant [sûr′vənt] *noun*, one who works for another especially in a home to perform chores

serve [sûrv] *verb*, 1) to do work for other people, to give assistance or help 2) to offer food to someone 3) to answer a purpose

serv-ice [sûr′vĭs] *noun*, 1) a job that one performs for others 2) a church ceremony

ser-vile [sûr′vəl] *adjective*, subservient, groveling, cringing

ses-sion [sĕsh′ən] *noun*, the sitting of an organized body for the transaction of business, a term

set [sĕt] *noun*, 1) a group of things thought of together, *verb*, 2) to put in a place 3) to make something happen, to begin 4) to sink in the sky below the horizon

set-ting [sĕt′ĭng]] *noun*, 1) the position of something, as a dial, that has been set 2) time and place, environment, etc. of an event, story, play, etc. 3) actual physical surroundings, real or artificial

set-tle [sĕt′l] *verb*, 1) to go and live in a place 2) to make comfortable 3) to come to a mutual agreement, to decide

set-tle-ment [sĕt′l-mənt] *noun*, 1) an agreement 2) a new place for people to live, a colony

sev-en [sĕv′ən] *adjective, noun*, the number 7, one plus six

sev-en-teen [sĕv′ən-tēn′] *adjective, noun*, the number 17, 7 + 10

sev-en-teenth [sĕv′ən-tēnth′] *adjective, noun*, number 17 in order, written 17th

sev-enth [sĕv′ənth] *adjective, noun*, number 7 in order, 7th

sev-en-ti-eth [sĕv′ən-tē-ĭth] *adjective, noun*, number 70 in order, written 70th

sev-en-ty [sĕv′ən-tē] *noun, adjective*, the number 70, 7 X 10

sev-er [sĕv′ər] *verb*, to cut off, to separate, to disconnect

sev-er-al [sĕv′ər-əl] *adjective*, 1) separate or distinct, *pronoun*, 2) being more than two but fewer than many

se-vere [sə-vîr′] *adjective*, 1) strict in judgment or discipline, harsh 2) hard to deal with

se-ver-i-ty [sə-vĕr′ĭ-tē] *noun*, harshness, intensity

sew [sō] *verb*, to bind two pieces of cloth together with a needle and thread, to repair with a thread

sew-age [sōō′ĭj] *noun*, liquid waste from homes and businesses transported away by sewers

sew-er [sōō′ər] *noun*, 1) a gutter, a disposal system 2) one who works with needle and thread

sex [sĕks] *noun*, to be male or female

shab-by [shăb′ē] *adjective*, old, cheap, dirty, falling apart

shack-le [shăk′əl] *noun*, 1) chains, handcuffs, *verb*, 2) to confine, to restrain with chains

shade [shād] *noun, no plural*, 1) shelter from the sun or light, *verb*, 2) to cut off from a bright light 3) to dim or darken

shad-ow [shăd′ō] *noun*, 1) the image cast on a surface when something blocks the light 2) a faint indication

shaft [shăft] *noun*, 1) a long thin pole 2) a long hole leading to a mine 3) a ray or beam

shake [shāk] *verb*, 1) to move quickly up and down or from side to side 2) to tremble

shall [shăl] *verb*, 1) a word used instead of will with *I* and *we*, to indicate something is going to happen 2) used with *I* and *we* in questions when asking or offering to do something

shal-low [shăl'ō] *adjective*, 1) not deep 2) superficial, with little seriousness or deep thought

sham [shăm] *noun*, a farce

sham-bles [shăm'bəlz] *noun*, *plural*, a scene of disorder

shame [shām] *noun*, 1) dishonor, guilt, humiliation, *verb*, 2) to humiliate or embarrass

sham-poo [shăm-pōō'] *noun*, 1) a liquid soap used to wash hair, *verb*, 2) to wash hair with soap

shape [shāp] *noun*, 1) the outline or form of something, 2) a form or condition in which something exists, *verb*, 3) to mold or give form to something

share [shâr] *noun*, 1) a portion of something after it has been divided, *verb*, 2) to use, experience, or enjoy with others 3) to participate in 4) to disclose to others

shark [shärk] *noun*, a large predatory fish with a huge jaw

sharp [shärp] *adjective*, 1) having a thin cutting edge 2) the ability to see things far away that are small 3) severe or intense, having a strong odor or flavor 4) alert 5) quick and forceful

sharp-en [shär'pən] *verb*, 1) to make a pointed edge 2) to make acute or more sensitive to feeling

sharp-ly [sharp-lē] *adverb*, clearly, suddenly, distinctly

shat-ter [shăt'ər] *verb*, to break into many pieces or fragments

shave [shāv] *verb*, to cut very close

shawl [shôl] *noun*, a long piece of cloth worn over the shoulders and head

she [shē] *pronoun*, the female person or subject in the sentence

sheaf [shēf] *noun*, 1) a quantity of grain bound together 2) any bundle of things such as papers

shear [shîr] *verb*, to cut wool from a sheep, to cut hair, to clip

shears [shîrz] *noun*, *plural*, large-sized scissors

sheathe [shēth] *noun*, a case that holds a sword or dagger

shed [shĕd] *noun*, 1) a hut for tools, *verb*, 2) to let something fall or come off naturally 3) to pour forth, to stream out

sheep [shēp] *noun*, *no plural*, an animal that is kept for meat and wool from its thick, fleecy coat

sheep-ish-ly [shē'pĭsh-lē] *adverb*, with a feeling of embarrassment

sheer [shîr] *adjective*, 1) totally, entirely 2) transparent

sheet [shēt] *noun*, 1) a large flat piece of something such as paper or cloth 2) a rope used to secure a ship's sail

shelf [shĕlf] *noun*, *plural*, **shelves,** a board attached to a wall to put things on it

shell [shĕl] *noun*, the hard protective covering of fruit, eggs or some fish and reptiles

shel-lac [shə-lăk⁄] *noun*, a wood finishing such as varnish, lacquer or polyurethane

shell-fish [shĕl⁄fĭsh⁄] *noun*, any fish with a hard armor such as crabs, lobsters, or oysters

shel-ter [shĕl⁄tər] *noun*, 1) a safe place, a place to hide, *verb*, 2) to hide someone, to guard or keep safe from harm, to protect

shep-herd [shĕp⁄ərd] *noun*, a person who herds and tends sheep, goats, or livestock

sher-bet [shûr⁄bĭt] *noun*, flavored dessert ice

sher-iff [shĕr⁄ĭf] *noun*, a law enforcement officer of a county

shib-bo-leth [shĭb⁄ə-lĭth] *noun*, a slogan, a catchword

shield [shēld] *noun*, 1) a piece of defensive armor carried on the arm, protection, *verb*, 2) to defend or protect 3) to conceal

shift [shĭft] *noun*, 1) a set of people who work together at one time 2) the length of time that one group works, *verb*, 3) to move, to transfer, to displace

shil-ling [shĭl⁄ĭng] *noun*, English currency equal to a dollar

shim-mer [shĭm⁄ər] *verb*, to glimmer intermittently, to glisten

shin [shĭn] *noun*, the part of the leg between the knee and the ankle

shine [shīn] *verb*, to give off light

shin-gle [shĭng⁄gəl] *noun*, a tile made of wood or tar used to protect a roof or wall

ship [shĭp] *noun*, a boat which travels in deep water like the sea

ship-ment [shĭp⁄mənt] *noun*, the act of sending goods by air, water, or, on the road

shirt [shûrt] *noun*, a garment which covers the upper part of the body consisting of a collar, sleeves, and buttons, similar to a blouse

shiv-er [shĭv⁄ər] *verb*, to shake from being cold or afraid

shoal [shōl] *noun*, 1) a sandbar or piece of rising ground in shallow water 2) a school of fish

shock [shŏk] *noun*, 1) the feeling caused by a horrible unpleasant surprise 2) a pain caused by electricity going through the body, *verb*, 3) to startle, to disturb or surprise

shod-dy [shŏd⁄ē] *adjective*, not genuine, inferior quality

shoe [shoo] *noun*, an outer covering for the foot consisting of a sole and a covering made of leather, vinyl, or cloth

shoot [shoot] *noun*, 1) new growth, a sprout, *verb*, 2) to discharge a weapon 3) to move quickly, to dart 4) to photograph or film

shop [shŏp] *noun*, 1) a place to go and buy different things that you need, *verb*, 2) to visit stores to make purchases

shore [shôr] *noun*, 1) land bordering water such as a lake or the sea, *verb*, 2) to prop up

short [shôrt] *adjective*, 1) the opposite of tall, small 2) not long, brief, concise

short-age [shôr⁄tĭj] *noun*, not enough, a deficiency

short-en [shôr'tn] *verb*, to cut down

short-en-ing [shôr'tn-ĭng] *noun*, lard or oil used in cooking

shorts [shôrts] *noun*, *plural*, pants worn above the knee

shot [shŏt] *noun*, 1) injection with a hypodermic needle 2) a try, an attempt 3) lead for a shotgun

should [shŏŏd] *verb*, obligated to do something, ought to

shoul-der [shōl'dər] *noun*, 1) part of the body between the neck and the chest, connected to the arms, *verb*, 2) to carry a burden

shouldn't [shŏŏd'nt] the *contraction* of the words **should** and **not**

shout [shout] *noun*, 1) a sudden cry in a loud voice, *verb*, 2) to speak or yell in a loud voice

shove [shŭv] *noun*, 1) a push, *verb*, 2) to push roughly or rudely

shov-el [shŭv'əl] *noun*, 1) a broad scoop with a long handle for lifting dirt, *verb*, 2) to lift things from the ground or another surface with a shovel

show [shō] *noun*, 1) a display in which things are gathered for people to see 2) a performance for an audience, *verb*, 3) to let someone see something

show-er [shou'ər] *noun*, 1) precipitation from clouds in the form of rain 2) a bath in which water is sprayed from a nozzle, 3) a party to honor someone, *verb*, 4) to pour down or fall on 5) to bestow

shred [shrĕd] *noun*, 1) a small amount, *verb*, 2) to tear or cut into small pieces

shrew [shrōō] *noun*, 1) a scolding woman, a nag 2) a mouse-like rodent with a long snout

shrewd [shrōōd] *adjective*, clever in business, sharp-witted

shriek [shrēk] *noun*, 1) a high-pitched scream, *verb*, 2) to utter a shrill cry, to scream

shrill [shrĭl] *adjective*, having a high-pitched sound, piercing

shrimp [shrĭmp] *noun*, a shellfish that is considered a delicacy

shrine [shrīn] *noun*, 1) a place for worship and keeping sacred relics 2) a saint's tomb

shrink [shrĭngk] *verb*, 1) to withdraw, to pull away from 2) to lessen, to make smaller

shriv-el [shrĭv'əl] *verb*, to contract in size, to shrink and wrinkle

shrub [shrŭb] *noun*, a bush

shrug [shrŭg] *verb*, 1) to raise the shoulders to show uncertainty about something 2) to disregard

shud-der [shŭd'ər] *noun*, a quick, light shaking motion, a shiver

shuf-fle [shŭf'əl] *verb*, 1) to walk dragging your feet 2) to rearrange the order, to mix together like a deck of cards

shun [shŭn] *verb*, to deliberately avoid, to stay away from

shut [shŭt] *verb*, to close, to adjust something so that it is not open

shut-ter [shŭt'ər] *noun*, 1) a wooden cover for a window 2) a mechanical device for opening and closing the aperture of a camera lens to expose the film

shy [shī] *adjective*, bashful, wary

sib-ling [sĭb′lĭng] *noun*, a brother or sister

sick [sĭk] *adjective*, not feeling well

sick-ness [sĭk′nĭs] *noun*, illness, nausea, ailment, disease

side [sīd] *noun*, 1) the right or left portion of the body 2) the surface of something flat that has a top and bottom 3) the boundaries of a surface or image 4) a perspective, a way of looking at something, an aspect

siege [sēj] *noun*, a continued attempt of an army to gain possession around a fortified place to compel its surrender

sieve [sĭv] *noun*, a bowl with holes in the bottom to let water drain out, or used to separate fine matter from the coarser materials

sigh [sī] *noun*, 1) a deep breath indicating that you are tired, sad, etc, *verb*, 2) to let out a deep breath, to exhale

sight [sīt] *noun*, 1) the ability or power to see 2) something worth seeing 3) a scene, an incident

sign [sīn] *noun*, 1) a gesture which sends a message to the person who sees it 2) an indication 3) a plaque with a message, *verb*, 4) to write your name 5) to hire or transfer by written agreement

sig-nal [sĭg′nəl] *noun*, 1) a movement or thing which tells you what to do, *verb*, 2) to warn someone, or send another message through motions

sig-na-ture [sĭg′nə-chər] *noun*, 1) a name written in ink, in cursive, as an endorsement to an agreement 2) the printed sheet so marked as to leave an imprint

sig-net [sĭg′nĭt] *noun*, an emblem

sig-nif-i-cance [sĭg-nĭf′ĭ-kəns] *noun*, *no plural*, the meaning

sig-nif-i-cant [sĭg-nĭf′ĭ-kənt] *adjective*, expressive or suggestive, important

sig-ni-fy [sĭg′nə-fī′] *verb*, to indicate, to signal, to denote

si-lence [sī′ləns] *noun*, *no plural*, 1) complete quiet 2) secrecy

si-lent [sī′lənt] *adjective*, making no sound, quiet, speechless

si-lent-ly [sī′lənt-lē] *adverb*, quietly, without a sound

sil-hou-ette [sĭl′ōō-ĕt′] *noun*, an outline of something against a light background

sil-i-con [sĭl′ĭ-kən, -kŏn′] *noun*, a nonmetallic element, very abundant in nature

silk [sĭlk] *noun*, a fine fabric made by the threads from a silkworm

sill [sĭl] *noun*, the rim on a window

sil-ly [sĭl′ē] *adjective*, not serious, or reasonable, playful, foolish

silt [sĭlt] *noun*, sediment of fine particles that hangs in stagnant water or forms on the bottom left there by running water

sil-ver [sĭl′vər] *adjective*, 1) the color of this metal, *noun*, *no plural*, 2) a soft shiny gray metal used for jewelry, coins, and ornaments

sim-i-an [sĭm′ē-ən] *adjective*, like a monkey or an ape

sim-i-lar [sĭm′ə-lər] *adjective*, somewhat like, nearly, corresponding, resembling

sim-i-lar-i-ty [sĭm′ə-lăr′ĭ-tē] *noun*, likeness, resemblance

sim-i-le [sĭm′ə-lē] *noun*, a phrase comparing unlike subjects using like or as, i.e., *he is as slow as a turtle; she sings like a bird*

sim-ple [sĭm′pəl] *adjective*, 1) easy to understand 2) plain, common, not complicated, not showy

sim-plic-i-ty [sĭm-plĭs′ĭ-tē] *adjective*, freedom from duplicity, absence of excess

sim-pli-fy [sĭm′plə-fī′] *verb*, to make easier to understand

sim-ply [sĭm′plē] *adverb*, only, or merely, absolutely

sim-u-late [sĭm′yə-lāt′] *verb*, to feign, to pretend, to fake

si-mul-ta-ne-ous [sī′məl-tā′nē-əs] *adjective*, occurring at the same time, concurrent

si-mul-ta-ne-ous-ly [sī′məl-tā′nē-əs-lē] *adverb*, happening at the same time

sin [sĭn] *noun*, 1) an act that harms someone, *verb*, 2) to err, to violate a moral principle

since [sĭns] *adverb*, 1) between a moment in the past and now, *conjunction*, 2) because, *preposition*, 3) after, from a certain time until the present

sin-cere [sĭn-sîr′] *adjective*, being in reality what it appears to be, genuine 3) free of hypocrisy

sin-cere-ly [sĭn-sîr′lē] *adverb*, honestly, truly

sin-cer-i-ty [sĭn-sĕr′ĭ-tē] *adverb*, honesty, truthfulness

sin-ew [sĭn′yōō] *noun*, 1) a tendon, a muscle 2) strength, power

sing [sĭng] *verb*, to make music with the voice

singe [sĭnj] *verb*, to scorch or burn the surface or ends

sin-gle [sĭng′gəl] *adjective*, 1) consisting of only one person or thing, alone, *noun*, 2) in baseball, a hit in which the batter reaches first base

sin-gu-lar [sĭng′gyə-lər] *adjective*, 1) when speaking of one, *noun*, 2) unique, particular, individual

sin-is-ter [sĭn′ĭ-stər] *adjective*, dishonest, indicative of lurking evil, wicked, menacing

sink [sĭngk] *noun*, 1) a basin that holds water, *verb*, 2) to go down 3) to become submerged in water 4) to permeate the mind

sin-ner [sĭn′ər] *noun*, one who does wrong to others

sip [sĭp] *noun*, 1) a small amount of liquid swallowed, *verb*, 2) to drink a very small amount

si-phon [sī′fən] *noun*, a bent tube, having one end longer than the other, used for drawing liquids from a higher to a lower level

sir [sûr] *noun*, 1) the title of a knight 2) a respectful term to use when talking to a man

si-ren [sī′rən] *noun*, a device that makes a loud warning sound

sis-ter [sĭs′tər] *noun*, 1) a girl who shares the same parents with a sibling 2) the title for a nun

sit [sĭt] *verb*, to rest in a chair or on the floor, with the back straight

site [sīt] *noun*, a particular piece of land or a building whose location has a specific use

sit-u-ate [sĭch′ōō-āt′] *verb*, to put in place, to position, to locate

sit-u-a-tion [sĭch′ōō-ā′shən] *noun,*
1) circumstances, the state of
affairs, a case 2) a position

six [sĭks] *adjective, noun,* the
number 6, five plus one

six-teen [sĭk-stēn′] *adjective, noun,*
the number 16, six plus ten

six-teenth [sĭk-stēnth′] *adjective,
noun,* the number 16 in order,
written 16th

sixth [sĭksth] *adjective, noun,* the
number 6 in order, written 6th

six-ti-eth [sĭk′stē-ĭth] *adjective,
noun,* number 60 in order, 60th

six-ty [sĭks′tē] *adjective,* the
number 60, six times ten

size [sīz] *noun,*) the amount of
space that something takes up

skate [skāt] *noun,* 1) a runner or set
of wheels with a frame to fit the
shoe, *verb,* 2) to glide over the
ground with shoes fit with a
runner or wheels

skel-e-ton [skĕl′ĭ-tn] *noun,* the
bones of a person or animal that
show its size and structure

skep-tic [skĕp′tĭk] *noun,* a doubter,
a cynic, a questioner

skep-ti-cal [skĕp′tĭ-kəl] *adjective,*
distrustful, not convinced

sketch [skĕch] *noun,* 1) a drawing
that lacks detail, an image, *verb,*
2) to draw in a rough manner

ski [skē] *noun, plural,* **skis,** one of
a pair of long, flat, wood or
metal runners used for gliding on
snow or water *verb,* 2) to slide
over snow on blades using poles
for balance

skid [skĭd] *noun,* 1) a pallet to
elevate something off the

ground, *verb,* 2) to slip on a wet
surface 3) to lose traction

skill [skĭl] *noun,* having the ability
and knowledge to do something

skil-let [skĭl′ĭt] *noun,* a small metal
pan with a handle, a frying pan

skill-ful [skĭl′fəl] *adjective,* very
good at doing something

skill-ful-ly [skĭl′fə-lē] *adverb,*
intelligently, sensibly

skim [skĭm] *verb,* 1) to read over
quickly 2) to take off the floating
layer 3) to glide in a sail boat

skimp [skĭmp] *verb,* to hold back,
to offer small portions

skin [skĭn] *noun,* 1) the covering of
the body, or fruit, often covered
with hairs, *verb,* 2) to remove
the outer layer of something

skip [skĭp] *verb,* 1) to move by
alternately hopping or stepping,
to move with light steps 2) to
omit, to pass over, to miss

skirt [skûrt] *noun,* 1) woman's
clothing that hangs from the
waist, *verb,* 2) to avoid

skit [skĭt] *noun,* a short play or
theatrical performance

skit-tish [skĭt′ĭsh] *adjective,* lively,
frisky, nervous

skulk [skŭlk] *verb,* 1) to move
slyly and secretly in a sneaking
manner 2) to lie in hiding

skull [skŭl] *noun,* the bony
structure of the head enclosing
the brain

skunk [skŭngk] *noun,* a rodent
with black fur distinguished by a
white strip that goes down its
back and tail and sprays a
horrible smell when scared

sky [skī] *noun*, the space above the Earth which can be seen when you look up

sky-scrap-er [skī′skrā′pər] *noun*, a very tall building

slack [slăk] *adjective*, 1) lazy, slow, barely moving 2) a mixture of small pieces of coal, dust, and dirt left from screening coal

slacks [slăks] *noun, plural*, pants or trousers for casual wear

slain [slān] *past tense* of **slay**

slam [slăm] *verb*, 1) to fling or put down violently, with a loud noise 2) to shut, to close

slan-der [slăn′dər] *noun*, 1) a malicious, false statement made about a person, *verb*, 2) to lie about someone, to malign

slang [slăng] *noun, no plural*, language used in conversation, that is crude, disrespectful, or inappropriate, an expletive.

slant [slănt] *verb*, to lean or slope

slap [slăp] *noun*, 1) the blow or hit caused by something flat, *verb*, 2) to hit with something flat, such as an open hand

slate [slāt] *adjective*, 1) a gray color, *noun*, 2) a fine-grained metamorphic rock used as a roof tile or writing tablet with chalk

slaugh-ter [slô′tər] *noun, no plural*, 1) a killing of a large number of people or animals, *verb*, 2) to kill animals or people as a group

slave [slāv] *noun*, a person owned as property, subject to the will of his owner

slav-er-y [slā′və-rē] *noun, no plural*, the concept of owning people as property

slay [slā] *verb*, to kill or murder

slea-zy [slē′zē] *adjective*, low class

sled [slĕd] *noun*, a wooden device with runners on the bottom used to carry people or things on snow or ice as a vehicle

sleek [slēk] *adjective*, smooth, neat, glossy, well-groomed

sleep [slēp] *noun, no plural*, 1) a time of rest, when not awake and alert, *verb*, 2) to rest semi-unconscious with eyes closed

sleet [slēt] *noun*, 1) a combination of ice and rain falling from the sky, *verb*, 2) to shower frozen rain

sleeve [slēv] *noun*, the part of clothing that covers the arm

sleigh [slā] *noun*, a horse drawn vehicle with runners used for carrying people over snow

sleight [slīt] *noun*, skill, cunning

slen-der [slĕn′dər] *adjective*, 1) slim, thin, narrow 2) meager

slice [slīs] *noun*, 1) a piece cut from the whole, a share, *verb*, 2) to cut a flat piece off from a whole

slick [slĭk] *adjective*, 1) a surface that is slippery when wet 2) clever, deceitful

slide [slīd] *noun*, 1) a piece of playground equipment you can sit on and slip on the surface, an image for projection on a screen, *verb*, 3) to slide smoothly along a surface, to slip

slight [slīt] *adjective*, of a small degree, of little importance

slim [slĭm] *adjective*, slender, thin, lean, narrow, meager

slime [slīm] *noun*, mire, mud

sling [slĭng] *noun*, 1) a piece of cloth holding something in place, *verb*, 2) to throw

slip [slĭp] *noun*, 1) a piece of paper 2) a garment worn under a dress 3) a mistake 4) a stall to keep something 5) a cutting from a plant, *verb*, 6) to lose your balance and fall off your feet 7) to enter or exit unobserved 8) to escape, to pass from

slip-per [slĭp/ər] *noun*, a light shoe which may be slipped on easily

slip-per-y [slĭp/ə-rē] *adjective*, 1) smooth and slick or slimy, hard to grip 2) devious, not trustworthy, shifty

slit [slĭt] *noun*, 1) a long narrow opening, *verb*, 2) to make a small cut as an opening

slith-er [slĭth/ər] *verb*, to move, walk or slide like a snake

slo-gan [slō/gən] *noun*, a catch phrase, a motto

slope [slōp] *noun*, 1) a surface which is higher on one side than the other, *verb*, 2) to lean on an incline, to slant up or downward

slot [slŏt] *noun*, a long, narrow opening for receiving something

sloth [slôth] *noun*, a lazy person

slov-en-ly [slŭv/ən-lē] *adjective*, untidy, careless in work habits

slow [slō] *adjective*, 1) to move without much speed, not fast 2) behind others, sluggish

slow-ly [slō/lē] *adverb*, to crawl or move sluggishly, not quickly

slug [slŭg] *noun*, 1) a soft, slimy creature without bones or legs that eats plants 2) a false coin, *verb*, 3) to hit with a fist

sluice [slōōs] *noun*, an artificial channel for water with a gate

slum [slŭm] *noun*, a poor neighborhood, a ghetto

slum-ber [slŭm/bər] *noun*, 1) a deep sleep, a long nap, *verb*, 2) to sleep, to doze

slump [slŭmp] *noun*, 1) a drop, a decline, a decrease, *verb*, 2) to sink, to slouch, to stoop

slur [slûr] *noun*, 1) a disrespectful remark, *verb*, 2) to insult, to offend 3) to garble, to speak unintelligibly

slush [slŭsh] *noun*, partially melting snow or ice

sly [slī] *adjective*, clever and deceiving, calculating

smack [smăk] *noun*, 1) a kiss, a pat, a peck, *verb*, 2) to hit with a hand as a slap 3) to put the lips together after a tasty meal

small [smôl] *adjective*, 1) little, not big 2) mean-spirited, petty

small-er [smôl/ər] *adjective*, not as big, shorter, less, fewer

small-est [smôl/ĕst] *adjective*, tiny, very little

smart [smärt] *adjective*, 1) intelligent, bright 2) well dressed, attractive, fashionable, *verb*, 3) to feel a painful, stinging sensation

smash [smăsh] *verb*, to break violently into many pieces

smat-ter-ing [smăt/ər-ĭng] *noun*, slight knowledge, a few facts

smell [smĕl] *noun*, 1) the identifying scent that distinguishes something, *verb*, 2) to use one of the five senses to recognize a scent

smelt [smĕlt] *verb*, to melt in a furnace, to purify an ore

smile [smīl] *noun*, 1) an expression formed by the upward curve of the mouth, to show pleasure, amusement, etc., 2) to look pleased, happy, or amused

smirk [smûrk] *noun*, a twisted smile, a smug expression

smog [smŏg] *noun*, a mixture of pollutants, principally ground-level ozone, produced by chemical reactions in the air

smoke [smōk] *noun*, 1) visible fumes, *verb*, 2) to puff or inhale the vapor from a lit cigarette, 3) to make fumes come from fire

smol-der [smōl′dər] *verb*, 1) to burn without flame 2) anger, liable to break out at any moment

smooth [smōōth] *adjective*, 1) even, level, without bumps 2) calm, composed, unruffled

smoth-er [smŭth′ər] *verb*, to hide or suppress, to suffocate

smudge [smŭj] *noun*, 1) a dirty mark, a smear, *verb*, 2) to make dirty with streaks, to blur

smug-gle [smŭg′əl] *verb*, to bring things across borders secretly or illegally to avoid tariffs or border police

snack [snăk] *noun*, 1) food eaten between meals, *verb*, 2) to eat when you are hungry

snail [snāl] *noun*, a slug in a spirally coiled shell

snake [snāk] *noun*, 1) a cold-blooded reptile without legs that slithers on the ground, *verb*, 2) to move like a snake by slithering and sliding

snap [snăp] *noun*, 1) the sharp sound of something breaking 2) a clothing fastener like a button that locks together, *verb*, 3) to make a crackling sound 4) to try to nip or bite someone

snare [snâr] *noun*, 1) a trap that entangles its victim, *verb*, 2) to trap with a noose, to entangle

snarl [snärl] *verb*, 1) to make an angry noise with bared teeth 2) to talk in a vicious tone

snatch [snăch] *verb*, to take something directly from someone in a rough manner

sneak [snēk] *noun*, 1) a cheater, a rascal, *verb*, 2) to creep, to slink

sneer [snîr] *verb*, to laugh at someone to make fun of them

sneeze [snēz] *noun*, to blow air through the nose and mouth without warning

sniff [snĭf] *verb*, to breathe in, to inhale, to get a whiff, to smell

snif-fle [snĭf′əl] *verb*, to gasp as if to hold back tears

snob [snŏb] *noun*, someone who thinks he is better than others

snore [snôr] *verb*, to make a loud guttural noise in the nose or throat when sleeping

snout [snout] *noun*, the part of an animal's head projecting forward containing the nose and jaws

snow [snō] *noun*, *no plural*, 1) precipitation that forms in the cloud as ice and falls to the ground as white crystals, *verb*, 2) a flurry of crystals or snowflakes falling to the earth from the sky

snug [snŭg] *adjective*, close fitting, comfortable, cozy, compact

so [sō] *adverb*, 1) in such a way, to such a point 2) also 3) very, very much 4) therefore 5) in order that 6) the same thing 7) used to show agreement 8) factual

soak [sōk] *verb*, to leave something immersed in liquid for awhile

soap [sōp] *noun*, a substance used for cleaning, manufactured as bars, flakes, or liquid, mixed with water

soar [sôr] *verb*, to fly or ascend quickly and easily upward

sob [sŏb] *verb*, to cry aloud in large gasps, to weep convulsively

so-ber [sō'bər] *adjective*, serious, somber, not gay or laughing

so-bri-e-ty [sə-brī'ĭ-tē] *noun*, self restraint, recovery from abusing alcohol, not drunk

so-bri-quet [sō'brĭ-kā'] *noun*, a nickname, a pet name

soc-cer [sŏk'ər] *noun, no plural*, a game of football as played in South America and Europe

so-cial [sō'shəl] *adjective*, pertaining to men as living in society, friendly, gregarious

so-cial-ism [sō'shə-lĭz'əm] *adjective*, a communist philosophy of equal sharing

so-ci-e-ty [sə-sī'ĭ-tē] *noun*, a group of persons associated together

so-ci-ol-o-gy [sō'sē-ŏl'ə-jē] *noun*, the science of the development of human society

sock [sŏk] *noun*, 1) a short stocking made of soft material to cover the foot, *verb*, 2) to punch

sock-et [sŏk'ĭt] *noun*, any device that holds a complementary part

sod [sŏd] *noun*, earth, dirt, soil

so-da [sō'də] *noun*, a carbonated beverage flavored with syrup

so-di-um [sō'dē-əm] *noun*, a silver-white, metallic element of the alkali group, also known as salt

so-fa [sō'fə] *noun*, a long couch, usually upholstered and having a back and arms

soft [sôft] *adjective*, 1) tender 2) not hard 3) low volume, not loud 4) smooth or silky

soft-en [sô'fən] *verb*, 1) to ease, to relax, 2) to melt

soft-ly [sôft'lē] *adverb*, 1) quietly 2) mildly, gently

soft-ware [sôft'wâr'] *noun*, instructions that allow a computer to do specific tasks

soil [soil] *noun*, 1) the earth where plants and organisms grow, the top layer of the earth, *verb*, 2) to make something dirty

so-journ [sō'jûrn'] *noun*, 1) a brief stay, *verb*, 2) to stay temporarily

sol-ace [sŏl'ĭs] *noun*, comfort in trouble, or sorrow, or distress

so-lar [sō'lər] *adjective*, referring to or relating to the sun

sold [sōld] *verb, past tense* of **sell**

sol-der [sŏd'ər] *noun*, a metal or a metallic alloy used to join by fusing metallic surfaces together

sol-dier [sōl'jər] *noun*, a man or woman enlisted in the army

sole [sōl] *adjective*, 1) single, one *noun*, 2) the part of the shoe on which the bottom of the foot rests 3) an edible flat fish

sole-ly [sōl′lē] *adverb*, the only one

sol-emn [sŏl′əm] *adjective*, serious, grave, formal and dignified

so-le-noid [sō′lə-noid′] *noun*, a cylindrical round coil

so-lic-it [sə-lĭs′ĭt] *verb*, to ask someone to buy something or commit themselves

so-lic-i-tor [sə-lĭs′ĭ-tər] *noun*, the law officer of a city or government

sol-id [sŏl′ĭd] *adjective*, 1) not hollow, hard, firm, *noun*, 2) any substance that cannot flow, takes up space and has a definite shape and volume

sol-id-ify [sə-lĭd′ə-fī′] *verb*, to change from liquid to solid

so-lil-o-quy [sə-lĭl′ə-kwē] *noun*, the act of talking to one's self, a monologue in a drama

sol-i-taire [sŏl′ĭ-târ′] *noun*, 1) a gem set by itself 2) a card game involving one person

sol-i-tar-y [sŏl′ĭ-tĕr′ē] *adjective*, living or being by one's self, single, alone, secluded

sol-i-tude [sŏl′ĭ-tōōd′] *noun*, state of being alone, a lonely place

so-lo [sō′lō] *noun*, 1) something accomplished by one person 2) an unaccompanied performance

sol-stice [sŏl′stĭs] *noun*, either of two times a year when the sun is farthest from the equator, June 21 and December 22

sol-u-ble [sŏl′yə-bəl] *adjective*, something that dissolves

so-lu-tion [sə-lōō′shən] *noun*, 1) a liquid containing another substance dissolved in it 2) the answer found

solve [sŏlv] *verb*, to find the answer by studying the problem

sol-vent [sŏl′vənt] *adjective*, 1) debt free, able to pay one's debts, *noun*, 2) a usually liquid substance in which another substance can dissolve

som-ber [sŏm′bər] *adjective*, gloomy, serious, melancholy

some [sŭm] *adjective,* 1) an amount of, not all, *pronoun,* 2) referring to people or things without saying exactly who or what

some-bod-y [sŭm′bŏd′ē] *pronoun*, any person, an unknown or unnamed individual

some-how [sŭm′hou′] *adverb*, in some unknown way

some-one [sŭm′wŭn′] *pronoun*, a person or an individual

some-place [sŭm′plās′] *noun*, a location, somewhere

som-er-sault [sŭm′ər-sôlt′] *noun*, the act of turning upside down with your head between your legs as though rolling in a ball

some-thing [sŭm′thĭng] *pronoun*, an unknown amount or identity

some-time [sŭm′tīm′] *adverb*, a time in the past or future

some-times [sŭm′tīmz′] *adverb*, occasionally, not always

some-what [sŭm′hwŏt′] *adverb*, slightly, to some degree

some-where [sŭm′hwâr′] *adverb*, in or to, in an unspecified space

som-nam-bu-list [sŏm-năm′byə-lĭst] *noun*, a sleepwalker

son [sŭn] *noun*, a male child, or offspring

song [sông] *noun*, 1) a piece of music with words 2) poetry

son-net [sŏn′ĭt] *noun*, a poem, fourteen lines in iambic pentameter

soon [so͞on] *adverb*, something that will happen in a short time from now, promptly, quickly

soon-er [so͞o′nər] *adjective*, before long, earlier than

soot [so͝ot] *noun*, *no plural*, a black powder separated from fuel during combustion, smoke residue, cinders, ash

soothe [so͞oth] *verb*, 1) to ease or comfort 2) to quiet, to pacify

so-phis-ti-ca-tion [sə-fĭs′tĭ-kā′shən] *noun*, intelligence, social grace, elegance, style, good taste

soph-o-more [sŏf′ə-môr] *noun*, a student in his second year of a four-year course

so-pran-o [sə-prăn′ō] *noun*, a singer who can reach the high notes in music

sor-cer-ess [sôr′sər-ĭs] *noun*, a magician, a witch

sor-did [sôr′dĭd] *adjective*, filthy, base, vile, squalid, selfish

sore [sôr, sōr] *adjective*, 1) hurting, painful, *noun*, 2) a painful, injured place on the body

so-ror-i-ty [sə-rôr′ĭ-tē] *noun*, a society or club of girls or women

sor-row [sŏr′ō] *noun*, sadness

sor-ry [sŏr′ē] *adjective*, feeling pity or sorrow, regret

sort [sôrt] *noun*, 1) a special kind, *verb*, 2) to separate into different categories, to classify

sought [sôt] *past tense* of **seek**

soul [sōl] *noun*, the part of you that is not body, and that some people think does not die with your body, the spirit of a person

sound [sound] *adjective*, 1) healthy, strong 2) deep or undisturbed, *noun*, 3) something heard from transmitted vibrations, *verb*, 4) to make a noise

soup [so͞op] *noun*, a liquid food made by boiling meat, fish, or vegetables and seasonings

sour [sour] *adjective*, 1) having a sharp, biting, acid taste, tart, tangy, 2) soured, curdled

source [sôrs] *noun*, 1) the thing or place from which something comes 2) someone who provides information 3) a reference book

south [south] *adjective*, just opposite the north

South America [south-ə-mĕr′ĭ-kə] *noun*, one of the seven continents, containing 5.9% of the world's population

South Carolina [south-kăr′ə-lī′nə] *noun*, one of the 50 United States, located in the Southeast, the capital is Columbia. The state flower of **South Carolina** is the yellow jasmine, and the motto is "Prepared in mind and resources." or "While I breathe I hope."

South Dakota [south-də-kō′tə] *noun*, one of the 50 United States, located in the Northwest, the capital is Pierre. The state flower of **South Dakota** is the pasque flower and the motto is "Under God the people rule."

sou-ve-nir [sōō′və-nîr′] *noun*, that which serves as a reminder, a keepsake, a memento

sov-er-eign [sŏv′ər-ĭn] *adjective*, highest in power, chief

sow *noun*, 1) [sou] *noun*, an adult female pig, [sō]*verb*, 2) to scatter seeds over the ground where they will grow to produce a crop

soy-bean [soi′bēn′] *noun*, a bean plant grown for its edible, nutritious seeds

space [spās] *noun*, 1) the limitless three-dimensional area all around 2) an empty place or unoccupied time

space-ship [spās′shĭp′] *noun*, a rocket orbiting the earth

spa-cious [spā′shəs] *adjective*, vast in extent, roomy, sizeable

spade [spād] *noun*, 1) a small hand-held shovel 2) one of the four suits in a deck of cards

spa-ghet-ti [spə-gĕt′ē] *noun*, a variety of macaroni made in cords of small diameter

span [spăn] *noun*, a stretch, the measure, the distance

spare [spâr] *adjective*, 1) kept in addition to what is already available, *verb*, 2) to give something extra, to share 3) to omit, to leave out

spark [spärk] *noun*, 1) a tiny burning particle, *verb*, 2) to stimulate, to set in motion

spar-kle [spär′kəl] *verb*, to shine with bright points of light

spark plug [spärk′plŭg′] *noun*, a device with two electrodes

between which an electric jump spark is made

spar-row [spăr′ō] *noun*, a small brownish-gray bird

sparse [spärs] *adjective*, not thick, thinly scattered or distributed

spasm [spăz′əm] *noun*, a seizure, a fit, a convulsive movement

spa-tial [spā′shəl] *adjective*, relating to space

spat-u-la [spăch′ə-lə] *noun*, an instrument with a broad blade used for spreading or mixing

spawn [spôn] *verb*, to lay eggs

spay [spā] *verb*, to remove the reproductive organs, to castrate

speak [spēk] *verb*, to say words aloud, to talk, to express ideas

speak-er [spē′kər] *noun*, 1) the one talking 2) an orator, a lecturer

spear [spîr] *noun*, a long thin weapon with a pointed end

spe-cial [spĕsh′əl] *adjective*, 1) individual, peculiar, particular, different from the others 2) extra nice, distinct 3) having a particular function or purpose

spe-cial-ist [spĕsh′ə-lĭst] *noun*, one who studies a subject at great length, an expert, an authority

spe-cial-ize [spĕsh′ə-līz′] *verb*, to focus on a particular profession

spe-cies [spē′shēz] *noun*, *plural*, 1) a distinct sort, kind, or variety 2) a group of living things that can breed together

spe-cif-ic [spĭ-sĭf′ĭk] *noun*, special, explicit, precise, peculiar

spec-i-fy [spĕs′ə-fī′] *verb*, to designate, to name explicitly, to indicate, to point out in detail

spec-i-men [spĕs′ə-mən] *noun*, a part of anything to show the quality of the whole

spe-cious [spē′shəs] *adjective*, something false that appears to be true, deceptively attractive

speck [spĕk] *noun*, a small piece or particle of something

spec-ta-cle [spĕk′tə-kəl] *noun*, 1) a public scene that attracts a lot of attention 2) a display, a show

spec-ta-cles [spĕk′tə-kəlz] *noun*, *plural*, glasses for the eyes to improve vision set in a frame that rests on the nose and ears

spec-tac-u-lar [spĕk-tăk′yə-lər] *adjective*, impressive, amazing, breath-taking, dramatic

spec-ta-tor [spĕk′tā′tər] *noun*, one who looks on and watches, an observer, a bystander

spec-ter [spĕk′tər] *noun*, any object of dread, a ghost, an apparition

spec-tro-scope [spĕk′trə-skōp′] *noun*, an optical instrument

spec-trum [spĕk′trəm] *noun*, a broad range or sequence, especially of light separated into its constituent colors

spec-u-late [spĕk′yə-lāt′] *verb*, 1) to gamble, to buy and sell on the market 2) to consider, to contemplate, to hypothesize

spec-u-la-tion [spĕk′yə-lā′shən] *noun*, theory, hypothesis, conjecture, contemplation

speech [spēch] *noun*, 1) a long talk usually prepared in advance 2) language, words, dialect

speed [spēd] *noun*, 1) the rate at which something moves, *verb*, 2) to quicken, to hasten

speed-om-e-ter [spĭ-dŏm′ĭ-tər] *noun*, an instrument for indicating speed or velocity

spell [spĕl] *noun*, 1) a charm that captivates some and holds their attention 2) a short period of time, *verb*, 3) to indicate the correct arrangement of letters in a word 4) to be a sign of

spell-ing [spĕl′ĭng] *noun*, the correct use of the proper letters composing a word

spend [spĕnd] *verb*, 1) to give money for something 2) to use or consume energy or time

spent [spĕnt] *past tense* of **spend**

sphere [sfĭr] *adjective*, 1) a social position, *noun*, 2) a ball or globe

spher-i-cal [sfĭr′ĭ-kəl] *adjective*, globular, round like a ball

spice [spīs] *noun*, a seed or root of a plant used to add flavor to food

spi-der [spī′dər] *noun*, a bug that uses threads from its body to make a web to capture insects

spill [spĭl] *noun*, 1) a fall, *verb*, 2) to accidentally allow a liquid to flow out of a container

spin [spĭn] *verb*, 1) to whirl quickly 2) to twist into a thread from wool or other natural fibers

spin-ach [spĭn′ĭch] *noun*, an edible green leafy vegetable

spine [spīn] *noun*, the long row of bones in your back

spi-ral [spī′rəl] *noun*, helical, like the thread of a screw

spire [spīr] *noun*, the pointed top of a tower or steeple

spir-it [spĭr′ĭt] *noun*, 1) a mysterious part of you which is not the body, the soul 2) an eager state of mind, enthusiasm 3) a supernatural being such as a ghost or a fairy 4) an alcoholic drink such as liquor

spir-it-u-al [spĭr′ĭ-chōō-əl] *adjective*, airy, motivated by the soul, holy, religious

spit [spĭt] *noun*, 1) saliva, *verb*, 2) to spray water or saliva out of the mouth

spite [spīt] *noun*, *no plural*, hatred, feelings of malice, wanting to hurt or annoy another person

splash [splăsh] *noun*, 1) the sound made when a solid falls into liquid, *verb*, 2) to make a wave of water in a pool

splen-did [splĕn′dĭd] *adjective*, excellent, magnificent, very fine

splice [splīs] *verb*, to insert a shoot, to join, to graft, to unite

splint [splĭnt] *noun*, a board used to keep a thing from bending, a way of protecting a broken limb

splin-ter [splĭn′tər] *noun*, a thin piece of wood split off from a larger piece, a sliver

split [splĭt] *noun*, 1) a tear or a break, *verb*, 2) to break lengthwise 3) to share

spoil [spoil] *verb*, 1) to damage or injure, to ruin 2) to become rotten or decayed 3) to overindulge or corrupt by coddling someone

spoke [spōk] *noun*, 1) one of the bars joining the rim of a wheel to the center to support weight, *verb*, 2) *past tense* of **speak**

sponge [spŭnj] *noun*, 1) a substance that absorbs water, used to clean and wipe 2) a primitive marine animal having a soft elastic skeleton with many pores, *verb*, 3) to live off the generosity of others

spon-sor [spŏn′sər] *noun*, 1) a patron, supporter, mentor, backer, *verb*, 2) to offer financial support for a program

spon-ta-ne-i-ty [spŏn′tə-nē′ĭ-tē] *noun*, acting at the spur of the moment, impromptu

spon-ta-ne-ous [spŏn-tā′nē-əs] *adjective*, 1) acting on impulse, a result of natural law 2) energy

spool [spōōl] *noun*, a round object used to wind thread or wire

spoon [spōōn] *noun*, a utensil consisting of a shallow bowl with a long handle attached to it, used for eating or stirring

spoon-ful [spōōn′fŏŏl′] *noun*, the quantity that sits in a spoon

spo-rad-ic [spə-răd′ĭk] *adjective*, occurring irregularly

spore [spōr] *noun*, a cell that reproduces itself such as fungus, fern, or bacterium

sport [spōrt] *noun*, 1) games and exercises done for pleasure 2) a rascal 3) a teammate

spot [spŏt] *noun*, 1) a small mark, drop, or blemish 2) a location, *verb*, 3) to see something

spouse [spous] *noun*, a partner in marriage, husband or wife

spout [spout] *noun*, 1) the lip of a container from which liquid is poured, *verb*, 2) to spurt, to discharge, to gush forth

sprain [sprān] *verb*, to strain a body part by twisting it, causing it to swell

sprawl [sprôl] *verb*, to stretch, to spread out, to extend

spray [sprā] *noun*, 1) liquid dispersed in very fine drops 2) a small branch of flowers or foliage, *verb*, 3) to blow or scatter liquid in very fine drops

spread [sprĕd] *verb*, 1) to cover a surface with a thin layer 2) to unfold or stretch out 3) to circulate, to disseminate 4) to extend over a large area

spring [sprĭng] *noun*, 1) a river or pond coming up from the ground 2) a piece of wire twisted into a spiral 3) the season following winter, when plants begin to grow, *verb*, 4) to jump 5) to come from 6) to grow

sprin-kle [sprĭng′kəl] *verb*, 1) to spatter, to disperse in drops 2) to drizzle 3) to dust lightly

sprint [sprĭnt] *noun*, 1) a short fast run, *verb*, 2) to dash at top speed

sprock-et [sprŏk′ĭt] *noun*, a projection shaped so as to engage with a chain

sprout [sprout] *verb*, to grow out of a seed, to start to grow

spruce [sprōōs] *noun*, one of the softwood evergreen trees

sprung [sprŭng] *past tense* of **spring**

spry [sprī] *adjective*, vigorous, quick, energetic, agile

spun [spŭn] *past tense* of **spin**

spur [spûr] *noun*, 1) a short side track connecting with the main railroad 2) a sharp blade on the back of a boot used to urge

horses to run faster 3) an impetus, a cause to action, *verb*, 4) to urge, to goad, to stimulate

spu-ri-ous [spyŏŏr′ē-əs] *adjective*, counterfeit, false, not genuine

spurn [spûrn] *verb*, to reject, to scorn, to despise, to shun

spy [spī] *noun*, *plural*, **spies** 1) an agent hired to secretly obtain information *verb*, 2) to see or catch sight of 3) to keep secret watch

squad [skwŏd] *noun*, a small group of soldiers who work, train, and fight together 2) a sports team

squad-ron [skwŏd′rən] *noun*, armed military aircraft

squal-id [skwŏl′ĭd] *adjective*, dirty through neglect, foul, filthy

squan-der [skwŏn′dər] *verb*, to spend money or resources without being accountable

square [skwâr] *noun*, 1) a surface with four equal sides and right angle corners 2) an open area in the center of town surrounded by stores and businesses

square number [skwâr- nŭm′bər] *noun*, the product of two equal factors, e.g., 12 x 12 = 144

squash [skwŏsh] *noun*, 1) a vegetable that grows on a vine 2) a game similar to racquetball, *verb*, 3) to repress 4) to flatten by pressing or from pressure

squat [skwŏt] *adjective*, 1) wide, stocky, *verb*, 2) to stoop

squeak [skwēk] *noun*, 1) a very sharp, high-pitched sound, *verb*, 2) to make a short high-pitched sound squeal [skwēl] *noun*, 1) a shrill cry, *verb*, 2) to make such a sound 3) to turn informer

squeeze [skwēz] *verb*, to press hard upon 2) to put pressure on to extract liquid 3) to force one's way 4) to crowd

squid [skwĭd] *noun*, a sea creature similar to an octopus

squint [skwĭnt] *verb*, to scrunch one's eyes to strain to see

squirm [skwûrm] *verb*, to wiggle

squir-rel [skwûr/əl, skwŭr/-] *noun*, a small rodent with a bushy tail that lives in trees

sta-bil-i-ty [stə-bĭl/ĭ-tē] *adjective*, firmness, constancy, strength

sta-ble [stā/bəl] *adjective*, 1) firm, steady, *noun*, 2) a building in which horses are kept

stac-ca-to [stə-kä/tō] *adjective*, music played in a quick, abrupt manner

stack [stăk] *noun*, 1) a large pile arranged in some sort of order 2) a chimney, *verb*, 3) to pile up

sta-di-um [stā/dē-əm] *noun*, an open arena where concerts, sports, or events are held

staff [stăf] *noun*, a long stick carried in the hand for support

stag [stăg] *noun*, a male deer

stage [stāj] *noun*, 1) a raised floor or platform in a theatre or auditorium 2) a period of time or a step in development

stage-coach [stāj/kōch/] *noun*, a carriage on wheels pulled by horses on a fixed route

stag-ger [stăg/ər] *verb*, to stand or walk unsteadily, to reel

stag-nant [stăg/nənt] *adjective*, not moving or flowing, motionless

stag-nate [stăg/nāt/] *verb*, to be or become stagnant, motionless, to become impure or foul

staid [stād] *adjective*, sober, sedate

stain [stān] *noun*, 1) a mark that changes the appearance of something, a blot, *verb*, 2) to make a strong mark that cannot be removed 3) to disgrace

stair [stâr] *noun*, a step connecting different levels, *plural*, **stairs,** a series or flight of steps

stake [stāk] *noun*, 1) a pointed post in the ground 2) a gamble, a risk

stale [stāl] *adjective*, 1) old, dry, not fresh, tasteless 2) dull, bored

stale-mate [stāl/māt/] *noun*, a deadlock, a situation in which no side may take action

stalk [stôk] *noun*, 1) the long part of a plant that supports leaves or flowers, *verb*, 2) to follow someone with the intention of harming them 3) to pursue prey

stall [stôl] *noun*, 1) a small open room, as in a barn or a market place, *verb*, 2) to stop due to a mechanical failure

stal-lion [stăl/yən] *noun*, a male horse used for breeding

stal-wart [stôl/wərt] *adjective*, 1) sturdy, strong 2) brave 3) firm, steadfast

stam-i-na [stăm/ə-nə] *noun*, the power to endure, strength

stamp [stămp] *noun*, 1) a small piece of paper purchased to put on an envelope or package to send it through the mail 2) the imprint left from a device used to leave a mark, *verb*, 3) to mark with a special sign or design 4) to set the foot down heavily

stam-pede [stăm-pēd'] *verb*, to rush wildly in a group

stance [stăns] *noun*, 1) posture 2) political or social position

stand [stănd] *verb*, 1) to be your feet 2) to take a position 3) to mean or signify, to represent

stand-ard [stăn'dərd] *adjective*, 1) regular, official, basic, *noun*, 2) a fixed quality by which things are compared

stands [stăndz] *noun*, *plural*, the bleachers where spectators watch sports events

stan-za [stăn'zə] *noun*, a verse in a poem, a song, or a refrain

sta-ple [stā'pəl] *noun*, 1) principle commodity, an essential element 2) a wire used to attach things together such as cloth or paper, *verb*, 3) to bond two things together with staples applied by a stapler

star [stär] *noun*, 1) a point of light that can be seen in the sky at night 2) a five-pointed shape, *verb*, 3) to stand out in a positive way, to be outstanding

star-board [stär'bərd] *adjective*, the right-hand side of a ship as one faces the bow

starch [stärch] *noun*, a carbohydrate, that turns into sugar in the body

stare [stâr] *verb*, to look at someone or something with a steady gaze, to glare

stark [stärk] *adjective*, extremely simple or severe, bleak

start [stärt] *noun*, 1) an act of beginning, *verb*, 2) to begin

star-tle [stär'tl] *verb*, to surprise, to greet unexpectedly, to shock

star-va-tion [stär-vā'shən] *noun*, to suffer from hunger and lack of food or nourishment

starve [stärv] *verb*, to be hungry, unfed, deprived of food

state [stāt] *noun*, 1) the condition of something 2) a mood 3) a group of people living under an independent government, that is part of a country or federal union which governs itself as a republic or commonwealth, *verb*, 5) to say, to declare

state-ment [stāt'mənt] *noun*, 1) a spoken or written commitment 2) a summary of an account showing the balance

states-man [stāts'mən] *noun*, a leader of government

stat-ic [stăt'ĭk] *noun*, applicable to electricity not in motion

sta-tion [stā'shən] *noun*, a stopping place for the convenience of passengers, a depot

sta-tion-ar-y [stā'shə-nĕr'ē] *adjective*, fixed in a place, not changing, not moving

sta-tion-er-y [stā'shə-nĕr'ē] *noun*, writing paper, pens, and ink

sta-tis-tic [stə-tĭs'tĭk] *noun*, a fact stated as a number or in tables

stat-ue [stăch'ōō] *noun*, replica of a figure, real or imaginary made of plaster, bronze, marble, etc.

stat-ure [stăch'ər] *noun*, 1) a person's status or place in the

community 2) the height of a
person or animal

sta-tus [stā′təs] *noun*, position,
high standing, prestige

stat-ute [stăch′o͞ot] *noun*, a law
enacted by a legislature

stat-u-to-ry [stăch′ə-tôr′ē]
adjective, authorized, made as a
law, regulated by statute

stay [stā] *verb*, to continue to be

stead-fast [stĕd′făst′] *adjective*,
firmly fixed or established,
unwavering, constant

stead-i-ly [stĕd′ə-lē] *adverb*,
constantly, continually, regularly

stead-y [stĕd′ē] *adjective*,
1) regular 2) firm, immovable

steak [stāk] *noun*, a thick flat piece
of meat or fish

steal [stēl] *verb*, 1) to take or carry
away without permission 2) to
move or pass very quietly
without making noise

stealth [stĕlth] *noun*, secrecy,
sneakiness, surreptitious

steam [stēm] *noun*, 1) the vapor
created by boiling water, *verb*,
2) to cook using the intense heat
of steam 3) to expose to steam

steel [stēl] *noun*, a hard metal made
of specially treated iron, used in
machines, knives, hardware, etc.

steep [stēp] *adjective*, 1) having a
sharp incline or slope, *verb*, 2) to
soak in liquid, to saturate

stee-ple [stē′pəl] *noun*, a free-
standing column or tower

steer [stîr] *noun*, 1) a form of long
horned cattle, *verb*, 2) to drive,
to fly, to conduct, or navigate

stel-lar [stĕl′ər] *adjective*, 1) star-
like, referring to heavenly
bodies, celestial 2) outstanding

stem [stĕm] *noun*, 1) the stalk of a
plant that supports the flower
and leaves, *verb*, 2) to develop
from 3) to stop the flow of

sten-cil [stĕn′səl] *noun*, a thin sheet
with perforations in the form of
a design through which ink or
paint may be forced

step [stĕp] *noun*, 1) a stair 2) the
movement with a foot 3) one of
a series of events in a program,
verb, 4) to walk or go on foot

ster-e-o [stĕr′ē-ō′] *noun*, an
electronic device that makes
sounds or plays music

ster-e-o-type [stĕr′ē-ə-tīp′] *noun*,
1) a typical example or pattern
2) a conventional, oversimplified
conception

ste-rile [stĕr′əl, -īl′] *adjective*,
clean, antiseptic, germ free

ster-i-lize [stĕr′ə-līz′] *verb*, 1) to
render incapable of germination,
2) to disinfect, to clean

ster-ling [stûr′lĭng] *adjective*,
1) genuine, superior, excellent,
of the highest quality *noun*,
2) made of pure silver

stern [stûrn] *adjective*,
1) unsympathetic, firm, strict
2) the back of the boat

steth-o-scope [stĕth′ə-skōp′] *noun*,
an instrument used to convey to
the ear, sounds produced by the
body, especially in the chest

stew [sto͞o] *noun*, 1) a thick soup,
verb, 2) to cook in liquid

stew-ard [sto͞o′ərd] *noun*, 1) one
who watches over something

2) one in charge of provisions and dinner arrangements

stew-ard-ess [stoo′ər-dĭs] *noun*, a woman who serves passengers on an airplane, a flight attendant

stick [stĭk] *noun*, 1) a short branch or twig, *verb*, 2) to make something adhere to a surface 3) to push in or out 4) to stay with something, to persevere

stiff [stĭf] *adjective*, 1) something that cannot be moved or bent easily 2) difficult or hard to accomplish 3) sore

stiff-en [stĭf′ən] *verb*, to harden, to brace, to become rigid

stig-ma [stĭg′mə] *noun*, 1) the apex of a flower pistil where pollen is placed 2) a disgraceful blot

stig-ma-tize [stĭg′mə-tīz′] *verb*, to brand, to mark as wicked

still [stĭl] *adjective*, 1) without movement, *adverb*, 2) up to this or that time 3) even so

still-ness [stĭl′nĭs] *noun*, the state of being still or without sound

stim-u-late [stĭm′yə-lāt′] *verb*, to rouse to action, to excite

stim-u-lus [stĭm′yə-ləs] *noun*, an incentive, an impetus

sting [stĭng] *noun*, 1) the pain or wound of an insect or bug bite 2) a sharp or smarting pain 3) the attack of an insect on its prey or an enemy

stin-gy [stĭn′jē] *adjective*, not generous, miserly

stink [stĭngk] *noun*, 1) an unpleasant or awful odor, *verb*, 2) to give off a bad smell

sti-pend [stī′pĕnd′] *noun*, payment given for services

stip-u-late [stĭp′yə-lāt′] *verb*, to bargain, to specify as a condition of an agreement

stir [stûr] *verb*, to mix or blend

stir-ring [stûr′ĭng] *adjective*, moving, touching, exciting

stitch [stĭch] *noun*, 1) a needle and thread, piercing cloth and then coming out again to form a link of thread in a fabric 2) a loop added to a knitting needle, *verb*, 3) to sew, to mend

stock [stŏk] *noun*, goods kept on hand, merchandise

stock-ade [stŏ-kād′] *noun*, a barricade, a fence, an obstacle

stock-hold-er [stŏk′hōl′dər] *noun*, an owner of stocks or shares in a corporation

stock-ing [stŏk′ĭng] *noun*, a sheer leg covering made of nylon

sto-ic [stō′ĭk] *noun*, one who is indifferent to pleasure or pain, stern, impassive, cold

stoke [stōk] *verb*, to provide with fuel, to feed abundantly

stole [stōl] *past tense* of **steal**

stom-ach [stŭm′ək] *noun*, a large muscular bag in the body that receives food, digests some of it, and passes it on, to the intestines

stone [stōn] *noun*, 1) a small piece of rock, *verb*, 2) to pelt or kill

stool [stool] *noun*, 1) a seat with three or four legs and no back 2) a bowel movement

stoop [stoop] *verb*, 1) to bend or squat the body over forwards 2) to lower oneself, to condescend

stop [stŏp] *verb*, 1) to end, to make something come to an end 2) to prevent something from happening, moving, etc. 3) to complete the action

stor-age [stôr'ĭj] *noun*, the act of keeping things for future use

store [stōr] *noun*, 1) supply of things saved for use later 2) a shop, a place to buy things, *verb*, 3) to put away for later use

stork [stôrk] *noun*, a large bird with long legs and a large beak

storm [stôrm] *noun*, a period of high winds, possibly thunder and lightning, rain, or snow

sto-ry [stōr'ē] *noun*, 1) telling of events with words spoken or written in a book 2) an account of something either true or fictitious, a report, a description 3) the floor of a building

stout [stout] *adjective*, 1) short, heavy-set 2) resolute, firm

stove [stōv] *noun*, an appliance which is heated and used for cooking or heating

stow [stō] *verb*, to store, to put away for future use

straight [strāt] *adjective*, 1) not curved, *adverb*, 2) without going anywhere else or doing anything else 3) moving on a path that is unchanged 4) without delay, *noun*, 5) a poker hand of 5 cards in consecutive order

straight-en [strāt'n] *verb*, to fix or arrange in order

strain [strān] *noun*, 1) the change of a body produced by an external force 2) a new species or breed 3) a suggestion, a hint, a trace, *verb*, 4) to cause stress, to stretch to reach

strait [strāt] *noun*, a narrow channel between two bodies of water, an inlet

strand [strănd] *noun*, 1) seashore, waterfront 2) a piece of something long and thin like a rope or a piece of hair

strange [strānj] *adjective*, unusual, odd, unfamiliar, exotic

strange-ly [strānj'lē] *adverb*, unusually, seldom, rarely

stran-ger [strān'jər] *noun*, a person you do not know, an outsider

stran-gle [străng'gəl] *verb*, 1) to kill by suffocating 2) to suppress

strap [străp] *noun*, 1) a narrow piece of leather, plastic, cloth, etc, used for fastening something, *verb*, 2) to fasten something on with a tie

strat-e-gy [străt'ə-jē] *noun*, a plan

strat-o-sphere [străt'ə-sfîr'] *noun*, the upper atmosphere extending 12-30 miles above the earth's surface, the ozone

stra-tum [strā'təm] *noun*, *plural* **strata**, a layer of the earth's surface, sedimentary rock

straw [strô] *noun*, 1) a dry stem 2) something that people use to suck a drink out of a glass

straw-ber-ry [strô'bĕr'ē] *noun*, the edible red berry of a small plant, that grows on the ground

stray [strā] *adjective*, 1) anything that does not seem to be part of a group, *verb*, 2) to wander away from home or the rest of the group 3) to digress

streak [strēk] *noun*, 1) a long mark like a band or a stripe, *verb*, 2) to draw stripes on something in a wild pattern

stream [strēm] *noun*, 1) a small river, a small body of running water 2) a steady or continuous flow, *verb*, 3) to flow, to pour

street [strēt] *noun*, a public paved road as in a town or city

strength [strĕngkth] *noun*, power, capacity for exertion or endurance, force in numbers

strength-en [strĕngk'thən] *verb*, to reinforce, to make stronger

stren-u-ous [strĕn'yo͞o-əs] *adjective*, characterized by vigorous exertion, difficult

stress [strĕs] *noun*, 1) anxiety, tension, *verb*, 2) to apply force to cause strain 3) to emphasize

stretch [strĕch] *noun*, 1) an expanse, a range or reach, *verb*, 2) to exaggerate 3) to extend across a given space 4) to extend one's body or limbs to feel limber

stretch-er [strĕch'ər] *noun*, a framework consisting of two poles with a cloth fastened between them used to carry an injured person

strict [strĭkt] *adjective*, close adherence to the rules

stride [strīd] *noun*, 1) a large step or movement, *verb*, 2) to step

stri-dent [strīd'nt] *adjective*, loud and harsh in sound, grating

strike [strīk] *noun*, 1) an unsuccessful attempt by a batter to hit a ball 2) a protest of wages that stops work in order to bargain for better working conditions, *verb*, 3) to hit or attack 4) to refuse to work because of a pay dispute 5) to discover, to uncover 6) to eliminate 7) to find, to reach

string [strĭng] *noun*, 1) a thin twine made by twisting several threads together 2) a fine piece of wire used in some musical instruments, *verb*, 3) to thread a bead onto a string

strin-gent [strĭn'jənt] *adjective*, strict, inflexible, exacting

stripe [strīp] *noun*, a long thin line

strive [strīv] *verb*, to exert oneself, to try, to make a strenuous effort

stroke [strōk] *noun*, 1) a mild heart attack, *verb*, 2) to caress, to rub

stroll [strōl] *verb*, to walk leisurely

strong [st rŏng] *adjective*, 1) able to take stress or strain 2) intense in degree 3) physically powerful

struck [strŭk]*verb*, *past tense* of **strike**

struc-ture [strŭk'chər] *noun*, 1) the framework of something, 2) a complete building

strug-gle [strŭg'əl] *noun*, 1) the fight, the effort, *verb*, 2) to continue to endure set backs

strut [strŭt] *verb*, to swagger, to walk with bravado

stub-born [stŭb'ərn] *adjective*, unwilling to give in or compromise, obstinate

stuck [stŭk]*verb*, *past tense* of **stick**

stu-dent [sto͞od'nt] *noun*, a person enrolled at a school or college

stud-y [stŭd'ē] *noun*, 1) a room to read and write 2) a subject or area of learning, *verb*, 3) to apply the mind to the effort to learn by reading and thinking

stuff [stŭf] *noun*, 1) substance, material, *verb*, 2) to fill by crowding, to push or crowd in

stum-ble [stŭm′bəl] *verb*, to walk unsteadily so that you appear to be about to fall, to trip while running 2) to come upon unexpectedly 3) to stammer

stump [stŭmp] *noun*, 1) what is left of a tree after it has been cut down, *verb*, 2) to perplex

stun [stŭn] *verb*, to astonish, to amaze, to confound, to shock

stunt [stŭnt] *noun*, 1) a performance, a skit, an act, *verb*, 2) to suppress, to retard the growth of something

stu-pen-dous [stoō-pĕn′dəs] *adjective*, astonishing, wonderful, amazing

stu-por [stoō′pər] *noun*, a state of apathy, daze, a lack of awareness

stur-dy [stûr′dē] *adjective*, very strongly built, durable

stut-ter [stə′tər] *verb*, to speak with difficulty, to stammer

sty [stī] *noun*, 1) a painful red swelling on the end of an eyelid 2) a pig pen

style [stīl] *noun*, 1) the fashion or design 2) elegance or flair

sty-mie [stī′mē] *verb*, to present an obstacle, to stump, to hinder

suave [swäv] *adjective*, smoothly, agreeable, courteous, polite

sub-due [səb-doō′] *verb*, to calm down, to bring under control

sub-ject [sŭb′jĭkt] *adjective*, 1) owing obedience to 2) likely to

be affected by, *noun*, 3) an area of study 4) a person under the authority or control of another 5) in a sentence the word about which the predicate makes a statement, *verb*, 6) to expose to

sub-jec-tive [səb-jĕk′tĭv] *adjective*, based on personal feelings or opinions

sub-lime [sə-blīm′] *adjective*, great, noble, majestic, superior

sub-lim-i-nal [sŭb-lĭm′ə-nəl] *adjective*, affecting the subconscious, below the threshold of consciousness

sub-ma-rine [sŭb′mə-rēn′] *noun*, a naval warship armed with torpedoes and missiles that operates under water

sub-merge [səb-mûrj′] *verb*, to put or sink under water

sub-mis-sive [səb-mĭs′ĭv] *adjective*, to take orders without questioning authority

sub-mit [səb-mĭt′] *verb*, 1) to put something forward for someone else's reaction 2) to give in to someone or something

sub-or-di-nate [sə-bôr′dn-ĭt] *adjective*, 1) being in a lower rank or class, subject to another's authority *noun*, 2) one lower in rank, inferior

sub-poe-na [sə-pē′nə] *noun*, a writ commanding a person listed in it to appear in court

sub-scribe [səb-scrīb′] *verb*, 1) to sign up for something 2) to give permission or consent

sub-scrip-tion [səb-skrĭp′shən] *noun*, money paid as a form of membership for service

sub-se-quent [sŭb′sĭ-kwĕnt′]
adjective, following, after

sub-ser-vi-ent [səb-sûr′vē-ənt]
adjective, useful in an inferior
capacity, subordinate

sub-side [səb-sīd′] *verb*, to settle
down to become calm

sub-si-dize [sŭb′sĭ-dīz′] *verb*, 1) to
add to 2) to provide financial aid

sub-si-dy [sŭb′sĭ-dē] *noun*, direct
financial aid by the government

sub-stance [sŭb′stəns] *noun*, the
material something is made of

sub-stan-tial [səb-stăn′shəl]
adjective, 1) strong 2) having
considerable property

sub-stan-ti-ate [səb-stăn′shē-āt′]
verb, to verify, to support

sub-stan-tive [sŭb′stən-tĭv]
adjective, essential, pertaining to

sub-sti-tute [sŭb′stĭ-tōōt′] *noun*,
1) a person or thing put in place
of another, a replacement *verb*,
2) to act in place of another

sub-ter-fuge [sŭb′tər-fyōōj′] *noun*,
a device or plan by which one
can hide an objective

sub-ter-ra-ne-an [sŭb′tə-rā′nē-ən]
adjective, 1) under the earth's
surface 2) hidden, secret

sub-tle [sŭt′l] *adjective*, difficult to
to detect, not obvious, slight

sub-tle-ty [sŭt′l-tē] *noun*, cunning,
delicately understated

sub-tract [səb-trăkt′] *verb*, to take
away one number from another

sub-trac-tion [səb-trăk′shən] *noun*,
an equation in which one
number is taken from another

sub-urb [sŭb′ûrb′] *noun*, a
residential community on the
outskirts of a city or town

sub-ur-ban [sə-bûr′bən] *adjective*,
pertaining to a smaller district
next to a city or town

sub-ver-sive [səb-vûr′sĭv]
adjective, tending to overthrow
or ruin, corruption

sub-way [sŭb′wā′] *noun*, an
underground electric train or
urban transit system

suc-ceed [sək-sēd′] *adjective*, to
follow in order, to be successful

suc-cess [sək-sĕs′] *noun*,
accomplishment, achievement

suc-cess-ful [sək-sĕs′fəl] *adjective*,
prosperous, enjoying abundance

suc-ces-sion [sək-sĕsh′ən] *noun*,
sequence, order, descent

suc-ces-sive [sək-sĕs′ĭv] *adjective*,
following one after another in a
line or series, consecutive

suc-ces-sor [sək-sĕs′ər] *noun*,
someone appointed to a title or
position to replace another

suc-cinct [sək-sĭngkt′] *adjective*,
concise, terse, brief, to the point

suc-cor [sŭk′ər] *noun*, aid, help,
assistance, relief

suc-cul-ent [sŭk′yə-lənt] *adjective*,
1) juicy 2) delicious, tasty

suc-cumb [sə-kŭm′] *verb*, 1) to
yield, to give way 2) to die

such [sŭch] *pronoun*, 1) of this or
that kind 2) used in some
phrases to mean like

suck [sŭk] *verb*, to draw into the
mouth by action of the lips and
tongue when inhaling

suc-tion [sŭk′shən] *noun*, the
pulling force of a partial vacuum

sud-den [sŭd′n] *adjective*, when something happens unexpectedly

sud-den-ly [sŭd′n-lē] *adverb*, happening at once without warning, unexpectedly

sue [sōō] *verb*, to ask a court to solve a problem legally

suede [swād] *noun*, a leather made when the flesh, or underside of the leather is buffed or sandpapered to produce a nap

suf-fer [sŭf′ər] *verb*, 1) to feel pain or hurt 2) to tolerate, to allow

suf-fer-ing [sŭf′ər-ĭng] *noun*, enduring pain and sadness

suf-fice [sə-fīs′] *verb*, 1) to be enough for 2) to satisfy a need

suf-fi-cient [sə-fĭsh′ənt] *adjective*, adequate for the purpose

suf-fix [sŭf′ĭks] *noun*, letters added to the end of a word, to change the meaning

suf-fo-cate [sŭf′ə-kāt′] *verb*, 1) to smother, to choke 2) to kill by depriving of oxygen

suf-frage [sŭf′rĭj] *noun*, the right to vote, a vote

sug-ar [shŏŏg′ər] *noun*, a sweet substance made from sugar cane or sugar beets and used in food products

sug-gest [səg-jĕst′] *verb*, 1) to bring up or call to mind, to propose for consideration 2) to imply, to indicate

sug-ges-tion [səg-jĕs′chən] *noun*, 1) a proposal, an idea, advice, a recommendation 2) a slight trace, a hint, an implication

su-i-cide [sōō′ĭ-sīd′] *noun*, the act of taking one's own life

suit [sōōt] *noun*, 1) a set of clothes made from the same fabric, *verb*, 2) to adapt, to perform

suit-a-ble [sōō′tə-bəl] *adjective*, fitting, proper, appropriate

suit-case [sōōt′kās′] *noun*, a rectangular piece of luggage

suite [swēt] *noun*, a number of rooms connected together

suit-or [sōō′tər] *noun*, a beau, a man who courts a woman

sul-fur [sŭl′fər] *noun*, a nonmetallic yellow element used in gunpowder, matches and medicine

sulk [sŭlk] *verb*, to pout and feel angry or sorry for yourself

sul-len [sŭl′ən] *adjective*, silent from anger or hurt, moody, indulging in self-pity

sul-ly [sŭl′ē] *verb*, 1) to disgrace, to tarnish someone's character 2) to soil, to stain

sul-try [sŭl′trē] *adjective*, sweltering, hot and humid

sum [sŭm] *noun*, the total of different amounts added together

sum-ma-ry [sŭm′ə-rē] *noun*, a shorter version of an article

sum-ma-tion [sə-mā′shən] *noun*, the act of finding the total

sum-mer [sŭm′ər] *noun*, the third season of the year, between spring and autumn

sum-mit [sŭm′ĭt] *noun*, 1) the top leaders, the highest point 2) the top of a mountain

sum-mon [sŭm′ən] *verb*, 1) to call, to send for by command 2) to gather, to call forth

sum-mons [sŭm'ənz] *noun*, a formal letter requesting a response in court

sump-tu-ous [sŭmp'choo-əs] *adjective*, luxurious, splendid

sun [sŭn] *noun*, the central star of the solar system around which the planets revolve which gives off light, heat and energy

sun-dae [sŭn'dē] *noun*, a dish of ice cream covered with toppings such as chocolate syrup, nuts and whipped cream

Sun-day [sŭn'dē] *noun*, the first day of the week, observed as the Sabbath by most Christians

sun-dry [sŭn'drē] *adjective*, various, more than one or two

sun-flow-er [sŭn'flou'ər] *noun*, a plant with large yellow-rayed flower heads that produces edible seeds that yield an oil

sun-rise [sŭn'rīz'] *noun*, the early morning, the crack of dawn

sun-set [sŭn'sĕt'] *noun*, close of the day, twilight

sun-shine [sŭn'shīn'] *noun*, *no plural*, bright light, day light

su-per [soo'pər] *adjective*,
1) outstanding, exceptionally fine,
2) great, extreme or excessive

su-perb [soo-pûrb'] *adjective*, exceptional, extraordinary

su-per-cil-i-ous [soo'pər-sĭl'ē-əs] *adjective*, lofty with pride, haughty, contemptuous

su-per-fi-cial [soo'pər-fĭsh'əl] *adjective*, 1) relating to the surface or appearance only
2) actions thoughtlessly done, insincere, shallow

su-per-flu-ous [soo-pûr'floo-əs] *adjective*, excessive, more than needed, unnecessary

su-per-in-tend-ent [soo'pər-ĭn-tĕn'dənt] *noun*, one having oversight and direction of some place or agency

su-pe-ri-or [soo-pîr'ē-ər] *adjective*, 1) beyond power or influence of another 2) greater in number or amount 3) above average

su-per-mar-ket [soo'pər-mär'kĭt] *noun*, a large store with shelves that have a variety of household products, a large grocery store

su-per-nat-u-ral [soo'pər-năch'ər-əl] *adjective*, beyond what is explainable by natural law, metaphysical

su-per-sede [soo'pər-sēd'] *adjective*, to come to take the place of something that is not as modern, efficient,or appropriate

su-per-son-ic [soo'pər-sŏn'ĭk] *adjective*, faster than sound

su-per-sti-tion [soo'pər-stĭsh'ən] *noun*, reverence for that which is unknown or mysterious

su-per-sti-tious [soo'pər-stĭsh'əs] *adjective*, awe of that which is unknown or mysterious based on an irrational belief

su-per-vise [soo'pər-vīz'] *verb*, to direct, to watch over

su-per-vi-sion [soo'pər-vĭzh'ən] *noun*, *no plural*, overseeing someone's work

su-per-vi-sor [soo'pər-vī'zər] *noun*, a person who oversees a department of workers

sup-per [sŭp′ər] *noun*, dinner, a meal eaten in the evening

sup-ple [sŭp′əl] *adjective*, 1) flexible, pliant, bending easily without breaking 2) limber

sup-ple-ment [sŭp′lə-mənt] *noun*, a part added, an appendix

sup-ply [sə-plī′] *noun*, 1) a resource, *verb*, 2) to provide something needed

sup-port [sə-pôrt′, -pōrt′] *noun*, 1) aid, assistance 2) an abutment, a brace, a stay, *verb*, 3) to advocate, to back, to uphold 4) to provide food and clothing and other necessities

sup-pose [sə-pōz′] *verb*, to hold that something is true, to assume that something is true

sup-posi-tion [sŭp′ə-zĭsh′ən] *noun*, presumption, theory, principle

sup-press [sə-prĕs′] *verb*, to subdue, to quell, to inhibit, to keep from being known

su-preme [sŏŏ-prēm′] *adjective*, highest in authority, highest in degree, above all

Su-preme Court [sŏŏ-prēm′kôrt] *noun*, the most important court in the United States, consisting of 9 members appointed by the President

sure [shŏŏr] *adjective*, best, convinced, certain beyond question, having no doubt

sure-ly [shŏŏr′lē] *adverb*, certainly

surf [sûrf] *noun*, *no plural*, 1) the waves of the sea as they hit the shores, *verb*, 2) to ride a surfboard 3) to search the Internet on a computer

sur-face [sûr′fəs] *noun*, 1) a plane, the outside or topside face 2) the top of the water, *verb*, 3) to rise to the top of a body of water

sur-feit [sûr′fĭt] *noun*, 1) excess *verb*, 2) to over-indulge, to give to use in excess

surge [sûrj] *noun*, 1) a rush, a flow, *verb*, 2) to swell, to pour out

sur-geon [sûr′jən] *noun*, one whose profession it is to cure diseases or injuries by performing an operation

sur-ger-y [sûr′jə-rē] *noun*, an operation when a doctor cuts into a person's body with instruments to help cure them

sur-ly [sûr′lē] *adjective*, rude, cross, bad-tempered, grumpy

sur-mise [sər-mīz′] *noun*, 1) a guess, speculation, likelihood, *verb*, 2) to assume, to guess, to suppose, to conjecture

sur-mount [sər-mount′] *verb*, to be overcome, to prevail over

sur-name [sûr′nām′] *noun*, a person's last name

sur-pass [sər-păs′] *verb*, to exceed, to do better, to go beyond

sur-plus [sûr′pləs, -plŭs′] *noun*, the amount that is more than needed

sur-prise [sər-prīz′] *noun*, 1) something sudden and unexpected, *verb*, 2) to cause to feel astonished

sur-ren-der [sə-rĕn′dər] *verb*, to give up, to yield

sur-rep-ti-tious [sûr′əp-tĭsh′əs] *adjective*, kept secret (especially if it would not be approved of), hidden, unauthorized

sur-ro-gate [sûr′ə-gĭt] *adjective*, substitute, replacement

sur-round [sə-round′] *verb*, to encircle, to enclose on all sides

sur-round-ings [sə-roundĭngs] *noun, plural,* the conditions or things around a person or place

sur-veil-lance [sər-vā′ləns] *noun*, a close watch over something

sur-vey [sər-vā′] *noun*, 1) a study, a poll, a review, *verb*, 2) to examine, to inspect, to watch

sur-vey-or [sər-vā′ər] *noun*, 1) one who collects data 2) one whose business it is to measure land

sur-viv-al [sər-vī′vəl] *noun, no plural,* what one needs to stay alive or exist

sur-vive [sər-vīv′] *verb*, to continue to exist, to live longer

sur-vi-vor [sər-vīv′ər] *noun*, the one to make it when the others died or failed

sus-cep-ti-ble [sə-sĕp′tə-bəl] *adjective*, capable of being affected emotionally

sus-pect [sə-spĕkt′] *noun*, 1) a person who is believed to have done something wrong, *verb*, 2) to suppose that something is true

sus-pend [sə-spĕnd′] *verb*, 1) to hang 2) to stop temporarily

sus-pend-ers [sə-spĕn′dərz] *noun*, two adjustable bands or straps arranged to pass over the shoulders to hold the trousers up

sus-pense [sə-spĕns′] *noun, no plural,* a pause or delay which leaves people anxious

sus-pen-sion [sə-spĕn′shən] *noun*, a delay, postponement

sus-pi-cion [sə-spĭsh′ən] *noun*, 1) distrust, doubt, 2) trace

sus-pi-cious [sə-spĭsh′əs] *adjective*, having a feeling that something is wrong, distrustful

sus-tain [sə-stān′] *verb*, to bear, to hold up, to keep going

sus-te-nance [sŭs′tə-nəns] *noun*, that which supports life, a food or nourishment

su-ture [sōō′chər] *noun*, stitches sewn to hold the cut edges of a wound or incision

swag-ger [swăg′ər] *verb*, to walk in a boastful and proud manner

swal-low [swŏl′ō] *noun*, 1) a small bird with a tail split into two parts, *verb*, 2) to consume food through the mouth into the stomach, to take in

swamp [swŏmp, swômp] *noun*, 1) wet, boggy ground which is always soft, wet land, *verb*, 2) to overwhelm with too much of something, to inundate

swan [swŏn] *noun*, a large white bird with a long neck that lives in the water and on land

swap [swŏp] *verb*, to exchange

swarm [swôrm] *noun*, 1) a large group of insects or bugs, *verb*, 2) to travel in a large group, to teem, to crowd

swarth-y [swôr′thē] *adjective*, having a dark complexion

swat [swŏt] *verb*, to hit, to whack

sway [swā] *verb*, to swing gently

swear [swâr] *verb*, 1) to curse 2) to promise, to make a solemn declaration

sweat [swĕt] *noun*, 1) moisture which comes out of the skin due to exertion, *verb*, 2) to give off water through the skin

sweat-er [swĕt'ər] *noun*, a wool or woven garment worn over the top of the body

sweep [swēp] *noun*, 1) a continuous search, *verb*, 2) to clean or clear with a brush or broom

sweet [swēt] *adjective*, 1) tasting like sugar or honey 2) a pleasant or kind personality 3) having a pleasant smell

swell [swĕl] *verb*, to become larger

swel-ter [swĕl'tər] *verb*, to be tired by the heat, to perspire, to sweat

swept [swĕpt] *past tense* of **sweep**

swerve [swûrv] *verb*, to move suddenly to one side when you are moving along

swift [swĭft] *adjective*, very fast or quick to act, nimble, prompt

swim [swĭm] *noun*, 1) the act of staying afloat or traveling in water, *verb*, 2) to move through the water by using movements of the body

swin-dle [swĭn'dl] *verb*, to cheat, to deceive or defraud

swing [swĭng] *noun*, 1) a seat hanging on ropes or chains, *verb*, 2) to move freely from a fixed point, to pivot, to turn

swirl [swûrl] *noun*, 1) a spiral, *verb*, 2) to turn in a circular motion

switch [swĭch] *noun*, 1) a device that can be used to turn something on or off, *verb*, 2) to exchange 3) to turn something on or off 4) to change as in direction, to shift, to transfer

swiv-el [swĭv'əl] *verb*, to turn or pivot on a bolt or pin

swol-len [swō'lən] *adjective*, inflamed, puffed up, enlarged

swoon [swoon] *noun*, 1) a fainting spell, *verb*, 2) to faint

swoop [swoop] *verb*, to fly down very quickly like a bird

sword [sôrd] *noun*, a weapon similar to a knife with a very long blade

swore [swôr] *past tense* of **swear**

syl-la-ble [sĭl'ə-bəl] *noun*, a combination of letters indicating a sound in a word

syl-lo-gism [sĭl'ə-jĭz'əm] *noun*, logical formula using a major premise, a minor premise leading to a conclusion

sym-bol [sĭm'bəl] *noun*, anything that stands for or represents something else

sym-met-ri-cal [sĭ-mĕt'rĭ-kəl] *adjective*, alike on both sides, proportional

sym-me-try [sĭm'ĭ-trē] *noun*, the balance of things on opposite sides, excellence of proportion

sym-pa-thet-ic [sĭm'pə-thĕt'ĭk] *adjective*, kind, warm, compassionate, tender

sym-pa-thize [sĭm'pə-thīz'] *verb*, to feel sorry for another, to share in a feeling

sym-pa-thy [sĭm'pə-thē] *noun*, the understanding of another person's feelings, pity

sym-pho-ny [sĭm'fə-nē] *noun*, a musical composition performed by an orchestra

symp-tom [sǐm′təm] *noun*, a sign indicating the presence of an illness or something

syn-a-gogue [sǐn′ə-gŏg′] *noun*, a house of worship, a temple

syn-chro-nic-i-ty [sǐng′krə-nǐs′ǐ-tē] *noun*, to do something that is similarly timed

syn-chro-nize [sǐng′krə-nīz′] *verb*, to agree in time, to move together, simultaneously

syn-di-cate [sǐn′dǐ-kǐt] *verb*, a network of businesses that sell news to the media

syn-o-nym [sǐn′ə-nǐm′].*noun*, a word that means the same as another

syn-op-sis [sǐ-nŏp′sǐs] *noun*, a general view of a whole, an abstract or summary

syn-the-sis [sǐn′thǐ-sǐs] *noun*, combining parts into a whole

syn-thet-ic [sǐn-thĕt′ǐk] *adjective*, produced by artificial processes, not real or genuine

sy-ringe [sə-rǐnj′] *noun*, an instrument with a needle used to inject a fluid into the blood stream through a vein

syr-up [sǐr′əp] *noun*, a sugar liquid

sys-tem [sǐs′təm] *noun*, a network of things working together as a functioning unit

sys-tem-at-ic [sǐs′tə-măt′ǐk] *adjective*, methodical, proceeding according to method

T

ta-ble [tā′bəl] *noun*, 1) a piece of furniture with a flat top and legs used for placing things on or using as a work space 2) a list, often using lines or boxes to arrange facts

tab-leau [tăb′lō′] *noun*, a scene of persons in costume remaining silent and motionless

ta-ble-cloth [tā′bəl-klôth′] *noun*, a decorative cloth spread over the top of a table

tab-let [tăb′lǐt] *noun*, a hard flat piece or block of something

ta-boo [tə-boo′] *adjective*, 1) forbidden, banned by religion or custom, *noun*, 2) a restriction, a ban or prohibition

tab-u-late [tăb′yə-lāt′] *verb*, to arrange in column forms

tac-it [tăs′ǐt] *adjective*, implied or indicated, but not expressed

tac-i-tur-ni-ty [tăs′ǐ-tûr′ nǐ-tē] *adjective*, habitually silent, not given to conversation

tack [tăk] *noun*, a small nail with a broad, flat head on it

tack-le [tăk′əl] *noun*, 1) ropes and pulleys arranged for hoisting or pulling 2) equipment used for fishing 3) downing a player 4) a football player, *verb*, 5) to undertake, to get down to business to solve a problem 6) to bring to the ground

tact [tăkt] *noun*, *no plural*, to do or say the right thing at the right time, diplomacy

tact-ful [tăkt′fəl] *adjective*, discreet, careful, prudent

tac-tic [tăk′tǐk] *noun*, a maneuver

tac-tile [tăk′təl, -tīl′] *adjective*, referring to the sense of touch

tag [tăg] *noun*, 1) a small identifying card or label 2) a game children play in which one player chases the others, *verb*, 3) to follow along

tail [tāl] *adjective*, 1) coming from behind, *noun*, 2) the part of an animal which sticks out at the end of its back

tai-lor [tā′lər] *noun*, one who cuts out and makes clothes

taint [tānt] *noun*, 1) a trace of something bad, *verb*, 2) to contaminate, to corrupt

take [tāk] *verb*, 1) to get hold of something 2) to carry something or go with someone to another place 3) to swallow something 4) to travel 5) to accept

tak-en [tā′kən] *adjective*, 1)held, seized 2) accepted

tale [tāl] *noun*, a story

tal-ent [tăl′ənt] *noun*, a natural ability, aptitude

tal-is-man [tăl′ĭs-mən] *noun*, an amulet or lucky charm

talk [tôk] *verb*, to speak or be able to speak, to consult or confer

talk-a-tive [tô′kə-tĭv] *adjective*, inclined to talk a lot, loquacious

tall [tôl] *adjective*, above average height, high

tal-ly [tăl′ē] *noun*, 1) a mark made to keep score or to count, *verb*, 2) to keep track of an account

tal-on [tăl′ən] *noun*, a claw, especially of a bird of prey

tame [tām] *adjective*, 1) trained to live with man, not wild, *verb*, 2) to make a wild animal obedient and friendly to people

tan [tăn] *adjective*, 1) light brown, tawny 2) to convert into leather

tan-gent [tăn′jənt] *noun*, a straight line that touches a curve without intersecting it

tan-ge-rine [tăn′jə-rēn′] *noun*, a variety of a small-sized orange

tan-gi-ble [tăn′jə-bəl] *adjective*, capable of being touched, real

tank [tăngk] *noun*, 1) a large container to hold liquid or gas fuel 2) an armed vehicle used in combat 3) the metal box in the back of the car to hold gasoline

tan-ta-lize [tăn′tə-līz′] *verb*, to tease, to tempt, to promise by offering a reward

tan-ta-mount [tăn′tə-mount′] *adjective*, equal in value

tan-trum [tăn′trəm] *noun*, an exaggerated display of anger, a fit of irritability, bad temper

tap [tăp] *noun*, 1) the faucet attached to a pipe to release liquid or gas, *verb*, 2) to hit or touch lightly 3) to drain by making a hole 4) to draw from

tape [tāp] *noun*, 1) a narrow piece of cloth or other material, *verb*, 2) to bind or secure with an adhesive material 3) to record

tap-er [tā′pər] *verb*, to decrease in amount or size by becoming narrower or smaller

tap-es-try [tăp′ĭ-strē] *noun*, a heavy, decorative, woven fabric used especially for wall hangings

tap-i-o-ca [tăp′ē-ō′kə] *noun*, cassava, a coarse granular preparation used in puddings

tar [tär] *noun*, a thick black liquid made from heating coal or wood

ta-ran-tu-la [tə-răn′chə-lə] *noun*, a hairy, large, poisonous spider

tar-get [tär′gĭt] *noun*, 1) somebody or something aimed at 2) an objective, a goal, *verb*, 3) to make the focus or object of something

tar-iff [tăr′ĭf] *noun*, a tax on goods exported or imported

tar-nish [tär′nĭsh] *verb*, 1) to dull the luster of metal 2) to taint

tart [tärt] *adjective*, 1) sour to the taste, *noun*, 2) a piece of pastry with fruit cooked on top of it

task [tăsk] *noun*, a chore or small job that must be done

tas-sel [tăs′əl] *noun*, a pendant ornament ending in a tuft of loose threads

taste [tāst] *noun*, 1) a preference, liking 2) the sense that distinguishes the flavor of things placed in the mouth 3) a flavor itself, *verb*, 4) to sample a food by taking it in the mouth

tat-too [tă-tōo′] *noun*, a design on the skin made using a needle filled with dye

taught [tôt] *past tense* of **teach**

taunt [tônt] *verb*, to tease or make fun of someone, to ridicule

taut [tôt] *adjective*, stretched tight

tau-tol-o-gy [tô-tŏl′ə-jē] *noun*, needless repetition of an idea in different words

taw-dry [tô′drē] *adjective*, cheap and showy or flashy, gaudy

tax [tăks] *noun*, 1) a sum of money to be paid to the government imposed by the elected leaders, *verb*, 2) to put a fee on service or goods that are given to the government

tax-i [tăk′sē] *noun*, a car for hire to take people from one place to another

tax-i-der-mist [tăk′sĭ-dûr′mĭst] *noun*, one who prepares dead animals to look life-like

tea [tē] *noun*, 1) prepared dried leaves of a plant 2) a small meal or snack in the afternoon 3) a cup of a beverage made with leaves steeped in hot water

teach [tēch] *verb*, to show someone how to do something

teach-er [tē′chər] *noun*, a person whose occupation is to instruct

team [tēm] *noun*, 1) persons working or playing together as a group 2) two or more animals harnessed together to pull a vehicle

tear [tîr] *noun*, 1) a drop of water that comes out of the eye 2) a hole or cut in material, *verb*, 3) to make a hole in material by pulling on it

tease [tēz] *verb*, to make fun of someone, to annoy

tea-spoon [tē′spōōn′] *noun*, a small spoon used to measure

tech-ni-cal [tĕk′nĭ-kəl] *adjective*, having knowledge of a mechanical or scientific subject

tech-ni-cian [tĕk-nĭsh′ən] *noun*, a person who works with machines or instruments

tech-nique [tĕk-nēk′] *noun*, a procedure used to perform a task

tech-nol-o-gy [tĕk-nŏl′ə-jē] *noun*, the use of science to produce useful things for practical purposes that improve life

te-di-ous [tē′dē-əs] *adjective*, tiresome, dull, boring

tel-e-phone [tĕl′ə-fōn′] *noun*, 1) an instrument for reproducing sounds at a distance, *verb*, 2) to call to someone on an instrument that communicates voices through airwaves or wires

tel-e-scope [tĕl′ĭ-skōp′] *noun*, an optical instrument for viewing distant objects

tel-e-vi-sion [tĕl′ə-vĭzh′ən] *noun*, a set used to transmit visual images onto a screen

tell [tĕl] *verb*, 1) to speak to someone, to inform, to narrate 2) to deduce, to differentiate

tell-er [tĕl′ər] *noun*, a bank employee who handles customer transactions

tem-per [tĕm′pər] *noun*, 1) a person's state of mind, mood, *verb*, 2) to tone down, to moderate, to bring under control

tem-per-a-ment [tĕm′prə-mənt] *noun*, the physical and mental character of an individual

tem-per-ance [tĕm′pər-əns] *noun*, habitual moderation of the appetites and passions

tem-per-a-ture [tĕm′pər-ə-chŏŏr′] *noun*, the degree of heat or cold

tem-ple [tĕm′pəl] *noun*, 1) a holy building 2) the part of the head above and in front of the ear

tem-po [tĕm′pō] *noun*, the rate of speed of a musical passage

tem-po-ral [tĕm′pər-əl] *adjective*, not lasting forever, limited by time, the present

tem-po-rar-y [tĕm′pə-rĕr′ē] *adjective*, intended to last a short period of time, not permanent

tempt [tĕmpt] *verb*, to entice someone to do something unwise or wrong, to provoke

temp-ta-tion [tĕmp-tā′shən] *noun*, an instant urge or desire

ten [tĕn] *noun*, the number 10, one plus nine

te-na-cious [tə-nā′shəs] *adjective*, holding fast, stubborn

te-nac-i-ty [tə-năs′ĭ-tē] *noun*, firmness, persistency

ten-ant [tĕn′ənt] *noun*, someone who lives in a house or apartment, an occupant

tend [tĕnd] *verb*, 1) to be likely to, to do something habitually 2) to take care of something

ten-den-cy [tĕn′dən-sē] *noun*, inclination, propensity, leaning

tend-er [tĕn′dər] *adjective*, 1) kind and gentle 2) sensitive to touch or movement 3) cooked so that the food is easy to eat, *noun*, 4) a car attached to a train for carrying food and water

ten-der-ness [tĕn′dər-nĭs] *noun*, affection, gentleness

ten-e-ment [tĕn′ə-mənt] *noun*, a building divided into flats

ten-et [tĕn′ĭt] *noun*, doctrine, dogma, belief, conviction

Ten-nes-see [tĕn′ĭ-sē′] *noun*, one of the 50 United States located in the South, the capital city is Nashville. The state flower of **Tennessee** is the iris, and the motto is "Agriculture and commerce."

ten-nis [tĕn′ĭs] *noun*, a game played on a court by two or four people in which a ball is hit over a net with rackets

ten-or [tĕn′ər] *noun*, 1) a tendency, a trend 2) the highest range of the male singing voice

tense [tĕns] *adjective*, 1) full of excitement 2) tightly stretched, taut, *noun*, 3) the form of a verb that shows when the action happens – past, present, or future

ten-sion [tĕn′shən] *noun*, 1) act of stretching, 2) mental or nervous state or condition of strain

tent [tĕnt] *noun*, a shelter of canvas or nylon, supported by poles

ten-ta-cle [tĕn′tə-kəl] *noun*, a long, arm-like structure growing out of an animal's body, used for movement or catching food

ten-ta-tive [tĕn′tə-tĭv] *adjective*, experimental, based on trials

tenth [tĕnth] *adjective*, the number after nine in series, written 10th

ten-u-ous [tĕn′yōō-əs] *adjective*, weak and unconvincing

ten-ure [tĕn′yər] *noun*, the period of time during which an office is held, occupation

te-pee [tē′pē] *noun*, a cone shaped tent in which some Indians live

tep-id [tĕp′ĭd] *adjective*, 1) not hot or cold, lukewarm 2) showing little enthusiasm

term [tûrm] *noun*, 1) a fixed amount of time 2) an expression or form of language 3) a condition or stipulation

ter-min-al [tûr′mə-nəl] *adjective*, 1) end, final, concluding, *noun*, 2) a depot where buses or trains make connections 3) a

conducting circuit arranged for connection in an electrical circuit

ter-mi-nate [tûr′mə-nāt′] *verb*, to end, to finish, to cancel

ter-mi-na-tion [tûr′mə-nā′shən] *noun*, the ending

ter-mi-nol-o-gy [tûr′mə-nŏl′ə-jē] *noun*, vocabulary used in a specialized subject

ter-race [tĕr′ĭs] *noun*, 1) a level area cut out from the side of a hill 2) a flat area outside a house

ter-rain [tə-rān′] *noun*, the features of an area of land

ter-rar-i-um [tə-râr′ē-əm] *noun*, a transparent container in which land animals or plants are kept

ter-res-tri-al [tə-rĕs′trē-əl] *adjective*, of the earth

ter-ri-ble [tĕr′ə-bəl] *adjective*, appalling, dreadful

ter-rif-ic [tə-rĭf′ĭk] *adjective*, awesome, wonderful

ter-ri-fy [tĕr′ə-fī′] *verb*, to fill or overwhelm with fear or horror

ter-ri-to-ry [tĕr′ĭ-tôr′ē] *noun*, a portion of land belonging to someone else, a region

ter-ror [tĕr′ər] *adjective*, fear

terse [tûrs] *adjective*, concise, abrupt, a short answer

ter-ror-ist [tĕr′ər] *noun*, one who uses violence to intimidate

tes-sel-la-tion [tĕs′ə-lā′shən] *adjective*, a mosaic pattern

test [tĕst] *noun*, 1) a trial 2) an examination to assess the level of knowledge of a subject, *verb*,

3) to try something out to see how it works 4) to examine

tes-ta-ment [těs/tə-mənt] *noun*,1) a will 2) scripture from the Bible

tes-ti-fy [těs/tə-fī/] *verb*, to establish some fact, under oath to serve as evidence

tes-ti-mo-ny [těs/tə-mō/nē] *noun*, the statement of a witness under oath, evidence or proof

tet-a-nus [tět/n-əs] *noun*, a painful, often fatal, infectious disease, marked by painful spasms of the muscles, frequently of the jaw

teth-er [těth/ər] *noun*, 1) a cord, a link, a supply line, *verb*, 2) to tie up with a rope, to hitch, to fasten

Tex-as [těk/səs] *noun*, one of the 50 United States located in the Southwest, the capital city is Austin. The state flower of **Texas**, is the bluebonnet, and the motto is "Friendship."

text [těkst] *noun*, the words used in a book, a written work

text-book [těkst/boŏk/] *noun*, an instruction book, a manual

tex-tile [těks/tīl/] *noun*, fabrics such as cotton, wool, linen, silk, rayon, and polyester

tex-ture [těks/chər] *noun*, the feel or appearance of something – soft, smooth, rough, etc.

than [thăn] used as a *conjunction*, to introduce the second part of a comparison

thank [thăngk] *verb*, to express gratitude and appreciation

thank-ful [thăngk/fəl] *adjective*, to be grateful, to show appreciation or praise

thanks [thăngks] *noun*, an acknowledgment of a kindness, favor, or the like

Thanks-giv-ing [thăngks-gǐv/ǐng] *noun*, a national holiday celebrated the fourth Thursday in November

that [thăt] *pronoun, plural,* **those,** 1) the one singled out 2) used instead of which 3) used to join two parts of a sentence 4) so 5) used to show the result

that's [thăts] the *contraction* of the words **that** and **is**

thatch [thăch] *noun*, bundles of straw woven together

thaw [thô] *verb*, to pass from a frozen to a liquid state

the [thē before a vowel, thə before a consonant] *article*, a word that usually goes before a noun

the-a-ter [thē/ə-tər] *noun*, a building where dramatic performances are presented

the-at-ri-cal [thē-ăt/rǐ-kəl] *adjective*, dramatic, eloquent

thee [thē] *pronoun*, the objective case of thou

theft [thěft] *noun*, the act or instance of stealing

their [thâr] *pronoun*, belonging to them, a form of the possessive case of **they** used attributively, e.g., *their school*

theirs [thârz] *pronoun*, showing personal ownership

them [thěm] *pronoun*, the objective case of **they** , *plural,* **them-selves,** the same people, animals, or things mentioned in the sentence as the subject

theme [thēm] *noun*, the subject on which one writes or speaks

then [thĕn] *adverb*, 1) at another time, not now 2) afterwards, next 3) if that is true

the-ol-o-gy [thē-ŏl'ə-jē] *noun*, the science of God or of religion

the-o-rem [thē'ər-əm] *noun*, a principle, a theoretical proposition, a thesis

the-o-ret-i-cal [thē'ə-rĕt'ĭ-kəl] *adjective*, depending on conjecture, speculative

the-o-ry [thē'ə-rē] *noun*, an abstract plan, an hypothesis

ther-a-peu-tic [thĕr'ə-pyōo'tĭk] *adjective*, curative, healing, good for personal growth and health

ther-a-py [thĕr'ə-pē] *noun*, exercises and treatment designed to rehabilitate a person

there [thâr] *adverb*, 1) referring to that place 2) referring to at that moment

there's [thârz] the *contraction* of the words **there** and **is**

there-fore [thâr'fôr'] *adverb*, for that reason, as a result

ther-mal [thûr'məl] *adjective*, pertaining to heat

ther-mo-dy-nam-ics [thûr'mō-dī-năm'ĭks] *noun*, the relationship between heat and other forms of energy

ther-mom-e-ter [thər-mŏm'ĭ-tər] *noun*, a device for measuring how hot or cold something is

ther-mos [thûr'məs] *noun*, a vacuum bottle for keeping liquids hot or cold for hours

ther-mos-tat [thûr'mə-stăt'] *noun*, a mechanical device used to control temperature

the-sau-rus [thĭ-sôr'əs] *noun*, a dictionary of synonyms and antonyms

these [thēz] *pronoun, adjective,* the *plural* of **this**

the-sis [thē'sĭs] *noun*, an essay presented by a candidate for a degree or diploma

they [thā] *pronoun*, the *plural* of **he**, **she** or **it**

they'll [thāl] the *contraction* of the words **they** and **will**

they're [thâr] the *contraction* of the words **they** and **are**

thick [thĭk] *adjective*, 1)occupying much space in depth or from side to side, measuring between sides 2) a dense fluid

thief [thēf] *noun, plural,* **thieves,** one who steals

thigh [thī] *noun*, the thick part of the leg above the knee and below the hip

thim-ble [thĭm'bəl] *noun*, a metal cap put over the finger to keep it from being pricked by a needle

thin [thĭn] *adjective*, 1) not thick, slender 2) lacking volume or density 3) sparse, insufficient, inadequate, flimsy

thing [thĭng] *noun*, 1) an object, a creature, a form of life 2) conditions 3) an act or event

think [thĭngk] *verb*, 1) to form or have on the mind 2) to use the power of reason 3) to believe, to suppose

third [thûrd] *adjective, noun*, the number three in order after second, written 3rd

thirst [thûrst] *noun, no plural*, the need to drink something

thirst-y [thûr/stē] *adjective*, needing something to drink

thir-teen [thûr-tēn/] *adjective, noun*, the number 13, 3+10

thir-teenth [thûr-tēnth/] *adjective, noun*, number 13 in order, 13th

thir-ti-eth [thûr/tē-ĭth] *adjective, noun*, number 30 in order, 30th

thir-ty [thûr/tē] *adjective, noun*, the number 30, ten times three

this [thĭs] *adjective*, 1) being the one present, near or just mentioned 2) being the one nearer or last mentioned, *adverb* 3) the thing the speaker is talking about, *pronoun*, 4) the one nearer than that one in time or space 5) what is in the present or being talked about

this-tle [thĭs/əl] *noun*, a plant with prickly leaves and stems and a purple flower

thorn [thôrn] *noun*, a sharp projection on a stem

thor-ough [thûr/ō] *adjective*, complete, perfect, absolute

thor-ough-ly [thûr/ō-lē] *adverb*, completely done

those [thōz] *pronoun*, the ones over there, the ones further away than this one

thou [thou] you

though [thō] *adverb*, 1) however, *conjunction*, 2) although

thought [thôt] *noun*, 1) an idea, the process of thinking 2) intention 3) attention, *verb*, 4) the *past tense* of **think**

thought-ful [thôt/fəl] *adjective*, showing consideration for others, kind, discreet

thou-sand [thou/zənd] *noun, adjective*, the number 1,000, ten times 100

thread [thrĕd] *noun*, 1) a fine string made of cotton, linen, or silk, *verb*, 2) to wind through openings 3) to pass a thread through the eye of a needle

threat [thrĕt] *noun*, a warning, that one may do harm

threat-en [thrĕt/n] *verb*, to torment, to scare, to pose a danger

three [thrē] *adjective, noun*, the number 3, one plus two, 3

thresh-old [thrĕsh/ōld/] *noun*, a piece of timber which lies under a door, an entrance

thrift [thrĭft] *noun*, the practice of being careful with money

thrift-y [thrĭf/tē] *adjective*, careful about money, economical

thrill [thrĭl] *noun*, 1) an excited feeling, *verb*, 2) to fill with excitement

thrive [thrīv] *verb*, 1) to grow abundantly 2) to prosper, to flourish, to succeed

throat [thrōt] *noun*, the passage inside of the neck attached to the mouth, lungs, and stomach

throb [thrŏb] *verb*, to beat strongly, to pulsate steadily

throne [thrōn] *noun*, a special chair for a king or queen

throng [thrông, thrŏng] *noun*, a crowd of people, a multitude

throt-tle [thrŏt′l] *noun,* 1) a lever or pedal that helps an engine start and run, *verb,* 2) to strangle, to suppress 3) to regulate the speed of an engine

through [thrōo] *adjective,* 1) finished, *adverb,* 2) from one side or end of something to the other, *preposition,* 3) in one side and out the other 4) by the agency of, by way of, via 5) among or between 6) past or beyond, in the midst of

through-out [thrōo-out′] *preposition,* all over, from end to end, from inside and out

throw [thrō] *noun,* 1) the distance something is tossed, cast or projected, *verb,* 2) to toss, fling, or hurl something through the air

thrust [thrŭst] *verb,* to push suddenly and hard

thud [thŭd] *noun,* a dull sound made when something heavy falls and lands

thumb [thŭm] *noun,* the short, thick finger on the hand which is separate from the others

thun-der [thŭn′dər] *noun, no plural,* the loud sound heard in the sky during a storm

Thurs-day [thûrz′dē] *noun,* the fifth day of the week

thus [thŭs] *adverb,* in this way

thy [thī] *pronoun,* your

thyme [tīm] *noun,* a pungent aromatic plant used in seasoning

tick [tĭk] *noun,* 1) the sound made by a clock 2) a check mark 3) a small parasite that sucks blood from animals and people, *verb,* 4) to make a soft, steady, rhythmic sound 5) to check off

things on a list that fit a certain criteria

tick-et [tĭk′ĭt] *noun,* 1) the ballot of a political party 2) an admission 3) a fine 4) a price tag

tick-le [tĭk′əl] *noun,* 1) a tingling sensation, *verb,* 2) to touch a person lightly to make them laugh 3) to delight, to amuse

tid-al [tīd′l] *adjective,* action of the sea caused by the tides

tide [tīd] *noun,* regular rise and fall of the ocean caused by the pull of the sun and the moon

ti-dy [tī′dē] *adjective,* 1) neat and orderly 2) substantial, more than enough, *verb,* 3) to make neat and well organized

tie [tī] *noun,* 1) a narrow piece of cloth used as a man's dress accessory worn around the neck with a shirt, a necktie 2) a bond 3) a standoff, *verb,* 4) to fasten something with string or rope 5) to come out equal in a contest

tier [tîr] *noun,* one of several levels

ti-ger [tī′gər] *noun,* a fierce animal, one of the big cats, which has yellow fur with black stripes

tight [tīt] *adjective,* 1) so close in structure that air cannot pass through 2) drawn close together

tight-en [tīt′n] *verb,* to draw closer together, to squeeze

tight-ly [tīt′lē] *adverb,* pulled closely together, tautly

tile [tīl] *noun,* a flat piece of baked clay that has been painted with glaze or linoleum used as a floor covering

till [tĭl] *adverb,* 1) before, up to, *noun,* 2) a cash box, a place to store money, *verb,* 3) to plow

till-er [tĭl′ər] *noun*, a handle used to steer a boat

tilt [tĭlt] *verb*, to make something lean so that it is not straight

tim-ber [tĭm′bər] *noun*, a piece of wood, lumber, hardwood

tim-bre [tăm′bər] *noun*, quality of a musical tone produced by a musical instrument

time [tīm] *noun*, 1) minutes, hours, days, weeks, months, years, etc. 2) a limited duration 3) a period or event 4) a certain hour or part of the day 5) a moment, *verb*, 6) to measure how long it takes to do something 7) a number multiplied by another

time-ly [tīm′lē] *adjective*, prompt, well-timed, favorable

tim-id [tĭm′ĭd] *adjective*, shy, afraid, uncertain, hesitant

tim-id-i-ty [tĭm′ĭ-dĭ-tē] *noun*, lack of self-confidence or courage

tim-or-ous [tĭm′ər-əs] *adjective*, fearful and hesitant

tin [tĭn] *noun*, *no plural*, a soft white metal mixed with alloys

tinc-ture [tĭngk′chər] *noun*, a slight quality added to anything, a trace or tinge, pigment

tin-gle [tĭng′gəl] *verb*, 1) to get excited 2) to have a prickling sensation

tin-ker [tĭng′kər] *verb*, to fool around, to dabble, to putter

tin-sel [tĭn′səl] *noun*, showy or flashy decorations

tint [tĭnt] *noun*, 1) the color, shade, hue, *verb*, 2) to color, to shade

ti-ny [tī′nē] *adjective*, very small

tip [tĭp] *noun*, 1) a point, a peak 2) a hint, advice, a pointer 3)

compensation for a service, gratuity, *verb*, 4) to tilt, to list, to lean to one side, to slant 5) to give someone money for a small service 6) to cause something to fall over and become unbalanced

tip-toe [tĭp′tō′] *noun*, 1) the tip of the toe, *verb*, 2) to walk on toes so that the step is not heard

ti-rade [tī′rād′] *noun*, extended scolding, denunciation

tire [tīr] *noun*, 1) a rubber, air-filled part of a car or bicycle wheel that cushions the ride, *verb*, 2) to make someone feel that he needs to rest 3) to become bored, fatigued

tir-ed [tīrd] *adjective*, feeling sleepy, needing rest

tis-sue [tĭsh′oo] *noun*, very thin paper that feels soft

ti-tan-ic [tī-tăn′ĭk] *adjective*, gigantic, of great size or power

tithe [tīth] *noun*, a payment of one tenth of an income given to the church

ti-tle [tīt′l] *noun*, 1) the name of a story, a book, a film, etc. 2) a word used in front of a person's name 3) a sport's championship

to [too; tə when unstressed] *adverb*, 1) in a direction toward *preposition*, 2) in the direction of 3) as far as 4) on or against 5) until 6) used to show why 7) used with the infinitive of a verb 8) for the purpose of, in order to 9) belonging to

toad [tōd] *noun*, an animal that looks like a frog but does not live in water

toast [tōst] *noun*, 1) sliced bread broiled to make it crisp, *verb*, 2) to praise someone when raising your drink in a glass 3) to brown by the heat of a fire

to-bac-co [tə-băk′ō] *noun*, the dried leaves of a plant used for smoking and chewing

to-bog-gan [tə-bŏg′ən] *noun*, a very long, flat-bottomed sled used to glide on snow

to-day [tə-dā′] *adverb*, 1) on or for this very day, *noun*, 2) modern times, present day, contemporary

toe [tō] *noun*, 1) one of the five digits at the end of the foot 2) the part of a shoe or sock that covers this end of the foot

tof-fee [tô′fē] *noun*, a hard, chewy candy made of caramel candy, brown sugar and butter

to-ga [tō′gə] *noun*, Roman outer robe of free born men

to-geth-er [tə-gĕth′ər] *adverb*, 1) at the same time 2) in conjunction, with each other, in cooperation

toil [toil] *verb*, to work very hard

toi-let [toi′lĭt] *noun*, an instrument to flush human waste into a sewage system, a bathroom

to-ken [tō′kən] *noun*, 1) a sign or symbol or gesture to indicate something 2) a souvenir 3) a coin used as a currency for travel

told [tōld] *past tense* of **tell**

tol-er-ance [tŏl′ər-əns] *noun*, compassion, open-mindedness

tol-er-ant [tŏl′ər-ənt] *noun*, broad minded, liberal, accepting

toll [tōl] *noun*, 1) the charge for a privilege or a service 2) the number lost or taken, *verb*, 3) to ring a bell slowly

to-ma-to [tə-mā′tō] *noun*, a red berry with seeds and a pulpy fruit eaten as a vegetable

tomb [tōōm] *noun*, a sacred place where a dead person is buried

tomb-stone [tōōm′stōn′] *noun*, the carved stone with an inscription identifying the person on a grave

tome [tōm] *noun*, a large volume

to-mor-row [tə-môr′ō] *adverb* 1) the day after today, *noun*, 2) sometime in the future

ton [tŭn] *noun*, the weight of measure of a very heavy quantity, e.g., 2,000 pounds

tone [tōn] *noun*, 1) the sound of a voice or a musical instrument 2) manner, expression

tongs [tôngz] *noun*, *plural*, (pair of) a tool with two legs used to pick up or to hold something

tongue [tŭng] *noun*, 1) the organ of speech covered by taste buds 2) the flap of leather or cloth under the lacing of a shoe 3) the language spoken 4) dialect

ton-ic [tŏn′ĭk] *noun*, a refreshing drink that invigorates

to-night [tə-nīt′] *adverb*, 1) the night following today, *noun*, 2) on or during the night of today

too [tōō] *adverb*, 1) also 2) more than is needed or wanted

took [tōōk] *past tense* of **take**

tool [tōōl] *noun*, an instrument used to do work or make repairs

tooth [tōōth] *noun*, *plural* **teeth**, 1) a white bony material that grows in the mouth, set in sockets around the jaw, used for chewing 2) the projections on a blade

tooth-ache [tŏŏth′āk′] *noun*, a pain in the mouth due to an infection from a tooth

top [tŏp] *adjective*, 1) best, first, chief, *noun*, 2) the highest part of something 3) the lid or cover of something 4) a toy that spins quickly on a point

to-paz [tō′păz′] *noun*, a precious stone, usually yellow or tan

top-ic [tŏp′ĭk] *noun*, the subject of a conversation, speech, or essay

to-pog-ra-phy [tə-pŏg′rə-fē] *noun*, detailed representation of the features of a region

top-ple [tŏp′əl] *verb*, to make or become unsteady and fall over

torch [tôrch] *noun*, an instrument that gives off a very hot flame

tor-ment [tôr′mĕnt′] *noun*, 1) abuse, agony, chaos, *verb*, 2) to torture, to annoy, to abuse, to afflict with mental suffering

tor-na-do [tôr-nā′dō] *noun*, a storm with a strong wind which spins very fast, a violent windstorm

tor-pe-do [tôr-pē′dō] *noun*, a self-propelled underwater missile containing explosives fired through the water from a ship to destroy another ship

tor-pid [tôr′pĭd] *adjective*, dormant, dull, lethargic

tor-rent [tôr′ənt] *noun*, a fast flow of water or energy

tor-ren-tial [tô-rĕn′shəl] *adjective*, a rushing, violent stream of water

tor-rid [tôr′ĭd] *adjective*, 1) passionate 2) tropical, sweltering, oppressively hot

tor-so [tôr′sō] *noun*, the trunk of a statue with head and limbs missing, the upper part of the human body

tort [tôrt] *noun*, a civil wrong, independent of a contract

tor-toise [tôr′tĭs] *noun*, a very large turtle that lives on the land

tor-tu-ous [tôr′chŏŏ-əs] *adjective*, winding, full of curves

tor-ture [tôr′chər] noun1) 1) the act of causing great pain or suffering 2) distress of mind or body, *verb*, 3) to inflict pain on someone mercilessly, in order to dominate and control

toss [tôs, tŏs] *verb*, 1) to throw 2) to move about up and down

to-tal [tōt′l] *adjective*, 1) making up the whole, *noun*, 2) the sum of numbers in addition, entire

to-tal-ly [tōt′l-ē] *adverb*, wholly, entirely, completely

touch [tŭch] *noun*, 1) one of the five senses that communicates texture, temperature, and density to the brain through feeling, *verb*, 2) to make physical contact with something or someone

tough [tŭf] *adjective*, 1) yielding to force without breaking, strong 2) brave 3) difficult to chew

tour [tŏŏr] *noun*, 1) a journey that ends where it starts, *verb*, 2) to make a trip through a place

tour-ist [tŏŏr′ĭst] *noun*, a person traveling for pleasure

tour-na-ment [tŏŏr′nə-mənt] *noun*, a set number of contests that includes many teams or players and produces one winner

tow [tō] *verb*, to pull or haul with a rope or a chain

to-ward [tôrd] *preposition*, 1) in the direction of, in relation to 2) facing from the opposite direction

tow-el [tou′əl] *noun*, a piece of cloth or paper used for wiping or drying

tow-er [tou′ər] *noun*, 1) a tall building or structure that stands above the rest 2) a turret or spire attached to a building or fortress, *verb*, 3) to stand or reach above everything

town [toun] *noun*, buildings creating a hamlet, larger than a village and smaller than a city

tox-ic [tŏk′sĭk] *adjective*, poisonous, harmful

toy [toi] *noun*, an ornament or article that children play with

trace [trās] *noun*, 1) a small amount of something, *verb*, 2) to draw an image using paper to duplicate it 3) to try to follow the path of someone by using evidence that indicates what they are doing or have done

track [trăk] *noun*, 1) a mark left by something that has passed 2) a path or roadway, *verb*, 3) to follow or trace, to trail

trac-ta-ble [trăk′tə-bəl] *adjective*, 1) obedient, willing, compliant 2) easily shaped, malleable

trac-tion [trăk′shən] *noun*, adhesive friction of being drawn or pulled, the grip of the wheels on the ground

trac-tor [trăk′tər] *noun*, a machine used to plow and to till soil

trade [trād] *noun, no plural,* 1) the exchange of goods 2) a form of business or enterprise 3) a specific type of work that requires training, *verb*, 4) to buy and sell goods, to barter

tra-di-tion [trə-dĭsh′ən] *noun*, a custom or belief passed within families or other groups from one generation to another

tra-di-tion-al [trə-dĭsh′ə-nəl] *adjective*, following a custom that has been handed down through generations

traf-fic [trăf′ĭk] *noun*, 1) commerce, trade, the interchange of goods 2) the movement of cars and people on streets or of planes and ships

trag-e-dy [trăj′ĭ-dē] *noun*, 1) drama that deals with sad or terrible themes, as opposed to comedy 2) a fatal or unfortunate event

trag-ic [trăj′ĭk] *adjective*, very sad, dreadful, unfortunate

trail [trāl] *noun*, 1) the marks or evidence left behind in a place by someone or something that was there earlier, *verb*, 2) to follow someone, to track

train [trān] *noun*, 1) railroad cars for people or freight pulled by an engine, *verb*, 2) to teach someone or yourself to do something difficult that is considered a skill

train-ing [trā′nĭng] *noun*, preparation, instruction

trait [trāt] *noun*, a distinguishing characteristic or feature

trai-tor [trā′tər] *noun*, one who betrays a cause or any trust

tra-jec-to-ry [trə-jĕk′tə-rē] *noun*, a path taken by a projectile, or a flying object in its flight

tramp [trămp] *noun*, a person with no home or job who travels from place to place begging, a vagrant

tram-ple [trăm′pəl] *verb*, to crush into the ground, to walk heavily on something

trance [trăns] *noun*, a dream-like state of deep relaxation

tran-quil [trăng′kwəl] *adjective*, calm, peaceful, quiet, serene

tran-quil-li-ty [trăng-kwĭl′ĭ-tē] *noun*, calmness, composure

tran-quil-iz-er [trăng′kwə-līz′ər] *noun*, a sleeping pill, sedative

trans-ac-tion [trăn-săk′shən] *noun*, the doing of any business

tran-scend [trăn-sĕnd′] *verb*, to rise above and beyond the ordinary limits, to surpass, to exist independent of

tran-scen-den-tal [trăn′sĕn-dĕn′tl] *adjective*, beyond understanding, supernatural, spiritual

trans-con-ti-nen-tal [trăns′kŏn-tə-nĕn′tl] *adjective*, spanning a continent

tran-scribe [trăn-skrīb′] *verb*, to write out a spoken message

tran-script [trăn′skrĭpt′] *noun*, a written copy of a broadcast or a student's academic record

trans-fer [trăns-fûr′] *noun*, 1) the act of moving something from one place to another, *verb*, 2) to convey from one place to another

trans-fer-a-ble [trăns-fûr′ə-bəl] *noun*, capable of being moved from one place to another

trans-form [trăns-fôrm′] *verb*, 1) to change the form or appearance of something 2) to glorify

trans-form-er [trăns-fôr′mər] *noun*, a device that transfers electrical energy from one circuit to another

trans-fu-sion [trăns-fyōō′zhən] *noun*, the introduction into a person's bloodstream of blood from another

trans-gres-sion [trăns-grĕsh′ən] *noun*, violation of law, a going beyond some limit

tran-sient [trăn′shənt] *adjective*, of short duration, not permanent

tran-sis-tor [trăn-zĭs′tər] *noun*, an electrical device like a radio that sends and amplifies voices

tran-sit [trăn′sĭt] *noun*, 1) a passage 2) the state of being carried 3) a surveyor's instrument for measuring angles

tran-si-tion [trăn-zĭsh′ən] *noun*, going from one state of action or position to another

tran-si-tive [trăn′sĭ-tĭv] *adjective*, when the action of a verb is done to something or somebody

tran-si-to-ry [trăn′sĭ-tôr′ē] *adjective*, temporary, brief, lasting only a short time

trans-late [trăns-lāt′] *verb*, to pass along the message from one language to another

trans-la-tion [trăns-lā′shən] *noun*, the conversion of a message into another language

trans-lu-cent [trăns-lōō′sənt] *adjective*, a material that lets light in diffusively, but cannot be seen through

trans-mis-sion [trăns-mĭsh′ən] *noun*, 1) the apparatus by which the power is transmitted from high-speed motor power to the wheels 2) the sending of pictures or sounds through the air, as by radio or television

trans-mit [trăns-mĭt′] *verb*, 1) to send information over wires or air waves 2) to convey or send from one person or place to another 3) to pass along

trans-mit-ter [trăns-mĭt′ər] *noun*, the part of a telegraph or telephone instrument used to send a message

trans-mute [trăns-myo͞ot′] *verb*, to change, to convert from one substance to another

trans-par-ent [trăns-pâr′ənt] *adjective*, easily or capable of being seen through, clear

tran-spire [trăn-spīr′] *verb*, 1) to exhale 2) to happen, to occur

trans-plant [trăns-plănt′] *verb*, 1) to take out of the ground to plant somewhere else 2) a medical operation that exchanges a body organ

trans-port [trăns-pôrt′] *noun*, 1) a means of carrying people or goods, *verb*, 2) to carry

trans-por-ta-tion [trăns′pər-tā′shən] *noun*, the act of carrying things from one place to another

trans-pose [trăns-pōz′] *verb*, 1) to switch 2) to put into a different key in music

trap [trăp] *noun*, 1) a device used

to capture someone or something 2) a strategy used to capture or entrap someone, *verb*, 3) to capture something or someone so that they cannot escape

tra-peze [tră-pēz′] *noun*, a short horizontal bar suspended by two parallel ropes, one at each end

trap-e-zoid [trăp′ĭ-zoid′] *noun*, a closed figure of four sides, two sides are parallel but unequal in length

trash [trăsh] *noun*, something considered worthless that is thrown away, garbage

trau-mat-ic [trou′măt′ĭk] *adjective*, upsetting, stressful, disturbing

tra-vail [trə-vāl′] *noun*, 1) painful labor, hard work 2) anguish

trav-el [trăv′əl] *noun*, 1) taking a trip, seeing the world, *verb*, 2) to go from one place to another 3) to be transmitted

trav-erse [trə-vûrs′] *verb*, to cross in traveling, to pass over

trawl-er [trô′lər] *noun*, a fishing boat which drags a cone-shaped net across the floor of the ocean

tray [trā] *noun*, a flat shallow receptacle with raised edges on which things can be carried

treach-er-ous [trĕch′ər-əs] *adjective*, dangerous

trea-cle [trē′kəl] *noun*, syrup obtained in refining sugar

tread [trĕd] *noun*, 1) the part touching the ground, *verb*, 2) to stand on, to walk on, to step

trea-son [trē′zən] *noun*, *no plural*, the crime of helping the enemy of a group or country one is loyal to

treas-ure [trĕzh'ər] *noun,* 1) an accumulation of wealth such as money or jewels, *verb,* 2) to regard as precious, to cherish

treas-ur-er [trĕzh'ər-ər] *noun,* one who is in charge of the disbursement of money

treas-ur-y [trĕzh'ə-rē] *noun,* a place to store and control money such as a bank

treat [trēt] *noun,* 1) something that gives pleasure or enjoyment, *verb,* 2) to behave toward 3) to deal with, to serve 4) to give medicine as a doctor

trea-tise [trē'tĭs] *noun,* an article treating a subject systematically and thoroughly

treat-ment [trēt'mənt] *noun,* 1) handling, processing 2) therapeutic care

trea-ty [trē'tē] *noun,* a formal agreement between two or more nations

tree [trē] *noun,* a large plant with a trunk, branches, and leaves

trek [trĕk] *verb,* to travel with hardship, a difficult journey

trem-ble [trĕm'bəl] *verb,* to shake, to feel nervous, to quiver

tre-men-dous [trĭ-mĕn'dəs] *adjective,* 1) marvelously great 2) very large 3) extraordinary

trem-or [trĕm'ər] *noun,* trembling, involuntary shaking of the body

trem-u-lous [trĕm'yə-ləs] *adjective,* quivering, wavering

trench [trĕnch] *noun,* a long narrow ditch, dug into the earth

trench-ant [trĕn'chənt]*adjective,* 1) keen, cutting 2) sarcastic, critical, mean-spirited

trench-er-man [trĕn'chər-mən] *noun,* a person with a hearty appetite

trend [trĕnd] *noun,* the popular course, direction, tendency

trep-i-da-tion [trĕp'ĭ-dā'shən] *noun,* fear, apprehension

tres-pass [trĕs'pəs] *noun,* 1) an intrusion, *verb,* 2) to encroach on another's right 3) to unlawfully enter property of another

tri-al [trī'əl] *noun,* 1) when people in a court of law decide whether a person is guilty of a crime 2) a test to see if something is good or bad 3) suffering or adversity

tri-an-gle [trī'ăng'gəl] *noun,* a plane figure with three sides and three angles

tri-an-gu-lar [trī-ăng'gyə-lər] *adjective,* having three points like a triangle

tribe [trīb] *noun,* a group of people descended from a common ancestor who practice the same traditions, customs, and rituals, lead by a chief, a clan

trib-u-la-tion [trĭb'yə-lā'shən] *noun,* distress, suffering

tri-bu-nal [trī-byōō'nəl] *noun,* a court or forum for justice

trib-u-tar-y [trĭb'yə-tĕr'ē] *adjective,* 1) subsidiary, *noun,* 2) a stream or river that flows into a larger river

trib-ute [trĭb'yōōt] *noun,* a gesture to show respect for someone, an accolade

trick [trĭk] *noun,* 1) a clever prank, a sly or ingenious feat, *verb,* 2) to deceive by cunning

trick-le [trĭk′əl] *verb*, to flow in a small, gentle stream

tri-cy-cle [trī′sĭk′əl] *noun*, a light three-wheeled vehicle

tried [trīd] *past tense* of **try**

tri-fle [trī′fəl] *noun*, 1) a small amount, *verb*, 2) to play or toy

tri-fling [trī′flĭng] *adjective*, of little value or importance

trig-ger [trĭg′ər] *noun*, 1) the firing mechanism on a gun, *verb*, 2) to set something off

trig-o-nom-e-try [trĭg′ə-nŏm′ĭ-trē] *noun*, measuring the sides and angles of triangles

tril-lion [trĭl′yən] *noun*, one million million: 1,000,000,000,000

tril-o-gy [trĭl′ə-jē] *noun*, a novel or play in three separate works that are closely related

trim [trĭm] *noun*, 1) ornaments or decorations, *verb*, 2) to decorate 3) to cut back to make tidy

tri-o [trē′ō] *noun*, a set of three

trip [trĭp] *noun*, 1) a journey, a jaunt, an excursion, a pilgrimage, *verb*, 2) to skip, to stumble 3) to release a lever suddenly

tri-ple [trĭp′əl] *adjective*, three-way, multiplied three times

tri-pod [trī′pŏd′] *noun*, a stand or support with three legs

trite [trīt] *adjective*, 1) trivial, insignificant 2) hackneyed

tri-umph [trī′əmf] *noun*, 1) exultation over success, *verb*, 2) to gain victory

tri-um-phant [trī-ŭm′fənt] *adjective*, feeling thrilled and happy about winning

triv-i-a [trĭv′ē-ə] *noun*, trifles, unimportant matters

triv-i-al [trĭv′ē-əl] *adjective*, of little worth or importance

trol-ley [trŏl′ē] *noun*, a public bus that travels on a train track

troop [tro͞op] *noun*, 1) a collection of people 2) a body of cavalry

tro-phy [trō′fē] *noun*, something as a prize or award, given to show success in an activity

trop-ic [trŏp′ĭk] *noun*, a place between the two imaginary lines that run parallel above and below the equator, where it is hot and humid all year long

trop-i-cal [trŏp′ĭ-kəl] *adjective*, temperatures of a jungle or warm climate near the equator

trot [trŏt] *verb*, to keep at a steady pace, to canter, to gallop

trou-ble [trŭb′əl] *noun*, 1) a problem, a difficulty 2) a dangerous or difficult situation 3) extra work or effort, *verb*, 4) to impose on 5) to distress

troupe [tro͞op] *noun*, a troop or company of musicians or performers

trou-sers [trou′zərz] *noun*, *plural*, loose fitting pants

trout [trout] *noun*, a small fresh-water fish in the salmon family

trow-el [trou′əl] *noun*, 1) a hand-held spade 2) a tool with a flat blade used to apply mortar or cement

tru-ant [tro͞o′ənt] *noun*, 1) absent from school without good reason or permission 2) neglectful

truce [tr$\overline{oo}$s] *noun*, a peace agreement, cease-fire

truck [trŭk] *noun*, a large, heavy vehicle with at least four wheels used to transport heavy materials or large quantities

true [tr$\overline{oo}$] *adjective*, 1) honest, real, based on fact 2) loyal

tru-ism [tr$\overline{oo}$′ĭz′əm] *noun*, a self-evident obvious truth

tru-ly [(tr$\overline{oo}$′lē] *adverb*, in fact or in truth, sincerely, really

trump [trŭmp] *verb*, 1) to fabricate or invent 2) to beat someone's hand in bridge

trum-pet [trŭm′pĭt] *noun*, a horn, one of the brass instruments with several keys and a flaring bell

trunk [trŭngk] *noun*, 1) a chest, a storage box 2) the main stem of a tree 3) a compartment in a car 4) the snout of an elephant

trust [trŭst] *noun*, 1) belief in someone's goodness and integrity, *verb*, 2) to believe that someone will do as they say

trust-ee [trŭ-stē′] *noun*, one entrusted to administer the property of another

truth [tr$\overline{oo}$th] *noun*, the facts, what actually happened, reality

try [trī] *verb*, 1) to attempt, to make an effort 2) to sample

try-ing [trī′ĭng] *adjective*, difficult, straining one's patience

tryst [trĭst] *noun*, an appointed meeting, a rendezvous

tsu-nami [ts$\overline{oo}$-nä′mē] *noun*, a giant, fast-moving ocean wave produced by an earthquake

tub [tŭb] *noun*, a container used to take a bath or wash clothes

tu-ba [t$\overline{oo}$′bə] *noun*, the lowest-pitched of the brass instruments

tube [t$\overline{oo}$b] *noun*, 1) a pipe made of metal, plastic 2) a glass usually used to conduct liquids or gases

tu-ber-cu-lo-sis [t$\overline{oo}$-bûr′kyə-lō′sĭs] *noun*, a disease due to the presence of small granular tumors in an organ marked by coughing

tuck [tŭk] *noun*, 1) a pleat, fold or gather, *verb*, 2) to wrap snugly

Tues-day [t$\overline{oo}$z′dē] *noun*, the third day of the week

tuft [tŭft] *noun*, a cluster, a clump

tug [tŭg] *verb*, to jerk, to yank, to pull with force or effort

tu-i-tion [t$\overline{oo}$-ĭsh′ən] *noun*, the price paid for instruction

tu-lip [t$\overline{oo}$′lĭp] *noun*, a flower grown from a bulb in a variety of colors, in the shape of a cup

tulle [t$\overline{oo}$l] *noun*, a thin, fine net of acetate, silk or rayon, often used for veils or a tutu

tum-ble [tŭm′bəl] *verb*, 1) to turn over and over 2) to fall down

tu-mult [t$\overline{oo}$′mŭlt′] *noun*, commotion, a riot, noise

tu-mul-tu-ous [t$\overline{oo}$-mŭl′ch$\overline{oo}$-əs] *adjective*, wild, chaotic

tu-na [t$\overline{oo}$′nə] *noun*, a large fish that lives in the ocean

tun-dra [tŭn′drə] *noun*, the vast treeless plains in Siberia and arctic North America

tune [t$\overline{oo}$n] *noun*, 1) musical notes arranged as a medley, *verb*, 2) to put the right amount of tension on a stringed instrument so that it gives a certain sound 3) to be in sync, to put in harmony

tung-sten [tŭng′stən] *noun*, a hard, brittle, whitish-gray metal with an extremely high melting point at 6100 degrees Fahrenheit

tun-nel [tŭn′əl] *noun*, 1) a long passageway dug underground, *verb*, 2) to dig, to burrow

tur-ban [tûr′bən] *noun*, a man's headdress having no brim

tur-bid [tûr′bĭd] *adjective*, muddy, having the sediment disturbed

tur-bine [tûr′bĭn] *noun*, a machine that uses the gas from liquid to turn a shaft

tur-bu-lence [tûr′byə-ləns] *noun*, 1) wind currents that move very quickly 2) confusion, excited activity

tur-bu-lent [tûr′byə-lənt] *adjective*, 1) agitated, violent, stormy 2) full of disorder

tu-reen [tŏŏ-rēn′] *noun*, a deep table dish for holding soup

tur-key [tûr′kē] *noun*, a bird of the pheasant family, originally found wild in North America

tur-moil [tûr′moil′] *adjective*, a state of great confusion, agitation or disturbance

turn [tûrn] *noun*, 1) a chance or opportunity to participate 2) a bend, a twist or a bend in the road 3) a reversal, *verb*, 4) to cause to rotate or revolve 5) to change or to transform

tur-nip [tûr′nĭp] *noun*, a thick, edible, roundish root in the mustard family, eaten when boiled

tur-pen-tine [tûr′pən-tīn′] *noun*, a thin flammable oil made from certain pine trees used as a solvent to thin paint

tur-quoise [tûr′kwoiz′] *noun*, a bluish green or greenish gray mineral used as a gem

tur-tle [tûr′tl] *noun*, a reptile with a soft body protected by a hard shell covering, it carries his house on his back

tusk [tŭsk] *noun*, a long pointed tooth, as of an elephant or walrus

tu-tor [tŏŏ′tər] *noun*, a private teacher

tweed [twēd] *noun*, a soft, flexible fabric made of wool

tweez-ers [twē′zərz] *noun*, *plural*, a pincer-like tool for picking up small things

twelfth [twĕlfth] *adjective*, the ordinal of twelve, written 12th

twelve [twĕlv] *noun*, *adjective*, the number 12, the number after eleven

twen-ti-eth [twĕn′tē-ĭth] *adjective*, the number 20 in order, 20th, the ordinal of 20

twen-ty [twĕn′tē] *adjective, noun*, the number 20, ten times two

twice [twīs] *adverb*, two times, in double amount or degree

twig [twĭg] *noun*, a small outshoot of a branch or stem

twi-light [twī′līt′] *noun*, the light as the sun sets from the west

twin [twĭn] *adjective*, 1) two of the same, matched 2) an identical couple 3) either of two offspring brought forth at birth

twine [twīn] *noun*, 1) a strong cord of threads twisted together, *verb*, 2) to twist together

twinge [twĭnj] *verb*, to feel a sharp physical or mental pain

twin-kle [twĭng′kəl] *verb*, to sparkle, to shimmer, to flicker

twins [twĭnz] *noun, plural*, two children born at the same time from the same mother

twirl [twûrl] *verb*, to whirl or spin in a circle, to rotate rapidly

twitch [twĭch] *verb*, to jerk or make spastic movements

two [tōō] *adjective, noun*, the number that follow one, written 2, one plus one

type [tīp] *noun*, 1) the letters in different fonts used to print words 2) category, sort, *verb*, 3) to use a keyboard to write words printed on a computer

type-writ-er [tīp′rī′tər] *noun*, an instrument for writing by means of type

ty-phoid [tī′foid′] *noun*, a fever which eats up the walls of the intestines causing internal bleeding

ty-phoon [tī-fōōn′] *noun*, a cyclone in the region of the Philippines or the China Sea

typ-i-cal [tĭp′ĭ-kəl] *adjective*, representing something by a model, characteristic

ty-rant [tī′rənt] *noun*, an absolute ruler who is usually cruel

U

u-biq-ui-tous [yōō-bĭk′wĭ-təs] *adjective*, being everywhere at the same time, omnipresent

UFO [yōō′ĕf-ō′] *noun*, Unidentified Flying Object, a thing in the sky that seems too strange to be real

ug-ly [ŭg′lē] *adjective*, revolting to look at, unattractive

ul-cer [ŭl′sər] *noun*, a sore on the skin filled with pus and infection that is painful, a lesion

ul-te-ri-or [ŭl-tîr′ē-ər] *adjective*, intentionally concealed

ul-ti-mate [ŭl′tə-mĭt] *adjective*, 1) final, supreme 2) farthest

ul-ti-mate-ly [ŭl′tə-mĭt-lē] *adverb*, finally, at the end, totally

ul-ti-ma-tum [ŭl′tə-mā′təm] *noun*, a final proposition or condition offered to end a dispute

um-brage [ŭm′brĭj] *noun*, resentment, anger, a sense of injury or insult, offense

um-brel-la [ŭm-brĕl′ə] *noun*, a covering held in the hand as protection from the rain

um-pire [ŭm′pīr′] *noun*, the judge or referee in a baseball game

un-a-ble [ŭn-ā′bəl] *adjective*, not capable of doing something

un-alienable [ŭn-āl′yə-nə-bəl] *adjective*, cannot be taken away

u-nan-i-mous [yōō-năn′ə-məs] *adjective*, being of one mind, showing complete agreement

u-nan-i-mous-ly [yōō-năn′ə-məs-lē] *adverb*, with all voters voting the same way

un-as-sum-ing [ŭn′ə-sōō′mĭng] *adjective*, modest, simple, plain

un-a-void-a-ble [ŭn′ə-voi′də-bəl] *adjective*, inevitable

un-bear-a-ble [ŭn-bâr′ə-bəl]
adjective, not capable of being
endured, intolerable

un-bri-dled [ŭn-brīd′ld] *adjective*,
not restrained, uninhibited

un-can-ny [ŭn-kăn′ē] *adjective*,
strange, mysterious, seeming to
have a supernatural basis

un-cer-tain-ty [ŭn-sûr′tn-tē] *noun*,
doubtfulness, not reliable

un-cle [ŭng′kəl] *noun*, the brother
of one of your parents, or the
husband of the sister of one of
your parents

un-com-fort-a-ble
[ŭn-kŭm′fər-tə-bəl] *adjective*,
uneasy, causing discomfort

un-com-mon [ŭn-kŏm′ən]
adjective, not usual, unique, odd

un-con-cern [ŭn′kən-sûrn′]
adjective, indifference, lack of
interest, freedom from anxiety

un-con-scion-a-ble
[ŭn-kŏn′shə-nə-bəl] *adjective*,
unscrupulous, something done
that shows no conscience,
excessive, unreasonable

un-con-scious [ŭn-kŏn′shəs]
adjective, not knowing what is
happening, lacking awareness

un-cov-er [ŭn-kŭv′ər] *verb*, 1) to
take something from on top of
something 2) to find out

un-der [ŭn′dər] *adjective*, 1) less
than 2) working for or obeying,
preposition, 3) below, beneath
the surface

un-der-es-ti-mate
[ŭn′dər-ĕs′tə-māt′] *verb*, to
undervalue, to minimize

un-der-go [ŭn′dər-gō′] *verb*, 1) to
experience 2) to suffer or endure

un-der-grad-u-ate
[ŭn′dər-grăj′ōō-ĭt] *noun*, a
student at a college who has not
received a bachelor's degree

un-der-ground [ŭn′dər-ground′]
adjective, 1) in the recesses of
the earth 2) in secrecy

un-der-growth [ŭn′dər-grōth′]
noun, *no plural*, thickly growing
plants underneath trees

un-der-line [ŭn′dər-līn′] *verb*, to
put a line under a word or words

un-der-neath [ŭn′dər-nēth′]
adverb, down from below

un-der-rate [ŭn′dər-rāt′] *verb*, to
evaluate too low, to undervalue

un-der-stand [ŭn′dər-stănd′] *verb*,
1) to grasp the nature of 2) to
know what something means

un-der-take [ŭn′dər-tāk′] *verb*, to
take upon oneself as a task

un-der-tak-er [ŭn′dər-tā′kər]
noun, one whose business is to
take charge of funerals

un-der-tak-ing [ŭn′dər-tā′kĭng]
noun, a duty, an obligation, a
job, a task

un-der-wear [ŭn′dər-wâr′] *noun*,
the garments worn next to the
skin under outside clothing

un-der-write [ŭn′dər-rīt′] *verb*, to
insure, to guarantee

un-do [ŭn-dōō′] *verb*, 1) to untie or
unfasten 2) to reverse or annul

un-doubt-ed-ly [ŭn-dou′tĭd-lē]
adverb, certainly, indeed

un-du-late [ŭn′jə-lāt′] *verb*, to
move with a wave-like motion

un-earth [ŭn-ûrth′] *verb*, to dig up

un-eas-y [ŭn-ē′zē] *adjective*, a little
afraid, worried, uncomfortable

un-em-ployed [ŭn′ĕm-ploid′]
adjective, having no paid work

un-equal [ŭn-ē′kwəl] *adjective*,
unmatched, unparalleled

un-e-quiv-o-cal [ŭn′ĭ-kwĭv′ə-kəl]
adjective, plain, obvious

un-err-ing-ly [ŭn-ûr′ĭng-lē]
adverb, correctly, precisely,
infallibly, accurately

un-e-ven [ŭn-ē′vən] *adjective*, not
level or flat, not uniform

un-ex-pect-ed [ŭn′ĭk-spĕk′tĭd]
adjective, sudden, coming
without warning, unforeseen

un-fair [ŭn-fâr′] *adjective*, unjust,
unethical, biased, dishonest

un-faltering [ŭn-fôl′tər-ĭng]
adjective, steadfast

un-fas-ten [ŭn-făs′ən] *verb*, to
undo, to detach, to separate

un-fit [ŭn-fĭt′] *adjective*, made
unsuitable, not prepared or
adapted, not competent

un-fold [ŭn-fōld′] *verb*, 1) to open
out 2) to explain, to evolve

un-for-tu-nate [ŭn-fôr′chə-nĭt]
adjective, unlucky, regrettable

un-for-tu-nate-ly
[ŭn-fôr′chə-nĭt-lē] *adverb*,
having bad luck, unsuccessful

un-friend-ly [ŭn-frĕnd′lē]
adjective, not nice, unkind

un-grate-ful [ŭn-grāt′fəl]
adjective, thankless

un-hap-py [ŭn-hăp′ē] *adjective*,
dissatisfied, not content, sad

un-health-y [ŭn-hĕl′thē] *adjective*,
1) ill, sickly 2) food or habits
that make a person feel tired

u-ni-form [yōō′nə-fôrm′]
adjective, 1) unvaried, regular,

constant, *noun*, 2) clothes worn
for a special job or school

u-ni-form-i-ty [yōō′nə-fôrm′ĭ-tē]
noun, sameness, consistency,
identical with others

u-ni-fy [yōō′nə-fī′] *verb*, to
combine, to integrate, to connect

u-ni-lat-er-al [yōō′nə-lăt′ər-əl]
adjective, one sided

un-im-ag-i-na-tive
[ŭn-ĭ-măj′ə-nə-tĭv] *adjective*,
uninspired, common, everyday

un-impeach-a-ble
[ŭn′ĭm-pē′chə-bəl] *adjective*,
blameless and exemplary

un-im-por-tant [ŭn′ĭm-pôr′tnt]
adjective, 1) trivial, trite
2) extraneous, irrelevant

un-in-hib-it-ed [ŭn′ĭn-hĭb′ĭ-tĭd]
adjective, not restrained by
convention, free and easy

un-in-tel-li-gi-ble
[ŭn′ĭn-tĕl′ĭ-jə-bəl] *adjective*, not
capable of being understood

un-ion [yōōn′yən] *noun*, 1) a
coming together 2) a group of
people who join to support a
cause 3) a combination, **Union**
4) the army fighting for northern
states during the Civil War

u-nique [yōō-nēk′] *adjective*,
single in kind or excellence

u-ni-son [yōō′nĭ-sən] *noun*, unity
of pitch, complete accord

u-nit [yōō′nĭt] *noun*, 1) a complete
set 2) a specific amount, a form of
measurement 3) a single entity

u-nite [yōō-nīt′] *verb*, to join, to
connect, to put together as one

United States
[yōō-nī′tǐd-stāts-ŭv-ə-mĕr′ǐ-kə]
noun, the country made up of the
land between the Pacific Ocean
and the Atlantic Ocean, between
Canada and Mexico, including
Alaska and Hawaii, the capital,
is the District of Columbia

u-ni-ver-sal [yōō′nə-vûr′səl]
adjective, mutual understanding,
totally accepted everywhere

u-ni-verse [yōō′nə-vûrs′] *noun*, all
existing things including the
earth and all of space

u-ni-ver-si-ty [yōō′nə-vûr′sǐ-tē]
noun, an institution of higher
learning empowered to confer
degrees in the arts and sciences

un-just [ŭn-jŭst′] *adjective*, unfair,
biased, unworthy

un-kempt [ŭn-kĕmpt′] *adjective*, a
messy, uncared for appearance

un-kind [ŭn-kīnd′] *adjective*,
indifferent, unfeeling, rude

un-known [ŭn-nōn′] *adjective*,
1) unfamiliar 2) unexplored

un-less [ŭn-lĕs′] *adjective*, under
different conditions, or else

un-like [ŭn-līk′] *adjective*,
dissimilar, different

un-load [ŭn-lōd′] *verb*, 1) to take
something off a vehicle such as
cargo 2) to dispose of

un-luck-y [ŭn-lŭk′ē] *adjective*,
unsuccessful, unfortunate

un-mis-tak-a-ble [ŭn′mǐ-stā′kə-
bəl] *adjective*, clear, obvious

un-mis-take-a-bly
[ŭn′mǐ-stā′kə-blē] *adverb*,
undoubtedly, obviously

un-nec-es-sar-y [ŭn-nĕs′ǐ-sĕr′ē]
adjective, uncalled for, needless

un-ob-tru-sive [ŭn′əb-trōō′sǐv]
adjective, not noticeable

un-pleas-ant [ŭn-plĕz′ənt]
adjective, disagreeable

un-prec-e-dent-ed
[ŭn-prĕs′ǐ-dĕn′tǐd] *adjective*,
novel, unparalleled

un-pre-pare-ed [ŭn′prǐ-pârd′]
adjective, unaware, not ready

un-rav-el [ŭn-răv′əl] *verb*, to
untangle, to unwind, to unfold

un-rea-son-a-ble [ŭn-rē′zə-nə-bəl]
adjective, absurd, illogical, not
guided by sound judgment

un-re-li-a-ble [ŭn′rǐ-lǐ′ə-bəl]
adjective, not dependable

un-ru-ly [ŭn-rōō′lē] *adjective*,
disobedient, lawless

un-safe [ŭn-sāf′] *adjective*,
hazardous, dangerous, risky

un-sat-is-fac-to-ry
[ŭn-săt′ǐs-făk′tə-rē] *adjective*,
not good enough, inadequate

un-scru-pu-lous
[ŭn-skrōō′pyə-ləs] *adjective*,
unprincipled, devious, deceptive

un-seem-ly [ŭn-sēm′lē] *adjective*,
unbecoming, inappropriate

un-so-phis-ti-cat-ed
[ŭn′sə-fǐs′tǐ-kā′tǐd] *adjective*,
innocent, showing inexperience

un-stead-y [ŭn-stĕd′ē] *adjective*,
1) not safe 2) unsure, wavering

un-suit-a-ble [ŭn-sōō′tə-bəl]
adjective, inappropriate,
unsatisfactory, something that
does not fit in, irregular

un-sure [ŭn-shŏŏr'] *adjective,* uncertain, doubtful

un-ten-a-ble [ŭn-tĕn'ə-bəl] *adjective,* not able to be maintained or supported against criticism

un-ti-dy [ŭn-tī'dē] *adjective,* messy, cluttered, not orderly

un-tie [ŭn-tī'] *verb,* to unfasten a string or rope, to loosen

un-til [ŭn-tĭl'] *conjunction,* 1) up to the time that, or when, *preposition,* 2) up to the time of, as far as, before

un-to-ward [ŭn-tôrd'] *adjective,* unfortunate, annoying

un-true [ŭn-trōō'] *adjective,* false, incorrect, deceptive, disloyal

un-u-su-al [ŭn-yōō'zhōō-əl] *adjective,* strange, odd

un-veil [ŭn-vāl'] *verb,* to remove the covering from something

un-well [ŭn-wĕl'] *adjective,* ill, sick, upset, ailing

un-wield-y [ŭn-wēl'dē] *adjective,* not easily carried, bulky

un-will-ing [ŭn-wĭl'ĭng] *adjective,* reluctant, resistant, averse

un-wind [ŭn-wīnd'] *verb,* 1) to undo something, to loosen 2) to relax, to get rid of tension

un-wise [ŭn-wīz'] *adjective,* not reasonable or sensible

un-wit-ting [ŭn-wĭt'ĭng] *adjective,* unintentional, not knowing

un-wrap [ŭn-răp'] *verb,* to remove the protective covering on a package or product

up [ŭp] *adverb,* 1) to put in a higher place, *preposition,* 2) to position something so that it is standing 3) toward

up-braid [ŭp-brād'] *verb,* to scold, to reproach, to criticize

up-heav-al [ŭp-hē'vəl] *noun,* an eruption, a change, a quake

up-hold [ŭp-hōld'] *verb,* to maintain, to support, to sustain

up-hol-ster-y [ŭp-hōl'stə-rē] *noun,* furniture with stuffing, springs, covers or trim

up-lift [ŭp-lĭft'] *noun,* 1) upgrade, restoration, *verb,* 2) to raise up 3) to improve socially or morally

up-on [ə-pŏn'] *adverb,* 1) on, *preposition,* 2) on top of something

up-per [ŭp'ər] *adjective,* 1) in a higher position, further up 2) the part of the shoe above the sole

up-right [ŭp'rīt'] *adjective,* 1) straight up and down 2) righteous, honest, honorable

up-set [ŭp-sĕt'] *verb,* 1) to knock over 2) to make unhappy or worried 3) to spoil something that was planned, to disrupt

up-stairs [ŭp'stârz'] *adverb,* 1) up the steps, *noun, plural,* 2) the next level, the upper level

up-ward [ŭp'wərd] *adjective,* to a higher place or position

u-ra-ni-um [yŏŏ-rā'nē-əm] *noun,* a rare radioactive, metallic element found in certain minerals used in nuclear weapons

ur-ban [ûr'bən] *noun,* characteristic of a city

ur-bane [ûr-bān'] *adjective,* suave, refined, elegant, sophisticated, charming, courteous, polite

ur-chin [ûr'chĭn] *noun*, a needy or mischievous child

urge [ûrj] *noun*, 1) a strong wish, *verb*, 2) to try to make someone do something, to push along

ur-gen-cy [ûr'jən-sē] *adverb*, calling for quick action

ur-gent [ûr'jənt] *adjective*, pressing, calling for immediate attention or action, insistent

us [ŭs] *pronoun*, the person who is speaking, and the others mentioned in the sentence, the objective case of **we**

us-age [yōō'sĭj] *noun*, a long continued practice, a custom

use [yōōz] *noun*, 1) a purpose, *verb*, 2) to find a purpose for something, to utilize

used to [yōōst-tōō] *adjective*, 1) knowing what something or someone is like, familiar 2) something done in the past but is not done now

use-ful [yōōs'fəl] *adjective*, helpful, serviceable

use-less [yōōs'lĭs] *adjective*, hopeless, valueless, vain

u-su-al [yōō'zhōō-əl] *adjective*, something that happens regularly, not uncommon

u-su-al-ly [yōō'zhōō-əl-lē] *adverb*, almost always, frequently

u-surp [yōō-sûrp'] *verb*, to seize, to take possession of by force or without right or authority

u-sur-pa-tion [yōō'sər-pā'shən] *noun*, the act of seizing power and rank of another

u-su-ry [yōō'zhə-rē] *noun*, interest in excess of a legal rate

Utah [yōō'tô'] *noun*, one of the 50 United States, the capital is Salt Lake City. The state flower of **Utah** is the sego lily; and the motto is "Industry."

u-ten-sil [yōō-tĕn'səl] *noun*, a tool, a dining instrument

u-til-i-ty [yōō-tĭl'ĭ-tē] *noun*, a company that provides products such as gas, water, or electricity

u-ti-lize [yōōt'l-īz'] *verb*, to make use of something

ut-most [ŭt'mōst'] *adjective*, the furthest or most extreme

u-to-pi-a [yōō-tō'pē-ə] *noun*, heaven on earth, an ideal place

ut-ter [ŭt'ər] *verb*, to speak

ut-ter-ance [ŭt'ər-əns] *noun*, vocal expression, articulation, speech

ut-ter-ly [ŭt'ər-lē] *adverb*, completely, entirely, without doubt, totally, absolutely

V

va-can-cy [vā'kən-sē] *noun*, 1) emptiness 2) an unfilled place, job or position 3) an opening

va-cant [vā'kənt] *adjective*, empty

va-cate [vā'kāt'] *verb*, 1) to leave, to empty, to abandon 2) to annul

va-ca-tion [vā-kā'shən] *noun*, time away from work for rest, amusement, and relaxation

vac-ci-nate [văk'sə-nāt'] *verb*, to inoculate with a vaccine as a form of protection

vac-ci-na-tion [văk'sə-nā'shən] *noun*, a remedy which is the injection of the virus itself

vac-cine [văk-sēn] *noun*, a weakened germ of a virus used to protect a person from the often fatal or debilitating effects of a virus

vac-il-late [văs'ə-lāt'] *verb*, to change one's mind often, to waffle, to waver

vac-u-um [văk'yōō-əm] *noun*, 1) the absolute absence of matter 2) an appliance used to rid carpets of dust and litter 3) a kind of bottle that keeps liquids hot or cold, such as a thermos

vag-a-bond [văg'ə-bŏnd'] *noun*, a tramp, an outcast, a vagrant

va-grant [vā'grənt] *adjective*, 1) wandering, begging, *noun*, 2) one who wanders around outside from place to place

vague [vāg] *adjective*, not clearly understood, indistinct

vain [vān] *adjective*, 1) conceited, too proud of the way one looks 2) fruitless, unsuccessful

vale [vāl] *noun*, valley, lowland

val-en-tine [văl'ən-tīn'] *noun*, a love poem, a card expressing love and affection

val-et [văl'ĭt] *noun*, a manservant who takes care of the clothes and personal needs of his employer

val-iant[văl'yənt]*adjective*, full of courage, brave

val-iant-ly [văl'yənt-lē] *adverb*, unafraid of danger, boldly, courageously, bravely

val-id [văl'ĭd] *adjective*, 1) significant, sound 2) legally effective or binding

val-i-date [văl'ĭ-dāt'] *verb*, to confirm, to ratify, to substantiate

va-lid-i-ty [və-lĭ'dĭ-tē] *noun*, confirmation that proves something is what it says it is

val-ley [văl'ē] *noun*, a region of low land situated between hills or mountains, a dale

val-or [văl'ər] *noun*, bravery, courage, boldness

val-u-a-ble [văl'yōō-ə-bəl] *adjective*, precious, of considerable worth, costly

val-ue [văl'yōō] *noun*, 1) what something is worth, what someone will pay, *verb*, 2) to think that something is important and meaningful 3) to say how much something is worth on the market, to rate

valve [vălv] *noun*, any device by which the flow of liquid, air, or gas may be regulated

van [văn] *noun*, a small, covered truck carrying goods or passengers or animals

van-dal-ism [văn'dl-ĭz'əm] *noun*, willful destruction of property

vane [vān] *noun*, a piece of metal or cloth set up high to swing with the wind to tell which way the wind is blowing

va-nil-la [və-nĭl'ə] *noun*, a flavoring made from the beans of the vanilla plant

van-ish [văn'ĭsh] *verb*, to disappear, to dissolve, to end

van-i-ty [văn'ĭ-tē] *noun*, 1) too proud of oneself 2) a small table for putting on makeup

van-quish [văng'kwĭsh] *verb*, to conquer, to overcome, to overpower in battle

van-tage [văn′tĭj] *noun*, the position giving an advantage

va-por [vā′pər] *noun*, 1) condensation 2) a substance in the gaseous state such as fog

var-i-a-ble [vâr′ē-ə-bəl] *noun*, changeable, liable to vary

var-i-ance [vâr′ē-əns] *noun*, degree of difference, disagreement

var-i-a-tion [vâr′ē-ā′shən] *noun*, a change in form, position, or condition

vari-ed [vâr′ēd] *adjective*, changing, various, mixed

va-ri-e-ty [və-rī′ĭ-tē] *noun*, many different things, assortment

var-i-ous [vâr′ē-əs] *adjective*, , several different kinds, diverse

var-nish [vär′nĭsh] *noun*, 1) a liquid that hardens into a clear, tough film, *verb*, 2) to paint with a clear protective sealant

var-si-ty [vär′sĭ-tē] *adjective*, a principal team in sports representing a school or college

var-y [vâr′ē] *verb*, to change

vase [vās] *noun*, a decorated pot for cut flowers or for decoration

vas-sal [văs′əl] *noun*, 1) in feudalism, one who held land of a superior lord 2) one subordinate to another

vast [văst] *adjective*, limitless, expansive, very great in size, quantity or degree, widespread

vat [văt] *noun*, a large container for liquids, a barrel

vaude-ville [vôd′vĭl′] *noun*, a theatrical performance with music, songs, and dance

vault [vôlt] *noun*, 1) a room constructed to protect its contents, *verb*, 2) to jump or leap over with hands holding a pole

veer [vîr] *verb*, to change in direction or position

veg-e-ta-ble [vĕj′tə-bəl] *noun*, an edible plant grown for food

veg-e-tate [vĕj′ĭ-tāt′] *verb*, to live in a monotonous, inactive way

veg-e-ta-tion [vĕj′ĭ-tā′shən] *noun*, plant growth, foliage, flowers

ve-he-ment [vē′ə-mənt] *adjective*, fervent, impassioned, fiery

ve-hi-cle [vē′ĭ-kəl] *noun*, something used to carry or transport people or things

veil [vāl] *noun*, a piece of transparent material worn to hide or protect the face, a cover

vein [vān] *noun*, 1) one of the vessels which conveys blood back to the heart 2) a crack in a rock filled with mineral matter

vel-lum [vĕl′əm] *noun*, a form of paper made out of animal skin that will hold ink

ve-loc-i-ty [və-lŏs′ĭ-tē] *noun*, speed, rapidity of motion

vel-vet [vĕl′vĭt] *noun*, *no plural*, a type of cloth with a soft surface

ven-det-ta [vĕn-dĕt′ə] *noun*, revenge for a dispute

ven-dor [vĕn′dər] *noun*, someone who sells something, a merchant

ve-neer [və-nîr′] *noun*, 1) a thin layer of finished wood, glued on a cheap surface 2) a superficial show of quality

ven-er-a-ble [vĕn′ər-ə-bəl] *adjective*, deserving high respect

ven-er-a-tion [věn′ə-rā′shən] *noun*, deep, respectful love, adoration

venge-ance [věn′jəns] *noun*, retribution, revenge, reprisal

ve-ni-al [vē′nē-əl] *adjective*, capable of being forgiven

ven-i-son [věn′ĭ-sən] *noun*, deer meat used for food

venn di-a-gram [věn-dī′ə-grăm′] *noun*, a tool to indicate the relationship of elements

ven-om [věn′əm] *noun*, poison stored in some animals

ven-om-ous [věn′ə-məs] *adjective*, poisonous, deadly, toxic

vent [věnt] *noun*, a small opening or outlet to let out air

ven-ti-late [věn′tl-āt′] *verb*, to cause fresh air to circulate through, to admit air into

ven-tril-o-quist [věn-trĭl′ə-kwĭst] *noun*, one who can make a voice seem to come from another person or thing

ven-ture [věn′chər] *noun*, 1) doing something that involves the risk of a loss *verb*, 2) to dare to go, to do or to say

ven-tur-ous [věn′chər-əs] *adjective*, daring, bold

ven-ue [věn′yōō] *noun*, an agreed place where something will take place, the scene of an event

ve-rac-i-ty [və-răs′ĭ-tē] *noun*, habitual observance of truth, truthfulness, accuracy

ve-ran-da [və-răn′də] *noun*, a long porch with a roof along the outside of a building

verb [vûrb] *noun*, the word expressing action in a sentence

ver-ba-tim [vər-bā′tĭm] *adverb*, word for word, literal

ver-bi-age [vûr′bē-ĭj] *noun*, a pompous array of words

ver-dant [vûr′dnt] *adjective*, green with vegetation

ver-dict [vûr′dĭkt] *noun*, the decision of a jury given to the court, a judgment or decision

verge [vûrj] *noun*, 1) the point beyond which something begins, the brink, *verb*, 2) to tend to incline

ver-i-fy [věr′ə-fī′] *verb*, to prove to be true, to confirm, to ascertain

ver-i-si-mil-i-tude [věr′ə-sĭ-mĭl′ĭ-tōōd′] *noun*, appearance of truth, likelihood

ver-i-ty [věr′ĭ-tē] *noun*, truth, reality, a statement that is true

ver-mi-cel-li [vûr′mĭ-chĕl′ē] *noun*, a pasta dried in a slender tube form, like spaghetti

ver-mic-u-lite [vər-mĭk′yə-līt′] *noun*, slivers of mica that expand when heated, used for insulation, and water absorption

Ver-mont [vər-mŏnt′] *noun*, one of the 50 United States located in New England, the capital is Montpelier. The state flower of **Vermont** is the red clover, the motto is "Freedom and unity."

ver-nal [vûr′nəl] *adjective*, of or occurring in spring

ver-sa-tile [vûr′sə-təl′] *adjective*, having the capability of doing many different things

verse [vûrs] *noun*, 1) lines of writing which have a rhythm often a rhyme 2) a few lines of this from a longer piece called a poem 3) a small part of the Bible, the Jewish Koran, or Talmud

ver-sion [vûr′zhən] *noun*, a description from a particular point of view, a standpoint

ver-sus [vûr′səs] *preposition*, against, in contrast with

ver-te-brate [vûr′tə-brĭt] *noun*, an animal with a backbone

ver-tex [vûr′tĕks′] *noun*, 1) the point where two planes intersect to form an angle 2) the highest point

ver-ti-cal [vûr′tĭ-kəl] *adjective*, straight up and down, perpendicular to the horizon

verve [vûrv] *noun*, enthusiasm, liveliness, energy, vitality

ver-y [vĕr′ē] *adjective*, 1) the same 2) the right or appropriate one, *adverb*, 3) to emphasize the word to make it stronger

ves-sel [vĕs′əl] *noun*, 1) a hollow utensil for holding anything 2) a boat 3) a channel for delivering blood, a vein or capillary

vest [vĕst] *noun*, a sleeveless top worn over a shirt with pockets

ves-ti-bule [vĕs′tə-byo͞ol′] *noun*, foyer, lobby, entry way

ves-tige [vĕs′tĭj] *noun*, a trace or visible sign of something gone

vet-er-an [vĕt′ər-ən] *noun*, experienced, old in service, especially in military life

vet-er-i-nar-i-an [vĕt′ər-ə-nâr′ē-ən] *noun*, a doctor who specializes in animal health and surgery

ve-to [vē′tō] *noun*, 1) a denial, a rejection, *verb*, 2) to deny, to reject, to turn down

vex [vĕks] *verb*, to annoy, to distress, to irritate

vex-a-tion [vĕk-sā′shən] *noun*, irritation, a cause of trouble or disquiet, annoyance

vi-a [vī′ə, vē′ə] *preposition*, traveling through, by way of

vi-a-ble [vī′ə-bəl] *adjective*, capable of maintaining life

vi-a-duct [vī′ə-dŭkt′] *noun*, a bridge for carrying a road, resting on masonry arches, often in water to allow boats through

vi-and [vī′ənd] *noun*, food, provision

vi-brate [vī′brāt′] *verb*, 1) to shake, to quiver or tremble 2) to echo, to reverberate, to move to and fro

vi-bra-tion [vī-brā′shən] *noun*, shaking, quivering, pulsation

vi-car-i-ous-ly [vī-kâr′ē-əs-lē] *adverb*, acting as a substitute, done in place of another

vice [vīs] *noun*, corruption, weakness, faults, foible

vice president [vīs′prĕz′ĭ-dənt] *noun*, the person chosen to replace the president

vi-cin-i-ty [vĭ-sĭn′ĭ-tē] *noun*, the region near or close by

vi-cious [vĭsh′əs] *adjective*, corrupt, wicked, mean

vi-cis-si-tude [vĭ-sĭs′ĭ-to͞od′] *noun*, change or succession from one thing to another

vic-tim [vĭk′tĭm] *noun*, 1) someone who suffers from an illness or action 2) a person who is deceived or cheated

vic-to-ri-ous [vĭk-tôr′ē-əs] *adjective*, conquering, triumphant in war, winning

vic-to-ry [vĭk′tə-rē] *noun*, winning
a contest or a battle, a triumph

vict-uals [vĭt′lz] *noun*, *plural*, food
for human beings, provisions

vid-e-o [vĭd′ē-ō′] *noun*, film for
showing on a television set

vie [vī] *verb*, to contend, to strive
in competition, to struggle

view [vyōō] *noun*, 1) ideas, beliefs,
opinion 2) something you see

vig-i-lance [vĭj′ə-ləns] *noun*,
watchfulness, caution

vi-gnette [vĭn-yĕt′] *noun*, a scene
depicting a moment in time

vig-or [vĭg′ər] *noun*, physical or
mental strength, stamina, energy

vig-or-ous [vĭg′ər-əs] *adjective*,
exhibiting strength, powerful,
energetic, intense, robust

vig-or-ous-ly [vĭg′ər-əs-lē] *adverb*,
very fast, with a great deal of
energy, healthy, spirited

vile [vīl] *adjective*, disgusting

vil-i-fy [vĭl′ə-fī′] *verb*, to slander,
to malign, to slur, to revile

vil-lage [vĭl′ĭj] *noun*, a group of
houses that form a community,
usually smaller than a town

vil-lain [vĭl′ən] *noun*, one capable
or guilty of great crimes, a rascal

vin-di-cate [vĭn′dĭ-kāt′] *verb*, to
support or maintain as true, to
free from suspicion

vin-dic-tive [vĭn-dĭk′tĭv] *adjective*,
revengeful, retaliatory, mean

vine [vīn] *noun*, a name given to
some plants with climbing stems

vin-e-gar [vĭn′ĭ-gər] *noun*, a sour
liquid made by fermentation of
wine or cider

vi-o-late [vī′ə-lāt′] *verb*, 1) to break
the rules, to disregard as a
promise 2) to break in on

vi-o-lence [vī′ə-ləns] *noun*,
commotion, disorder, outrage,
brutality, intense force

vi-o-lent [vī′ə-lənt] *adjective*,
brutal, vicious, forceful, rough

vi-o-lent-ly [vī′ə-lənt-lē] *adverb*,
harshly, with destructive force

vi-o-let [vī′ə-lĭt]) *adjective*, 1) the
color that is a combination of
blue and red, *noun*, 2) a purple
flower that grows wild as a
ground cover

vi-o-lin [vī′ə-lĭn′] *noun*, one of the
small stringed instruments
played with a bow

vi-o-lin-ist [vī′ə-lĭn′ĭst] *noun*, a
person who plays a violin

vi-per [vī′pər] *noun*, a poisonous
snake, a serpent

vir-gin [vûr′jĭn] *adjective*, pure,
chaste, unused

Vir-gin-i-a [vər-jĭn′yə] *noun*, one
of the 50 United States located
in the Southeast, the capital is
Richmond. The state flower of
Virginia is the flowering
dogwood and the motto is "Ever
thus to tyrants."

vir-ile [vîr′əl] *adjective*, manly,
showing masculine strength

vir-tue [vûr′chōō] *noun*,
uprightness, moral excellence

vir-tu-ous [vûr′chōō-əs] *adjective*,
righteous, honest, moral

vi-rus [vī′rəs] *noun*, an group of
infectious submicroscopic agents
that cause various diseases in
plants or animals

vis-age [vĭz′ĭj] *noun*, the face, countenance, or look of a person.

vis-cer-al [vĭs′ər-əl] *adjective*, felt in one's inner organs

vis-cous [vĭs′kəs] *adjective*, thick and sticky in consistency

vise [vīs] *noun*, a clamp, clasp, grip

vis-i-ble [vĭz′ə-bəl] *adjective*, as seen by the eye, in view

vi-sion [vĭzh′ən] *noun*, 1) something imagined, as in a dream, 2) a look into the future, unusual foresight 3) eyesight

vi-sion-ar-y [vĭzh′ə-nĕr′ē] *noun*, existing only in the imagination

vis-it [vĭz′ĭt] *noun*, 1) a social call, an appointment, *verb*, 2) to go to see someone 3) to chat casually

vis-i-tor [vĭz′ĭ-tər] *noun*, one who comes and goes to see another

vi-sor [vī′zər] *noun*, a sunshade or shield to block out glare

vi-su-al [vĭzh′ōō-ə-l] *adjective*, of or used in seeing, pleasing to the sight

vi-su-al-ize [vĭzh′ōō-ə-līz′] *verb*, 1) to imagine 2) to see something in the mind

vi-tal [vīt′l] *adjective*, necessary to life, important, indispensable

vi-tal-i-ty [vī-tăl′ĭ-tē] *noun*, spirit, energy, the capacity to develop

vi-ta-min [vī′tə-mĭn] *noun*, nutrients that give the body nourishment to help balance the metabolism

vi-ti-ate [vĭsh′ē-āt′] *verb*, to spoil the effect of something, to make less effective or imperfect

vit-ri-ol-ic [vĭt′rē-ŏl′ĭk] *adjective*, mean, causing bad feelings

vi-tu-per-a-tive [vī-tōō′pər-ə-tĭv] *adjective*, abusive, scolding

vi-va-cious [vĭ-vā′shəs] *adjective*, lively, sprightly, energetic

viv-id [vĭv′ĭd] *adjective*, easy to see, life-like, bright, colorful

vo-cab-u-lar-y [vō-kăb′yə-lĕr′ē] *noun*, the words of a language

vo-cal [vō′kəl] *adjective*, 1) voiced, outspoken 2) expressed by singing 3) relating to the sound made by the voice

vo-ca-tion [vō-kā′shən] *noun*, a job, employment or occupation, a profession

vogue [vōg] *adjective*, fashionable, in style, popular

voice [vois] *noun*, 1) the sounds coming through a person's mouth made by the respiratory system 2) to express an idea in writing or speaking

void [void] *noun*, an empty space

vol-ca-no [vŏl-kā′nō] *noun*, an opening in the earth's crust where melted rock, lava, gases, and ash are thrust onto the land

vo-li-tion [və-lĭsh′ən] *noun*, the act of making a conscious choice

vol-ley [vŏl′ē] *noun*, 1) a barrage, a bombardment, *verb*, 2) to return a ball before it hits the ground

vol-ley-ball [vŏl′ē-bôl′] *noun*, no plural, a game in which a large ball is knocked back and forth across a net, by hand

volt [vōlt] *noun*, 1) a measure of electricity, the unit of electromotive force 2) a turning movement of a horse, sideways around a center

vol-ume [vŏl′yōōm] *noun*, 1) a single book, *no plural*, 2) the space something occupies 3) the amount of sound something makes, loudness of a sound

vo-lu-mi-nous [və-lōō′mə-nəs] *adjective*, bulky, large

vol-un-tar-y [vŏl′ən-tĕr′ē] *adjective*, proceeding from the will, to give or perform freely

vol-un-teer [vŏl′ən-tîr′] *noun*, 1) one who offers his services of his own free will, *verb*, 2) to give freely of your time

vo-lup-tu-ous [və-lŭp′chōō-əs] *adjective*, shapely, full in form

vom-it [vŏm′ĭt] *noun,* 1) something from the stomach that comes out of the mouth, *verb*, 2) to throw up, to regurgitate food

vo-ra-cious [vô-rā′shəs] *adjective*, 1) someone who has a large appetite 2) exceedingly eager

vor-tex [vôr′tĕks′] *noun*, whirlpool, a whirling mass of water

vote [vōt] *noun*, 1) a choice made during an election, *verb*, 2) to decide by general consent

vot-er [vōt′ər] *noun*, a person registered to participate in an election

vouch [vouch] *verb*, to certify, to assure, to provide proof

vouch-er [vou′chər] *noun*, a document exchangeable for certain goods or services

vow [vou] *noun*, 1) an oath, a solemn plédge, *verb*, 2) to promise something important

vow-el [vou′əl] *noun*, the letters – **a,e,i,o,u**, and sometimes **y**

voy-age [voi′ĭj] *noun*, a long journey by sea, water, air, or space from one place to another

vul-gar [vŭl′gər] *adjective*, rude or rough in behavior, taste, etc, lacking good taste or refinement

vul-ner-a-ble [vŭl′nər-ə-bəl] *adjective*, capable of being easily harmed or injured

vul-ture [vŭl′chər] *noun*, a large bird that eats as a scavenger of dead animals

W

wade [wād] *verb*, to walk through a substance such as water or snow

waf-fle [wŏf′əl] *noun*, 1) a cake baked in an iron skillet, *verb*, 2) to change one's mind often

waft [wäft] *verb*, to move or be moved lightly over water or air, to drift

wag [wăg] *verb*, to move or cause to move briskly from side to side or up and down

wage [wāj] *noun*, 1) money paid for work or services, salary, *verb*, 2) to carry on (a war or campaign)

wa-ger [wā′jər] *noun*, the amount of money or property risked in an uncertain event, a bet

wag-on [wăg′ən] *noun*, a vehicle with four wheels that is pulled

waif [wāf] *noun*, a homeless child or animal, an orphan

wail [wāl] *verb*, to make a long cry showing sadness or pain, to sob

waist [wāst] *noun*, the part of the body between the ribs and the hips where the stomach is

wait [wāt] *noun*, 1) a time of anticipation, *verb*, 2) to expect, to anticipate, to be ready

wait-er [wā'tər] *noun*, a person hired to serve meals

waive [wāv] *verb*, to give up temporarily, to yield

waiv-er [wā'vər] *noun*, the act of giving up a right or claim

wake [wāk] *noun*, 1) the ripple of waves created by the motion of a boat, *verb*, 2) to stop sleeping, to be aroused from sleep

walk [wôk] *noun*, 1) a journey on foot, *verb*, 2) to take one step at a time, to proceed along

wall [wôl] *noun*, 1) a partition made of bricks or stone that separates space 2) one of the sides of a room or building, *verb*, 3) to divide, to partition

wal-let [wŏl'ĭt] *noun*, a small flat case for money, cards, etc., usually carried in a pocket

wal-low [wŏl'ō] *verb*, to tumble in the mud 2) move slowly

wall-pa-per [wôl'pā'pər] *noun*, *no plural*, decorative paper used to cover walls of a room

wal-nut [wôl'nŭt'] *noun*, 1) a hard, dark-colored wood, valuable for furniture 2) the nut or seed from the walnut tree in a hard shell

wal-rus [wôl'rəs] *noun*, a sea animal like the sea lion and the seal, with outside ears and tusks

waltz [wôlts] *verb*, a dance with four beats per measure

wand [wŏnd] *noun*, a baton, a rod, a fairy's magic stick

wan-der [wŏn'dər] *verb*, 1) to travel from place to place with no plan or purpose in mind 2) to slip easily off the subject

wane [wān] *verb*, to grow gradually smaller or decrease in strength, to decline, to dwindle

wan-gle [wăng'gəl] *verb*, to bring about by manipulation or trickery, to scheme

want [wŏnt] *noun*, 1) a need, lack, not having something necessary, *verb*, 2) to desire or feel a need for something, to require

wan-ton [wŏn'tən] *adjective*, unruly, wild, excessive

war [wôr] *noun*, a deadly conflict

war-ble [wôr'bəl] *verb*, to sing melodiously, to trill as a bird

ward [wôrd] *noun*, 1) a child in the care of someone other than his family 2) a district, a division, *verb*, 3) to fend off, to avert

war-den [wôrd'n] *noun*, the chief administrator of a prison

ward-robe [wôr'drōb'] *noun*, a closet of clothes

ware [wâr] *noun*, a product, merchandise, stock

ware-house [wâr'hous'] *noun*, a storehouse for wares or goods

war-i-ly [wâr'ĭ-lē] *adverb*, in a watchful and suspicious way

warm [wôrm] *adjective*, 1) a temperature between hot and cold, moderately hot, *verb*, 2) to add heat to make something no longer cold

warmth [wôrmth] *noun,*
1) friendship, 2) bodily heat

warn [wôrn] *verb,* 1) to inform
someone that something bad will
happen or of impending danger
2) to admonish, to exhort

warn-ing [wôr'nĭng] *noun,* the act
of telling someone to proceed
with caution, notification

warp [wôrp] *verb,* 1) to twist out of
shape, to distort 2) to pervert

war-rant [wôr'ənt] *noun,* 1) a
written request by a judge to
make an arrest, *verb,* 2) to be
sure of something, to justify

war-ran-ty [wôr'ən-tē] *noun,* a
guarantee that a contract will be
carried out by a manufacturer

war-ri-or [wôr'ē-ər] *noun,* a man
engaged in war, a soldier

wart [wôrt] *noun,* a small growth
or lump that looks like a blemish
on skin often caused by a virus

war-y [wâr'ē] *adjective,* very
cautious, on guard, watchful

was [wŭz] *verb, past tense* of **be,**
used in the 3rd singular, **he, she**
or **it**

wash [wŏsh] *noun,* 1) a batch of
clothes that are to be or have
been washed, *verb,* 2) to clean
with soap and water

wash-er [wŏsh'ər] *noun,* 1) a
machine for washing clothes or
dishes 2) a round piece of metal
put under a bolt to reinforce it

Wash-ing-ton [wŏsh'ĭng-tən]
noun, one of the 50 United
States located in the Northwest,
the capital is Olympia. The state
flower of **Washington** is the
coast rhododendron and the
motto is "By and by."

wasn't [wŭz'ənt] the *contraction* of
the words **was** and **not**

wasp [wŏsp] *noun,* a flying insect
like a bee, the female inflicts the
sting

waste [wāst] *adjective,* 1) useless,
noun, 2) anything discarded that
is not considered useful, *verb,*
3) to throw away, to spend or
use carelessly, to squander

waste-ful [wāst'fəl] *adjective,*
squandering or spending in a
needless manner

waste-wa-ter [wāst'wô'tər] *noun,*
water that has been used either
to manufacture a product or in
the home, which requires
treatment and purification before
it can be used again

watch [wŏch] *noun,* 1) a small
clock worn on the wrist or hung
from a chain, *verb,* 2) to observe,
to look at attentively 3) to guard,
to be on the lookout

wa-ter [wô'tər] *noun,* 1) a
molecule made of one oxygen
atom and two hydrogen atoms,
that covers 75% of the earth's
surface, *verb,* 2) to moisten or
soak with water 3) to dilute

wa-ter-fall [wô'tər-fôl'] *noun,* a
cascade of water coming down
from a precipice or cliff

wa-ter-way [wô'tər-wā'] *noun,* a
body of water that ships can use

wa-ter-wheel [wô'tər-hwēl] *noun,*
a wheel turned by water running
against or falling on paddles or
steps, used as a source of power

watt [wŏt] *noun*, a measure of electrical power equivalent to one joule per second

wave [wāv] *noun*, 1) a breaker, a surge, surf, *verb*, 2) to greet

wa-ver [wā′vər] *verb*, 1) to be unsteady and show signs of falling or giving way 2) to be indecisive

wax [wăks] *noun*, a substance made from fats and oils that melts when heated

way [wā] *noun*, 1) the manner, custom, style 2) means, process 3) a passage, a road

way-ward [wā′wərd] *adjective*, unruly, disobedient, willful

we [wē] *plural*, *pronoun*, referring to one or more people, including oneself and others

weak [wēk] *adjective*, not strong, fragile, feeble, lacking strength

weak-ness [wēk′nĭs] *noun*, inclination, tendency

wealth [wĕlth] *noun*, riches, abundance of property

wealth-y [wĕl′thē] *adjective*, rich

wean [wēn] *verb*, 1) to accustom a baby not to nurse 2) to give up a cherished activity or habit

weap-on [wĕp′ən] *noun*, an instrument used for attack or defense in combat

wear [wâr] *noun*, 1) the diminished value caused by use, *verb*, 2) to put on, to carry on the body or over the body 3) to exhibit a certain expression on the face 4) to diminish through friction 5) to cause someone to be weary or exhausted 6) to impair by use

wear-y [wîr′ē] *adjective*, 1) tired, fatigued, physically or mentally exhausted 2) bored or resigned

weath-er [wĕth′ər] *noun*, 1) the condition of the atmosphere with regard to temperature, moisture, wind, etc., *verb*, 2) to endure the elements and the conditions outside in the atmosphere

weath-er-ing [wĕth′ər-ĭng] *noun*, the effects of the elements such as wind and water on rock surfaces, and homes or buildings

weave [wēv] *verb*, 1) to interlace threads into cloth 2) to wind or curve in and out

web [wĕb] *noun*, an entanglement, a mesh, an intricate network

web-li-og-ra-phy [wĕb′lē-ŏg′rə-fē] a bibliography of Internet sites used for research

we'd [wēd] the *contraction* of the words **we** and **would**

wed [wĕd] *verb*, to join in marriage

wed-ding [wĕd′ĭng] *noun*, the ceremony when two people are married

wedge [wĕj] *noun*, 1) a flat edge used to split objects or to lift them up 2) a chunk or a block of something, *verb*, 3) to force something to split apart 4) to press in closely, to cramp

Wednes-day [wĕnz′dē, -dā′] *noun*, the fourth day of the week

weed [wēd] *noun*, 1) an unwanted or unwelcome plant, *verb*, 2) to remove as being undesirable

week [wēk] *noun*, the seven days between Sunday and Saturday

weep [wēp] *verb*, 1) to cry, to shed tears 2) to grieve, to mourn 3) to exude liquid

weigh [wāt] *verb*, to measure the heaviness of someone or something by use of a scale

weight [wāt] *noun*, 1) the force with which a body is attracted to the earth or other celestial bodies 2) how heavy a thing is

weight-less [wāt′lĭs] *adjective*, having little or no weight

weird [wîrd] *adjective*, strange

wel-come [wĕl′kəm] *verb*, to receive gladly or hospitably

weld [wĕld] *verb*, 1) to join or connect by fusing two metals with heat 2) to unite

wel-fare [wĕl′fâr′] *noun*, assistance from the government, a state of well-being, health, happiness

well [wĕl] *adjective*, 1) healthy, strong, fit, *adverb*, 2) in a thoroughly manner, *noun*, 3) a narrow, deep hole made in the ground to reach water, oil, or natural gas, *verb*, 4) to rise to the surface and flow out

welt [wĕlt] *noun*, a large blister caused by heat or a beating

went [wĕnt] past participle of **go**

were [wûr] *past tense* of the *verb* **to be** used with **we**, **you** and **they**

west [wĕst] *noun*, the direction in which the sunsets

west-ern [wĕs′tərn] *adjective*, of or typical of Europe and the Americas

West Vir-gin-i-a [wĕst- vər-jĭn′yə] *noun*, one of the 50 United States, located in the Southeast, the capital is Charleston. The state flower of **West Virginia** is the great rhododendron, and the motto is "Mountaineers are always free."

wet [wĕt] *adjective*, 1) covered with water, moistened, *verb*, 2) to soak with water

wet-lands [wĕt′lăndz′] *noun*, *plural*, a habitat of swamps and marshes for wildlife

whale [hwāl] *noun*, the largest animal in the sea, it is not a fish, it feeds its young with milk

wharf [hwôrf] *noun*, a dock along a shore where boats moor and wait to load or unload

what [hwŏt, hwŭt, wŏt] *adjective*, 1) used to ask about the identity of a person, object, or matter 2) how remarkable, *adverb*, 3) how, in what way? *pronoun*, 4) which thing, an event, etc. 5) used to ask a question

what-ev-er [hwŏt-ĕv′ər] *pronoun*, anything that, so what

what's [hwŏts] the *contraction* of the words **what** and **is**

wheat [hwēt] *noun*, one of the cereal plants used to make flour

whee-dle [hwēd′l] *verb*, to coax

wheel [hwēl] *noun*, 1) a circular frame or disk attached to an axis that rolls, *verb*, 2) to move on rollers or wheels, to turn

wheel-bar-row [hwēl′băr′ō] *noun*, a hand cart with three wheels

when [hwĕn] *adverb*, at what time

when-ev-er [hwĕn-ĕv′ər] *adjective*, any time, no matter when

where

where [hwâr] *adverb*, 1) to or toward a certain place 2) at or in what place

wher-ev-er [hwâr-ĕv′ər] *adjective*, at or any place at all

whet [hwĕt] *verb*, 1) to sharpen by friction 2) to stimulate, to stir

wheth-er [hwĕth′ər] *conjunction*, used to express two choices

which [hwĭch] *noun*, the one, that

while [hwīl] *noun*, a period of time

whim-per [hwĭm′pər] *verb*, to pout, to whine, to cry

whim-si-cal [hwĭm′zĭ-kəl] *adjective*, capricious, given to fanciful notions, playful

whine [hwīn] *verb*, 1) to make a high and sad sound 2) to complain in an annoying manner

whip [hwĭp] *noun*, 1) an instrument made with a handle attached to a long lash made of leather or rope used to hit animals, *verb*, 2) to strike with a lash, to flog 3) to beat to a froth 4) to defeat

whirl [hwûrl] *verb*, to move or make something move around and around very fast

whisk [hwĭsk] *noun*, 1) a cooking utensil used to mix ingredients, *verb*, 2) to move quickly

whisk-er [hwĭs′kər] *noun*, 1) hair growing on the sides of a man's face 2) one of the long stiff hairs that grow near the mouth of dogs, cats, rats, etc.

whis-per [hwĭs′pər] *noun*, 1) a murmur, *verb*, 2) to speak very softly, to murmur quietly

whis-tle [hwĭs′əl] *noun*, 1) an instrument that makes a shrill, musical sound, *verb*, 2) to make a clear, high-pitched sound by

forcing breath through the teeth or by pursing the lips, or using a device

white [hwīt] *adjective*, the color of snow, the absence of pigment

whit-tle [hwĭt′l] *verb*, 1) to shape by carving or sculpting 2) to reduce gradually, to diminish

who [hoo] *pronoun*, 1) the person or people 2) that 3) what persons?

who-ev-er [hoo-ĕv′ər] *pronoun*, any one that

whole [hōl] *adjective*, 1) total, complete, *noun*, 2) the total amount of a thing or entity

whole-some [hōl′səm] *adjective*, sound, healthy, beneficial

whom [hoom] *pronoun*, objective case for **who**

whose [hooz] *pronoun*, of whom, possessive case of who

why [hwī] *adverb*, 1) for what reason or purpose, *noun*, 2) the cause or interaction

wick [wĭk] *noun*, the string in a candle or oil lamp that burns the flame, the fuse

wick-ed [wĭk′ĭd] *adjective*, evil, very bad, sinful, vicious

wide [wīd] *adjective*, 1) broad, expansive 2) to be fully open or accessible, of great scope

wid-ow [wĭd′ō] *noun*, a woman whose husband is dead

wid-ow-er [wĭd′ō-ər] *noun*, a man whose wife is dead

width [wĭdth] *noun*, the distance across, the breadth

wield [wēld] *verb*, to control, to sway, to manage, to use

wife [wīf] *noun*, *plural*, **wives,** a married woman

wig [wĭg] *noun*, a covering for the head, hair from other people or animals, a toupee, a hairpiece

wig-gle [wĭg'əl] *verb*, to move around, to squirm

wild [wīld] *adjective*, untamed or domesticated, a natural state

wil-der-ness [wĭl'dər-nĭs] *noun*, a tract of land undeveloped and uninhabited by people

wild-life [wīld'lĭf'] *noun*, any species of animals living in their natural habitat

will [wĭl] *noun*, 1) power in the mind or character, what we want to do 2) a declaration by a person concerning their estate, *verb*, 3) used with other verbs to show something is going to happen 4) used in questions when asking to do something

will-ful [wĭl'fəl] *adjective*, 1) determined, intentional, deliberate 2) obstinate, stubborn

will-ing [wĭl'ĭng] *adjective*, ready, given or done gladly

wil-low [wĭl'ō] *noun*, a tree with long drooping branches

wilt [wĭlt] *verb*, 1) to wither, to lose freshness 2) to lose strength

wil-y [wī'lē] *adjective*, sly, clever

win [wĭn] *verb*, 1) to achieve victory over others 2) to receive an award for a performance

wind [wĭnd] *noun*, 1) currents of air moving quickly with force, [wīnd] *verb*, 2) to wrap around over and over 3) to turn round

and round, to move in curves and bends, not a straight line

win-dow [wĭn'dō] *noun*, 1) a pane of glass 2) an opening with a transparent cover that allows light in

win-dow-sill [wĭn'dō-sĭl'] *noun*, a shelf or ledge below a window

wine [wīn] *noun*, an alcoholic drink made from fermented grapes

wing [wĭng] *noun*, 1) one of the two limbs of a bird or insect with which it flies 2) a side projection of an airplane 3) an extension of a building

wink [wĭngk] *noun*, 1) one eye closed and one eye open as a gesture of approval, *verb*, 2) to close and open one eye quickly

win-now [wĭn'ō] *verb*, to sift, to separate good parts from bad

win-some [wĭn'səm] *adjective*, agreeable, gracious, engaging

win-ter [wĭn'tər] *noun*, the first season of the year, between autumn and spring, when the earth is farthest from the sun

wipe [wīp] *verb*, to make dry or clean with a cloth

wire [wīr] *noun*, 1) a metal thread or strand, *verb*, 2) to connect

Wis-con-sin [wĭs-kŏn'sĭn] *noun*, one of the 50 United States located in the North, the capital city is Madison. The state flower of **Wisconsin** is the violet, and the motto is "Forward."

wis-dom [wĭz'dəm] *noun*, learning and the capacity to use it

wise [wīz] *adjective*, showing good judgment, intelligent

wish [wĭsh] *noun*, 1) a desire that is beyond your reach, *verb*, 2) to desire, to long for, to want

wist-ful [wĭst′fəl] *adjective*, hopeful, yearning, longing

wit [wĭt] *noun*, cleverness, quickness of mind, ingenuity

witch [wĭch] *noun*, a woman who is believed to have magic powers

with [wĭth] *preposition*, 1) in the company of 2) using it 3) having 4) because of 5) next to

with-draw [wĭth-drô′] *verb*, to retreat, to go back on or to take back an offer, to remove

with-drawn [wĭth-drôn′] *adjective*, 1) taken back, removed 2) shy, introverted, retiring

with-er [wĭth′ər] *verb*, to shrivel, to fade, to lose freshness

with-hold [wĭth-hōld′] *verb*, to restrain, to hold back

with-in [wĭth-ĭn′] *adverb*, 1)inside, *preposition*, 2) in, not beyond

with-out [wĭth-out′] *adverb*, 1) outside, *preposition*, 2) lacking, wanting, not having

wit-ness [wĭt′nĭs] *noun*, 1) a spectator, an onlooker, a person who sees something, *verb*, 2) to see, to observe, to hear

wiz-ard [wĭz′ərd] *noun*, someone who performs sorcery and magic

woe [wō] *noun*, self-pity, sadness

wolf [wŏŏlf] *noun*, *plural*, **wolves,** a wild dog similar to a coyote

wom-an [wŏŏm′ən] *noun*, *plural*, **women**, a female, a lady

won-der [wŭn′dər] *noun*, 1) a feeling of surprise and admiration, amazement, *verb*, 2) to express a wish to know

won-der-ful [wŭn′dər-fəl] *adjective*, extra special, very good, remarkable, marvelous

won-drous [wŭn′drəs] *adjective*, amazing, astonishing, marvelous

wont [wônt] *adjective,* 1) apt or likely, *noun,* 2) custom, habitual procedure

won't [wōnt] the *contraction* of the words **will** and **not**

wood [wŏŏd] *noun*, 1) the material which comes from trees 2) a small forest

wood-land [wŏŏd′lənd] *noun*, the forest, land covered with trees

wood-peck-er [wŏŏd′pĕk′ər] *noun*, a black and white bird with a red head that pecks at wood with its bill to find bugs to eat

wood-winds [wŏŏd′wĭndz′] *noun*, musical instruments, usually made of wood or metal, that you blow into or use a reed to play such as a clarinet

wool [wŏŏl] *noun*, the, soft, thick fur on a sheep often used for yarn or fabric

word [wûrd] *noun*, 1) speech, sound or symbol used to communicate 2) a message 3) a promise 4) news, information

work [wûrk] *noun*, 1) a job, a form of labor, a duty 2) a deed, an accomplishment, *verb,* 3) to do a job, to labor, to perform a duty

world [wûrld] *noun*, the Earth and its people and all living things

world-ly [wûrld′lē] *adjective*, known all over, cosmopolitan

worm [wûrm] *noun*, a thin creature without bones or legs that lives in the earth

wor-ry [wûr′ē] *verb*, to fret, to show concern, to feel anxious

worse [wûrs] *adjective*, to go from bad to a more damaged condition, inferior, less good or well

wor-ship [wûr′shĭp] *noun*, 1) ardent devotion, *verb*, 2) to pray to or show reverence or respect for someone

worth [wûrth] *noun*, the value or importance of something

worth-less [wûrth′lĭs] *adjective*, without worth, valueless

wor-thy [wûr′thē] *adjective*, admirable, deserving, noble

would [wŏŏd] future perfect tense of the *verb* **be**

wouldn't [wŏŏd′nt] the *contraction* of the words **would** and **not**

wound [wŏŏnd] *noun*, 1) an injury, *verb*, 2) to injure, to hurt 3) to disturb or upset someone

wrap [răp] *noun*, 1) a removable covering, *verb*, 2) to cover with a substance usually to protect something, to enclose

wrath [răth] *noun*, anger, fury

wreak [rēk] *verb*, to produce rage, to perpetuate, to inflict

wreath [rēth] *noun*, a ring of flowers and leaves

wreck [rĕk] *noun*, 1) the remains of something partially destroyed like a car, building, or ship, *verb*, 2) to destroy or damage something, to tear down

wren [rĕn] *noun*, a brown-grey bird that lives in the south

wrench [rĕnch] *noun*, 1) a tool used to grip a bolt or a nut 2) a forcible twist, *verb*, 3) to pull or turn suddenly with a violent twist, to damage or injure

wrest [rĕst] *verb*, 1) to pull away 2) to take away by force, to seize, to wrench away

wres-tle [rĕs′əl] *verb*, to struggle hand to hand, to grapple

wretch [rĕch] *noun*, a vile, disgusting person

wrig-gle [rĭg′əl] *verb*, to squirm or twist like a worm, to writhe

wring [rĭng] *verb*, to twist, to squeeze by twisting tightly

wrin-kle [rĭng′kəl] *noun*, 1) a crease or fold, *verb*, 2) to pucker into folds and creases

wrist [rĭst] *noun*, the joint between the hand and the forearm

write [rīt] *verb*, to use an instrument such as a pencil to draw symbols to communicate

writer [rī′tər] *noun*, author, journalist, newsperson

writhe [rīth] *verb*, to twist or move as if in pain, to thrash

wrong [rông *adjective*, 1) in error, mistaken, incorrect 2) contrary to morality or laws

wrote [rĭt′n] *past tense* of **write**

Wy-o-ming [wī-ō′mĭng] *noun*, one of the 50 United States, located in the Northwest, the capital is Cheyenne. The state flower of **Wyoming** is the indian paintbrush and the motto is "Equal rights."

X

xeno-phile [zĕn'ə-fīl'] *noun*, one attracted to foreign people, manners, and styles

xeno-pho-bi-a [zĕn'ə-fō'bē-ə] *noun*, fear and hatred of foreigners or strangers

xy-lem [zī'ləm] *noun*, the system of a woody tissue that transports water in a plant

xy-log-ra-phy [zī-lŏg'rə-fē] *noun*, the art of engraving on wood

x-ray [ĕks'rā'] *noun*, 1) a photograph of a part of the inside of your body, *verb*, 2) to take a picture of the inside of the body

xy-lo-phone [zailəfoun] *noun*, a percussion instrument played by striking horizontal wooden bars with small wooden hammers

Y

yacht [yät] *noun*, a boat used either for private pleasure or as a vessel of state to convey people from one place to another

yam [yăm] *noun*, a sweet potato, the root of a potato plant

yard [yärd] *noun*, 1) a length of measure equal to 36 inches 2) the lawn or property around someone's house

yarn [yärn] *noun*, 1) knitting thread, spun wool 2) a story, a fictional account

yawn [yôn] *verb*, to open the mouth wide and breathe deeply as if tired or bored

year [yîr] *noun*, 365 days, or each cycle that the earth rotates around the sun divided, into 12 months, 52 weeks, and 4 seasons

yearn [yûrn] *verb*, to strive, to long for, to desire something

yeast [yēst] *noun*, a fungus which produces fermentation, used as a leavening agent in dough

yell [yĕl] *verb*, to shout, to scream

yel-low [yĕl'ō] *noun*, one of the primary colors, the color of corn

yen [yĕn] *noun*, a longing, an urge

yes [yĕs] *interjection*, a word of agreement, an affirmative reply

yes-ter-day [yĕs'tər-dā'] *adverb*, 1) on the day before today, *noun*, 2) the day before today

yet [yĕt] *conjunctionb*, until now

yield [yēld] *verb*, 1) to give way to, to submit, to surrender 2) to produce, to supply, to give forth

yo-gurt [yō'gərt] *noun*, a dairy product that is thicker than milk and has a slightly sour taste

yolk [yōk] *noun*, the yellow and principal part inside an egg

yon-der [yŏn'dər] *adjective*, distant, far-off, faraway

you [yo͞o] *pronoun*, the person or persons spoken to

you'd [yo͞od] the *contraction* of the words **you** and **would**

you'll [yo͞ol] the *contraction* of the words **you** and **will**

young [yŭng] *adjective*, the early stage of life, not old

young-ster [yŭng'stər] *noun*, a very young person, a child

your [yŏŏr] *pronoun*, belonging to you

you're [yŏŏr] the *contraction* of the words, **you** and **are**

yours [yŏŏrz, yôrz, yōrz] *pronoun*, belonging to you

your-self [yŏŏr-sĕlf′] *pronoun*, a form of you for emphasis when the object of a verb and the subject are the same

youth [yōōth] *noun*, a young person, an adolescent

Z

za-ny [zā′nē] *adjective*, crazy, whimsically comical

zeal [zēl] *noun*, ardor in pursuit of anything, fervor, eagerness

zeal-ous [zĕl′əs] *adjective*, enthusiastic, eager, devoted

ze-bra [zē′brə] *noun*, an African wild animal like a horse which has brown and white stripes all over its body

Zen Buddhism [zĕn- bōō′dĭz′əm] *noun*, a faith in which Buddha is the embodiment of the superior man and followers seek enlightenment through meditation and intuition instead of the traditional scriptures

ze-nith [zē′nĭth] *noun*, the point directly overhead in the sky, the summit, the highest point

zeph-yr [zĕf′ər] *noun*, a gentle breeze, the west wind

ze-ro [zîr′ō] *noun, plural*, **zeros** or **zeroes**, 1) the numberical symbol 0 2) nothing 3) the temperature on a scale indicated by this symbol

zest [zĕst] *noun*, feeling of enjoyment, excitement

zinc [zĭngk] *noun*, a bluish white metallic element often mixed with other metals

zip-per [zĭp′ər] *noun*, a slide fastener for clothing, briefcases, and other objects, with two sets of interlocking teeth

zone [zōn] *noun*, a division of an area that differs or is distinguished in some respect from adjoining areas

zoo [zōō] *noun*, a place where different animals are kept for people to look at

zo-ol-o-gy [zō-ŏl′ə-jē] *noun*, the science of animals

zy-gote [zī′gōt′] *noun*, the single cell resulting from the union of an egg and a sperm

Punctuation

Punctuation marks and pauses are used to separate written or printed information into sentences and parts of sentences to assist the reader in understanding the meaning of the writer.

A **Period** (.) is placed at the end of a sentence; as,
God gives every bird his food but He doesn't throw it in the nest.

Nathan Hale, 1776

Or is used after an abbreviation; as
Dr. Johnson   Jan. 1, 2007

A **question mark** (?) indicates a question; as
Did you know that the average acre of lawn can use more than 3,000 gallons of water a week?
An **Exclamation Point** (!) denotes humor or strong feeling; as,
Forgive us our trespasses, Little creatures everywhere!

James Stephans

The **Comma** (,), **Semicolon** (;), and **Colon** (:) mark grammatical division in a sentence; as,
There are three kinds of water: freshwater, saltwater, and brackish water; a combination of saltwater and freshwater in tributaries at the mouth of the ocean.
A **comma** is used to list items in a series. The **colon** may separate two clauses when the second explains the first, and is also used before an explanatory list. The **semicolon** is used to separate two independent clauses when there is no conjunction. Sometimes it is called a weak period.

A **Hyphen** (-) is used between syllables in a word divided at the end of a line; as,
na-ture   wat-er
And between the parts of a compound word, as
self-improvement   absent-minded

The **Dash** (--) is used where there is a sudden break or pause in a sentence; as,

Apprentice yourself to nature—not a day will pass without her opening a new and wondrous world of experience to learn from and enjoy. Richard Langer

Quotation marks (" ") denote the words of another; as

"My name is Margalo," said the little bird softly in a musical voice. "I come from fields once tall with wheat, from pastures deep in fern and thistle; I come from vales of meadow-sweet, and I love to whistle." Stuart Little, E.B. White, 1985

An **apostrophe** (') denotes that a letter or letters are left out; as,

Whether it's on the farm or in the city, there's something inspirational about common folk banding together to work as a community to better their lives. E.E. Strickland

And is also used to show ownership; as

I feel I have a responsibility while I'm on this earth to preserve some beauty and pass it on to the next generation, because if I do not pass something on, these children and the children's children will have a barren world. Studs Terkel

Pronunciation Key

a̞,	for	ŏ,	as in	want	y̆,	for ĭ,	as in	chlorophyll
ê,	"	â,	"	tear	e,	" k,	"	character
e̞,	"	ā,	"	eight	ç,	" s,	"	city
ï,	"	ē,	"	police	çh,	" sh,	"	chivalry
ī̞,	"	ē,	"	sir	eh,	" k,	"	chorus
ȯ,	"	ŭ,	"	ton	ǧ,	" j,	"	general
o̞,	"	o͞o,	"	do	n̠,	" ng,	"	sang
ọ,	"	o͝o,	"	book	s̠,	" z,	"	hands
ô,	"	a̞,	"	pork	s,	" sh,	"	sure
õ,	"	û,	"	worm	x̠,	" ḡz,	"	example
u̞,	"	o͝o,	"	pull	gh,	" f,	"	laugh
u̠,	"	o͞o,	"	rule	ph,	" f,	"	phone
y̆,	"	ī,	"	try	qu,	" k.	"	plaque

qu, for kw, as in quiet

357

Weights and Measures

__ENGLISH__

__Length__
12 inches	=	1 foot
3 feet	=	1 yard
5280 feet	=	1 mile
1760 yards	=	1 mile

__Area__
144 square inches	=	1 square foot
9 square feet	=	1 square yard
4840 square yards	=	1 acre
640 acres	=	1 square mile

__Volume__
1728 cubic inches	=	1 cubic foot
27 cubic feet	=	1 cubic yard

__Capacity__ (Dry)
2 pints	=	1 quart
8 quarts	=	1 peck
4 pecks	=	1 bushel

__Capacity__ (Liquid)
16 fluid ounces	=	1 pint
2 pints	=	1 quart
4 quarts	=	1 gallon (8 pints)

__Mass__
16 ounces	=	1 pound (7000 grains)
20 cwt	=	1 ton
2000 lbs	=	1 ton

__Troy Weights__
12 ounces	=	1 pound (5760 grains)

__Measures__
16 fluid ounces	=	1 pint

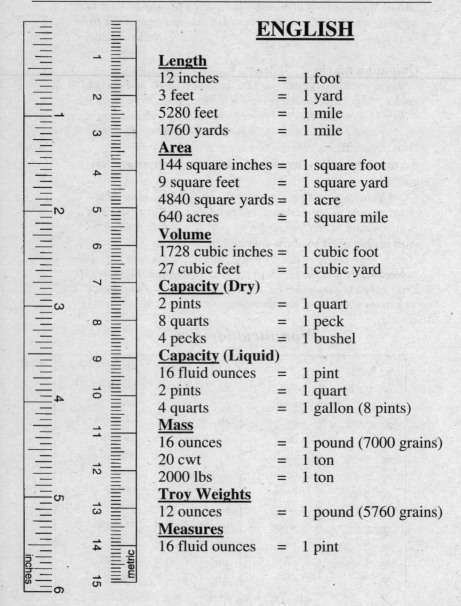

METRIC

Length

1 millimeter	=	1000 micrometers
1 centimeter	=	10 millimeters
1 meter	=	1000 millimeters
1 meter	=	100 centimeters
1 kilometer	=	1000 meters

Area

1 square centimeter	=	100 square millimeters
1 square meter	=	10,000 square centimeters
1 square meter	=	1,000,000 square millimeters
1 square kilometer	=	1,000,000 square meters

Volume

1 milliliter	=	1 cubic centimeter
1 liter	=	1000 milliliters
1 liter	=	0.001 cubic meter

Mass

1 gram	=	1000 milligrams
1 kilogram	=	1000 grams
1 metric ton	=	1000 kilograms

Volume

1 cubic inch (in^3) = 16.39 cubic centimeters (cm^3)

1,728 cubic inches = 1 cubic foot = 0.02832 cubic meters (m^3)

27 cubic feet (ft^3) = 1 cubic yard (y^3) = 0.7646 cubic meters

Temperature Conversions

°C Celsius = (5/9 °F) –32   °F Fahrenheit = (9/5 °C) +32

Square Measure

100 sq. meters = 1 sq. decameter = 119.6 sq. yards

100 sq. decameters = 1 sq. hectometer = 2.471 acres

100 sq. hectometers = 1 sq. kilometer = 0.386 sq. miles or
247.1 acres

Periodic Table of the Elements

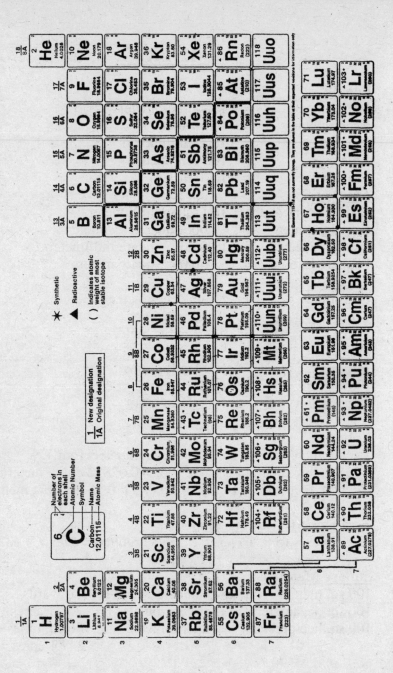

Alabama (AL)

The Yellowhammer State

Capital	Montgomery
Size	52,419 square miles
Population	4,486,508

Amphibian	*Red Hills Salamander*	*2000*
Bird	*Yellowhammer*	*1927*
Freshwater Fish	*Largemouth Bass*	*1975*
Saltwater Fish	*Tarpon*	*1955-*
Insect	*Monarch Butterfly*	*1989*
Mammal	*Racking Horse*	
Reptile	*Red-Bellied Turtle*	*1990*

Zoo Location: Birmingham; Montgomery

Alaska (AK)

The Last Frontier

Capital	Juneau
Size	663,267 square miles
Population	643,786

Amphibian	*none*	
Bird	*Willow Ptarmigan*	*1955*
Fish	*King Salmon*	*1962*
Insect	*Four Spot Skimmer Dragonfly*	*1995*
Land Mammal	*Moose*	*1998*
Marine Mammal	*Bowhead Whale*	*1983*
Reptile	*none*	

Arizona (AZ)

The Grand Canyon State

Capital	Phoenix
Size	114,006 square miles
Population	5,456,453

Amphibian	*Arizona Tree Frog*	*1986*
Bird	*Cactus Wren*	*1931*
Fish	*Apache Trout*	*1986*
Insect	*Two-Tailed Swallowtail*	*2001*
Mammal	*Ringtail*	*1986*
Reptile	*Arizona Ridge-Nosed Rattlesnake*	*1986*

Zoo Locations: Arizona Sonora Desert Museum (Tucson)
The Phoenix Zoo
Reid Park Zoo (Tucson)
Wildlife World Zoo (Litchfield Park)

Arkansas (AR)

The Land of Opportunity

Capital	Little Rock
Size	53,182 square miles
Population	2,710,079

Amphibian	*none*	
Bird	*Mockingbird*	*1929*
Fish	*none*	
Insect	*Honeybee*	*1973*
Mammal	*White-Tailed Deer*	*1993*
Reptile	*none*	

Zoo Location: Little Rock Zoological Garden

California (CA)

The Golden State

Capital	Sacramento
Size	163,696 square miles
Population	35,116,033

Amphibian	*none*	
Bird	*California Valley Quail*	*1931*
Freshwater Fish	*California Golden Trout*	*1947*
Saltwater Fish	*Garibaldi*	
Insect	*California Dogface Butterfly*	*1972*
Land Mammal	*California Grizzly Bear*	*1953*
Marine Mammal	*California Gray Whale*	*1975*
Reptile	*Desert Tortoise*	*1972*

Aquariums: Aquarium of the Bay (San Francisco), Aquarium of the Pacific (Long Beach), Birch Aquarium at Scripps (LaJolla), Cabrillo Marine Aquarium (San Pedro), Monterey Bay Aquarium, Steinhart Aquarium(San Francisco)

Zoo Locations: Chaffee Zoological Gardens (Fresno), Charles Paddock Zoo (Atascadero), Coyote Point Museum (San Mateo), Happy Hollow Zoo (San Jose), The Living Desert (Palm Desert), Los Angeles Zoo, Micke Grove Zoo (Lodi),Oakland Zoo, Sacramento Zoo, San Diego Wild Animal Park, San Diego Zoo, San Francisco Zoological Gardens, Santa Ana Zoo, Santa Barbara Zoological Gardens, Sea World San Diego, Sequoia Park Zoo, Six Flags Marine World/Africa USA (Vallejo)

Colorado (CO)

The Centennial State

Capital	Denver
Size	104,100 square miles
Population	4,506,542

Amphibian	*none*	
Bird	*Lark Bunting*	*1931*
Fish	*Greenback Cutthroat Trout*	*1994*
Insect	*Colorado Hairstreak Butterfly*	*1996*
Mammal	*Rocky Mountain Bighorn Sheep*	*1961*
Reptile	*none*	

Aquarium: Landry's Downtown Aquarium (Denver)

Zoo Locations: Cheyenne Mountain Zoological Park (Colorado Springs) Denver Zoological Gardens, Pueblo Zoo

Connecticut (CT)

The Constitution State

Capital	Hartford
Size	5,544 square miles
Population	3,460,503

Amphibian	*none*	
Bird	*American Robin*	*1943*
Fish	*American Shad*	
Insect	*Praying Mantis*	*1997*
Mammal	*Sperm Whale*	*1975*
Reptile	*none*	

Aquarium: Mystic Aquarium & Institute for Exploration

Zoo Locations: Connecticut's Beardsley Zoo (Bridgeport), Denver Zoological Gardens

Delaware (DE)

The First State

Capital	Dover
Size	2,489 square miles
Population	807,385

Amphibian	*none*	
Marine Animal	*Horseshoe Crab*	*2002*
Bird	*Blue Hen Chicken*	*1939*
Insect	*Ladybug*	*1974*
Fish	*Weakfish*	*1981*
Mammal	*none*	
Reptile	*none*	

Zoo Location: Brandywine Zoo (Wilmington)

Florida (FL)

The Sunshine State

Capital	Tallahassee
Size	65,755 square miles
Population	16,713,149

Amphibian	*none*	
Bird	*Mockingbird*	1927
Freshwater Fish	*Largemouth Bass*	1975
Saltwater Fish	*Atlantic Sailfish*	1975
Insect	*Zebra Long Wing Butterfly*	1996
Land Mammal	*Florida Panther*	1982
Marine Mammal	*Manatee(sea cow)*	1975
Reptile	*American Alligator*	1987

Aquariums: The Florida Aquarium (Tampa Bay), Living Seas (Lake Buena Vista), Mote Marine Lab (Sarasota), Sea World (Orlando)

Zoo Locations: Brevard Zoo (Melbourne), Busch Gardens (Tampa), Caribbean Gardens (Naples) Central Florida Zoological Park (Lake Monroe), Disney's Animal Kingdom, (Orlando) Jacksonville Zoological Park, Lion Country Safari (west Palm Beach) Lowry Park Zoological Garden (Tampa), Miami Metrozoo, Palm Beach Zoo at Dreher Park (West Palm Beach) Santa Fe Community College Teaching Zoo (Gainesville) St Augustine Alligator Farm, The Zoo (Gulf Breeze)

Georgia (GA)

The Peach State

Capital	Atlanta
Size	59,425 square miles
Population	8,560,310

Amphibian	*Green Tree Frog*	
Bird	*Brown Thrasher*	1970
Fish	*Largemouth Bass*	1970
Insect	*Honeybee*	1975
Mammal	*Right Whale*	1985
Reptile	*Gopher Tortoise*	1989

Aquarium: Georgia Aquarium, Atlanta
Zoo Locations: Chehaw Wild Animal Park (Albany)
Zoo, Atlanta

Hawaii (HI)

The Aloha State

Capital	Honolulu
Size	10,931 square miles
Population	1,244,898

Amphibian	none	
Bird	Nene (Hawaiian Goose)	1988
Fish	Humuhumunukunukuapua'a (Hawaiian Trigger Fish)	1985
Insect	none	
Mammal	Humpback Whale	1979
Reptile	none	

Aquarium: Waikiki Aquarium (Honolulu)

Zoo Locations: Honolulu Zoo, Sea Life Park (Waimanalo)

Idaho (ID)

The Gem State

Capital	Boise
Size	83,574 square miles
Population	1,341,131

Amphibian	none	
Bird	Mountain Bluebird	1931
Fish	Cutthroat Trout	1990
Insect	Monarch Butterfly	1992
Mammal	Appaloosa Horse	
Reptile	none	

Zoo Locations: Tautphaus Park Zoo, Zoo Boise

Illinois (IL)

Capital	Springfield
Size	57,918 square miles
Population	12,600,620

Amphibian	*none*	
Bird	*Cardinal*	*1929*
Fish	*Bluegill*	*1986*
Insect	*Monarch Butterfly*	*1975*
Mammal	*White-Tailed Deer*	*1982*
Reptile	*none*	

Aquarium: John G. Shedd Aquarium

Zoo Locations: Brookfield Zoo, Cosley Zoo (Wheaton), Glen Oak Zoo (Peoria), Henson Robinson Zoo (Springfield), Lincoln Park Zoological Gardens (Chicago), Miller Park Zoo(Bloomington), Scovill Zoo (Decatur)

Indiana (IN)

Capital	Indianapolis
Size	36,420 square miles
Population	6,159,068

Amphibian	*none*	
Bird	*Cardinal*	*1933*
Fish	*none*	
Insect	*none*	
Mammal	*none*	
Reptile	*none*	

Zoo Locations: Fort Wayne Children's Zoo, Indianapolis Zoological Society, Inc., Mesker Park, Zoo & Botanical Garden (Evansville), Potawatomi Zoo (South Bend)

Iowa (IA)

The Hawkeye State

Capital	Des Moines
Size	56,276 square miles
Population	2,936,760

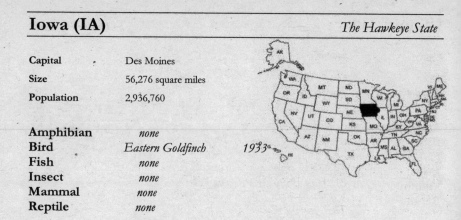

Amphibian	*none*	
Bird	*Eastern Goldfinch*	*1933*
Fish	*none*	
Insect	*none*	
Mammal	*none*	
Reptile	*none*	

Zoo Location: Blank Park Zoo (Des Moines)

Kansas (KS)

The Sunflower State

Capital	Topeka
Size	82,282 square miles
Population	2,715,884

Amphibian	*Barred Tiger Salamander*	*1994*
Bird	*Western Meadowlark*	*1937*
Fish	*Channel Catfish*	*2003*
Insect	*Honeybee*	*1976*
Mammal	*American Buffalo (Bison)*	*1955*
Reptile	*Ornate Box Turtle*	*1986*

Zoo Locations: Emporia Zoo, Hutchinson Zoo,
Lee Richardson Zoo (Garden City), Rolling Hills Refuge Wildlife
Conservation Center (Salina), Sedgwick County Zoo (Wichita),
Sunset Zoological Park (Manhattan), Topeka Zoo

Kentucky (KY)

Capital	Frankfort
Size	40,411 square miles
Population	4,092,891

Amphibian	*none*	
Bird	*Cardinal*	*1926*
Fish	*Kentucky Spotted Bass*	*1956*
Insect	*Viceroy Butterfly*	*1990*
Mammal	*Thoroughbred Horse*	
Reptile	*none*	

Aquarium: Newport Aquarium

Zoo Location: Louisville Zoological Park

Louisiana (LA)

The Pelican State

Capital	Baton Rouge
Size	51,840 square miles
Population	4,482,646

Amphibian	*Green Tree Frog*	*1993*
Bird	*Brown Pelican*	*1966*
Saltwater Fish:	*Spotted Sea Trout or Speckled Trout*	*2001*
Freshwater Fish	*White Perch*	*1993*
Insect	*Honeybee*	*1977*
Mammal	*Black Bear*	*1992*
Reptile	*Alligator*	*1983*

Aquarium: Aquarium of the Americas (New Orleans)

Zoo Locations: Alexandria Zoological Park, Audubon Park and Zoological Garden (New Orleans), Brec's Baton Rouge Zoo

Maine (ME)

The Pine Tree State

Capital	Augusta
Size	35,385 square miles
Population	1,294,464

Amphibian	*none*	
Bird	*Black-Capped Chickadee*	*1927*
Fish	*Landlocked Salmon*	*1969*
Insect	*Honeybee*	*1975*
Mammal	*Moose*	*1979*
Reptile	*none*	

Maryland (MD)

The Old Line State

Capital	Annapolis
Size	12,407 square miles
Population	5,458,137

Amphibian	*none*	
Bird	*Baltimore Oriole*	*1947*
Fish	*Rockfish (Striped Bass)*	*1965*
Insect	*Baltimore Checkerspot Butterfly*	*1973*
Mammal	*Thoroughbred Horse*	
Reptile	*Diamondback Terrapin*	*1994*

Aquarium: National Aquarium in Baltimore

Zoo Locations: Baltimore Zoo
Salisbury Zoological Zoo

Massachusetts (MA)

The Bay State

Capital	Boston
Size	10,555 square miles
Population	6,427,801

Amphibian	*none*	
Bird	*Black-Capped Chickadee*	*1941*
Fish	*Atlantic Cod*	*1974*
Insect	*Ladybug*	*1974*
Mammal	*Right Whale*	*1980*
Reptile	*Bushmaster Viper*	

Zoo Locations: Butterwood Park Zoo (New Bedford), Capron Park Zoo (Attleboro), Franklin Park Zoo (Boston), Museum of Science (Boston)

Michigan (MI)

The Wolverine State

Capital	Lansing
Size	96,705 square miles
Population	10,050,446

Amphibian	*none*	
Bird	*Robin*	*1931*
Fish	*Brook Trout*	*1988*
Insect	*none*	
Mammal	*White-Tailed Deer*	*1997*
	Wolverine	
Reptile	*Painted Turtle*	*1995*

Aquarium: Belle Isle Aquarium (Detroit)

Zoo Locations: Binder Park Zoo(Battle Creek), Detroit Zoological Gardens(Grand Rapids), Potter Park Zoological Gardens (Lansing)

Minnesota (MN)

The Land of 10, 000 Lakes

Capital	Saint Paul
Size	86,943 square miles
Population	5,019,720

Amphibian	*none*	
Bird	*Common Loon*	*1961*
Insect	*Monarch Butterfly*	*2000*
Fish	*Walleye Pike*	*1965*
Mammal	*none*	
Reptile	*Blanding's Turtle*	

Zoo Locations: Lake Superior Zoological Gardens (Duluth)
Minnesota Zoological Garden (Apple Valley),
St. Paul's Como Zoo

Mississippi (MS)

The Magnolia State

Capital	Jackson
Size	48,430 square miles
Population	2,871,782

Amphibian	*none*	
Bird	*Mockingbird*	*1944*
Fish	*Largemouth Bass*	*1974*
Insect	*Honeybee*	*1980*
Land Mammal	*White-Tailed Deer*	*1974*
	Red Fox	*1997*
Marine Mammal	*Bottlenose Dolphin*	*1974*
Reptile	*none*	

Zoo Location: Jackson Zoological Park

Missouri (MO)

Capital	Jefferson City
Size	69,709 square miles
Population	5,672,579

Amphibian	*North American Bullfrog*	
Aquatic Animal	*Paddlefish or Spoonbill*	*1997*
Bird	*Bluebird*	*1927*
Fish	*Channel Catfish*	*1997*
Insect	*Honeybee*	*1985*
Mammal	*Missouri Mule*	*1995*
Reptile	*none*	

Zoo Locations: American National Fish and Wildlife Museum (Springfield) The Butterfly House (Chesterfield), Dickerson Park Zoo(Springfield) Kansas City Zoo, St. Louis Zoological Park

Montana (MT)

Capital	Helena
Size	147,046 square miles
Population	909,453

Amphibian	*none*	
Bird	*Western Meadowlark*	*1931*
Fish	*Black Spotted Cutthroat Trout*	*1977*
Insect	*Mourning Cloak Butterfly*	
Mammal	*Grizzly Bear*	*1983*
Reptile	*none*	

Zoo Locations: Grizzly Discovery Center (West Yellowstone) Zoo Montana (Billings)

Nebraska (NE)

The Cornhusker State

Capital	Lincoln
Size	77,358 square miles
Population	1,729,180

Amphibian	*none*	
Bird	*Western Meadowlark*	*1931*
Fish	*Channel Catfish*	*1997*
Insect	*Honeybee*	*1975*
Mammal	*White-Tailed Deer*	*1981*
Reptile	*none*	

Zoo Locations: Folsom Children' Zoo (Lincoln)
Omaha's Henry Doorly Zoo
Riverside Zoo (Scottsbluff)

Nevada (NV)

The Silver State

Capital	Carson City
Size	110,567 square miles
Population	2,173,491

Amphibian	*none*	
Bird	*Mountain Bluebird*	*1967*
Fish	*Lahontan Cutthroat Trout*	*1981*
Insect	*none*	
Mammal	*Desert Bighorn Sheep*	*1973*
Reptile	*Desert Tortoise*	*1989*

Aquarium Shark Reef at Mandalay Bay (Las Vegas)

New Hampshire (NH)

The Granite State

Capital	Concord	
Size	9,283 square miles	
Population	1,275,056	

Amphibian	*Spotted Newt*	*1985*
Bird	*Purple Finch*	*1957*
Freshwater Fish	*Brook Trout*	*1994*
Saltwater Fish	*Striped Bass*	*1994*
Insect	*Ladybug*	*1977*
Mammal	*White Tailed Deer*	*1983*
Reptile	*none*	

New Jersey (NJ)

The Garden State

Capital	Trenton	
Size	8,721 square miles	
Population	8,590,300	

Amphibian	*none*	
Bird	*Eastern Goldfinch*	*1935*
Fish	*Brook Trout*	*1991*
Insect	*Honeybee*	*1974*
Mammal	*Horse*	*1977*
Reptile	*none*	

Aquarium: New Jersey Aquarium (Camden)

Zoo Locations: Bergen County Zoological Park (Paramus)
Cape May County Park Zoo (Cape May)

New Mexico (NM)

Land of Enchantment

Capital	Santa Fe
Size	121,598 square miles
Population	1,855,059

Amphibian *New Mexico Spadefoot Toad*

Bird	*Road Runner (or Chaparral Bird)*	1949
Fish	*New Mexico Cutthroat Trout*	1955
Insect	*Tarantula Hawk Wasp*	1989
Mammal	*Black Bear*	1963
Reptile	*none*	

Zoo Locations: Alameda Park Zoo
Albuquerque Biological Park (Alamogordo)
The Living Desert Zoo (Carlsbad)

New York (NY)

The Empire State

Capital	Albany
Size	54,556 square miles
Population	19,157,532

Amphibian	*none*	
Bird	*Eastern Bluebird*	1970
Fish	*Brook Trout or Speckled Trout*	1975
Insect	*Ladybug*	1989
Mammal	*Beaver*	1975
Reptile	*none*	

Aquarium: New York Aquarium

Zoo Locations: Bronx Zoo/Wildlife Conservation Society (WCS)Buffalo Zoological Gardens, Central Park Zoo, New York State Living Museum (Watertown), Prospect Park Wildlife Center (Brooklyn), Queens Zoo, Rosamond Gifford Zoo at Burnet Park Zoo (Syracuse), Ross Park Zoo (Binghamton) Seneca Park Zoo (Rochester), Staten Park Zoo, Trevor Zoo (Millbrook), Utica Zoo

North Carolina (NC)

The Tar Heel State

Capital	Raleigh	
Size	53,819 square miles	
Population	8,320,146	

Amphibian	*none*	
Bird	*Cardinal*	*1943*
Fish	*Channel Bass (Red Drum)*	*1971*
Insect	*Honeybee*	*1973*
Mammal	*Gray Squirrel*	*1969*
Reptile	*Eastern Box Turtle*	*1979*

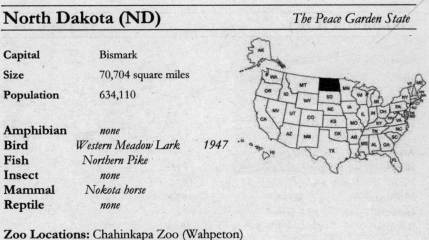

Aquariums: North Carolina Aquarium at Fort Fisher (Kure Beach), North Carolina Aquarium at Pine Knoll Shores, North Carolina Aquarium on Roanoke Island (Manteo)

Zoo Locations: North Carolina Zoological Park (Asheboro), western North Carolina Nature Center (Ashville)

North Dakota (ND)

The Peace Garden State

Capital	Bismark	
Size	70,704 square miles	
Population	634,110	

Amphibian	*none*	
Bird	*Western Meadow Lark*	*1947*
Fish	*Northern Pike*	
Insect	*none*	
Mammal	*Nokota horse*	
Reptile	*none*	

Zoo Locations: Chahinkapa Zoo (Wahpeton)
Dakota Zoo (Bismarck)
Roosevelt Park Zoo (Minot)

Ohio (OH)

The Buckeye State

Capital	Columbus
Size	44,828 square miles
Population	11,421,267

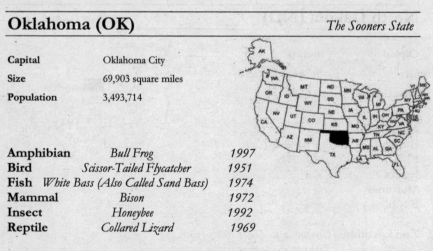

Amphibian	*none*	
Bird	*Cardinal*	*1933*
Fish	*none*	
Insect	*Ladybug*	*1975*
Mammal	*White-Tailed Deer*	*1988*
Reptile	*Black Racer Snake*	*1995*

Zoo Locations: African Safari Wildlife Park (Port Clinton)
Akron Zoological Park, Boonshoft Museum of Discovery (Dayton)
Cincinnati Zoo and Botanical Garden, Cleveland Metroparks Zoo,
Columbus Zoological Gardens, Six Flags Worlds of Adventure (Aurora),
Toledo Zoological Gardens, The Wilds (Cumberland)

Oklahoma (OK)

The Sooners State

Capital	Oklahoma City
Size	69,903 square miles
Population	3,493,714

Amphibian	*Bull Frog*	*1997*
Bird	*Scissor-Tailed Flycatcher*	*1951*
Fish	*White Bass (Also Called Sand Bass)*	*1974*
Mammal	*Bison*	*1972*
Insect	*Honeybee*	*1992*
Reptile	*Collared Lizard*	*1969*

Zoo Locations: Oklahoma City Zoological Park
Tulsa Zoo and Living Museum

Oregon (OR)

The Beaver State

Capital	Salem
Size	98,381 square miles
Population	3,521,515

Amphibian	*none*	
Bird	*Western Meadow Lark*	*1927*
Fish	*Chinook Salmon*	*1961*
Insect	*Oregon Swallowtail Butterfly*	*1979*
Mammal	*Beaver*	*1969*

Aquarium: Oregon Coast Aquarium (Newport)

Zoo Locations: Oregon Zoo
Wildlife Safari (Winston)

Pennsylvania (PA)

The Keystone State

Capital	Harrisburg
Size	46,058 square miles
Population	12,335,091

Amphibian	*none*	
Bird	*Ruffed Grouse*	*1931*
Fish	*Brook Trout*	*1970*
Insect	*Firefly*	*1974*
Mammal	*White Tailed Deer*	*1959*
Reptile	*none*	

Aquarium: Pittsburgh Zoo and PPG Aquarium

Zoo Locations: Clyde Peeling's Reptiland (Allenwood)
Elmwood Park Zoo (Norristown), Erie Zoo, National Aviary in Pittsburgh,
Philadelphia Zoo, Zooamerica North America Wildlife Park (Hershey)

Rhode Island (RI)   *The Ocean State*

Capital   Providence

Size   1,545 square miles

Population   1,069,725

Amphibian	*none*	
Bird	*Rhode Island Red*	*1954*
Fish	*Stripped Bass*	*2000*
Insect	*none*	
Mammal	*none*	
Reptile	*none*	

Zoo Location: Roger Williams Park Zoo (Providence)

South Carolina (SC)   *The Palmetto State*

Capital   Columbia

Size   32,020 square miles

Population   4,107,183

Amphibian	*Spotted Salamander*	*1999*
Bird	*Carolina Wren*	*1948*
Fish	*Striped Bass*	*1972*
Insect	*Carolina Mantid (Praying Mantis)*	*1988*
Mammal	*White Tailed Deer*	*1972*
Reptile	*Loggerhead Sea Turtle*	*1988*

Aquariums: Ripley's Aquarium at Myrtle Beach
South Carolina Aquarium (Charleston)

Zoo Locations: Brookgreen Gardens (Pawley's Island)
Greenville Zoo
Riverbanks Zoological Park (Columbia)

South Dakota (SD)

The Mount Rushmore State

Capital	Pierre
Size	77,121 square miles
Population	761,063

Amphibian	*none*	
Bird	*Chinese Ring-Necked Pheasant*	*1943*
Fish	*Walleye*	*1982*
Insect	*Honeybee*	*1978*
Mammal	*Coyote*	*1949*
Reptile	*none*	

Zoo Locations: Bramble Park Zoo (Watertown)
Great Plains Zoo and Delbridge Museum (Sioux Falls)

Tennessee (TN)

The Volunteer State

Capital	Nashville
Size	42,146 square miles
Population	5,797,280

Amphibian	*Tennessee Cave Salamander*	*1995*
Bird	*Mockingbird*	*1933*
Fish	*Largemouth Bass*	*1988*
Insect	*Firefly, Ladybug and Honeybee*	*1975*
Mammal	*Raccoon*	*1972*
Reptile	*Eastern Box Turtle*	*1995*

Aquariums: Ripley's Aquarium of the Smokies (Gatlinburg)
Tennessee Aquarium (Chattanooga)

Zoo Locations: Chattanooga Zoo at Warner Park, Knoxville Zoological
Gardens, Memphis Zoological Garden and Aquarium

Texas (TX)

Capital	Austin
Size	268,581 square miles
Population	21,779,893

Amphibian	*none*	
Bird	*Mockingbird*	1927
Fish	*Guadalupe Bass*	1989
Insect	*Monarch Butterfly*	1995
Mammal (Large)	*Texas Longhorn*	1995
Mammal (Small)	*Nine-Banded Armadillo*	1995
Flying Mammal	*Mexican Free-Tailed Bat*	1995
Reptile	*Horned Lizard*	1993

Aquariums: Dallas World Aquarium, Moody Gardens Rainforest and   Aquarium (Galveston Island), SeaWorld San Antonio, Texas State Aquarium (Corpus Christi)

Zoo Locations: Abilene Zoological Gardens, Caldwell Zoo (Tyler), Cameron Park Zoo (Waco), Dallas Zoo, El Paso Zoo, Ellen Trout Zoo (Lufkin), Fort Worth Zoological Park, Fossil Rim Wildlife Center (Glen Rose), Gladys Porter Zoo (Brownsville), Houston Zoological Gardens, San Antonio Zoo and Aquarium, The Texas Zoo (Victoria)

Utah (UT)

Capital	Salt Lake City
Size	84,904 square miles
Population	2,316,256

Amphibian	*none*	
Bird	*California Gull*	1955
Fish	*Bonneville Cutthroat Trout*	1997
Insect	*Honeybee*	1983
Mammal	*Rocky Mountain Elk*	1971
Reptile	*none*	

Zoo Locations: Tracy Aviary (Salt Lake City)
Utah's Hogle Zoo (Salt Lake City)

Vermont (VT)

The Green Mountain State

Capital	Montpelier
Size	9,615 square miles
Population	616,592

Amphibian	*Northern Leopard Frog*	*1997*
Bird	*Hermit Thrush*	*1941*
Cold Water Fish	*Brook Trout*	*1978*
Warm water Fish	*Walleye Pike*	*1978*
Insect	*Honeybee*	*1977*
Mammal	*Morgan Horse*	*1961*
Reptile	*none*	

Virginia (VA)

Old Dominion State

Capital	Richmond
Size	42,774 square miles
Population	7,293,542

Amphibian	*none*	
Bird	*Cardinal*	*1950*
Fish	*Brook Trout*	*1993*
Insect	*Tiger Swallowtail butterfly*	*1991*
Mammal	*American Fox Hound*	
Reptile	*none*	

Aquarium: Virginia Marine Science Museum (Virginia Beach)

Zoo Locations: Mill Mountain Zoo (Roanoke),
Virginia Zoological Park (Norfolk)

383

Washington (WA)

Evergreen State

Capital	Olympia
Size	71,300 square miles
Population	6,068,996

Amphibian	*none*	
Bird	*Willow Goldfinch*	*1951*
Fish	*Steelhead Trout*	*1969*
Insect	*Green Darner Dragonfly*	*1997*
Mammal	*none*	
Reptile	*none*	

Aquarium: Seattle Aquarium

Zoo Locations: Northwest Trek Wildlife Park (Eatonville), Point Defiance Zoo and Aquarium (Tacoma), Woodland Park Zoological Gardens (Seattle)

West Virginia (WV)

Mountain State

Capital	Charleston
Size	24,231 square miles
Population	1,801,873

Amphibian	*none*	
Bird	*Cardinal*	*1949*
Fish	*Brook Trout*	*1973*
Insect	*Honeybee*	
Mammal	*Black Bear*	*1973*
Reptile	*none*	

Zoo Location: Oglebay's Good Zoo (Wheeling)

Wisconsin (WI)

The Badger State

Capital	Madison
Size	65,499 square miles
Population	5,441,196

Amphibian	*none*	
Bird	*Robin*	*1949*
Fish	*Muskellunge*	*1955*
Insect	*Honeybee*	*1977*
Mammal	*Dairy Cow*	*1971*
Reptile	*none*	

Zoo Locations: International Crane Foundation (Baraboo)
Racine Zoological Gardens, Henry Vilas Zoo (Madison)
Milwaukee County Zoological Gardens
Northeastern Wisconsin (NEW) Zoo (Green Bay)

Wyoming (WY)

The Equality State

Capital	Cheyenne
Size	97,818 square miles
Population	498,703

Amphibian	*none*	
Bird	*Western Meadowlark*	*1927*
Fish	*Cutthroat Trout*	*1987*
Insect	*none*	
Mammal	*Buffalo (Bison)*	*1985*
Reptile	*Horned Toad*	*1993*

MAPS OF THE WORLD

The World

Total area: 510.072 million sq km (316.96 million sq mi).

Land area: 148.94 million sq km (92.55 million sq mi).

Water area: 361.132 million sq km (224.41 million sq mi).
Note: 70.8% of the world is water, 29.2% is land.

The Four Oceans:
Pacific Ocean: 64,186,300 square miles; 12,925 feet deep
Atlantic Ocean: 33,420,000 square miles; 11,730 feet deep
Indian Ocean: 28,350,500 square miles; 12,598 feet deep
Arctic Ocean: 5,105,700 square miles; 3,407 feet deep

- **Terrain:** Highest elevation is Mt. Everest at 8,850 m (29,035 ft) and lowest land depression is the Dead Sea at −411 m (−1,349 ft) below sea level.

- **Land use:** Arable land: 10%. Permanent crops: 1%. Meadows and pastures: 26%. Forests and woodlands: 32%. Other: 31% (1993 est.). Irrigated land: 2,481,250 sq km (1,541,849 sq mi).

* **Note**: *The maps of the world and the seven continents are from The World Factbook 2003.*

ASIA

Asia measures 16,990,000 square miles and holds 61% of the world's population. Asia is comprised of many countries including Russia, China, Mongolia, Iran and India.

AUSTRALIA

Australia, the only continent that is also a country, measures 2,978,000 square miles. It is in the Southern Hemisphere and holds .5% of the world's population.

AFRICA

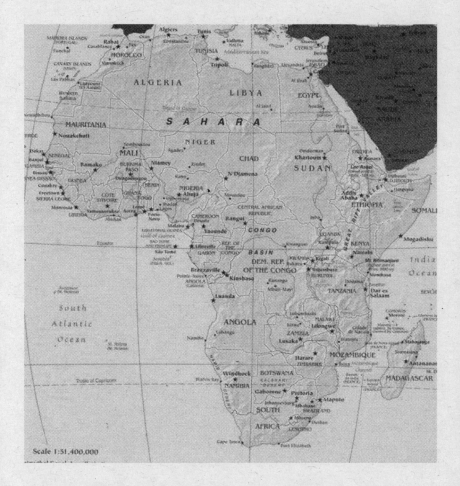

Scale 1:51,400,000

Africa measures 11,657,000 square miles and holds 12.7% of the world's population. The equator goes right through the middle of Africa.

NORTH AMERICA

North America measures 9,348,000 square miles. The United States and Canada are the only two countries in North America which holds 7.9% of the world's population.

SOUTH AMERICA

South America measures 6,885,000 square miles and is in the
Southern Hemisphere. South America contains 5.9% of the world's
population.

ANTARCTICA

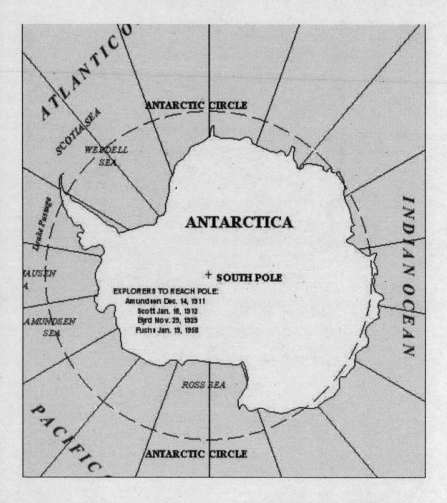

Located south of the Antarctic Circle, Antarctica is 5,404,000 square miles. Antarctica the coldest and windiest place on earth, there are no indigenous inhabitants, but there are seasonally staffed research stations. The Antarctic Treaty governs the continent of Antarctica.

EUROPE

Europe is 4,051,000 square miles and holds 12% of the world's population. Many countries make up the continent of Europe including France, Italy and Germany.

The World

Area: 510.072 million sq km
        land: 148.94 million sq km
       water: 361.132 million sq km
Note: 70.8% of the world's surface is *water*, 29.2% is *land*.
Area-comparative:
  land area about 16 times the size of the US

Population: 6,379,157,361

Population growth rate:1.14%

Climate: two large areas of polar climates separated by two rather narrow temperate zones form a wide equatorial band of tropical to subtropical climates.

Environmental – current issues: large areas subject to overpopulation, industrial disasters, pollution (air, water, acid rain, toxic substances), loss of vegetation (overgrazing, deforestation, desertification), loss of wildlife, soil degradation, soil depletion, erosion.

Selected International Environmental Agreements

Air Pollution

(Convention on Long-Range Trans-boundary Air Pollution)

Opened for signature: November 13, 1979

Entered into force: March 16, 1983

Objective: to protect the human environment against air pollution and to gradually reduce and prevent air pollution, including long range trans-boundary air pollution.

Air Pollution-Nitrogen Oxides

(Protocol to the 1979 Convention on Long-Range Trans-boundary Air Pollution Concerning the Control of Emissions of Nitrogen Oxides or Their Trans-boundary Fluxes)

Opened for signature: October 31, 1988

Entered into force: February 14, 1991

Objective: to provide for the control or reduction of nitrogen oxides and their trans-boundary fluxes.

Air Pollution-Persistent Organic Pollutants

(Protocol to the 1979 Convention on Long-Range Trans-boundary Air Pollution on Persistent Organic Pollutants)

Opened for signature: June 24, 1998

Entered into force: October 23, 2003

Objective: to provide for the control and reduction of emissions of persistent organic pollutants in order to reduce their trans-boundary fluxes so as to protect human health and the environment from adverse effects.

Air Pollution – Sulfur 85
(Protocol to the 1979 Convention on Long-Range Trans-boundary Air Pollution on the Reduction of Sulfur Emissions or their Trans-boundary Fluxes by at Least 30%)

Opened for signature : July 8, 1985

Entered into force: September 2, 1987

Objective: to provide for a 30% reduction in sulfur emissions or trans-boundary fluxes by 1993.

Air Pollution – Sulfur 94
(Protocol to the 1979 Convention on Long-Range Trans-boundary Air Pollution on Further Reduction of Sulfur Emissions)

Opened for signature: June 14, 1994

Entered into force: August 5, 1998

Objective: to provide for a further reduction in sulfur emissions or trans-boundary fluxes.

Air Pollution-
Volatile Organic Compounds
(Protocol to the 1979 Convention on Long-Range Trans-boundary Air Pollution Concerning the Control of Emissions of Volatile Organic Compounds or Their Trans-boundary Fluxes)

Opened for signature: November 18, 1991

Entered into force: September 29, 1997

Objective: to provide for the control and reduction of emissions of volatile organic compounds in order to reduce their trans-boundary fluxes so as to protect human health and the environment from adverse effects.

Antarctic-Environmental Protocol
(Protocol on Environmental Protection to the Antarctic Treaty)

Opened for signature: October 4, 1991

Entered into force: January 14, 1998

Objective: to provide for comprehensive protection of the Antarctic environment and dependent and associated ecosystems; applies to the area covered by the Antarctic Treaty.

Antarctic Treaty

Opened for signature: December 1, 1959
Entered into force: June 23, 1961
Objective: to ensure that Antarctic is used for peaceful purposes only (such as international cooperation in scientific research); to defer the question of territorial claims asserted by some nations and not recognized by others; to provide an international forum for management of the region; applies to land and ice shelves south of 60 degrees South Latitude.

Basil Convention
on the Control of Trans-boundary
Movements of Hazardous Wastes and Their
Disposal
(Hazardous Wastes)

Opened for signature: March 22, 1989
Entered into force: May 5, 1992
Objective: to reduce trans-boundary movements of wastes subject to the Convention to a minimum consistent with the environmentally sound and efficient management of such wastes; to minimize the amount and toxicity of wastes generated and ensure their environmentally sound management of the hazardous and other wastes they generate.

Biodiversity
(Convention on Biological Diversity)

Opened for signature: June 5, 1992
Entered into force: December 29, 1993
Objective: to develop national strategies for the conservation and sustainable use of biological diversity.

Climate Change
(United Nations Framework Convention on Climate Change)

Opened for signature: May 9, 1992
Entered into force: March 21, 1994
Objective: to achieve stabilization of greenhouse gas concentrations in the atmosphere at low enough level to prevent dangerous anthropogenic interference with the climate system.

Climate Change-Kyoto Protocol
(Kyoto Protocol to the United Nations Framework Convention on Climate Change)
Opened for signature: March 16, 1998
Entered into force: February 23, 2005
Objective: to further reduce greenhouse gas emissions by enhancing the national programs of developed countries aimed at this goal and by establishing percentage reduction targets for the developed countries.

Convention for the Conservation of Antarctic Seals
Opened for signature: June 1, 1972
Entered into force: March 11, 1978
Objective: to promote and achieve the protection, scientific study, and rational use of Antarctic seals, and to maintain a satisfactory balance within the ecological system of Antarctica.

Convention on Fishing and Conversation of Living Resources of the High Seas
(Marine Life Conservation)
Opened for signature: April 29, 1958
Entered into force: March 20, 1966
Objective: to solve through international cooperation the problems involved in the conservation of living resources of the high seas, considering that because of the development of modern technology some of these resources are in danger of being overexploited.

Convention on Wetlands of International Importance Especially As Waterfowl Habitat
(Ramsar)   (Wetlands)
Opened for signature: February 2, 1971
Entered into force: December 21, 1975
Objective: to stem the progressive encroachment on and loss of wetlands now and in the future, recognizing the fundamental ecological functions of wetlands and their economic, cultural, scientific, and recreational value.

Convention on the Conservation of Antarctic Marine Living Resources

Opened for signature: May 5, 1980
Entered into force: April 7, 1982
Objective: to safeguard the environment and protect the integrity of the ecosystem of the seas surrounding Antarctica, and to conserve Antarctic marine living resources.

Convention on the International Trade in Endangered Species of Wild Flora & Fauna

Opened for signature: March 3, 1973
Entered into force: July 1, 1975
Objective: to protect certain endangered species from overexploitation by means of a system of import/export permits.

Convention on the Prevention of Marine Pollution by Dumping Wastes and Other Matter
(London Convention)   (Marine Dumping)

Opened for signature: December 29, 1972
Entered into force: August 30, 1975
Objective: to control pollution of the sea by dumping and to encourage regional agreements supplementary to the Convention.

Convention on the Prohibition of Military or Any Other Hostile Use of Environmental Modification Techniques

Opened for signature: December 10, 1976
Entered into force: October 5, 1978
Objective: to prohibit the military or other hostile use of environmental modification techniques in order to further world peace and trust among nations.

Desertification
(United Nations Convention to Combat Desertification in Those Countries Experiencing Serious Drought and /or Desertification Particularly in Africa)

Opened for signature: October 14, 1994
Entered into force: December 26, 1996
Objective: to combat desertification and mitigate the effects of drought through national action programs that incorporate long-term strategies supported by international cooperation and partnership arrangements.

International Convention for the Regulation of Whaling

Opened for signature: December 2, 1946
Entered into force: November 10, 1948
Objective: to protect all species of whales from over hunting; to establish a system of international regulation for the whale fisheries to ensure proper conservation and development of whale stocks; and to safeguard for future generations the great natural resources represented by whale stocks.

International Tropical Timber Agreement, 1983

Opened for signature: November 18, 1983
Entered into force: April 1, 1985
Expired - 1 January 1997, when Tropical Timber 94 went into effect.
Objective: to provide an effective framework for cooperation between tropical timber producers and consumers and to encourage the development of natural policies aimed at sustainable utilization and conservation of tropical forests and their genetic resources.

International Tropical Timber Agreement, 1994

Opened for signature: January 26, 1994
Entered into force: January 1, 1997
Objective: to ensure that by year 2000 exports of tropical timber originate from sustainably managed sources; to establish a fund to assist tropical timber producers in obtaining the resources necessary to reach this objective.

Law of the Sea
(United Nations Convention on the Law of the Sea)

Opened for signature: December 10, 1982
Entered into force: November 16, 1994
Objective: to set up a comprehensive new legal regime for the sea and oceans; to include rules concerning environmental standards as well as enforcement provisions dealing with pollution of the marine environment.

Montreal Protocol on Substances That Deplete the Ozone Layer
(Ozone Layer Protection)

Opened for signature: September 16, 1987
Entered into force: January 1, 1989
Objective: to protect the ozone layer by controlling emissions of substances that deplete it.

Nuclear Test Ban
(Treaty Banning Nuclear weapon Tests in the Atmosphere, in Outer Space, and Under Water)

Opened for signature: August 5, 1963
Entered into force: October 10, 1963
Objective: to obtain an agreement on general and complete disarmament under strict international control in accordance with the objectives of the United Nations; to put an end to the armaments race and eliminate incentives for the production and testing of all kinds of weapons, including nuclear weapons.

Protocol of 1978 Relating to the International Convention for the Prevention of Pollution from Ships, 1973
(Ship Pollution)

Opened for signature: February 17, 1978
Entered into force: October 2, 1983
Objective: to preserve the marine environment through the complete elimination of pollution by oil and other harmful substance and the minimization of accidental discharge of such substances.

FACTS ABOUT COUNTRIES

This data is derived from The World Factbook 2004 compiled by the Central Intelligence Agency

AFGHANISTAN

Location: Southern Asia, north and west of Pakistan, east of Iran.
Area: 250,000 sq mi (647,500 sq km).
Area – comparative: slightly smaller than Texas.
Population: 28,513,677.
Population growth rate: 4.92%.
Climate: arid to semi-arid; cold winters and hot summers.
Environment - current issues: limited natural fresh water resources; inadequate supplies of potable water; soil degradation; overgrazing ; deforestation (much of the remaining forests are being cut down for fuel and building materials); desertification; air and water pollution.
Land Use: *arable land:* 12.13%.
　　　　　permanent crops: 0.22%.
　　　　　other: 87.65%.
International Agreements *party to:* Biodiversity, Desertification, Endangered Species, Environmental Modification, Marine Dumping.
Signed, but not ratified: Climate Change, Hazardous Wastes, Law of the Sea, Marine Life Conservation.

ALBANIA

Location: Southeastern Europe, bordering the Adriatic Sea and Ionian Sea, between Greece and Serbia and Montenegro.
Area: 11,099 sq mi (28,748 sq km).
Area – comparative: slightly smaller than Maryland.
Population: 3,544,808.
Population growth rate: 0.51%.
Climate: mild temperate; cool, cloudy, wet winters; hot clear dry summers; interior is cool and wet.
Environment - current issues: deforestation, soil erosion; water pollution from industrial and domestic effluents.
Land Use: *arable land:* 21.09%
　　　　　permanent crops: 4.45%
　　　　　other: 74.46%
International Agreements: *party to:* Biodiversity, Climate Change, Desertification, Endangered Species, Hazardous Waste, Law of the Sea, Ozone Layer Protection, Wetlands.
Signed, but not ratified: none of the selected agreements.

ALGERIA

Location: Northern Africa, bordering Mediterranean Sea, between Morocco and Tunisia.
Area: 919,590 sq mi (2,381,740 sq km).

Area- comparative: slightly less than 3.5 times the size of Texas.
Population: 32,129,324.
Population growth rate: 1.28%.
Climate: arid to semiarid; mild, wet winters with hot, dry summers along the coast; drier with cold winters and hot summers on high plateau; sirocco is a hot, dust/sand-laden wind, especially common in summer.
Environment – current issues: soil erosion from overgrazing and poor farming practices; desertification; dumping of raw sewage, petroleum refining wastes and other industrial effluents is leading to the pollution of rivers and coastal waters; Mediterranean Sea, in particular, becoming polluted from oil wastes, soil erosion, and fertilizer runoff; inadequate supply of potable water.
Land Use: *arable land*: 3.21%
permanent crops:0.21%
other: 96.58%
International Agreements: *party to*: Biodiversity, Climate Change, Desertification, Endangered Species, Environmental Modification, Hazardous Wastes, Law of the Sea, Ozone Layer Protection, Ship Pollution, Wetlands.
Signed, but not ratified: none of the selected agreements.

AMERICAN SAMOA
Location: Oceania, group of islands in the South Pacific Ocean approximately half way between Hawaii and New Zealand.
Area: 77 sq mi (199 sq km).
Area-comparative: slightly larger than Washington, D.C.
Population: 57,902.
Population growth rate: 0.04%.
Climate: tropical marine, moderated by southeast trade winds; annual rainfall averages about 3 m; rainy season from November to April, dry season from May to October; little seasonal temperature variation.
Environment - current issues: limited natural fresh water resources; the water division of the Government has spent substantial funds in the past few years to improve water catchments and pipelines.
Land Use: *arable land*: 5%
permanent crops: 10%
other :85%
No listing for signed but not ratified

ANDORRA
Location: Southwestern Europe, between France and Spain.
Area: 180 sq mi (468 sq km).
Area–comparative: 2.5 times the size of Washington, D.C.
Population: 69,865.
Population growth rate: 1%.
Climate: temperate; snowy, cold winters and warm dry summers.
Environment– current issues: deforestation; overgrazing of mountain meadows contributes to soil erosion; air pollution; wastewater treatment and solid waste disposal.
Land Use: *arable land: 2.22%*
permanent crops: 0%
other: 97.78%
International Agreements: *party to*: Hazardous Wastes.

ANGOLA

Location: Southern Africa, bordering the South Atlantic Ocean, between Namibia and the Democratic Republic of the Congo.
Area: 481,351 sq mi (1,246,700 sq km).
Area-comparative: slightly less than twice the size of Texas.
Population: 10,978,552.
Population growth rate: 1.93%.
Climate: semiarid in south and along coast to Luanda; north has cool, dry season (May to October) and hot, rainy season (November to April).
Environment – current issues: overuse of pastures and subsequent soil erosion attributable to population pressures; desertification; deforestation of tropical rain forest, in response to both international demand for tropical timber and to domestic use as fuel, resulting in loss of biodiversity; soil erosion contributing to water pollution and situation of rivers and dams; inadequate supplies of potable water.
Land Use: *arable land: 2.41%*
   permanent crops: 0.4%
   other: 97.19%
International Agreements: *party to*: Biodiversity, Climate Change, Desertification, Law of the Sea, Ozone Layer Protection, Ship Pollution.
Signed but not ratified: none of the selected agreements.

ANGUILLA (overseas territory of the UK)

Location: islands between Caribbean Sea & North Atlantic Ocean, east of Puerto Rico.
Area: 39 sq mi (102 sq km).
Area-comparative: about one half the size of Washington, D.C.
Population: 13,008.
Population growth rate: 1.98%.
Climate: tropical; moderated by northeast trade winds.
Environment – current issues: supplies of potable water sometimes cannot meet increasing demand largely because of poor distribution system.
Land Use: *arable land: 0%*
   permanent crops: 0%
   other: 100% (mostly rock with sparse scrub oak, few trees, some commercial salt ponds)
No listings for agreements signed or not signed

ANTIGUA AND BARBUDA

Location: islands between the Caribbean Sea and North Atlantic Ocean, east-southeast of Puerto-Rico.
Area: 171 sq mi (total 443 sq km).
Area-comparative: 2.5 times the size of Washington, D.C.
Population: 68,320.
Population growth rate: 0.6%.
Climate: tropical; little seasonal temperature variation.
Environment – current issues: water management a major concern because of limited natural fresh water resources – is further hampered by the clearing of trees to increase crop production, causing rainfall to run off quickly.
Land Use: *arable land*: 18.18%
   permanent crops: 0%
   other: 81.82%

International Agreements: *party to:* Biodiversity, Climate Change, Kyoto Protocol, Desertification, Endangered Species, Environmental Modification, Hazardous Wastes, Law of the Sea, Marine Dumping, Ozone Layer Protection, Ship Pollution, Whaling.
Signed, but not ratified: none of the selected agreements.

ARGENTINA

Location: Southern South America, bordering the South Atlantic Ocean, between Chile and Uruguay.
Area: 1,068,297 sq mi (2,766,890 sq km).
Area-comparative: slightly less than three tenths the size of the US.
Population: 39,144,753.
Population growth rate: 1.02%
Climate: mostly temperate; arid in the Southeast, subantarctic in Southwest
Environment – current issues: environmental problems (urban and rural) typical of industrializing economy such as deforestation, soil degradation, desertification, air pollution, and water pollution.
   Note: Argentina is a world leader in setting voluntary greenhouse gas targets
Land Use: *arable land:* 9.14%
      permanent crops: 0.8%
      other: 90.06%
International Agreements: *party to :*Antarctic-Environmental Protocol, Antarctic-Marine Living Resources, Antarctic Seals, Antarctic Treaty, Biodiversity, Climate Change, Kyoto Protocol, Desertification, Endangered Species, Environmental Modification, Hazardous Wastes, Law of the Sea, Marine Dumping, Ozone Layer Protection, Ship Pollution, Wetlands, Whaling.
Signed but not ratified: Marine Life Conservation.

ARMENIA

Location: Southwestern Asia, east of Turkey.
Area: 11,505 sq mi (29,800 sq km).
Area-comparative: slightly smaller than Maryland.
Population: 2,991,360
Population growth rate: -0.32%
Climate: highland continental, hot summers, cold winters.
Environment – current issues: soil pollution from toxic chemicals such as DDT; the energy crisis of the 1990s led to deforestation when citizens scavenged for firewood; pollution of Hrazdan (Razdan) and Aras Rivers; the draining of Sevana Lich (Lake Sevan), a result of its use as a source for hydropower, threatens drinking water supplies; restart of Metsamor nuclear power plant in spite of its location in seismically active zone.
Land Use: *arable land:* 17.52 %
      permanent crops: 2.3%
      other: 80.18%
International Agreements: *party to:* Air Pollution, Biodiversity, Climate Change, Kyoto Protocol, Desertification, Hazardous Wastes, Law of the Sea, Ozone Layer Protection, Wetlands.
Signed but not ratified: Air-Pollution-Persistent Organic Pollutants.

ARUBA (part of the Kingdom of the Netherlands).
Location: Caribbean, island in the Caribbean Sea, north of Venezuela.
Area: 74.5 sq mi (193 sq km)
Area-comparative: slightly larger than Washington, D.C.
Population: 71,218
Population growth rate: 0.51%
Climate: tropical marine; little seasonal temperature variation.
Environment – current issues: NA
Land Use: *arable land*: 10.53%
     permanent crops: 0%
     other: 89.47%
No international agreements listed.

AUSTRALIA
Location: Oceania, continent between the Indian Ocean and the South Pacific Ocean.
Area: 2,967,895 sq mi (7,686,850 sq km)
Area-comparative: slightly smaller than the US contiguous 48 states.
Population: 19,913,144
Population growth rate: 0.9%
Climate: Generally arid to semi-arid; temperate in south and east; tropical in north.
Environment – current issues: soil erosion from overgrazing; industrial development; and poor farming practices; soil salinity rising due to the use of poor quality water; desertification; clearing for agricultural purposes threatens the habitat of many unique animal and plant species; the great Barrier Reef off the Northeast coast, the largest coral reef in the world, is threatened by increased shipping and its popularity as a tourist site; limited natural fresh water resources.
Land Use: *arable land* 6.88%
     permanent crops: 0.03%
     other: 93.09%
International Agreements: *party to:* Antarctic-Environmental Protocol, Antarctic-Marine Living Resources, Antarctic Seals, Antarctic Treaty, Biodiversity, Climate Change, Desertification, Endangered Species, Environmental Modification, Hazardous Wastes, Law of the Sea, Marine Dumping; Marine Life Conservation, Ozone Layer Protection, Ship Pollution, Tropical Timber 83, Tropical Timber 94, Wetlands, Whaling.
Signed but not ratified: Climate Change-Kyoto Protocol.

AUSTRIA
Location: Central Europe, north of Italy and Slovenia.
Area: 32,377 sq mi (83,858 sq km)
Area-comparative: slightly smaller than Maine.
Population: 8,174,762
Population growth rate: 0.14%
Climate: temperate; cloudy; cold winters with frequent rain and some snow   in lowlands and snow in mountains; moderate summers with occasional   showers.
Environment – current issues: some forest degradation caused by air and soil pollution; soil pollution results from the use of agricultural chemicals; air pollution results from emissions by coal-and oil-fired power stations and industrial plants and from trucks transiting Austria between northern and southern Europe.

Land Use: *arable land*: 16.89%
        permanent crops: 0.99%
        other: 82.12%

International Agreements *party to*: Air Pollution, Air Pollution-Nitrogen Oxides, Air Pollution-Sulfur 85 Air Pollution-Sulfur 94,Air Pollution-Volatile Organic Compounds, Antarctic Treaty, Biodiversity, Climate Change, Climate Change-Kyoto Protocol, Desertification, Endangered Species, Environmental Modification, Hazardous Wastes, Law of the Sea, Ozone Layer Protection ,Ship Pollution, Tropical Timber 85, Tropical Timber 94, Wetlands, Whaling.
Signed but not ratified: Air Pollution-Persistent Organic Pollutants.

AZERBAIJAN

Location: Southwestern Asia, bordering the Caspian Sea, between Iran and Russia.
Area: 33,436 sq mi (86,600 sq km)
Area-comparative: slightly smaller than Maine.
Population: 7,868,385
Population growth rate: 0.52%
Climate: dry, semiarid steppe.
Environment – current issues: local scientists consider the Abseron Yasaqliqi (Apsheron Peninsula including Bakuand Sumqayit) and the Caspian Sea to be the most ecologically devastated area in the World due to severe air, soil and water pollution; soil pollution from oil spills, from the use of DDT as a pesticide, and from toxic defoliants used in the production of cotton.
Land use: *arable land*: 19.31%
        permanent crops: 3.04%
        other: 77.65%

International Agreements:*party to*: Air Pollution, Biodiversity, Climate Change, Climate Change-Kyoto Protocol, Desertification, Endangered Species, Hazardous Wastes, Marine Dumping, Ozone Layer Protection, Wetlands.
Signed but not ratified: none of the selected agreements.

THE BAHAMAS

Location: Caribbean, chain of islands in the North Atlantic Ocean, northeast of Cuba.
Area: 5,382 sq mi (13,940 sq km)
Area-comparative: slightly smaller than Connecticut.
Population: 299,697
Population growth rate: 0.72%
Climate: tropical marine; moderated by warm waters.
Environment – current issues: coral reef decay; solid waste disposal.
Land use: *arable land*: 0.6%
        permanent crops: 0.04%
        other: 99%

International Agreements: *party to*: Biodiversity, Climate Change, Climate Change-Kyoto Protocol, Desertification, Endangered Species, Hazardous Wastes, Law of the Sea, Ozone Layer Protection, Ship Pollution, Wetlands.
Signed but not ratified: none of the selected agreements.

BAHRAIN

Location: Middle East, east of Saudi Arabia.
Area: 257 sq mi (665 sq km)
Area-comparative: 3.5 times the size of Washington, D.C.
Population: 677,886
Population growth rate: 1.56%
Climate: arid, mild, pleasant winters; very hot humid summers.
Environment –current issues: desertification resulting from the degradation of limited
arable land, periods of drought, and dust storms; coastal degradation
(damage to coastlines, coral reefs and sea vegetation) resulting from oil
spills and other discharges from large tankers, oil refineries, and distribution
stations; lack of freshwater resources, groundwater and seawater are the
only sources for all water needs.
Land use: *arable land*: 4.35%
permanent crops: 4.35%
other: 91.3%
International agreements: *party to*: Biodiversity, Climate Change, Desertification,
Hazardous Waste, Law of the Sea, Ozone Layer Protection, Wetlands.
Signed but not ratified: none of the selected agreements.

BANGLADESH

Location: Southern Asia, bordering the Bay of Bengal, between Burma and India.
Area: 55,598 sq mi (144,000 sq km)
Area-comparative: slightly smaller than Iowa.
Population: 141,340,476
Population growth rate: 2.08%
Climate: tropical; mild winter (October to March); hot, humid summer (March to June);
warm rainy monsoon (June to October).
Environment – current issues: many people are landless and forced to live on and
cultivate flood-prone land; water-borne diseases prevalent in surface water
pollution, especially of fishing areas, results from the use of commercial
pesticides; ground water contaminated by naturally occurring arsenic;
intermittent water shortages because of falling water tables in the northern
and central parts of the country; soil degradation and erosion; deforestation;
severe overpopulation.
Land use: *arable land*: 60.7%
permanent crops: 2.61%
other: 36.69%
International agreements: *party to*: Biodiversity, Climate Change, Climate Change-
Kyoto Protocol, Desertification, Endangered Species, Environmental
Modification, Hazardous Wastes, Law of the Sea, Ozone Layer Protection,
Wetlands.
Signed but not ratified: none of the selected agreements.

BARBADOS

Location: Caribbean, island in the North Atlantic Ocean, northeast of Venezuela.
Area: 166 sq mi (430 sq km)
Area-comparative: 2.5 times the size of Washington, D.C.
Population: 278,289
Population growth rate: 0.36%
Climate: tropical; rainy season (June to October).

Environment – current issues: pollution of coastal waters from waste disposal from ships; soil erosion; illegal solid waste disposal threatens contamination of aquifers.

Land use: *arable land*: 37.21%
  permanent crops: 2.33%
  other: 60.46%

International agreements: *party to*: Biodiversity, Climate Change, Climate Change-Kyoto Protocol, Desertification, Endangered Species, Hazardous Wastes, Law of the Sea, Marine Dumping, Ozone Layer Protection, Ship Pollution.

Signed but not ratified: none of the selected agreements.

BELARUS

Location: Eastern Europe, east of Poland.
Area: 80,154 sq mi (207,600 sq km)
Area-comparative: slightly smaller than Kansas.
Population: 10,310,520
Population growth rate: -0.11%
Climate: cold winters, cool and moist summers; transitional between continental and maritime.
Environmental – current issues: soil pollution from pesticide use; southern part of country contaminated with fallout from 1986 nuclear reactor accident at Chernobyl' in northern Ukraine.
Land use: *arable land*: 29.76%
  permanent crops: 0.69%
  other: 69.55%

International Agreements: *party to:* Air Pollution, Air Pollution-Nitrogen Oxides, Air Pollution Sulfur 83, Biodiversity, Climate Change, Desertification, Endangered Species, Environmental Modification, Hazardous Wastes, Marine Dumping, Ozone Layer Protection, Ship Pollution, Wetlands.

Signed but not ratified: Law of the Sea.

BELGIUM

Location: Western Europe, bordering the North Sea, between France and Netherlands.
Area: 11,779 sq mi (30,510 sq km)
Area-comparative: about the size of Maryland.
Population: 10,348,276
Population growth rate: 0.16%
Climate: temperate; mild winters, cool summers; rainy, humid, cloudy.
Environment – current issues: the environment is exposed to intense pressures from human activities: urbanization, dense transportation network, industry, extensive animal breeding and crop cultivation; air and water pollution also have repercussions for neighboring countries; uncertainties regarding federal and regional responsibilities (now resolved) have slowed progress in tackling environmental challenges.
Land Use: *arable land*: 25%
  permanent crops: 0%
  other: 75%

International Agreements: *party to*: Air Pollution, Air Pollution-Nitrogen Oxides ,Air Pollution-Sulfur 85,Air Pollution-Sulfur 94, Air Pollution-Volatile Organic Compounds, Antarctic-Environmental Protocol, Antarctic Treaty Biodiversity, Climate Change, Climate Change-Kyoto Protocol, Desertification,

Endangered Species, Environmental Modification, Hazardous Wastes, Law of the Sea, Marine Dumping, Marine Life Conservation, Ozone Layer Protection, Ship Pollution, Tropical Timber 83, Tropical Timber 94, Wetlands.
Signed, but not ratified: Air Pollution-Persistent Organic Pollutants.

BELIZE

Location: bordering the Caribbean Sea, between Guatemala and Mexico.
Area: 8,867 sq mi (22,966 sq km)
Area-comparative: slightly smaller than Massachusetts.
Population: 272,945
Population growth rate: 2.39%
Climate: tropical; very hot and humid; rainy season (May to November); dry season (February to May).
Environment – current issues: deforestation; water pollution from sewage, industrial effluents, agricultural runoff; solid and sewage waste disposal.
Land Use: *arable land*: 2.81%
　　　　permanent crops:1.1%
　　　　other: 96.09%
International Agreements: *party to*: Biodiversity, Climate Change, Climate Change-Kyoto Protocol, Desertification, Endangered Species, Hazardous Wastes, Law of the Sea, Ozone Layer Protection, Ship Pollution, Wetlands.
Signed but not ratified: none of the selected agreements.

BENIN

Location: Western Africa, bordering the Bight of Benin, between Nigeria and Togo.
Area: 43,482 sq mi (112,620 sq km)
Area-comparative: slightly smaller than Pennsylvania.
Population: 7,250,033
Population growth rate: 2.89%
Climate: tropical; hot, humid in South; semi-arid in north.
Environment – current issues: inadequate supplies of potable water; poaching threatens wildlife population deforestation, desertification.
Land use: *arable land*: 15.28%
　　　　permanent crops: 1.36%
　　　　other: 83.36%
International agreements: *party to*: Biodiversity, Climate Change, Climate Change-Kyoto Protocol, Desertification, Endangered Species, Environmental Modification, Hazardous Wastes, Law of the Sea, Ozone Layer Protection, Ship Pollution, Wetlands.
Signed, but not ratified: none of the selected agreements.

BERMUDA *(overseas territory of the UK)*

Location: North America, group of islands in the North Atlantic Ocean, east of North Carolina (US).
Area: 20.5 sq mi (53.3 sq km)
Area-comparative: about one third the size of Washington, D.C.
Population: 64,935
Population growth rate: 0.68%
Climate: subtropical; mild, humid; gales, strong winds common in winter.
Environment – current issues: asbestos disposal; water pollution; preservation of

open space; sustainable development
Land use: *arable land*: 6%
    permanent crops: 0%
    other: 94%
International agreements: *none liste.d*

BHUTAN
Location: Southern Asia, between China and India.
Area: 18,146 sq mi (47,000 sq km)
Area-comparative: about half the size of Indiana.
Population: 2,185,569
Population growth rate: 2.12%
Climate: varies; tropical in southern plains; cool winters and hot summers in central valleys; severe winters and cool summers in Himalayas.
Environment – current issues: soil erosion; limited access to potable water.
Land use: *arable land*: 2.98%
    permanent crops: 0.43%
    other: 96.59%
International agreements: *party to:* Climate Change, Climate Change-Kyoto Protocol, Endangered Species, Hazardous Wastes.
Signed but not ratified: Law of the Sea.

BOLIVIA
Location: Central South America, southwest of Brazil.
Area: 424,162 sq mi (1,098,580 sq km)
Area-comparative: slightly less than three times the size of Montana.
Population: 8,724,156
Population growth rate: 1.56%
Climate: varies with altitude; humid and tropical to cold and semiarid.
Environment – current issues: the clearing of land for agricultural purposes and the international demand for tropical timber are contributing to deforestation; soil erosion from over grazing and poor cultivation methods (including slash-and-burn agriculture); desertification; loss of biodiversity; industrial pollution of water supplies used for drinking and irrigation.
Land use: *arable land*: 1.73%
    permanent crops: 0.21%
    other: 98.06%
International agreements: *party to*: Biodiversity, Climate Change, Climate Change-Kyoto Protocol, Desertification, Endangered Species, Hazardous Wastes, Law of the Sea, Marine Dumping, Ozone Layer Protection, Ship Pollution, Tropical Timber 83, Tropical Timber 94, Wetlands.
Signed but not ratified: Environmental Modification, Marine Life Conservation, Ozone Layer Protection.

BOSNIA AND HERZEGOVINA
Location: Southeastern Europe, bordering the Adriatic Sea and Croatia.
Area: 19,740 sq mi (51,129 sq km)
Area-comparative: slightly smaller than West Virginia.
Population: 4,007,608
Population growth rate: 0.45%
Climate: hot summers and cold winters; areas of high elevation have short cool

summers and long severe winters; mild rainy winters along the coast.

Environment – current issues: air pollution from metallurgical plants; sites for disposing of urban waste are limited; water shortages and destruction of infrastructure because of the 1992-95 civil strife; deforestation.

Land use: *arable land*: 9.8%
  permanent crops: 2.94%
  other: 87.26%

International agreements: *party to*: Air Pollution, Biodiversity, Climate Change, Hazardous Wastes, Law of the Sea, Marine Life Conservation, Ozone Layer Protection, Wetlands.
Signed but not ratified: none of the selected agreements.

BOTSWANA

Location: Southern Africa, north of South Africa.
Area: 231,803 sq mi (600,370 sq km)
Area-comparative: slightly smaller than Texas.
Population: 1,561,973
Population growth rate: -0.89%
Climate: semiarid; warm winters and hot summers.
Environment – current issues: overgrazing; desertification; limited fresh water.
Land use*: arable land*: 0.61%
  permanent crops: 0.01%
  other: 99.38%

International agreements:*party to*: Biodiversity, Climate Change, Climate Change-Kyoto Protocol, Desertification, Endangered Species , Hazardous Wastes, Law of the Sea, Ozone Layer Protection, Wetlands.

BRAZIL

Location: Eastern South America, bordering the Atlantic Ocean.
Area: 3,285,618 sq mi (8,511,965 sq km)
Area-comparative: slightly smaller than the US.
Population: 184,101,109
Population rate growth: 1.11%
Climate: mostly tropical, but temperate in the South.

Environment – current issues: deforestation in Amazon Basin destroys the habitat and endangers a multitude of plant and animal species indigenous to the area; there is a lucrative illegal wildlife trade; air and water pollution in Rio de Janeiro, San Palo, and several other large cities; land degradation and water pollution caused by improper mining activities; wetland degradation; severe oil spills.

Land Use: *arable land*: 6.3%
  permanent crops: 1.42%
  other: 92.28%

International agreements: *party to:* Antarctic-Environmental Protocol; Antarctic-Marine Living Resources, Antarctic Seals, Antarctic Treaty, Biodiversity, Climate Change, Climate Change-Kyoto Protocol, Desertification, Endangered Species, Environmental Modification, Hazardous Wastes, Law of the Sea, Marine Dumping, Ozone Layer Protection, Ship Pollution, Tropical Timber 83, Tropical Timber 94, Wetlands, Whaling.
Signed but not ratified: none of the selected agreements.

BRITISH VIRGIN ISLANDS (overseas territory of the UK)

Location: east of Puerto Rico, between the Caribbean Sea and North Atlantic Ocean.
Area: 59 sq mi (153 sq km)
Area-comparative: about 0.9 times the size of Washington, D.C.
Population: 22,187
Population growth rate: 2.06%
Climate: subtropical; humid; temperatures moderated by trade winds.
Environment – current issues: limited natural fresh water resources (except for a few seasonal streams and springs on Tortola, most of the islands' water supply comes from wells and rainwater catchments).
Land use: *arable land*: 20%
  permanent crops: 6.67%
  other: 73.33%
International agreements: no listing.

BRUNEI

Location: Southeastern Asia, bordering the South China Sea and Malaysia.
Area: 2,227 sq mi (5,770 sq km)
Area-comparative: slightly smaller than Delaware.
Population: 365,251
Population growth rate: 1.95%
Climate: tropical; hot humid, rainy.
Environment – current issues: seasonal smoke/haze resulting from forest fires in Indonesia.
Land use: *arable land*: 0.57%
  permanent crops: 0.76
  other: 98.67%
International agreements: *party to:* Endangered Species, Hazardous Wastes, Law of the Sea, Ozone Layer Protection, Ship Pollution.
Signed but not ratified; none of the selected agreements.

BULGARIA

Location: Southeastern Europe, bordering the Black Sea, between Romania and Turkey.
Area: 42,811 sq mi (110,910 sq km)
Area-comparative: slightly larger than Tennessee.
Population: 7,517,973
Population growth rate: -0.92%
Climate: temperate; cold damp winters; hot dry summers.
Environment – current issues: air pollution from industrial emissions; rivers polluted from raw sewage, heavy metals, detergents, deforestation, forest damage from air pollution and resulting acid rain; soil contamination from heavy metals from metallurgical plants and industrial wastes.
Land use: *arable land*: 39%
  permanent crops: 1.8%
  other: 59.2%
  International agreements: *party to*: Air Pollution, Air Pollution-Nitrogen Oxides, Air Pollution-Persistent Organic Pollutants, Air Pollution- Sulfur 85, Air Pollution-Volatile Organic Compounds Antarctic-Environmental Protocol, Antarctic- Marine Living Resources, Antarctic Treaty, Biodiversity, Climate Change, Climate Change-Kyoto Protocol, Desertification, Endangered

Species, Environmental Modification, Hazardous Wastes, Law of the Sea, Ozone Layer Protection, Ship Pollution, Wetlands.
Signed but not ratified: Air Pollution Sulfur 94.

BURKINA FASO

Location: Western Africa, north of Ghana.
Area: 105,841 sq mi (274,200 sq km)
Area-comparative: slightly larger than Colorado.
Population:13,574,820
Population growth rate: 2.57%
Climate: tropical; warm, dry winters; hot, wet summers.
Environment – current issues: recent droughts and desertification severely affecting agricultural activities; overgrazing; soil degradation; deforestation.
Land use: *arable land*: 12.43%
  permanent crops: 0.18%
  other: 87.39%
International agreements: *party to:* Biodiversity; Climate Change; Desertification; Endangered Species, Hazardous Wastes; Marine Life Conservation; Ozone Layer Protection; Wetlands.
Signed but not ratified: Law of the Sea

BURMA

Location: Southeastern Asia, bordering the Andaman Sea and the Bay of Bengal.
Area: 261,901 sq mi (678,500 sq km)
Area-comparative: slightly smaller than Texas.
Population: 42,720,196
Population growth rate: 0.47%
Climate: tropical monsoon; cloudy, rainy, hot, humid summers (southwest monsoon, June to September); less cloudy, scant rainfall, mild temperatures, lower humidity during winter (northeast monsoon, December to April).
Environment – current issues: deforestation; industrial pollution of air, soil, and water; inadequate sanitation and water treatment contribute to disease.
Land use: *arable land*: 14.53%
  permanent crops: 0.9%
  other: 84.57%
International agreements: *party to:* Biodiversity, Climate Change, Climate Change-Kyoto Protocol, Desertification, Endangered Species, Law of the Sea, Ozone Layer Protection, Ship Pollution, Tropical Timber 85, Tropical Timber 94.
Signed but not ratified: none of the selected agreements.

BURUNDI

Location: Central Africa, east of Democratic Republic of the Congo.
Area: 10,742 sq mi (27,830 sq km)
Area-comparative: slightly smaller than Maryland.
Population: 6,231,221
Population growth rate: 2.2%
Climate: high plateau with considerable altitude variation (772 m to 2,670 m above sea level); average annual temperature varies with altitude from 23 to17 degrees centigrade but is generally moderate; the average annual rainfall is about 150 cm; wet seasons from February to May and September to November, and dry seasons from June to August and December to January.

Environment – current issues: soil erosion as a result of overgrazing and the expansion of agriculture into marginal lands; deforestation (little forested land remains because of uncontrolled cutting of trees for fuel); habitat loss threatens wildlife populations.

Land use: *arable land*; 29.98%
  permanent crops: 12.85%
  other. 57.17%

International agreements: *party to*: Biodiversity, Climate Change, Climate Change-Kyoto Protocol, Desertification, Endangered Species, Hazardous Wastes, Ozone Layer Protection.
Signed but not ratified: Law of the Sea.

CAMBODIA

Location: Southeastern Asia, bordering the Gulf of Thailand, between Thailand, Vietnam, and Laos.

Area: 69,881 sq mi (181,040 sq km)

Area-comparative: slightly smaller than Oklahoma.

Population: 13,363,421

Population growth rate: 1.8%

Climate: tropical; rainy, monsoon season (May to November); dry season (December to April); little seasonal temperature variation.

Environment – current issues: illegal logging activities throughout the country and strip-mining for gems in western region along the border with Thailand have resulted in habitat loss and declining biodiversity (in particular, destruction of mangrove swamps threatens natural fisheries); soil erosion; in rural areas, most of the population does not have access to potable water; declining fish stocks because of illegal fishing and over fishing.

Land use: *arable land*: 20.96%
  permanent crops: 0.61%
  other. 78.43%

International agreements: *party to*: Biodiversity, Climate Change, Climate Change-Protocol, Desertification, Endangered Species, Hazardous Wastes, Marine Life Conservation, Ozone Layer Protection, Ship Pollution, Tropical Timber 94, Wetlands.
Signed but not ratified: Law of the sea.

CAMEROON

Location: Western Africa, bordering the Bight of Biafra, between Equatorial Guinea and Nigeria.

Area: 183,519 sq mi (475,440 sq km)

Area-comparative: slightly larger than California.

Population: 16,063,678

Population growth rate: 1.97%

Climate: varies with terrain, from tropical along coast to semiarid and hot north

Environment – current issues: water-borne diseases are prevalent; deforestation; over grazing; desertification, poaching; over fishing.

Land use: *arable land*: 12.81%
  permanent crops: 2.58%
  other. 84.61%

International agreements: *party to:* Biodiversity, Climate Change, Climate Change-

Kyoto Protocol, Desertification, Endangered Species, Hazardous Wastes, Law of the Sea, Ozone Layer Protection, Tropical Timber 83, Tropical Timber 94.
Signed but not ratified: none of the selected agreements.

CANADA

Location: Northern North America, bordering the North Atlantic Ocean, Arctic Ocean and North Pacific Ocean, north of the 48 mainland states of the U.S.
Area: 3,850,790 sq mi (9,984,670 sq km)
Area-comparative: somewhat larger than the U.S.
Population: 32,507,874
Population growth rate: 0.92%
Climate: varies from temperate in south to sub arctic and arctic north.
Environment - current issues: air pollution and resulting acid rain severely affecting lakes and damaging forests; metal smelting, coal-burning utilities; and vehicle emissions impacting on agricultural and forest productivity; ocean waters becoming contaminated due to agricultural, industrial mining, and forestry activities.
Land use: *arable land*: 4.94%
    permanent crops: 0.02%
    other: 95.04%
International agreements: *party to:* Air Pollution, Air Pollution-Nitrogen Oxides, Air-Pollution-Persistent Organic Pollutants, Air-Pollution-Sulfur 85, Air-Pollution 94, Antarctic-Environmental Protocol, Antarctic-Marine Living Resources, Antarctic Seals ,Antarctic Treaty, Biodiversity, Climate Change, Climate Change-Kyoto Protocol, Desertification, Endangered Species, Environmental Modification, Hazardous Wastes ,Law of the Sea, Marine Dumping, Ozone Layer Protection, Ship Pollution, Tropical Timber 83, Tropical Timber 94, Wetlands.

CAPE VERDE

Location: Western Africa, group of islands in the North Atlantic Ocean, west of Senegal.
Area: 1,556 sq mi (4,033 sq km)
Area-comparative: slightly larger than Rhode Island.
Population: 415,294
Population growth rate: 0.73%
Climate: temperate; warm, dry summer; precipitation meager and very erratic.
Environment – current issues: soil erosion; demand for wood used as fuel has resulted in deforestation; desertification; environmental damage has threatened several species of birds and reptiles; illegal beach sand extraction; over fishing.
Land use: *arable land*: 9.68%
    permanent crops: 0.5%
    other: 89.82%
International agreements: *party to:* Biodiversity, Climate Change, Desertification, Environmental Modification, Hazardous Wastes, Law of the Sea, Marine Dumping, Ozone Layer Protection.

CAYMAN ISLANDS (overseas territory of the UK)

Location: Caribbean, island group in Caribbean Sea, nearly one half of the way from

Cuba to Honduras.
Area: 101 sq mi (262 sq km)
Area-comparative: 1.5 times the size of Washington, D.C.
Population: 43,103
Population growth rate: 2.71%
Climate: tropical marine; warm, rainy summers (May to October) and cool; relatively
        dry winters (November to April).
Environment – current issues: no natural fresh water resources; drinking water
        supplies must be me by rainwater catchments.
Land use*: arable land* : 0%
        permanent crop: 0%
        other: 100%
International agreements: *none listed.*

CENTRAL AFRICAN REPUBLIC
Location: Central Africa, north of Democratic Republic of the Congo.
Area: 240,471 sq mi (622,984 sq km)
Area-comparative: slightly smaller than Texas.
Population: 3,742,482
Population growth rate: 1.56%
Climate: tropical; hot dry winters; mild to hot, wet summers.
Environment – current issues: tap water is not potable; poaching has diminished the
        country's reputation as one of the last great wildlife refuges; desertification;
        deforestation.
Land use: *arable land*: 3.1%
        permanent crops: 0.14%
        other: 96.76%
International agreements: *party to:* Biodiversity, Climate Change, Desertification,
        Endangered Species, Ozone Layer Protection, Tropical Tjmber 94.
 Signed but not ratified: Law of the Sea.

CHAD
Location: Central Africa, south of Libya.
Area: 495,624 sq mi (1,284,000 sq km)
Area-comparative: slightly more than 3 times the size of California.
Population: 9,538,544
Population growth rate: 3%
Climate: tropical in the South, desert in the North.
Environment – current issues: inadequate supplies of potable water; improper waster
        disposal in rural areas contributes to soil and water pollution; desertification.
Land use: *arable land*: 2.78%
        permanent crops:0.02%
        other: 97.2%
International agreements: *party to*: Biodiversity, Climate Change, Desertification,
        Endangered Species, Ozone Layer Protection, Wetlands.
Signed but not ratified: Law of the Sea, Marine Dumping.

CHILE
Location: Southern South America, bordering the South Atlantic Ocean and South
Pacific Ocean, between Argentina and Peru.

Area: 292,182 sq mi (756,950 sq km)
Area-comparative: slightly smaller than twice the size of Montana.
Population: 15,823,957
Population growth rate: 1.01%
Climate: temperate; desert in north; Mediterranean in central region; cool and damp in south.
Environment – current issues: widespread deforestation and mining threaten natural resources; air pollution from industrial and vehicle emissions; water pollution from raw sewage.
Land use: *arable land*: 2.65%
  permanent crops: 0.42%
  other: 96.93%
International agreements: *party to:* Antarctic-Environmental Protocol, Antarctic-Marine Living Resources, Antarctic Seals, Antarctic Treaty, Biodiversity, Climate Change, Climate Change-Kyoto Protocol, Desertification, Endangered Species, Environmental Modification, Hazardous Wastes, Law of the Sea, Marine Dumping, Ozone Layer Protection, Ship Pollution, Wetlands, Whaling.
Signed but not ratified: none of the selected agreements.

CHINA

Location: Eastern Asia, bordering the East China Sea, Korea Bay, Yellow Sea, and South China Sea, between North Korea and Vietnam.
Area: 3,704,426 sq mi (9,596,960 sq km)
Area-comparative: slightly smaller than the U.S.
Population: 1,298,847,624
Population growth rate: 0.57%
Climate: extremely diverse; tropical in the South to sub arctic the North.
Environment – current issues: air pollution (greenhouse gases, sulfur dioxide particulates) from reliance on coal produces acid rain; water shortages, particularly in north; water pollution from untreated wastes; deforestation, estimated loss of one-fifth of agricultural land since 1949 to soil erosion and economic development desertification; trade in endangered species.
Land use: *arable land*: 13.31%
  permanent crops: 1.2%
  other: 85.49%
International agreements: *party to:* Antarctic-Environmental Protocol, Antarctic Treaty, Biodiversity, Climate Change, Climate Change-Kyoto Protocol, Desertification, Endangered Species, Hazardous Wastes, Law of the Sea, Marine Dumping, Ozone Layer Protection, Ship Pollution, Tropical Timber 83, Tropical Timber 94, Wetlands, Whaling.
Signed but not ratified: none of the selected agreements.

COLOMBIA

Location: Northern South America, bordering the Caribbean Sea, between Panama and Venezuela, bordering the North Pacific Ocean, between Ecuador and Panama.
Area: 439,619 sq mi (1,138,910 sq km)
Area-comparative: slightly less than 3 times the size of Montana.
Population: 42,310,775
Population growth rate: 1.53%
Climate: tropical along coast and eastern plains; cooler in highlands.

Environment – current issues: deforestation; soil and water quality damage from overuse of pesticides; air pollution, especially in Bogota, from vehicle emissions.
Land use: *arable land*: 1.9%
   permanent crops: 1.96%
   other: 96.14%
International agreements: *party to:* Antarctic Treaty, Biodiversity, Climate Change, Climate Change-Kyoto Protocol, desertification, Endangered Species, Hazardous Wastes, Marine Life Conservation, Ozone Layer Protection, Ship Pollution, Tropical Timber 83, Tropical Timber 94, Wetlands,
Signed but not ratified: Law of the Sea.

COMOROS

Location: southern Africa, group of islands in the Mozambique Channel, about two-thirds of the way between northern Madagascar and northern Mozambique.
Area: 838 sq mi (2,170 sq km)
Area-comparative: slightly more than 12 times the size of Washington, D.C.
Population: 651,901
Population growth rate: 2.94%
Climate: tropical marine; rainy season (November to May).
Environment –current issues: soil degradation and erosion results from crop cultivation on slopes without proper terracing deforestation.
Land use: *arable land*: 34.98%
   permanent crops: 17.94%
   other: 47.08%
International agreements: *party to:* Biodiversity, Climate Change, Desertification, Endangered Species, Hazardous Wastes, Law of the Sea, Ozone Layer Protection, Ship Pollution, Wetlands.
Signed but not ratified: none of the selected agreements.

CONGO, DEMOCRATIC REPUBLIC OF THE (ZAIRE)

Location: Central Africa, northeast of Angola
Area: 905,328 sq mi (2,345,410 sq km)
Area-comparative: slightly less than one-fourth the size of the U.S.
Population: 58,317,930
Population growth rate: 2.99%
Climate: tropical; hot and humid in equatorial river basin,; cooler and dryer in southern highlands; north of Equator – wet season April to October, dry season December to February; south of Equator –wet season November to March, dry season April to October.
Environment – current issues: poaching threatens wildlife populations; water pollution; deforestation, refugees responsible for significant deforestation, soil erosion, and wildlife poaching; mining of minerals (coltan –a mineral used in creating capacitors, diamonds, and gold) causing environmental damage.
Land use: *arable land*: 2.96%
   permanent crops: 0.52%
   other: 96.52%
International agreements: *party to*: Biodiversity, Climate Change, Desertification, Endangered Species, Hazardous Wastes, Law of the Sea, Marine Dumping, Ozone Layer Protection, Tropical Timber 83, Tropical Timber 94, Wetlands.
Signed but not ratified: Environmental Modification.

CONGO, REPUBLIC OF THE

Location: Western Africa, bordering the South Atlantic Ocean, between Angola and Gabon.
Area: 132,012 sq mi (342,000 sq km)
Area-comparative: slightly smaller than Montana.
Population: 2,998,040
Population growth rate: 1.42%
Climate: tropical; rainy season (March to June); dry season (June to October) constantly high temperatures and humidity; particularly enervating climate astride the Equator.
Environmental – current issues: air pollution from vehicle emissions; water pollution from the dumping of raw sewage; tap water is not potable; deforestation.
Land use: *arable land:* 0.5%
   permanent crops: 0.13%
   other: 99.37%
International agreements: *party to:* Biodiversity, Climate Change, Desertification, Endangered Species, Ozone Layer Protection, Tropical Timber 83, Tropical Timber 94, Wetlands.
Signed but not ratified: Law of the Sea.

COSTA RICA

Location: Central America, bordering both the Caribbean Sea and the North Pacific Ocean, between Nicaragua and Panama.
Area: 19,724 sq mi (51,100 sq km)
Area-comparative: slightly smaller than West Virginia.
Population: 3,956,507
Population growth rate: 1.52%
Climate: tropical and sub tropical; dry season (December to April); rainy season (May to November); cooler in Highlands.
Environment – current issues: deforestation and land use change, largely a result of the clearing of land for cattle ranching and agriculture; soil erosion, coastal marine pollution; fisheries protection; solid waste management; air pollution.
Land use: *arable land:* 4.41%
   permanent crops: 5.48%
   other: 90.11%
International agreements: *party to:* Biodiversity, Climate Change, Climate Change-Kyoto Protocol ,Desertification, Endangered Species, Environmental Modification, Hazardous Wastes, Law of the Sea, Marine Dumping, Ozone Layer Protection, Wetlands Whaling.
Signed, but not ratified: Marine Life Conservation.

COTE d'IVOIRE

Location: Western Africa, bordering the North Atlantic Ocean, between Ghana and Liberia.
Area: 124,469 sq mi (322,460 sq km)
Area-comparative: slightly larger than New Mexico.
Population: 17,327,724
Population growth rate: 2.11%
Climate: tropical along coast, semiarid in far north; three seasons – warm and dry (November to March), hot and dry (March to May), hot and wet (June to October).

Environment – current issues: deforestation (most of country's forests – once the largest in West Africa – have been heavily logged); water pollution from sewage and industrial and agricultural effluents.

Land use: *arable land*: 9.28%
 permanent crops: 13.84%
 other: 76.88%

International agreements: *party to:* Biodiversity, Climate Change, Desertification, Endangered Species, Hazardous Wastes, Law of the Sea, Marine Dumping, Ozone Layer Protection, Ship Pollution, Tropical Timber 83, Tropical Timber 94, Wetlands.
Signed, but not ratified: none of the selected agreements.

CROATIA

Location: Southeastern Europe, bordering the Adriatic Sea, between Bosnia, Herzegovina, and Slovenia.

Area: 21,824 sq mi (56,542 sq km)

Area-comparative: slightly smaller than West Virginia.

Population: 4,496,869

Population growth rate: -0.02%

Climate: Mediterranean and continental, continental climate predominant with hot summers and cold winters; mild winters, dry summers along coast.

Environment – current – issues: air pollution (from metallurgical plants) and resulting acid rain is damaging the forest; coastal pollution from industrial and domestic waste; landmine removal and reconstruction of infrastructure consequent to 1992-95 civil strife.

Land use: *arable land*: 23.55%
 permanent crops: 2.24%
 other: 74.21%

International agreements: *party to*: Air Pollution, Air Pollution-Sulfur 94, Biodiversity, Climate Change, Desertification, Endangered Species, Hazardous Wastes, Law of the Sea, Marine Dumping, Ozone Layer Protection, Shop Pollution, Wetlands.
Signed but not ratified: Air Pollution-Persistent Organic Pollutants, Climate Change-Kyoto Protocol.

CUBA

Location: Caribbean, island between the Caribbean Sea and the North Atlantic Ocean, south of Florida.

Area: 42,791 sq mi (110,860 sq km)

Area-comparative: slightly smaller than Pennsylvania.

Population: 11,308,764

Population growth rate: 0.34%

Climate: tropical; moderated by trade winds; dry season (November to April); rainy season (May to October).

Environment – current issues: air and water pollution; biodiversity loss, deforestation.

Land use: *arable land*: 33.04%
 permanent crops: 7.61%
 other: 59.35%

International agreements: *party to*: Antarctic Treaty, Biodiversity, Climate Change, Climate Change-Kyoto Protocol, Desertification, Endangered Species,

Environmental Modification, Hazardous Wastes, Law of the Sea, Marine Dumping, Ozone Layer Protection, Ship Pollution, Wetlands.
Signed, but not ratified: Marine Life Conservation.

CYPRUS

Location: Middle East, island in the Mediterranean Sea, south of Turkey.
Area: 3,571 sq mi (9,250 sq km)
Area-comparative: about 0.6 times the size of Connecticut.
Population: 775,927
Population growth rate: 0.55%
Climate: temperate; Mediterranean with hot, dry summers and cool winters
Environment – current issues: water resource problems (no natural reservoir catchments, seasonal disparity in rainfall, seawater intrusion to island's largest aquifer, increased salination in the north); water pollution from sewage and industrial wastes; coastal degradation, loss of wildlife habitats from urbanization.
Land use: *arable land*: 14.4%
  permanent crops: 4.5%
  other: 81.1%
International agreements: *party to*: Air Pollution, Biodiversity, Climate Change, Climate Change-Kyoto Protocol, Desertification, Endangered Species, Environmental Modification, Hazardous Wastes, Law of the Sea, Marine Dumping, Ozone Layer Protection, Ship Pollution.
Signed but not ratified: Air Pollution-Persistent Organic Pollutants.

CZECH REPUBLIC

Location: Central Europe, southeast of Germany.
Area: 30,403 sq mi (78,866 sq km)
Area-comparative: slightly smaller than South Carolina.
Population: 10,246,178
Population growth rate: -0.05%
Climate: temperate; cool summers; cold cloudy humid winters.
Environmental – current issues: air and water pollution in areas of northwest Bohemia and in northern Moravia around Ostrava present health risks; acid rain damaging forests; efforts to bring industry up to EU code should improve domestic pollution.
Land use: *arable land*: 40%
  permanent crops:3.04%
  other: 56.96%
International agreements: *party to:* Air Pollution, Air Pollution-Nitrogen Oxides, Air Pollution-Sulfur-85, Air Pollution-Sulfur 94, Air Pollution-Volatile Organic Compounds, Antarctic Treaty, Biodiversity, Climate Change, Climate Change-Kyoto Protocol, Desertification, Endangered Species, Environmental Modification, Hazardous Wastes, Law of the Sea, Ozone Layer Protection, Ship Pollution, Wetlands.
Signed but not ratified; Air Pollution-Persistent Organic Pollutants.

Denmark

Location: Northern Europe, bordering the Baltic Sea and the North Sea, on a peninsula north of Germany.
Area: 16,634 sq mi (43,094 sq km)

Area-comparative: slightly less than twice the size of Massachusetts.
Population: 5,413,392
Population growth rate: 0.35%
Climate: temperate; humid and overcast; mild, windy winters and cool summers.
Environment – current issues: air pollution, principally from vehicle and power plant emissions; nitrogen and phosphorus pollution of the North Sea; drinking and surface water becoming polluted from animal wastes and pesticides.
Land use: *arable land*: 55.74%
    permanent crops: 0.19%
    other: 44.07%
International agreements: *party to:* Air Pollution, Air Pollution-Nitrogen Oxides, Air Pollution-Persistent Organic Pollutants, Air Pollution-Sulfur 85, Air Pollution-Sulfur 94, Air Pollution-Volatile Organic Compounds, Antarctic Treaty, Biodiversity, Climate Change, Climate Change-Kyoto Protocol, Desertification, Endangered Species, Environmental Modification, Hazardous Wastes, Marine Dumping, Marine Life Conservation, Ozone Layer Protection, Ship Pollution, Tropical Timber 83, Tropical Timber 94, Wetlands, Whaling.
Signed but not ratified: Law of the Sea.

DJIBOUTI

Location: Eastern Africa, bordering the Gulf of Aden and the Red Sea, between Eritrea and Somalia.
Area: 8,878 sq mi (23,000 sq km)
Area-comparative: slightly smaller than Massachusetts.
Population: 466,900
Population growth rate: 2.1%
Climate: desert; torrid, dry.
Environment – current issues: inadequate supplies of potable water; limited arable land; desertification; endangered species.
Land use: *arable land*: 0%
    permanent crop: 0%
    other :100%
International agreements: *party to*: Biodiversity, Climate Change, Climate Change-Kyoto Protocol, Desertification, Endangered Species, Hazardous Wastes, Law of the Sea, Ozone Layer Protection, Ship Pollution.
Signed but not ratified; none of the selected agreements.

DOMINICA

Location: Caribbean, island between the Caribbean Sea and the North Atlantic Ocean, about one-half of the way from Puerto Rico to Trinidad and Tobago.
Area: 290 sq mi (754 sq km)
Area-comparative: slightly more than 4 times the size of Washington, D.C.
Population: 69,278
Population growth rate: -0.45%
Climate: tropical; moderated by northeast trade winds; heavy rainfall.
Environment – current issues: NA
Land use: *arable land*: 4%
    permanent crops: 16%
    other: 80%
International agreements: *party to*: Biodiversity, Climate Change, Desertification,

Endangered Species, Environmental Modification, Hazardous Wastes, Law of the Sea, Ozone Layer Protection, Ship Pollution, Whaling.
Signed but not ratified: none of the selected agreements.

DOMINICAN REPUBLIC

Location: Caribbean, eastern two-thirds of the island of Hispaniola, between the Caribbean Sea and the North Atlantic Ocean, east of Haiti.
Area: 18,810 sq mi (48,730 sq km)
Area-comparative: slightly more than twice the size of New Hampshire.
Population: 8,833,634
Population growth rate: 1.33%
Climate: tropical maritime; little seasonal variation in temperature and rainfall.
Environment – current issues: water shortages; soil eroding into the sea damages coral reefs; deforestation.
Land use: *arable land*: 21.08%
　　　　　permanent crops: 9.92%
　　　　　other: 69%
International agreements: *party to*: Biodiversity, Climate Change, Climate Change-Kyoto Protocol, Desertification, Endangered Species, Hazardous Wastes, Marine Dumping, Marine Life Conservation, Ozone Layer Protection, Ship Pollution.
Signed but not ratified: Law of the Sea.

ECUADOR

Location: Western South America, bordering the Pacific Ocean at the Equator.
Area: 109,454 sq mi (283,560 sq km)
Area-comparative: slightly smaller than Nevada.
Population: 13,212,742
Population growth rate: 1.03%
Climate: tropical along coast, becoming cooler inland at higher elevations; tropical in Amazonian jungle lowlands.
Environment – current issues: deforestation; soil erosion, desertification; water pollution; pollution from oil production wastes in ecologically sensitive areas of the Amazon Basin and Galapagos Islands.
Land use: *arable lands*: 5.69%
　　　　　permanent crops: 5.15%
　　　　　other: 89.16%
International agreements: *party to :* Antarctic-Environmental Protocol, Antarctic Treaty, Biodiversity, Climate Change, Climate Change-Kyoto Protocol, Desertification, Endangered Species, Hazardous Wastes, Ozone Layer Protection, Ship Pollution, Tropical Timber 83, Tropical Timber 94, Wetlands.
Signed but not ratified; none of the selected agreements.

EGYPT

Location: Northern Africa, bordering the Mediterranean Sea, between Libya and the Gaza Strip.
Area: 386,560 sq mi (1,001,450 sq km)
Area-comparative: slightly more than three times the size of New Mexico.
Population: 76,117,421
Population growth rate: 1.83%
Climate: desert; hot dry summers with moderate winters.

Environment – current issues: agricultural land being lost to urbanization and windblown sands; increasing soil salination below Aswan High Dam; desertification; oil pollution threatening coral reefs, beaches, and marine habitats; other water pollution from agricultural pesticides, raw sewage, and industrial effluents; very limited natural fresh water resources away from the Nile which is the only perennial water source; rapid growth in population overstraining the Nile and natural resources.

Land use: *arable land*: 2.85%
 permanent crops: 0.47%
 other: 96.68%

International agreements: *party to:* Biodiversity, Climate Change, Desertification, Endangered Species, Environmental Modification, Hazardous Wastes, Law of the Sea, Marine Dumping, Ozone Layer Protection, Ship Pollution, Tropical Timber 83, Tropical Timber 94, Wetlands.
 Signed but not ratified: Climate Change-Kyoto Protocol.

EL SALVADOR

Location: Central America, bordering the North Pacific Ocean, between Guatemala and Honduras.

Area: 8,121 sq mi (21,040 sq km)

Area-comparative: slightly smaller than Massachusetts.

Population: 6,587,541

Population growth rate: 1.78%

Climate: tropical; rainy season (May to October); dry season (November to April); tropical on coast; temperate in uplands.

Environment – current issues: deforestation; soil erosion, water pollution; contamination of soils from disposal of toxic wastes.

Land use: *arable land*: 27.27%
 permanent crops:12.11%
 other: 60.62%

International agreements: *party to*: Biodiversity, Climate Change, Climate Change-Kyoto Protocol, Desertification, Endangered Species, Hazardous Wastes, Ozone Layer Protection, Wetlands.
 Signed but not ratified: Law of the Sea.

EQUATORIAL GUINEA

Location: Western Africa, bordering Bight of Biafra, between Cameroon and Gabon.

Area: 10,827 sq mi (28,051 sq km)

Area-comparative: slightly smaller than Maryland.

Population: 523,051

Population growth rate: 2.43%

Climate: tropical; always hot, humid

Environment – current issues: tap water is not potable; deforestation.

Land use: *arable land*: 4.63%
 permanent crop: 3.57%
 other: 91.8%

International agreements: *party to:* Biodiversity, Climate Change, Climate Change-Kyoto Protocol, Desertification, Endangered Species, Hazardous Wastes, Law of the Sea, Ship Pollution.

ERITREA

Location: Eastern Africa, bordering the Red Sea, between Djibouti and Sudan.
Area: 46,830 sq mi (121,320 sq km)
Area-comparative: slightly larger than Pennsylvania.
Population: 4,447,307
Population growth rate: 2.57%
Climate: hot, dry desert strip along Red Sea coast; cooler and wetter in central highlands (up to 61 cm of rainfall annually); semiarid in western hills and lowlands; rainfall heaviest during June-September except in coastal desert.
Environment – current issues: deforestation; desertification; soil erosion; overgrazing; loss of infrastructure from civil warfare.
Land use: *arable land*: 3.87%
　　　permanent crops: 0.02%
　　　other: 96.11%
International agreements: *party to:* Biodiversity; Climate Change, Desertification, Endangered Species.
Signed but not ratified: none of the selected agreements.

ESTONIA

Location: Eastern Europe, bordering the Baltic Sea and Gulf of Finland, between Latvia and Russia.
Area: 17,457 sq mi (45,226 sq km)
Area-comparative: slightly smaller than New Hampshire and Vermont combined.
Population: 1,341,664
Population growth rate: -0.66%
Climate: maritime, wet, moderate winters, cool summers.
Environment – current issues: air polluted with sulfur dioxide from oil-shale burning power plants in northeast; however, the amount of pollutants emitted to the air has fallen steadily, the emissions of 2000 were 80%less than in 1980; the amount of unpurified wastewater discharged to water bodies in 2000 was one twentieth the level of 1980; in connection with the start-up of new water purification plants, the pollution load of wastewater decreased; Estonia has more than 1,400 natural and manmade lakes, the smaller of which in agricultural areas need to be monitored; coastal seawater is polluted in certain locations.
Land use: *arable land*: 26.5%
:　　　*permanent crops*: 0.35%
　　　other: 73.15%
International agreements: *party to:* Air Pollution, Air Pollution-Nitrogen Oxides, Air Pollution-Sulfur 85, Air Pollution-Volatile Organic Compounds, Antarctic Treaty, Biodiversity, Climate Change, Climate Change-Kyoto Protocol, Endangered Species, Hazardous Wastes, Ship Pollution, Ozone Layer Protection, Wetlands.
Signed but not ratified: none of the selected agreements.

ETHIOPIA

Location: Eastern Africa, west of Somalia.
Area: 435,071 sq mi (1,127,127 sq km)
Area-comparative: slightly less than twice the size of Texas.
Population: 67,851,281
Population growth rate: 1.89%

Climate: tropical monsoon with wide topographic-induced variation.
Environment – current issues: deforestation; overgrazing; soil erosion;
desertification; water shortages in some areas from water-intense farming
and poor management.
Land use: *arable land*: 9.9%
     permanent crops: 0.65%
     other: 89.45%
International agreements: *party to:* Biodiversity, Climate Change, Desertification,
endangered Species, Hazardous Wastes, Ozone Layer Protection
Signed but not ratified: Environmental Modification, Law of the Sea.

FIJI

Location: Oceania, island group in the South Pacific Ocean, 2/3's of the way from
Hawaii to New Zealand.
Area: 7,052 sq mi (18,270 sq km)
Area-comparative: slightly smaller than New Jersey.
Population: 880,874
Population growth rate: 1.41%
Climate: tropical marine; only seasonal temperature variation.
Environment – current issues: deforestation; soil erosion.
Land use: *arable land*: 10.95%
     permanent crops: 4.65%
     other: 84.4%
International agreements: *party to*: Biodiversity, Climate Change, Climate Change-
Kyoto Protocol, Desertification, Endangered Species, Law of the Sea, Marine
Life Conservation, Ozone Layer Protection, Tropical Timber 83, Tropical
Timber 94.
Signed but not ratified: none of the selected agreements.

FINLAND

Location: Northern Europe, bordering Baltic Sea, Gulf of Bothnia, and Gulf of Finland.
Area: 130,094 sq mi (337,030 sq km)
Area-comparative: slightly smaller than Montana.
Population: 5,214,512
Population growth rate: 0.18%
Climate: cold temperate; potentially sub-artic but comparatively mild because of
moderating influence of the North Atlantic Current, Baltic Sea, and more than
60,000 lakes.
Environment – current issues: air pollution from manufacturing and power plants
contributing to acid rain; water pollution from industrial wastes, agricultural
chemicals; habitat loss threatens wildlife populations.
Land use: *arable land*: 6.98%
     permanent crops: 0.01%
     other: 93.01%
International agreements: *party to:* Air Pollution, Air Pollution-Nitrogen Oxides, Air
Pollution-Sulfur 85, Air Pollution-Sulfur 94, Air Pollution-Volatile Organic
Compounds, Antarctic-Environment Protocol, Antarctic-Marine Living
Resources, Antarctic Treaty, Biodiversity, Climate Change, Climate Change
Kyoto Protocol, Desertification, Endangered Species, Environmental
Modification, Hazardous Wastes, Law of the Sea, Marine Dumping, Marine
Life Conservation, Ozone Layer Protection, Ship Pollution, Tropical Timber

83, Tropical Timber 94, Wetlands, Whaling.
Signed but not ratified: Air Pollution-Persistent Organic Pollutants.

FRANCE

Location: Western Europe, bordering the Bay of Biscay and English Channel, between Belgium and Spain, southeast of the UK; bordering the Mediterranean Sea, between Italy and Spain.
Area: 211,153 sq mi (547,030 sq km)
Area-comparative: slightly less than twice the size of Colorado.
Population: 60,424,213
Population growth rate: 0.39%
Climate: generally cool winters and mild summers, but mild winters and hot summers along the Mediterranean; occasional strong, cold, dry, north-to-northwesterly wind known as mistral.
Environment – current issues: some forest damage from acid rain; air pollution from industrial and vehicle emissions; water pollution from urban wastes, agricultural runoff.
Land use: *arable land*: 33.3%
　　　　permanent crops: 2.11%
　　　　other: 64.59%
International agreements: *party to:* Air Pollution, Air Pollution-Nitrogen Oxides, Air Pollution-Sulfur 85, Air Pollution-Sulfur 94, Air Pollution-Volatile Organic Compounds, Antarctic-Environmental Protocol, Antarctic-Marine Living Resources, Antarctic Seals, Antarctic Treaty, Biodiversity, Climate Change, Climate Change-Kyoto Protocol, Desertification, Endangered Species, Hazardous Wastes, Law of the Sea, Marine Dumping, Marine Life Conservation, Ozone Layer Protection, Ship Pollution, Tropical Timber 83, Tropical Timber 94, Wetlands Whaling.
Signed but not ratified: Air Pollution-Persistent Organic Pollutants.

GABON

Location: Western Africa, bordering the Atlantic Ocean at the Equator, between Republic of the Congo and Equatorial Guinea.
Area: 103,319 sq mi (267,667 sq km)
Area-comparative: slightly smaller than Colorado.
Population: 1,355,246
Population growth rate: 2.5%
Climate: tropical; always hot, humid.
Environment – current issues: deforestation; poaching.
Land use: *arable land*: 1.26%
　　　　permanent crops: 0.66%
　　　　other: 98.08%
International agreements: *party to:* Biodiversity, Climate Change, Desertification, Endangered Species, Law of the Sea, Marine Dumping, Ozone Layer Protection, Ship Pollution, Tropical Timber 83, Tropical Timber 94, Wetlands.
Signed but not ratified: none of the selected agreements.

GAMBIA

Location: Western Africa, bordering the North Atlantic Ocean and Senegal.
Area: 4,362 sq mi (11,300 sq km)
Area-comparative: slightly less than twice the size of Delaware.

Population: 1,546,848
Population growth rate: 2.98%
Climate: tropical; hot, rainy season (June to November); cooler, dry season (November to May).
Environment – current issues: deforestation; desertification, water-borne diseases prevalent.
Land use: arable land:19.5%
       permanent crops: 0.5%
       other: 80%
International agreements: *party to:* Biodiversity, Climate Change, Climate Change-Kyoto Protocol, Desertification, Endangered Species, Hazardous Wastes, Law of the Sea, Ozone Layer Protection, Ship Pollution, Wetlands
Signed but not ratified: none of the selected agreements.

GAZA STRIP

Location: Middle East, bordering the Mediterranean Sea, between Egypt and Israel.
Area: 360 sq km
Area-comparative: slightly more than twice the size of Washington, D.C.
Population: 1,324,991
Population growth rate: 3.83%
Climate: temperate, mild winters, dry and warm to hot summers.
Environment – current issues: desertification; salination of fresh water; sewage treatment; water-borne disease; soil degradation; depletion and contamination of underground water resources.
Land use: *arable land:* 26.32%
       permanent crops: 39.47%
       other: 34.21%
International agreements; none listed.

GEORGIA

Location: Southwestern Asia, bordering the Black Sea, between Turkey and Russia.
Area: 26,904 sq mi (69,700 sq km)
Area-comparative: slightly smaller than South Carolina.
Population: 4,693,892
Population growth rate: -0.36%
Climate: warm and pleasant; Mediterranean-like on Black Sea coast.
Environment – current issues: air pollution, particularly in Rust'avi; heavy pollution of Mtkvari River and Black Sea, inadequate supplies of potable water; soil pollution from toxic chemicals.
Land use: *arable land:* 11.21%
       permanent crops: 4.09%
       other: 84.7%
    International agreements: *party to:* Air Pollution, Biodiversity, Climate Change, Climate Change-Kyoto Protocol, Desertification, Endangered Species, HazardousWastes, Law of the Sea, Ozone Layer Protection, Ship pollution, Wetlands.
Signed but not ratified: none of the selected agreements.

GERMANY

Location: Central Europe, bordering the Baltic Sea and North Sea, between the Netherlands and Poland.
Area: 137,810 sq mi (357,021 sq km)
Area-comparative: slightly smaller than Montana.
Population: 82,424,609
Population growth rate: 0.02%
Climate: temperate and marine; cool, cloudy, wet winters and summers; occasional warm mountain (foehn wind).
Environment – current issues: emissions from coal-burning utilities and industries contribute to air pollution; acid rain, resulting from sulfur dioxide emissions, is damaging forests; pollution in the Baltic Sea from raw sewage and industrial effluents from rivers in eastern Germany; hazardous waste disposal; government established a mechanism for ending the use of nuclear power over the next 15 years; government working to meet EU commitment to identify nature preservation areas in line with the EU's Flora, Fauna, and Habitat directive.
Land use: *arable land*: 33.88%
   permanent crops: 0.65%
   other: 65.47%
International agreements: *party to*: Air Pollution, Air Pollution-Nitrogen Oxides, Air Pollution-Sulfur 85, Air Pollution-Sulfur 94, Air Pollution-Volatile Organic Compounds, Antarctic-Environmental Protocol, Antarctic-Marine Living Resources, Antarctic Seals, Antarctic Treaty, Biodiversity, Climate Change, Climate Change-Kyoto Protocol , Desertification, Endangered Species, Environmental Modification, Hazardous Wastes, Law of the Sea, Marine Dumping, Ozone Layer Protection, Ship Pollution, Tropical Timber 83, Tropical Timber 94, Wetlands, Whaling.
Signed but not ratified: Air Pollution-Persistent Organic Pollutants.

GHANA

Location: Western Africa, bordering Gulf of Guinea, between Cote d'Ivoire and Togo.
Area: 92,431 sq mi (239,460 sq km)
Area-comparative: slightly smaller than Oregon.
Population: 20,757,032
Population growth rate: 1.36%
Climate: tropical; warm and comparatively dry along southeast coast; hot and humid in southwest; hot and dry in north.
Environment – current issues: recurrent drought in north severely affects agricultura activities; deforestation; overgrazing; soil erosion, poaching and habitat destruction threatens wildlife populations; water pollutions; inadequate supplies of potable water.
Land use: *arable land*: 15.82%
   permanent crops: 7.47%
   other: 76.71%
International agreements: *party to:* Biodiversity, Climate Change, Climate Change-Kyoto Protocol, Desertification, Endangered Species, Environmental Modification, Hazardous Wastes, Law of the Sea, Ozone Layer Protection, Ship Pollution, Tropical Timber 83, Tropical Timber 94, Wetlands.
Signed but not ratified: Marine Life Conservation.

GREECE

Location: Southern Europe, bordering the Aegean Sea, Ionian Sea, and the Mediterranean Sea.
Area: 50,929 sq mi (131,940 sq km)
Area-comparative: slightly smaller than Alabama.
Population: 10,647,529
Population growth rate: 0.2%
Climate: temperate; mild, wet winters; hot, dry summers.
Environment – current issues: air pollution; water pollution.
Land use: *arable land*: 22%
　　　　　permanent crops: 8%
　　　　　other: 70%
International agreements: *party to:* Air Pollution, Air Pollution-Nitrogen Oxides, Air Pollution-Sulfur 94, Antarctic-Environmental Protocol, Antarctic-Marine Life Resources, Antarctic Treaty, Biodiversity, Climate Change, Climate Change-Kyoto Protocol, Desertification, Endangered Species, Environmental Modification, Hazardous Wastes, Law of the Sea, Marine Dumping, Ozone Layer Protection, Ship Pollution, Tropical timber 83, Tropical Timber 94, Wetlands.
Signed but not ratified: Air Pollution-Persistent Organic Pollutants, Air Pollution-Volatile Organic Compounds.

GRENADA

Location: Caribbean island between the Caribbean Sea and Atlantic Ocean, north of Trinidad and Tobago.
Area: 133 sq mi (344 sq km)
Area-comparative: twice the size of Washington, D.C.
Population: 89,357
Population growth rate: 0.14%
Climate: tropical; tempered by northeast trade winds.
Environment – current issues: NA
Land use: *arable land*: 5.88%
　　　　　permanent crops: 26.47%
　　　　　other: 67.65%
International agreements: *party to:* Biodiversity, Climate Change Climate Change-Kyoto Protocol, Desertification, Endangered Species, Law of the Sea, Ozone Layer Protection, Whaling.
Signed but not ratified: none of the selected agreements.

GUATEMALA

Location: Central America, bordering North Pacific Ocean, between El Salvador and Mexico, bordering Gulf of Honduras (Caribbean Sea) between Honduras and Belize.
Area: 42,031 sq mi (108,890 sq km)
Area-comparative: slightly smaller than Tennessee.
Population: 14,280,596
Population growth rate: 2.61%
Climate: tropical; hot, humid in lowlands; cooler in highlands.
Environment – current issues: deforestation in the rainforest, erosion, water pollution.
Land use: *arable land*: 12.54 %
　　　　　permanent crops: 5.03%
　　　　　other: 82.43%

International agreements: *party to:* Antarctic Treaty, Biodiversity, Climate Change, Climate Change-Kyoto Protocol, Desertification, Endangered Species, Environmental Modification, Hazardous Wastes, Law of the Sea, Marine Dumping, Ozone Layer Protection, Ship Pollution, Wetlands.
Signed but not ratified: none of the selected agreements.

GUINEA

Location: Western Africa, bordering the North Atlantic Ocean, between Guinea-Bissau and Sierra Leone.
Area: 94,901 sq mi (245,857 sq km)
Area-comparative: slightly smaller than Oregon.
Population: 9,246,462
Population growth rate: 2.37%
Climate: generally hot and humid; monsoonal-type rainy season (June to November) with southwesterly winds; dry season (December to May) with northeasterly harmattan winds
Environment – current issues: deforestation; inadequate supplies of potable water; desertification; soil contamination and erosion; over fishing, over population in forest region; poor mining practices have led to environmental damage.
Land use: *arable land:* 3.6%
permanent crops: 2.44%
other: 93.96%
International agreements: *party to:* Biodiversity, Climate Change, Climate Change-Kyoto Protocol, Desertification, Endangered Species, Hazardous Wastes, Law of the Sea, Ozone Layer Protection, Wetlands, Whaling.
Signed but not ratified: none of the selected agreements.

GUINEA-BISSAU

Location: Western Africa, bordering the North Atlantic Ocean, between Guinea and Senegal.
Area: 13,942 sq mi (36,120 sq km)
Area-comparative: slightly less than three times the size of Connecticut.
Population: 1,388,363
Population growth rate: 1.99%
Climate: tropical; generally hot and humid; monsoonal-type rainy season (June to November) with southwesterly winds; dry season (December to May) with northeasterly harmatten winds.
Environment – current issues: deforestation; soil erosion; overgrazing; over fishing.
Land use: *arable land:* 10.67%
permanent crops: 1.78%
other: 87.55%
International agreements: *party to:* Biodiversity, Climate Change, Desertification, Endangered Species, Law of the Sea, Wetlands.
Signed but not ratified: none of the selected agreements.

GUYANA

Location: Northern South America, bordering North Atlantic Ocean, between Suriname and Venezuela.
Area: 82,978 sq mi (214,970 sq km)
Area-comparative: slightly smaller than Idaho.
Population: 705,803

Population growth rate: 0.61%
Climate: tropical; hot, humid, moderated by northeast trade winds; two rainy
   seasons (May to mid-August, mid-November to mid-January).
Environment – current issues: water pollution from sewage and agricultural and
   industrial chemicals; deforestation.
Land use: *arable land*: 2.44%
         permanent crops: 0.08%
         other: 97.48%
International agreements: *party to:* Biodiversity, Climate Change, Climate Change-
   Kyoto Protocol, Desertification, Endangered Species, Hazardous Wastes,
   Law of the Sea, ozone Layer Protection, Ship Pollution, Tropical Timber 83,
   Tropical Timber 94.
Signed, but not ratified: none of the selected agreements.

HAITI

Location: Caribbean, western one-third of the island of Hispaniola, west of the
Dominican Republic.
Area: 10,711 sq mi (27,750 sq km)
Area-comparative: slightly smaller than Maryland.
Population: 7,656,166
Population growth rate: 1.71%
Climate: tropical; semiarid where mountains in east cut off trade winds
Environment – current issues: extensive deforestation (much of the remaining
      forested land is being cleared for agriculture and used as fuel); soil erosion;
      inadequate supplies of potable water.
Land use: arable land: 20.3%
         permanent crops: 12.7%
         other: 67%
International agreements: *party to:* Biodiversity, Climate Change, Desertification, Law
   of the Sea, Marine Dumping, Marine Life Conservation, Ozone Layer
   Protection.
Signed but not ratified: Hazardous Wastes.

HONDURAS

Location: Central America, bordering the Caribbean Sea, between El Salvador and
Nicaragua.
Area: 43,267 sq mi (112,090 sq km)
Area-comparative: slightly larger than Tennessee.
Population: 6,823,568
Population growth rate: 2.24%
Climate: subtropical in lowlands, temperate in mountains.
Environment – current issues: urban population expanding; deforestation results
      from logging and the clearing of land for agricultural purposes; further land
      degradation and soil erosion hastened by uncontrolled development and
      improper land use practices such as farming of marginal lands; mining
      activities polluting Lago de Yojoa (the country's largest source of fresh
      water), as well as several rivers and streams, with heavy metals.
Land use: *arable land*: 15.15%
         permanent crops: 3.13%
         other: 81.72%
International agreements: *party to:* Biodiversity, Climate Change, Climate Change-

Kyoto Protocol, Desertification, Endangered Species, Hazardous Wastes, Law of the Sea, Marine Dumping, Ozone Layer Protection, Ship Pollution, Tropical Timber 83, Tropical Timber 94, Wetlands.
Signed but not ratified: none of the selected agreements.

HUNGARY

Location: Central Europe, northwest of Romania.
Area: 35,910 sq mi (93,030 sq km)
Area-comparative: slightly smaller than Indiana.
Population: 10,032,375
Population growth rate: - 0.25%
Climate: temperate; cold, cloudy, humid winters warm summers.
Environment – current issues: the upgrading of Hungary's standards in waste management, energy efficiency and air, soil, and water pollution with environmental requirements for EU accession will require large investments.
Land use: arable land: 52.2%
   permanent crops: 2.46%
   other: 45.34%
International agreements: *party to:* Air Pollution, Air Pollution-Nitrogen Oxides, Air Pollution –Sulfur 85, Air Pollution-Volatile Organic Compounds, Antarctic Treaty, Biodiversity, Climate Change, Climate Change-Kyoto Protocol, Desertification, Endangered Species, Environmental Modification, Hazardous Wastes, Law of the Sea, Marine Dumping, ozone Layer Protection, Ship Pollution, Wetlands.
Signed but not ratified: Air Pollution-Persistent Organic Pollutants, Air Pollution-Sulfur94.

ICELAND

Location: Northern Europe, island between the Greenland Sea and the North Atlantic Ocean.
Area: 39,758 sq mi (103,000 sq km)
Area-comparative: slightly smaller than Kentucky.
Population: 293,966
Population growth rate: 0.97%
Climate: temperate; moderated by North Atlantic Current; mild windy winters; damp, cool summers.
Environment – current issues: water pollution from fertilizer runoff; inadequate wastewater treatment.
Land use: *arable land:* 1%
   permanent crops: 0%
   permanent pastures: 28%
   forest and woodlands: 1%
   other: 70%
International agreements: *party to:* Air Pollution, Biodiversity, Climate Change, Climate Change-Kyoto Protocol; Desertification, Endangered Species, Hazardous Wastes, Kyoto Protocol, Law of the Sea, Marine Dumping, Ozone Layer Protection, Ship Pollution, Transboundary Air Pollution, Wetlands.
Signed but not ratified: Air Pollution-Persistent Organic Pollutants, Environmental Modification, Marine Life Conservation.

INDIA

Location: Southern Asia, bordering the Arabian Sea and the Bay of Bengal, between Burma and Pakistan.
Area: 1,269,009 sq mi (3,287,590 sq km)
Area-comparative: slightly more than one-third the size of the United States.
Population: 1,065,070,607
Population growth-rate: 1.44%
Climate: varies from tropical monsoon in south to temperate in north.
Environment – current issues: deforestation; soil erosion; overgrazing; desertification; air pollution from industrial effluents and vehicle emissions; water pollution from raw sewage and runoff of agricultural pesticides; tap water is not potable throughout the country; huge and growing population is overstraining natural resources.
Land use: *arable land*: 54.35%
　　　　permanent crops: 2.66%
　　　　other: 42.99%
International agreements: *party to:* Antarctic-Environmental Protocol, Antarctic-Marine Living Resources, Antarctic Treaty, Biodiversity, Climate Change, Kyoto Protocol, Desertification, Endangered Species, Environmental Modification, Hazardous Wastes, Law of the Sea, Ozone Layer Protection, Ship Pollution, Tropical Timber 83, Tropical Timber 94, Wetlands, Whaling.
Signed but not ratified: none of the selected agreements.

INDONESIA

Location: Southeastern Asia, group of islands between the Indian Ocean and the Pacific Ocean.
Area: 740,904 sq mi (1,919,440 sq km)
Area-comparative: slightly less than three times the size of Texas.
Population: 238,452,952
Population growth rate: 1.49%
Climate: tropical; hot, humid; moderate in highlands.
Environments – current issues: deforestation; water pollution from industrial wastes, sewage; air pollution in urban areas; smoke and haze from forest fires.
Land use: *arable land*: 9.9%
　　　　permanent crops: 7.2%
　　　　other: 82.9%
International agreements: *party to:* Biodiversity, Climate Change, Desertification, Endangered Species, Hazardous Wastes, Law of the Sea, Ozone Layer Protection, Ship Pollution, Tropical Timber 83, Tropical Timber 94, Wetlands.
Signed but not ratified: Climate Change-Kyoto Protocol, Marine Life Conservation.

IRAN

Location: Middle East, bordering the Gulf of Oman, the Persian Gulf, and the Caspian Sea, between Iraq and Pakistan.
Area: 636,128 sq mi (1,648,000 sq km)
Area-comparative: slightly larger than Alaska.
Population: 69,018,924
Population growth rate: 1.07%
Climate: mostly arid and semiarid; subtropical along Caspian coast.
Environment – current issues: air pollution, especially in urban areas, from vehicle

emissions, refinery operations, and industrial effluents; deforestation; overgrazing; desertification; oil pollution in Persian Gulf; wetland losses from drought; soil degradation; (salination); inadequate supplies of potable water; water pollution from raw sewage and industrial waste; urbanization.

Land use: *arable land*: 10.17%
     permanent crops: 1.16%
     other: 88.67%

International agreements: *party to:* Biodiversity, Climate Change, Desertification, Endangered Species, Hazardous Wastes, Marine Dumping, Ozone Layer Protection, Wetlands.
Signed but not ratified: Environmental Modification, Law of the Sea, Marine Life Conservation.

IRAQ

Location: Middle East, bordering the Persian Gulf, between Iran and Kuwait.
Area: 168,710 sq mi (437,072 sq km)
Area-comparative: slightly more than twice the size of Idaho.
Population: 25,374,691
Population growth rate: 2.74%
Climate: mostly desert; mild to cool winters with dry hot summers; northern mountainous regions along Iranian and Turkish borders experience cold winters with occasionally heavy snows that melt in early spring, sometimes causing extensive flooding in central and southern Iraq.
Environment – current issues: government water control projects have drained most of the inhabited marsh areas east of An Nasiriyah by drying up or diverting the feeder streams and rivers; a once sizable population of Marsh Arabs, who inhabited these areas for thousands of years, has been displaced; furthermore, the destruction of natural habitat poses serious threats to the area's wildlife populations; inadequate supplies of potable water; development for the Tigris and Euphrates rivers system contingent upon agreements with upstream riparian Turkey; air and water pollution; soil degradation (salination) and erosion; desertification.

Land use: *arable land*: 11.89%
     permanent crops: 0.78%
     other: 87.33%

International agreements: *party to*: Law of the Sea.
Signed but not ratified: Environmental Modification.

IRELAND

Location: Western Europe, island in the North Atlantic Ocean, west of Great Britain.
Area: 27,128 sq mi (70,280 sq km)
Area-comparative: slightly larger than West Virginia.
Population: 3,969,558
Population growth rate: 1.16%
Climate: temperate maritime; modified by North Atlantic Current; mild winters, cool summers; consistently humid; overcast about half the time.
Environment – current issues: water pollution, especially of lakes, from agricultural runoff.

Land use: *arable land*: 19.49%
     permanent crops: 0.04%
     other: 80.47%

International agreements: *party to*: Air Pollution, Air Pollution-Nitrogen Oxides, Air Pollution-Sulfur 94, Biodiversity, Climate Change, Climate Change-Kyoto Protocol, Desertification, Endangered Species, Environment Modification, Hazardous Wastes, Law of the Sea, Marine Dumping, Ozone Layer Protection, Ship Pollution, Tropical Timber 83, Tropical Timber 94, Wetlands, Whaling.
Signed but not ratified: Air Pollution-Persistent Organic Pollutants, Marine Life Conservation.

ISRAEL

Location: Middle East, bordering the Mediterranean Sea, between Egypt and Lebanon.
Area: 8,017 sq mi (20,770 sq km)
Area-comparative: slightly smaller than New Jersey.
Population: 6,199,008
Population growth rate: 1.29%
Climate: temperate; hot and dry in southern and eastern desert areas.
Environment – current issues: limited arable land and natural fresh water resources pose serious constraints; desertification; air pollution from industrial and vehicle emissions; groundwater pollution from industrial and vehicle emissions; groundwater pollution from industrial and domestic waste, chemical fertilizers, and pesticides.
Land use: *arable land*: 17.02%
    permanent crops: 4.17%
    other: 78.81%
International agreements: *party to:* Biodiversity, Climate Change, Desertification, Endangered Species, Hazardous Wastes, Ozone Layer Protection, Ship Pollution, Wetlands.
Signed but not ratified: Climate Change-Kyoto Protocol, Marine Life Conservation.

ITALY

Location: Southern Europe, peninsula extending into the central Mediterranean Sea, northeast of Tunisia.
Area: 116,275 sq mi (301,230 sq km)
Area-comparative: slightly larger than Arizona.
Population: 58,057,477
Population growth rate: 0.09%
Climate: predominantly Mediterranean; Alpine in far north; hot dry in south.
Environment – current issues: air pollution from industrial emissions such as sulfur dioxide; coastal and inland rivers polluted from industrial and agricultural effluents; inadequate industrial waste treatment and disposal facilities.
Land use: *arable land*: 28.07%
    permanent crops: 9.25%
    other: 62.68%
International agreements: *party to:* Air Pollution, Air Pollution-Nitrogen Oxides, Air Pollution-Sulfur 85, Air Pollution-Sulfur 94, Air Pollution-Volatile Organic Compounds, Antarctic-Environmental Protocol, Antarctic-Marine Living Resources, Antarctic Seals, Antarctic Treaty, Biodiversity, Climate Change, Climate Change-Kyoto Protocol, Desertification, Endangered Species, Environmental Modification, Hazardous Wastes, Law of the Sea, Marine Dumping, Ozone Layer Protection, Ship Pollution, Tropical Timber 83, Tropical Timber 94, Wetlands, Whaling.
Signed but not ratified: Air Pollution-Persistent Organic Pollutants.

JAMAICA

Location: Caribbean, island in the Caribbean Sea, south of Cuba.
Area: 4,242 sq mi (10,991 sq km)
Area-comparative: slightly smaller than Connecticut.
Population: 2,713,130
Population growth rate: 0.66%
Climate: tropical; hot, humid; temperate interior.
Environment – current issues: heavy rates of deforestation; coastal waters polluted by industrial wastes, sewage, and oil spills; damage to corral reefs; air pollution in Kingston results from vehicle emissions.
Land use: *arable land*: 16.07%
  permanent crops: 9.23%
  other: 74.7%
International agreements: *party to:* Biodiversity, Climate Change, Climate Change-Kyoto Protocol, Desertification, Endangered Species, Hazardous Wastes, Law of the Sea, Marine Dumping, Marine Life Conservation, Ozone Layer Protection, Ship Pollution, Wetlands.
Signed but not ratified: none of the selected agreements.

JAPAN

Location: Eastern Asia, island chain between the North Pacific Ocean and the Sea of Japan, east of the Korean Peninsula.
Area: 145,844 sq mi (377,835 sq km)
Area-comparative: slightly smaller than California.
Population: 127,333,002
Population growth rate: 0.08%
Climate: varies from tropical in south to cool temperate in north.
Environment – current issues: air pollution from power plant emissions results in acid rain; acidification of lakes and reservoirs degrading water quality and threatening aquatic life; Japan is one of the largest consumers of fish and tropical timber, contributing to the depletion of these resources in Asia.
Land use: *arable land*: 12.13%
  permanent crops: 1.01%
  other: 86.86%
International agreements: party to: Antarctic-Environmental Protocol, Antarctic-Marine Living Resources; Antarctic Seals, Antarctic Treaty, Biodiversity, Climate Change, Climate Change-Kyoto Protocol, Desertification, Endangered Species, Environmental Modification, Hazardous Wastes, Law of the Sea, Marine Dumping, Ozone Layer Protection, Ship Pollution, Tropical Timber 83, Tropical Timber 94, Wetlands, Whaling.

JORDAN

Location: Southwestern Asia, northwest of Saudi Arabia.
Area: 35,628 sq mi (92,300 sq km)
Area-comparative: slightly smaller than Indiana.
Population: 5,611,202
Population growth rate: 2.67%
Climate: mostly arid desert; rainy season in west (November to April).
Environment – current issues: limited natural fresh water resources; deforestation; overgrazing; soil erosion; desertification.

Land use: *arable land*: 2.87%
    permanent crops: 1.52%
    other: 95.61%
International agreements: *party to:* Biodiversity, Climate Change, Climate Change-
    Kyoto Protocol, Desertification, Endangered Species, Hazardous Wastes,
    Law of the Sea, Marine Dumping, Ozone Layer Protection, Wetlands.
Signed but not ratified: none of the selected agreements.

KAZAKHSTAN

Location: Central Asia, northwest of China.
Area: 1,048,877 sq mi (2,717,300 sq km)
Area-comparative: slightly less than four times the size of Texas.
Population: 15,143,704
Population growth rate: 0.26%
Climate: continental, cold winters and hot summers, arid and semiarid.
Environment – current issues: radioactive or toxic chemical sites associated with
    former defense industries and test ranges scattered throughout the country
    pose health risks for humans and animals; industrial pollution is severe in
    some cities; because the two main rivers which flowed into the Aral Sea have
    been diverted for irrigation, it is drying up and leaving behind chemical
    pesticides and natural salts; these substances are then picked up by the
    wind and blown into noxious dust storms; pollution in the Caspian Sea; soil
    pollution from overuse of agricultural chemicals and salination from poor
    infrastructure and wasteful irrigation practices.
Land use: *arable land*: 11.23%
    permanent crops: 0.05%
    other: 88.72%
International agreements: *party to:* Air Pollution, Biodiversity, Climate Change,
    Desertification, Endangered Species, Hazardous Wastes, Ozone Layer
    Protection, Ship Pollution.
Signed but not ratified: Climate Change-Kyoto Protocol.

KENYA

Location: Eastern Africa, bordering the Indian Ocean, between Somalia and Tanzania.
Area: 224,903 sq mi (582,650 sq km)
Area-comparative: slightly more than twice the size of Nevada.
Population: 32,021,856
Population growth rate: 1.14%
Climate: varies from tropical along coast to arid in interior.
Environment – current issues: water pollution from urban and industrial wastes;
    degradation of water quality from increased use of pesticides and fertilizers;
    water hyacinth infestation in Lake Victoria; deforestation; soil erosion;
    desertification; poaching.
Land use: *arable land*: 7.03%
    permanent crops: 0.91%
    other: 92.06%
International Agreements: *party to:* Biodiversity, Climate Change, Desertification,
    Endangered Species, Hazardous Wastes, Law of the Sea, Marine Dumping,
    Marine Life Conservation, Ozone Layer Pollution, Ship Pollution, Wetlands,
    Whaling.
Signed but not ratified: none of the selected agreements.

KIRIBATI

Location: a group of islands in the Pacific Ocean, about one-half of the way from Hawaii to Australia.

Area: 313 sq mi (811 sq km)

Area-comparative: four times the size of Washington, D.C.

Population: 100,798

Population growth rate: 2.25%

Climate: tropical; marine, hot humid, moderated by trade winds.

Environment – current issues: heavy pollution in lagoon of south Tarawa atoll due to heavy migration mixed with traditional practices such as lagoon latrines and open-pit dumping; ground water at risk.

Land use: *arable land:* 0%

*permanent crops:*50.68%

other: 49.32%

International Agreements: *party to:* Biodiversity, Climate Change, Climate Change-Kyoto Protocol, Desertification, Hazardous Wastes, Law of the Sea, Marine Dumping, Ozone Layer Protection.

Signed but not ratified: none of the selected agreements.

KOREA, NORTH

Location: Eastern Asia, northern half of the Korean Peninsula bordering the Korea Bay and the Sea of Japan, between China and South Korea.

Area: 46,541 sq mi (120,540 sq km)

Area-comparative: slightly smaller than Mississippi.

Population: 22,697,553

Population growth rate: 0.98%

Climate: temperate with rainfall concentrated in summer.

Environment – current issues: water pollution; inadequate supplies of potable water; water-borne disease; deforestation; soil erosion and degradation.

Land use: *arable land:* 14.12%

permanent crops: 2.49%

other: 83.39%

International Agreements: *party to:* Antarctic Treaty, Biodiversity, Climate Change, Environmental Modification, Ozone Layer Protection, Ship Pollution

Signed but ratified: Law of the Sea.

KOREA, SOUTH

Location: Eastern Asia, southern half of the Korean Peninsula bordering Yellow Sea and Sea of Japan.

Area: 38,013 sq mi (98,480 sq km)

Area-comparative: slightly larger than Indiana.

Population: 48,598,175

Population growth rate: 0.62%

Climate: temperate, with rainfall heavier in summer than winter.

Environment – current issues: air pollution in large cities; acid rain; water pollution from the discharge of sewage and industrial effluents; drift net fishing.

Land use: *arable land:* 17.44%

permanent crops: 2.05%

other: 80.51%

International Agreements: *party to:* Antarctic-Environmental Protocol, Antarctic-Marine Living Resources, Antarctic Treaty, Biodiversity, Climate Change,

Climate Change-Kyoto Protocol, Desertification, Endangered Species, Environmental Modification, Hazardous Wastes, Law of the Sea, Marine Dumping, Ozone Layer Protection, Ship Pollution, Tropical Timber 83, Tropical Timber 94, Wetlands, Whaling.
Signed but not ratified: none of the selected agreements.

KUWAIT
Location: Southwestern Asia, the Middle East, bordering the Persian Gulf, between Iraq and Saudi Arabia.
Area: 6,878 sq mi (17,820 sq km)
Area-comparative: slightly smaller than New Jersey.
Population: 2,257,549
Population growth rate: 3.36%
Climate: dry desert; intensely hot summers; short cool winters.
Environment – current issues: limited natural fresh water resources; some of the world's largest and most sophisticated desalination facilities provide much of the water; air and water pollution; desertification.
Land use: *arable land*: 0.34%
permanent crops: 0.06%
other: 99.6%
International Agreements: *party to:* Biodiversity, Climate Change, Desertification, Endangered Species, Environmental Modification, Hazardous Wastes, Law of the Sea, Ozone Layer Protection.
Signed but not ratified: Marine Dumping.

KYRGYZSTAN
Location: Central Asia, west of China.
Area: 76,621 sq mi (198,500 sq km)
Area-comparative: slightly smaller than South Dakota.
Population: 5,081,429
Population growth rate: 1.25%
Climate: dry continental to polar in high Tien Shan; subtropical in southwest (Fergana Valley); temperate in northern foothill zone.
Environment – current issues: water pollution; many people get their water directly from contaminated streams and wells; as a result water-borne diseases are prevalent; increasing soil salinity from faulty irrigation practices.
Land use: *arable land*: 7.04%
permanent crops: 0.39%
other: 92.57%
International Agreements: *party to:* Air Pollution, Biodiversity, Climate Change, Climate Change-Kyoto Protocol, Desertification, Hazardous Wastes, Ozone Layer Protection.
Signed but not ratified: none of the selected agreements.

LAOS
Location: Southeastern Asia, northeast of Thailand, west of Vietnam.
Area: 91,405 sq mi (236,800 sq km)
Area-comparative: slightly larger than Utah.
Population: 6,068,117
Population growth rate: 2.44%
Climate: tropical; rainy season (May to November); dry season (December to April)

Environment – current issues: unexploded ordnance; deforestation; soil erosion; most of the population does not have access to potable water.
Land use: *arable land*: 3.47%
      permanent crops: 0.23%
      other: 96.3%
International Agreements: *party to:* Biodiversity, Climate Change, Climate Change-Kyoto Protocol, Desertification, Endangered Species, Environment Modification, Law of the Sea, Ozone Layer Protection.
Signed but not ratified; none of the selected agreements.

LATVIA

Location: Eastern Europe, bordering the Baltic Sea, between Estonia and Lithuania.
Area: 24,931 sq mi (64,589 sq km)
Area-comparative: slightly larger than West Virginia.
Population: 2,306,306
Population growth rate: -0.71%
Climate: maritime; wet, moderate winters.
Environment – current issues: Latvia's environment has benefited from a shift to service industries after the country regained independence; the main environmental priorities are improvement of drinking water quality and sewage system, household and hazardous waste management, and reduction of air pollution; in 2001, Latvia closed the EU accession negotiation chapter on environment committing to full enforcement directives by 2010.
Land use: *arable land*: 29.01%
      permanent crops: 0.48%
      other: 70.51%
International Agreements: *party to:* Air Pollution, Biodiversity, Climate Change, Climate Change-Kyoto Protocol, Endangered Species, Hazardous Wastes, Ozone Layer Protection, Ship Pollution, Wetlands.
Signed but not ratified: Air Pollution-Persistent Organic Pollutants.

LEBANON

Location: Middle East, bordering the Mediterranean Sea, between Israel and Syria.
Area: 4,015 sq mi (10,400 sq km)
Area-comparative: about 0.7 times the size of Connecticut.
Population: 3,777,218
Population growth rate: 1.3%
Climate: Mediterranean; mild to cool, wet winters with hot, dry summers; Lebanon mountains experience heavy winter snows.
Environment – current issues: deforestation; soil erosion; desertification; air pollution in Beirut from vehicle traffic and the burning of industrial wastes; pollution of coastal waters from raw sewage and oil spills.
Land use: *arable land*: 17.6%
      permanent crops: 12.51%
      other: 69.89%
International Agreements: *party to*: Biodiversity, Climate Change, Desertification, Hazardous Wastes, Law of the Sea, Ozone Layer Protection, Ship Pollution, Wetlands.
Signed but not ratified: Environmental Modification, Marine Life Conservation.

LESOTHO

Location: Southern Africa, an enclave of South Africa.
Area: 11,717 sq mi (30,355 sq km)
Area-comparative: slightly smaller than Maryland.
Population: 1,865,040
Population growth rate: 0.14%
Climate: temperate; cool to cold, dry winters; hot wet summers.
Environment – current issues: population pressure forcing settlement in marginal areas results in overgrazing; severe soil erosion, and soil exhaustion; desertification; Highlands Water Project controls, stores, and redirects water to South Africa.
Land use: *arable land*: 10.71%
    permanent crops: 0%
    other: 89.29%
International Agreements: *party to*: Biodiversity, Climate Change, Climate Change-Kyoto Protocol, Desertification, Endangered Species, Hazardous Wastes, Marine Life Conservation, Ozone Layer Protection.
Signed but not ratified: Law of the Sea.

LIBERIA

Location: Western Africa, bordering the North Atlantic Ocean, between Cote d'Ivorie and Sierra Leone.
Area: 42,989 sq mi (111,370 sq km)
Area-comparative: slightly larger than Tennessee.
Population: 3,390,635
Population growth rate: 2.7%
Climate: tropical; hot, humid; dry winters with hot days and cool to cold nights; wet, cloudy summers with frequent heavy showers.
Environment – current issues: tropical rain forest deforestation; soil erosion; loss of biodiversity; pollution of coastal waters from oil residue and raw sewage.
Land use: *arable land*: 1.97%
    permanent crops: 2.08%
    other: 95.95%
International Agreements: *party to:* Biodiversity, Climate Change-Kyoto Protocol, Desertification, Endangered Species, Ozone Layer Protection, Ship Pollution, Tropical Timber 83, Tropical Timber 94.
Signed but not ratified: Climate Change, Environmental Modification, Law of the Sea, Marine Life Conservation.

LIBYA

Location: Northern Africa, bordering the Mediterranean Sea, between Egypt and Tunisia.
Area: 679,182 sq mi (1,759,540 sq km)
Area-comparative: slightly larger than Alaska.
Population: 5,631,585
Population growth rate: 2.37%
Climate: Mediterranean along coast; dry extreme desert interior.
Environment – current issues: desertification; very limited natural fresh water resources; the Great Manmade River Project, the largest water development scheme in the world, is being built to bring water from large aquifers under the Sahara to coastal cities.

Land use: *arable land*: 1.03%
        permanent crops: 0.17%
        other: 98.8%
International Agreements: *party to:* Biodiversity; Climate Change; Desertification, Endangered Species, Hazardous Wastes, Marine Dumping, Ozone Layer Protection.
Signed but not ratified: Law of the Sea.

LIECHTENSTEIN

Location: Central Europe, between Austria and Switzerland.
Area: 62 sq mi (160 sq km)
Area-comparative: about 0.9 times the size of Washington D.C.
Population: 33,436
Population growth rate: 0.86%
Climate: continental; cold cloudy winters with frequent snow or rain; cool to moderately warm, cloudy, humid summers.
Environment – current issues: NA
Land use: *arable land*: 25%
        permanent crops: 0%
        other: 75%
International Agreements: *party to:* Air Pollution, Air Pollution-Nitrogen Oxides, Air Pollution-Sulfur 85, Air Pollution-Sulfur 94, Air Pollution-Volatile Organic Compounds, Biodiversity, Climate Change, Desertification, Endangered Species, Hazardous Wastes, Ozone Layer Protection, Wetlands.
Signed but not ratified: Air Pollution-Persistent Organic Pollutants, Climate Change-Kyoto Protocol, Law of the Sea.

LITHUANIA

Location: Eastern Europe, bordering the Baltic Sea, between Latvia and Russia.
Area: 25,167 sq mi (65,200 sq km)
Area-comparative: slightly larger than West Virginia.
Population: 3,607,899
Population growth rate: -0.33%
Climate: transitional, between maritime and continental; wet, moderate winters and Summers.
Environment – current issues: contamination of soil and groundwater with petroleum products and chemicals at military bases
Land use: *arable land*: 45.46%
        permanent crops: 0.93%
        other: 53.61%
International Agreements: *party to*: Air Pollution, Biodiversity, Climate Change, Climate Change-Kyoto Protocol, Endangered Species, Hazardous Wastes, Law of the Sea, Ozone Layer Protection, Ship Pollution, Wetlands.
Signed but not ratified: Air pollution-Persistent Organic Pollutants.

LUXEMBOURG

Location: Western Europe, between France and Germany.
Area: 998 sq mi (2,586 sq km)
Area-comparative: slightly smaller than Rhode Island.
Population: 462,690

Population growth rate: 1.28%
Climate: modified continental with mild winters, cool summers.
Environment – current issues: air and water pollution in urban areas, soil pollution of farmland.
Land use: *arable land*: 25%
　　　　　permanent crops: 0%
　　　　　other: 75%
International agreements: *party to:* Air Pollution, Air Pollution-Nitrogen Oxides, Air Pollution-Persistent Organic Pollutants, Air Pollution-Sulfur 83, Air Pollution-Sulfur 94, Air Pollution—Volatile Organic Compounds, Biodiversity, Climate Change, Climate Change-Kyoto Protocol, Desertification, Endangered Species, Hazardous Wastes, Law of the Sea, Marine Dumping, Ozone Layer Protection, Ship Pollution, Tropical Timber 83, Tropical Timber 94, Wetlands.
Signed but not ratified: Environmental Modification.

MACEDONIA
Location: Southeastern Europe, north of Greece.
Area: 9,778 sq mi (25,333 sq km)
Area-comparative: slightly larger than Vermont.
Population: 2,071,210
Population growth rate: 0.39%
Climate: warm, dry summers and autumns and relatively cold winters with heavy snowfall.
Environment – current issues: air pollution from metallurgical plants
Land use: *arable land*: 23.59%
　　　　　permanent crops: 1.85%
　　　　　other: 74.56%
International Agreements: *party to*: Air Pollution, Biodiversity, Climate Change, Endangered Species, Hazardous Wastes, Law of the Sea, Ozone Layer Protection, Wetlands.
Signed but not ratified; none of the selected agreements.

MADAGASCAR
Location: Southern Africa, island in the Indian Ocean, east of Mozambique.
Area: 226,597 sq mi (587,040 sq km)
Area-comparative: slightly less than twice the size of Arizona.
Population: 17,501,871
Population growth rate: 3.03%
Climate: tropical along coast, temperate inland, and in south.
Environment – current issues: soil erosion results from deforestation and overgrazing; desertification; surface water contaminated with raw sewage and other organic wastes; several species of flora and fauna unique to the island is endangered.
Land use: *arable land*: 4.99%
　　　　　permanent crops: 1.03%
　　　　　other: 93.98%
International Agreements: *party to*: Biodiversity, Climate Change, Climate Change-Kyoto Protocol, Desertification, Endangered Species, Hazardous Wastes Law of the Sea, Marine Life Conservation, Ozone Layer Protection, Wetlands
Signed but not ratified: none of the selected agreements.

MALAWI

Location: Southern Africa, east of Zambia.
Area: 45,733 sq mi (118,480 sq km)
Area-comparative: slightly smaller than Pennsylvania.
Population: 11,906,855
Population growth rate: 2.14%
Climate: sub-tropical; rainy season (November to May); dry season (May to November)
Environment – current issues: deforestation; land degradation; water pollution from agricultural runoff, sewage, industrial wastes; situation of spawning grounds endangers fish populations.
Land use: *arable land*: 19.93%
　　　permanent crops: 1.33%
　　　other: 78.74%
International Agreements: *party to:* Biodiversity, Climate Change, Climate Change-Kyoto Protocol, Desertification, Endangered Species, Environmental Modification, Hazardous Wastes, Marine Life Conservation, Ozone Layer Protection, Ship Pollution, Wetlands.
Signed but not ratified: Law of the Sea.

MALAYSIA

Location: Southeastern Asia, peninsula and northern one-third of the island of Borneo, south of Vietnam.
Area: 127,283 sq mi (329,750 sq km)
Area-comparative: slightly larger than New Mexico.
Population: 23,522,482
Population growth rate: 1.83%
Climate: tropical; annual southwest (April to October) and northeast (October to February) monsoons.
Environment – current issues: air pollution from industrial and vehicular emissions; water pollution from raw sewage; deforestation; smoke/haze from forest fires.
Land use: *arable land*: 5.54%
　　　permanent crops: 17.61%
　　　other: 76.85%
International agreements: *party to*: Biodiversity, Climate Change, Climate Change-Kyoto Protocol, Desertification, Endangered Species, Hazardous Wastes, Law of the Sea, Marine Life Conservation, zone Layer Protection, Ship Pollution, Tropical Timber 83, Tropical Timber 94, Wetlands.

MALDIVES

Location: Southern Asia, group of atolls in the Indian Ocean, south-southwest of India.
Area: 116 sq mi (300 sq km)
Area-comparative: about 1.7 times the size of Washington D.C.
Population: 339,330
Population growth rate: 2.86%
Climate: tropical; hot, humid; dry, northeast monsoon (November to March); rainy, southwest monsoon (June to August).
Environment – Current issues depletion of freshwater aquifers threatens water supplies; global warming and sea level rise; coral reef bleaching.
Land use: *arable land*: 3.33%
　　　permanent crops: 6.67%
　　　other: 90%

International agreements: *party to:* Biodiversity, Climate Change, Climate Change-Kyoto Protocol, Hazardous Wastes, Law of the Sea, Ozone Layer Protection
Signed but not ratified: none of the selected agreements.

MALI
Location: Western Africa, southwest of Algeria.
Area: 478,640 sq mi (1,240,000 sq km)
Area-comparative: slightly less than twice the size of Texas.
Population: 11,956,788
Population growth rate: 2.78%
Climate: subtropical to arid; hot and dry February to June; rainy, humid, and mild June to November; cool and dry November to February.
Environment – current Issues: deforestation; soil erosion; desertification; inadequate supplies of potable water; poaching.
Land use: *arable land*: 3.77%
      permanent crops: 0.04%
      other: 96.19%
International Agreements: *party to*: Biodiversity, Climate Change, Climate Change-Kyoto Protocol, Desertification, Endangered Species, Hazardous Wastes, Law of the Sea, Ozone Layer Protection, Wetlands.
Signed but not ratified: none of the selected agreements.

MALTA
Location: Southern Europe, islands in the Mediterranean Sea, south of Italy.
Area: 122 sq mi (316 sq km)
Area-comparative: slightly less than twice the size of Washington, D.C.
Population: 396,851
Population growth rate: 0.42%
Climate: Mediterranean with mild, rainy winters and hot, dry summers.
Environment – current issues: very limited natural fresh water resources; increasing reliance on desalination.
Land use: *arable land*: 31.25%
      permanent crops: 3.13%
      other: 65.62%
International Agreements: *party to*: Air Pollution, Biodiversity, Climate Change, Climate Change-Kyoto Protocol, Desertification, Endangered Species, Hazardous Wastes, Law of the Sea, Marine Dumping, Ozone Layer Protection, Ship Pollution, Wetlands.
Signed but not ratified: none of the selected agreements.

MARSHALL ISLANDS
Location: Oceania, group of atolls and reefs in the North Pacific Ocean, about one-half of the way from Hawaii to Australia.
Area: 70 sq mi (181.3 sq km)
Area-comparative: about the size of Washington D.C.
Population: 57,738
Population growth rate: 2.29%
Climate: tropical; hot and humid; wet season from May to November; islands border typhoon belt.
Environment – current issues: inadequate supplies of potable water; pollution of Majuro lagoon from household wastes and discharges from fishing vessels.

Land use: *arable land*: 16.67%
       permanent crops: 0%
       other: 83.33%
International Agreements: *party to*: Biodiversity, Climate Change, Climate Change-Kyoto Protocol, Desertification, Hazardous Wastes, Law of the Sea, Ozone Layer Protection, Ship Pollution.
Signed but not ratified: none of the selected agreements.

MAURITANIA

Location: Northern Africa, bordering the North Atlantic Ocean, between Senegal and Western Sahara.
Area: 397,850 sq mi (1,030,700 sq km)
Area-comparative: slightly larger than three times the size of New Mexico.
Population: 2,998,563
Population growth rate: 2.91%
Climate: desert; constantly hot, dry, dusty.
Environment – current issues: overgrazing, deforestation, and soil erosion aggravated by drought are contributing to desertification; very limited natural fresh water resources away from Senegal, which is the only perennial river.
Land use: *arable land*: 0.48%
       permanent crops: 0.01%
       other: 99.51%
International Agreements: *party to*: Biodiversity, Climate Change, Desertification, Endangered Species, Hazardous Wastes, Law of the Sea, Ozone Layer Protection, Ship Pollution, Wetland.
Signed but not ratified: none of the selected agreements.

MAURITIUS

Location: Southern Africa, island in the Indian Ocean, east of Madagascar.
Area: 787 sq mi (2,040 sq km)
Area-comparative: almost 11 times the size of Washington D.C.
Population: 1,220,481
Population growth rate: 0.81%
Climate: tropical, modified by southeast trade winds; warm, dry winter (May to November); hot, wet, humid summer (November to May).
Environment – current issues: water pollution, degradation of coral reefs.
Land use: *arable land*: 49.26%
       permanent crops: 2.96%
       other: 47.78%
International Agreements: *party to:* Biodiversity, Climate Change, Climate Change-Kyoto Protocol, Desertification, Endangered Species, Environmental Modification, Hazardous Wastes, Law of the Sea, Marine Life Conservation, Ozone Layer Protection, Ship Pollution, Wetlands.
Signed but not ratified: none of the selected agreements.

MEXICO

Location: located in the southern part of North America, bordering the Caribbean Sea and the Gulf of Mexico, between Guatemala and the United States.
Area: 761,404 sq mi (1,972,550 sq km)
Area-comparative: slightly less than three times the size of Texas.
Population: 104,959,594

Population growth rate: 1.18%
Climate: varies from tropical to desert.
Environment – current issues: scarcity of hazardous waste disposal facilities, natural fresh water resources scarce and polluted in north, inaccessible and poor quality in center and extreme Southeast; raw sewage and industrial effluents polluting rivers in urban areas; deforestation, widespread erosion; desertification; deteriorating agricultural lands; serious air and water pollution in national capital and urban centers along US-Mexico border.
Land use: *arable land*: 13.2%
    permanent crops: 1.1%
    other: 85.7%
International Agreements: *party to*: Biodiversity, Climate Change, Climate Change-Kyoto Protocol, Desertification, Endangered Species, Hazardous Wastes, Law of the Sea, Marine Dumping, Marine Life Conservation, Ozone Layer Protection, Ship Pollution, Wetlands, Whaling.
Signed but not ratified: none of the selected agreements.

MICRONESIA

Location: Federated state of Oceania, island group in the North Pacific Ocean, about three-quarters of the way from Hawaii to Indonesia.
Area: 271 sq mi (702 sq km)
Area-comparative: four times the size of Washington D.C.
Population: 108,155
Population growth rate: -0.02%
Climate: tropical; heavy year-round rainfall, especially in eastern islands; located on southern edge of the typhoon belt with occasionally severe damage.
Environment – current issues: over fishing, climate change, pollution.
Land use: *arable land*: 5.71%
    permanent crops: 45.71%
    other: 48.58%
International Agreements: *party to*: Biodiversity, Climate Change, Climate Change-Kyoto Protocol, Desertification, Hazardous Wastes, Law of the Sea, Ozone Layer Protection.
Signed but not ratified: none of the selected agreements.

MOLDOVA

Location: Eastern Europe, northeast of Romania.
Area: 13,060 sq mi (33,843 sq km)
Area-comparative: slightly larger than Maryland.
Population: 4,446,455
Population growth rate: 0.18%
Climate: moderate winters, warm summers.
Environment – current issues: heavy use of agricultural chemicals, has contaminated soil and groundwater; extensive soil erosion from poor farming methods.
Land Use: *arable land*: 54.08%
    permanent crops: 12.1%
    other: 33.82%
International Agreements: *party to*: Air Pollution, Biodiversity, Climate Change, Climate Change-Kyoto Protocol, Desertification, Endangered Species, Hazardous Wastes, Ozone Layer Protection.
Signed but not ratified: Air Pollution-Persistent Organic Pollutants.

MONACO

Location: Western Europe, bordering the Mediterranean Sea, on the southern coast of France, near the border with Italy.
Area: .75 sq mi (1.95 sq km)
Area-comparative: about 3 times the size of The Mall in Washington, D.C.
Population: 32,270
Population growth rate: 0.44%
Climate: Mediterranean with mild, wet winters and hot, dry summers.
Environment – current issues: NA
Land use: *arable land* 0%
  permanent crops: 0%
  other: 100%
International Agreements: *party to:* Air Pollution, Air Pollution-Volatile Organic Compounds, Biodiversity, Climate Change, Desertification, Endangered Species, Hazardous Wastes, Law of the Sea, Marine Dumping, Ozone Layer Protection, Ship Pollution, wetlands, Whaling.
Signed but not ratified: Climate Change-Kyoto Protocol.

MONGOLIA

Location: Northern Asia, between China and Russia.
Area: 604,090 sq mi (1,565,000 sq km)
Area-comparative: slightly smaller than Alaska.
Population: 2,751,314
Population growth rate: 1.43%
Climate: desert; continental (large daily and seasonal temperature ranges).
Environment – current issues: limited natural fresh water resources in some areas; the policies of former Communists regimes promoted rapid urbanization and industrial growth that had negative effects on the environment; the burning of soft coal in power plants and the lack of enforcement of environmental laws severely polluted the air in Ulaanbaatar; deforestation, overgrazing, and the converting of virgin land to agricultural production increased soil erosion from wind and rain; desertification and mining activities had a deleterious effect on the environment.
Land use: *arable land*: 0.84%
  permanent crops: 0%
  other: 99.16%
International agreements: *party to:* Biodiversity, Climate Change, Climate Change-Kyoto Protocol, Desertification, Endangered Species, Environmental Modification, Hazardous Wastes, Law of the Sea, Ozone Layer Protection, Wetlands.
Signed but not ratified: none of the selected agreements.

MOROCCO

Location: Northern Africa, bordering the North Atlantic Ocean and the Mediterranean Sea, between Algeria and Western Sahara.
Area: 172,368 sq mi (446,550 sq km)
Area-comparative: slightly larger than California.
Population: 32,209,101
Population growth rate: 1.61%
Climate: Mediterranean, becoming more extreme in the interior.

Environment – current issues: land degradation/desertification (soil erosion resulting from farming of marginal areas, overgrazing, destruction of vegetation); water supplies contaminated by raw sewage; siltation of reservoirs; oil pollution of coastal waters.

Land use: *arable land*: 20.12%
  permanent crops: 2.05%
  other: 77.83%

International agreements: *party to:* Biodiversity, Climate Change, Climate Change-Kyoto Protocol, Desertification, Endangered Species Hazardous Wastes, Marine Dumping, Ozone Layer Protection, Ship Pollution, Wetlands, Whaling
Signed but not ratified: Environmental Modification, Law of the Sea.

MOZAMBIQUE

Location: South-eastern Africa, bordering the Mozambique Channel, between South Africa and Tanzania.

Area: 309,414 sq mi (801,590 sq km)

Area-comparative: slightly less than twice the size of California.

Population: 18,811,731

Population growth rate: 1.22%

Climate: tropical to subtropical.

Environment current issues: a long civil war recurrent drought in the hinterlands have resulted in increased migration of the population to urban and coastal areas with adverse environmental consequences; desertification; pollution of surface and coastal waters; elephant poaching for ivory is a problem.

Land use: *arable land*: 3.98%
  permanent crops: 0.29%
  other: 95.73%

International Agreements: *party to*: Biodiversity, Climate Change, Desertification, Endangered Species, Hazardous Wastes, Law of the Sea, Ozone Layer Protection.
Signed but not ratified: none of the selected agreements.

NAMIBIA

Location: Southern Africa, bordering the South Atlantic Ocean, between Angola and South Africa.

Area: 318,611 sq mi (825,418 sq km)

Area-comparative: slightly more than half the size of Alaska.

Population: 1,954,033

Population growth rate: 1.25%

Climate: desert; hot, dry; rainfall sparse and erratic.

Environment – current issues: very limited natural fresh water resources; desertification; wildlife poaching; land degradation has led to few conservation areas.

Land use: *arable lands*: 0.99%
  permanent crops: 0%
  other: 99.01%

International Agreements: *party to:* Antarctic-Marine Living Resources, Biodiversity, Climate Change, Climate Change-Kyoto Protocol, Desertification, Endangered Species, Hazardous Wastes, Law of the Sea, Ozone Layer Protection, Wetlands.
Signed but not ratified: none of the selected agreements.

NAURU

Location: Oceania, island in the South Pacific Ocean, south of the Marshall Islands.
Area: 8 sq mi (21 sq km)
Area-comparative: about 0.1 times the size of Washington D.C.
Population: 12,809
Population growth rate: 1.87%
Climate: tropical with a monsoonal pattern; rainy season (November to February).
Environment – current issues: limited natural fresh water resources, roof storage tanks collect rainwater, but mostly dependent on a single, aging desalination plant; intense phosphate mining during the past 90 years-mainly by the UK, Australia, and NZ consortium- has left the central 90% of Nauru a wasteland and threatens limited remaining land resources.
Land use: *arable land*: 0%
  permanent crops: 0%
  other: 100%
International agreements: *party to:* Biodiversity, Climate Change, Climate Change-Kyoto Protocol, Desertification, Hazardous Wastes, Law of the Sea, Marine Dumping, Ozone Layer Protection.
Signed but not ratified: none of the selected agreements.

NEPAL

Location: Southern Asia, between China and India.
Area: 54,349 sq mi (140,800 sq km)
Area-comparative: slightly larger than Arkansas.
Population: 27,070,666
Population growth rate: 2.23%
Climate: varies from cool summers and severe winters in north to subtropical summers and mild winters in south.
Environment – current issues: deforestation (overuse of wood for fuel); contaminated water (with human and animal wastes, agricultural runoff, industrial effluents); wildlife conservation; vehicular emissions.
Land Use: *arable land*: 20.27%
  permanent crops: 0.49%
  other: 79.24%
International Agreements: *party to:* Biodiversity, Climate change, Desertification, Endangered Species, Hazardous Wastes, Law of the Sea, Ozone Layer Protection, Tropical Timber 83, Tropical Timber 94, Wetlands.
Signed but not ratified: Marine Life Conservation.

NETHERLANDS

Location: Western Europe, bordering the North Sea, between Belgium and Germany.
Area: 16,029 sq mi (41,526 sq km)
Area-comparative: slightly less than twice the size of New Jersey.
Population: 16,318,199
Population growth rate: 0.57%
Climate: temperate; marine; cool summers and mild winters.
Environment – current issues: water pollution in the form of heavy metals, organic compounds, and nutrients such as nitrates and phosphates; air pollution from vehicles and refining activities; acid rain.
Land use: *arable land*: 26.53%
  permanent crops: 1.03%   *other*: 72.44%

452

International Agreements: *party to:* Air pollution Air Pollution-Nitrogen Oxides, Air Pollution-Persistent Organic Pollutants, Air Pollution-Sulfur 85, Air Pollution-Sulfur 94, Air Pollution-Volatile Organic Compounds, Antarctic-Environment Protocol, Antarctic-Marine Living Resources, Antarctic Treaty, Biodiversity, Climate Change, Climate Change-Kyoto Protocol, Desertification, Endangered Species, Environmental Modification, Hazardous Wastes, Kyoto Protocol, Law of the Sea, Marine Dumping, Marine Life Conservation, Ozone Layer Protection, Ship Pollution, Tropical Timber 83, Tropical Timber 94, Wetlands, Whaling.

NEW ZEALAND

Location: Oceania, islands in the South Pacific Ocean, southeast of Australia.
Area: 103,710 sq mi (268,680 sq km)
Area-comparative: about the size of Colorado.
Population: 3,993,817
Population growth rate: 1.05%
Climate: temperate with sharp regional contrasts.
Environment – current issues: deforestation; soil erosion; native flora and fauna hard hit by species introduced from outside.
Land Use: *arable land*: 5.8%
      permanent crops: 6.44%
      other: 87.76%
International Agreements: *party to:* Antarctic-Environmental Protocol, Antarctic-Marine Living Resources, Antarctic Treaty, Biodiversity, Climate Change, Climate Change-Kyoto Protocol, Desertification, Endangered Species, Environmental Modification, Hazardous Wastes, Law of the Sea, Marine Dumping, Ozone Layer Protection, Ship Pollution, Tropical Timber 83, Tropical Timber 94, Wetlands, Whaling.
Signed but not ratified: Antarctic Seals, Marine Life Conservation.

NICARAGUA

Location: Central America, bordering both the Caribbean Sea and the North Pacific Ocean, between Costa Rica and Honduras.
Area: 49,985 sq mi (129,494 sq km)
Area-comparative: slightly smaller than the state of New York.
Population: 5,359,759
Population growth rate: 1.97%
Climate: tropical in lowlands; cooler in highlands.
Environment – current issues: deforestation; soil erosion; water pollution.
Land use: *arable land*: 20.24%
      permanent crops: 2.38%
      other: 77.38%
International Agreements: *party to:* Biodiversity, Climate Change, Climate Change-Kyoto Protocol, Desertification, Endangered Species, Hazardous Wastes, Law of the Sea, Ozone Layer Protection, Ship Pollution, Wetlands.
Signed but not ratified: Environmental Modification.

NIGER

Location: Western Africa, southeast of Algeria.
Area: 489,062 sq mi (1,267,000 sq km)
Area-comparative: slightly less than twice the size of Texas.

Population: 11,360,538
Population growth rate: 2.67%
Climate: desert; mostly hot dry, dusty; tropical in extreme south.
Environment – current issues: overgrazing; soil erosion; deforestation; desertification; wildlife populations (such as elephant, hippopotamus, giraffe, and lion) threatened because of poaching and habitat destruction.
Land use: *arable lands*: 3.94%
    permanent crops: 0%
    other: 96.06%
International Agreements: *party to:* Biodiversity, Climate Change, Desertification, Endangered Species, Environmental Modification, Hazardous Wastes, Ozone Layer Protection, Wetlands.
Signed but not ratified: Climate Change-Kyoto Protocol, Law of the Sea.

NIGERIA

Location: Western Africa, bordering the Gulf of Guinea, between Benin and Cameroon
Area: 356,574 sq mi (923,768 sq km)
Area-comparative: slightly more than twice the size of California.
Population: 137,253,133
Population growth rate: 2.45%
Climate: varies; equatorial in south, tropical in center, arid in north.
Environment – current issues: soil degradation; rapid deforestation; urban air and water pollution; desertification; oil pollution-water, air and soil; has suffered serious damage from oil spills; loss of arable land; rapid urbanization.
Land use: *arable land*: 30.96%
    permanent crops: 2.79%
    other: 66.25%
International Agreements: *party to:* Biodiversity, Climate Change, Desertification, Endangered Species, Hazardous Wastes, Law of the Sea, Marine Dumping, Marine Life Conservation, Ozone Layer Protection, Wetlands.
Signed but not ratified: none of the selected agreements.

NORWAY

Location: Northern Europe, bordering the North Sea and the North Atlantic Ocean, west of Sweden
Area: 125,149 sq mi (324,220 sq km)
Area-comparative: slightly larger than New Mexico.
Population: 4,574,560
Population growth rate: 0.41%
Climate: temperate along the coast, modified by North Atlantic Current; colder interior with increased precipitation and colder summers; rainy year-round on west coast.
Environment – current issues: water pollution; acid rain damaging forests and adversely affecting lakes, threatening fish stocks; air pollution from vehicle emissions.
Land use: *arable land*: 2.94%
    permanent crops: 0%
    other: 97.06%
International Agreements: *party to*: Air Pollution, Air Pollution-Nitrogen Oxides, Air Pollution-Persistent Organic Pollutants, Air Pollution-Sulfur 85, Air Pollution-Sulfur 94, Air Pollution-Volatile Organic Compounds, Antarctic-Environmental

Protocol, Antarctic-Marine Living Resources, Antarctic seals, Antarctic Treaty, Biodiversity, Climate Change, Climate Change-Kyoto Protocol, Desertification, Endangered Species, Environmental Modification, Hazardous Wastes, Law of the Sea, Marine Dumping, Ozone Layer Protection, Ship Pollution, Tropical Timber 83, Tropical Timber 94, wetlands, Whaling.
Signed but not ratified: none of the selected agreements.

OMAN

Location: Middle East, bordering the Arabian Sea, Gulf of Oman, and the Persian Gulf, between Yemen and United Arab Emirates.
Area: 82,010 sq mi (212,460 sq km)
Area-comparative: slightly smaller than Kansas.
Population: 2,903,165
Population growth rate: 3.35%
Climate: dry desert; hot, humid along coast; hot, dry interior; strong southwest summer monsoon (May to September) in far south.
Environment – current issues: rising soil salinity; beach pollution from oil spills; very limited natural fresh water resources.
Land use: *arable land*: 0.08%
　　　　　　permanent crops: 0.22%
　　　　　　other: 99.7%
International Agreements: *party to:* Biodiversity, Climate Change, Desertification, Hazardous Wastes, Law of the Sea, Marine Dumping, Ozone Layer Protection, Ship Pollution, Whaling.
Signed but not ratified: none of the selected agreements.

PAKISTAN

Location: Southern Asia, bordering the Arabian Sea, between India on the east and Iran and Afghanistan on the west and China in the north.
Area: 310, 321 sq mi (803,940 sq km)
Area-comparative: slightly less than twice the size of California.
Population: 159,196,336
Population growth rate: 1.98%
Climate: mostly hot, dry desert; temperate in northwest; arctic in north.
Environment – current issues: water pollution from raw sewage, industrial wastes, and agricultural run off; limited natural fresh water resources; a majority of the population does not have access to potable water; deforestation; soil erosion, desertification.
Land use: *arable land*: 27.81%
　　　　　　permanent crops:0.79%
　　　　　　other: 71.4%
International Agreements: *party to:* Biodiversity, Climate Change, Desertification, Endangered Species, Environmental Modification, Hazardous Wastes, Law of the Sea, Marine Dumping, Ozone Layer Protection, Ship Pollution, Wetlands.
Signed but not ratified: Marine Life Conservation

PALAU

Location: Oceania, group of islands in the North Pacific Ocean, southeast of the Philippines.
Area: 177 sq mi (458 sq km)

Area-comparative: slightly more than 2.5 times the size of Washington, D.C.
Population: 20,016
Population growth rate: 1.46%
Climate: tropical; hot and humid; wet season May to November
Environment – current issues: inadequate facilities for disposal of solid waste; threats to the marine ecosystem from sand and coral dredging, illegal fishing practices, and over fishing.
Land use: *arable land:* 21.74%
      permanent crops: 0%
      other: 78.26%
International Agreements: *party to:* Biodiversity, Climate Change, Climate Change-Kyoto Protocol, Desertification, Law of the Sea, Ozone Layer Protection.
Signed but not ratified: none of the selected agreements.

PANAMA

Location: Central America, bordering both the Caribbean Sea and the North Pacific Ocean, between Colombia and Costa Rica.
Area: 30,185 sq mi (78,200 sq km)
Area-comparative: slightly smaller than South Carolina.
Population: 3,000,463
Population growth rate: 1.31%
Climate: tropical maritime; hot, humid, cloudy: prolonged rainy season (May to January), short dry season (January to May).
Environment – current issues: water pollution from agricultural runoff threatens fishery resources; deforestation of tropical rain forest; land degradation and soil erosion threatens siltation of Panama Canal; air pollution in urban areas; mining threatens natural resources.
Land use: *arable land:* 6.72%
      permanent crops: 2.08%
      other: 91.2%
International Agreements: *party to:* biodiversity, Climate Change, Climate Change-Kyoto Protocol, Desertification, Endangered Species, Hazardous Wastes, Law of the Sea, Marine Dumping, Ozone Layer Protection, Ship Pollution, Tropical Timber 83, Tropical Timber 94, Wetlands, Whaling.
Signed, but not ratified: Marine Life Conservation

PAPUA NEW GUINEA

Location: Oceania, group of islands including the eastern half of the island of New Guinea, east of Indonesia.
Area: 178,656 sq mi (462,840 sq km)
Area-comparative: slightly larger than California.
Population: 5,420,280
Population growth rate: 2.3%
Climate: tropical; northwest monsoon (December to March), southeast monsoon (May to October); slight seasonal temperature variation.
Environment – current issues: rain forest subject to deforestation as a result of growing commercial demand for tropical timber; pollution from mining projects; severe drought.
Land use: *arable land:* 0.13%
      permanent crops: 1.35%
      other: 98.52%

International Agreements: *party to:* Antarctic Treaty, Biodiversity, Climate Change, Climate Change-Kyoto Protocol, Desertification, Endangered Species, Environmental Modification, Hazardous Wastes, Law of the Sea, Marine Dumping, Ozone Layer Protection, Ship Pollution, Tropical Timber 83, Tropical Timber 94, Wetlands.
Signed but not ratified: none of the selected agreements.

PARAGUAY

Location: Central South America, northeast of Argentina.
Area: 157,005 sq mi (406,750 sq km)
Area-comparative: slightly smaller than California.
Population: 6,191,368
Population growth rate: 2.51%
Climate: subtropical to temperate; substantial rainfall in the eastern portions, becoming semiarid in the far west.
Environment – current issues: deforestation; water pollution; inadequate means for waste disposal present health risks for many urban residents; loss of wetlands.
Land use: *arable land:* 5.54%
     permanent crops: 0.21%
     other: 94.25%
International Agreements: *party to:* Biodiversity, Climate Change, Climate Change-Kyoto Protocol, Desertification, Endangered Species, Hazardous Wastes, Law of the Sea, Ozone Layer Protection, Wetlands.
Signed but not ratified: none of the selected agreements.

PERU

Location: Western South America, bordering the South Pacific Ocean, between Chile and Ecuador.
Area: 496,094 sq mi (1,285,220 sq km)
Area-comparative: slightly smaller than Alaska.
Population: 27,544,305
Population growth rate: 1.39%
Climate: varies from tropical in east to dry desert in west; temperate to frigid in Andes.
Environment – Current issues: deforestation (some the result of illegal logging); overgrazing of the slopes of the costa and sierra leading to soil erosion; desertification; air pollution in Lima; pollution of rivers and coastal waters from municipal and mining wastes.
Land Use: *arable land:* 2.85%
     permanent crops: 0.38%
     other: 96.77%
International Agreements: *party to:* Antarctic-Environmental Protocol, Antarctic-Marine Living Resources, Antarctic Treaty, Biodiversity, Climate Change, Climate Change-Kyoto Protocol, Desertification, Endangered Species, Hazardous Wastes, Marine Dumping, Ozone Layer Protection, Ship Pollution, Tropical Timber 83, Tropical Timber 94, Wetlands, Whaling.
Signed but not ratified: none of the selected agreements.

PHILIPPINES

Location: Southeastern Asia, group of islands between the Philippine Sea and the South China Sea, east of Vietnam.

Area: 115,800 sq mi (300,000 sq km)
Area-comparative: slightly larger than Arizona.
Population: 86,241,697
Population growth rate: 1.88%
Climate: tropical marine; northeast monsoon (November to April); southwest monsoon (May to October).
Environment – current issues: uncontrolled deforestation especially in watershed areas; soil erosion; air and water pollution in major urban centers; coral reef degradation; increasing pollution of coastal mangrove swamps that are important breeding grounds for fish.
Land use: *arable land*: 18.45%
　　　 permanent crops: 14.76%
　　　 other: 66.79%
International Agreements: *party to*: Biodiversity, Climate Change, Climate Change-Kyoto Protocol, Desertification, Endangered Species, Hazardous Wastes, Law of the Sea, Marine Dumping, Ozone Layer Protection, Ship Pollution, Tropical Timber 83, Tropical Timber 94, Wetlands, Whaling.
Signed but not ratified: Air pollution-Persistent Organic Pollutants.

POLAND

Location: Central Europe, east of Germany.
Area: 120,696 sq mi (312,685 sq km)
Area-comparative: slightly smaller than New Mexico.
Population: 38,626,349
Population growth rate: 0.02%
Climate: temperate with cold, cloudy, moderately severe winters with frequent precipitation; mild summers with frequent showers and thunderstorms.
Environment – current issues: situation has improved since 1989 due to decline in heavy industry and increased environmental concern by post-Communist governments; air pollution nonetheless remains serious because of sulfur dioxide emissions from coal-fired power plants, and the resulting acid rain has caused forest damage; water pollution from industrial and municipal sources is also a problem, as is disposal of hazardous wastes; pollution levels should continue to decrease as industrial establishments bring their facilities up to European Union code, but at substantial cost to business and the government.
Land use: *arable land*: 45.81%
　　　 permanent crops: 1.23%
　　　 other: 52.96%
International Agreements: *party to:* Air Pollution, Antarctic-Environmental Protocol, Antarctic-Marine Living Resources, Antarctic Seals, Antarctic Treaty, Biodiversity, Climate Change, Climate Change-Kyoto Protocol, Desertification, Endangered Species, Environmental Modification, Hazardous Wastes, Kyoto Protocol, Law of the Sea, Marine Dumping, Ozone Layer Protection, Ship Pollution, Wetlands.
Signed but not ratified: Air Pollution-Nitrogen Oxides, Air Pollution-Persistent Organic Pollutants, Air Pollution-Sulfur 94.

PORTUGAL

Location: Southwestern Europe, bordering the North Atlantic Ocean, west of Spain.
Area: 35,663 sq mi (92,391 sq km)

Area-comparative: slightly smaller than Indiana.
Population: 10,524,145
Population growth rate: 0.41%
Climate: maritime temperate; cool and rainy in north, warmer and drier in south
Environment – current issues: soil erosion; air pollution caused by industrial and vehicle emissions; water pollution, especially in coastal areas.
Land use: *arable land*: 20.57%
  permanent crops: 7.74%
  other: 71.69%
International Agreements: *party to*: Air Pollution, Biodiversity, Climate Change, Climate Change-Kyoto Protocol, Desertification Endangered Species, Hazardous Wastes, Law of the Sea, Marine Dumping, Marine Life Conservation, Ozone Layer Protection, Ship Pollution, Tropical Timber 83, Tropical Timber 94, Wetlands.
Signed but not ratified: Air Pollution Persistent- Organic Pollutants, Air Pollution-Volatile Organic Compounds, Environmental Modification.

PUERTO RICO (commonwealth associated with the US)
Location: Caribbean, island between the Caribbean Sea and the North Atlantic Ocean, east of the Dominican Republic.
Area: 3514 sq mi (9,104 sq km)
Area-comparative: slightly less than three times the size of Rhode Island.
Population: 3,897,960
Population growth rate: 0.49%
Climate: tropical marine, mild; seasonal temperature variation.
Environment – current issues: erosion; occasional drought caused by water shortages.
Land use: *arable land*: 3.7%
  permanent crops: 5.1%
  other: 91.2%
International Agreements: *party to*: Biodiversity, Climate Changes, Desertification, Endangered Species, Hazardous Wastes, Law of the Sea, Ozone Layer Protection.
Signed but not ratified: none of the selected agreements.

QATAR
Location: Middle East, peninsula bordering the Persian Gulf and Saudi Arabia.
Area: 4,415 sq mi (11,437 sq km)
Area-comparative: slightly smaller than Connecticut.
Population: 840,290
Population growth rate: 2.74%
Climate: arid; mild pleasant winters; very hot, humid summers.
Environment – current issues: limited natural fresh water resources are increasing dependence on large-scale desalination facilities.
Land use: *arable land*: 1.27%
  permanent crops: 0.27%
  other: 98.46%
International Agreements: *party to:* Biodiversity, Climate Change, Desertification, Endangered Species, Hazardous Wastes, Law of the Sea, Ozone Layer Protection.
Signed but not ratified: none of the selected agreements.

ROMANIA

Location: Southeastern Europe, bordering the Black Sea, between Bulgaria and Ukraine.
Area: 91,675 sq mi (237,500 sq km)
Area-comparative: slightly smaller than Oregon.
Population: 22,355,551
Population growth rate: -0.11%
Climate: temperate; cold cloudy winters with frequent snow and fog; sunny summers with frequent showers and thunderstorms.
Environment – current issues: soil erosion and degradation, water pollution; air pollution in south from industrial effluents; contamination of Danube delta wetlands.
Land use: *arable land*: 40.57%
   permanent crops: 2.4%
   other: 57.03%
International Agreements: *party to* Air pollution, Antarctic Treaty, Biodiversity, Climate Change, climate Change-Kyoto Protocol, Desertification, Endangered Species, Environmental Modification, Hazardous Wastes, Law of the Sea, Ozone Layer Protection, Ship Pollution, Wetlands.
Signed but not ratified: Air Pollution-Persistent Organic Pollutants.

RUSSIA

Location: Northern Asia, bordering the Arctic Ocean, between Europe and the North Pacific Ocean.
Area: 6,591,027sq mi (17,075,200 sq km)
Area-comparative: approximately 1.8 times the size of the United States.
Population: 143,782,338
Population growth rate: -0.45%
Climate: ranges from steppes in the south through humid continental in much of European Russia; sub-arctic in Siberia to tundra climate in polar north; winters vary from cool along Black Sea coast to frigid in Siberia; summers vary from warm in the steppes to cool along the Arctic coast.
Environment – current issues: air pollution from heavy industry, emissions of coal-fired electric plants, and transportation in major cities; industrial, municipal, and agricultural pollution of inland water ways and seacoast; deforestation; soil erosion; soil contamination from improper application of agricultural chemicals; scattered areas of sometimes intense radioactive contamination; groundwater contamination from toxic wastes; urban solid waste management; abandoned stocks of obsolete pesticides.
Land use: *arable land*: 7.46%
   permanent crops: 0.11%
   other: 92.43%
International Agreements: *party to:* Air Pollution, Air Pollution-Nitrogen Oxides, Air pollution-Sulfur 85, Antarctic-Environmental Protocol, Antarctic-Marine Living Resources, Antarctic Seals, Antarctic Treaty, Biodiversity, Climate Change, Endangered Species, Environmental Modification, Hazardous Wastes, Law of the Sea, Maine Dumping, Ozone Layer Protection, Ship Pollution, Tropical Timber 83, Wetlands, Whaling.
Signed but not ratified: Air Pollution-Sulfur 94, Climate Change-Kyoto Protocol.

RWANDA

Location: Central Africa, east of Democratic Republic of the Congo.
Area: 10,166 sq mi (26,338 sq km)
Area-comparative: slightly smaller than Maryland.
Population: 7,954,013
Population growth rate: 1.82%
Climate: temperate; two rainy seasons (February to April, November to January); mild in mountains with frost and snow possible.
Environment – current issues: deforestation results from uncontrolled cutting of trees for fuel; over grazing; soil exhaustion; soil erosion; widespread poaching.
Land use: *arable land:* 32.43%
   permanent crops: 10.13%
   other: 57.44%
International Agreements: *party to:* Biodiversity, Climate Change, Desertification, Endangered Species, Hazardous Wastes, Ozone Layer Protection.
Signed but not ratified: Law of the Sea.

SAINT KITTS AND NEVIS

Location: Caribbean, islands in the Caribbean Sea, about one-third of the way from Puerto Rico to Trinidad and Tobago.
Area: 101 sq mi (261 sq km)
Area-comparative: 1.5 times the size of Washington, D.C.
Population: 38,836
Population growth rate: 0.25%
Climate: tropical tempered by constant sea breezes; little seasonal temperature variation; rainy season (May to November).
Environment – current issues: NA
Land use: *arable land:* 16.67%
   permanent crops: 2.78%
   other: 80.55%
International Agreements: *party to:* Biodiversity, Climate change, Desertification, Endangered Species, Hazardous Wastes, Law of the sea, Ozone Layer Protection, Ship Pollution, Whaling.
Signed but nor ratified: none of the selected agreements.

SAINT LUCIA

Location: island between the Caribbean Sea and North Atlantic Ocean, north of Trinidad and Tobago.
Area: 238 sq mi (616 sq km)
Area-comparative: 3.5 times the size of Washington, D.C.
Population: 164,213
Population growth rate: 1.27%
Climate: tropical, moderated by northeast trade winds; dry season from January to April, rainy season May to August.
Environment – current issues: deforestation, soil erosion, particularly in northern region.
Land use: *arable land:* 4.9%
   permanent crops: 23%
   other: 72.1%
International Agreements: *party to:* Biodiversity, Climate Change, Climate Change-Kyoto Protocol, Desertification, Endangered Species, Environmental

461

Modification, Hazardous Wastes, Law of the sea, Marine Dumping, Ozone Layer Protection, Ship Pollution, Whaling.
Signed but not ratified: none of the selected agreements.

SAINT VINCENT AND THE GRENADINES

Location: Caribbean, islands in the Caribbean Sea, north of Trinidad and Tobago.
Area: 150 sq mi (389 sq km)
Area-comparative: twice the size of Washington D.C.
Population: 117,193
Population growth rate: 0.31%
Climate: tropical; little seasonal temperature variation; rainy season (May to November).
Environmental – current issues: pollution of coastal waters and shorelines from discharges from pleasure yachts and other effluents; in some areas pollution is serious enough to make swimming prohibitive.
Land use: arable land: 10.3%
　　　　　permanent crops: 17.9%
　　　　　other: 71.8%
International Agreements: *party to*: biodiversity, Climate Change, Desertification, Endangered Species, Environmental Modification, Hazardous Wastes, Law of the Sea, Marine Dumping, Ozone Layer Protection, Ship Pollution, Whaling.
Signed but not ratified: Climate Change-Kyoto Protocol.

SAMOA

Location: Oceania, group of islands in the South Pacific Ocean, about one-half of the way from Hawaii to New Zealand.
Area: 1,136 sq mi (2,944 sq km)
Area-comparative: slightly smaller than Rhode Island.
Population: 177,714
Population growth rate: -0.25%
Climate: tropical; rainy season (November to April) dry season (May to October).
Environment – current issues: soil erosion, deforestation, invasive species, over- fishing.
Land use: *arable land*: 19.43%
　　　　　permanent crops: 23.67%
　　　　　other: 56.9%
International Agreements: *party to:* Biodiversity, Climate Change, Climate Change-Kyoto Protocol, Desertification, Hazardous Wastes, Law of the Sea, Ozone Layer Protection.
Signed but not ratified: none of the selected agreements.

SAN MARINO

Location: Southern Europe, an enclave in central Italy.
Area: 24 sq mi (61 sq km)
Area-comparative: about 0.3 times the size of Washington, D.C.
Population: 28,503
Population growth rate: 1.33%
Climate: Mediterranean; mild to cool winters; warm sunny summers.
Environment – current issues: NA
Land use: *arable land*:16.67%

> *permanent crops*: 0%
> *other*: 83.33%

International Agreements: *party to:* Biodiversity, Climate Change, Desertification
Signed but not ratified: Air Pollution.

SAO TOME AND PRINCIPE

Location: Western Africa, islands straddling the Equator in the Gulf of Guinea, west of Gabon.
Area: 386 sq mi (1,001 sq km)
Area-comparative: more than 5 times the size of Washington, D.C.
Population: 181,565
Population growth rate: 3.18%
Climate: tropical; hot, humid; one rainy season (October-May).
Environment – current issues: deforestation; soil erosion and exhaustion.
Land use: *arable land:* 2%
> *permanent crops:* 41%
> *other:* 57%

International Agreements: *party to:* Biodiversity, Climate Change, Desertification, Endangered Species, Environmental Modification, Law of the Sea, Ozone Layer Protection, Ship Pollution.
Signed but not ratified: none of the selected agreements.

SAUDI ARABIA

Location: Middle East, bordering the Persian Gulf and the Red Sea, north of Yemen.
Area: 756,785 sq mi (1,960,582 sq km)
Area-comparative: slightly more than one-fifth the size of the U.S.
Population: 25,795,938
Population growth rate: 2.44%
Climate: harsh, dry desert with great temperature extremes.
Environment – current issues: desertification, depletion of under ground water resources; the lack of perennial rivers or permanent water bodies has prompted the development of extensive seawater desalination facilities; coastal pollution from oil spills.
Lane use: *arable land:* 1.72%
> *permanent crops:* 0.06%
> *other:* 98.22%

International agreements: *party to:* Biodiversity, Climate Change, Desertification, Endangered Species, Hazardous Wastes, Law of the Sea, Ozone Layer Protection.
Signed but not ratified: none of the selected agreement.

Senegal

Location: Western Africa, bordering the North Atlantic Ocean, between Guinea-Bissau and Mauritania.
Area: 75,729 sq mi (196,190 sq km)
Area-comparative: slightly smaller than South Dakota.
Population: 10,852,147
Population rate growth: 2.52%
Climate: tropical: hot humid; rainy season (May to November) has strong southeast winds; dry season (December to April) dominated by hot, dry, harmattan wind.

Environment – current issues: wildlife populations threatened by poaching; deforestation; over grazing; soil erosion; desertification; over fishing
Land use: *arable land*: 11.58%
  permanent crops: 0.19%
  other: 88.23%
International Agreements: *party to:* Biodiversity, Climate Change, climate Change-Kyoto Protocol, Desertification, Endangered Species, Hazardous Wastes, Law of the Sea, Marine Life Conservation, Ozone Layer Protection, Ship Pollution, Wetlands, Whaling.

SEYCHELLES

Location: Eastern Africa, group of islands in the Indian Ocean, northeast of Madagascar.
Area: 176 sq mi (455 sq km)
Area-comparative: 2.5 times the size of Washington, D.C.
Population: 80,832
Population growth rate: 0.45%
Climate: tropical marine; humid; cooler season during southeast monsoon (late May to September); warmer season during northwest monsoon (March to May).
Environment – current issues: water supply depends on catchments to collect rainwater.
Land use: *arable land*: 2.22%
  permanent crops: 13.33%
  other: 84.45%
International Agreements: *party to:* Biodiversity, Climate Change, Climate Change-Kyoto Protocol, Desertification, Endangered Species, Hazardous Wastes, Law of the Sea, Marine Dumping, Ozone Layer Protection, Ship Pollution
Signed but not ratified: none of the selected agreements.

SIERRA LEONE

Location: Western Africa, bordering the North Atlantic Ocean, between Guinea and Liberia.
Area: 27,692 sq mi (71,740 sq km)
Area-comparative: slightly smaller than South Carolina.
Population: 5,883,889
Population growth rate: 2.27%
Climate: tropical; hot, humid; summer rainy season (May to December); winter dry season (December to April).
Environment – current issues: rapid population growth pressuring the environment; over harvesting of timber, expansion of cattle grazing, and slash-and –burn agriculture have resulted in deforestation and soil exhaustion; civil war depleting natural resources; over fishing.
Land use: *arable land*: 6.76%
  permanent crops: 0.78%
  other: 92.46%
International Agreements: *party to:* Biodiversity, Climate Change, Desertification, Endangered Species, Law of the Sea, Marine Life Conservation, Ozone Layer Protection, Ship Pollution, wetlands
Signed but not ratified: Environmental Modification

SINGAPORE

Location: Southeastern Asia, islands between Malaysia and Indonesia.
Area: 267 sq mi (692.7 sq km)
Area-comparative: slightly more than 3.5 times the size of Washington, D.C.
Population: 4,353,893
Population growth rate: 1.71%
Climate: tropical; hot, humid, rainy; two distinct monsoon seasons – Northeastern monsoon from December to March and southwestern monsoon from June to September; inter-monsoon – frequent afternoon and evening thunderstorms.
Environment – current issues: industrial pollution; limited natural fresh water resources; limited land availability presents waste disposal problems; seasonal smoke/haze resulting from forest fires in Indonesia.
Land use: *arable land*: 1.64%
    permanent crops: 0%
    other: 98.36%
International Agreements: *party to:* Biodiversity, Climate Change, Desertification, Endangered Species, Hazardous Wastes, Law of the Sea, Ozone Layer Protection, Ship Pollution.
Signed but not ratified: none of the selected agreements.

SLOVAKIA

Location: Central Europe, south of Poland.
Area: 18,854 sq mi (48,845 sq km)
Area-comparative: about twice the size of New Hampshire.
Population: 5,423,567
Population growth rate: 0.14%
Climate: temperate; cool summers; cold, cloudy, humid winters.
Environment – current issues: air pollution from metallurgical plants presents human health risks; acid rain damaging forest.
Land use: *arable land*: 30.74%
    permanent crops: 2.64%
    other: 66.62%
International Agreements: *party to:* Air Pollution, Air Pollution-Nitrogen oxides, Air Pollution-Sulfur 85, Air Pollution-Sulfur 94, Air Pollution-Volatile Organic Compounds, Antarctic Treaty, Biodiversity, Climate Change, Climate Change-Kyoto Protocol, Desertification, Endangered Species, Environmental Modification, Hazardous Wastes, Law of the Sea, Ozone Layer Protection, Ship Pollution, Wetlands.
Signed but not ratified: Air Pollution-Persistent Organic Pollutants.

SLOVENIA

Location: Central Europe, eastern Alps bordering the Adriatic Sea, between Austria and Croatia.
Area: 7,825 sq mi (20,273 sq km)
Area-comparative: slightly smaller than New Jersey.
Population: 2,011,473
Population growth rate: -0.01%
Climate: Mediterranean Climate on the coast, continental climate with mild to hot summers and cold winters in the plateaus and valleys east.
Environment – current issues: Sava River polluted with domestic and industrial waste; pollution of coastal waters with heavy metals and toxic chemicals;

forest damage near Koper from air pollution (originating at metallurgical and chemical plants) and resulting acid rain.

Land use: *arable land*: 11.48%
      permanent crops: 2.68%
      other: 85.84%

International Agreements: *party to:* Air Pollution, Air Pollution-Sulfur 94, Biodiversity, Climate Change, Climate Change-Kyoto Protocol, Desertification, endangered Species, Hazardous Wastes, Law of the Sea, Marine Dumping, Ozone Layer Protection, Ship Pollution, Wetlands.
Signed but not ratified: Air Pollution-Persistent Organic Pollutants.

SOLOMON ISLANDS

Location: Oceania, group of islands in the South Pacific Ocean, east of Papua New Guinea.

Area: 10,981 sq mi (28,450 sq km)

Area-comparative: slightly smaller than Maryland.

Population: 523,617

Population growth rate: 2.76%

Climate: tropical monsoon; few extremes of temperature and weather

Environment – current issues: deforestation; soil erosion; many of the surrounding coral reefs are dead or dying.

Land Use: *arable land*: 1.5%
      permanent crops: 0.64%
      other: 97.86%

International Agreements: *party to*: Biodiversity, Climate Control, Climate Control Kyoto Protocol, Desertification, Environment Modification, Law of the Sea, Marine Dump, Marine Life Conservation, Ozone Layer Protection, Whaling
Signed but not ratified: none of the selected agreements.

SOMALIA

Location: Eastern Africa, bordering the Gulf of Aden and the Indian Ocean, east of Ethiopia.

Area: 246,135 sq mi (637,657 sq km)

Area-comparative: slightly smaller than Texas.

Population: 8,304,601

Population growth rate: 3.41%

Climate: principally desert; December to February northeast monsoon, moderate temperatures in north and very hot in south; May to October- southwest monsoon, torrid in the north and hot in south, irregular rainfall, hot and humid periods (tangambili) between monsoons.

Environment – current issues: famine; use of contaminated water contributes to human health problems; deforestation; overgrazing; soil erosion; desertification.

Land use: *arable land*: 1.66%
      permanent crops: 0.04%
      other: 98.3%

International Agreements: *party to*: Endangered Species, Law of the Sea, Ozone Layer Protection.

SOUTH AFRICA

Location: Southern Africa, at the southern tip of the continent of Africa.
Area: 470,886 sq mi (1,219,912 sq km)
Area-comparative: slightly less than twice the size of Texas
Population: 42,718,530
Population growth rate: -0.25%
Climate: mostly semiarid; subtropical along east coast; sunny days, cool nights
Environment – current issues: lack of important arterial rivers or lakes requires extensive water conservation and control measures; growth in water usage outpacing supply; pollution of rivers from agricultural run off and urban discharge; air pollution resulting in acid rain; soil erosion, desertification.
Land use: *arable land*: 12.13%
Permanent crops: 0.77%
Other: 87.1%
International Agreements: *party to*: Antarctic Environmental Protocol, Antarctic-Marine Living Resources, Antarctic Seals, Antarctic Treaty, Biodiversity, Climate Control, Climate Control-Kyoto Protocol, Desertification, Endangered Species, Hazardous Wastes, Law of the Sea, Marine Dumping, Marine Life Conservation, Ozone Layer Protection, Ship Pollution, Wetlands, Whaling.
Signed but not ratified: none of the selected agreements.

SPAIN

Location: Southwestern Europe, bordering the Bay of Biscay, Mediterranean Sea, North Atlantic Ocean, and Pyrenees Mountains, southwest of France.
Area: 194,846 sq mi (504,782 sq km)
Area-comparative: slightly more than twice the size of Oregon.
Population: 40,280,780
Population growth rate: 0.16%
Climate: temperate; clear, hot summers in interior, more moderate and cloudy along the coast; cloudy, cold winters in interior, partly cloudy and cool along the coast.
Environment – current issues: pollution of the Mediterranean Sea from raw sewage and effluents from off shore production of oil and gas; water quality and quantity nationwide; air pollution; deforestation; desertification.
Land use: *arable land*: 28.6%
    permanent crops: 9.56%
    other: 61.84%
International Agreements: *party to*: Air Pollution, Air Pollution-Nitrogen Oxides, Air Pollution-Sulfur 94, Air Pollution-Volatile Organic Compounds, Antarctic-Environmental Protocol, Antarctic-Marine Living Resources, Antarctic Treaty, Biodiversity, Climate Control, Climate Control-Kyoto Protocol, Desertification, Endangered Species, Environmental Modification, Hazardous Wastes, Law of the Sea, Marine Dumping, Marine Life Conservation, Ozone Layer Protection, Ship Pollution, Tropical Timber 83, Tropical Timber 94, Wetlands, Whaling.
Signed but not ratified: Air Pollution-Persistent Organic Pollutants.

SRI LANKA

Location: Southern Asia, island in the Indian Ocean, south of India.
Area: 25,325 sq mi (65,610 sq km)
Area-comparative: slightly larger than West Virginia.
Population: 19,905,165

Population growth rate: 0.81%
Climate: tropical monsoon; northeast monsoon (December to March); southwest monsoon (June to October).
Environment – current issues: deforestation; soil erosion, wildlife populations threatened by poaching and urbanization; coastal degradation from mining activities and increased pollution; freshwater resources being polluted by industrial wastes and sewage runoff; waste disposal; air pollution in Colombo
Land use: *arable land*: 13.43%
   permanent crops: 15.78%
   other: 70.79%
International Agreements: *party to*: Biodiversity, Climate Control, Climate Control-Kyoto Protocol, Desertification, Endangered Species, Environmental Modification, Hazardous Wastes, Law of the Sea, Ozone Layer Protection, Ship Pollution, Wetlands.
Signed but not ratified: Marine Life Conservation.

SUDAN

Location: Northern Africa, bordering the Red Sea, between Egypt and Eritrea.
Area: 967,242 sq mi (2,505,810 sq km)
Area-comparative: slightly more than one-quarter the size of the US.
Population: 39,148,162
Population growth rate: 2.64%
Climate: tropical in south; arid desert in north; rainy season varies by region (April to November).
Environment – current issues: inadequate supplies of potable water; wildlife population threatened by excessive hunting; soil erosion; desertification; periodic drought.
Land use: *arable land*: 7.03%
   permanent crops: 0.08%
   other: 92.89%
International Agreements: *party to*: Climate Control, Desertification, Endangered Species, Law of the Sea, Ozone Layer Protection.
Signed but not ratified: none.

SURINAME

Location: Northern South America, bordering the North Atlantic Ocean, between French Guiana and Guyana.
Area: 63,022 sq mi (163,270 sq km)
Area-comparative: slightly larger than Georgia.
Population: 436,935
Population growth rate: 0.31%
Climate: tropical; moderated by trade winds.
Environment – current issues: deforestation as timber is cut for export; pollution of inland waterways by small-scale mining activities.
Land use: *arable land*: 0.37%
   permanent crops: 0.06%
   other: 99.57%
International Agreements: *party to*: Biodiversity, Climate Control, Desertification, Endangered Species, Law of the Sea, Marine Dumping, Ozone Layer Protection, Ship Pollution, Tropical Timber 94, Wetlands.

SWAZILAND

Location: Southern Africa, between Mozambique and South Africa.
Area: 6,702 sq mi (17,363 sq km)
Area-comparative: slightly smaller than New Jersey.
Population: 1,169,241
Population growth rate: 0.55%
Climate: varies from tropical to near temperate.
Environment – current issues: limited supplies of potable water; wildlife supplies
being depleted because of excessive hunting; overgrazing; soil degradation,
soil erosion.
Land use: *arable land:* 9.77%
permanent crops: 0.7%
other: 89.53%
International Agreements: *party to:* Climate Control, Desertification, Endangered
Species, Ozone Layer Protection.
Signed but not ratified: Law of the Sea.

SWEDEN

Location: Northern Europe, bordering the Baltic Sea, Gulf of Bothnia, Kattegat, and
Skagerrak, between Finland and Norway.
Area: 173,686 sq mi (449,964 sq km)
Area-comparative: slightly larger than California.
Population: 8,986,400
Population growth rate: 0.18%
Climate: temperate in south with cold, cloudy winters and cool partly cloudy summers;
sub-arctic in north.
Environment – current issues: acid rain damage to soils and lakes; pollution of the
North Sea and the Baltic Sea.
Land use: *arable land:* 6.8%
permanent crops: 0%
other: 93.2%
International Agreements: *party to:* Air Pollution, Air Pollution-Nitrogen Oxides, Air
Pollution-Persistent Organic Pollutants, Air Pollution-Sulfur 85, Air Pollution-
Sulfur 94, Air Pollution-Volatile Organic Compounds, Antarctic-Environmental
Protocol, Antarctic-Marine Living Resources, Antarctic Treaty, Biodiversity,
Climate Control, Climate Control-Kyoto Protocol, Desertification, Endangered
Species, Hazardous Wastes, Law of the Sea, Marine Dumping, Ozone Layer
Protection, Ship Pollution, Tropical Timber 83, Tropical Timber 94, Wetlands,
Whaling.
Signed but not ratified: none.

SWITZERLAND

Location: Central Europe, east of France, north of Italy.
Area: 15,938 sq mi (41,290 sq km)
Area-comparative: slightly less than twice the size of New Jersey.
Population: 7,450,867
Population growth rate: 0.54%
Climate: temperate, but varies with altitude; cold, cloudy, rainy/snowy winters; cool to
warm, cloudy humid summers with occasional showers.
Environment – current issues: air pollution from vehicle emissions and open-air
burning; loss of biodiversity, water pollution from increased use of fertilizers.

Land use: *arable land*: 10.57%
    permanent crops: 0.61%
    other: 88.82%
International agreements: *party to*: Air Pollution, Air Pollution-Nitrogen Oxides, Air Pollution-Persistent Organic Pollutants, Air Pollution-Sulfur 85, Air Pollution-Sulfur 94, Air Pollution-Volatile Organic Compounds, Antarctic Treaty, Biodiversity, Climate Control, Climate Control-Kyoto Protocol, Desertification, Endangered Species, Environmental Modification, Hazardous Wastes, Marine Dumping, Marine Life Conservation, Ozone Layer Protection, Ship Pollution, Tropical Timber 83, Tropical Timber 94, Wetlands, Whaling.
Signed but not ratified: law of the Sea.

SYRIA

Location: Middle East, bordering the Mediterranean Sea, between Lebanon and Turkey.
Area: 71,479 sq mi (185,180 sq km)
Area comparative: slightly larger than North Dakota.
Population: 18,056,874
Population growth rate: 2.4%
Climate: mostly desert; hot, dry, sunny summers (June to August) and mild rainy winters (December to February) along coast; cold weather with snow or sleet periodically in Damascus.
Environment – current issues: deforestation; overgrazing; soil erosion, desertification, water pollution from raw sewage and petroleum refining wastes, inadequate potable water.
Land use*: arable land:* 25.96%
    permanent crops: 4.08%
    other: 69.96%
International Agreements: party to: Biodiversity, Climate Control, Desertification, Endangered Species, Hazardous Wastes, Ozone Layer Protection, Ship Pollution, Wetlands.
Signed but not ratified: Environmental Modification.

TAJIKISTAN

Location: Central Asia, west of China.
Area: 55,237 sq mi (143,100 sq km)
Area-comparative: slightly smaller than Wisconsin.
Population: 7,011,556
Population growth rate: 2.14%
Climate: hot summers, mild winters; semiarid to polar in Pamir Mountains.
Environment – current issues: inadequate sanitation facilities; increasing levels of soil salinity; industrial pollution; excessive pesticides.
Land Use: *arable land*: 5.4%
    permanent crops: 0.9%
    other: 93.7%
International Agreements: *party to*: Biodiversity, Climate Change, Desertification, Environmental Modification, Ozone Layer Protection, Wetlands
Signed but ratified: none of the selected agreements.

TANZANIA

Location: East Africa, bordering the Indian Ocean, between Kenya and Mozambique.
Area: 364,804 sq mi (945,087 sq km)
Area-comparative: slightly larger than twice the size of California.
Population: 36,588,225
Population growth rate: 1.95%
Climate: varies from tropical along coast to temperate in highlands.
Environment – current issues: soil degradation, deforestation; desertification; destruction of coral reefs threatens marine habitats; recent droughts affected marginal agriculture; wildlife threatened by illegal hunting and trade, especially ivory.
Land use: *arable land*: 4.24%
 permanent crops: 1.02%
 other: 94.74%
International Agreements: *party to*: Climate Control, Climate Control-Kyoto Protocol, Desertification, Endangered Species, Hazardous Wastes, Law of the Sea, Ozone Layer Protection, Wetlands.
Signed but ratified: none of the selected agreements.

THAILAND

Location: southeastern Asia, bordering the Andaman Sea and the Gulf of Thailand, southeast of Myanmar.
Area: 198,404 sq mi (514,000 sq km)
Area-comparative: slightly more than twice the size of Wyoming.
Population: 64,865,523
Population growth rate: 0.91%
Climate: tropical; rainy, warm, cloudy southwest monsoon (mid-May to September); dry, cool northeast monsoon (November to mid-March); southern isthmus always hot and humid.
Environment- current issues: air pollution from vehicle emissions; water pollution from organic and factory wastes; deforestation; soil erosion; wildlife populations threatened by illegal hunting.
Land use: *arable land*: 32.88%
 permanent crops: 7%
 other: 60.12%
International Agreements: *party to*: Biodiversity, Climate Control, Climate Control-Kyoto Protocol, Desertification, Endangered Species, Hazardous Wastes, Marine Life Conservation, Ozone Layer Protection, Tropical Timber 83, Tropical Timber 94.
Signed but not ratified: Law of the Sea.

TOGO

Location: Western Africa, bordering the Bight of Benin, between Benin and Ghana.
Area: 21,919 sq mi (56,785 sq km)
Area-comparative: slightly smaller than West Virginia.
Population: 5,556,812
Population growth rate: 2.27%
Climate: tropical; hot, humid in south; semiarid in north.
Environment – current issues: deforestation attributable to slash-and –burn agriculture and the use of wood for fuel; water pollution presents health hazards and hinders the fishing industry; air pollution rising in urban areas.

Land use: *arable land*: 41.37%
　　　　　permanent crops: 1.84%
　　　　　other: 56.79%
International Agreements: *party to*: Biodiversity, Climate Control, Desertification, Endangered Species, Law of the Sea, Ozone Layer Protection, Ship Pollution, Tropical Timber 83, Tropical Timber 94, Wetlands.
Signed but not ratified: none of the selected agreements.

TONGA

Location: Oceania, group of islands in the South Pacific Ocean, about two-thirds of the way from Hawaii to New Zealand.
Area: 289 sq mi (748 sq km)
Area-comparative: four times the size of Washington, D.C.
Population: 110,237
Population growth rate: 1.94%
Climate: tropical; modified by trade winds; warm season (December to May), cool season (May to December).
Environment – current issues: deforestation results as more and more land is being cleared for agriculture and settlement; some damage to coral reefs from starfish and indiscriminate coral and shell collectors; over-hunting threatens native sea turtle populations.
Land use: *arable land*: 23.61%
　　　　　permanent crops: 43.06%
　　　　　other: 33.33%
International Agreements: *party to*: Biodiversity, Climate Control, Desertification, Law of the Sea, Marine Dumping, Marine Life Conservation, Ozone Layer Protection, Ship Pollution.
Signed but not ratified: none of the selected agreements.

TRINIDAD AND TOBAGO

Location: Caribbean, islands between the Caribbean Sea and the North Atlantic Ocean, northeast of Venezuela.
Area: 1,979 sq mi (5,128 sq km)
Area-comparative: slightly smaller than Delaware.
Population: 1,096,585
Population growth rate: -0.71%
Climate: tropical; rainy season (June to December).
Environment – current issues: water pollution from agricultural chemicals, industrial wastes, and raw sewage; oil pollution of beaches; deforestation; soil erosion.
Land use: *arable land*: 14.6%
　　　　　permanent crops: 9.2%
　　　　　other: 76.2%
International Agreements: *party to*: Biodiversity, Climate Control, Climate Control-Kyoto Protocol, Desertification, Endangered Species, Hazardous Wastes, Law of the Sea, Marine Life Conservation, Ozone Layer Protection, Ship Pollution, Tropical Timber 83, Tropical Timber 94, Wetlands.
Signed but not ratified: none of the selected agreements.

TUNISIA

Location: Northern Africa bordering the Mediterranean Sea between Algeria and Libya
Area: 63,153 sq mi (163,610 sq km)

Area-comparative: slightly larger than Georgia.
Population: 9,974,722
Population growth rate: 1.01%
Climate: temperate in the north with rainy winters and hot dry summers; desert in south
Environment – current issues: toxic and hazardous waste disposal is ineffective and poses health risks; water pollution from raw sewage: limited natural fresh water resources; deforestation; overgrazing, soil erosion; desertification.
Land use: *arable land:* 18.67%
    permanent crops: 12.87%
    other: 68.46%
International Agreements: *party to:* Biodiversity, Climate Change, Climate Change-Kyoto Protocol, Desertification, Endangered Species, Environmental Modification, Hazardous Wastes, Law of the Sea, Marine Dumping, Ozone Layer Protection, Ship Pollution, Wetlands.
Signed but not ratified: Marine Life Conservation.

TURKEY
Location: Southeastern Europe, Southwestern Asia, bordering the Black Sea, between Bulgaria and Georgia, between Greece and Syria.
Area: 301,304 sq mi (780,580 sq km)
Area-comparative: slightly larger than Texas.
Population: 68,893,918
Population growth rate: 1.13%
Climate: temperate; hot, dry summers with mild, wet winters; harsher in interior.
Environment – current issues: water pollution from dumping of chemicals and detergents; air pollution, particularly in urban areas; deforestation, concern for oil spills from increasing Bosporus ship traffic.
Land use: *arable land:* 34.53%
    permanent crops: 3.36%
    other: 62.11%
International Agreements: *party to:* Air Pollution, Antarctic Treaty, Biodiversity, Desertification, Endangered Species, Hazardous Wastes, Ozone Layer Protection, Ozone Layer Protection, Ship Pollution; Wetlands.
Signed but not ratified: Environmental Modification.

TURKMENISTAN
Location: Central Asia, bordering the Caspian Sea, between Iran and Kazakhstan.
Area: 188,406 sq mi (488,100 sq km)
Area-comparative: slightly larger than California.
Population: 4,863,169
Population growth rate: 1.81%
Climate: subtropical desert.
Environment – current issues: contamination of soil and groundwater with chemicals, pesticides; salination, water-logging of soil due to poor irrigation methods; Caspian Sea pollution; diversion of a large share of the flow of the Amu Darya into irrigation contributes to that river's inability to replenish the Aral Sea; desertification.
Land use: *arable land:* 3.6%
    permanent crops: 0.1%
    other: 96.3%
International Agreements: *party to:* Biodiversity, Climate Change, Climate Change-

Kyoto Protocol, Desertification, Hazardous Wastes, Ozone Layer Protection.
Signed but not ratified: none of the selected agreements.

UGANDA

Location: Eastern Africa, west of Kenya.
Area: 91,111 sq mi (236,040 sq km)
Area-comparative: slightly smaller than Oregon.
Population: 26,404,543
Population growth rate: 2.97%
Climate: tropical; generally rainy with two dry seasons (December to February, June to August); semiarid in northeast.
Environment – current issues: draining of wetlands for agricultural use; deforestation; over-grazing, soil erosion; poaching is widespread.
Land Use: *arable land*: 25.34%
     permanent crops: 8.77%
     other: 65.89%
International Agreements: *party to*: Biodiversity, Climate Change, Climate Change-Kyoto Protocol, Desertification, Endangered Species, Hazardous Wastes, Law of the Sea, Marine Life Conservation, Ozone Layer Protection, Wetlands
Signed but not ratified: Environmental Modification.

UKRAINE

Location: Eastern Europe, bordering the Black Sea, between Poland and Russia.
Area: 233,028 sq mi (603,700 sq km)
Area-comparative: slightly smaller than Texas.
Population: 47,732,079
Population growth rate: -0.66%
Climate: temperate continental; Mediterranean only on the southern Crimean coast; precipitation disproportionately distributed, highest in west and north, lesser in east and southeast; winters vary from cool along the Black Sea to cold further inland; summers are warm across the greater part of the country, hot in the south.
Environment – current issues: inadequate supplies of potable water; air and water pollution; deforestation; radiation contamination in then in the northeast from 1986 accident at Chernobyl Nuclear Power Plant.
Land use: *arable land*: 57.1%
     permanent crops: 1.73%
     other: 41.17%
International Agreements: *party to*: Air Pollution, Air Pollution-Nitrogen Oxides, Air Pollution-Sulfur 85, Antarctic-Environmental Protocol, Antarctic Marine Living Resources, Antarctic Treaty, Biodiversity, Climate Control, Climate-Kyoto Protocol, Endangered Species, Environmental Modification, Hazardous Wastes, Law of the Sea, Marine Dumping, Ozone Layer Protection, Ship Pollution, Wetlands.
Signed but not ratified: Air Pollution-Persistent Organic Pollutants, Air Pollution-Sulfur 94, Air Pollution-Volatile Organic Compounds.

UNITED ARAB EMIRATES

Location: Middle East, bordering the Gulf of Oman and the Persian Gulf, between Oman and Saudi Arabia.
Area: 31,992 sq mi (82,880 sq km)

474

Area-comparative: slightly smaller than Maine.
Population: 2,523,915
Population growth rate: 1.57%
Climate: desert; cooler in eastern mountains.
Environmental – current issues: lack of freshwater resources compensated by desalination plants; desertification; beach pollution from oil spills.
Land use: *arable land*: 0.48%
    permanent crops: 0.49%
    other: 99.03%
International Agreements: *party to*: Biodiversity, Climate Control, Desertification, Endangered Species, Hazardous Wastes, Marine Dumping, Ozone Layer Protection.
Signed but not ratified: Law of the Sea.

UNITED KINGDOM

Location: Western Europe, between the North Atlantic Ocean and the North Sea, northwest of France.
Area: 94,500 sq mi (244,820 sq km)
Area-comparative: slightly smaller than Oregon.
Population: 60,270,708
Population growth rate: 0.29%
Climate: temperate; moderated by prevailing southwest winds over North Atlantic current; more than one-half of the days are overcast.
Environment – current issues :continues to reduce greenhouse gas emissions (has met Kyoto Protocol target of a 12.5% reduction from 1990 levels and intends to meet the legally binding target and move towards a domestic goal of a 20% cut in emissions by 2010); by 2005 the government aims to reduce the amount of industrial and commercial waste disposed of in landfill sites to 85% of 1998 levels and to recycle or compost at least 25% of household wastes, increasing to 33% by 2015; between 1998-99 and 1999-2000, household recycling increased from 8.8% to 10.3%.
Land use: *arable land*: 26.41%
    permanent crops: 0.18%
    other: 73.41%

International Agreements: *party to*: Air Pollution, Air Pollution-Nitrogen Oxides, Air Pollution-Sulfur 94, Air Pollution-Volatile Organic Compounds, Antarctic-Marine Living Resources, Antarctic Seals, Antarctic Treaty, Biodiversity, Climate Control, Climate Control-Kyoto Protocol, Desertification, Endangered Species, Environmental Modification, Hazardous Wastes, Law of the Sea, Marine Dumping, Marine Life Conservation, Ozone Layer Protection, Ship Pollution, Tropical Timber 83, Tropical Timber 94, Wetlands, Whaling.
Signed but not ratified: Air Pollution-Persistent Organic Pollutants.

UNITED STATES OF AMERICA

Location: North America, bordering both the North Atlantic Ocean and the North Pacific Ocean, between Canada and Mexico.
Area: 3,716,829 sq mi (9,631,418 sq km)
Area-comparative: about half the size of Russia; about three-tenths the size of Africa; about half the size of South America (or slightly larger than Brazil); slightly larger than China; about two and half times the size of western Europe.

Population: 293,027,571
Population growth rate: 0.92%
Climate mostly temperate, but tropical in Hawaii and Florida, arctic in Alaska, semiarid in the great plains west of the Mississippi River, and arid in the Great Basin of the Southwest; low winter temperature in the Northwest are ameliorated occasionally in January and February by warm Chinook winds from the eastern slopes of the Rocky Mountains.
Environment – current issues: air pollution resulting in acid rain in both the US and Canada; the US is the largest single emitter of carbon dioxide from the burning of fossil fuels; water pollution from runoff of pesticides and fertilizers; limited natural fresh water resources in much of the western part of the country require careful management; desertification.
Land use: *arable land*: 19.3%
　　permanent crops: 0.2%
　　other: 80.5%
International Agreements: *party to*: Air Pollution, Air Pollution-Nitrogen Oxides, Antarctic-Environmental Protocol, Antarctic Marine Living Resources, Antarctic Seals, Antarctic Treaty, Climate Change, Desertification, Endangered Species, Environmental Modification, Marine Dumping, Marine Life Conservation, Ozone Layer Protection, Ship Pollution, Tropical Timber 83, Tropical Timber 94, Wetlands, Whaling.
Signed but not ratified: Air Pollution-Persistent Organic Pollutants, Air Pollution-Volatile Organic Compound, Biodiversity, Climate Change-Kyoto Protocol, Hazardous Wastes.

URUGUAY

Location: Southern South America, bordering the South Atlantic Ocean, between Argentina and Brazil.
Area: 68,021 sq mi (176,220 sq km)
Area-comparative: slightly smaller than the state of Washington.
Population: 3,399,237
Population growth rate: 0.51%
Climate: warm temperate; freezing temperatures almost unknown.
Environment – current issues: water pollution from meat packing/tannery industry; inadequate solid/hazardous waste disposal.
Land use: *arable land*: 7.21%
　　permanent crops: 0.27%
　　other: 92.52%
International Agreements: *party to*: Antarctic –Environmental Protocol, Antarctic-Marine Living Resources, Antarctic Treaty, Biodiversity, Climate Control, Climate Control-Kyoto Protocol, Desertification, Endangered Species, Environmental Modification, Hazardous Wastes, Law of the Sea, Ozone Layer Protection, Ship Pollution, Tropical Timber 94, Wetlands.
Signed but not ratified: Marine Dumping, Marine Life Conservation.

UZBEKISTAN

Location: Central Asia, north of Afghanistan.
Area: 172,696 sq mi (447,400 sq km)
Area-comparative: slightly larger than California.
Population: 26,410,416
Population growth rate: 1.65%

Climate: mostly mid-latitude desert, long, hot summers, mild winters; semiarid grassland in east.

Environment – current issues: shrinkage of the Aral Sea is resulting in growing concentrations of chemical pesticides and natural salts, these substances are then blown from the increasingly exposed lake bed and contribute to desertification; water pollution from industrial wastes and the heavy use of fertilizers and pesticides is the cause of many human health disorders; soil contamination from buried nuclear processing and agricultural chemicals.

Land use: *arable land*: 10.8%
     permanent crops: 0.91%
     other: 88.29%

International Agreements: *party to*: Biodiversity, Climate Change, Climate Change-Kyoto Protocol, Desertification, Endangered Species, Environmental Modification, Hazardous Wastes, Ozone Layer Protection, Wetlands.
Signed but not ratified: none of the selected agreements.

VENEZUELA

Location: Northern South America, bordering the Caribbean Sea and the North Atlantic Ocean, between Colombia and Guyana.
Area: 352,051 sq mi (912,050 sq km)
Area-comparative: slightly more than twice the size of California.
Population: 25,017,387
Population growth rate: 1.44%
Climate: tropical; hot, humid; more moderate in highlands.
Environment – current issues: sewage pollution of Lago de Valencia; oil and urban pollution of Lago de Maracaibo; deforestation; soil degradation; urban and industrial pollution, especially along the Caribbean coast; threat to the rainforest ecosystem from irresponsible mining operations.
Land use: *arable land*: 2.99%
     permanent crops: 0.96%
     other: 96.05%
International Agreements: *party to*: Antarctic Treaty, Biodiversity, Climate Change, Desertification, Endangered Species, Hazardous Wastes, Marine Life Conservation, Ozone Layer Protection, Ship Pollution, Tropical Timber 83, Tropical Timber 94, Wetlands.

VIETNAM

Location: Southeastern Asia, bordering the Gulf of Thailand, Gulf of Tonkin, and South China Sea, alongside China, Laos, and Cambodia.
Area: 127,210 sq mi (329,560 sq km)
Area-comparative: slightly larger than New Mexico.
Population: 82,689,518
Population growth rate: 1.3%
Climate: tropical in south; monsoonal in north with hot, rainy season (mid-May to mid-September) and warm dry season (mid-October to mid-March).
Environment: - current issues: logging and slash-and-burn agricultural practices contribute to deforestation and soil degradation; water pollution and over-fishing threaten marine life populations; groundwater contamination limits potable water supply; growing urban industrialization and population migration are rapidly degrading environment in Haoi and Ho Chi Minh City.
Land use: *arable land*: 17.41%

>*permanent crops*: 4.71%
>*other*: 77.88%

International Agreements: *party to*: Biodiversity, Climate Control, Climate Control-Kyoto Protocol, Desertification, Endangered Species, Environmental Modification, Hazardous Wastes, Law of the Sea, Ozone Layer Protection, Ship Pollution, Wetlands.

Signed but not ratified: none of the selected agreements

VIRGIN ISLANDS

Location: islands between the Caribbean Sea and the North Atlantic Ocean, east of Puerto Rico.
Area: 136 sq mi (352 sq km)
Area-comparative: twice the size of Washington, D.C.
Population: 108,775
Population growth rate: -0.05%

Climate: subtropical, tempered by easterly trade winds, relatively low humidity, little seasonal temperature variation; rainy season May to November.
Environment- current issues: lack of natural freshwater resources.
Land use: *arable land*: 15%
>*permanent crops*: 6%
>*other*: 79%
International Agreements: NA

WEST BANK

Location: Middle East, west of Jordan
Area: 2,262 sq mi (5,860 sq km)`
Area-comparative: slightly smaller than Delaware
Population: 2,311,204
Population growth rate: 3.21%
Climate: temperate; temperature and precipitation very with altitude, warm to hot summers, cool to mild winters
Environment – current issues: adequacy of fresh water supply; sewage treatment
Land use: *arable land*: NEGL%
>*permanent crops*: 0%
>*other*: 100%
International Agreements: NA

YEMEN

Location: Middle East, bordering the Arabian Sea, Gulf of Aden, and Red Sea, between Oman and Saudi Arabia
Area: 203,796 sq mi (527,970 sq km)
Area-comparative: slightly larger than twice the size of Wyoming
Population: 20,024,867
Population growth rate: 3.44%
Climate: mostly desert; hot and humid along west coast; temperate in western mountains affected by seasonal monsoon; extraordinarily hot, dry, harsh desert in east
Environment – current issues: very limited fresh natural fresh water resources; inadequate supplies of potable water; overgrazing; soil erosion;

desertification
Land use: *arable land*: 2.75%
     permanent crops: 0.21%
     other: 97.04%
International Agreements: *party to*: Biodiversity, Climate Control, Desertification, Endangered Species, Environmental Modification, Hazardous Wastes, Law of the Sea, Ozone Layer Protection
Signed but not ratified: none of the selected agreements.

ZAMBIA

Location: Southern Africa, east of Angola.
Area: 290,509 sq mi (752,614 sq km)
Area-comparative: slightly larger than Texas.
Population: 10,462,436
Population growth rate: 1.47%
Climate: tropical; modified by altitude; rainy season (October to April).
Environment – current issues: air pollution and resulting acid rain in the mineral extraction and refining region; chemical runoff into watersheds; poaching seriously threatens rhinoceros, elephant, antelope, and large cat populations; deforestation; soil erosion; desertification, lack of adequate water treatment presents human health hazards.
Land use: *arable land*: 7.08%
     permanent crops: 0.03%
     other: 92.89%
International Agreements: *party to*: Biodiversity, Climate Change, Desertification, Endangered Species, Hazardous Wastes, Law of the Sea, Ozone Layer Protection, Wetlands.
Signed but not ratified: Climate Change-Kyoto Protocol.

ZIMBABWE

Location: Southern Africa, between South Africia and Zambia.
Area: 150,764 sq mi (390,580 sq km)
Area-comparative: slightly larger than Montana.
Population: 12,671,860
Population growth rate: 0.68%
Climate: tropical; moderated by altitude; rainy season (November to March).
Environment – current issues: deforestation; soil erosion; land degradation; air and water pollution; the black rhinoceros herd – once the largest concentration of the species in the world – has been significantly reduced by poaching; poor mining practices have led to toxic waste and heavy metal pollution.
Land use: *arable land*: 8.4%
     permanent crops: 0.34%
     other: 91.26%
International Agreements: *party to*: Biodiversity, Climate Control, Desertification, Endangered Species, Law of the Sea, Ozone Layer Protection.
Signed but not ratified: none of the selected agreements.

The Savanna Animals

Patas Monkey *(Erythrocebus patas)*
Weight: 7-13 kg.
Length: 50-70 cm.
Speed: 55 km/h.
Number on the Planet: 1.5 individuals/sq.km (though limited range and highly hunted). Considered threatened.
Number in a litter: 1 (infant).
Life Span: up to 24 years.
Location: across sub-Saharan Africa from the western tip of Senegal to East Africa and as far south as Cameroon.
Calories: 790-2,400 kcal/day.
Diet: fruits, insects, leaves, roots and bird eggs.
What they are called in a group: troop.

Grevy's Zebra *(Equus grevyi)*
Weight: 405 kg.
Height: 1,250-1,500 mm at the shoulder.
Length: 2.1-2.3 m.
Speed: 64 km/h.
Number on the Planet: ~6,000.
"Grevy's zebra is of special concern for conservationists. It is considered endangered by IUCN.
Number in a litter: 1 (colt/foal).
Life Span: 18-30 years.
Location: southeastern Ethiopia, Kenya and Somalia.
Calories: 12,600-38,000 kcal/day.
Diet: grasses, leaves, bark, buds, fruit.
What they are called in a group: herd.

Golden-Rumped Lion Tamaran *(Leontopithecus chrysopygus)*
Weight: 300-700 g.
Length: 20-33.5 cm.
Speed: 30 km/h arboreal locomotion.
Number on the Planet: 700, considered critically endangered.
Number in a litter: 2 most commonly- though sometimes triplets and quadruplets, (infants).
Life Span: average 10 years, up to 28.

Location: 375 square kilometer *Morro do Diabo State Forest Reserve* in southwestern Sao Paulo. The other is the *Caiteus Reserve*, a 23 square kilometer reserve in central Sao Paulo.
Calories: 100-300 kcal/day.
Diet: insects, fruits, small lizards, small birds, bird eggs, and small vertebrates.
What they are called in a group: troop.

Dama Gazelle *(Gazella dama)*
Weight: 35-75 kg.
Height: 90-120 cm at the shoulder.
Length: 140-168 cm.
Speed: 80 km/h.
Number on the Planet: possibly less than 250 mature individuals-- no estimates of overall population size are available. Known remnant populations are all very small and fragmented.
Number in a litter: 1-2 (calves).
Life Span: up to 12 years.
Location: countries of the African Sahel and Sahara Desert.
Calories: 2,800-8,400 kcal/day
Diet: shrubs, herbs, coarse desert grasses, and *Acacia* tree leaves.
What they are called in a group: herd.

Senegal Bush Baby *(Galago senegalensis)*
Weight: 95-300 g.
Length: 130 mm.
Speed: ~16 km/h.
Number on the Planet: not available.
Number in a litter: 1-3 (pup)
Life Span: average 3-4, up to ~10 years.
Location: throughout sub-Saharan and East Africa.
Calories: 45-131 kcal/day.
Diet: grasshoppers, small birds, eggs, fruits, seeds, tree gum and flowers.
What they are called in a group: troop.

The Savanna Animals

African Wild Dog *(Lycaon pictus)*
Weight: 17-36 kg.
Height: 61-78 cm at the shoulder.
Length: 76-112 cm.
Speed: 65 km/h.
Number on the Planet: 3,000-5,500.
Number in a litter: up to 16 (pups).
Life Span: up to 10 years.
Location: southern Africa; northern
Botswana, north-east Namibia,
western Zimbabwe, *Kruger National
Park* in South Africa, *Kafue National
Park* and the Luangwa valley in
Zambia, southern Tanzania, Kenya,
Ethiopia, Sénégal and Cameroon.
Calories: 1,600-4,900 kcal/day.
Diet: antelope, zebras, wildebeest,
springboks, gazelles, impala, lizards,
eggs, hares and livestock (sheep,
goats, cattle).
What they are called in a group: pack.

Black Rhinoceros
(Diceros bicornis)
Weight: 800-1,400 kg.
Height: 140-180 cm at the shoulder.
Length: 300-375 cm.
Speed: 48-64 km/h.
Number on the Planet: 3,600.
Number in a litter: 1 (calf).
Life Span: up to 45 years.
Location: eastern and central areas of
Africa including Kenya, Tanzania,
Cameroon, South Africa, Namibia and
Zimbabwe.
Calories: 27,000-80,000 kcal/day
Diet: leaf and woody plant browse.
What they are called in a group:
crash.

Cheetah *(Acinonyx jubatus)*
Weight: 40-65 kg.
Height: 73 cm.
Length: 112-135 cm.
Speed: 110 km/h.
Number on the Planet: 9,000-13,000.
Number in a litter: average 3-5 and up
to 9 (cubs).
Life Span: 12-20 years.
Location: Iran and various countries in
sub-Saharan Africa.

Calories: 2,700-8,200 kcal/day.
Diet: gazelles, impala, wildebeest,
calves, Guinea fowl and hares (most
small mammals).
What they are called in a group:
coalition.

Malabar Large Spotted Civet
(Viverra civettina)
Weight: 8-9 kg.
Length: 76-85 cm.
Speed: up to 40 km/h in short bursts.
Number on the Planet: less than 250
mature individuals.
Number in a litter: 1-4 (average 2-3)
(pups).
Life Span: 10-20 years.
Location: coastal districts of Malabar.
and Travancore in southwest India.
Calories: 700-2,100 kcal/day.
Diet: small animals, eggs and
vegetable matter.
What they are called in a group:
pack/solitary.

Ossabaw Island Pig
(Sus scrofa domesticus)
Weight: ~45kg.
Height: 55-110cm at the shoulder.
Length: ~90cm.
Speed: up to 48 km/h.
Number on the Planet: less than 200.
Number in a litter: average 6 (4-12)
(piglets/shoats/farrows).
Life Span: 15-20 years.
Location: Ossabaw Island, off the
coast of Georgia.
Calories: 2,400-7,300
Diet: acorns, corn, oats and roots (+
farm slop).
What they are called in a group:
drove/herd.

Ethiopian Wolf (Canis simensis)
Weight: 11-19 kg.
Height: 50 cm.
Length: 1m.
Speed: up to 60 km/h.
Number on the Planet: less than 250
mature individuals.
Number in a litter: 2-6 (pups/whelps).

The Savanna Animals

Life Span: 8-9 years.
Location: mountain ranges of Ethiopia;
Arssi and Bale mountains of southeast
Ethiopia, the Simien mountains,
northeast Shoa, Gojjam, and Mt.
Guna, largest population existing in
Bale Mountains National Park.
Calories: 1,100-3,200 kcal/day.
Diet: moles, goslings, eggs, and
young ungulates.
What they are called in a group: pack.

Komodo Dragon
(Varanus komodensis)
Weight: 70-166 kg.
Length: 2-3 m.
Speed: 20 km/h.
Number on the Planet: 1,000-6,000.
Number in a litter: 20.
eggs.(hatchlings).
Life Span: 25-30 years.
Location: Indonesian islands of
Komodo, Rintja, Padar, and Flores.
Calories: 560-1,700 kcal/day.
Diet: insects, smaller reptiles, birds
and their eggs and chicks, small
mammals, wild pigs, goats, deer,
macaques, horses, water buffaloes
and smaller dragons, occasionally
humans and human corpses.
What they are called in a group:
solitary.

Banded Hare Wallaby
(Lagostrophus fasciatus)
Weight: 1.3-3 kg.
Height: 40-45 cm.
Length: 40-45 cm, 35-40 cm tail.
Speed: up to ~55 km/h.
Number on the Planet:considered
vulnerable by the IUCN.
Number in a litter: 1-2 (joey).
Life Span: 5-6 years.
Location: Dorre Island and Bernier
Island in Shark Bay, 50-60 km west of
the Australian mainland.
Calories: 174-522 kcal/day.
Diet: foliage and grasses.
What they are called in a group: mob.

Asian Elephants
(Elephas maximus)
Weight: 3,000-5,000 kg.
Height: 2.5-3 m.
Length: 2-4 m.
Speed: up to 40-48 km/h.
Number on the Planet: 38,000-51,000.
Number in a litter: 1-2 (usually 1)
(calf).
Life Span: 60-80 years.
Location: India, Sri Lanka, Indochina
peninsula and parts of Indonesia.
Calories: 35,000-211,000 kcal/day.
Diet: grasses, leaves, tree and shrubs.
What they are called in a group: herd.

African Wild Ass *(Equus africanus)*
Weight: 200 kg.
Height: 125-145 cm at the shoulder.
Length: 2 m.
Speed: 50 km/h.
Number on the Planet: less than 570.
Number in a litter: 1 (foal/yearling).
Life Span: up to 40 years.
Location: Eritria, Somalia and
Ethiopia.
Calories: 7,400-22,000 kcal/day.
Diet: grasses.
What they are called in a group:
drove/herd.

Attwater's Prairie-Chicken
(Tympanuchus cupido attwateri)
Weight: 0.7-0.9 kg.
Height: 70cm wingspan.
Length: 43-45.5 cm.
Speed: up to 80 km/h.
Number on the Planet: ~260.
Number in a litter: 12 eggs (chicks).
Life Span: 2-3 years.
Location: *Attwater Prairie Chicken
National Wildlife Refuge* near Eagle
Lake, Texas.
Calories: 125-375 kcal/day.
Diet: leaves, seeds and insects (e.g.
grasshoppers).
What they are called in a group: flock.

The Savanna Animals

Mississippi Sandhill Crane
(Grus canadensis pulla)
<u>Weight:</u> 3-6.5 kg.
<u>Height:</u> 80 cm-1.2 m.
<u>Length:</u> 2 m wingspan.
<u>Speed:</u> 40-48 km/h.
<u>Number on the Planet:</u> 100.
<u>Number in a litter:</u> 1-2 eggs (chicks).
<u>Life Span:</u> 15-20 years.
<u>Location:</u> *Mississippi Sandhill Crane National Wildlife Refuge.*
<u>Calories:</u> 500-1,500 kcal/day.
<u>Diet:</u> edible tubers, roots, berries, nuts, fruits, insects, worms, crustaceans, and other invertebrates, occasionally small vertebrates such as small fish or amphibians.
<u>What they are called in a group:</u> solitary.

Florida Panther
(Puma concolor coryi)
<u>Weight:</u> 30-57 kg.
<u>Height:</u> 60-70 cm at the shoulder.
<u>Length:</u> 1.8-2.1 m.
<u>Speed:</u> 56 km/h.
<u>Number on the Planet:</u> 20-50.
<u>Number in a litter:</u> 1-3 (cubs).
<u>Life Span:</u> average 10-12, up to 20 years.
<u>Location:</u> southern Florida.
<u>Calories:</u> 2,400-7,100 kcal/day.
<u>Diet:</u> white-tailed deer, rabbit, raccoon, wild hog, armadillo, birds.
<u>What they are called in a group:</u> solitary.

African Buffalo *(Syncerus caffer)*
<u>Weight:</u> 500-900 kg.
<u>Height:</u> 1-1.7 m at the shoulder.
<u>Length:</u> 2.1-3 m.
<u>Speed:</u> 57km/h.
<u>Number on the Planet:</u> 900,000.
<u>Number in a litter:</u> 1 (calf).
<u>Life Span:</u> 15-30 years.
<u>Location:</u> middle of the African continent; range stretches from south of the Sahara to north of South Africa.
<u>Calories:</u> 9,500-28,500 kcal/day.
<u>Diet:</u> grasses.
<u>What they are called in a group:</u> herd.

Meerkat *(Suricata suricatta)*
<u>Weight:</u> 720-731 g.
<u>Height:</u> 15 cm at the shoulder.
<u>Length:</u> 42.5-60 cm.
<u>Speed:</u> up to 40 km/h.
<u>Number on the Planet:</u> meerkats are not considered a threatened or endangered species, but beyond that, there do not appear to be readily available population estimates for these creatures.
<u>Number in a litter:</u> 3 (pups).
<u>Life Span:</u> 5-15 years.
<u>Location:</u> South African, Botswanan, Zimbabwe and Mozambique savannas.
<u>Calories:</u> 110-330 kcal/day.
<u>Diet:</u> bugs, lizards, eggs, plant-matter and small rodents.
<u>What they are called in a group:</u> mob/gang.

Riverine Rabbit
(Bunolagus monticularis)
<u>Weight:</u> 1.5-1.8 kg.
<u>Length:</u> 337-470 mm.
<u>Speed:</u> up to 50 km/h.
<u>Number on the Planet:</u> less than 250.
<u>Number in a litter:</u> 1 (kitten/bunny/kit).
<u>Life Span:</u> up to 10 years.
<u>Location:</u> South Africa.
<u>Calories:</u> 200-600 kcal/day.
<u>Diet:</u> salt-loving plants, flowers and leaves from boegoe, and ink bushes, and grasses.
<u>What they are called in a group:</u> nest/colony.

American Kestrel
(Falco sparverius)
<u>Weight:</u> 120-166 g.
<u>Height:</u> 50-60 cm wingspan.
<u>Length:</u> 19-21 cm.
<u>Speed:</u> 97 km/h.
<u>Number on the Planet:</u> 100,000+.
<u>Number in a litter:</u> 3-7 (average 4-5) eggs (chicks/fledglings).
<u>Life Span:</u> average 3-5, up to 15 years.
<u>Location:</u> North and South America from Alaska and Canada south to

The Savanna Animals

Tierra del Fuego, also found in the West Indies, the Juan Fernandez Islands and Chile.
Calories: 36-110 kcal/day.
Diet: large insects (mainly grasshoppers), small mammals (mice and sparrow-sized birds), sandpiper chicks, lizards, scorpions and amphibians.
What they are called in a group: pair/solitary.

Przewalski's Gazelle
(Procapra Przewalskii)
Weight: 21-32 kg.
Height: 54-84 cm at the shoulder.
Length: 1m.
Speed: up to 100 km/h.
Number on the Planet: less than 300.
Number in a litter: 1 (calf).
Life Span: 10-12 years.
Location: Qinghai Lake basin, in northeast China's Qinghai Province
Calories: 1,600-4,900 kcal/day.
Diet: plants of the sedge family, the grass family and other sands plants.
What they are called in a group: herd.

Southern White Rhinoceros
(Ceratotherium simum)
Weight: 1,440-3,600 kg.
Height: 150-185 cm at the shoulder.
Length: 335-420 cm.
Speed: up to 50 km/h.
Number on the Planet: ~4,000.
Number in a litter: 1 (calf).
Life Span: 35-40 years.
Location: restricted to game preserves and national parks in Africa.
Calories: 25,000-75,000 kcal/day.
Diet: grasses.
What they are called in a group: herd.

Lesser Florican
(Sypheotides indica)
Weight: 0.99-1.45 kg.
Length: 46-51 cm.
Speed: up to ~30 km/h.
Number on the Planet: ~ 2,200.
Number in a litter: 3-4 eggs (chicks).
Life Span: 4 years or more.

Location: Pakistan and occasionally Nepal.
Calories: 180-543 kcal/day.
Diet: many types of invertebrates and various plant parts: grasshoppers, beetles, flying ants, hairy caterpillars, centipedes, worms, frogs, small lizards (e.g. *Agama*), crop shoots, leaves (e.g. soybean), herbs and berries.
What they are called in a group: flock.

African Elephant
(Loxodonta africana)
Weight: 3,600-6,000 kg.
Height: 3-3.75 m.
Length: 5.4-7.5 m.
Speed: up to 40 km/h.
Number on the Planet: 400,000-660,000
Number in a litter: 1-2 (average 1) (calf).
Life Span: up to ~70 years.
Location: limited to several national parks and game reserves in southern Africa.
Calories: 40,000-240,000 kcal/day.
Diet: leaves, roots, fruit, grasses and bark.
What they are called in a group: herd.

Sumatran Tiger
(Panthera tigris sumatrae)
Weight: 100 kg.
Height: 60 cm at the shoulder.
Length: 2.55 m.
Speed: up to 70 km/h.
Number on the Planet: 400-500.
Number in a litter: 2-3, up to 6 (cubs/whelps).
Life Span: 15-20 years.
Location: Indonesian island of Sumatra.
Calories: 4,400-13,200 kcal/day.
Diet: wild boar, deer, fowl, and fish.
What they are called in a group: solitary/streak.

The Savanna Animals

White-Rumped Vulture
(*Gyps bengalensis*)
Weight: 3.5-7.5 kg.
Height: 75-85 cm.
Length: 180-210 cm wingspan.
Speed: up to 144 km/h.
Number on the Planet: ~ 1,000.
Number in a litter: 1 (fledgling).
Life Span: up to ~30 years.
Location: Pakistan, India, Bangladesh, Nepal, Bhutan, Myanmar (Burma), Thailand, Laos, Cambodia, Afghanistan and southern Vietnam.
Calories: 560-1,680 kcal/day.
Diet: carrion.
What they are called in a group: mob/colony.

Demoiselle Crane
(*Anthropoides virgo*)
Weight: 2-2.70 kg.
Height: 51-59 cm wingspan.
Length: 90 cm.
Speed: 48-56 km/h.
Number on the Planet:~ 250,000.
Number in a litter: 2 eggs (chick).
Life Span: up to 67 years.
Location: wide range of the Ethiopian, Palearctic, and Oriental regions; winter migration to northeastern Africa, Pakistan, and India.
Calories: 300-900 kcal/day.
Diet: seeds, leaves, acorns, nuts, berries, fruits, waste grains, small mammals, birds, insects, worms, snails, grasshoppers, beetles, snakes, lizards, and rodents.
What they are called in a group: flock.

Bengal Monitor
(*Varanus bengalensis*)
Weight: 1.5-2.7, up to 10 kg.
Length: 75cm, 100 cm tail.
Speed: 18-56 km/h.
Number on the Planet: endangered (less than 10,000 mature individuals).
Number in a litter: up to 30 eggs (hatchlings).
Life Span: up to 50 years.
Location: throughout Bangladesh and India.

Calories: 35-105, up to 112-337 kcal/day (depending on body mass of lizard).
Diet: small terrestrial vertebrates, ground birds and their eggs, arthropods and fish.
What they are called in a group: solitary.

Chimpanzee (*Pan troglodytes*)
Weight: 35-70 kg.
Height: 0.6-1.2 m.
Length: 635-25 mm.
Speed: 2.9 km/h knuckle-walking.
Number on the Planet: less than 2,500 mature individuals, vulnerable.
Number in a litter: 1-2 (infants).
Life Span: 40 years in the wild, up to 60-74 years in captivity.
Location: west and central Africa.
Calories: 2,750-8,250 kcal/day.
Diet: ripe fruits and young leaves, stems, buds, bark, seeds, and resins, a variety of insects, small vertebrates, eggs and sometimes soil.
What they are called in a group: society.

Hispid Hare (*Caprolagus hispidus*)
Weight: 2.5 kg.
Length: 405-538 mm.
Speed: ~48 km/h.
Number on the Planet: less than 110.
Number in a litter: 1-5, up to 15 (leverets).
Life Span: 1-7 years.
Location: northwestern Assam, and a few areas in Nepal.
Calories: 280-835 kcal/day.
Diet: bark, roots, shoots, grasses and crops.
What they are called in a group: solitary/nest.

Ball Python (*Python regius*)
Weight: ~1 kg.
Length: 1-2 m.
Speed: ~1 km/h.
Number on the Planet: endangered (less than 2,500 mature individuals).
Number in a litter: 4-10 eggs.

The Savanna Animals

Life Span: 20-40 years and up to 48.
Location: southern Sudan in the Bahrel Ghazal and in region of Nuba Mountains(Southern Kordofan); in West Africa from Senegal to Sierra Africa.
Calories: 20-60 kcal/day.
Diet: rodents (gerbils, jerboas and rats).
What they are called in a group: solitary/nest.

Bali Mynah *(Leucopsar rothschildi)*
Weight: 75-95 g.
Length: 25 cm.
Speed: 29-64 km/h.
Number on the Planet: ~ 1,000.
Number in a litter: 1-2 (chicks).
Life Span: 3 years in the wild, up to 20 years in captivity.
Location: island of Bali in Indonesia, zoos and breeding centers around the world.
Calories: 40-120 kcal/day.
Diet: insects and fruit
What they are called in a group: flock.

Savanna Hawk
(Heterospizias meridionalis)
Weight: 845 g.
Height: 89-92 cm wingspan.
Length: 46-61 cm.
Speed: ~48-64 km/h.
Number on the Planet: 100,000-1,000,000.
Number in a litter: 1 egg (eyas).
Life Span: up to ~15 years.
Location: throughout South America.
Calories: 136-408 kcal/day.
Diet: small mammals, lizards, snakes, crabs and large insects.
What they are called in a group: cast/kettle.

Swift Fox *(Vulpes velox)*
Weight: 2-3 kg.
Height: 30 cm at the shoulder.
Length: 37-53 cm.
Speed: 40 km/h.
Number on the Planet: 120-150.
Number in a litter: 2-10 (kit/cub/pup).

Life Span: up to 14 years.
Location: Great Plains of North America.
Calories: 280-835 kcal/day.
Diet: mainly carrion (compete scavenging with coyotes).
What they are called in a group: skulk/leash.

Baringo Giraffe *(Giraffa camelopardalis Rothschild)*
Weight: 1,360-2,000 kg.
Height: 4.8-5.5 m.
Length: 3.8-4.7 m.
Speed: 48-58 km/h.
Number on the Planet: less than 110,000.
Number in a litter: 1 (calf).
Life Span: 25-28 years.
Location: Africa, south of the Sahara, specifically northern Kenya and Uganda.
Calories: 18,300-55,100 kcal/day.
Diet: leaves and buds of acacia, mimosa, and wild apricot trees, as well as lower vegetation.
What they are called in a group: herd.

Golden Eagle *(Aquila chrysaetos)*
Weight: 3-6 kg.
Height: 185-220 cm wingspan.
Length: 70-84 cm.
Speed: up to 129 km/h, though the average speed is 45-51 km/h, and may reach speeds up to 322 km/h in a dive.
Number on the Planet: 250,000.
Number in a litter: 1-4, average 2 eggs (fledglings/eaglets).
Life Span: up to 32-46 years.
Location: Eurasia, in northern Africa, and in North America.
Calories: 490-1,460 kcal/day.
Diet: rabbits, ground squirrels, prairie dogs, marmots, birds, reptiles, fish; occasionally capture large prey, including seals, coyotes and badgers, also known to capture large flying birds such as geese or cranes.
What they are called in a group: solitary/pairs.

The Savanna Animals

Scimitar-Horned Oryx
(Oryx dammah)
Weight: 67 kg.
Height: 1.2 m at the shoulder.
Length: 1.7 m.
Speed: up to 48 km/h in short bursts.
Number on the Planet: (extinct in the wild) at least 1,250 captive animals held in zoos and parks around the world, and 2,145 on ranches in Texas.
Number in a litter: 1 (calf).
Life Span: up to 20 years.
Location: region of Africa known as the "Great Steppe," a strip of arid grassland extending from Senegal to central Sudan (borders the southern edge of the Sahara Desert).
Calories: 3,300-9,800 kcal/day
Diet: grasses, herbs, juicy roots, buds, and (when water is scarce) fruits and vegetables.
What they are called in a group: herd.

Crowned Lemur
(Eulemur coronatus)
Weight: 2 kg.
Length: 33 cm, 42-51 cm tail.
Speed: up to 40 km/h arboreal locomotion.
Number on the Planet: 1,000-10,000.
Number in a litter: 1-2 (pups).
Life Span: 20 years.
Location: Madagascar (from savanna and dry bush regions of both northeastern and northwestern Madagascar).
Calories: 235-706 kcal/day.
Diet: fruit, flowers, young leaves and occasional invertebrate.
What they are called in a group: aggregation.

Wrentit *(Chamaea fasciata)*
Weight: 13-16 g.
Height: 25 cm wingspan.
Length: 15 cm.
Speed: ~up to 30 km/h.
Number on the Planet: 1,500,000.
Number in a litter: 1-5, average 3-4 eggs (chicks).

Life Span: 2-3 years.
Location: narrow strip of coastal habitat in western coast of North America, from southern Washington to Baja California.
Calories: 11-35 kcal/day.
Diet: caterpillars, ants, beetles, bugs, berries and seeds.
What they are called in a group: flock.

Northern White Rhinoceros
(Ceratotherium simum cottoni)
Weight: 1800-3000 kg.
Height: 150-185 cm at the shoulder.
Length: 3.35-4.2 m.
Speed: up to 48 km/h.
Number on the Planet: 5-10.
Number in a litter: 1 (calf).
Life Span: 35-40 years.
Location: Garamba National Park, Democratic Republic of the Congo.
Calories: 48,000-144,000 kcal/day.
Diet: grasses.
What they are called in a group: crash.

Indian Rhinoceros
(Rhinoceros unicornis)
Weight: 1,500-2,000 kg.
Height: 1.75-2.0 m at the shoulder.
Length: 3-3.8 m.
Speed: 64 km/h.
Number on the Planet: 1,700-2,400.
Number in a litter: 1 (calf).
Life Span: ~40 years.
Location: northern Pakistan, India, Nepal, Bangladesh, and Assam.
Calories: 38,000-114,000 kcal/day.
Diet: grass, fruit, leaves, branches, aquatic plants, and cultivated crops.
What they are called in a group: crash.

Javan Rhinoceros
(Rhinoceros sondaicus)
Weight: 900-2,300 kg.
Height: 1.5-1.7 m at the shoulder.
Length: 2-4 m.
Speed: 48k m/h.
Number on the Planet: 60.
Number in a litter: 1 (calf).

The Savanna Animals

Life Span: up to 21 years.
Location: lowlands of Indonesia and Vietnam.
Calories: 35,000-106,000 kcal/day.
Diet: shoots, twigs, young foliage and fallen fruit.
What they are called in a group: crash.

Arabian Oryx (*Oryx leucoryx*)
Weight: 100-210 kg.
Height: 900-1,400 cm at the shoulder.
Length: 1.53-2.53 m.
Speed: up to 80 km/h.
Number on the Planet: ~2,800.
Number in a litter: 1 (calf).
Life Span: 20 years.
Location: originally found in Syria, Iraq, Israel, Jordan, Sinai, and the Arabian Peninsula.
Calories: 6,200-18,500 kcal/day.
Diet: grasses and shrubs.
What they are called in a group: herd.

Fringed-Eared Oryx
(*Oryx beisa callotis*)
Weight: 175-210 kg.
Height: 110-120 cm at the shoulder.
Length: 160-190 cm.
Speed: up to ~100 km/h.
Number on the Planet: they are abundant in their region and have at least 100,000+ mature individuals in existence.
Number in a litter: 1 (calf).
Life Span: up to ~18 years.
Location: Kenya (South of the Tana river) and northeastern Tanzania.
Calories: 7,200-21,700 kcal/day.
Diet: grass, leaves, fruit and buds.
What they are called in a group: herd.

Plains Zebra/Burchell's Zebra
(*Equus burchellii*)
Weight: 290-340 kg.
Height: 127-140 cm at the shoulder.
Length: 1.3 m.
Speed: 64 km/h.
Number on the Planet: almost extinct.
Number in a litter: 1 (colt/foal).
Life Span: ~20 + years.

Location: southeastern Africa, from southern Ethiopia in the north to eastern South Africa in the south.
Calories: 10,500-31,400 kcal/day.
Diet: herbs, leaves and many different species of grasses.
What they are called in a group: herd.

Reticulated Giraffe
(*Giraffa camelopardalis reticulata*)
Weight: 544-1,814 kg.
Height: 4.2-5.1 m, up to 5.8 m.
Length: 3.8-4.7 m.
Speed: 56 km/h.
Number on the Planet: listed as low risk on the World Conservation Union's (IUCN's) list of Threatened Animals.
Number in a litter: 1 (calf).
Life Span: 25-30 years.
Location: eastern Africa.
Calories: 28,000-84,500 kcal/day.
Diet: leaves, fruits, and seedpods from acacia, mimosa, and wild apricot trees.
What they are called in a group: herd.

Lesser Kudu
(*Tragelaphus imberbis*)
Weight: 56-105 kg.
Height: 90-110 cm at the shoulder.
Length: 110-140 cm, 25-40 cm tail.
Speed: rather than run from predators, Kudu leap vertically at ~1.8-2.1m to escape over brush.
Number on the Planet: abundant in the region.
Number in a litter: 1 (calf).
Life Span: 15 years.
Location: East Africa and (possibly) the southern Arabian Peninsula.
Calories: 3,700-11,300 kcal/day.
Diet: leaves, grasses and fruits.
What they are called in a group: herd/troop.

The Desert Animals

Desert Rosy Boa
(Lichanura trivigata)
Weight: 311-595 g.
Length: 43-112 cm.
Speed: ~1.6 km/h.
Number on the Planet: listed neither Endangered nor Vulnerable by the IUCN.
Number in a litter: 2 to 15 neonates.
Life Span: over 18 years.
Location: located in the Mojave and Colorado Desert, and in Northern Baja Peninsula and Southwestern Arizona.
Calories: 1200 kcal/week.
Diet: small mammals, rodents, lizards, small birds, amphibians.
What they are called in a group:nest.

Addax *(Addax nasomaculatus)*
Weight: 135 kg.
Height: 93-114 cm at the shoulder.
Length: 150-170 cm.
Speed: up to 100 km/h.
Number on the Planet: a few hundred + ~900 in captivity.
Number in a litter: 1 calf.
Life Span: average age of 25 years.
Location: Dune regions of the Sahara Desert, e.g. Mauritania, W. Mali; patchy distribution in Algeria, Chad, Niger and Sudan.
Calories: ~2,000 kcal/day.
Diet: herbs, coarse desert grasses, most plant life (derives all moisture from plants rather than drinking water).
What they are called in a group: herd

Arabian Oryx *(Oryx leucoryx)*
Weight: 65-75 kg.
Height: 1m at the shoulder.
Length: 72-91 cm.
Speed: 97 km/h.
Number on the Planet: ~900.
Number in a litter: 1 calf.
Life Span: 20 years.

Location: Saudi Arabia, Bahrain, Oman, Israel.
Calories: 3400-10,160 calories/ day.
Diet: grasses, herbs, seedpods, fruit, fresh growth on trees, tubers and roots.
What they are called in a group:herd.

Leopard Gecko *(Buteo regalis)*
Weight: 45-60 g.
Length: 15-23 cm.
Speed: 11 km/h.
Number on the Planet: exact number unknown, but plentiful.
Number in a litter: 1 to 2 eggs (hatchlings).
Life Span: 30 years.
Location: Western India, Pakistan and Afghanistan.
Calories: ~2-7 calories/ day.
Diet: insects, fruit, small birds, eggs, small lizards, and baby mice.
What they are called in a group: flange.

Ferruginous Hawk *(Buteo regalis)*
Weight: 980-2030 g.
Height: 134-152 cm wingspan.
Length: 50-66 cm.
Speed: up to 64 km/hr.
Number on the Planet: 3400.
Number in a litter: 3 to 5 eggs (eyas)
Life Span: 5-20 years.
Location: Western Great Basin and Great Plains; Washington, Southern Canada, Oregon, Nevada, Arizona, New Mexico, Texas, Nebraska, Kansas, Oklahoma—winters migrate to southern Baja California and Mexico.
Calories: ~350-1050 calories/ day.
Diet: gophers, mice, rabbits, prairie dogs.
What they are called in a group: cast or a parade.

489

The Desert Animals

Central Chinese Goral
**((Nemorhaedus caudatus
arnouxianus)**
Weight: 22-32 kilograms.
Height: 50-70 cm at the shoulder.
Length: 80-120 cm.
Speed: ~40 km/h.
Number on the Planet: less than
3000.
Number in a litter: 1-2 calves.
Life Span: 8-10 years.
Location: Southeastern Tibet,
Yunnan, China, Northeast India,
Northern Myanmar, North Pakistan,
Bhutan, Nepal, China and Eastern
Russia.
Calories: ~1600 calories/ day.
Diet: grasses, leaves, twigs, nuts,
stems, fruit and vegetables.
What they are called in a group:herd.

Aruba Island Rattlesnake
(Crotalus unicolor)
Weight: 0.9-1.4 kg.
Length: 95 cm.
Speed: up to 4.8 km/h.
Number on the Planet: less than 300
in the wild.
Number in a litter: 5-15 neonates.
Life Span: 15-20 years.
Location: Desert Island of Aruba off
of the coast of Venezuela.
Calories: ~22-66 kcal/day.
Diet: rodents, lizards, birds.
What they are called in a group:
rhumba.

Nubian Ibex (Capra ibex nubiana)
Weight: 50 kg.
Height: 60 cm at the shoulder.
Length: 30 cm (female)- 1m (male).
Speed: up to 72 km/hr.
Number on the Planet: ~1200.
Number in a litter: 1-2.
Life Span: 15-20 years.
Location: mountainous regions of
Israel, Saudi Arabia, Oman, Egypt
and Sudan.

Calories: 2 kg dry food/day (~2,600
kcal/day).
Diet: grasses and leaves.
What they are called in a group:herd.

Inland Bearded Dragon
(Pogona vitticeps)
Weight: 1.7 kg.
Length: 33-61 cm.
Speed: 1 m/s running.
Number on the Planet: not
endangered, though exact count
unavailable.
Number in a litter: 24 eggs
(hatchlings).
Life Span: 10 years.
Location: Australia.
Calories: ~30-90 kcal/day
Diet: plants, insects, lizards and
rodents.
What they are called in a group:
flange.

Red-Tailed Hawk
(Buteo jamaicensis)
Weight: 0.9-1.8 kg.
Height: wingspan up to 1.47 m.
Length: 56 cm.
Speed: Aerial dives up to 193 km/h,
average flight 32-64 km/h.
Number on the Planet: increasing in
numbers (though exact number not
known).
Number in a litter: 1 to 3 eggs.
Life Span: 10 to 21 years.
Location: North America.
Calories: ~97-300 k-calories/ day.
Diet: rodents, snakes, birds and
lizards.
What they are called in a group: cast
or kettle.

Great-Horned Owl
(Bubo virginianus)
Weight: 1.4 kg.
Height: wingspan ~1.4 m.
Length: 45-62 cm.
Speed: on average 64 km/h.
Number on the Planet: abundant.

The Desert Animals

Number in a litter: 2 to 3 eggs (fledglings/owlets)
Life Span: ~13 years, though much longer in captivity (~29-38).
Location: forests of North, Central and South America.
Calories: ~100-600 kcal/ day.
Diet: frogs, fish, birds, rodents, and rabbits and other small mammals.
What they are called in a group: parliament.

Cactus Ferruginous Pygmy-Owl (Aucidium brasilianum cactorum)
Weight: 62-75 g.
Height: 36-41cm wingspan.
Length: 17 cm.
Speed: 48 km/h.
Number on the Planet: only 18.
Number in a litter: 4 to 5 eggs (fledglings/owlets).
Life Span: 6-7 years.
Location: Arizona, Texas and Mexico
Calories: ~87-261 k-calories /day.
Diet: insects, birds, frogs, earthworms.
What they are called in a group: parliament.

Desert *Tortoise* (Gopherus agassizii)
Weight: 3.6-6.8 kg.
Height: 10-15 cm.
Length: 23-38 cm.
Speed: 0.21-0.48 km/h.
Number on the Planet: threatened species (low numbers though exact count unknown).
Number in a litter: 4-8 eggs (hatchlings).
Life Span: 80-100 years.
Location: southwestern Arizona.
Calories: ~69-200 kcal/day.
Diet: herbs, grasses and wildflowers.
What they are called in a group:herd.

Wild Bactrian Camel (Camelus bactrianus)
Weight: 830-1140kg (females), 810-930kg (males).
Height: 2.13 m.
Length: 225-345 cm.
Speed: 30 km/h.
Number on the Planet: 250-950.
Number in a litter: 1-2 calves.
Life Span: 35-50 years.
Location: Mongolia, China and Kazakhstan.
Calories: ~25,000-74,000 kcal/day.
Diet: shrubs.
What they are called in a group:herd.

Eastern Screech Owl (Otus asio)
Weight: ~200 g.
Height: wingspan up to 61cm.
Length: 16-25 cm.
Speed: 42 km/h.
Number on the Planet: 770,000.
Number in a litter: 2-7 eggs (fledglings/owlets).
Life Span: up to 14 years in the wild, 20 years in captivity.
Location: eastern North America from eastern Montana and the Great Lakes to the Gulf of Mexico, South to Tamaulipas in Northeast Mexico as well as southern Ontario down to Florida.
Calories: ~46-140 kcalories/day.
Diet: rodents and deer mice, small mammals, wood and Norway rats, chipmunks, cotton rats, squirrels, shrews, bats, and moles, large flying insects such as beetles, katydids, grasshoppers, locusts, crickets, roaches, cicadas, moths, horseflies, and dragonflies. Birds, including many species of small songbirds, and larger birds such as Northern Bobwhite, Rock Dove, Ruffed Grouse, and other screech-Owls. Other prey include small fish, small snakes, lizards, and soft-shelled turtles, small frogs, toads, and salamanders, and invertebrates such

The Desert Animals

as crayfish, snails, spiders, earthworms, scorpions, centipedes.
What they are called in a group: parliament.

Elf Owl *(Micrathene whitneyi)*
Weight: 42 g.
Height: wingspan 34-41 cm.
Length: 13-14 cm.
Speed: ~40 km/h.
Number on the Planet: not threatened, an exact count is not available.
Number in a litter: 1-5 eggs (fledglings/owlets)
Life Span: ~5 years.
Location: Texas, California, Arizona and New Mexico (migrating to Mexico for winter).
Calories: ~15-45 kcal/day.
Diet: insects, mice and lizards.
What they are called in a group: parliament.

Emu *(Dromaius novaehollandiae)*
Weight: 30-45 kg.
Height: 1-2 m.
Speed: 50 km/h sprinting (non-flying bird).
Number on the Planet: 625,000-725,000.
Number in a litter: 11 average (up to 20) (young = chicks).
Life Span: 10-20 years in the wild, longer in captivity.
Location: Australia.
Calories: consume up to 1kg of food/day (~2,480-7,440 kcal/day).
Diet: variety of plant life and insects.
What they are called in a group: solitary (rare grouping: "flock").

Cream-Colored Courser
(Cursorius cursor)
Weight: 110 g.
Height: 54 cm. wingspan.
Length: 23 cm.
Speed: up to 25 km/h.

Number on the Planet: 56,000-210,000.
Number in a litter: 2 eggs (fledglings)
Life Span: up to ~40 years.
Location: Southern Asia, Northern Africa (winter migrate to India, Arabia, along southern edges of the Sahara Desert)—also Finland, Ireland and Great Britain.
Calories: ~30-90 kcal/day.
Diet: mostly insects, small invertebrates and vertebrates.
What they are called in a group:flock.

Lappet-Faced Vulture
(Torgos tracheliotus)
Weight: 14 kg.
Height: 3 m wingspan.
Length: 1.15 m.
Speed: 70 km/h.
Number on the Planet: 8,500.
Number in a litter: 1 egg (fledgling).
Life Span: up to 40 years.
Location: Africa and Arabian Peninsula.
Calories: up to 5 kg/day of food (~1,100-3,300).
Diet: mostly carrion but occasionally live prey.
What they are called in a group: usually solitary.

Dromedary "Arabian Camel"
(Camelus dromedaries)
Weight: 300-690 kg.
Height: 1.8-2.0 m.
Length: 3 m.
Speed: 16 km/h average speed.
Number on the Planet: 13 million domesticated, ~300,000 feral population in Australia.
Number in a litter: 1-2 calves.
Life Span: 25-50 years.
Location: Arabian Peninsula.
Calories: ~15,000-44,000 kcal/day.
Diet: plants, fish, meat, bones and skin.
What they are called in a group:flock.

The Desert Animals

Pronghorn
(Antilacapra americana)
Weight: 36-70 kg.
Height: 1.1m at the shoulder.
Length: 1-1.5 m.
Speed: 97 km/h.
Number on the Planet: 252 in USA, 220 in Mexico (less than 150 in the wild).
Number in a litter: 2 fawns.
Life Span: 9 to 10 years in the wild, up to 12 in captivity.
Location: American southwest running from Saskatchewan, Canada down to Mexico).
Calories: ~2,750-8,250 kcal/day.
Diet: shrubs, grasses, juniper, cacti, domestic crops and sagebrush.
What they are called in a group:herd.

Gerenuk *(Litocranius wallen)*
Weight: 29-51 kg.
Height: 0.9-1.1 m at the shoulder.
Length: 1.2-1.5 m.
Speed: up to 100 km/h.
Number on the Planet: not available.
Number in a litter: 1 calf.
Life Span: 6-12 years.
Location: East Africa.
Calories: ~2,226-6,680 kcal/day.
Diet: leaves and shoots of prickly bushes and trees mix of buds, flowers, fruit and climbing plants.
What they are called in a group:herd.

Mulgara *(Dasycercus cristicauda)*
Weight: 130 g.
Height: 12.5-22 cm.
Length: 12.5-22 cm
Speed: can attack at "lightening speed".
Number on the Planet: less than 2,500.
Number in a litter: 6-7 pups.
Life Span: 6 years.
Location: Australia.
Calories: ~21-64 kcal/day.
Diet: small rodents, reptiles, insects.

What they are called in a group: troop or horde.

Kowari (*Dasycercus byrnei*)
Weight: 70-137 g.
Length: 15-18 cm.
Speed: 41 km/h.
Number on the Planet: less than 10,000.
Number in a litter: 3-7 pups.
Life Span: up to 6.5 years.
Location: Australia.
Calories: ~50-150 kcal/day.
Diet: insects, arachnids, birds, rodents and lizards.
What they are called in a group: colonies.

Southern Marsupial Mole
(*Notoryctes typhlops*)
Weight: 35-70 g.
Length: 10 cm.
Speed: 0.3 m/s.
Number on the Planet: listed as endangered.
Number in a litter: 1-2 pups.
Life Span: longevity unknown.
Location: Central Australia.
Calories: ~11-34 kcal/day.
Diet: ants and their eggs, termites, larvae pupae.
What they are called in a group: labor.

Spectacled Hare Wallaby
(*Lagorchestes conspicillatus*)
Weight: 1.6-4.5 kg.
Length: 40-50 cm.
Speed: up to 40 km/h.
Number on the Planet: 10,000.
Number in a litter: 1-2 joeys.
Life Span: 6-10 years.
Location: northern Territory and western Australia.
Calories: ~226-668 kcal/day.
Diet: grass and herb foliage, seeds and fruit.
What they are called in a group: solitary.

The Desert Animals

Northern Grasshopper Mouse
(*Onychomys leucogaster*)
Weight: 22-51 g.
Height: 1.5-2.5 cm.
Length: 13-19 cm.
Speed: 0.4 m/s.
Number on the Planet: abundant
(exact count not available).
Number in a litter: 2-6 pups.
Life Span: 4-5 years.
Location: arid and semiarid regions
ranging from Mexico through central
and western United States and into
Canada. Dry, sandy grasslands of
western Kansas.
Calories: ~10-65 kcal/day.
Diet: grasshoppers, beetles,
caterpillars, scorpions and spiders.
They also eat forbs, grasses, sedges
and seeds.
What they are called in a group:
horde.

Gila Monster
(*Heloderma suspectum*)
Weight: 1.8 kg.
Length: up to 56 cm.
Speed: 0.5 m/s running.
Number on the Planet: not available
Number in a litter: 1-12 eggs
(hatchlings)
Life Span: 20-30 years.
Location: ranges from southwestern
Utah, to southern Nevada, and
adjacent San Bernadino County,
California, southwestern Arizona and
southwestern New Mexico.
Calories: 31-93 kcal/day.
Diet: small mammals (young rabbits,
mice and squirrels), birds, lizards,
and eggs (of birds, lizards, snakes,
turtles, and tortoises).
What they are called in a group:
pack or herd.

Fat-Tailed Gerbil
(*Pachyuromys duprasi*)
Weight: 40 g.
Height: 10 cm.

Length: 10 cm.
Speed: up to 13 km/h.
Number on the Planet: exact count
not kept due to widespread
availability as they are bred as pets
and sold all over the world.
Number in a litter: 3 to 6 pups.
Life Span: 5-7 years.
Location: originally found in the
Northern Sahara (North-western
Egypt, Libya, Tunisia, and Algeria).
Currently spreading to all parts of the
world where they are bred and sold
as pets (particularly in the
Netherlands).
Calories: ~13-41 kcal/day.
Diet: insects and a variety of plants.
Mealworms, crickets, moth, beetles
and most other insects.
What they are called in a group:
horde.

Large North African Gerbil
(*Gerbillus campestris*)
Weight: 28 g.
Length: 25 cm.
Speed: up to 12km/h
Number on the Planet: count not
kept, while among the world's small
mammals, this species is one of the
most abundant.
Number in a litter: 4-5 pups.
Life Span: up to 4 years.
Location: North Africa.
Calories: ~10-32 kcal/day.
Diet: seeds, roots, nuts, grasses and
insects.
What they are called in a group:
horde.

African Pygmy *Mouse*
(*Mus minutoides*)
Weight: 3-12 g.
Length: 30-80 mm; 20- 40 mm tail.
Speed: 3-6 km/h.
Number on the Planet: abundant.
Number in a litter: ~3.
Life Span: 2-4 years.

The Desert Animals

Location: originated in South Africa, sub-Saharan Africa.
Calories: ~4-12 kcal/day.
Diet: seeds, grains and mealworms, insects.
What they are called in a group: horde.

Desert Dormouse
(Selevinia betpakdalaensis)
Weight: 28 g.
Length: 8 to 10 cm.
Speed: ambling gait (can jump 20 cm in the air).
Number on the Planet: less than 10,000.
Number in a litter: 6-8 pups.
Life Span: up to 5 years.
Location: Kazhakstan.
Calories: 21g/day (up to three quarters own body weight)(~11-32 kcal/day).
Diet: fruit, berries, flowers, nuts and insects, spiders, small invertebrates.
What they are called in a group: horde.

Desert Hedgehog
(Hemiechinus aethiopicus)
Weight: 300-500 g.
Length: 14-28 cm.
Speed: up to 10 km/h.
Number on the Planet: actual count is unavailable. Species is not endangered, but rather quite common within its range.
Number in a litter: 3-5 piglets/pups.
Life Span: 3-10 years.
Location: deserts of northern Africa, south to Mali, Niger, Sudan, northern Ethiopia, northern Somalia, and the Arabian Peninsula.
Calories: ~125-375 kcal/day.
Diet: insects, small invertebrates, the eggs of ground-nesting birds, frogs, snakes and scorpions.
What they are called in a group: array.

Dingo (Canis lupus dingo)
Weight: 10-24 kg.
Height: 44-63 cm at the shoulder.
Length: 86-122 cm.
Speed: 19km/h trots and up to 40km/h in short spurts.
Number on the Planet: under threat of extinction. In South-Eastern highlands of Australia, one third of populations are cross-breeds, and unless there is a radical change the extinction of pure Dingoes seems inevitable due to human negligence.
Number in a litter: 1-10 (average 5).
Life Span: 3-7 years (up to 14 in captivity).
Location: southeast Asia and Australia.
Calories: ~1,300-4,000 kcal/day.
Diet: rats, kangaroos, birds, rabbits, lizards and some farm animals.
What they are called in a group: pack.

Fennec Fox (Fennecus zerda)
Weight: 0.8-1.5 kg.
Height: 20 cm.
Length: 24-40 cm. + tail of 25 cm.
Speed: 4km/h
Number on the Planet: unavailable.
Number in a litter: 2-5 kits/cubs/pups
Life Span: up to 12 years.
Location: northern Africa, the Sahara, the Sinai Peninsula and Arabia.
Calories: ~175-520 kcal/day.
Diet: large insects (beetles and locusts), small rodents, lizards and occasionally birds; some plant material (berries and leaves).
What they are called in a group: skulk or leash.

Indian Mongoose
(Herpestes javanicus)
Weight: 430-650 g.
Height: 30-40 cm.
Length: 45-106 cm.
Speed: quick to attack.

The Desert Animals

Number on the Planet: exact count
unknown, although it is sought after
to control the population as they are
destructive to other species.
Number in a litter: 2-5 pups.
Life Span: up to 4 years.
Location: Africa, South America,
West Indies, several Pacific islands,
southern Europe, and Asia
Calories: ~98-295 kcal/day.
Diet: rats, mice, snakes, lizards,
eggs, insects.
What they are called in a group: mob
or gang.

Striped Hyena *(Hyaena hyaena)*
Weight: 25-55 kg.
Height: 80 cm at the shoulder.
Length: 121-152 cm.
Speed: 64 km/h.
Number on the Planet: not available.
Number in a litter: 2 to 4 cubs.
Life Span: up to 24 years.
Location: northern and eastern
Africa, Arabia, Asia Minor and India.
Calories: ~2,000-6,000 kcal/day.
Diet: insects, small mammals, birds,
and eggs.
What they are called in a group: clan
or cackle.

Caracal *(Caracal caracal)*
Weight: 11-20 kg.
Height: 40-50 cm at the shoulder.
Length: 600 to 950 mm.
Speed: up to 70 km/h.
Number on the Planet: less than
10,000.
Number in a litter: 1 to 6 (average 3)
kittens.
Life Span: 19 years.
Location: northern Africa, the
Arabian peninsula, and southwestern
Asia.
Calories: ~1,100-3,280 kcal/day.
Diet: birds, rodents, and small
antelopes.
What they are called in a group:
clan/ pack.

Cheetah *(Acinonyx jubatus)*
Weight: 36-64 kg.
Height: 81 cm.
Length: 121-142 cm.
Speed: up to 96 km/h.
Number on the Planet: 10,000-
15,000.
Number in a litter: 2 to 4 cubs.
Life Span: 10 to 12 years.
Location: Botswana, Zimbabwe,
South Africa, Kenya and Tanzania,
Namibia + Eastern and
Southwestern Asia.
Calories: ~2,600-7,900 kcal/day.
Diet: gazelles, antelopes, and
impalas.
What they are called in a group:
coalition.

Palla's Cat (*Otocolobus manul***)**
Weight: 4.5 kg.
Height: 30 cm at the shoulder.
Length: 50-62 cm.
Speed:~32 km/h.
Number on the Planet: 3000-3650.
Number in a litter: 2 to 4 kittens.
Life Span: 8-10 years. (up to 12 in
captivity).
Location: Asia.
Calories: ~430-1,300 kcal/day.
Diet: small animals, rodents, and
birds.
What they are called in a group:
clowder.

Turkey Vulture (*Cathartes aura***)**
Weight: 2000 g.
Height: 183 cm wingspan.
Length: 63 cm.
Speed: 51-72 km/h.
Number on the Planet: overall North
American populations increased over
the last few decades.
Number in a litter: 1-3 eggs
(fledglings)
Life Span: depending on
environment, broad range 5-32 years
Location: deserts of the Southwest,
and most of North America.

The Desert Animals

Calories: ~260-790 kcal/day.
Diet: carrion and small mammals.
What they are called in a group:
kettle.

Great Gray Owl (*Strix nebulosa*)
Weight: 790-1454 g.
Height: wingspan up to 152 cm.
Length: 61-84 cm.
Speed: up to 100 km/h when
"swooping" down on prey.
Number on the Planet: not available,
but not threatened or endangered.
Number in a litter: 2-5 (average 3)
(fledglings/owlets).
Life Span: up to 40 years.
Location: Alaska across Canada,
down the Northern Rocky Mountains,
and northern Minnesota. Also found
in northern Europe and Asia.
Calories: ~170-510 kcal/day.
Diet: voles, rats, mice, shrews,
squirrels, rabbits, chipmunks, moles,
and weasels. Sometimes crows,
small hawks, American Robin,
ducks, grouse, frogs, toads, snakes,
and insects.
What they are called in a group:
parliament.

**Cactus Wren (*Campylorhynchus
brunneicapillus*)**
Weight: 33-45 g.
Height: 5 cm.
Length: 21 cm.
Speed: 40-50 km/h.
Number on the Planet: less than
1000.
Number in a litter: 3 to 6 eggs
(fledglings)
Life Span: ~7 years.
Location: southern California,
southern Nevada, southwest Utah,
central New Mexico, and central and
southern Texas to central Mexico.
Calories: ~14-41 kcal/day.
Diet: ants, beetles, grasshoppers,
wasps, fruit, seeds and frogs and
lizards.

What they are called in a group:
herd/flock.

**Greater Road Runner
(*Geococcyx californianus*)**
Weight: 226-680 g.
Height: 25-30 cm.
Length: 51-63 cm.
Speed: 27 km/h.
Number on the Planet: not available;
reduction in numbers due to
urbanization.
Number in a litter: 2-12 eggs
(fledglings)
Life Span: 7-8 years.
Location: Mojave, Sonoran,
Chihuahuan and southern Great
Basin deserts, and all the
southwestern states.
Calories: ~86-260 kcal/day.
Diet: insects, lizards, bugs
What they are called in a group:flock.

Desert Lark (*Ammomenes deserti*)
Weight: 80-115 g.
Length: 15–16.5 cm.
Speed: 20 km/h.
Number on the Planet: 60,600.
Number in a litter: 3-4 eggs
(fledglings).
Life Span: average 2-5, up to 8 years
Location: Africa, Middle East, and
Northwest India, Arabian Peninsula,
Afghanistan.
Calories: ~45-135 kcal/day.
Diet: seeds and insects.
What they are called in a group:
exaltation.

**Thick-Billed /Clotbey Lark
(*Rhamphocoris clotbey*)**
Weight: 45-55 g.
Length: 17 cm.
Speed: ~20 km/h.
Number on the Planet: not
threatened.
Number in a litter: 2-3 eggs.
Life Span: 2-5 years.

The Desert Animals

Location: North Africa, the Sahara from Mauritania and Morocco to Algeria, Tunisia, and Libya, Egypt, Syria, Jordan, and Arabia.
Calories: ~27-82 kcal/day.
Diet: seeds, green plant-life, insects.
What they are called in a group: exaltation.

Greater Hoopoe Lark/ Bifasciated Lark *(Alaemon alaudipes)*
Weight: 30-47 g.
Length: 19-22.5 cm.
Speed: ~20 km/h.
Number on the Planet: not available.
Number in a litter: 2-4 eggs (fledglings).
Life Span: ~7 years.
Location: Cape Verde Archipelago, Sahara to Middle East, and Western India.
Calories: ~22-67 kcal/day.
Diet: grubs, locust pupae, anthropods, snails and seeds.
What they are called in a group: exaltation.

Chuckwalla *(Sauromalus)*
Weight: 0.9 kg.
Length: 28-46 cm.
Speed: up to 1 m/s.
Number on the Planet: estimate not available.
Number in a litter: 5-16 eggs (hatchlings).
Life Span: up to 25 years.
Location: Mojave and Sonoran deserts (southern California, Nevada, Utah, Arizona, islands of Baja and Mexico).
Calories: ~18-55 kcal/day.
Diet: seeds, leaves, buds, fruit and flowers.
What they are called in a group: herd

Desert Horned Lizard
(Phrynosoma platyrhinos)
Weight: 4.5 g.
Length: 140 mm.

Speed: currently unknown.
Number on the Planet: abundant.
Number in a litter: 2-16 eggs
Life Span: ~5 years.
Location: western USA and Mexico.
Calories: over 200 ants /day (~1 kcal/day).
Diet: ants, spiders, beetles and other slow-moving terrestrial insects, and some plant-life.
What they are called in a group:pack

Yellow-footed Rock Wallaby
(Petrogale xanthopus)
Weight: 3-9 kg.
Height: 0.5 m.
Length: 51-76 cm.
Speed: up to 28 km/h.
Number on the Planet: vulnerable
Number in a litter: 1 joey
Life Span: up to 14 years
Location: South Australia, Western New Wales, Queensland.
Calories: ~258-774 kcal/day
Diet: grass, plants and bark
What they are called in a group: herd

Coyote *(Canis latrans)*
Weight: 9-22kg
Height: 0.6m
Length: 1-1.5m
Speed: up to 64km/h
Number on the Planet: hundreds of thousands
Number in a litter: 4-6 pups
Life Span: 6-10 years
Location: throughout North America from eastern Alaska to New England and south through Mexico to Panama
Calories: ~1,000-3,200 kcal/day
Diet: rabbits, mice, shrews, voles, foxes, fruits, grasses, and vegetables
What they are called in a group: pack or rout.

The Freshwater Animals

Vaquita *(Phocoena sinus)*
Weight: up to 55 kg.
Length: females: up to 1.5 m; males: up to 1.4 m.
Speed: ~20 km/h (not very active, swim slowly).
Number on the Planet: less than 600.
Number in a litter: 1 (calf).
Life Span: up to 21 years.
Location: Sea of Cortez (northern end of Gulf of California).
Calories: ~1,400-8,400 kcal/day.
Diet: small fish and squid.
What they are called in a group: solitary/pod.

Irrawaddy Dolphin
(Orcaella brevirostris)
Weight: 90-150 kg.
Length: 2.15-2.75 m.
Speed: slow-moving (~20-25km/h top speed).
Number on the Planet: only a few hundred.
Number in a litter: 1 (pup/calf).
Life Span: approximately 30 years.
Location: coastal waters and large rivers of southeast Asia, northern Australia, and Papua New Guinea.
Calories: ~2,500-15,000 kcal/day.
Diet: fish, squid and crustaceans.
What they are called in a group: pod.

Yangtze River Finless Porpoise
(Neophocaena phocaenoides)
Weight: 30-45 kg.
Length: up to 1.9 m.
Speed: most porpoises, up to ~50 km/h.
Number on the Planet: fewer than 100.
Number in a litter: 1 (calf).
Life Span: 10-20 years.
Location: Yangtze River, China
Calories: ~1,100-6,400 kcal/day
.Diet: fish, shrimp, prawns and octopus.
What they are called in a group: herd/pod.

Ganges River Dolphin
(Platanista gangetica gangetica)
Weight: 70-90 kg.
Length: 1.5-2.5 m.
Speed: ~30-40 km/h.
Number on the Planet: 1,200-2,500.
Number in a litter: 1 (calf/pup).
Life Span: 26 + years.
Location: India, Bangladesh and Nepal.
Calories: ~1,900-11,000 kcal/day
Diet: fish and crustaceans, invertebrates, sometimes turtles and birds.
What they are called in a group: school.

Ash Meadows Amargosa Pupfish
(Cyprinodon nevadensis mionectes)
Weight: av. 1.7 g.
Length: 3-6 cm.
Speed: up to 0.6 m/s
Number on the Planet: ~400 endangered and limited range.
Number in a litter: one egg at a time (up to 25 times/day) (fry/fingerlings).
Life Span: 1-3 years.
Location: Ash Meadows area of Amargosa Valley, Nye County, Nevada.
Calories: 0.17-0.5 kcal/day
Diet: algae.
What they are called in a group: school.

Smoky Madtom *(Noturus baileyi)*
Weight: 17 g.
Length: 59-73 mm.
Speed: up to 10 km/h.
Number on the Planet: 500-1,000.
Number in a litter: 35-42 eggs (fry/fingerlings).
Life Span: up to 2-3 years.
Location: Tennessee.
Calories: 0.94-2.8 kcal/day.
Diet: aquatic insects.
What they are called in a group: school.

Coho Salmon (Silver Salmon)
(Oncorhynchus kisutch)
Weight: 3.6-5.5 kg.
Length: 61-76 cm.
Speed: 1.3-2.7 km/h.

Number on the Planet: abundant
(hundreds of thousands).
Number in a litter: 2,400-4,500 eggs
(fry/fingerlings).
Life Span: 3-5 years.
Location: coastal waters of Alaska from
the Southeast to Point Hope on the
Chukchi Sea and in the Yukon River to
the Alaska-Yukon border.
Calories: 62-186 kcal/day.
Diet: aquatic insects, zooplankton and
small fish.
What they are called in a group: school.

Red-legged Frog
(Rana aurora draytonii)
Weight: 1.5-7 g.
Length: 3.8-12.7 cm.
Speed: up to 60 cm/s swimming.
Number on the Planet: endangered
species (less than 10,000).
Number in a litter: 300-5,000 eggs
(average 2,000) (tadpoles/polliwogs).
Life Span: 12-13 years.
Location: Sonoma and Butte Counties in
the north to Riverside County in the
south, primarily in the western counties
of California, USA.
Calories: 0.33-0.99 kcal/day.
Diet: beetles, caterpillars, isopods and
other invertebrates (young eat algae).
What they are called in a group:
army/knot.

Delta Smelt
(Hypomesus transpacificus)
Weight: up to 16 g.
Length: 55-70 mm, and up to 130mm.
Speed: 30 cm/s.
Number on the Planet: number unknown
since population fluctuates (species
highly sensitive to environmental
changes); declined 80% in past 3 years.
Number in a litter: 1000-2600 eggs
(fry/fingerlings).
Life Span: 9 months- 2 years.
Location: Sacramento- San Joaquin
Sanctuary.
Calories: 0.9-2.7 kcal/day.

Diet: zooplankton.
What they are called in a group: school.

Gila Trout *(Oncorhynchus gilae gilae)*
Weight: 2 kg.
Length: 180-220 mm.
Speed: 1.33 m/s.
Number on the Planet: 50,000-60,000
Number in a litter: 96-196 eggs,
maximum 696 eggs (fry/fingerlings).
Life Span: ~5-9 years.
Location: USA (Arizona and New
Mexico).
Calories: at least 40 g of food/day.
Diet: aquatic invertebrates, small fish.
What they are called in a group: hoover.

Cutthroat Trout
(Oncorhynchus clarki)
Weight: 0.2-7.7 kg.
Length: 0.3-0.4 m.
Speed: ~1-1.5 m/s.
Number on the Planet: less than
100,000 mature individuals.
Number in a litter: 1100-1700 eggs
(fry/fingerlings).
Life Span: 9-10 years.
Location: fresh, brackish and salt waters
of North America, mainly west of the
Rocky Mountains.
Calories: up to 154 g of food/day (56-
168 kcal/day).
Diet: smaller fish
What they are called in a group: hoover.

Rainbow Trout
(Oncorhynchus mykiss)
Weight: up to 25.4 kg.
Length: 30-45 cm.
Speed: 7.4 km/h.
Number on the Planet: abundant in
numbers (not quantified)—assumed
hundreds of thousands.
Number in a litter: 800-1000 eggs
(fry/fingerlings).
Life Span: 6-8 average, up to 11 years.
Location: mainly Pacific Ocean in Asia
and North America but has been
introduced into New Zealand, Australia,

The Freshwater Animals

South America, Africa, Japan, southern Asia, Europe and Hawaii.
Calories: up to 508 g of food/day (226-678 kcal/day).
Diet: plankton, insects, crustaceans and other fish.
What they are called in a group: hoover.

The Amazon Manatee
(Trichechus inunguis)
Weight: 300-500 kg.
Length: 3 m.
Speed: 3-8 and up to 32 km/h.
Number on the Planet: ~10,000.
Number in a litter: 1 (calf).
Life Span: up to 12.5 years.
Location: Amazon River Base of northern South America.
Calories: ~6,260-37,000 kcal/day.
Diet: aquatic vegetation (aquatic grasses and floating plants like water lilies).
What they are called in a group: solitary/herd.

Chinook Salmon
(Oncorhynchus tshawytscha)
Weight: 5-25 kg, up to 50 kg.
Length: 840 to 910 mm, up to 1.47 m.
Speed: 22 km/h.
Number on the Planet: ~ 10,000, considered threatened.
Number in a litter: 1,000-14,000 eggs (fry/fingerlings).
Life Span: 4-5 years.
Location: range from San Francisco Bay in California to north of the Bering Strait in Alaska, and arctic waters of Canada and Russia (the Chukchi Sea), including the entire Pacific coast in between. Occur in Asia as far south as the islands of Japan. Found in Russia in Kamchatka and the Kuril Islands. Species established itself in the waters of the Patagonia in South America. Fresh water populations also introduced into the Great Lakes of North America.
Calories: up to 750 g of food/day (240-720 kcal/day).

Diet: planktonic diatoms, copepods, kelps, seaweeds, jellyfish, sea stars, insects, amphipods, and other crustaceans, and primarily other fish.
What they are called in a group: school.

Common Shiner *(Luxilus cornutus)*
Weight: av. 0.68 kg.
Length: 13-17 cm.
Speed: 0.5-0.9 m/s.
Number on the Planet: very common and abundant.
Number in a litter: 3,000-4,000 eggs (fry/fingerlings).
Life Span: 4-6, up to 9 years.
Location: Minnesota, USA.
Calories: 14-42 kcal/day.
Diet: insects (larvae) and plant-life (algae) and small fish.
What they are called in a group: school.

Fallfish *(Semotilus corporalis)*
Weight: 2.7 g.
Length: 150-300 mm.
Speed: 30 cm/s.
Number on the Planet: less than 100,000.
Number in a litter: 2,000-12,000 eggs (fry/fingerlings).
Life Span: 9-10 growing seasons.
Location: northeast USA.
Calories: 0.2-0.7 kcal/day.
Diet: phytoplankton, zooplankton, insect, crayfish, fish, algae, and detritus.
What they are called in a group: school.

White Sucker
(Catostomus commersonii)
Weight: ½-1 kg.
Length: 30-50 cm.
Speed: 10 km/h.
Number on the Planet: extremely common in eastern North America (abundant in numbers).
Number in a litter: 20,000-50,000 eggs (fry/fingerlings).
Life Span: 17 years.
Location: Canada, Ohio and Lake Erie.
Calories: 16-48 kcal/day.

Diet: aquatic plants, algae, and small invertebrate animals (especially worms and crustaceans) as well as eggs of other fish species.
What they are called in a group: school.

Shorthead Redhorse
(Moxostoma macrolepidotum)
Weight: 3.99 kg.
Length: 75 cm.
Speed: 0.5 m/s.
Number on the Planet: common and abundant in numbers (hundreds of thousands to millions).
Number in a litter: 13,000-45,000 eggs (fry/fingerlings).
Life Span: 12 + years.
Location: North America: Great Lakes-St. Lawrence River, Hudson Bay and Mississippi River basins from Quebec to Alberta in Canada and south to northern Alabama and Oklahoma in the USA; Atlantic Slope drainages from Hudson River in New York to Santee River in South Carolina, USA.
Calories: 56-169 kcal/day.
Diet: copepods, water-fleas, insect larvae, side-swimmers, worms and very little plant-life.
What they are called in a group: school.

Bigmouth Buffalo
(Ictiobus cyprinellus)
Weight: 22.7 kg and up to 18.5 kg.
Length: 350-600 mm.
Speed: up to 35km/h.
Number on the Planet: declining but quite common (hundreds of thousands).
Number in a litter: 100,000-750,000 eggs (fry/fingerlings).
Life Span: 10-15 years.
Location: Apache and Roosevelt Lakes in North America.
Calories: 178-535 kcal/day.
Diet: plankton, copepods, cladocerans, bottom plants, aquatic insects, mollusks, small fish and fish eggs.
What they are called in a group: school.

Pacu (Colossoma macroponum)
Weight: up to 30 kg.
Length: up to 76 cm.
Speed: 10 km/h.
Number on the Planet: population status "exotic"—(established but unknown numbers in reproduction).
Number in a litter: up to several hundred thousand eggs (fry/fingerlings).
Life Span: 10-20 years +
Location: native South America, illegally introduced into United States.
Calories: 183-384 kcal/day.
Diet: plant-life and small insects.
What they are called in a group: school.

Neon Tetra (Paracheirodon innesi)
Weight: 0.2-0.4 g.
Length: 4 cm.
Speed: 30 cm/s.
Number on the Planet: abundant.
Number in a litter: ~130 eggs (fry/fingerlings).
Life Span: 5-10 years.
Location: Northern South America (Peru) and now widespread in the pet market.
Calories: 0.05-0.14 kcal/day.
Diet: shrimp, worms and plant-life.
What they are called in a group: school/shoal.

Giant Tigerfish (Hydrocynus goliath)
Weight: 50 kg.
Length: 133 cm.
Speed: up to 12 km/h.
Number on the Planet: not considered endangered, vulnerable or limited.
Number in a litter: hundreds to thousands of eggs per spawning (fry/fingerlings).
Life Span: 8 years.
Location: rivers and streams of central and northern Africa.
Calories: 376-1128 kcal/day.
Diet: smaller fish.
What they are called in a group: school.

The Freshwater Animals

Red-Bellied Piranha
(Pygocentrus nattereri)
Weight: 3.85 kg.
Length: 30 cm.
Speed: "lightening speed" swimmers
Number on the Planet: unknown; reported by Lachner et al in 1970, to be the most common and widely distributed pirhana in tropical fish stores and public aquaria of the United States.
Number in a litter: 5,000 eggs (fry).
Life Span: 8-10 years.
Location: Northern South America (Amazon and its tributaries).
Calories: 4.585-176.5 kcal/day.
Diet: fish (live and dead), mollusks, insects, crustaceans, spermatophytes, and algae.
What they are called in a group: school.

Chinese Mitten Crab
(Eriocheir sinensis)
Weight: ~169 g.
Length: 53-88 mm.
Speed: can migrate downstream 11.5 km/day.
Number on the Planet: population expanding at alarming rate (detrimental to environment).
Number in a litter: 250,000-1 million eggs (larvae).
Life Span: 2-5 years.
Location: native distribution is coastal rivers and estuaries of the Yellow Sea in Korea and China. Recently established on the west coast of the U.S. in the San Francisco Bay/Delta watershed in California.
Calories: 5-16 kcal/day.
Diet: worms, clams, ghost shrimp, shad and plant-life.
What they are called in a group: solitary.

Curimbata *(Prochilodus lineatus)*
Weight: up to 6-8 kg.
Length: 50-60 cm and up to 1 m.
Speed: up to 0.6m/s.
Number on the Planet: dwindling population.

Number in a litter: hundreds of thousands of eggs (fry/fingerlings).
Life Span: up to 5 years.
Location: South America.
Calories: 43-129 kcal/day.
Diet: seaweed and other plant-life, small organisms found in organic mud.
What they are called in a group: shoal/school.

Green Sunfish *(Lepomis cyanellus)*
Weight: 85-680 g.
Length: 7.6-17.7 cm.
Speed: 20-25 cm/s.
Number on the Planet: not listed endangered or threatened either nationally or internationally. They are common and abundant throughout their range.
Number in a litter: 2,000-26,000 eggs (fry/fingerlings).
Life Span: 4-6 years.
Location: native rivers in Ohio, USA.
Calories: 0.97-2.9 kcal/day.
Diet: insects, mollusks, small fishes.
What they are called in a group: solitary/schools during breeding.

Electric Eel
(Electrophorus electricus)
Weight: 20 kg.
Length: up to 2.5 m (though ~1m is most common).
Speed: 37cm/s
Number on the Planet: they are common throughout their range of distribution but at low densities.
Number in a litter: average 1,200, documented as many as 17,000 eggs (elver).
Life Span: 10-22 years.
Location: Amazon River Basin, South America.
Calories: 94-283 kcal/day.
Diet: smaller fish and bottom-dwelling invertebrates.
What they are called in a group: school/swarm.

The Freshwater Animals

Butterfish (*Poronotus triacanthus*)
Weight: 57-793 g.
Length: 30 cm.
Speed: 15-20 cm/s.
Number on the Planet: between 560,000 and million individual fish (more exact estimates not available) common, abundant, or highly abundant on the Atlantic coast.
Number in a litter: thousands (fry/fingerling).
Life Span: up to 12 years.
Location: Atlantic coast of North America (mainly New England).
Calories: 1.77-5 kcal/day.
Diet: small fish, squid and other crustaceans.
What they are called in a group: school/shoal.

African Glass Catfish (*Pareutropius buffei*)
Weight: 10 g.
Length: 8 cm.
Speed: 10 cm/s.
Number on the Planet: less than 100,000.
Number in a litter: up to 100 eggs (fry/fingerlings).
Life Span: 8 years.
Location: Central Africa, Southern Nigeria, Niger River.
Calories: 0.6-1.8 kcal/day.
Diet: omnivorous (eats plant-life and small fish, etc.).
What they are called in a group: school.

Blue Catfish (*Ictalurus furcatus*)
Weight: 23-52 kg.
Length: 1.5 m.
Speed: 10 cm/s.
Number on the Planet: common and abundant
Number in a litter: up to tens of thousands of eggs (fry).
Life Span: 20-25 years.
Location: native to major rivers of the Ohio, Missouri, and Mississippi river basins. The range also extends south through Texas, Mexico, and into northern Guatemala.
Calories: 303-909 kcal/day.
Diet: any species of fish they can catch, along with crayfish, freshwater mussels, frogs, and other readily available aquatic food sources.
What they are called in a group: school.

Tadpole Madtom (*Noturus gyrinus*)
Weight: 17 g.
Length: 50-56 mm, up to 115 mm.
Speed: 0.45 m/s.
Number on the Planet: widespread and abundant.
Number in a litter: 80-180 eggs (fry/fingerlings).
Life Span: 2-3 years.
Location: North America in the Atlantic and Gulf slope drainages from New Hampshire to east Texas, the St. Lawrence River and Great Lakes, the Mississippi basin from southern Quebec to southern Saskatchewan, and south to the Gulf of Mexico.
Calories: 0.94-2.8 kcal/day.
Diet: eats small fish, midge, mayfly and caddisfly larvae, isopods and amphipods.
What they are called in a group: school.

Brown Bullhead Catfish (*Ameiurus nebulosus*)
Weight: average 0.45 kg, up to 2.7-3.6 kg.
Length: 36 cm.
Speed: 10 cm/s.
Number on the Planet: abundant and common in its regions.
Number in a litter: 2,000-10,000 eggs (fry).
Life Span: 6-8 years.
Location: southern Canada, eastern USA to Florida also western USA, New Zealand and Europe.
Calories: 33-99 kcal/day.
Diet: algae, plants, mollusks, insects, fish eggs and fish.
What they are called in a group: school.

The Freshwater Animals

Electric Catfish
(Malapterurus electricus)
Weight: 20-24 kg
Length: up to 90 cm.
Speed: 10 cm/s.
Number on the Planet: plentiful, not endangered or threatened.
Number in a litter: nothing much is known of the reproductive biology of *M. electricus*, breeding pairs nest in holes 3 meters in length, excavated in clay banks in water 1 to 3 meters (young are called "fry").
Life Span: 15 years.
Location: Nile River and Lake Chad, Africa.
Calories: 200-600 kcal/day.
Diet: primarily other fish.
What they are called in a group: school/solitary.

Doria's Bumblebee Goby/Golden-Banded Goby
(Brachygobius doriae)
Weight: up to 25 g.
Length: 5 cm.
Speed: 9 cm/s.
Number on the Planet: common and abundant.
Number in a litter: 150-200 eggs (fry/fingerlings).
Life Span: 5 years.
Location: Asia; fresh and brackish water in Borneo, Java, India, Malaysia, Sumatra, and Thailand.
Calories: 1.25-3.75 kcal/day.
Diet: insect larvae, worms, crustaceans
What they are called in a group: school.

Pungas Catfish *(Pangasius sutchi)*
Weight: up to 20-30 kg.
Length: 60+cm up to 120 cm.
Speed: 10 cm/s.
Number on the Planet: relatively abundant in numbers- not quantified, though considered to be decreasing in numbers.
Number in a litter: over 100,000 (fry).
Life Span: 10 years.

Location: Thailand.
Calories: 222-667 kcal/day.
Diet: smaller fish (e.g. carp).
What they are called in a group: school/solitary.

Giant Mekong Catfish
(Pangasianodon gigas)
Weight: up to 293 kg.
Length: up to 2.74 m.
Speed: 8 cm/s.
Number on the Planet: less than 10,000.
Number in a litter: little known about reproduction, but they are called "fry" as young.
Life Span: 60 + years.
Location: China and Southeast Asia.
Calories: 1,400-4,250 kcal/day.
Diet: worms and plant-life.
What they are called in a group: school/solitary.

Tiger Catfish
(Pseudoplatystoma fasciatum)
Weight: 17 kg.
Length: up to 130 cm.
Speed: 10 cm/s.
Number on the Planet: abundant; not threatened.
Number in a litter: 150,000-8 million+ eggs (fry).
Life Span: 5-10 years.
Location: Bolivia, Brazil, Colombia, Ecuador, French Guiana, Peru, Venezuela.
Calories: 167-502 kcal/day.
Diet: crustaceans and fish.
What they are called in a group: school.

Upside-Down Catfish
(Synodontis nigriventris)
Weight: 2.0-2.2 g.
Length: up to 10 cm.
Speed: 7 cm/s.
Number on the Planet: relatively widespread and abundant.
Number in a litter: up to 450 eggs (fry).
Life Span: over 5 years.
Location: Zaire and Niger River basin.

The Freshwater Animals

Calories: 0.2-0.6 kcal/day.
Diet: algae, insect larvae, fry, amphibian eggs, tiny crustaceans, minnows, invertebrates, and insects.
What they are called in a group: school.

Apple Snail *(Pomacea maculata)*
Weight: up to 120 g.
Height: 155 mm.
Length: 135 mm.
Speed: 0.2 cm/s.
Number on the Planet: abundant, not threatened- exact number unknown.
Number in a litter: 200-500 (larva).
Life Span: 1-5 years.
Location: South America (specifically Brazil and Peru).
Calories: 4-12 kcal/day.
Diet: fruit, seeds, old leaves and invertebrates.
What they are called in a group: solitary.

Australian Freshwater Catfish (*Tandanus tandanus*)
Weight: up to 7 kg.
Length: 61cm.
Speed: 10 cm/s.
Number on the Planet: considered a vulnerable, species, less than 100,000.
Number in a litter: 20,000 eggs (fry).
Life Span: up to 22 years.
Location: southern Australia
Calories: 86-258 kcal/day.
Diet: insect larvae, prawns, crayfish, mollusks and small fish.
What they are called in a group: school.

Dwarf Livebearer/Least Killifish (*Heterandria Formosa*)
Weight: 1-2.5 g.
Length: 1.5-3 cm.
Speed: 15 cm/s.
Number on the Planet: population size not quantified.
Number in a litter: 2-3 young in random "batches" (up to 20 in 2-3 week period) (fry).
Life Span: 3-5 years.

Location: Louisiana, Florida and North Carolina.
Calories: 0.13-0.4 kcal/day.
Diet: water fleas, brine shrimp, white worms, micro worms.
What they are called in a group: school.

Northern Pike *(Esox lucius)*
Weight: ~25 kg.
Length: ~150 cm.
Speed: ~6 km/h.
Number on the Planet: common and abundant in their native regions- so much so that they pose a threat to other endangered species. An exact count is unavailable because of their great numbers.
Number in a litter: 2,000-600,000 eggs (fry/fingerlings).
Life Span: 10-30 years.
Location: freshwaters of the northern hemisphere (Britain, northern Europe, Russia, Alaska, Canada and Northern USA).
Calories: 223-669 kcal/day.
Diet: frogs, smaller fish, crayfish, small mammals and birds.
What they are called in a group: school.

Elephant-nose Fish (*Gnathonemus petersii*)
Weight: up to 500 g.
Length: 23 cm.
Speed: 18 cm/s
Number on the Planet:abundant; a well-known species in the international aquarium trade.
Number in a litter: nothing is currently known about reproduction (litter size included) about Elephant-nose Fish (young are called "fry").
Life Span: 6-10 years.
Location: West and Central Africa; Nigeria, Cameroon and Zaire.
Calories: 11-33 kcal/day.
Diet: worms and insect larvae.
What they are called in a group: school.

The Freshwater Animals

Lake Trout *(Salvelinus namaycush)*
Weight: up to 46 kg (average 4.54 kg).
Length: 126 cm (average 43-68 cm).
Speed: 9.9-117.8 cm/s.
Number on the Planet: at risk because of over-fishing and predation.
Number in a litter: 3,600-8,200+ eggs (fry/fingerlings).
Life Span: ~20 years.
Location: Lakes in northern North America (Canada and northern USA).
Calories: 112-338 kcal/day.
Diet: fish, insects, crustaceans and plankton.
What they are called in a group: hoover.

Arctic Charr *(Salvelinus alpinus)*
Weight: 900 g-2.3 kg and up to 9 kg.
Length: 25-97 cm.
Speed: up to 40 km/h in short bursts.
Number on the Planet: over 100,000.
Number in a litter: 100-500 eggs (fry).
Life Span: up to 10 years.
Location: Arctic and North Atlantic freshwater; Britain, Europe, Russia and North America.
Calories: 86-258 kcal/day.
Diet: Capelin, Arctic Cod, mollusks and crustaceans.
What they are called in a group: school.

Northern Cavefish
(Amblyopsis spelea)
Weight: 0.1-0.3 kg.
Length: 11 cm.
Speed: up to 1 m/s.
Number on the Planet:~1,000-10,000; considered vulnerable.
Number in a litter: a few hundred (fry).
Life Span: 5-10 years.
Location: Kentucky and Indiana.
Calories: 5.9-17.9 kcal/day
Diet: Benthic crustaceans (amphipods), isopods, decapods non-annelids worms and flatworms.
What they are called in a group: school.

Burbot *(Lota lota)*
Weight: 1.36 kg, up to 34 kg.
Length: 51-99 cm, up to 152 cm.
Speed: 25 cm/s.
Number on the Planet: exact count unavailable. Considerable numbers in many inland lakes, but has declined over past levels in the Great Lakes, where it had been considered a nuisance species.
Number in a litter: 1 million+ eggs.
Life Span: 20 + years.
Location: Canada, North USA, North Europe and Asia.
Calories: 172-517 kcal/day.
Diet: fish, crustaceans, and insects.
What they are called in a group: school.

American Mink *(Mustela vison)*
Weight: 0.7-1.6 kg.
Length: 46-70 cm.
Speed: up to 2.4 km/h surface swimming.
Number on the Planet: plentiful, listed as "least concern" by IUCN.
Number in a litter: 1-8 (pups).
Life Span: ~10 years.
Location: throughout the United States, appearing in parts of every state except Arizona. They are also present in most of Canada, including an introduced population on Newfoundland. Only along the Arctic coast and some offshore islands are they absent.
Calories: 155-566 kcal/day.
Diet: crayfish and small frogs, along with small mammals such as shrews, rabbits, mice, and muskrats. Fish, ducks and other water fowl provide additional food choices. In the winter, they primarily prey on mammals.
What they are called in a group: solitary.

The Tundra Animals

Northern Chinese Leopard
(Panthera pardus japonensis)
Weight: 28-90 kg.
Height: 46-76 cm at the shoulder.
Length: 91-191 cm.
Speed: 58 km/h.
Number on the Planet: 2500, 100 in captivity.
Number in a litter: 1-6, average 2-3 (cubs).
Life Span: 12-20 years.
Location: Northern China.
Calories: 3,000-9,000 kcal/day.
Diet: carnivorous; monkeys, baboons, rodents, reptiles, amphibians, large birds, fish, antelope, and porcupines.
What they are called in a group: leap/prowl.

Amur Leopard
(Panthera pardus orientalis)
Weight: 25-75 kg.
Height: 46-77 cm at the shoulder.
Length: 0.9-1.8 m.
Speed: over 36 miles per hour.
Number on the Planet: ~250 (~50 in wild, ~200 captive).
Number in a litter: 1-4, average 2 (cubs).
Life Span: 10-15 in the wild, up to 20 years in captivity.
Location: Siberia, Manchuria, Amur-Usssi region of China and North Korea.
Calories: 2,600-7,900 kcal/day.
Diet: antelope, ibex, bush hyrax, alpine hare, deer and wild sheep.
What they are called in a group: solitary.

Snow Leopard *(Uncia uncia)*
Weight: 50-70 kg.
Height: 60 cm at the shoulder.
Length: 1.3 m.
Speed: 65 km/h.
Number on the Planet: 3,000-7,400.

Number in a litter: 2-3 (cubs).
Life Span: 15-18 years.
Location: mountainous regions of central Asia, ranging in the North from Russia and Mongolia down through China and Tibet into the Himalayan regions of Afghanistan, Pakistan and India.
Calories: 3,000-9,000 kcal/day.
Diet: wild sheep, wild boars, gazelles, hares, markhor, bobak, tahr, marmots, mice and deer.
What they are called in a group: solitary/pair.

Tundra Wolf *(Canis lupus albus)*
Weight: 45-57 kg.
Height: 60-90 cm at the shoulder.
Length: 150-200 cm.
Speed: 8-10 km/h average; 15-20 km/h hunting pace; up to 70 km/h.
Number on the Planet: less than 50,000, though declining.
Number in a litter: 2-11 (pups/whelps).
Life Span: 8-16 years in the wild, more than 20 years in captivity.
Location: northern Europe and Asia, primarily in the northern arctic and boreal regions of Russia.
Calories: 1,000-3,000 kcal/day.
Diet: deer, elk, moose, caribou, musk-ox, bison, mountain sheep, rabbits, hares, beaver, and small rodents.
What they are called in a group: pack.

Brown Bear *(Ursus arctos)*
Weight: 80-600 kg.
Height: 90-150 cm at the shoulder.
Length: 1-2.8 m.
Speed: 30 mph.
Number on the Planet: ~131,000. (1,000 USA; 30,000 Canada and Alaska; 100,000 Eurasia).
Number in a litter: 1-4, average 2-3 (cubs).
Life Span: 20-30 years and up to 50 years.

The Tundra Animals

Location: North America, eastern and western Europe, northern Asia and Japan.
Calories: 22,200-66,900 kcal/day.
Diet: a variety of plant foods, including grasses, sedges, roots, moss, and bulbs, fruits, nuts, berries, bulbs, and tubers, insects, fungi, and roots, mice, ground squirrels, marmots, larvae, moose, elk, mountain sheep, and mountain goats, occasionally black bears, carrion, young calves of caribou and moose, vulnerable populations of breeding salmon.
What they are called in a group: sleuth/sloth.

Peale's Peregrine Falcon
(Falco peregrinus pealei)
Weight: 453-952 g.
Height: 94-116 cm wingspan.
Length: 37-46 cm.
Speed: 55-97 km/h, ~300 km/h diving top-speed.
Number on the Planet: ~60 pairs, considered vulnerable.
Number in a litter: 4 eggs (chicks).
Life Span: up to 18-20 years.
Location: Alaska coastline from the Southeast to the Aleutians.
Calories: 120-360 kcal/day.
Diet: small seabirds and mammals.
What they are called in a group: cast.

Snowy Owl *(Bubo scandiacus)*
Weight: 1.13-2.0 kg.
Height: 137-164 cm wingspan.
Length: 51-68.5 cm.
Speed: 56 km/h.
Number on the Planet: 290,000.
Number in a litter: 5-8, up to 14 eggs (fledglings/owlets).
Life Span: 10-35 years.
Location: North America; western Aleutian Islands, and from northern Alaska, northern Yukon, and Prince Patrick and northern Ellesmere islands south to coastal western Alaska, northern Mackenzie, southern

Keewatin, extreme northeastern Manitoba, Southampton and Belcher islands, northern Quebec and northern Labrador.
Calories: 218-655 kcal/day.
Diet: small birds, small mammals (mice, hares, muskrats, marmots, squirrels, rabbits, prairie dogs, rats, moles), and eggs of other birds.
What they are called in a group: parliament.

Mountain Goat
(Oreamnos americanus)
Weight: 46-136 kg.
Height: 35 to 45 inches.
Length: 1.25-1.79m, 84-203 mm tail.
Speed: up to 64 km/h.
Number on the Planet: 100,000.
Number in a litter: 1-3 (kids/billies).
Life Span: 12-15 years.
Location: southeast Alaska to Washington, western Montana, and central Idaho; introduced into sections of South Dakota, Colorado, and Washington.
Calories: 4,100-12,400 kcal/day.
Diet: sedges, grasses, herbs, mosses.
What they are called in a group: herd.

Canada Lynx *(Lynx canadensis)*
Weight: 4.50-17.30 kg.
Height: 50-75 cm at the shoulder.
Length: 65-100 cm.
Speed: up to ~50 km/h.
Number on the Planet: ~ 50,000.
Number in a litter: 1-5, average 2-3 (cubs/kittens).
Life Span: 14-27 years.
Location: throughout Canada, in western Montana, and in nearby parts of Idaho and Washington; small populations in New England and Utah; Oregon, Wyoming and Colorado.
Calories: 840-2,500 kcal/day.
Diet: hares, grouse, rabbits, small rodents, foxes and carrion.
What they are called in a group: solitary.

The Tundra Animals

Eurasian Lynx *(Lynx lynx)*
Weight: 18-20 kg.
Height: 65-75 cm at the shoulder.
Length: 80-130 cm.
Speed: up to ~48 km/h.
Number on the Planet: less than 50,000.
Number in a litter: 1-5, 2-3 average (cubs/kittens),
Life Span: 10-12 years.
Location: throughout Europe and Siberia.
Calories: 1,300-3,800 kcal/day.
Diet: small mammals (roe deer, chamois, hares, marmots, foxes, and squirrels), small rodents, birds and carrion.
What they are called in a group: solitary.

American Golden Plover
(Pluvialis dominica)
Weight: 99-198 g.
Height: 180 mm wingspan.
Length: 24-28 cm.
Speed: up to 180 km/h.
Number on the Planet: 150,000.
Number in a litter: 3-4 eggs (fledglings/chicks).
Life Span: up to 15 years.
Location: arctic tundra of Alaska and Canada, migrate to South America; occurrences along western African coast, the Netherlands, Ireland, Okinawa, New Guinea, and New Zealand.
Calories: 36-110 kcal/day.
Diet: flying insects, spiders, crustaceans, berries, worms, and seeds.
What they are called in a group: flock.

Chamois *(Rupicapra pyrenaica)*
Weight: 24-50 kg.
Height: 760-810 mm at the shoulder.
Length: 900-1300 mm.
Speed: up to 50 km/h.
Number on the Planet: 31,000.

Number in a litter: 1-2 (kids).
Life Span: 14-22 years.
Location: northwestern Spain, the Pyrenees, and the Apennines of central Italy
Calories: 2,100-6,300 kcal/day.
Diet: grasses, leaves, buds, shoots and fungi.
What they are called in a group: herd.

Siberian Ibex *(Capra sibirica)*
Weight: 35-130 kg.
Height: 67-110 cm at the shoulder.
Length: 130-165 cm.
Speed: up to 56 km/h.
Number on the Planet: ~250,000.
Number in a litter: 1-2 (kids).
Life Span: up to 16 years.
Location: Russia, Siberia, Sayan Mountains, near Munku Sardyx.
Calories: 3,800-11,500 kcal/day.
Diet: plants, leaves, buds, shoots, sprouts.
What they are called in a group: herd.

Emperor Penguin
(Aptenodytes forsteri)
Weight: 30 kg.
Height: 1.1 m.
Speed: 6-9, up to 19 km/h swimming.
Number on the Planet: 150,000-200,000 breeding pairs.
Number in a litter: 1 (chick).
Life Span: 20-40 years.
Location: Antarctic tundra.
Calories: 2,000-6,000 kcal/day.
Diet:crustaceans, small fish and squid.
What they are called in a group: colony.

Muskox *(Ovibos moschatus)*
Weight: 180-400 kg.
Height: 120 cm at the shoulder.
Length: 135-250 cm.
Speed: up to 40 km/h.
Number on the Planet: ~ 60,000.
Number in a litter: 1-2 (stots/calves).
Life Span: 10-20 years.

The Tundra Animals

Location: Canada, Greenland, and reintroduced to Alaska from animals captured in Greenland; also introduced into Russia, Svalbard, Norway, and Siberia with some herds finding their own way into Sweden.
Calories: 9,700-29,100 kcal/day.
Diet: grasses, leafy plants, sedges, mosses, shrubs, herbs, and other vegetation.
What they are called in a group: herd.

Arctic Tern *(Sterna paradisaea)*
Weight: 86-127 g.
Height: 76-85 cm wingspan.
Length: 33-39 cm.
Speed: 22,500 km in one flight without resting.
Number on the Planet: 1,000,000.
Number in a litter: 1-3 (average 2).
Life Span: 20-34 years.
Location: northern hemisphere, Arctic (Europe, Asia and North America).
Calories: 29-87 kcal/day.
Diet: small fish, shrimp, krill, or insects and small invertebrates.
What they are called in a group: colony.

Dall's Sheep *(Ovis dalli)*
Weight: 46-113 kg.
Height: 94 cm at the shoulder.
Length: 1.3-1.8 m.
Speed: 48 km/h.
Number on the Planet: ~ 30,000.
Number in a litter: 1 (lamb/ lambkin/ cosset).
Life Span: up to 12-15 years.
Location: northeast, central and southern Alaska, as well as in the Yukon Territory, the northwest corner of British Columbia, and southwest of the Mackenzie River in the Northwest Territories.
Calories: 3,700-11,100 kcal/day.
Diet: grasses, sedges, lichen, forbes and mosses.
What they are called in a group: flock/herd.

Tundra Swan
(Cygnus columbianus)
Weight: 6.3-7.5 kg.
Height: 215 cm wingspan.
Length: 1.2-1.4 m.
Speed: 82 km/h.
Number on the Planet: 300,000.
Number in a litter: 3-6 eggs (cygnets/ flappers).
Life Span: up to 20 years.
Location: North America; summer range in Arctic regions of northern Alaska and Canada, winter range along west coast of US (Texas, New Mexico, and along the eastern seaboard).
Calories: 664-1,992 kcal/day.
Diet: tubers, roots of aquatic plants, mussels and clams.
What they are called in a group: bevy/ flock.

Canada Goose *(Branta canadensis)*
Weight: 3.0-6.5 kg.
Height: 160-175 cm wingspan.
Length: 90-100 cm.
Speed: 16-80 km/h.
Number on the Planet: 1,000,000-10,000,000.
Number in a litter: 4-8 eggs (goslings).
Life Span: av. 10-25 years, and up to over 40 years.
Location: Canada, U.S, Britain and Scandinavia.
Calories: 500-1,500 kcal/day.
Diet: aquatic plants and field plant-material.
What they are called in a group: flock/ gaggle.

Ptarmigan/Snow Grouse
(Lagopus muta)
Weight: 0.3-0.7 kg.
Height: 54-60 cm wingspan.
Length: 31-35 cm.
Speed: 32 km/h.
Number on the Planet: 8,200,000.
Number in a litter: 7-10 eggs (fledglings/ chicks).

The Tundra Animals

Life Span: ~3-4 years.
Location: arctic and subarctic Eurasia and North America (including Greenland) on rocky mountainsides and tundra; isolated populations in Scotland, the Pyrenees, the Alps, Bulgaria, the Urals, the Pamir Mountains, the Altay Mountains, and Japan.
Calories: 156-468 kcal/day.
Diet: leaves, buds, seeds, berries, stems and insects.
What they are called in a group:covey.

Polar Bear (*Ursus maritimus*)
Weight: 150-800 kg.
Height: 1.6 m at the shoulder.
Length: 1.8-2.5 m.
Speed: 40 km/h running, 16km/h swimming.
Number on the Planet: 21,470-28,370.
Number in a litter: 1-4, average 2 (cubs).
Life Span: 25-30 years.
Location: throughout the arctic region surrounding the North Pole.
Calories: 7,100-21,366 kcal/day.
Diet: ringed seals, bearded seals, harp seals, hooded seals, walruses, sea birds (and their eggs), small mammals, fish and scavenge on carrion of seals, walruses, or whales.
What they are called in a group: solitary.

Whimbrel *(Numenius phaeopus)*
Weight: 270-450 g.
Height: 71-81 cm wingspan.
Length: 37-45 cm.
Speed: ~64 km/h.
Number on the Planet: 1,000,000-2,100,000.
Number in a litter: 3-5 eggs (chicks/fledglings).
Life Span: up to ~16 years.
Location: North America, Europe, Africa, South America and Australia and Asia.
Calories: 326-978 kcal/day.

Diet: insects, snails, slugs, crabs, shrimps, mollusks and worms.
What they are called in a group: flock.

Ruff (*Philomachus pugnax*)
Weight: 70-150 g.
Height: 46-58 cm wingspan.
Length: 20-32 cm.
Speed: 40 km/h.
Number on the Planet: 2,000,000.
Number in a litter: 4 eggs (chicks/fledglings).
Life Span: up to 10 years.
Location: Europe (particularly on the eastern and southern coasts of the United Kingdom).
Calories: 30-90 kcal/day.
Diet: insects, larvae, small fish and seeds.
What they are called in a group: flock.

Red Phalarope
(*Phalaropus lobatus*)
Weight: 20-48 g.
Height: 31-34 cm wingspan.
Length: 18-19 cm.
Speed: 16-27 km/h.
Number on the Planet: ~ 1,000,000
Number in a litter: 3-4 eggs (chicks).
Life Span: up to 5 years.
Location: coastal regions of the Arctic Ocean, south to Aleutians and northwest to Britain; can be found off central-western South America, in the Arabian Sea and from central Indonesia to western Melanesia.
Calories: 12-37 kcal/day.
Diet: insects, mollusks and crustaceans.
What they are called in a group: flock.

Kodiak Bear
(*Ursus arctos middendorffi*)
Weight: up to 680 kg.
Height: 1.5 m at the shoulder (and up to 3 m on hind legs).
Length: 170-280 cm.
Speed: 50 km/h.
Number on the Planet: 3,500.

The Tundra Animals

Number in a litter: 3-6 (cubs).
Life Span: up to 34 years.
Location: islands in the Kodiak Archipelago (Alaska).
Calories: 18,600-55,900 kcal/day.
Diet: grass, plants, berries, specific parts of salmon, elk, deer and cattle.
What they are called in a group: sleuth/ sloth.

Brown Lemming
(*Lemmus sibiricus*)
Weight: 45-130 g.
Length: 130-180 mm.
Speed: 3.6-5 km/h, 1km/h swimming.
Number on the Planet: ~ 100,000.
Number in a litter: 2-13 (pups).
Life Span: less than 2 years.
Location: tundra regions of Siberia and North America.
Calories: 23-68 kcal/day.
Diet: fresh sedges, grasses, mosses, leaves and monocot.
What they are called in a group: solitary.

Arctic Redpol   l
(*Carduelis hornemanni*)
Weight: 10-18 g.
Height: 13.5-15.5 cm wingspan.
Length: 11.5 cm.
Speed: up to 48 km/h.
Number on the Planet: unknown
Number in a litter: 4-7 eggs (chicks).
Life Span: up to 8 years.
Location: Greenland and Canada.
Calories: 11-32 kcal/day.
Diet: small seeds and insects.
What they are called in a group: flock.

Arctic Loon (*Gavia arctica*)
Weight: 1.0-2.5 kg.
Height: 100-122 cm wingspan.
Length: 63-75 cm.
Speed: 88-97 km/h.
Number on the Planet: 130,000-2,000,000.
Number in a litter: 1-2 eggs (chicks).
Life Span: 25-30 years.

Location: Eurasia and western Alaska.
Calories: 240-712 kcal/day.
Diet: fish, mollusks and crustaceans.
What they are called in a group: flock.

Porcupine Caribou
(*Rangifer tarandus grantii*)
Weight: 65-100 kg.
Height: 102-113 cm at the shoulder.
Length: 170-201 cm.
Speed: up to 80 km/h.
Number on the Planet: 129,000.
Number in a litter: 1 (calf).
Life Span: average 8-10 years.
Location: northern Yukon and Alaska.
Calories: 3,800-11,400 kcal/day.
Diet: lichen, ever-green low-brush cranberry shrub, moss, grasses, equisetum and other small shrubs.
What they are called in a group: herd.

Ermine/Short-tailed Weasel
(*Mustela erminea*)
Weight: 200 g.
Length: 25cm and the tail is 8cm.l
Speed: up to 32km/h.
Number on the Planet: ~ 100,000.
Number in a litter: 3-18, average 4-9 (kits).
Life Span: 1-2 average; up to 7 years.
Location: Arctic tundra of North America and Europe.
Calories: 42-125 kcal/day.
Diet: small mammals (mice, squirrels, rabbits, and hares), birds, insects, carrion and berries.
What they are called in a group: gang.

Snow Bunting
(*Plectrophenax nivalis*)
Weight: 40 g.
Height: 30.48-33.02 cm wingspan.
Length: 16.51-19.05 cm.
Speed: average 32-48 km/h.
Number on the Planet: 39,000,000.
Number in a litter: 4-6 eggs (chicks).
Life Span: 3-6 years.
Location: northern Europe, Russia, Canada and northern United States.

The Tundra Animals

Calories: 14-42 kcal/day.
Diet: seeds, leaf buds and insects.
What they are called in a group: flock.

Meadow Pipit
(Anthus pratensis)
Weight: 16-25 g.
Height: 22-25 cm wingspan.
Length: 14-15 cm.
Speed: up to 53 km/h in short bursts.
Number on the Planet: 14,000,000–32,000,000.
Number in a litter: 3-5 eggs (chicks).
Life Span: up to 7 years.
Location: Central Asia, Europe and Greenland.
Calories: 14-41 kcal/day.
Diet: flies, beetles, moths and spiders.
What they are called in a group: flock.

Water Pipit (Anthus spinoletta)
Weight: 19-26 g.
Height: 22-28 cm wingspan.
Length: 14-17 cm.
Speed: up to ~50 km/h in short bursts.
Number on the Planet: 1,500,000-4,200,000.
Number in a litter: 4-6 eggs (chicks).
Life Span: up to 7 years.
Location: southern Europe and Asia.
Calories: 15-45 kcal/day.
Diet: insects and larvae.
What they are called in a group: flock.

Horned Lark (Eremophila alpestris)
Weight: 28-48 g.
Height: 31.12-35.56 cm wingspan.
Length: 18-20 cm.
Speed: 45 km/h.
Number on the Planet: 140,000,000.
Number in a litter: 3-4 eggs (chicks).
Life Span: average 2-5 years, up to 8 years.
Location: across North America, and also inhabits Asia and northern Europe. It lives throughout the western, central, and eastern United States, including Alaska, and

throughout northern and southern Canada.
Calories: 22-67 kcal/day.
Diet: weeds, grass seeds and insects.
What they are called in a group: flock.

Tundra Moose (Alces alces gigas)
Weight: 270-600 kg.
Height: 2.3 m at the shoulder.
Length: 2.4-3.2 m.
Speed: 56 km/h.
Number on the Planet: 175,000.
Number in a litter: 1-2 (calves).
Life Span: average 8-12 years, up to 22 years.
Location: throughout northern North America and Eurasia.
Calories: 6,700-20,000 kcal/day.
Diet: twigs, bark, roots, shoots of woody plants (willows and aspens), water plants (water lilies, pondweed, horsetails, bladderworts, and bur-reed), conifers (balsam fir).
What they are called in a group: herd.

Long-tailed Chinchilla
(Chinchilla lanigera)
Weight: 400-750 g.
Length: 38-55 cm.
Speed: up to 25 km/h in short bursts
Number on the Planet: ~5,500.
Number in a litter: 1-4 (pups).
Life Span: 10-22 years.
Location: South America.
Calories: 77-231 kcal/day.
Diet: grasses, bushes, fruit and plants.
What they are called in a group: colony.

Northern Wheatear
(Oenanthe oenanthe)
Weight: 24 g.
Height: 29 cm wingspan.
Length: 15 cm.
Speed: ~30-40 km/h.
Number on the Planet: 2,900,000.
Number in a litter: 3-8, average 5-6 eggs (chicks).
Life Span: up to 7 years.

The Tundra Animals

Location: Europe, Asia, Eastern Canada, India and Greenland.
Calories: 18-54 kcal/day.
Diet: insects, berries, centipedes and snails.
What they are called in a group: flock.

Snares Penguin
(*Eudyptes robustus*)
Weight: 3-4 kg.
Height: 50-60 cm.
Speed: average 24 km/h.
Number on the Planet: 25,000-35,000 breeding pairs.
Number in a litter: 2 eggs (chicks).
Life Span: 15-20 years.
Location: Snares Island, south of New Zealand.
Calories: 400-1,200 kcal/day.
Diet: krill, squid and fish.
What they are called in a group: rookery.

Wolverine (*Gulo gulo*)
Weight: 7-32 kg.
Height: 35-45 cm at the shoulder.
Length: 65-105 cm and a 17-26 cm tail.
Speed: 15km/h.
Number on the Planet: ~ 50,000.
Number in a litter: 1-6, average 2-3 (cubs).
Life Span: 8-10 years, and up to 17 years in captivity.
Location: Scandinavia, Siberia, Alaska, Canada and Northern USA.
Calories: 1,300-3,900 kcal/day.
Diet: small mammals, eggs, deer and sheep.
What they are called in a Group: pack.

Gray Seal (*Halichoerus grypus*)
Weight: 150-300 kg.
Length: 2.3-3 m.
Speed: 19 km/h.
Number on the Planet: 290,000-300,000.
Number in a litter: 1 (pup).
Life Span: 35-40 years.

Location: Labrador, Canada to New England, Norway to France and the Baltic Sea (found on both shores of the North Atlantic Ocean).
Calories: 4,100-12,200 kcal/day.
Diet: pollock, haddock, skates, flatfish capelin, cod, flounder, whiting, squid, lobster and octopus.
What they are called in a group: herd.

Leopard Seal (*Hydrurga leptonyx*)
Weight: 200-590 kg.
Length: 2.4-4 m.
Speed: 40 km/h.
Number on the Planet: 220,000-440,000.
Number in a litter: 1 (pup).
Life Span: 12-15 years in the wild, over 25 years in captivity.
Location: along the coast of Antarctica and on most subantarctic islands; some can be found on the coasts of South Africa, southern Australia, Tasmania, New Zealand, Lord Howe Island, the Cook Islands, Tierra del Fuego, and the Atlantic coast of South America.
Calories: 12,400-37,200 kcal/day.
Diet: Adelie penguins, krill, squid and other seals.
What they are called in a group: herd.

Barren-Ground Caribou
(*Rangifer tarandus groenlandicus*)
Weight: 90-150 kg.
Height: 120 cm at the shoulder.
Length: 150-230 cm.
Speed: up to 80 k/h.
Number on the Planet: 160,000.
Number in a litter: 1-2 (calves).
Life Span: 5 years in the wild, 10-15 years in captivity.
Location: Canadian territories Nunavut and the Northwest Territories and western Greenland.
Calories: 5,100-15,200 kcal/day.
Diet: grass, moss, lichen, sedges, mushrooms.
What they are called in a group: herd.

The Tundra Animals

Snowshoe Hare
(Lepus americanus)
Weight: 1.2-1.6 kg.
Length: 413-518 mm.
Speed: 43 km/h.
Number on the Planet: abundant.
Number in a litter: average 2-4, up to 8 (leverets).
Life Span: ~1year, up to 6 years in captivity.
Location: throughout Canada and in the northern United States.
Calories: 180-540 kcal/day.
Diet: green grasses, forbs, bluegrass, brome, vetches, asters, jewelweed, wild strawberry, pussy-toes, dandelions, clovers, daisies, horsetails, aspen, birches and willows.
What they are called in a group: down.

Northern Pika
(Ochotona hyperborea)
Weight: 140 g.
Length: 12.7-18.6 cm, 0.5-1.2cm tail.
Speed: up to 18 km/h.
Number on the Planet: abundant.
Number in a litter: 2-6 (pups).
Life Span: 3 years.
Location: across northern Asia, from the Ural Mountains to northern Japan and south through Mongolia, Manchuria, and northern Korea.
Calories: 32-96 kcal/day.
Diet: stems and leaves of grass, weeds.
What they are called in a group: pack.

Sumatran Short-Eared Rabbit
(Nesolagus netscheri)
Weight: 1.5 kg.
Length: 350-400 mm, 15mm tail.
Speed: up to 56 km/h.
Number on the Planet: less than 100.
Number in a litter: 1-8 (kitten/ bunny)
Life Span: up to 9 years.
Location: West and Southwest Sumatra (Indonesia).
Calories: 190-570 kcal/day.
Diet: stalks and leaves.

What they are called in a group:
colony/ drove.

Gelada Baboon
(Theropithecus gelada)
Weight: 13-21 kg.
Length: 50-74 cm.
Speed: up to 56-64 km/h.
Number on the Planet: 50,000-60,000.
Number in a litter: 1 (infant).
Life Span: up to over 30 years.
Location: Africa (highlands of Ethiopia and Eritrea; majority living in Gich and Sankaber areas of *Semien Mountains National Park* in Ethiopia).
Calories: 1,200-3,500 kcal/day.
Diet: grasses, fruits, tubers, insects and flowers.
What they are called in a group: troop.

Juan Fernandez Fur Seal
(Arctocephalus philippii)
Weight: 140 kg.
Length: 1.42-2.0 m.
Speed: 24 km/h.
Number on the Planet: 4,000-12,000.
Number in a litter: 1 (pup).
Life Span: 13-23 years.
Location: Juan Fernandez Islands (off coast of Chile).
Calories: 5,700-17,100 kcal/day.
Diet: fish and cephalopods (octopuses and squid).
What they are called in a group: herd.

Mediterranean Monk Seal
(Monachus monachus)
Weight: 300-315 kg.
Length: 2.4-2.8 m.
Speed: up to ~38 km/h.
Number on the Planet: less than 500.
Number in a litter: 1 (pup)
Life Span: 20-30 years.
Location: Eastern Mediterranean and Northwest Atlantic near Africa.
Calories: 10,300-30,800 kcal/day.
Diet: fish, octopus and squid.
What they are called in a group: herd/ pod.

The Rainforest Animals

Giant Panda Bear
(Ailuropoda melanoleuca)
Weight: 80-125 kg.
Height: 65-70 cm at the shoulder.
Length: 1.5-1.8 m.
Speed: up to 50 km/h in short bursts (though they tend not to run to conserve energy).
Number on Planet: less than 2,000.
Number in Litter: 5-6 (cubs).
Lifespan: 26-30 years in the wild, 34 years in captivity.
Location: limited to the provinces of Sichuan, Gansu, and Shanxi in the central part of China.
Calories:4,500-13,530 kcal/day.
Diet: bamboo stems and shoots, fruits of plant matter like kiwi, small mammals, fish and insects.
What they are called in a Group:solitary.

Siamang Gibbon
(Hylobates syndactylus)
Weight: 10-12 kg.
Height: 185-234 cm arm-span.
Length: 71-90 cm.
Speed: can leap 9m in one jump, up to 56 km/h.
Number on Planet: 22,390.
Number in Litter: 1-2 (though twins are rare) (infants).
Lifespan: 30-40yrs.
Location: Malaysia, Thailand and Sumatra.
Calories: 845-2,500 kcal/day.
Diet: leaves, fruit, insects, small invertebrates and bird eggs.
What they are called in a Group: band.

Long-nosed Bandicoot
(Perameles nasuta)
Weight: 0.85 kg-1.1 kg.
Length: 31-43 cm, 12-15 cm tail.
Speed: 4 m/s.
Number on Planet: 130-160.

Number in Litter: 1-7, average 2-4 (pups).
Lifespan: 3-5 years., average 2.5 years.
Location: Eastern Australia, in Queensland, New South Wales and Victoria.
Calories: 96-288 kcal/day.
Diet: insects, larvae, roots, tubers, mice and other small rodents.
What they are called in a Group:solitary.

Keel-billed Toucan
(Ramphastos Sulfuratus)
Weight: 400 g.
Length: 50 cm.
Speed: up to ~48 km/h.
Number on Planet: considered to be a look-alike of threatened species, and therefore needs to be monitored. The species is a common resident in areas where it occurs (its range), except where there is heavy deforestation. There are some areas where they are locally scarce due to hunting (to eat or/and for ornaments). Toucan feathers are used as ornaments.
Number in Litter: 1-4 eggs (chicks).
Lifespan: 15-20 years.
Location: Central and South America.
Calories: 78-235 kcal/day.
Diet: fruits (primarily berries), some insects, bird eggs, and tree frogs
What they are called in a Group: flock.

Giant Anteater
(Myrmecophaga tridactyla)
Weight: 29-65 kg.
Height: 60 cm at the shoulder.
Length: 1.8-2.4 m.
Speed: moves rapidly through the trees, using its forelimbs and even its tail.
Number on Planet: less than 10,000 mature individuals.
Number in Litter: 1 (puggle).
Lifespan: ~14 years in the wild, 26 years in captivity.
Location: southern Mexico, through Central America, and South America

The Rainforest Animals

east of the Andes through Uruguay and
northern Argentina.
Calories: 2,500-7,500 kcal/day.
Diet: ants, termites, grubs, eggs, larvae
and insects.
What they are called in a Group:solitary.

Jaguar (*Panthera onca*)
Weight: 45-114 kg.
Height: 0.8-1.0 m at the shoulder.
Length: 1.2 m.
Speed: up to ~96 km/h (in short bursts).
Number on Planet: less than 50,000.
Number in Litter: 1-4 (cubs).
Lifespan: 15-20 years average, up to 22
years.
Location: southwestern United States to
Argentina.
Calories: 5,600-16,700 kcal/day.
Diet: deer, peccaries, agoutis, pacas,
fish, frogs, turtles, and small alligators.
What they are called in a Group:solitary.

Mantled Howler Monkey
(*Alouatta palliata*)
Weight: 3-9 kg.
Length: 380-580 mm, 520-670 mm tail.
Speed: up to 48 km/h arboreal
locomotion.
Number on Planet: less than 20,000.
Number in Litter: 1 (infant).
Lifespan: males 7 years average,
females 11-12 years average.
Location: southern Mexico, from
Honduras in Central America to
Colombia and western Ecuador in South
America, and southern Guatemala.
Calories: 536-1,600 kcal/day.
Diet: leaves, fruit and flowers.
What they are called in a Group: troop.

Northern Muriqui
(*Brachyteles* hypoxanthus)
Weight: 12-15 kg.
Length: 61 cm.
Speed: up to 50 km/h arboreal
locomotion.
Number on Planet: less than 300.
Number in Litter: 1 (infant).

Lifespan: 10-50 years (environment
dependent).
Location: Atlantic coastal forests of
Brazil.
Calories: 1,100-3,200 kcal/day.
Diet: leaves, fruit and flowers.
What they are called in a Group: troop.

Military Macaw (*Ara militaris*)
Weight: 800g-1.1 kg.
Height: 71 cm wingspan.
Length: 71 cm.
Speed: up to 56 km/h.
Number on Planet: 10,000-12,000.
Number in Litter: 2-4 eggs (chicks).
Lifespan: up to 60 years.
Location: limited ranges from Mexico to
Argentina.
Calories: 150-450 kcal/day.
Diet: fruit, vegetable matter, nuts and
seeds.
What they are called in a Group: flock.

Goliath Birdeater Tarantula
(*Theraphosa blondi*)
Weight: 70-120 g.
Length: 30 cm.
Speed: 2 m/min.
Number on Planet: population status
unknown, though believed to be
abundant within range.
Number in Litter: 50 eggs (spiderlings).
Lifespan: male 3-6 years, females 6-14
years, up to 25 years.
Location: northern South America.
Calories: 3.4-10.3 kcal/day.
Diet: invertebrates such as crickets,
mealworms and moths, and small
vertebrates such as frogs, mice, and
lizards.
What they are called in a Group:solitary.

Laughing Kookaburra
(*Dacelo novaeguineae*)
Weight: 453 g.
Height: 64-66 cm wingspan.
Length: 40-45 cm.
Speed: up to ~48 km/h.

The Rainforest Animals

Number on Planet: the global population size has not been quantified, but it is believed to be large as the species is described as 'common' in at least parts of its range.
Number in Litter: 2-4 eggs (chicks).
Lifespan: up to 20 years.
Location: eastern and southeastern Australia and New Zealand.
Calories: 142-427 kcal/day.
Diet: insects, worms and crustaceans, small snakes, mammals, frogs and birds.
What they are called in a Group: flock.

Leopard *(Panthera pardus)*
Weight: 30-90 kg.
Height: 45-78 cm.
Length: 91-243 cm, 58-97 cm tail.
Speed: 64 km/h.
Number on Planet: 500,000.
Number in Litter: 1-2 (cubs).
Lifespan: 7-9 years in the wild, 21-23 years in captivity.
Location: sub-Saharan Africa, Asia Minor, the Middle East, India, Pakistan, China, Siberia, much of mainland South-East Asia, and the islands of Java and Sri Lanka.
Calories: 3,000-9,000 kcal/day.
Diet: monkeys, rodents, reptiles, amphibians, birds, fish, wild pigs, and ungulates.
What they are called in a Group: leap.

Sumatran Orangutan *(Pongo abelii)*
Weight: 30-90 kg.
Height: 2.2 arm span.
Length: 1.5 m.
Speed: the orangutan has to move slowly and cautiously because it has to burn a lot of energy to move its great mass.
Number on Planet: 7,500.
Number in Litter: 1-2 (infants).
Lifespan: 35-40 years in the wild, 50-60 years in captivity.
Location: Sumatran tropical forests.
Calories: 3,000-9,000 kcal/day.

Diet: fruit, honey, leaves, flowers, seeds, bark and insects.
What they are called in a Group:solitary.

Emerald Tree Boa *(Corallus caninus)*
Weight: up to ~15 kg.
Length: 1.8-2.2 m.
Speed: 1.6 km/h.
Number on Planet: population status and size unknown.
Number in Litter: up to 20 (live) (neonates).
Lifespan: 15-20 years.
Location: lower Amazon basin (in Brazil) and in Guyana and Suriname (rainforests of South America).
Calories: 76-228 kcal/day (though they will consume this or more about once a week or so rather than eating daily portions).
Diet: birds and rodents.
What they are called in a Group: solitary/ nest.

**Western Lowland Gorilla
*(Gorilla gorilla gorilla)***
Weight: 135-275 kg.
Height/Length: males 165-175 cm, females 140 cm.
Speed: up to 40 km/h in short bursts.
Number on Planet: 94,000.
Number in Litter: 1 infant.
Lifespan: 30-50 years in the wild, up to ~54 years captivity.
Location: tropical rainforest of mid-west Africa.
Calories: 14,350-43,050 kcal/day.
Diet: fruit, shoots, bulbs, a little tree bark, and leaves.
What they are called in a Group: band.

**Yellow-eared Parrot
*(Ognorhynchus icterotis)***
Weight: up to 700 g.
Length: 42 cm.
Speed: up to 48 km/h.
Number on Planet: 75-144.
Number in Litter: 2-4 eggs (chicks).
Lifespan: up to 50 years.

The Rainforest Animals

Location: cloud forests of the northern Andes, Colombia.
Calories: 120-360 kcal/day.
Diet: fruit, bark, flowers, shoots of various trees and seeds.
What they are called in a Group: company/ flock.

Scarlet Macaw (Ara macao)
Weight: 1.2 kg.
Height: 112-120 cm wingspan.
Length: 89cm.
Speed: up to 56-60 km/h.
Number on Planet: the global population size has not been quantified, but it is believed to be large as the species is described as 'common' in at least parts of its range.
Number in Litter: 2-4 eggs (chicks).
Lifespan: 40-50 and up to 75 years.
Location: southern Mexico, Central America, and South America (as far south as northeastern Argentina).
Calories: 18-55 kcal/day.
Diet: fruit, nuts, seeds, grains, nectar and flowers.
What they are called in a Group: monogamous pair/company/flock.

Goodfellow's Tree Kangaroo (Dendrolagus goodfellowi)
Weight: 6.7-7.7 kg.
Length: 51-76 cm, 43-91cm tail.
Speed: 9 m/s leaps.
Number on Planet: less than 250.
Number in Litter: 1 joey.
Lifespan: up to 14 years.
Location: rainforests of central and eastern New Guinea.
Calories: 424-1,265 kcal/day.
Diet: leaves, fruit, grains, flower, sap, bark and eggs.
What they are called in a Group:solitary.

Proboscis Monkey (Nasalis larvatus)
Weight: 7-22 kg.
Length: 60-70 cm.
Speed: up to ~50 km/h (swinging).
Number on Planet: 7,000-10,000.

Number in Litter: 1 infant.
Lifespan: up to ~23 years.
Location: island of Borneo.
Calories: 1,040-3,120 kcal/day.
Diet: fruits, seeds, leaves, shoots of mangrove and small invertebrates (caterpillars and larvae).
What they are called in a Group: troop.

Blue Poison Arrow Frog (Dendrobates azureus)
Weight: ~3 g.
Length: 3-4.5 cm.
Speed: up to 0.7 m/s.
Number on Planet: the destruction of rainforest habitat by fires and by humans for farmland has contributed to the decreasing numbers of in the wild. The illegal pet trade has also negatively impacted its existence by smuggling hundreds of these frogs out of Suriname into pet stores worldwide. With this pressure from illegal trade and shrinking habitat, it has become one of the most threatened of all the poison dart frogs.
Number in Litter: 5-10. (tadpoles/polliwogs).
Lifespan: 4-6 years in the wild, 10-12 years in captivity.
Location: southern part of Suriname (or Surinam), South America.
Calories: 0.26-0.77 kcal/day.
Diet: termites, crickets, ants and fruit flies.
What they are called in a Group: army.

Giant Armadillo (Priodontes maximus)
Weight: 18.70-32.30 kg.
Length: 832-960 mm.
Speed: 0.24-1 km/h.
Number on Planet: less than 10,000 mature individuals; vulnerable.
Number in Litter: 1-2 (pups).
Lifespan: 12-15 years.
Location: found from southeastern Venezuela and the Guianas in the North through northeastern Brazil, Paraguay, and the extreme north of Argentina.

The Rainforest Animals

Calories: 1,650-4,950 kcal/day.
Diet: termites, ants, carrion, worms and other small invertebrates.
What they are called in a Group:solitary.

White-bellied Spider Monkey (*Ateles belzebuth*)
Weight: 5.9-10.4 kg.
Length: 34-59 cm.
Speed: up to ~50 km/h swinging.
Number on Planet: less than 10,000 mature individuals; vulnerable.
Number in Litter: 1 infant.
Lifespan: 30-40 years.
Location: northeastern portion of the Amazon in South America (Colombia, Venezuela, Peru, Ecuador, and Brazil).
Calories: 370-1,110 kcal/day.
Diet: fruit, seeds, leaves and sometimes dead wood.
What they are called in a Group: troop.

Baird's Tapir (*Tapirus bairdii*)
Weight: 150-250 kg.
Height: 77-108 at the shoulder.
Length: 204-221 cm.
Speed: up to 40 km/h.
Number on Planet: 4,530-15,250.
Number in Litter: 1-2 (average 1) (infants).
Lifespan: up to 28-35 years.
Location: dense jungles of Central America, including southeastern Mexico, Belize, Guatemala, Honduras, Costa Rica, and Panama, and possibly Nicaragua, Colombia and Ecuador.
Calories: 3,700-11,168 kcal/day.
Diet: fruits, leaves, stems, sprouts, small branches, grasses, aquatic plants, tree bark, aquatic organisms, and cane, melon, cocoa, rice, and corn from plantations.
What they are called in a Group: herd.

White-faced Capuchin (*Cebus capucinus*)
Weight: 2.5-3.5 kg.
Length: 435 mm, 551mm tail.
Speed: up to 56 km/h swinging.

Number on Planet: considered abundant, with distribution larger than 20,000 km^2. The species adapts well to modified environments and there is no indication that the situation may change in the near future.
Number in Litter: 1-2 (average 1) (infants).
Lifespan: 15-25 years and almost 50 years in captivity.
Location: Central America, range extending from Belize to extreme northern Colombia.
Calories: 320-960 kcal/day.
Diet: fruits and insects.
What they are called in a Group: troop.

Ring-tailed Lemur (*Lemur catta*)
Weight: 2.3-3.5 kg.
Length: 385-455 mm, 560-624 mm tail.
Speed: up to ~48 km/h arboreal locomotion.
Number on Planet: 10,000-100,000.
Number in Litter: 1-2 (infants).
Lifespan: up to 33 years.
Location: southern and southwestern Madagascar, with an additional population on the southeastern plateau of the Andringita Mountains.
Calories: 311-933 kcal/day.
Diet: plants, leaves, flowers, fruit, insects, sap and bark.
What they are called in a Group: troop.

Prehensile-tailed Porcupine (*Coendou prehensilis*)
Weight: 2-5 kg.
Length: 300-600 mm, 330-485 mm tail.
Speed: slow arboreal animal.
Number on Planet: abundant and widespread throughout its range despite possibility of declining numbers.
Number in Litter: 1 porcupette.
Lifespan: 17+ years.
Location: Venezuela, Guiana, Brazil, Bolivia, Paraguay, Trinidad, and some extreme northern sections of Argentina.
Calories: 460-1,074 kcal/day.

The Rainforest Animals

Diet: leaves, tender stems, fruits, blossoms, and roots.
What they are called in a Group: pair.

Pale-throated Three-toed Sloth (*Bradypus tridactylus*)
Weight: 2.25-5.5 kg.
Length: 46-76 cm.
Speed: ~0.88 km/h characterized by its excessively slow locomotion.
Number on Planet: unknown.
Number in Litter: 1 pup.
Lifespan: up to 30-40 years.
Location: tropical rain forests from southern Central America to north-eastern Argentina.
Calories: 386-1,160 kcal/day.
Diet: twigs, buds, and leaves of trees of the genus Cecropia.
What they are called in a Group:solitary.

Blue Morpho Butterfly (*Morpho menelaus*)
Weight: 2 g.
Length: 13-17 cm wingspan.
Speed: 8-19 km/h.
Number on Planet: unknown.
Number in Litter: one egg at a time throughout lifespan (up to ~100 eggs in total) (larvae).
Lifespan: ~1 month.
Location: rainforests of South and Central America, including Brazil, Costa Rica, and Venezuela.
Calories: 0.19-0.56 kcal/day.
Diet: fermented juices of fruit, bodily fluids of dead animals and fungi.
What they are called in a Group: swarm.

White's Tree Frog (*Litoria caerulea*)
Weight: 40-50 g.
Length: 7-11.5 cm.
Speed: 5.7 cm/s.
Number on Planet: tolerance of a broad range of habitats, presumed large population, and because it is unlikely to be declining fast enough to qualify for listing in a more threatened category.

Number in Litter: 200-300 eggs (tadpole/polliwogs).
Lifespan: up to 16 years.
Location: Australia and New Guinea, with introduced populations in New Zealand and the United States.
Calories: 1.9-5.9 kcal/day.
Diet: insects, spiders, smaller frogs and small vertebrates.
What they are called in a Group: army

Blue & Yellow Macaw (*Ara ararauna*)
Weight: 900-1,300 g.
Height: 115 cm wingspan.
Length: 76-86 cm.
Speed: flight is direct with slow shallow wing beats. They are quite fast for such a large bird.
Number on Planet: less than 100,000.
Number in Litter: 2 eggs (chicks).
Lifespan: up to 30-50 years.
Location: tropical South America from Panama, south to Brazil, Bolivia and Paraguay.
Calories: 84-251 kcal/day.
Diet: fruits, seeds, nuts and vegetable matter.
What they are called in a Group: flock.

Goliath Beetle (*Goliathus goliatus*)
Weight: 42g-100 g.
Length: 128-150 mm.
Speed: up to 0.6 m/s.
Number on Planet: unknown.
Number in Litter: up to several thousand eggs (low fecundity) (larvae).
Lifespan: up to 1 year.
Location: rainforests of Africa near the equator.
Calories: 2.75-8.25 kcal/day.
Diet: nectar and pollen of flowering plant *Vernonia conferta*.
What they are called in a Group: swarm.

Red-eyed Tree Frog (*Agalychnis callidryas*)
Weight: 4-8 g.
Length: 4-7 cm.
Speed: up to 0.7 m/s.

The Rainforest Animals

Number on Planet: not considered threatened in their natural environment, however there has been much concern about the overall condition of the rain forest habitat in which *A. callidryas* resides. Global warming, deforestation, climatic and atmospheric changes, wetland drainage, and pollution have caused dramatic declines in the amphibian population in, and among the rainforests of Central and South America."

Number in Litter: 30-50 eggs (tadpoles/polliwogs).
Lifespan: 3-4 years up to 5 years.
Location: throughout most of Central America, as far north as southern Mexico.
Calories: 1.28-3.86 kcal/day.
Diet: crickets, moths, flies, grasshoppers, sometimes smaller frogs, fruit flies and pinhead crickets.
What they are called in a Group: army.

Ocelot (*Leopardus pardalis*)
Weight: 10-11.5 kg.
Height: 40-50 cm at the shoulder.
Length: 550-1000 mm, 300-450 mm tail.
Speed: 64-80 km/h.
Number on Planet: 50,000 or more.
Number in Litter: 1-3 (1-2 average) (cubs).
Lifespan: 7-10 years in the wild, 20 years in captivity.
Location: southwestern Texas to northern Argentina.
Calories: 831-2,493 kcal/day.
Diet: small to medium-sized mammals and birds, amphibians, fish, and reptiles (rabbits, rodents, agouti, young peccaries, monkeys, lesser anteaters, iguanas, tree lizards, frogs, crabs, and small turtles).
What they are called in a Group: pack.

Imperial Amazon
(*Amazona imperialis*)
Weight: 800 g.
Height: 284-286 mm wingspan.

Length: 45 cm, 166-169mm tail.
Speed: up to ~60 km/h.
Number on Planet: less than 200.
Number in Litter: 2 eggs (chicks).
Lifespan: 50-60 years, up to 100 years.
Location: island of Dominica in the Lesser Antilles.
Calories: 131-395 kcal/day.
Diet: fruits, seeds, nuts, berries, blossoms and shoots.
What they are called in a Group: flock.

Gray Hawk (*Buteo nitidus*)
Weight: 378-660 g.
Height: 89-91 cm.
Length: 46-61 cm.
Speed: 30-70 km/h.
Number on Planet: 500,000-5,000,000.
Number in Litter: 1-3 eggs (2 average) (eyas).
Lifespan: 15-20 years.
Location: southwestern USA and Mexico, south to Bolivia, Brazil and central Argentina.
Calories: 82-246 kcal/day.
Diet: reptiles, small mammals, birds, and some insects.
What they are called in a Group: cast.

Kinkajou (*Potos flavus*)
Weight: 2-3 kg.
Length: 40-75 cm, 40-60 cm tail.
Speed: extremely agile and fast, traveling quickly along the tree tops.
Number on Planet: considered widespread and common throughout range.
Number in Litter: 1-2 (average 1) (infants).
Lifespan: up to 20-24 years.
Location: forests throughout the neotropics (in Central and South America).
Calories: 139-417 kcal/day.
Diet: fruit, honey, insects, flowers and leaves.
What they are called in a Group:solitary.

The Rainforest Animals

White-Tufted-Ear Marmoset
(Callithrix jacchus)
Weight: 300-360 g.
Length: 12-15 cm, 29.5-35 cm tail.
Speed: up to ~48km/h arboreal locomotion.
Number on Planet: in the low thousands.
Number in Litter: twins (average 2) (infants).
Lifespan: 1-20 years.
Location: southeastern Brazilian coastal rainforest.
Calories: 60-182 kcal/day.
Diet: tree sap, insects, spiders, fruit, flowers, and nectar, small lizards, bird's eggs, nestlings, and frogs.
What they are called in a Group: troop.

Grey-cheeked Hornbill
(Ceratogymna subcylindricus)
Weight: 1.31 kg.
Length: 60-70 cm.
Speed: up to ~28 km/h.
Number on Planet: has a large range, with an estimated global extent of occurrence of 960,000 km^2. The global population size has not been quantified, but it is believed to be large as the species is described as 'frequent' in at least parts of its range.
Number in Litter: average 2 eggs (chicks).
Lifespan: up to 31 years.
Location: Central and western Africa, including Congo and the Ivory Coast.
Calories: 191-573 kcal/day.
Diet: insects, arachnids, small birds, bats, lizards and their eggs, snails and millipedes.
What they are called in a Group: flock.

Okapi *(Okapia johnstoni)*
Weight: 200-250 kg.
Height: 1.5-2.0 m at the shoulder.
Length: 1.9-2.5 m.
Speed: up to 56 km/h.
Number on Planet: 10,000-20,000.
Number in Litter: 1 (calf).

Lifespan: 15-30 + years.
Location: Ituri Rainforest in central Africa.
Calories: 8,100-24,400 kcal/day.
Diet: tree leaves and buds, grass, ferns, fruit, and fungi.
What they are called in a Group: herd.

Bongo Antelope
(Tragelaphus euryceros)
Weight: 210-405 kg.
Height: 1.1-1.3 m at the shoulder.
Length: 1.7-2.5 m.
Speed: up to 80 km/h in short bursts.
Number on Planet: 28,000.
Number in Litter: 1 (calf).
Lifespan: up to 19 years.
Location: Kenya and western Africa.
Calories: 10,280-30,841 kcal/day.
Diet: leaves, flowers, garden produce and twigs.
What they are called in a Group: herd.

Mandrill *(Mandrillus sphinx)*
Weight: 11-27 kg.
Height: up to 80 cm at the shoulder.
Length: 56-81 cm.
Speed: slow-moving on the ground, able to leap 2-5 m at once.
Number on Planet: less than 10,000 mature individuals.
Number in Litter: 1 (infant).
Lifespan: up to 20 years in the wild, up to 46 years in captivity.
Location: Cameroon, Gabon, Equatorial Guinea, and Congo.
Calories: 1,274-3,822 kcal/day.
Diet: grasses, herbs, shoots, bark, tubers, roots, fruit, small animals, including spiders, snails, worms, ants, and small ground vertebrates.
What they are called in a Group: troop.

Drill *(Mandrillus leucophaeus)*
Weight: 11.5-25 kg.
Length: 610-764 mm, 52-76 mm tail.
Speed: up to 35 km/h.
Number on Planet: 3,000.
Number in Litter: 1 (infant).

Lifespan: up to 46 years.
Location: Cameroon, north of the Sanaga river and on the coastal island of Fernando Poo.
Calories: 1,236-3,708 kcal/day.
Diet: fruit, leaves and invertebrates.
What they are called in a Group: troop.

Red-shanked Douc Langur (Pygathrix nemaeus nemaeus)
Weight: 5-7 kg.
Length: 61-76 cm, 56-76 cm tail.
Speed: up to 48 km/h arboreal locomotion.
Number on Planet: less than 2,500 mature individuals; considered endangered.
Number in Litter: 1 (infant)
Lifespan: up to 25 years.
Location: Cambodia, Laos and Vietnam.
Calories: 536-1,610 kcal/day.
Diet: small, young and tender leaves, fruit (like figs), buds, flowers and bamboo shoots.
What they are called in a Group: troop.

Slender Loris (Loris tardigradus)
Weight: 86-348 g.
Length: 175-264 mm.
Speed: 0.16-0.48 km/h arboreal.
Number on Planet: less than 2,500 mature individuals; considered endangered.
Number in Litter: 1-2 (infants).
Lifespan: up to ~15 years.
Location: India and Sri Lanka.
Calories: 44-133 kcal/day.
Diet: shoots, young leaves, fruits with hard rinds, bird's eggs, and small vertebrates.
What they are called in a Group: pair.

Linnaeus's Two-toed Sloth (Choloepus didactylus)
Weight: 4-8.5 kg.
Length: 540-740 mm.
Speed: 0.88km/h crawling (they are arboreal).

Number on Planet: in view of its wide distribution, presumed large population, its occurrence in a number of protected areas, and because it is unlikely to be declining fast enough to qualify for listing in a more threatened category.
Number in Litter: 1 pup.
Lifespan: up to 30 years.
Location: South America (Venezuela, the Guineas and Brazil north of the Amazon River).
Calories: 276-830 kcal/day.
Diet: stems, leaves and fruits.
What they are called in a Group: solitary.

Jambu Fruit Dove (Ptilinopus jambu)
Weight: 42 g.
Height: 7.6-15.2 cm wingspan.
Length: 23-27 cm.
Speed: up to 48 km/h.
Number on Planet: its numbers are declining, though there is no quantification of existing numbers.
Number in Litter: 2 eggs (chicks).
Lifespan: 5-15 years.
Location: southern Thailand, Malaysia and the Indonesian islands of Kalimantan, Sumatra west Java and Brunei.
Calories: 24-72 kcal/day.
Diet: fruit.
What they are called in a Group: flock.

Silvery Gibbon (Hylobates moloch)
Weight: 4-9 kg.
Length: 44-64 cm.
Speed: up to 56 km/h; they have adopted a rapid form of locomotion, brachiation, in which they swing by their long arms from branch to branch.
Number on Planet: less than 2,000.
Number in Litter: 1 infant.
Lifespan: up to 44 years.
Location: Indonesian island of Java (southeast Asia).
Calories: 569-1709 kcal/day.
Diet: fruits, leaves and flowers.
What they are called in a Group: troop.

The Deciduous Animals

Mallee Fowl *(Leipoocellata)*
Weight: 15k grams.
Height: 90 cm wingspan.
Length: 60 cm.
Speed: 15 km/h running speed
(clumsy in flight).
Number on Planet: less than 10,000
mature individuals; considered
vulnerable.
Number in Litter: 36 eggs (chicks).
Life Span: 25-30 years.
Location: Australia.
Calories: ~1,200-3,500 kcal/day.
Diet: acacia and cassia Seeds along
with various insects, vegetation.
What they are called in a group: flock.

Ruby-crowned Kinglet
(Regulus calendula)
Weight: 7 grams.
Height: 16-18 cm wingspan.
Length: 10 cm.
Speed: 45-50 km/h.
Number on the Planet: 72,000,000.
Number in a litter: 8-12 eggs
(fledglings/ chicks).
Life Span: 3-6 years.
Location: North America.
Calories: 6.2-18.6 kcal/day.
Diet: spiders, insects and their eggs,
weed seeds, fruits, berries of wax
myrtle, small arthropods, ants and
sap.
What they are called in a group: flock.

Greater Long-Eared Bat
(Nyctophilus timoriensis)
Weight: 11-20 grams.
Height: 26-30 cm.
Length: 5-7 cm.
Speed: up to 97 km/h.
Number on the Planet: less than
10,000 mature individuals; considered
vulnerable.
Number in a Litter: 1-2 pups.
Life Span: up to 14 years.
Location: Australia.

Calories: ~6-18 kcal/day.
Diet: moths, beetles, caterpillars.
What they are called in a group:
colony.

Grizzly Bear *(Ursus Arctos)*
Weight: males: 145-363 kg, females:
94-236 kg.
Height: 90-150 cm at the shoulder.
Length: 1.98 m.
Speed: 48-56 km/h.
Number on the Planet: 343,200
bears.
Number in a litter: 1 to 5 cubs.
Life Span: 25 to 30 years.
Location: mountain regions of
Wyoming, Montana, Idaho and
Washington; also found throughout
Western Canada and Alaska.
Calories: ~8,000-20,000 kcal/day.
Diet: salmon, grass, roots, berries,
ground squirrels, insects, deer, elk,
moose and bison.
What they are called in a Group:
sleuth or sloth.

Black Bear *(Ursus anericanus)*
Weight: males: 68-272 kg, females:
40-68 kg.
Height: 0.9 m at the shoulder.
Length: 1.2-1.8 m.
Speed: 48 km/h.
Number on the Planet: 600,000
bears.
Number in a Litter: one to four cubs.
Life Span: 20 to 25 years.
Location: throughout North America.
Calories: ~6,000-20,000 kcal/day.
Diet: plants, insects, small mammals,
carrion and fish.
What they are called in a group:
sleuth/ sloth.

Red-Cockaded Woodpecker
(Picoides borealis)
Weight: 45 g.
Height: 18-20 cm.
Length: 18-20 cm, wingspan 35-38
cm.

The Deciduous Animals

Speed: 0.268 m/sec.
Number on the Planet: 12,500 birds.
Number in a litter: 2 to 5 eggs (fledglings).
Life Span: up to 15 years.
Location: Alabama, Arkansas, Florida, Georgia, Louisiana, Mississippi, North Carolina, South Carolina and Texas.
Calories: ~25-75 kcal/day.
Diet: ants, beetles, wood boring insects, caterpillars, corn ear worms, and seasonal wild fruit.
What they are called in a Group: clan.

Mountain Weasel (Mustela altaica)
Weight: 122-220 g.
Length: 22-29 cm, 11-15 cm tail.
Speed: 29km/h.
Number on the Planet: abundant.
Number in a litter: 1-8 pups.
Life Span: 7-10 years.
Location: mountains of Asia, from Russia, Central Asia to Korea to northern India.
Calories: 37-111 kcal/day.
Diet: voles, pikas, muskrats, ground squirrels, young rabbits, small birds, lizards, frogs, fish, and insects.
What they are called in a Group: pack.

Western Chimpanzee (Pan troglodytes verus)
Weight: males: 43-60 kg, females: 33-47 kg.
Height: 70-100 cm.
Length: 1.25-1.5 m.
Speed: ~up to 40 km/h.
Number on the Planet: 21,000-55,000.
Number in a litter: 1 infant.
Life Span: 40-50 years.
Location: central and west Africa.
Calories: ~1200-7000 kcal/day.
Diet: fruit, Seeds, nuts, flowers, leaves, insects, eggs and other vertebrates.
What they are called in a Group: community.

Eurasian Beaver (Castor fiber)
Weight: 17-32 kg.
Height: 30-40 cm at the shoulder.
Length: 0.79-1.1 m, 30-35 cm tail.
Speed: 8km/h swimming.
Number on the Planet: original population species "near threatened" with declining numbers; subspecies increasing in population.
Number in a litter: 1-5, average 3 pups/kitten.
Life Span: 10-17 average, and up to 35 years.
Location: Norway, France, Poland, Germany, Eastern Europe, Siberia, and other Scandinavian countries.
Calories: 1500-4500 kcal/day.
Diet: hundreds of species of water and river bank plants such as tubers and the rootstocks of myrtles, cattails, and water lilies. Beavers also eat trees. They prefer aspen trees but also eat hazels, black poplars, lime trees, and other softwood barks.
What they are called in a Group: colony.

Cross River Gorilla (Gorilla gorilla diehli)
Weight: 75-160 kg.
Height: 1.3-1.9 m.
Speed: up to 30 km/h in short bursts.
Number on the Planet: 100-300.
Number in a litter: 1 infant.
Life Span: up to 50 years.
Location: Central Africa.
Calories: ~2,500-7,500 kcal/day.
Diet: leaves, fruit, seeds, flowers, roots, herbs, insects and clay.
What they are called in a Group:troop.

Western Lowland Gorilla (Gorilla gorilla gorilla)
Weight: females: 70-140 kg, males: 135-275 kg.
Height: 1.25-1.75 m.
Speed: up to 30 km/h in short bursts.
Number on the Planet: 94,500.
Number in a litter: 1 infant.

Life Span: 30 to 40 years in the wild; 40 to 50 years in captivity.
Location: Central Africa. (southeastern Nigeria and western Cameroon).
Calories: ~3,100-11,100 kcal/day.
Diet: plants, rotten wood, small animals and fleshy fruit.
What they are called in a Group:troop.

Eastern Lowland Gorilla
(Gorilla beringei graueri)
Weight: male: 140-275 kg, female: 70-140 kg.
Height: male: 1.8 m, female: 1.5 m.
Speed: up to 30 km/h in short bursts.
Number on the planet: 16,000.
Number in a Litter: 1 infant
Life Span: up to 30 years.
Location: Central Africa.
Calories: 6,600-19,300 kcal/day.
Diet: leaves, stems and fruit of plants such as bamboo. Eastern lowland gorillas also eat insects and small invertebrates.
What they are called in a group:troop.

Mountain Gorilla
(Gorilla gorilla beringei)
Weight: 135-220 kg.
Height: 122-183 cm.
Speed: up to 30 km/h in short bursts.
Number on the Planet: 600 gorillas.
Number in a litter: 1 infant.
Life Span: up to 50 years.
Location: Rwanda, Zaire and Uganda.
Calories: 6,800-20,400 kcal/day.
Diet: stems, bamboo shoots, fruits, bark and invertebrates.
What they are called in a group:troop.

Northern Bald Eagle (Haliaeetus leucocephalus alascanus)
Weight: 2.7-7.2 kg.
Height: 76-93 cm wingspan.
Length: 76-101 cm.
Speed: up to 160 km/h diving.
Number on the Planet: 80,000 to 110,000.

Number in a litter: 2-3 eggs (eaglets).
Life Span: up to and over 30 years.
Location: contiguous United States and Canada.
Calories: 772-2,316 kcal/day.
Diet: primarily fish but also ducks, rodents, snakes and carrion.
What they are called in a group: pair.

Northern Spotted Owl
(Strix occidentalis caurina)
Weight: 481-963 g.
Height: 43-48 cm wingspan.
Length: 40-50 cm.
Speed: up to 56 km/h.
Number on the Planet: considered threatened, though population estimates are unavailable due to lack of information.
Number in a Litter: 1-2 eggs (owlets).
Life Span: up to 15 + years.
Location: northwest mountains of California, Oregon, Washington and Southwest British Columbia.
Calories: 122-366 kcal/day.
Diet: In the wild rats, white-footed mice, deer mice, red tree mice, small bats, moths, crickets, large beetles and flying squirrels. In captivity, mice and small rats.
What they are called in a group: parliament.

Masked Bobwhite
(Colinus virginianus ridgewayi)
Weight: 140-170 grams.
Height: 25 cm wingspan.
Length: 20 cm.
Speed: run up to 19km/h and fly up to 40 km/h.
Number on the Planet: evaluated as near threatened.
Number in a Litter: 12-15 eggs (chicks).
Life Span: up to 5 years.
Location: Southern Arizona.
Calories: 38-115 kcal/day.
Diet: berries, insects and plants.
What they are called in a Group:bevy.

The Deciduous Animals

Southwestern Willow Flycatcher
(Empidonax traillii extimus)
Weight: 11 grams.
Height: 15 cm wingspan.
Length: 140 mm.
Speed: up to 36 km/h.
Number on the Planet: 900-1000 breeding pairs.
Number in a litter: 3 to 4 eggs (fledglings).
Life Span: 3-4 years.
Location: southwestern United States and Mexico.
Calories: 9-26 kcal/day.
Diet: insects, seeds and grains.
What they are called in a Group: flock.

Indiana Myotis Bat *(Myotis sodalis)*
Weight: 5-8 grams.
Height: 24-26 cm wingspan.
Length: 7-9 cm.
Speed: up to 64 km/h.
Number on the Planet: 13,000.
Number in a litter: 1 pup.
Life Span: 14-15 + years.
Location: Alabama, Arkansas, Georgia, Iowa, Illinois, Indiana, Kansas, Kentucky, Maryland, Michigan, Missouri, Mississippi, New Jersey, New York, North Carolina, Ohio, Oklahoma, Pennsylvania, South Carolina, Tennessee, Vermont, Virginia and West Virginia.
Calories: 3.2-9.6 kcal/day.
Diet: variety of flying insects found along rivers, lakes, and in up land areas.
What they are called in a Group: colony.

Red Panda *(Ailurus fulgens)*
Weight: 5.4-9 kg.
Height: 273-283 mm at the shoulder.
Length: 55 cm.
Speed: up to 40 km/h in short bursts.
Number on the Planet: less than 2,500 mature individuals; considered endangered.

Number in a litter: 1 to 4 cubs.
Life Span: 8-15 + years.
Location: Bhutan, China, India, Laos, Myanmar and Nepal.
Calories: 602-1,806 kcal/day.
Diet: bamboo shoots, leaves, grasses, roots, fruits, lichen and acorns. They also eat insects, eggs, young birds and small rodents.
What they are called in a Group: usually solitary.

Southern Pudu *(pudu pudu)*
Weight: 7.5-13 kg.
Height: 35-38 cm at the shoulder.
Length: 70-83 cm.
Speed: up to 64 km/h.
Number on the Planet: less than 10,000 mature individuals.
Number in a litter: 1-2 fawns.
Life Span: 8-10 years.
Location: ranges from southern Chile, southwestern Argentina, southern Columbia, northern Ecuador, and the Galapagos Islands.
Calories: 800-2,400 kcal/day.
Diet: leaves, flowers, fruit and buds, and seeds.
What they are called in a group: herd.

Lange's Metalmark Butterfly
(Apodemia morms langei)
Weight: 14-56 g.
Length: 2.4-3.8 cm wingspan.
Speed: 0.65 m/s.
Number on the Planet: ~1,000.
Number in a Litter: 1 larva (one/year).
Life Span: up to 2 weeks as adults.
Location: Antioch Dunes National Wildlife Refuge, California, and San Joaquin River.
Calories: 1.6-4.8 kcal/day.
Diet: buckwheat (larval food plant), butterweed and snake nectar.
What they are called in a group: swarm/ rabble.

The Deciduous Animals

Schaus Swallowtail *(Heraclides Aristodemus ponceanus)*
Weight: 30-90 g.
Length: 10-13 cm wingspan.
Speed: can stop mid-air and fly backwards (less than 1m/s).
Number on the Planet:700-850 adults.
Number in a Litter: several hundred.
Life Span: ~3 days.
Location: South Miami & Lower Matecumbe Key, Florida.
Calories: 2.4-7.2 kcal/day.
Diet: torch wood & cheese shrub, blue porter weed sea grape, wild sage, wild coffee, and guava nectars.
What they are called in a group: swarm/ rabble.

Indo-Chinese Tiger
(Panthera tigris corbetti)
Weight: 130-230 kg.
Height: 76-103 cm at the shoulder.
Length: 2.74 m.
Speed: up to 60 km/h.
Number on the Planet: 1227-1785.
Number in a litter: 2-4 cubs.
Life Span: 10-15 years.
Location: Southeast Asia.
Calories: 6,879-20,639 kcal/day.
Diet: wild pigs, cattle, deer, smaller mammals and birds.
What they are called in a Group: usually solitary.

Sumatran Tiger
(Panthera tigris sumatrae)
Weight: 75-140 kg.
Height: 60 cm at the shoulder.
Length: 2.5 m.
Speed: up to 56 km/h.
Number on the Planet: 400-500.
Number in a litter: 2-4 cubs.
Life Span: 10-20 years.
Location: western Indonesia.
Calories: 4,673-14,021 kcal/day.
Diet: wild pig, wild cattle, deer.
What they are called in a Group: streak; usually solitary.

Siberian Tiger
(Panthera tigris altaica)
Weight: 100-181 kg.
Height: up to 1 m at the shoulder.
Length: 3 m.
Speed: up to 60 km/h.
Number on the Planet: 360-406.
Number in a litter: 2-4 cubs.
Life Span: 20-25 years.
Location: far-eastern Asia.
Calories: 5,713-17,139 kcal/day.
Diet: deer and wild boar.
What they are called in a Group: streak; usually solitary.

Bengal Tiger *(Panthera tigris tigris)*
Weight: 110-220 kg.
Height: 0.9m at the shoulder.
Length: 2.4-2.9 m.
Speed: up to 60 km/h.
Number on the Planet: 3176-4556.
Number in a litter: 2-4 cubs.
Life Span: up to 15 + years.
Location: Indian subcontinent.
Calories: 6,445-19,335 kcal/day.
Diet: Rabbits, water buffalo, deer, goats, wild boar, gaur, peacocks and can climb trees to hunt primates.
What they are called in a Group: streak; usually solitary.

South China Tiger
(Panthera tigris amoyensis)
Weight: 110-150 kg.
Height: 95-110 cm at the shoulder.
Length: 2.3-2.5 m.
Speed: up to 50 km/h.
Number on the Planet: 20-30.
Number in a litter: 2-4 cubs.
Life Span: 15-20 years.
Location: China.
Calories: 5,389-16,169 kcal/day.
Diet: undulates.
What they are called in a Group: streak; usually solitary.

The Deciduous Animals

Western Screech Owl
(Megascops kennicottii)
Weight: 111-156 g.
Height: 54-56cm wingspan.
Length: 21-23 cm.
Speed: up to 45 km/h.
Number on the Planet: 740,000.
Number in a litter: 2-7 eggs (owlets).
Life Span: average 13 years.
Location: western North America.
Calories: 34-103 kcal/day.
Diet: small mammals, insects, snakes, lizards, frogs, small birds, crayfish, scorpions, ducks, pheasants and quail.
What they are called in a Group: parliament.

Mandrill *(Mandrillus Sphinx)*
Weight: 30 kg males, 15 kg females.
Height: ~50cm at the shoulder.
Length: 1 m.
Speed: up to 40 km/h in short bursts.
Number on the Planet: less than 10,000 mature individuals; considered vulnerable.
Number in a Litter: 1 infant.
Life Span: up to 46 years, but average around 25.
Location: tropical rainforests of west Africa.
Calories: 1,470-4,411 kcal/day.
Diet: plants, insects, smaller animals.
What they are called in a group:troop.

Domestic Rabbit
(Oryctolagus cuniculus)
Weight: 1-7 kg.
Length: 38-50 cm.
Speed: up to 50 km/h in short bursts.
Number on the Planet: abundant (on pet market and also as "pests" in nature).
Number in a Litter: 5-6 bunnies.
Life Span: 5-10 years.
Location: exists on every continent except Asia and Antarctica.
Calories: 432-1,297 kcal/day.

Diet: hay, fresh vegetables, pellets, and constant water supply.
What they are called in a group: herd.

Barn Owl *(Tyto alba)*
Weight: 396-708 g.
Height: 35 cm wingspan.
Length: 33-38 cm.
Speed: 14 km/h.
Number on the Planet: 4,900,000.
Number in a litter: 4-7 eggs (owlets).
Life Span: average 2 years.
Location: every continent but Antarctica.
Calories: 99-299 kcal/day.
Diet: mice, voles, shrews, young rabbits, birds, bats, frogs, large insects, small birds.
What they are called in a Group: parliament.

Roosevelt Elk
(Cervus canandensis roosevelti)
Weight: 450-591 kg.
Height: 1.5 m at the shoulder.
Length: 2.4 m.
Speed: up to 72 km/h.
Number on the Planet: approximately 1,200 mature individuals.
Number in a Litter: 1 calf.
Life Span: average 10-13, up to 20 years.
Location: Pacific Northwest.
Calories: 15,256-45,768 kcal/day.
Diet: weeds and grasses, shrubs, huckleberry, wild berry, vine maple.
What they are called in a group: herd.

Golden-Cheeked Warbler
(Dendroica chrysoparia)
Weight: 7-15 g.
Height: 20 cm wingspan.
Length: 11-14 cm.
Speed: up to 40 km/h.
Number on the Planet: 2200-4600.
Number in a Litter: 3-4 eggs (chicks).
Life Span: 2-10 years.
Location: for nesting Edwards Plateau and Palo Pinto County in Central

Texas. Also found in Mexico, Central America.
Calories: 8.6-26 kcal/day.
Diet: insects and spiders found on leaves and bark of oaks and other trees.
What they are called in a group: flock.

Barred Owl (Strix Varia)
Weight: 617-779 grams.
Height: 96-127 cm wingspan.
Length: 40-60 cm.
Speed: 20-30 mph.
Number on the Planet: 560,000 mature individuals.
Number in a litter:2 to 4 eggs (owlets).
Life Span: 10-25 years.
Location: widespread throughout North America from Florida to southern Canada on the eastern part and moving westward in Northern America. Also, parts of central America.
Calories: 119-357 kcal/day.
Diet: rats, mice, voles, chipmunks, lizards, frogs, fish, birds, large insects and quails.
What they are called in a group: parliament.

Great Horned Owl (Budo virginianus)
Weight: 900-1800 grams.
Height: 91-152 cm wingspan.
Length: 46-63 cm.
Speed: up to 64 km/h.
Number on the Planet: widespread and frequent.
Number in a Litter: 2-4 eggs.
Life Span: 29-38 years in captivity and 13 years in the wild.
Location: throughout northern tree-line in North America and in Central and South America.
Calories: 156-468 kcal/day.
Diet: rabbits, hares, rodents, squirrels, minks, skunks, raccoons, armadillos, porcupines, dogs and cats, turkeys, pigeons, young alligators, turtles,
snakes, crows, woodpeckers, other owls, lizards, frogs, toads, swans ducks, salamanders, shrews, porcupines, large insect, spiders, and crayfish.
What they are called in a group: parliament; usually solitary.

Gyrfalcon (Falco rusticolus)
Weight: 800-2100 grams.
Height: 122 cm wingspan.
Length: 48-63 cm.
Speed: up to 160 km/h.
Number on the Planet: 10,000-100,000 mature individuals.
Number in a litter: 3-5 eggs (chicks).
Life Span: up to 25 years.
Location: parts of Alaska, Canada, Greenland, Scandinavia, and Siberia.
Calories: 211-634 kcal/day.
Diet: birds and small mammals.
What they are called in a group: cast.

Visayan Spotted Deer (Cervus Alfredi)
Weight: 40-60 kg.
Height: 60-80 cm at the shoulder.
Length: 120-130 cm.
Speed: up to 50 km/h.
Number on the Planet: only a few hundred in the wild.
Number in Litter: 1-2 fawns.
Life Span: ~12-17 years.
Location: Panay and Negros islands which are located in the Visayan Archipelago.
Calories: 2,600-7,900 kcal/day.
Diet: grasses and other plant-life.
What they are called in a Group: herd.

Harris's Hawk (Parabuteo unicintus)
Weight: 0.68-1.13 kg.
Height: 91-121 cm wingspan.
Length: 45-60 cm.
Speed: up to 140 km/h.
Number on the Planet: 390,000.
Number in a Litter: 2-4 eggs (eyas).
Life Span: 11-15 + years.

The Deciduous Animals

Location: southwestern United States through Central America and into drier habitats in South America.
Calories: 144-434 kcal/day.
Diet: small mammals, birds, and retiles.
What they are called in a group: cast.

Red-Tailed Hawk
(Buteo Jamacicensis)
Weight: 1.8 kg.
Height: 1.2 m wingspan.
Length: 64 cm.
Speed: 120 km/h.
Number on the Planet: 100,000-1,000,000.
Number in a Litter: 1-3 eggs (eyas).
Life Span: up to 15 years.
Location: In forests near open country. Nests are usually built near the edge of a stream, lake, or field.
Calories: 242-727 kcal/day.
Diet: small mammals that include mice, voles, shrews, moles, squirrels, chipmunks, rats, rabbits, opossums, muskrats, cats, skunks, and bats.
What they are called in a group: cast.

Spectacled Owl
(Pulsatrix perspicillata)
Weight: 595-935 grams.
Height: 43-48 cm wingspan.
Length: 40-48 cm.
Speed: up to 40 km/h.
Number on the Planet: considered abundant.
Number in a litter: 2 eggs (owlets).
Life Span: up to 25 years.
Location: southern Mexico, Paraguay, southern Brazil and northern Argentina.
Calories: 127-382 kcal/day.
Diet: insects, tree frogs, reptiles, birds, small mammals and crabs.
What they are called in a Group: parliament.

North American Porcupine
(Erethizon dorsatum)
Weight: 3-18 kg.
Height: 30 cm at the shoulder.
Length: 95-129 cm.
Speed: 3 km/h.
Number on the Planet: not threatened or endangered.
Number in a litter: 1 pup.
Life Span: 10-25 years in captivity; 5-6 years in the wild.
Location: North American desert regions, the entire west, and north to Canada.
Calories: 816-2,449 kcal/day.
Diet: bark, grasses, buds, twigs, roots, leaves, flowers, seeds and other vegetation.
What they are called in a Group: usually solitary.

Gray Wolf *(Canis lupus)*
Weight: 20-75 kg.
Height: 60-90 cm at the shoulder.
Length: 1.17-1.3 m.
Speed: 56 km/h.
Number on the Planet: ~12,500 mature individuals.
Number in a Litter: 2-14 pups.
Life Span: 5-15 years.
Location: Michigan's Upper Peninsula, northern Minnesota, Wisconsin, Alaska, Canada, Europe, Middle East, and Asia.
Calories: 2,533-7,599 kcal/day
Diet: eat most meat without differentiating.
What they are called in a group: pack.

Giant Panda
(Ailuropoda melanoleuca)
Weight: 80-125 kg.
Height: 65-70 cm at the shoulder.
Length: 1.5-1.8 m.
Speed: up to 40 km/h in short bursts.
Number on the Planet: 1,600.
Number in a litter: 1-3 cubs.
Life Span: 20 years.

Location: provinces of Sichuan, Gansu, and Shanxi in the central part of China.
Calories: 4;500-13,529 kcal/day.
Diet: bamboo.
What they are called in a Group: usually solitary.

European Red Squirrel
(Sciurus vulgaris)
Weight: 350 g.
Length: 36.5c m (including tail).
Speed: up to 22.5 km/h.
Number on the Planet: not quantified, though considered threatened (high in numbers but beginning to decline rapidly).
Number in a Litter: 1-10 (average 3-7) pups/ kittens.
Life Span: 4-6 years.
Location: distributed from northern Portugal to southern Norway.
Calories: 63-191 kcal/day.
Diet: mostly seeds, acorns, fungi, chestnuts, hazelnuts and beech flowers.
What they are called in a group: dray.

Kirtland's Warbler
(Dendroica kirtlandii)
Weight: 14 g.
Height: 20-21cm wingspan.
Length: 12-14 cm.
Speed: 29-38 km/h.
Number on the Planet: over 1,000 singing males ("singing males" used to gauge population fluctuations).
Number in a Litter: 4-5 eggs (chicks).
Life Span: average 2 and up to 9 years.
Location: Michigan's northern lower and upper peninsulas, Wisconsin, Ontario, winter in Bahamas and in the Turks, Caicos and Hispaniola islands.
Calories: 10.4-31.2 kcal/day.
Diet: caterpillars, butterflies, moths, flies, grasshoppers, and blueberries.
What they are called in a group: flock.

Woodland Caribou
(Rangifer tarandus caribou)
Weight: 115-180 kg.
Height: 1.2 m at the shoulder.
Length: 1.8 m.
Speed: up to 80 km/h.
Number on the Planet: less than 100 mature individuals.
Number in a Litter: 1 calf.
Life Span: 10-15 years.
Location: Canadian forests.
Calories: 5,925-17,776 kcal/day.
Diet: lichens, grasses, leaves and other plant material.
What they are called in a group: herd.

Seychelles Scops-Owl
(Otus insularis)
Weight: 1-1.3 kg.
Height: 20 cm wingspan.
Length: 17 cm.
Speed: up to 50 km/h.
Number on the Planet: 360.
Number in a Litter: 1 egg (owlet).
Life Span: 20-60 years (in captivity).
Location: Highland Forests of Mahe, The islands of the Seychelles archipelago.
Calories: 173-591 kcal/day.
Diet: insects, spiders, frogs, and small lizards.
What they are called in a group: parliament.

Comoro Black Flying Fox
(Pteropus livingstonii)
Weight: 700 grams.
Height: 1.4 m wingspan.
Length: 30 cm.
Speed: up to 60 km/h.
Number on the Planet: 1,200.
Number in a Litter: 1 pup.
Life Span: 12-22 years.
Location: Comoros Islands.
Calories: 107-321 kcal/day.
Diet: forest fruits.
What they are called in a group: usually solitary.

The Prairie Animals

American Toad
(*Bufo americanus*)
Weight: 27-53 g.
Length: 50-100 mm.
Speed: 0.10-0.30 m/s.
Number on the Planet:no special
conservation status, as they are
still common in most of their
range. Some populations have
declined in recent years, possibly
due to pollution. American toads
are the most widespread toad
species in North America.
Number in a litter: 4,000-8,000
eggs (tadpoles/ polliwogs).
Life Span: 10 years on average
and up to 36 + years.
Location: throughout large
portions of North America; from
northern Chihuahua in Mexico,
northward to James Bay in
Canada and eastward from the
Imperial Valley of California and
the Columbia River Valley in
Washington and Oregon to the
Atlantic coast from Florida to
southern Quebec.
Calories: 2.2-6.7 kcal/day.
Diet: insects, spiders, earthworms,
snails and slugs.
What they are called in a Group:
knot.

American Badger
(*Taxidea taxus*)
Weight: 4-12 kg.
Length: 420-720 mm, tail 100-150
mm.
Speed: 16-24 km/h.
Number on the Planet: several
hundred thousand.
Number in a litter: 1-5 (kits/ cubs).
Life Span: 8-10 years and up to
26 years.
Location: western two-thirds of the
United States, and extends into

Canada in the North and Mexico
in the South.
Calories: 665-1,997 kcal/day.
Diet: ground squirrels, mice,
pocket gophers, kangaroo rats,
prairie dogs, cottontail rabbits,
marmots, chipmunks, deer mice,
voles, young skunks, larvae of
beetles, bees, wasps and hornets,
grasshoppers, crickets, beetles
and caterpillars.
What they are called in a Group:
cete.

Black-footed ferret
(*Mustela nigripes*)
Weight: 0.7-1.1 kg.
Length: 46-60 cm.
Speed: 8-11 km/h.
Number on the Planet: ~500.
Number in a litter: 3-4 (kits).
Life Span: average 3-4 years and
up to 12 years.
Location: once lived in the
southern and eastern Rockies and
in the Great Plains (now exists
almost solely in captivity).
Calories: 130-390 kcal/day.
Diet: prairie dogs, mice and small
animals.
What they are called in a Group:
business.

American Bison (*Bison bison*)
Weight: 408-1,000 kg.
Height: 2 m at the shoulder.
Length: 1.5-2 m.
Speed: up to 48 km/h.
Number on the Planet: 250,000.
Number in a litter: 1 (calf).
Life Span: 18-22 years.
Location: parts of Canada and
western United States.
Calories: 9,600-57,400 kcal/day.
Diet: grasses and sedges.
What they are called in a Group:
herd.

The Prairie Animals

Black-tailed jack rabbit
(Lepus californicus)
Weight: 1.5-4 kg.
Length: 47-112 cm.
Speed: up to 56 km/h.
Number on the Planet: population densities often reach 470 animals per square km, with densities as high as 1500 animals per square km recorded.
Number in a litter: 1-6 (bunny).
Life Span: 5-7 years.
Location: from the southwestern United States, east into Missouri and north to Washington.
Calories: 700-2,000 kcal/day.
Diet: grasses, twigs, herbs, young bark, leaves, roots, woods, stems and fruits.
What they are called in a Group: colony.

Black-tailed Prairie Dog
(Cynomys ludovicianus)
Weight: 0.68-1.36 kg.
Height: 7.6-10.1 cm.
Length: 7.6-12.7 cm.
Speed: up to 56 km/h (for short periods).
Number on the Planet: several million.
Number in a litter: 3-8 (pups).
Life Span: 3-5 years and up to 8.5 years.
Location: western United States, from Montana, south to Mexico.
Calories: 240-720 kcal/day.
Diet: grasses, roots, leaves and flowers.
What they are called in a Group: coterie/ town.

Bobcat (Felis rufus)
Weight: 4-15kg
Height: 45-58cm
Length: 63.5-104cm
Speed: 48km/h
Number on the Planet: 725,000-1,020,000.

Number in a litter: 1-6 (cubs).
Life Span: 12-13 years and up to 30 years.
Location: southern Canada to northern Mexico, throughout the Southwest of North America.
Calories: 760-2,275 kcal/day.
Diet: rabbits, rodents, birds, bats and adult deer.
What they are called in a Group: usually solitary.

Bull Snake
(Pituophis melanoleucus)
Weight: average 665 g.
Length: 1.25-2.54 m.
Speed: less than 13 km/h.
Number on the Planet: not available.
Number in a litter: 3-20 eggs (hatchlings).
Life Span: up to 30 years.
Location: throughout prairies of North America.
Calories: 15-88 kcal/day (or up to 1,200 kcal once every 1-2 weeks).
Diet: mice, gophers, ground squirrels, rabbits, ground-nesting birds and their eggs.
What they are called in a Group: bed/ nest.

Burrowing Owl
(Athene cunicularia)
Weight: 170.1-214 g.
Height: wingspan 50.8-61cm
Length: 21.6-28 cm.
Speed: 19 km/h.
Number on the Planet: ~ 100,000, but numbers are declining and nearing endangered status. Locally frequent, but otherwise rare.
Number in a litter: 6-9, up to 12 eggs (owlets/ fledglings).
Life Span: 9-10 + years.
Location: all states west of the Mississippi valley, western and midwestern states, and Florida.

The Prairie Animals

They are also found in Mexico, Central and South America.
Calories: 370-1,112 kcal/day.
Diet: small mammals, especially mice, rats, gophers, and ground squirrels, are also important food items. Reptiles and amphibians, scorpions, young cottontail rabbits, bats, and birds, such as sparrows and horned larks.
What they are called in a Group: parliament.

California condor
(Gymnogyps californianus)
Weight: 10 kg.
Height: 2.9 m wingspan.
Length: 45 inches.
Speed: 56-64 km/h.
Number on the Planet: 289.
Number in a litter: 1 egg (chick).
Life Span: up to 60 years.
Location: coastal mountains of south-central California and the Grand Canyon area of northern Arizona.
Calories: 877-2,631 kcal/day.
Diet: medium and large-sized dead mammals like cattle, sheep, deer, and horses in any state of decay.
What they are called in a Group: flock.

American Burying Beetle
(Nicrophorus americanus)
Weight: ~1 g.
Length: 1.8-3 cm.
Speed: ~0.5 m/s.
Number on the Planet: ~ 1,000.
Number in a litter: 10-30 eggs (larva).
Life Span: one season (less than a year).
Location: Nebraska, Rhode Island, Oklahoma, South Dakota, Kansas, and Arkansas. Ohio, and Massachusetts (where attempts are being made to re-introduce the species).
Calories: 0.63-1.9 kcal/day.
Diet: carrion and fly larvae.
What they are called in a Group: colony.

Common snipe
(Gallinago gallinago)
Weight: 170-226 g.
Height: 39-45 cm wingspan.
Length: 23-28 cm.
Speed: up to 12 km/h.
Number on the Planet: >5,400,000 - 7,500,000.
Number in a litter: 3-4 eggs (chicks).
Life Span: 4-5 years.
Location: North America, South America, Asia and Europe.
Calories: 129-386 kcal/day.
Diet: larvae, insects and crustaceans.
What they are called in a Group: flock.

Coyote (Canis latrans)
Weight: 9-23 kg.
Height: 31-51cm at the shoulder.
Length: 101-152 cm.
Speed: up to 64 km/h.
Number on the Planet: common and widespread.
Number in a litter: 2-12 (pup).
Life Span: average 6-10, up to 18 years.
Location: North America (mainly deserts of the Southwest).
Calories: 1,120-3,360 kcal/day.
Diet: small mammals, insects, reptiles, fruit and carrion.
What they are called in a Group: band.

Cougar (Felis concolor)
Weight: 90 + kg.
Height: 56-79 cm at the shoulder.
Length: 2.5 m.
Speed: 50 km/h.

The Prairie Animals

Number on the Planet: less than 2,500 mature individuals; considered endangered.
Number in a litter: 1-6 (cubs).
Life Span: 15-20 years.
Location: Canada, British Colombia and most coastal islands in North American northwest as well as throughout most of North America.
Calories: 2,000-12,200 kcal/day.
Diet: deer, bighorn sheep, mountain goats, mice, beaver and snowshoe hares.
What they are called in a Group: clowder.

White-tailed Deer
(Odocoileus virginianus)
Weight: 90-180 kg.
Height: 0.9-1 m at the shoulder.
Length: 150-200 cm.
Speed: 48 km/h.
Number on the Planet: 8-15 + million.
Number in a litter: 1-3 (fawns).
Life Span: average 2-3 years, and up to 20 years.
Location: most of North and Central America, northern South America.
Calories: 2,800-16,600 kcal/day.
Diet: leaves, grass, acorns, other plant-life.
What they are called in a Group: herd.

Common Green Darner Dragonfly (*Anax junius*)
Weight: ~1 g.
Height: 11.4 cm wingspan.
Length: 7.6 cm.
Speed: up to 56 km/h.
Number on the Planet: most abundant and widespread dragonfly species in North America.
Number in a litter: thousands of eggs (nymphs).

Life Span: 4-7 months.
Location: North America, West-Indies and South America.
Calories: up to 300 insects/day (0.63-1.9 kcal/day).
Diet: wasps, butterflies, mosquitoes, and other flying insects.
What they are called in a Group: swarm.

Prairie Falcon
(Falco mexicanus)
Weight: 420-1,100 g.
Height: 90-113 cm wingspan.
Length: 37-47 cm.
Speed: 72 km/h.
Number on the Planet: over 5,000 pairs.
Number in a litter: 3-6 eggs (chicks).
Life Span: average 2-3 years and up to 20 years.
Location: southwestern Canada, western United States, Baja California, and northern Mexico.
Calories: 126-760 kcal/day.
Diet: birds, reptiles, insects and ground squirrels).
What they are called in a Group: cast.

Eastern Cottontail
(Sylvilagus floridanus)
Weight: 0.9-1.8 kg.
Length: 400-490 mm.
Speed: Up to 24 km/h.
Number on the Planet: extremely common throughout their ranges.
Number in a litter: average 4-5 and up to 9 (kit/ kitten/ bunny).
Life Span: up to 3 years.
Location: most eastern United States except for New England.
Calories: 175-526 kcal/day.
Diet: grasses, clover, bark, twigs, fruit and vegetables.
What they are called in a Group: usually solitary.

The Prairie Animals

Elk *(Cervus canadensis)*
Weight: av. 225-315 kg, recorded up to 591 kg.
Height: 1.3-1.5 m at the shoulder.
Length: 2-2.4 m.
Speed: 45-47 km/h long distance, 56-61 km/h sprints.
Number on the Planet: over 1 million.
Number in a litter: 1 (2-3 rarely) (calves).
Life Span: av.10-15, up to over 20yrs.
Location: North America and regions above the Arctic Circle.
Calories: 4,600-28,000 kcal/day.
Diet: various grasses, bark, acorns, leaves, tender seedlings, twigs, saplings, berries and mushrooms.
What they are called in a Group: herd.

Ferruginous Hawk
(Buteo regalis)
Weight: 1-2 kg.
Height: 0.9-1.2 m wingspan.
Length: 56-61 cm.
Speed: ~48-64 km/h.
Number on the Planet: 2,800-3,400 breeding pairs.
Number in a litter: 3-5 eggs (eyas).
Life Span: up to 15-20 years.
Location: throughout western North America.
Calories: 211-634 kcal/day.
Diet: squirrels, voles, rabbits, gophers and rats.
What they are called in a Group: cast/ kettle though ferruginous hawks pair for reproduction).

Plains Garter Snake
(Thamnophis radix)
Weight: average 250 g.
Length: 36-109 cm.
Speed: ~17 km/h.

Number on the Planet: exact numbers unknown, though it is estimated between 10,000-20,000 mature individuals.
Number in a litter: 10-70 eggs (hatchlings).
Life Span: 3-10 years.
Location: throughout dry, prairie regions of North America.
Calories: 10-45 kcal/day.
Diet: earthworms, fish, frogs, toads, salamanders, mice, carrion and birds eggs.
What they are called in a Group: nest.

Short-eared Owl
(Asio flammeus)
Weight: 206-475 g.
Height: av.105-107 cm wingspan.
Length: 33-43 cm.
Speed: 32-48 km/h.
Number on the Planet: ~1,000 pairs worldwide. Fluctuations in the population, is most likely due to the cyclical variation in the population of voles, making it difficult to determine long-term trends.
Number in a litter: 4-14 eggs (average 5-7) (owlets/ fledglings).
Life Span: up to 13 years.
Location: occur widely in the Old World, in Iceland, the Hawaiian Islands, Galapagos Islands, and North and South America.
Calories: ~10 kcal/day.
Diet: meadow voles, deer mice, shrews, ground squirrels, pocket gophers, pocket mice, moles, rats, bats, rabbits, muskrats, shorebirds, terns, small gulls and seabirds, Horned Larks, meadowlarks, blackbirds, pipits, roaches, grasshoppers, beetles, katydids, and caterpillars.
What they are called in a Group: pair(reproduction)/ flock/ parliament.

The Prairie Animals

Great Basin Gopher Snake
(Pituophis catenifer deserticola)
Weight: 270-550 g.
Length: up to 1.8 m.
Speed: "slow-moving" (under 10 km/h).
Number on the Planet: exact number unknown; considered threatened.
Number in a litter: 2-24 eggs (hatchlings).
Life Span: ~10 years.
Location: Southern British Columbia, Canada and throughout much of western United States.
Calories: eat once every 10 days (average 6 Kcal/day).
Diet: small rodents, rabbits, lizards and other small mammals.
What they are called in a Group: nest.

Slant-faced Grasshopper
(Syrbula admirabilis)
Weight: 223-376 mg.
Length: 25-39 mm.
Speed: 2-9 km/h.
Number on the Planet: hundreds of thousands (50/ square mile in region).
Number in a litter: 2-10, average 5 eggs (nymphs).
Life Span: one season (about 6 months).
Location: found in prairies from Iowa to Pennsylvania, south to Florida, west to Arizona, and into Mexico.
Calories: 0.5-1.55 kcal/day.
Diet: big bluestem *(Adropogen gerardii)* and other grasses.
What they are called in a Group: swarm.

Gray Wolf *(Canis lupus)*
Weight: 25-52 kg.
Height: 66-81cm at the shoulder.
Length: 1.2-1.5 m.
Speed: up to 70 km/h.

Number on the Planet: ~212,500.
Number in a litter: 4-7 (pups/ whelps).
Life Span: 8-12 years.
Location: Alaska, Idaho, Michigan, Minnesota, Montana, Wisconsin and Wyoming.
Calories: 2,100-6,500 kcal/day.
Diet: deer, elk, beavers and rabbits.
What they are called in a Group: pack.

California Ground Squirrel
(Otospermophilus beecheyi)
Weight: 450g-1 kg.
Length: 30 cm, 15 cm tail (45 cm total length).
Speed: average 3.63 m/s.
Number on the Planet: overly abundant (considered pests).
Number in a litter: 3-15, average 4-5 (pups/ kits/ kittens).
Life Span: average 3-4 years, up to 6 years in the wild, 10 years in captivity.
Location: central Washington through western Oregon, California and into northern Baja California.
Calories: 110-660 kcal/day.
Diet: seeds, fruits, acorns, roots, mushrooms, grasshoppers, crickets, and caterpillars.
What they are called in a Group: dray.

Killdeer (*Charadrius vociferous*)
Weight: 75-128 g.
Height: 46-48 cm wingspan.
Length: 20-28 cm.
Speed: up to 89 km/h.
Number on the Planet: 1,000,000.
Number in a litter: 4-6 eggs (chicks).
Life Span: 10-11years.
Location: Central and South America, Alaska to Newfoundland and British Columbia and Utah.

Calories: 46-138 kcal/day.
Diet: insects, berries and crustaceans.
What they are called in a Group: flock.

Convergent Lady Beetle (Ladybird Beetle)
(Hippodamia convergens)
Weight: up to 2 g.
Length: 4-7 mm.
Speed: up to 24 km/h.
Number on the Planet: overly-abundant (considered pests)—millions+.
Number in a litter: 200-1000 eggs (larva).
Life Span: average, several months, up to 3 years.
Location: mainly North America from southern California to South America.
Calories: 50 aphids a day (0.19-0.56 kcal/day).
Diet: aphids (cotton, pea, melon, cabbage, potato, green peach, and corn leaf aphids). Small insect larvae, insect eggs, mites, nectar, and honeydew.
What they are called in a Group: colony.

Prairie Horned Lark
(Eremophila alpestris)
Weight: 31-32 g.
Height: 31-36 cm wingspan.
Length: 18-20 cm.
Speed: 35-45 km/h.
Number on the Planet: 1,000-2,000 pairs; considered threatened.
Number in a litter: average 4, 2-6 eggs (fledglings/chicks).
Life Span: 8 + years.
Location: North America; from Alaska and Canada, south to West Virginia, North Carolina, Missouri, Kansas and coastal Texas.

Calories: 19-57 kcal/day.
Diet: weed seeds, waste grains, caterpillars, ants, wasps, spiders, grasshoppers, and leafhoppers.
What they are called in a Group: flock.

Long-billed Curlew
(Numenius americanus)
Weight: 0.5-0.8 kg.
Height: 90-101cm wingspan.
Length: 45-66 cm.
Speed: 80 km/h.
Number on the Planet: 20,000.
Number in a litter: 4 eggs (chicks).
Life Span: up to 10 years.
Location: Southern Canada to Northern California, Utah, Northern New Mexico and Texas.
Calories: 96-278 kcal/day.
Diet: grasshoppers, beetles, amphibians, crickets, small crustaceans, mollusks, berries and seeds.
What they are called in a Group: flock.

Meadow Vole
(Microtus pennsylvanicus)
Weight: average 35.6 g.
Length: 128-195 mm.
Speed: 8-9.7 km/h.
Number on the Planet: very abundant. At population peak and in preferred habitat, vole populations may be as high as 400 voles/ acre or around 200 voles for an area as large as an average home lot.
Number in a litter: 2-9, 6-7 average (pups).
Life Span: ~1year.
Location: widespread in North America; east to west range continuous from central Alaska to the Atlantic coast. South of the Canadian border western limit is Rocky mountains, found as far

south as New Mexico and Georgia.

Calories: 65-194 kcal/day.

Diet: fresh grass, sedges, herbs, seeds, grains, bark and roots of shrubs and small trees, tubers and bulbs, cranberries and other types of fruit, flesh (sometimes feeding on new born young).

What they are called in a Group: labor.

Monarch Butterfly
(Danaus plexippus)

Weight: 0.27-0.75 g.

Length: 8.6-12.4 cm wingspan.

Speed: 10.8 km/h.

Number on the Planet: hundreds of millions.

Number in a litter: 400 eggs (larva).

Life Span: 2weeks - 9months.

Location: found on all continents save polar regions.

Calories: 0.2 kcal/day.

Diet: milkweed.

What they are called in a Group: swarm/ rabble.

Northern Grasshopper Mouse
(Onychomys leucogaster)

Weight: 27-52 g.

Height: 17-25 mm.

Length: 130-190mm.

Speed: 12 km/h.

Number on the Planet: unknown, restricted distribution.

Number in a litter: 2-6 (pups).

Life Span: up to only a few months in the wild, longest in captivity 4 years.

Location: Central and southwestern United States to northern Mexico.

Calories: 12-37 kcal/day.

Diet: insects, worms and smaller mice.

What they are called in a Group: horde.

Opossum (Didelphis virginiana)

Weight: 0.3-6.4 kg.

Length: 35-94 cm.

Speed: 11.2 km/h.

Number on the Planet: abundant.

Number in a litter: average 5-8, up to 14 (joeys).

Life Span: 2-4 years.

Location: found in most of the United States east of the Rocky Mountains and on the West Coast. Also found in Mexico, Central America and British Columbia, Canada.

Calories: 242-728 kcal/day.

Diet: insects, dead animals, birds and their eggs, frogs, snails, and earthworms. Fruits and berries and human leftovers thrown in the trash.

What they are called in a Group: usually solitary.

Greater Prairie Chicken
(Tympanuchus cupido)

Weight: 700-1,200 g.

Length: 350 mm.

Speed: 64 km/h.

Number on the Planet: 459,000.

Number in a litter: 5-17eggs, 10-12average (chicks).

Life Span: 2-8 years.

Location: Central North America.

Calories: 150-450 kcal/day.

Diet: seeds, fruit, green plants and insects.

What they are called in a Group: flock.

White-tailed Prairie dog
(Cynomys leucurus)

Weight: 0.68-1.36 kg.

Height: 7.6-10.1 cm.

Length: 7.6-12.7 cm.

Speed: up to 56 km/h.

Number on the Planet: ~10,000.

Number in a litter: 3-8 (pups).

Life Span: 3-5 years.

The Prairie Animals

Location: central and western Wyoming, northwestern Colorado, northeastern Utah, and south-central Montana.
Calories: 240-720 kcal/day.
Diet: grasses, roots, weeds, forbs and blossoms.
What they are called in a Group: town/ coterie.

Prairie Rattlesnake
(Crotalus viridis)
Weight: 0.5 kg.
Length: 89-114 cm.
Speed: less than 13 km/h.
Number on the Planet: exact number unavailable.
Number in a litter: 4-21 live young (neonates).
Life Span: 20-30 years.
Location: most of the United States west of Texas and the Dakotas, northern Mexico and southwest Canada.
Calories: 12-36 kcal/day.
Diet: mammals, birds (particularly meadow larks), ground nesting bird eggs, mice, young prairie dogs, cottontail rabbits, small reptiles and frogs.
What they are called in a Group: nest/ rhumba.

Prairie Skink
(Eumeces septentrionalis)
Weight: 14 g.
Length: 5-8.5 cm.
Speed: up to 10 km/h in short bursts.
Number on the Planet: less than 2,500 mature individuals; considered endangered.
Number in a litter: 8-10 eggs (hatchlings).
Life Span: 6-20 years.
Location: prairies east of the Rocky Mountains in North America (US and Canada).
Calories: 16-49 kcal/day.

Diet: small invertebrates (spiders, crickets, grasshoppers).
What they are called in a Group: usually solitary.

Pronghorn antelope
(Antilocapra Americana)
Weight: 35-60 kg.
Height: 81-104 cm at the shoulder.
Length: 1.0-1.5 m.
Speed: up to 97 km/h.
Number on the Planet: 500,000.
Number in a litter: 2 (calves).
Life Span: 10-12 years.
Location: southern Saskatchewan and Alberta in Canada to Sonora and Baja California in Mexico. They live on both sides of the Rocky Mountains. The eastern limit of their range is the Missouri River in the United States.
Calories: 2,500-7,600 kcal/day.
Diet: cacti, grasses, forbs.
What they are called in a Group: herd.

Red fox *(Vulpes vulpes)*
Weight: 3.6-6.8 kg.
Height: 35-40 cm at the shoulder.
Length: 90-112 cm.
Speed: up to 48 km/h.
Number on the Planet: 20 million .
Number in a litter: 1-13, average 5 (kit/ cub/ pup).
Life Span: average 3 years, up to 10-12 years.
Location: found throughout Canada, Alaska, almost all of United States, all of Europe and Britain, and almost all of Asia, including Japan, also several populations in North Africa.
Calories: 480-1,450 kcal/day.
Diet: rodents, eastern cottontail rabbits, insects, fruit and carrion.
What they are called in a Group: skulk/ leash.

The Prairie Animals

Red-tailed hawk
(Buteo jamaicensis)
Weight: 800-1,300 g.
Height: 120-141cm wingspan.
Length: 45-65 cm.
Speed: 30 km/h-65 km/h, up to
195 km/h.
Number on the Planet: estimated
to be 8,700.
Number in a litter: 4 eggs (eyas).
Life Span: average 2 years, up to
20-30 years.
Location: western Alaska and
northern Canada to Panama and
the West Indies.
Calories: 162-485 kcal/day.
Diet: rodents, rabbits, pheasant,
grouse, quail, rattle snakes,
copperheads, lizards, carp and
catfish.
What they are called in a Group:
cast/ kettle.

Prairie Shrew *(Sorex haydeni)*
Weight: 4 g.
Length: 8 cm.
Speed: up to 16 km/h.
Number on the Planet: the
population does not appear to be
in decline. Assessed as Least
Concern,
Number in a litter: 3-6 (pups).
Life Span: 1-1.5 years.
Location: Canadian prairies and
mid-western United States.
Calories: 13-38 kcal/day.
Diet: insects, worms, snails, small
mammals and seeds.
What they are called in a Group:
labor.

Striped Skunk
(*Mephitis mephitis*)
Weight: 1.2-5.3 kg.
Length: 575-800 mm.
Speed: 16 km/h.
Number on the Planet: abundant
and are not of any conservation
concern.

Number in a litter: 5-6 (kits).
Life Span: up to 2-3 years in the
wild, 15 years in captivity.
Location: North America, ranging
from central Canada, throughout
the United States, and south into
northern Mexico.
Calories: 340-1,000 kcal/day.
Diet: insects, small mammals,
fish, crustaceans, fruits, grasses,
leaves, buds, grains, nuts, and
carrion.
What they are called in a Group:
usually solitary.

Donkey (*Equus asinus*)
Weight: 250 kg.
Height: 125 cm at the shoulder.
Length: 200 cm, 45 cm tail.
Speed: up to 50 km/h.
Number on the Planet: abundant,
considered a nuisance, pests
(several reduction policies in
effect in the past for lowering their
numbers, especially in the
western United States).
Number in a litter: 1 (foal/colt).
Life Span: 25-30 years, up to 40-
50 years.
Location: native range extends
from Morocco to Somalia and
Mesopotamia to Oman, but they
have now spread all over the
world.
Calories: 8,800-26,400 kcal/day.
Diet: grasses, shrubs and other
plants.
What they are called in a Group:
herd.

Six-spotted Tiger Beetle
(*Cicindela sexuttata*)
Weight: 1 g.
Length: 12-14 mm.
Speed: 8 km/h.
Number on the Planet: population
size unknown but considered
widespread and abundant within
its range.

The Prairie Animals

Number in a litter: 1 egg at a time throughout breeding season (larva).
Life Span: 2 years.
Location: United States, found over much of the eastern and Great Plains states into southeastern Canada.
Calories: 0.1-0.3 kcal/day.
Diet: arthropods; caterpillars, ants and spiders.
What they are called in a Group: swarm.

Western Meadowlark
(Sturnella neglecta)
Weight: ~7 g.
Height: 41 cm wingspan.
Length: 25 cm.
Speed: up to 64 km/h.
Number on the Planet: ~ 32,000,000.
Number in a litter: 4-5 eggs (chicks/ fledglings).
Life Span: ~3-10 years.
Location: across western and central North America to northern Mexico.
Calories: 35-105 kcal/day.
Diet: insects, seeds and berries.
What they are called in a Group: flock.

Western Tiger Swallowtail
(Papilio rutulus)
Weight: 14 g.
Length: 7-10 cm wingspan.
Speed: 19 km/h.
Number on the Planet: generally common in its range.
Number in a litter: 100 eggs (larva).
Life Span: average 2 weeks.
Location: western North America (from eastern British Columbia to eastern North Dakota, and southern New Mexico).
Calories: 5-15 kcal/day.

Diet: leaves of a variety of trees (e.g. cottonwood, willow and quaking aspen trees).
What they are called in a Group: swarm/ rabble.

American Buffalo *(Bison bison)*
Weight: 450-900 kg.
Height: 2 m.
Length: 3 m.
Speed: 62 km/h.
Number on the Planet: 200,000-350,000.
Number in a litter: 1 (calf).
Life Span: 18-22 years, up to 35-40 years.
Location: North American Great Plains and prairie reservations.
Calories: 18,500-55,600 kcal/day.
Diet: grasses and other vegetation (ex. sagebrush).
What they are called in a Group: herd.

Big-Horn Sheep *(Ovis Canadensis)*
Weight: 63-135 kg.
Height: 81-100 cm.
Length: 1.3-1.6 m.
Speed: 24 km/h in the mountains, 48 km/h on flat-ground.
Number on the Planet: 280-1,000.
Number in a litter: 1-2 (lambs).
Life Span: 10-15 years.
Location: ranges from Nevada and California to west Texas and south into Mexico.
Calories: 4,400-13,000 kcal/day.
Diet: grasses, sedges and forbes.
What they are called in a Group: herd.

The Wetland Animals

Mission Blue Butterfly
(Icaricia icarioides missionensis)
Weight: 0.04 g.
Height: 2.5-3 cm wingspan.
Length: 21-33 mm.
Speed: ~8 km/h.
Number on the Planet: declared *endangered* by the Federal Government.
Number in a litter: (from late March to early July) female lays single egg at a time, continuously throughout season (larvae).
Life Span: 1 year.
Location: San Francisco (San Bruno Mountain, San Mateo County).
Calories: 0.01-0,03 kcal/day.
Diet: nectar from perennial lupines.
What they are called in a Group: swarm

Red Wolf (*Canis rufus*)
Weight: 20-40 kg.
Height: 660-790 mm.
Length: 1000-1300 mm, 300-420 mm tail.
Speed: up to 56 km/h.
Number on the Planet: 250 in captivity, 80-100 in the wild.
Number in a litter: average 3-6, up to 12 (pup/ whelp).
Life Span: average 4 years, up to 14.
Location: southeastern Texas and southwestern Louisiana; being reintroduced into North Carolina and Tennessee.
Calories: 1,800-5,400 kcal/day.
Diet: raccoons, white-tailed deer, swamp rabbits, cottontail rabbits, pigs, rice rats, nutria, muskrats and carrion.
What they are called in a Group: pack.

Indian Python
(Python molurus molurus)
Weight: 32-59 kg.
Length: up to 6 m.
Speed: 1.6 km/h.
Number on the Planet: considered an endangered species Fauna and Flora Protection Ordinance (FFPO).
Number in a litter: 20-60 eggs (neonates).
Life Span: 20 + years.
Location: southeast Asia (India).
Calories: 350-1,050 kcal/day (though they may consume a much larger amount all at once and then fast for a long period of time).
Diet: mammals, rodents, birds, insects and fish.
What they are called in a Group: usually solitary.

Yuma Clapper Rail
(Rallus longirostris yumanensis)
Weight: 160-400 g.
Height: 50 cm wingspan.
Length: 35-41 cm.
Speed: 32-48 km/h.
Number on the Planet: less than 1,000.
Number in a litter: 4-12 eggs (chicks).
Life Span: 7-8 years.
Location: marshlands along lower Colorado River, Salton Sea in California, and Salt and Gila Rivers in Arizona.
Calories: 100-300 kcal/day.
Diet: crayfish, fish, bird eggs, frogs, clams and insects.
What they are called in a Group: flock.

Roseate Spoonbill (*Ajaia ajaja*)
Weight: 1.36 kg.
Height: 120 cm wingspan.
Length: 80 cm.
Speed: ~45 km/h.
Number on the Planet:100,000-250;000.
Number in a litter: 2-5 eggs (chicks).
Life Span: average 10 years and up to ~16 years.
Location: throughout Florida and the Gulf Coast to Texas, South America and the Caribbean.
Calories: 196-590 kcal/day.
Diet: crayfish, shrimp, mollusks, slugs, aquatic insects, and fish.
What they are called in a Group: flock.

The Wetland Animals

San Francisco Garter Snake
(Thamnophis sirtalis tetrataenia)
Weight: 50-175 g.
Length: 0.3-0.9 m.
Speed: ~5-6 km/h.
Number on the Planet: ~1,500.
Number in a litter: 12-24 eggs
(hatchlings).
Life Span: average 2 years, and up to
10 years.
Location: San Mateo County on the San
Francisco Peninsula (California, United
States).
Calories: 7-21 kcal/day.
Diet: frogs, fish, toads, insects, small
mammals, and birds.
What they are called in a Group: nest.

Lotis Blue Butterfly
(Lycaeides idas lotis)
Weight: 0.5 g.
Height: 1.5-3.2 cm wingspan.
Length: 2.5-3 cm.
Speed: ~5-8 km/h.
Number on the Planet: unknown—
believed to possibly already be extinct.
Number in a litter: single egg at a time
throughout breeding period (larvae).
Life Span: several months up to a year.
Location: sites near Mendocino on
California's North Coast, United States.
Calories: 0.07-0.2 kcal/day.
Diet: plants (specifically *Seaside Bird's-
foot Trefoil*).
What they are called in a Group: swarm.

Red-Crowned Crane
(Grus japonensis)
Weight: 9.5 kg.
Height: 2.4 m wingspan.
Length: 1.6 m.
Speed: up to ~48 km/h.
Number on the Planet: 1,700-2,000.
Number in a litter: 2 eggs (chick).
Life Span: up to 30 years in the wild, up
to 65 years in captivity.
Location: southeast Asia and Russia.
Calories: 840-2,500 kcal/day.

Diet: insects, aquatic invertebrates, fish,
amphibians, rodents, reeds, grasses,
heath berries, corn, and other plants.
What they are called in a Group: herd.

Hooded Crane *(Grus monacha)*
Weight: ~3.75 kg.
Height: 185 cm wingspan.
Length: 96.5 cm.
Speed: up to ~48 km/h.
Number on the Planet: ~10,000
Number in a litter: 2 eggs (chicks)
Life Span: ~30 years.
Location: south-central and south-
eastern Siberia; also bred in Mongolia.
Winters in Izumi, southern Japan, South
Korea and China.
Calories: 420-1,300 kcal/day.
Diet: rice awns, seeds and roots of
grass, water plants, and small animals
such as insects and crustaceans.
What they are called in a Group: herd.

North American River Otter
(Lontra canadensis)
Weight: 5-14 kg.
Length: 66-127 cm.
Speed: 29 km/h.
Number on the Planet: 100,000.
Number in a litter: 1-6, average 2-3
(whelp/ pup).
Life Span: average 8-9 years, up to 21
years.
Location: North America (throughout
Canada and the United States, except
for areas of southern California, New
Mexico, and Texas, and the Mohave
desert of Nevada and Colorado. Areas
of the Rio Grande and Colorado River in
Mexico. They are, however, rare or
locally extinct throughout much of the
eastern, central, and southern US).
Calories: 760-2,300 kcal/day.
Diet: amphibians, fish, turtles, crayfish,
crabs, and other invertebrates, birds and
their eggs, small terrestrial mammals
and aquatic plants.
What they are called in a Group: family/
raft/ romp.

The Wetland Animals

White-Naped Crane *(Grus vipio)*
Weight: 5.6 kg.
Height: 2 m wingspan.
Length: 130 cm.
Speed: up to ~48 km/h.
Number on the Planet: 4,900-6,500.
Number in a litter: 2 eggs (chicks).
Life Span: up to 25 years.
Location: Dauria on the border of Russia, Mongolia and China, the Amur and Ussuri basins on the Sino-Russian border and the Songnen and Sanjiang plains, China.
Calories: 570-1,700 kcal/day.
Diet: insects, small vertebrates and plants.
What they are called in a Group: herd.

Cane Toad *(Bufo marinus)*
Weight: 0.5-1.5 kg, up to 2.65 kg.
Length: 10-20 cm, up to 38 cm.
Speed: 1.8 m/s.
Number on the Planet: 100,000,000+.
Number in a litter: 8,000-35,000 eggs (tadpoles).
Life Span: 10-15 years in the wild, up to 20 in captivity.
Location: Rio Grande Valley of Texas south to the Central Amazon and southeastern Peru; introduced into the Caribbean Islands, South Florida, the Hawaiian islands, and Australia's East Coast.
Calories: 20-60 kcal/day.
Diet: ants, beetles, earwigs, dragonflies, grasshoppers, true bugs, crustaceans, gastropods and plant matter.
What they are called in a Group: knot.

Wood Stork *(Mycteria americana)*
Weight: 2.1-2.6 kg.
Height: 1m.
Length: 1.5 + m wingspan.
Speed: 32-48 km/h.
Number on the Planet: 5,500 breeding pairs.
Number in a litter: 2-4 (chicks).
Life Span: 11-18 years in the wild.

Location: from North America to Argentina (in United States they nest in South Carolina, Georgia, and Florida).
Calories: 148-444 kcal/day.
Diet: small fish, tadpoles and crayfish.
What they are called in a Group: flock.

Tomato Frog *(Dyscophus antongilli)*
Weight: 28-226 g.
Length: 6-10.5 cm.
Speed: up to 0.4m/s
Number on the Planet: considered near threatened because its extent of occurrence is probably less than 20,000 km^2, but the species is adaptable and survives well in disturbed habitats.
Number in a litter: 1,500 eggs(tadpoles).
Life Span: 10 years.
Location: island of Madagascar and limited to the northeastern coast from Antongil Bay, south to Andevoranto.
Calories: 4-13 kcal/day.
Diet: invertebrates, larvae and insects.
What they are called in a Group: army.

Whooping Crane *(Grus Americana)*
Weight: 7.5 kg.
Height: 1.5 m.
Length: 2.5 m wingspan.
Speed: 45 km/h.
Number on the Planet: 471/
Number in a litter: 2 eggs (chicks).
Life Span: up to 24 years.
Location: North America.
Calories: 700-2,100 kcal/day.
Diet: snails, insects, berries, frogs and small fish.
What they are called in a group: siege.

Flatwoods Salamander
(Ambystoma cingulatum)
Weight: 4-10 g.
Length: 9-13 cm.
Speed: up to 0.2 m/s.
Number on the Planet: less than 10,000.
Number in a litter: 1-34 eggs (larval salamanders).
Life Span: 4-10 + years.

Location: Southern South Carolina and Georgia, in Florida and west into Alabama.
Calories: 2.7-8.1 kcal/day.
Diet: invertebrates, zooplankton, worms and insects.
What they are called in a Group: usually solitary.

Northern Leopard Frog
(Rana pipiens)
Weight: 1.2-8 g.
Length: 5-11.1 cm.
Speed: up to 0.6 m/s.
Number on the Planet: exact count unavailable; considered at risk because of extensive freshwater habitat loss in North America, estimated at 53% of wetlands lost in the 1980's since 1780.
Number in a litter: 300-6,500 eggs (tadpoles).
Life Span: up to 9 years.
Location: throughout much of North America, from as far north as the Hudson Bay, along the eastern seaboard to northern Virginia and west to British Columbia, eastern Washington, Oregon, New Mexico, Arizona, Colorado, Utah, and portions of California and Nevada.
Calories: 0.35-1.0 kcal/day
Diet: terrestrial invertebrates, including spiders, insects and their larvae, slugs, snails, earthworms and will sometimes consume other frogs.
What they are called in a Group: army.

Mudpuppy *(Necturus maculosus)*
Weight: 125-187 g.
Length: 20-33 cm.
Speed: up to 0.4 m/s.
Number on the Planet: locally common throughout its range. It has no special national conservation status. It is tolerant of a variety of aquatic habitats. However, habitat destruction from siltation and pollution, and habitat loss due to development is a threat to some populations. Listed as "endangered" in

Iowa and is "special concern" in Maryland and North Carolina.
Number in a litter: 18-180 eggs (hatchlings)
Life Span: 20 + years.
Location: southeast Manitoba to southern Quebec, south to south Missouri and northern Georgia.
Calories: 5-16 kcal/day.
Diet: crayfish, insects, worms, snails, fish.
What they are called in a Group: usually solitary.

Green Crested Basilisk
(Basilicus plumifrons)
Weight: 200 + g.
Length: 0.6-0.9 m.
Speed: 11km/h.
Number on the Planet: hundreds of thousands; common and widespread throughout its range).
Number in a litter: 1-7 eggs (hatchling).
Life Span: 5-10 years.
Location: Mexico to Ecuador.
Calories: 6-18 kcal/day.
Diet: insects and small fish.
What they are called in a Group: pack.

Least Bittern *(Txobrychus exilis)*
Weight: 47-113 g.
Height: 41-46 cm wingspan.
Length: 28-37 cm.
Speed: ~16-48 km/h.
Number on the Planet: less than 1,000 pairs.
Number in a litter: 2-6, average 4-5 eggs (chicks).
Life Span: unknown.
Location: from southern Canada, south to South America, and winter from California, Texas and Florida to Panama and Colombia.
Calories: 20-62 kcal/day.
Diet: small fishes, frogs, tadpoles, salamanders, leeches, slugs, crayfish, dragonflies, aquatic bugs and occasionally shrews and mice.
What they are called in a Group: flock.

The Wetland Animals

Jabiru *(Jabiru mycteria)*
Weight: up to 8 kg.
Height: 2.6 m wingspan.
Length: 1.15 m.
Speed: 1m/s running (when catching prey).
Number on the Planet: the global population size has not been quantified, but it is believed to be large, as the species is described as 'frequent' in at least parts of its range.
Number in a litter: 2-5 eggs (chicks).
Life Span: average 30 years, and up to 40 years.
Location: the Americas west of the Andes; as far north as Mexico and as far south as Argentina and most commonly in wetland regions of Brazil and Paraguay. Also spotted in Argentina, Belize, Bolivia, Brazil, Columbia, Costa Rica, Ecuador, El Salvador, French Guiana, Grenada, Guatemala, Guyana, Honduras, Mexico, Nicaragua, Panama, Paraguay, Peru, Suriname, Trinidad and Tobago, Uruguay, and Venezuela.
Calories: 665-2,000 kcal/day.
Diet: fish, mollusks, insects, amphibians, reptiles, small mammals and carrion.
What they are called in a Group: flock.

Marsh Deer
(Blastocerus dichotomus)
Weight: 89-125 kg.
Height: 1.0-1.2 m at the shoulder.
Length: ~2m, 15 cm tail.
Speed: up to 32 km/h.
Number on the Planet: less than 10,000.
Number in a litter: 1 (fawn).
Life Span: average 10-12 years.
Location: southern margins of Amazonian Peru and Brazil, south through northeastern Argentina.
Calories: 3,700-14,000 kcal/day.
Diet: aquatic and riparian vegetation (water lilies, leaves, and grasses).
What they are called in a Group: herd.

Big Brown Bat *(Eptesicus fuscus)*
Weight: 12 g.
Height: 330 mm wingspan.
Length: 110-130 mm.
Speed: up to 64 km/h.
Number on the Planet: abundant and common throughout its range, though perhaps beginning to decline in numbers.
Number in a litter: 1-2 (pups).
Life Span: up to 19 years.
Location: ranges from southern Canada, through temperate North America, down through Central America to extreme northern South America, and the West Indies
Calories: 5-15 kcal/day.
Diet: beetles, moths, flies, wasps, flying ants, lacewing flies, and dragonflies.
What they are called in a Group: colony.

Yellow Anaconda *(Eunectus notaeus)*
Weight: up to 250 kg.
Length: up to 3 m.
Speed: ~1 km/h.
Number on the Planet: although not necessarily threatened with extinction, may become so, unless trade is strictly regulated in order to avoid utilization incompatible with their survival.
Number in a litter: 20-40 (neonates).
Life Span: average 15-20 years, up to 50-60 years.
Location: southern Amazon Basin in Bolivia, Paraguay, Uruguay, western Brazil and northeastern Argentina.
Calories: 1,300-3,800 kcal/day.
Diet: fish, birds, small mammals and reptiles.
What they are called in a Group: nest.

Australian Pink-Tongued Skink
(Hemisphaeriodon gerrardii)
Weight: 283-510 g.
Length: 40-45 cm.
Speed: 13 m/min.
Number on the Planet: population status not quantified, believed to be somewhat rare in its range.

The Wetland Animals

Number in a litter: 12-25 (neonates).
Life Span: up to 20 years.
Location: New South Whales and Eastern Australia.
Calories: 10-30 kcal/day.
Diet: insects, snails and slugs.
What they are called in a Group: band.

Platypus *(Ornithorhynchus anatinus)*
Weight: 700g-2.4 kg.
Length: 43-50 cm.
Speed: 80 "dives" underwater/hour.
Number on the Planet: common throughout its original range, with the exception of South Australia. The species has recovered well from past reductions caused by over-hunting and accidental by-catch, thanks to an effective government conservation programme.
Number in a litter: 1-3 eggs (pups).
Life Span: 11-17 years.
Location: eastern Australia and Tanzania.
Calories: 193-583 kcal/day.
Diet: annelid worms and insect larvae, freshwater shrimps, and freshwater crayfish.
What they are called in a Group: usually solitary.

Palmate Newt *(Triturus helveticus)*
Weight: 1.5-3.5 g.
Length: 6.5-11 cm.
Speed: up to 10 cm/s.
Number on the Planet: not available.
Number in a litter: 100-300 eggs (larvae/tadpoles).
Life Span: 10 years.
Location: Great Britain, western and northern Europe.
Calories: 0.22-0.67 kcal/day.
Diet: worms, crustaceans, frog tadpoles, daphnia, planktonic animals, and other small invertebrates.
What they are called in a Group: usually solitary.

Annamese Pond Turtle *(Mauremys annamensis)*
Weight: 50-70 g.
Length: 29 cm.
Speed: ~0.26 km/h.
Number on the Planet: less than 1,000 (in captivity, no longer existing in the wild).
Number in a litter: 1-13 eggs (hatchlings).
Life Span: up to 30yrs. (in some cases 50-70yrs.)
Location: central Vietnam.
Calories: 2.4-7.3 kcal/day.
Diet: insects, worms and aquatic vegetation.
What they are called in a Group: bale.

Maud Island Frog *(Leiopelma pakeka)*
Weight: 5-12 g.
Length: 50 mm.
Speed: up to 0.8 m/s.
Number on the Planet: 27,700-39,700.
Number in a litter: 20 eggs (tadpoles/polliwogs).
Life Span: up to 30 years.
Location: New Zealand (Maud Island and Motuara Island).
Calories: 0.6-1.7 kcal/day.
Diet: terrestrial insects.
What they are called in a Group: army.

American White Pelican *[Pelecanus erythrorhynchos]*
Weight: 5-8 kg.
Height: 3 m wingspan.
Length: 1.5 m.
Speed: up to 50 km/h.
Number on the Planet: 1,000+ nesting pairs.
Number in a litter: 2-4 eggs (chicks).
Life Span: 12-14 years.
Location: North America (summer in northern California, western Nevada, Utah, Colorado, northeastern South Dakota, southwestern Minnesota, and occasionally on the central coast of Texas; winter in Florida and Mexico).
Calories: 635-1,900 kcal/day.

The Wetland Animals

Diet: fish (carp, chubs, shiners, yellow perch, catfish, and jackfish).
What they are called in a Group: flock.

Etruscan Shrew (Suncus etruscus)
Weight: 1.3-2 g.
Length: 36 mm.
Speed: up to 10 km/h.
Number on the Planet: exact number unknown, but considered unthreatened at this time.
Number in a litter: 4-6 (pups).
Life Span: ~15 months.
Location: from southern Asia throughout southern Europe.
Calories: 2-6 kcal/day.
Diet: insects, spiders and other invertebrates.
What they are called in a Group: usually solitary.

Giant Water Bug
(Lethocerus americanus)
Weight: 57 g.
Length: up to 10 cm.
Speed: 1.9 km/h.
Number on the Planet: exact number not known; considered not threatened.
Number in a litter: up to 100 eggs (larva).
Life Span: 1 year.
Location: North America, South Africa and India.
Calories: 1.16-3.49 kcal/day.
Diet: small insects, salamanders, tadpoles and small fish.
What they are called in a Group: colony.

Pond Skater
(Archispirostreptus gigas)
Weight: 0.02 g.
Length: 20 mm.
Speed: ~1.5 m/s.
Number on the Planet: considered abundant.
Number in a litter: 4-5 (larva).
Life Span: 2 + years.
Location: Britain and Europe.
Calories: 0.01-0.03 kcal/day.

Diet: insects.
What they are called in a Group: swarm.

Madagascar Hissing Cockroach
(Gromphadorhina portentosa)
Weight: up to 24 g.
Length: 5-7.6 cm.
Speed: 4.8 km/h.
Number on the Planet: exact number unknown; this species of cockroach is common in Madagascar and is restricted only to that island.
Number in a litter: 30-60 (larva).
Life Span: 2-5 years in captivity.
Location: Madagascar.
Calories: 1.2-3.7 kcal/day.
Diet: various plant and animal matter.
What they are called in a Group: colony.

Painted Turtle (Chrysemys picta)
Weight: 300-500 g.
Length: 10-18 cm.
Speed: 0.65 km/h.
Number on the Planet: hundreds of thousands; common and widespread across North America.
Number in a litter: 5-10 eggs (hatchlings).
Life Span: 5-10 years in the wild, 20 years in captivity.
Location: North America.
Calories: 10.5-31.5 kcal/day
Diet: insects, snails, slugs, crayfish, leeches, mussels, tadpoles, frogs, fish eggs, small fish, carrion, and plants (including duckweed, algae, and lily pads).
What they are called in a Group: bale.

Crawfish Frog (Rana areolata)
Weight: 5-12 g.
Length: 7.6 cm.
Speed: up to 0.6 m/s.
Number on the Planet: exact number unknown; listed as threatened because this species is in significant decline (at a rate of less than 30% over ten years) because of widespread habitat loss.

Number in a litter: Up to 7,000 eggs
(tadpoles/ polliwogs).
Life Span: up to 7 years.
Location: southern United States (west
Louisiana and east Texas, and drainage
systems of Arkansas, Missouri,
Mississippi, and Ohio rivers).
Calories: 0.6-1.7 kcal/day.
Diet: small organisms, mainly crayfish.
What they are called in a Group: army.

**Blue-spotted Salamander
(*Ambystoma laterale*)**
Weight: 7-12 g.
Length: 10-14 cm.
Speed: up to 10 cm/s.
Number on the Planet: exact count
unavailable. Due to the loss of wetlands
and the destruction of forests, the
salamanders are threatened. However,
there is no evidence of decline in the
blue-spotted salamander as of yet, they
are more tolerant of human
disturbances than other salamanders.
Number in a litter: 500 eggs
(hatchlings).
Life Span: possibly up to 30 years.
Location: moist woodlands in central
North America and stretch in a broad
band across to the Atlantic Provinces
and northern New England.
Calories: 0.6-1.8 kcal/day.
Diet: worms, snails, slugs, insects,
centipedes, spiders and other
invertebrates.
What they are called in a Group: solitary

Striped Cuckoo (*Tapera naevia*)
Weight: 40 g.
Length: 27 cm.
Speed: 35 km/h.
Number on the Planet: this species has
a large range, with an estimated global
extent of occurrence of 12,000,000 km^2.
The global population size has not been
quantified, but it is believed to be large
as the species is described as 'common'
in at least parts of its range.
Number in a litter: 1-2 eggs (fledglings).

Life Span: up to ~4 years.
Location: from Mexico and Trinidad
south to Bolivia and Argentina (South
and Central America).
Calories: 23-69 kcal/day.
Diet: insects.
What they are called in a Group: flock.

Map Turtle (*Graptemys geographica*)
Weight: 0.45-2.2 kg.
Length: 9-27 cm.
Speed: 4.8-6.4 km/h.
Number on the Planet: exact number
unavailable; the population has been
reduced or eliminated in some areas,
but they do still persist in suburban
rivers and agricultural lands.
Number in a litter: 6-20 eggs
(hatchlings).
Life Span: up to 60 + years.
Location: from southern Quebec and
northwestern Vermont, extends west
through the Great Lakes and into
southern Wisconsin and eastern
Minnesota, west of the Appalachians,
south to Kansas, northeastern
Oklahoma, Arkansas, Tennessee,
Alabama, northwestern Georgia, in the
Susquehanna River system in
Pennsylvania, Maryland and in the
Delaware River.
Calories: 25-74 kcal/day.
Diet: snails, clams, crayfish, aquatic
insects, snails, and smaller crustaceans,
dead fish and some plant material.
What they are called in a Group: bale.

Green Heron (*Butorides virescens*)
Weight: 240 g.
Height: 64-68 cm wingspan.
Length: 41-46 cm.
Speed: 28-56 km/h.
Number on the Planet: this species has
a large range, with an estimated global
extent of occurrence of 7,900,000 km^2.
The global population size has not been
quantified, but it is believed to be large
as the species is described as 'common'
in at least parts of its range.

Numb... ...ter: 3-5 eggs (chicks).
Life Span: up to ~8 years.
Location: wide range in North American wetlands; occur as far north as southern Canada and as far south as northern South America.
Calories: 53-160 kcal/day.
Diet: small fish, frogs and aquatic insects.
What they are called in a group: hedge.

Black-Winged Stilt
(Himantopus himantopus)
Weight: 166-205 g.
Length: 35-39 cm.
Speed: 40 km/h.
Number on the Planet: 21,000 pairs.
Number in a litter: 3-4 eggs (chicks).
Life Span: average 2-3 years, up to ~12 + years.
Location: France and Iberia, south to sub-Saharan Africa and Madagascar, east to central Asia and northern central China, Indochina, Taiwan, and Indian subcontinent.
Calories: 44-132 kcal/day.
Diet: aquatic invertebrates including insects, small mollusks, crustaceans, and worms, as well as small fish and their eggs, and tadpoles.
What they are called in a group: flock.

Eurasian Beaver *(Castor fiber)*
Weight: 17-32 kg.
Height: 0.3-0.35 m at the shoulder.
Length: 0.8-0.9 m.
Speed: can swim up to 8 km/h.
Number on the Planet: 430,000+
Number in a litter: 1-5 (pup/ kitten).
Life Span: 10-17 years in the wild, up to 35 years in captivity.
Location: on the Elbe, the Rhone, the Danube Rivers and in parts of Scandinavia; reintroduced in Bavaria and The Netherlands.
Calories: 770-2,300 kcal/day.
Diet: tubers and the rootstocks of myrtles, cattails, and water lilies, and

aspen, hazels, black poplars, lime, and other softwood bark trees.
What they are called in a group: lodge.

Black Legless Lizard
(Anniella pulchra nigra)
Weight: up to 8 g.
Length: 11-17 cm.
Speed: up to 0.7 m/s.
Number on the Planet: 1,000-2,500.
Number in a litter: 1-4 (neonates).
Life Span: 6-10 + years.
Location: California, United States.
Calories: 0.53-1.6 kcal/day.
Diet: larval insects, beetles, termites, and spiders.
What they are called in a Group: nest.

Caiman Lizard *(Dracaena guianesis)*
Weight: 1.4-2.7 kg.
Length: 122 cm.
Speed: up to 20 cm/s.
Number on the Planet: exact count unavailable.
Number in a litter: average 8 eggs (hatchlings).
Life Span: most less than one year, some up to 9 years.
Location: South America (Amazon Basin of Peru and Brazil).
Calories: 17-51 kcal/day.
Diet: insects, snails, clams and crawfish.
What they are called in a Group: herd, usually solitary.

Muskrat *(Ondatra zibethicus)*
Weight: up to 1.7 kg.
Length: 25-40 cm, 20-25 cm tail.
Speed: can swim 4.8 km/h.
Number on the Planet: exact count unavailable. Population appears to go through a regular pattern of rise and dramatic decline spread over a 6 to 10 year period. Muskrats are widespread and abundant. Populations remain stable even when they are being hunted for fur, affected by disease, or a target for large predator populations because

muskrats have the ability to reproduce quickly.
Number in a litter: 6-8 (pups).
Life Span: average 3 years in the wild, up to 10 years in captivity.
Location: Alaska, Canada, United States and Mexico; introduced into Europe.
Calories: 210-625 kcal/day.
Diet: cattails and other aquatic vegetation, freshwater mussels, frogs, crayfish and small turtles.
What they are called in a Group: pack.

Common Kingfisher *(Alcedo atthis)*
Weight: 26-39 g.
Height: average 26 cm wingspan.
Length: 17-19 cm.
Speed: ~58 km/h.
Number on the Planet: exact count unavailable; not listed as a concern for many of the top conservation sites. Common kingfishers do undergo large fluctuations in populations on a yearly basis, due mostly to severe cold. In one census, after a severe winter in Belgium there were 8 pairs, five years later there were 45, but reduced to 25 the following year.
Number in a litter: 4-10 eggs (chicks).
Life Span: average 7 years in the wild, up to 15 years in captivity.
Location: throughout Europe and Asia as far east as Japan. They are also found in Africa, south of the Sahara.
Calories: 20-60 kcal/day.
Diet: aquatic insects, small fish, small arthropods and crustaceans.
What they are called in a Group: flock.

Great Blue Heron *(Ardea herodias)*
Weight: 2.10-2.50 kg.
Height: 60 cm.
Length: 97-137 cm.
Speed: 30-47 km/h.
Number on the Planet: exact count unavailable; the most well-known and most widespread heron in North America. Human interference with the heron primarily involves destruction of habitat. Great blue herons are protected by the United States Migratory Bird Treaty Act.
Number in a litter: 2-7 eggs (chicks).
Life Span: 15 years in the wild, 23 years in captivity.
Location: Canada, United States, Mexico, West Indies and the Galapagos Islands.
Calories: 291-874 kcal/day.
Diet: fish, frogs, salamanders, lizards, snakes, birds, shrimp, crabs, crayfish, dragonflies, grasshoppers, and many other aquatic insects.
What they are called in a Group: usually solitary; colonies for breeding.

Black Rat Snake
(Elaphe obsoleta obsoleta)
Weight: 150 + g.
Height: 3.8 cm diameter.
Length: 106.7-183 cm.
Speed: up to 5.8 km/h (briefly).
Number on the Planet: exact count unavailable, however listed as special concern in the state of Michigan. Their habitat is slowly being reduced due to land development and the cutting of trees. They continue to maintain a healthy population in many areas.
Number in a litter: 12-20 eggs (hatchlings).
Life Span: 15 – 20 + years.
Location: from New England south through Georgia and west across the northern parts of Alabama, Mississippi, and Louisiana, and north through Oklahoma to southern Wisconsin.
Calories: 4.8-14.5 kcal/day.
Diet: birds, eggs, lizards, frogs, other snakes, chipmunks, squirrels, small rabbits, mice, rats, voles, shrews and other small mammals.
What they are called in a Group: nest.

The Ocean Animals

Short-Tailed Albatross
(Phoebastria albatrus)
Weight: 11 kg.
Height: wingspan: 213-229 cm.
Length: 84-91 cm.
Speed: up to 135 + km/h.
Number on the Planet: 2000 birds.
Number in a litter: one egg (fledgling).
Life Span: 12-45 years.
Location: Toroshima, Japan and Minami-Kojima in the Senkaku Islands of Southern Ryukyu Islands (most of northwestern and northeastern Pacific Ocean).
Calories: ~925-2826 kcal/day.
Diet: flying fish eggs, shrimp, squid, and crustaceans.
What they are called in a group: flock.

Olive Ridley Turtle
(Lepidochelys olivacea)
Weight: 35-45 kg.
Length: 75 cm.
Speed: up to 5 m/s (swimming).
Number on the Planet: 800,000 nesting females (and thought about as many males).
Number in a litter: 107 eggs(hatchlings).
Life Span: 50-60 years.
Location: Pacific, Indian and Southern Atlantic Oceans. Found around North America in the Caribbean Sea and along the Gulf of California. Largest nesting beach is at the Bhitar Kanika Wildlife Sanctuary on the Bay of Bengal in Orissa, India.
Calories: ~318-958 kcal/day
Diet: jellyfish, snails, shrimp and crabs (a wide variety of invertebrates and protochordates).
What they are called in a Group: bale.

Kemp's Ridley Turtle
(Depidochelys kempi)
Weight: up to (but averaging less than) 45 kg.
Length: 62-70 cm.

Speed: up to ~5 m/s.
Number on the Planet: 3,000 nesting females (and thought about as many males).
Number in a litter: 105 eggs(hatchlings).
Life Span: up to 50 years.
Location: Gulf of Mexico, but range through coastal waters along eastern seaboard as far north as Nova Scotia.
Calories: ~347-1042 kcal/day.
Diet: crustaceans, jellyfish, mollusks, crabs and small fish.
What they are called in a Group: bale.

Leatherback Turtle
(Dermochelys coriacea)
Weight: 900 kg.
Length: 2 m.
Speed: up to 6.7 m/s.
Number on the Planet: estimated 25,000-45,000 nesting females *males.
Number in a litter: up to 100 eggs (average 40-60) (hatchlings).
Life Span: have been known to live up to 150 years.
Location: coasts of northern South America and western Africa. The United States Caribbean, primarily Puerto Rico and the Virgin Islands, and southeastern Florida.
Calories: up to 90kg/day (~3286-9859 kcal/day).
Diet: jellyfish and salps (soft bodied animals) and often plants.
What they are called in a Group: bale.

Lion Fish *(Pterois volitans)*
Weight: 4.5 g.
Height: up to 76 cm pectoral fin span.
Length: 5.5 cm.
Speed: ~4.8 km/h.
Number on the Planet: exact couont unavailable; considered abundant; not threatened or endangered within their range.
Number in a litter: several thousand eggs.
Life Span: up to 10 years.

The Ocean Animals

Location: Indian Ocean and Pacific Ocean.
Calories: 0.34-1.0 kcal/day.
Diet: small ocean animals- crabs in particular and any fish and crustaceans.
What they are called in a Group: school.

Green Turtle (Chelonia mydas)
Weight: 136-180 kg (largest ever recorded: 395 kg).
Length: 76-91 cm (largest ever recorded: 150 cm).
Speed: 9m/s.
Number on the Planet: 88,520 nesting females (as many or fewer males).
Number in a litter: 110-115 eggs (hatchlings).
Life Span: 20 -5 0 years.
Location: worldwide in warm ocean waters.
Calories: ~891-2674 kcal/day, up to 5316 kcal/day.
Diet: eats worms, young crustaceans, aquatic insects, grasses and algae until it reaches 20-25 cm in length (when it then primarily eats sea grass and algae).
What they are called in a group: bale.

North Atlantic Right Whale (Eubalaena glacialis)
Weight: up to 100,000 kg.
Height: up to 7 m fluke-span, ~2.4 m in diameter.
Length: up to 17 m.
Speed: 6 miles an hour.
Number on the Planet: ~350.
Number in a litter: 1 (calf).
Life Span: more than 60 years.
Location: Atlantic Ocean.
Calories: 500,000-1 million kcal/day
Diet: Small marine crustaceans, krill and zooplankton.
What they are called in a Group: mainly solitary but may feed in small groups (gam/ grind/ herd/ pod/ school).

Bowhead Whale (Balaena mysticetus)
Weight: 72,000-95,000kg (72-91 tonnes).
Height: up to ~7m tall.
Length: 15-18.5 m.
Speed: up to 16-19.5 km/h.
Number on the Planet: 8000-12000.
Number in a litter: 1 calf.
Life Span: 40 years.+.
Location: Arctic.
Calories: 190,000 Kcal/day.
Diet: plankton, krill and other copepods.
What they are called in a Group: pod.

Blue Whale (Balaenoptera musculus)
Weight: 109,000 kg (109 tonnes).
Height: ~14.5 m body-circumference.
Length: 25 m.
Speed: up to 38-48 km/h.
Number on the Planet: 10,000-14,000.
Number in a litter: 1 calf.
Life Span: 35-40 years.
Location: all oceans of the world.
Calories: ~ 1 million kcal/day.
Diet: krill, copepods and small fish.
What they are called in a Group: pod.

Fin Whale (Balaenoptera physalus)
Weight: 45,360-63,500 kg.
Height: 60 cm tall dorsal fin.
Length: ~24-27 m.
Speed: up to 37 km/h.
Number on the Planet: 40,000 - 60,000.
Number in a litter: 1 calf.
Life Span: 80-100 years.
Location: all oceans of the world.
Calories: 1,814kg/day (~490,000-over 1 million kcal/day).
Diet: krill and schooling fish.
What they are called in a Group: pod.

Sei Whale (Balaenoptera borealis)
Weight: 36,000 kg.
Height: 25-61cm tall dorsal fin.
Length: 8-15 m.
Speed: up to 64 km/h.
Number on the Planet: 54,000.
Number in a litter: 1 calf.
Life Span: up to 70 years.

The Ocean Animals

Location: all oceans of the world.
Calories: ~366,000-1 million kcal/day.
Diet: copepods, krill, shrimp,
crustaceans and small fish.
What they are called in a Group: pod.

Gray Whale *(Eschrichtius robustus)*
Weight: 33,000 kg (33 tonnes).
Height: ~4.5m tall.
Length: 13.8-15 m.
Speed: up to 16-17.5 km/h.
Number on the Planet: 15,000-22,000.
Number in a litter: 1 calf.
Life Span: 50-60 years.
Location: eastern North Pacific.
Calories: ~343,000- 1 million kcal/day.
Diet: small crustaceans, amphipods,
krill, copepods, etc., plankton, mollusks,
squid and fish.
What they are called in a Group: pod.

Hector's Dolphin
(Cephalorhynchus hectori)
Weight: males: 35 kg, females: 45 kg.
Length: 1.2-1.4 m.
Speed: ~up to 110 km/h.
Number on the Planet: 3,00-4,000.
Number in a litter: 1 calf.
Life Span: up to 20 years.
Location: New Zealand.
Calories: ~2,226-6,680 kcal/day.
Diet: fish, crabs and squid.
What they are called in a Group: pod/
herd.

Maui's Dolphin
(Cephalorhynchus hectori maui)
Weight: 50 kg.
Length: 1.2-1.4 m.
Speed: ~100 km/h.
Number on the Planet: 150 or less.
Number in a litter: 1 calf.
Life Span: up to 20 years.
Location: New Zealand.
Calories: ~2,600-7,800 kcal/day.
Diet: fish, squid and sometimes
crustaceans.
What they are called in a Group: pod/
herd.

Humpback Whale
(Megaptera novaeangliae)
Weight: 27,000-45,000 kg (27-45
tonnes).
Height: 1.8 m tall/high.
Length: 16 m.
Speed: up to 24-26.5 km/h.
Number on the Planet: 30,000-40,000.
Number in a litter: 1 calf.
Life Span: 45-50 years.
Location: all of world's oceans.
Calories: 2000-2500 kg/day (~615,000-
over 1 million kcal/day).
Diet: krill, shrimp-like crustaceans and
various small fish.
What they are called in a Group: pods.

Northern Right Whale
(Eubalaena glacialis)
Weight: 20,000-30,000 kg.
Height: ~2.4m in diameter.
Length: 14-17 m.
Speed: 17 km/h.
Number on the Planet: 3,000-4,000.
Number in a litter: 1 calf.
Life Span: over 60 years.
Location: Pacific and Atlantic Oceans.
Calories: ~500,000-1 million kcal/day.
Diet: plankton and krill.
What they are called in a Group: pods.

Loggerhead Sea Turtle
(Caretta caretta)
Weight: 113 kg.
Length: 92 cm.
Speed: 4-5 m/s.
Number on the Planet: 68,000-90,000.
Number in a litter: 120/ clutch.
Life Span: 30 years.
Location: Along the Atlantic coast of
Florida, North Carolina, South Carolina
and Georgia. There are also some nests
along the Gulf of Mexico. (Atlantic,
Pacific and Indian Oceans).
Calories: ~700-2100 kcal/day.
Diet: conchs, clams, crabs, horseshoe
crabs, shrimp, sea urchins, sponges,
fish, squid, and octopus. During
migration through the open sea,

The Ocean Animals

Loggerheads eat jellyfishes, pteropods, floating mollusks, floating egg clusters.
What they are called in a Group: bale.

White Sturgeon
(Acipenser transmontanus)
Weight: up to 181 kg.
Length: up to 3 m.
Speed: 90 cm/s.
Number on the Planet: under 600.
Number in a litter: 100,000 to 4 million Eggs.
Life Span: over 100 years.
Location: Ensenada, Mexico to Cook Inlet, Alaska. Found in most estuaries along the Pacific coast.
Calories: 500-1,500 kcal/day.
Diet: algae, aquatic insects, fish, shellfish, crayfish, clams, amphipods and shrimp.
What they are called in a Group: school.

Greater Sage-Grouse
(Centrocercus urophasianus)
Weight: 1400-2900 g.
Height: ~10 cm.
Length: 56-75 cm.
Speed: ~1 m/s (clumsy flight).
Number on the Planet: 100,000-500,000, trends show population is declining.
Number in a litter: 6-8 eggs (chicks).
Life Span: up to 10 years though average is about 1-2 years.
Location: western North America (eastern Montana, Wyoming, northwestern Colorado, Utah, southern Idaho, Nevada, and northeastern California. There is also an isolated population in central Washington).
Calories: ~300-850 kcal/day.
Diet: sagebrush.
What they are called in a Group: flock.

Roseate Tern *(Sterna dougallii)*
Weight: 113 g.
Height: 76 cm wingspan.
Length: 36-43 cm.
Speed: up to 37 km/h.

Number on the Planet: 6,000-6,500.
Number in a litter: 2-3 eggs (chicks).
Life Span: 21+ years.
Location: North America (along the coasts of the Atlantic, Pacific and Indian oceans. From the Canadian Maritime Provinces south to Long Island).
Calories: ~40-100 kcal/day.
Diet: sand lance, white hake, juvenile herring, mackerel, gadids, cod, pollock and haddock.
What they are called in a Group: flock.

Whiskery Shark *(Furgaleus macki)*
Weight: 12.9 kg.
Length: up to 1.6 m.
Speed: up to ~28 km/h in short bursts.
Number on the Planet: exact numbers unknown; not endangered (stable population).
Number in a litter: 5-24 pups.
Life Span: up to 15 years.
Location: Australian waters (Indian Ocean).
Calories: 136-408 kcal/day.
Diet: cephalopods, octopus, squid, fish, rock lobsters, peanut worms, and sea grass.
What they are called in a Group: school.

Whale Shark *(Rhincodon typus)*
Weight: 13,600 kg.
Length: up to 14 m.
Speed: no more than 5 km/h.
Number on the Planet: exact count unavailable; there are no reliable population numbers or indices that can be used to assess this criterion.
Number in a litter: a pregnant female contains hundreds of live young at a time.
Life Span: 100 to 150 years.
Location: warm water, usually around the equator, except in the Mediterranean Sea.
Calories: 2,518-7,556 kcal/day.
Diet: plankton, krill, small fish and squid.
What they are called in a Group: usually solitary.

The Ocean Animals

Humphead Wrasse
(Cheilinus undulates)
Weight: up to 190.5 kg.
Length: 35-50 cm, one found up to 229 cm.
Speed: 1.8 km/h (long-distances).
Number on the Planet: severely declining numbers (less than 450).
Number in a litter: thousands of eggs though survival rate is very low.
Life Span: over 30 years.
Location: currently only found around the coast of Sabah, Malaysia at Pulau Sipadan and Pulau Layang Layang.
Calories: 512-1,538 kcal/day.
Diet: shellfish, fish, sea stars, sea urchins, crabs, mussels and worms.
What they are called in a Group: usually solitary.

Wandering Albatross
(Diomedea exulans)
Weight: 6-12 kg.
Height: 3.5 m wingspan.
Length: 1.35 meters.
Speed: 6000 km in 12 days (up to 80 km/h).
Number on the Planet: ~28,000 mature individuals.
Number in a litter: 1 chick.
Life Span: up to 80 years.
Location: mainly Australia (southern Ocean).
Calories: ~800-2400 kcal/day.
Diet: squid, fish and floating carrion.
What they are called in a Group: pair.

Dugong *(Dugong dugon)*
Weight: 400 kg.
Length: 2.4-4 m.
Speed: 10 km/h.
Number on the Planet: less than 10,000; considered to be endangered.
Number in a litter: 1 calf (twins rare).
Life Span: up to 70 years.
Location: Indo-Pacific Region. Coastal waters of east Africa from the Red Sea to northernmost South Africa, northeastern Indian, along the Malay peninsula, around the northern coast of Australia to New Guinea and many of the island groups of the South Pacific.
Calories: ~12,500-37,000 kcal/day.
Diet: sea grass, algae and occasional crabs.
What they are called in a Group: herd.

Shark Ray or Bowmouth Guitarfish
(Rhina ancylostoma)
Weight: up to 135 kg.
Length: up to 270 cm.
Speed: up to 30 km/h.
Number on the Planet: less than 100,000.
Number in a litter: 4 live young.
Life Span: 20-30 years.
Location: Indo-West Pacific: Red Sea and East Africa to Papua New Guinea, north to Japan, south to New South Wales, Australia.
Calories: 792-2,376 kcal/day.
Diet: crabs, shellfish, bottom crustaceans, mollusks.
What they are called in a group: school.

Black-Browed Albatross
(Diomedea melanophrys)
Weight: 3-5 kg.
Height: wing span of 210-250 cm.
Length: 80-95 cm.
Speed: up to 80 km/h.
Number on the Planet: 680,000 pairs.
Number in a litter: 1 egg (chick).
Life Span: 30 years or more.
Location: Antarctic and sub tropical waters.
Calories: ~400-1300 kcal/day.
Diet: krill, fish and jellyfish.
What they are called in a Group: colony.

Great White Shark
(Carcharodon carcharias)
Weight: up to 3200 kg.
Length: 3.7-4.9 m (and up to 7 m).
Speed: average 3 km/h, up to 24 km/h.
Number on the Planet: exact count is unavailable; the world population is unknown.

The Ocean Animals

Number in a litter: 2-14.
Life Span: up to 100 years.
Location: temperate coastlines worldwide (coastlines of California to Alaska, the East Coast of the United States and most of the Gulf Coast, Hawaii, most of South America, South Africa, Australia (except the North Coast), New Zealand, the Mediterranean Sea, West Africa to Scandinavia, Japan, and the eastern coastline of China and southern Russia).
Calories: 90-136kg of food (meat) at a time (8,500-25,527 kcal/day).
Diet: fish, manta rays, carrion, sea mammals and other sharks.
What they are called in a Group: pairs.

Blue-ringed Octopus *(Hapalochlaena)*
Weight: 10-100 g.
Length: 20 cm.
Speed: up to 10 cm/s.
Number on the Planet: exact count unavailable; common in range though heavily hunted and nearing population vulnerability.
Number in a litter: up to 30.
Life Span: 2 years.
Location: shallow reefs and tide pools from Japan to Australia.
Calories: 2.13-6.39 kcal/day.
Diet: primarily crabs and mollusks.
What they are called in a Group: usually solitary.

White-beaked Dolphin
(Lagenorhynchus albirostris)
Weight: 180 kg (and up to 270kg).
Length: up to 3.1 m.
Speed: up to 32 km/h.
Number on the Planet: a few hundred thousand (exact count not available).
Number in a litter: 1-2.
Life Span: unknown (~20 years).
Location: cool waters of North Atlantic and North Sea.
Calories: most dolphins consume ~8-15 kg/day (~6,900-20,000 kcal/day).

Diet: bottom-dwelling fish such as cod and whiting and squid.
What they are called in a Group: school.

Pantropical Spotted Dolphin
(Stenella attenuate)
Weight: 90-115 kg.
Length: up to 2.4 m.
Speed: 40 km/h.
Number on the Planet: 1.7 million.
Number in a litter: 1-2.
Life Span: up to 45 years.
Location: deep oceanic waters 22 degrees Celsius+ all over the world.
Calories: ~4,500-13,500 kcal/day.
Diet: fish, squid and crustaceans.
What they are called in a Group: school.

Largetooth Sawfish *(Pristis perotteti)*
Weight: 500-600 kg.
Length: 3 m.
Speed: ~8 km/h.
Number on the Planet: estimated 250 or less mature individuals; considered critically endangered.
Number in a litter: 1-13 (7-9 average).
Life Span: ~30 years.
Location: temperate and tropical waters throughout the world (mainly western Atlantic Ocean).
Calories: 2,271-6,813 kcal/day.
Diet: benthic crustaceans and other invertebrates, small schooling fish (mullet and smaller herrings).
What they are called in a Group: school.

Pacific Seahorse
(Hippocampus ingens)
Weight: 8 g.
Length: 30 cm.
Speed: slowest-moving animal in the ocean (it takes then about 2.5 days to travel 1km).
Number on the Planet: exact count unavailable; severely declining numbers.
Number in a litter: hundreds.
Life Span: 4 years.

The Ocean Animals

Location: Indo-Australian waters, Atlantic coasts of Europe, Africa and the Pacific coast of North America (from San Diego in California, United States to Peru including the Galápagos Islands).
Calories: 0.5-1.5 kcal/day.
Diet: bottom-swarming organisms such as mysids and other plankton.
What they are called in a Group: pair.

Nassau Grouper
(Epinephelus striatus)
Weight: ~180 g.
Length: 48 cm.
Speed: up to 38 km/h.
Number on the Planet: less than 10,000; candidate species for the Fish and Wildlife Service's Endangered Species List.
Number in a litter: over 785,000 eggs.
Life Span: ~25 years.
Location: tropical western Atlantic Ocean.
Calories: 8.5-25 kcal/day.
Diet: fish and crustaceans.
What they are called in a Group:solitary.

Box Jellyfish *(Chironex Fleckeri)*
Weight: 2 kg.
Length: 20 cm (body) 3 m tentacles.
Speed: 7.4 km/h.
Number on the Planet: exact count unavailable; numbers are increasing alarmingly (negative effect on environment).
Number in a litter: thousands of eggs (ephyra).
Life Span: maximum 2-6 months.
Location: Australia, Queensland, the Philippines and other tropical waters.
Calories: 33-99 kcal/day.
Diet: small fish and crustaceans.
What they are called in a Group: smack.

Hawksbill Turtle
(Eretmochelys imbricata)
Weight: 45-68 kg, up to 91 kg.
Length: 63-90 cm.
Speed: 1-3 km/h.

Number on the Planet: about 20,000 throughout its range; considered endangered.
Number in a litter: 130 eggs per nest (3-5 nests per season).
Life Span: 30-50 years.
Location: circum-tropical; usually occurring from 30° N to 30° S latitude in the Atlantic, Pacific, and Indian Oceans and associated bodies of water. Caribbean Sea and western Atlantic Ocean, southern Florida and the Gulf of Mexico (especially Texas), in the Greater and Lesser Antilles, and along the Central American mainland south to Brazil. Hawksbills do not occur in the Mediterranean Sea. Within the United States, hawksbills are most common in Puerto Rico and its associated islands and in the Virgin Islands.
Calories: ~400-1200 kcal/day, up to 1800.
Diet: sponges, sea jellies, mollusks, fish, marine algae and crustaceans.
What they are called in a Group: bale, usually solitary.

Strap-Toothed Whale
(Mesoplodon layardii)
Weight: at least 2,000 kg.
Length: 6.2 m.
Speed: up to 45km/h
Number on the Planet: no population estimates while strap-toothed whale seems to be fairly abundant in its non-hunted status.
Number in a litter: 1 calf.
Life Span: known to live 27-48 years.
Location: Australia, New Zealand, subantarctic islands, South Africa and South America.
Calories: ~210,000-630,000 kcal/day.
Diet: squid, deep-sea fish and crustaceans.
What they are called in a Group: solitary or in pairs.

The Ocean Animals

Minke Whale
(Balaenoptera acutorostrata)
Weight: 8,000-13,500 kg.
Length: 8-10 m.
Speed: 5-34 km/h.
Number on the Planet: 610,000-1,284,000.
Number in a litter: 1 pup/ calf.
Life Span: up to 60 years.
Location: polar, tropical and temperate waters all over the world.
Calories: ~150,000-440,000 kcal/day.
Diet: plankton, krill, (euphausiids) and small fish.
What they are called in a Group: pod.

Atlantic Spotted Dolphin
(Stenella frontalis)
Weight: 125 kg.
Length: 2.2 m.
Speed: 2.88 km/h.
Number on the Planet: 100,000.
Number in a litter: 1 (and sometimes 2) (pup/calf).
Life Span: 45 years.
Location: tropical and subtropical waters of the Atlantic.
Calories: ~5,600-15,600 kcal/day.
Diet: fish (herring, anchovies, flounder) and squid.
What they are called in a Group: pod

Common Dolphin
(Delphinus delphis/capensis)
Weight: 135 kg.
Length: 2.3-2.6 m.
Speed: up to 46km/h
Number on the Planet: depleted population, though estimated up to 3 million remaining.
Number in a litter: 1 (sometimes 2) (pup/calf).
Life Span: 25-30 years.
Location: all tropical and warm-temperate regions.
Calories: 2600 kcal/day (resting) ~5500-16,000 kcal/day.
Diet: squid and small schooling fish.
What they are called in a Group: herd.

White-Beaked Dolphin
(Lagenorhynchus albirostris)
Weight: 180 kg.
Length: 2.5-2.7 m, up to 3 m.
Speed: 29-35 mph.
Number on the Planet: a few hundred thousand.
Number in a litter: 1 calf/ pup.
Life Span: unknown though thought to be ~10-20 years on average.
Location: endemic to temperate and sub-arctic waters of North Atlantic as far north as the White Sea and as far south as Spanish coast. Common off the Norwegian coast and the North Sea and found in the Baltic Sea. Found less often in northwest Atlantic but are abundant off Labrador and as far south as Cape Cod.
Calories: 7.2-16.2 kg/day (~6,900-20,000 kcal/day).
Diet: fish, squid, octopus and small crustaceans.
What they are called in a Group: herd.

Striped-Dolphin
(Stenella coeruleoalba)
Weight: 90-150 kg.
Length: 1.8-2.5 m.
Speed: 15 km/h.
Number on the Planet: 2 million+.
Number in a litter: 1(pup/ calf).
Life Span: 55-60 years.
Location: tropical and sub-tropical waters of both Atlantic and Pacific Oceans.
Calories: 8-15 kg/day (~5,000-15,000 kcal/day).
Diet: small pelagic fish, crustaceans, squid and shrimp.
What they are called in a Group: herd.

Bryde's Whale *(Balaenoptera edeni)*
Weight: up to 26,000 kg.
Height: 2 m.
Length: 12.5-14 m.
Speed: ~up to 37 km/h.

The Ocean Animals

Number on the Planet: exact number and estimates are unavailable.
Number in a litter: 1 calf.
Life Span: up to 70 years.
Location: tropical and subtropical waters of all seas.
Calories: ~286,600-860,000 kcal/day.
Diet: fish and krill.
What they are called in a Group: pod.

Killer Whale *(Orcinus orca)*
Weight: up to 4500 kg.
Length: 8.5-9.5 m.
Speed: 48.4 km/h.
Number on the Planet: ~100,000.
Number in a litter: 1 calf.
Life Span: 45-90 years.
Location: In oceans all over the world.
Calories: ~77,000-231,000 kcal/day.
Diet: fish, squids, seals, sea lions, walruses, porpoises, birds, sea turtles, otters, penguins, cetaceans (both mysticete and odontocete), polar bears.
What they are called in a Group: pod.

Pig-Nosed Turtle
(Carettochelys insculpta)
Weight: 22.5 kg.
Length: 60 cm.
Speed: up to 0.3 m/minute.
Number on the Planet: over 3,000.
Number in a litter: 7-19 eggs on average, up to 39.
Life Span: minimum 25 years.
Location: Indonesia, Papa New Guinea, northwestern Northern Territory of Australia.
Calories: ~200-600 kcal/day.
Diet: leaves, flowers, fruit, fish, mollusks, crustaceans, carrion, worms, aquatic insect larvae.
What they are called in a Group: bale.

Pygmy Right Whale
(Caperea marginata)
Weight: 3,991 kg.
Length: 5.5-6.5 m.
Speed: up to 26 km/h.

Number on the Planet: several hundred tracked; considered at low-risk but not in danger of being depleted.
Number in a litter: 1-2 calves.
Life Span: 40-60 years.
Location: temperate waters of the southern hemisphere around Tasmania, New Zealand, southern Australia, South Africa, southeast and southwest Indian Ocean, western and eastern Pacific.
Calories: ~70,000-210,000 kcal/day
Diet: Tiny crustaceans (copepods)
What they are called in a Group: pairs.

Bottlenose Whale
(Hyperoodon ampullatus/planifrons)
Weight: 58,000-75,000 kg.
Length: 8-10 m.
Speed: up to 34 km/h.
Number on the Planet: 500,000.
Number in a litter: 1-2 calves.
Life Span: 37 years.
Location: endemic to North Atlantic Ocean and occurs in cool and subarctic waters.
Calories: 110,000 kcl/day (resting) ~500,000-1 million kcal/day.
Diet: squid and other invertebrates, small fish.
What they are called in a Group: herd.

Narwhal *(Monodon monoceros)*
Weight: 900 kg.
Length: 4.0-4.9 m.
Speed: ~18 km/h.
Number on the Planet: 10,000-45,000.
Number in a litter: 1 calf.
Life Span: ~50 years.
Location: Arctic Ocean.
Calories: ~23,000-69,000 kcal/day.
Diet: fish, squid, shrimp and other marine animals.
What they are called in a group: pod.

Beluga Whale
(Delphinapterus leucas)
Weight: 1,500 kg.
Length: 4.6 m.

The Ocean Animals

Speed: 3-9 km/h (on average) and up to 22 km/h.
Number on the Planet: 40,000-80,000.
Number in a litter: 1 (sometimes twins) calf/ calves.
Life Span: 25-30 years.
Location: Arctic Ocean and adjoining seas.
Calories: 18.2- 27.2 kg of food/ day (~34,000-100,000 kcal/ day).
Diet: octopus, squid, crab, shrimp, clams, snails, sandworms, capelin, cod, herring, smelt and flounder.
What they are called in a Group: pod.

Sperm Whale
(Physeter macrocephalus)
Weight: 36,000-45,000 kg.
Height: 9 m body-circumference
Length: 17-20 m.
Speed: 4.8-14.4 km/h is normal, 33.8-43.4 km/h highest speed.
Number on the Planet: 200,000.
Number in a litter: 1 calf.
Life Span: over 70 years.
Location: all regions of all seas and oceans excluding the polar region. Found in deep water, rarely coastal.
Calories: 1000 kg of food/day (~400,000-over 1 million kcal/day).
Diet: giant squid, fish, octopus, skate.
What they are called in a Group: pod.

Manatee *(Trichecus manatus)*
Weight: 680-816 kg.
Length: 3.7 m.
Speed: 6.4 km/h.
Number on the Planet: over 3,000.
Number in a litter: 1.
Life Span: 50-60 years.
Location: warm tropical and subtropical waters, primarily Floridian region and up to the Carolinas and in the Pacific.
Calories: ~20,000-60,000 kcal/day.
Diet: turtle grass, manatee grass, shoal grass, mangrove leaves, various algae, water hyacinth, and water hydrilla.
What they are called in a Group: herd.

Sea Otter *(Enhydra lutris)*
Weight: 20-37 kg.
Length: 1.3 m.
Speed: up to 9 km/h for short spurts, (average swimming speed: 0.8-2.4km/h).
Number on the Planet: ~70,000.
Number in a litter: 1 pup.
Life Span: 15-20 years.
Location: Pacific Ocean coasts, bays, and kelp beds, found from the coast of California through Alaska and along the eastern coast of Russia to northern Japan.
Calories: ~1,200-4,000 kcal/day.
Diet: crabs, clams, mussels, abalone,octopus, squid, sea urchins, and fish.
What they are called in a group: family/ raft/ romp.

The oceans are the planet's last great living wilderness.
John L. Culliney

565

Clouds

Luke Howard, died in 1864, used four terms to classify the clouds he saw in the sky. These terms still form the basis of cloud categories used today.

Cumulus=heap

Cumulus clouds are white and appear fluffy. They are generally seen in fair weather. The base of a cumulus cloud is relatively low, less than 2,000 meters above the earth's surface.

Cumulonimbus clouds are large cumulus clouds, high above the earth 2,000 -7,000 meters.

Altocumulus look like patches and sheets of rolled clouds- separate or sometimes merged at the height of at 5,000 - 13,700 meters, that produce thunderstorms. They look like ripples or grains of white clouds in regular patterns.

Stratus = layer

Stratus clouds are low, flat gray clouds. They often produce a steady rain. They are anywhere from the earth's surface to 460 meters high.

Stratocumulus are layers of white clouds with dark gray areas above the stratus clouds, 460- 2,000 meters, from the surface of the earth; often producing light rain or snow.

Altostratus clouds are 2,000 -7,000 meters above the earth. **They** are sheets of gray-blue clouds covering the sky, often covering the sun and the moon.

Cirrus=curl

Cirrus clouds are extremely high (more than 5,000 -13,700 meters above the earth's surface) and feathery. They are made of ice crystals and are seen in fair weather.

Cirriocumulus clouds look like grains or ripples of white clouds in regular patterns.

Cirrostratus clouds look like thin layers of clouds covering much of the sky like sheets. They are very high (5,000-13,700 meters).

Nimbus= rain

Nimbostratus are dark heavy clouds usually associated with rain and snow, they cover most of the sky at 900 to 3000 meters above the earth.

Fog is a cloud at ground or sea level.

Weather Proverbs

Red sky at night, sailors' delight, red sky at morning, sailors' take warning.

Rain before seven, fine by eleven.

The sudden storm lasts not three hours.

566

EXOSPHERE

THERMOSPHERE (to c.700km)

Appleton Layer[F2] (c.300km)

Heaviside Layer[E] (c.100km)

MESOSPHERE (to c.85km)

STRATOSPHERE (to c.50km)

Tropopause (17km)

TROPOSPHERE (to c.17km)

Ozone is a rare molecule consisting of three oxygen atoms. Ninety percent of the ozone in Earth's atmosphere is found in the stratosphere, the atmospheric layer that is between 15 and 50 kilometers above the Earth's surface. This stratospheric ozone is often referred to as the "ozone layer," and plays a vital role in protecting life on Earth by reflecting most of the harmful ultraviolet radiation that comes from the sun back into space. (In the late twentieth century, scientists discovered that the ozone layer was thinning and had even developed holes in some places as a result of human-made chemicals that destroyed the ozone molecules. The use of those chemicals is now strictly regulated, and it is expected that the ozone layer will recover in the twenty-first century.)

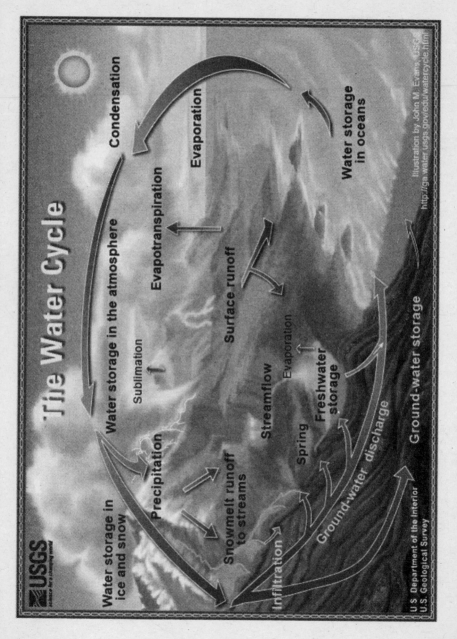

568